RHETORIC AND POETICS IN ANTIQUITY

Jeffrey Walker

OXFORD
UNIVERSITY PRESS
2000

OXFORD
UNIVERSITY PRESS

Oxford   New York
Athens   Auckland   Bangkok   Bogotá   Buenos Aires   Calcutta
Cape Town   Chennai   Dar es Salaam   Delhi   Florence   Hong Kong   Istanbul
Karachi   Kuala Lumpur   Madrid   Melbourne   Mexico City   Mumbai
Nairobi   Paris   São Paulo   Singapore   Taipei   Tokyo   Toronto   Warsaw

and associated companies in
Berlin   Ibadan

Copyright © 2000 by Oxford University Press, Inc.

Published by Oxford University Press, Inc.
198 Madison Avenue, New York, New York 10016

Oxford is a registered trademark of Oxford University Press

Library of Congress Cataloging-in-Publication Data
Walker, Jeffrey, 1949–
Rhetoric and poetics in antiquity / Jeffrey Walker.
p.   cm.
Includes bibliographical references and index.
ISBN 0-19-513035-9
1. Rhetoric, Ancient. 2. Classical literature—History and
criticism—Theory, etc. 3. Poetics. I. Title.
PA3265.W35   2000
808'.00938—dc21   99-27391

3 5 7 9 8 6 4 2

Printed in the United States of America
on acid-free paper

in memoriam
William S. Walker

Preface

In 1924, Charles Sears Baldwin published a volume entitled *Ancient Rhetoric and Poetic*, followed four years later by *Medieval Rhetoric and Poetic (to 1400)*. Baldwin's entire argument began, from the opening pages of *Ancient Rhetoric and Poetic*, with the inauspicious declaration that poetry and rhetoric were fundamentally different, even incompatible things, which the ancients had perversely persisted in confusing. One would like to dismiss that view as long since obsolete, but it has had surprising staying power. This is most apparent, on one hand, in what were to 1990 and to a great extent still are the received, standard histories of "classical" rhetoric; on the other hand, we see it persisting too in what remain the prevailing notions of "poetry" and poetics in contemporary culture.

What we might call the received, standard history of rhetoric typically presumes that "rhetoric" is and was originally, essentially, an art of practical civic oratory that emerged in the law courts and political assemblies of ancient Greece and Rome, while defining epideictic, literary, and poetic manifestations of this art as "secondary," derivative, and inferior. (This opposition often takes on a gendered tone as well: practical rhetoric is more manly.) Practical rhetoric is understood as an art of argumentation and persuasion suitable for deliberation, debate, discussion, and decision in the civic arena—or what Jürgen Habermas might call the "public sphere"—while epideictic, poetic, or literary rhetoric is understood as a "display" (or "*mere* display") of formal eloquence serving chiefly to provide aesthetic pleasure or diversion, or to provide occasions for elegant consumption and displays of high-class taste, or to rehearse, reconfirm, and intensify dominant ideologies. From this point of view, a conversion of "rhetorical" genres or techniques from practical to epideictic purposes is often seen as a step toward decadence, and is typically thought to reflect corruption of the civic sphere by autocratic or oppressive political regimes. The classic example is the emergence of declamation (the fictive imitation of a judicial or political oration, originally a school exercise) as a popular mode of epideictic literature and performance in the so-called Second Sophistic, accompanied by the seeming dearth of "great" practical oratory, and complaints about a "decline of rhetoric," when the Roman Empire was at its height.

At the same time, modern notions of 'poetry" and poetics (or literary theory more broadly) have typically appropriated "rhetoric" as a name for figurality, or "metaphor," while resisting a fuller notion of rhetoric as argumentation and persuasion. What we today call poetry continues generally to be thought of as a discourse that expresses, dramatizes, represents, or "models" states of subjectivity, or that adumbrates a complex "meaning," *rather than* offering argument/persuasion. This tends to be true even for contemporary critics, and poets, who want to envision (and practice) poetry as a viable medium of ideological contestation, or as a means of promoting social change. As I argue in part III (chapter 6), such views often depend on an extraordinarily narrow and inadequate conception of what "argumentation" is—a conception that is then rejected, reasonably enough—while leaving unaddressed the question of how a poetic discourse that wishes to challenge received belief, or to revise, critique, or overturn a dominant ideology (or some aspect of it), can do so *persuasively* for an audience not already committed to the position that the discourse represents. As I argue in part IV, such views have their origins in the grammatical tradition of late antiquity and in the subordination of "rhetoric" (and a rhetorical notion of poetics) to grammar and logic in the Middle Ages. The point I would note for now, however, is that the still dominant contemporary notion of "poetry" is closely related to, or is a version of, the notion of epideictic/"aesthetic" discourse inscribed in the received-standard history of rhetoric.

I began this book with an intention of responding to these interdependent and persistent lines of thought. I rather cheerfully imagined that I would write a revisionary tale about the notions of "rhetoric" and "poetics" in antiquity and modernity—and soon discovered how impossibly large that subject really was, and is. I have accordingly confined myself to rhetoric and poetics in antiquity, which already is a subject more than large enough, and indeed even here I have found it necessary to make selections. For now, I leave the rest of the tale to be worked out in subsequent volumes, or by other hands. I do, however, look toward modernity in my final chapter. (And my earlier book, *Bardic Ethos and the American Epic Poem*, can be understood as a "modern" chapter of the tale.)

What this book offers is, on one hand, a revised account of the history of rhetoric in antiquity, one that understands "rhetoric" in more or less sophistic terms as centrally and fundamentally an art of epideictic argumentation/persuasion *that derives originally from the poetic tradition* and that extends, in "applied" versions of itself, to the practical discourses of public and private life. This account participates in, and is a contribution to, recent revisionary discussions of the history of rhetoric, particularly those that have emerged since 1990, and particularly those that have sought to rehabilitate the sophists.[1] It is also a contribution to rhetorical theory, insofar as it defends a conception of "rhetoric" at variance with the more or less neo-Aristotelian notion embodied in the standard histories, and revises the conventional (and still widely prevalent) notion of epideictic discourse as mere display, or as limited to the ritual rehearsal of received beliefs and values. On the other hand, I also offer a "rhetorical poetics," grounded in an examination of ancient poetry—chiefly archaic Greek lyric—in which "poetry" is understood and practiced as epideictic argument that calls its audience to acts of judgment and response. This discussion speaks to contemporary poetics and, again, to rhetorical theory. I am, in

sum, offering what might be called a sophist's history of "rhetoric," one that includes "poetry" and "poetics" as essential, central parts of "rhetoric's" domain.

The general argument of this book might be summed up in the image presented
on its frontispiece, a vase painting from the fifth century B.C. The image shows Orpheus, singing to and charming a group of Thracian warriors. But it can be read as a
paradigmatic image of poetic-epideictic eloquence that lies at the root of what
came to be called the "rhetorical" tradition in antiquity. (One could change the
personnel, for example, by substituting Sappho and her circle, or the women of
Mytilene, for the all-male cast that appears on the pot.) In the scene we see, the
singer is immediately flanked by two listeners. One of them, on the left and behind
the singer, stands with his eyes shut and his posture slackened, carried away completely by the stream of the singer's discourse, as he leans on his spear. The other, on
the right and in front of the singer, may also have his eyes shut, but his posture is
more aggressive: he stands with a foot propped on the rock the singer sits on and he
leans forward into the stream of discourse, listening carefully. There is something
about which he must make up his mind. These two figures are flanked by two others, one of whom (on the far left) leans forward into the scene with open eyes, over
the transported listener's shoulder, as if to hear better, with an intent expression on
his face; the other (on the far right) stands with his head slightly bowed, apparently
listening carefully, interested but neither carried off nor puzzled nor brought to the
tension of judgment or decision. This is not simply an image of "music soothes the
savage heart," though it is partly that. It is also an image of variable responses to a
psychagogic, "soul-guiding" eloquence that calls its audience to acts of judgment
and ethical positioning: the poet, as prototypical rhetor, offers persuasion, and indeed offers arguments, while the audience is persuaded or not persuaded, transported and brought to puzzlements, in varying degrees and ways. Further, it is an
image of eloquence addressing power, of discourse (*logos*) addressing force (*bia*), of
discursive art (*logôn technê*) as a counterweight to mere coercion, asserting a force
and power of its own. Moreover, it is an image of power made willing to respond to
a discursive art that can effectively present itself as *wisdom-speaking eloquence;* and
this, if anything, may be the central dream of "rhetoric" from its earliest beginnings.
This image is, in short, a version of rhetoric's primal scene, and of poetry's primal
scene as well.

The discussion that follows is structured as four extended, multichapter essays—
or two pairs of extended essays. In the four chapters composing parts I and II, I discuss
the emergence of the terms "poetry" and "rhetoric" in the fifth and fourth centuries
B.C. and the subsequent evolution of "rhetoric" as a disciplinary concept in the Hellenistic and Roman periods. My central claims are, first, that what came to be called
rhetoric was neither originally nor essentially an art of practical civic oratory—
rather, that it originated from an expansion of the poetic/epideictic domain, from
"song" to "speech" to "discourse" generally—and second, that although there certainly were changes in sociopolitical conditions and rhetorical practices, there was
no "decline of rhetoric" in any meaningful sense in either the Hellenistic or the
Roman period. The Hellenistic and Roman republican periods may represent the
high-water mark of a more narrowly practical conception of "rhetoric," and of a
rhetorical practice that Cicero deemed destructive to the possibilities for civil com-

munity; but one also finds a persistent notion that "rhetoric" is a general, epideictic-centered, philosophico-literary discourse art such as Isocrates taught. This view comes to full flower in the Second Sophistic and remains predominant through late antiquity. Arguably, the persistence and eventual predominance of this conception represents not a collapse but a triumph of Cicero's rhetorical ideal. I conclude these chapters with reflections on the notion of rhetoric as an "amulet of justice," as Aelius Aristides called it, and on the relationship between "rhetoric" and democracy, about which so much has been presupposed. I suggest that "rhetoric" (as broadly conceived in the sophistic/Isocratean tradition) does not depend on, rise, or fall with democratic institutions, as is often assumed; rather, "rhetoric" (so conceived) may be democracy's condition of possibility.

In the seven chapters composing parts III and IV (the larger part of this volume), I develop a notion of rhetorical poetics that can be found embodied in archaic poetry and I discuss the gradual occlusion of this notion in the grammatical tradition and the "grammaticalized" rhetoric and poetics transmitted from the Middle Ages to early modernity. I examine archaic lyric as a "pretheoretical" discursive practice—preceding the emergence of "rhetoric" and "poetics" as systematic, disciplinary discourses—and as a synechdoche for "poetic" discourse generally. From an examination of the fundamentally rhetorical understanding of poetry reflected in Theognis's gnomic verse, the discussion proceeds to a general paradigm of "lyric" (broadly defined) as enthymematic argument, and to various exemplifications of this paradigm in the poetry of Pindar, Alcaeus, Sappho, and Solon, as well as its more "minimal" manifestations in epigrammatic poetry. I offer detailed rhetorical analyses of several poems with attention to their immediate historical/social contexts and performance circumstances (insofar as these can be reconstructed or conjectured with some degree of probability or plausibility). A major concern in these analyses is the capacity for "maximal" and "minimal" lyric argument to function as culturally significant public discourse able to speak persuasively beyond the boundaries of an immediate, "inside" audience, or to persuasively maintain counterhegemonic or controversial positions. I trace the later grammaticalization of poetics from what I call the double vision of Aristotle's *Poetics* to such figures as Neoptolemus of Parium, Plutarch, and the pseudo-Plutarchan *Essay on the Life and Poetry of Homer,* and I discuss the effects of this double vision in the "rhetorical poetics" of Horace, Dio Chrysostom, Hermogenes, and the so-called Menander Rhetor, as well as such late-antique poets as Claudian and Ausonius, who lived and wrote in the last decades before Alaric's sack of Rome in 410 A.D. Finally, I sketch the medieval-to-Renaissance grammaticalization of rhetoric and poetics as exemplified chiefly in Augustine's *De Doctrina Christiana* and Sidney's *Defense of Poetry.* In general, my claim is that archaic poetry embodies a rhetorical poetics that the "grammaticalized poetics" we inherit from late antiquity and the Middle Ages has made less thinkable, or more difficult to perceive, and sometimes more difficult to enact—even if it has never really gone away, or never ceased to be embodied in the suasive practices of poets, orators, writers, and all whom Hermes deigns to sponsor.

Plato and Aristotle play less central roles in my discussion of ancient rhetoric than some readers might expect—although they are by no means ignored (as they cannot be). This general shift of emphasis is, in part, an effect of telling that history from a "sophistic" or neosophistic rather than a neo-Aristotelian perspective: figures often relegated to "minor" status in traditional historiographies take on more prominence and centrality; and Plato and Aristotle, while still important, take on the look of faces in a crowd, voices in a wider conversation, and not always or necessarily the most important ones. Indeed from the perspective of my tale, the central tradition in "rhetoric" runs from Isocrates (and his older sophistic predecessors) through the likes of Dionysius of Halicarnassus to the leading figures of the Second Sophistic, and from Hellenistic Isocrateanism through Cicero to what might be called a Latin sophistic also.

Some readers may note as well that, in my discussion of "rhetorical poetics" and poetic argumentation in parts III and IV, I have short-shrifted such major figures as Callimachus or the great Latin poets of the Augustan and "silver" ages. Indeed at one point I did consider chapters on Callimachus, Horace, and Propertius. My general claim would be, in essence (and as I suggest in chapter 6), that the argument I advance about archaic lyric applies to them as well: they are practicing lyric poetry as a mode of enthymematic argument, and doing so with brilliant rhetorical skill, although they are doing so in a more explicitly "literary" mode and in (perhaps) more sophisticated and complex social and political contexts. In the end I chose not to include these chapters, partly from not wanting to make this book a great deal longer, and partly from a belief that they would largely be reiterations of the general argument I advance at length in chapters 5–9. The central point of my jump from archaic to late-antique poets such as Ausonius and Claudian is to highlight the effects of the "grammaticalized" poetics that dominates high culture in late antiquity. I do discuss Horace's *Ars Poetica* in chapter 10, and I do discuss Propertius (briefly) in chapter 6, but otherwise I have contented myself with more or less glancing references to Callimachus and the great Latin poets. Beyond this, I refer the reader to Alan Cameron's massive and impressive *Callimachus and His Critics*, and an excellent volume edited by Tony Woodman and David West, *Poetry and Politics in the Age of Augustus*— both of which (Cameron in particular) go a long way toward the sort of argument I would construct, though ultimately they are devoted to different issues and different claims than mine.

In my quotations of and references to primary materials, unless otherwise indicated, I have used the most recent available Loeb edition of the text (if there is one) as my "default" option. However, I have generally prepared—unless otherwise indicated—my own translations of the passages and poems I work with. Readers who know their Greek will see that I have not been completely consistent in my transliterations of Greek names. I have generally used the traditional, Anglicized spellings for well-known figures or canonic authors: Socrates rather than Sokrates, Alcaeus rather than Alkaios, Pittacus rather than Pittakos, and so forth. Otherwise, however, I have generally used the more direct transcription, for example, Kyrnos rather than Cyrnus, Melanippos rather than Melanippus, and so on, especially when (as with Kyrnos Polypaides, in Theognis's poems) the name itself seems significant. Likewise, in my citations of Greek or Latin terms, I have sometimes preferred the dictionary form, and sometimes an inflected form as it appears in quotation from some ancient writer. Here the principle of choice has generally been to prefer whatever will be most meaningful or accessible to the nonclassicist reader, especially when the inflected form differs sufficiently from the "basic" dictionary form as to be almost unrecognizable, and the coherence of my argument at that point depends on the reader being able to recognize the term. Readers may not agree with the judgment calls I have made in all these renderings of Greek and Latin names and terms, but I hope that, at least, my variations and inconsistencies will not seem wholly arbitrary.

Chapter 1 appeared originally as "Before the Beginnings of 'Poetry' and 'Rhetoric': Hesiod on Eloquence," in *Rhetorica* 14.3 (1996). Likewise, the discussion of enthymemes in chapter 6 reprises (with some revisions) material that appeared originally in "The Body of Persuasion: A Theory of the Enthymeme," in *College English* 56.1 (1994). Permission for the reuse of these materials is gratefully acknowledged. Further acknowledgment should be given, as well, for an earlier article, "Aristotle's Lyric: Re-Imagining the Rhetoric of Epideictic Song." in *College English* 51.1 (1989), which provided the kernels for several lines of argument in this book—though they are now greatly scattered, modified, and rearranged. Grateful acknowledgment is also made to the Staatliche Museen zu Berlin, for permission to reproduce the Orpheus image used in the frontispiece (© Bildarchiv Preussischer Kulturbesitz Berlin 1998; Antikensammlung V.I. 3172; photo by Ute Jung).

Finally, I have many personal acknowledgments to make. Over the years my colleagues in rhetoric at Penn State—in particular, Don Bialostosky, Marie Secor, and Jack Selzer—have given me stimulation and encouragement, and in particular with responses to drafts (early and late) of various chapters of this book. Likewise, my good friend and colleague Patrick Cheney has provided invaluable conversation (much of it while jogging through snow, in the long Pennsylvania winters). To the graduate students with whom I have worked in different iterations of my "rhetoric and poetics" seminar I owe a debt, for through discussions with them, in effect, this book began: I cannot here name them all, but in particular I wish to thank (in alphabetical order) Andrew Alexander, Edward Armstrong, Alan Bilansky, Benjamin Click, Richard Cunningham, Rosa Eberly, Linda Ferreira-Buckley, Ann George, Debra Hawhee, Jean Nienkamp, Fiona Paton, Blake Scott, Cynthia Miecznikowski Sheard, Christine Skolnik, Kakie Urch, and Janet Zepernick. To Leonard Nathan, who since my graduate student days at Berkeley continually has been my best reader and best mentor—and who made crucial comments on an early, very rough draft of what eventually became parts I and II, and on several other, later drafts as well—I owe more than I can possibly repay. I likewise thank Thomas Sloane and (in memoriam) Jeannette Richardson, whose voices are present here. I am grateful to Richard Leo Enos and Thomas Conley, for their generous readings of and incisive comments on the completed manuscript, which have helped me to sharpen and clarify several key points. (I hope they will be satisfied with my responses!) I thank the Fulbright Foundation in Greece for a one-semester fellowship in Athens in 1993, which galvanized my writing, and my thinking, in ways that still surprise me. To Susan Chang and the editorial staff at Oxford University Press I am grateful for the expeditious and skillful way this project has been brought to fruition. And last but far from least, to my wife, Yoko, and my son Eliot, who have constantly entertained my humors, obsessions, and absent-mindednesses, and who have kept me on task, I owe more than the usual debt of love.

Contents

PART I

THE BEGINNINGS OF "POETRY" AND "RHETORIC"

Before the Beginnings

Hesiod on Eloquence

A t the end of the 104-line hymn to the Muses that commences Hesiod's *Theogony*, we find what is probably the earliest account on record, at least in the West, of the relationship between the eloquence of prince and bard, or what most of us think of now as "rhetoric" and "poetry."[1] This is what he says:[2]

> Whomsoever the daughters of great Zeus honor
> and mark at his birth as a god-nurtured prince,
> on his tongue they pour sweet distillation,
> and words from his mouth flow honeyed: the people
> all look toward him discerning precedents
> with straight justice, and with unfaltering address
> he quickly and skillfully settles even a great dispute;
> thus there are sagacious princes, for when the people
> are misguided in assembly these end the wheeling recriminations
> easily, persuading with gentle words.
> He goes through the gathering, like a god admired
> with honeyed reverence, conspicuous amid the throng;
> such is the Muses' sacred gift to humankind.
> For from the Muses and far-shooting Apollo
> singer-men are on the earth, and harpers,
> and from Zeus princes: happy the one whom the Muses
> love; sweet from his mouth flows the voice.
> For even if one have sorrow fresh in his troubled soul
> and be stricken at heart with grief, when a singer
> the Muses' servant sounds the glories of ancient folk
> and hymns the blessed gods, on Olympos dwelling,
> soon the careworn one is made forgetful and no sorrow
> he recalls; the goddesses' gift soon turns his thought aside.
> Hail, children of Zeus! and grant me lovely song. (81–104)

As I will argue here and in the following chapters, Hesiod's account requires us to rethink some key assumptions on which our histories of rhetoric have traditionally been based—assumptions that, despite a number of recent reexaminations of rhetoric's early history, can fairly be said to retain wide currency. These assumptions are, to put the matter as briefly as possible, that the "primary" and most essential form of "rhetoric"—and the form in which it originates from the traditional, "pre-conceptual" or predisciplinary discourse practices of archaic Greek society—is the practical oratory of political assemblies and courts of law. And further, that poetic, epideictic, or "literaturized" forms of rhetoric are "secondary," derivative manifestations, in which the pristine virtue of the civic speech act is reduced to little more than genteel ornament, or decorative display, and made to serve the purposes of elegant consumption or entertainment or the reinforcement of existing values and beliefs.[3] What follows from these assumptions, generally, are histories of "rhetoric" in which the art is seen to "rise" and "fall" with the fortunes of practical civic oratory in Greek and Roman polities.

The basic position of this and the succeeding chapters is, as Stesichorus once said, *It is not true, that tale*: there is another and more persuasive tale that we might tell. In this chapter my argument rests on two main kinds of evidence. First, I call on Hesiod's account as my central witness, for Hesiod presents us with an image of archaic, "preconceptual" eloquence that is distinctly at odds with our traditional standard histories and at the same time is reasonably consistent with what is known about the discursive practices of oral or "traditional" societies worldwide (or, for that matter, with Homer's representations of those practices in archaic Greece). Second, my argument invokes from ancient sources a particular notion of "epideictic" and "pragmatic" discourse as the best, most effective way to frame what Hesiod describes, and perhaps indeed to frame the "realm of rhetoric" in general. As we will see in the chapters that follow, Hesiod's account—or the sophistic, Isocratean accounts descended from it—remains as the persisting and finally prevailing view of epideictic and pragmatic eloquence throughout antiquity.

But let us now turn to Hesiod.

Hesiod on Eloquence

In Hesiod's world of the eighth century B.C., of course, the words "poetry" and "rhetoric" do not exist. *Poiêsis, poiêtês,* and *rhêtôr* will not appear until the fifth century, and *rhêtorikê* will not emerge as a disciplinary term until the fourth, where its first known use is in Plato's *Gorgias*.[4] (*Poiêtikê* and *poiêma,* as terms for "poetry," seem to be fourth-century developments as well.) For Hesiod, there are only the "song" (*aoidê*) or the "hymns" (*hymnoi*) of the "singer" (*aoidos*) and the eloquent "words" (*epea*) of the wise prince (*basileus*) speaking in assembly. We can, of course, easily recognize the respective activities of *aoidos* and *basileus* as "poetry" and "rhetoric," but to do so is more than a little misleading, insofar as those terms imply for us an opposition or antithesis. It will, in fact, be helpful to forget awhile just what those words have meant in the last two centuries or so.

Significantly, Hesiod considers both the *aoidos* and the good *basileus* to be engaged in essentially the same activity. Both acquire their gift of eloquence from the Muses, and both are gifted with the power of persuasion, here figured as the ability to deflect or "turn aside" the listener's mind from its current state or path.[5] This is the explicit meaning of line 103, as the hymns of the *aoidos* deflect "the careworn one" from preoccupation with his troubles and lead him to contemplate glories both ancient and divine. Likewise, in line 89, the words of the *basileus* deflect the thinking (and the actions) of the people when they are "misguided in assembly." Hesiod's word for "misguided," *blaptomenois*, can also mean "caught" or tangled in a snare, "hindered" or "frustrated," or "deluded" and unwittingly doing harm—a state in which the people fall to what Hesiod calls *metatropa erga*, literally "turnabout works" or wrongful actions that provoke (or perhaps enact) revenge. The general sense of the line, in the larger context of settling "even a great dispute," is that of an assembled crowd becoming "tangled" in a cycle of recrimination and vendetta, or in a course of unjust action that will eventually bring everyone to grief. (Hesiod's term for "the people," *laoi*, is actually a plural—*laities*, peoples, groups of men or soldiers—suggesting not a homogenous folk but a heterogeneous set of competing factions.) The wise *basileus* brings this cycle of squabbling and vendetta to an end by means of eloquence, and he thus restores the people or peoples of his *polis* to the path of "straight justice" and intelligent decision. As Hesiod says in *Works and Days* (225—237), the ability of a *basileus* to do this is what enables a *polis* to live peacefully and in prosperity, and is what constitutes the essence of good rulership; the lack of such ability, conversely, constitutes the sort of bad rulership that Hesiod frequently complains about. Thus for Hesiod the peace and justice bringing power of eloquence, a power the good *basileus* and the *aoidos* share, is "the Muses' sacred gift to humankind."

This Muse-given eloquence is figured consistently by Hesiod as a voice (*audê*) that "flows sweetly" from the mouth, a sensually pleasing stream of words (*epea*) that carry off the listener's mind from one way of thinking to another. Both the *aoidos* and the eloquent *basileus*, in effect, are masters of what Gorgias of Leontini in the fifth century B.C. will call in his *Encomium of Helen* the verbal "witchcraft" (*goêteia*) that "merges with opinion in the soul" and "beguiles and persuades" it with druglike power, in his description of both "poetry" (*poiêsis*) and the "speeches" (*logoi*) made in public assemblies and philosophical debates (*Helen* 8–14). Plato, after Gorgias, will call this witchcraft a *technê psychagôgia*, a "psychagogic art" of enthralling and leading a listener's mind wherever one wills, in his description of what he names as "rhetoric" (*Phaedrus* 261).[6] If we allow ourselves to speak anachronistically, we might say that Hesiod sees both the eloquent *basileus* and the *aoidos* practicing "rhetoric," the psychagogic witchcraft of persuasion, though in the differing forums of civic debate and ritual celebration, and in the differing modalities of speech and song—the realms of Zeus and Apollo respectively. Indeed Hesiod's consistent word for the "flow" of eloquence in both realms, the verb *rheô*, is the root of such other words as *rhêsis* (a saying, speech, declaration, tale, or legend), *rhêtos* (stated, specified, or spoken of), and *rhêtra* (a verbal agreement, bargain or covenant), as well as the later words *rhêtôr* and *rhêtorikê*.

What relation then holds between the psychagogic eloquence, the rhetoric, of *aoidos* and *basileus* in Hesiod's account? Consider, again, the eloquence of the good *basileus*. His persuasive power arises from two sources. One is his skill in "discerning precedents" (*diakrinonta themistas*) that apply to the matter in dispute, in other words, his ability to resolve disputes by relating the present issue to established customs, codes, usages, oracles, decrees, or laws (all of which are possible meanings of *themistas*), the particular relevance of which he must "discern," determine, judge, or sort out (all of which are possible meanings of *diakrinô*), with "straight justice." The other source of persuasive power is his ability to articulate this judgment, and presumably the interpretation of "precedents" on which it is founded, with "unfaltering address," with steady and self-assured declaration, and in well-shaped, "honeyed" and fluent "words" or phrases (*epea*). Clearly, Hesiod offers a brief and compressed ur-theory of what rhetoric manuals would later describe as the faculties of invention, composition, and delivery in civic oratory.[7]

But what is perhaps most significant in Hesiod's account is the use of the term *epea* (words, tales, songs, or sayings)—rather than *logos* (word, speech, discourse) or *onoma* (name, utterance)—to signify the words of eloquence of the *basileus*. Both alternatives are certainly available to Hesiod. In *Works and Days*, for example, he uses *logos* to signify the gift of "wily words" (*aimylious logous*) that Hermes gave to "all-endowed" Pandora (78), and later *onomainô* (a verb formed from *onoma*) to signify this gift again (80). Hesiod's use of the word *epea* may signify, as Eric Havelock has suggested, the oral-formulaic phrases of *epos*, the "winged words" of gods and bards; indeed, as Bruno Gentili maintains, *epea* may signify "verses" or rhythmic formulae in general and is not necessarily limited to the hexameter verses of Homeric and Hesiodic poetry.[8] Likewise, Gorgias (*Encomium of Helen* 10) uses the word *epôidai* (songs, charms, refrains) to signify rhythmic or incantatory words, to which he ascribes a magical or druglike persuasive power; and, like Hesiod, he applies this notion not only to poetry but also to speech in civic and philosophical forums. The implication is that the eloquence of the *basileus* derives from his knowledge and command of the rhythmic formulae, the *epea*, of poetic discourse. This is not to say that Hesiod's *basileus* always orates in hexameters, or recites poems to settle a dispute (although he might); and there were, of course, bad kings who spoke badly. The point is that his knowledge of and skill at weaving together or composing with *epea*, the "sayings" of poetic discourse, is the basis of the good king's eloquence, and even of his ability to give "straight justice."

As Hesiod tells us, in the lines just preceding the passage I am examining (79–80), the Muse who chiefly attends an eloquent *basileus* is Kalliope ("Lovely-voice"), the Muse of *epos*. But *epos* here signifies something broader than the notion of heroic narrative that is typically attached to our conventional ideas of "epic." Here, in Hesiod's context, it simply means "verse" or rhythmic composition, in short poems or long, such as we see in the so-called Homeric Hymns and Epigrams, which are late examples of traditional Homeric/Hesiodic "epic" practice. *Epos* in this broader sense comprises the entire range of cultural lore an oral society cultivates, disseminates, and preserves in rhythmic discourse, in memorable *epea*, including not only mythological and heroic narratives but also discursive and/or catalogic representations of knowledge and belief—genealogies, hymns, prayers, curses, proverbs, instructions, "scientific" or technical information, ethical exhortation, praise and blame, and so on—such as we find abundantly in the works of Hesiod, as well as in the Indo-European (Sanskrit and early Iranian) precursors of archaic Greek poetry.[9] In the Greek world from Hesiod to Solon (from the eighth to the sixth centuries B.C.), the cultural lore encoded in the rhythms of *epea* would include the customary laws or "precedents," the *themistas*, on which the civic rhetoric of the

basileus is grounded. The two chief sources of princely eloquence thus resolve, in effect, into one source, and the good *basileus*'s dependence on Kalliope becomes fairly
clear. His ability to speak wisely and persuasively to the people in assembly depends
on his knowledge of both the lore and language of *epos:* he must be able to recall,
interpret, and apply to the question at issue the memorious lore encoded in rhythmic formulae; and he must be able to compose his own speech in rhythmic phrases
and formulae, sententious language resembling traditional *epea,* as he carries off the
mind of the fractious crowd on the stream of his "honeyed" discourse.[10]

Epideiktikon and Pragmatikon

At this point it is useful to introduce one more anachronism. What I am calling the
rhetoric of Hesiod's *aoidos* and *basileus* corresponds, more or less, to what later (and
especially late-sophistic) rhetorical theory would recognize as *epideiktikon* and *pragmatikon,* "the epideictic" and "the pragmatic." The category of the *pragmatikon* was
traditionally understood to include two main types of civic discourse: speeches of
accusation and defense in courts of law; and speeches proposing, supporting, or opposing laws or resolutions in political assemblies (or speeches of advice presented in
council or to a magistrate or ruler). This is the picture we consistently find from
Aristotle's *Rhetoric* and Anaximenes' *Rhetoric to Alexander* in the fourth century
B.C., through to the dominant Latin and Greek authorities for later antiquity,
namely Quintilian and Hermogenes of Tarsus. The category of the *epideiktikon,* in
contrast, was more amorphous and inclusive, though it was generally identified with
discourse delivered outside judicial and legislative forums, such as speeches performed at festivals and ceremonial or symposiastic occasions, and it was typically
conceived as the discourse of praise and blame. Its prototypes were frequently
thought to be the *Olympic Speech* of Gorgias and the *epitaphios,* the funeral oration,
particularly as modeled by Pericles (in Thucydides), or by Socrates' mock *epitaphios*
in Plato's *Menexenus* (a speech that Socrates claims was taught him by the female
sophist and teacher/companion of Pericles, Aspasia).[11] Probably the most influential model for epideictic, however, was the "panegyric" kind of discourse practiced
by the sophist Isocrates, which he described (in *Antidosis* 45–50) as akin to poetry:
logoi in a highly wrought style, dealing with "philosophical" questions of large cultural and political import, and suitable for presentation at panhellenic gatherings.
Thucydides, likewise, was to become a model for epideictic, as were the dialogues of
Plato, which Aristotle (in *Poetics* 1 1447b) considered a yet unclassified type of poetry. By later antiquity, a more or less Isocratean view seems to have prevailed: we
find the category of the *epideiktikon* understood by the writers of rhetoric manuals to
include not only various kinds of ceremonial or ritual discourse but also panegyric
speeches, epic and lyric poetry, philosophy, and history; this is the explicit view, for
example, of Hermogenes of Tarsus.[12] *Epideiktikon,* in sum, came to include everything that modernity has tended to describe as "literature," and more, and comprised a range of genres much greater and more various than the handful of speech-
types identified as *pragmatika.* It is this expanded, basically sophistic notion of
epideiktikon that I will develop and employ throughout this book.

It is important to recognize that what distinguishes the *epideiktikon* and the *pragmatikon* (in this view) has little to do with subject matter, a fact that is often obscured by the conventional translation of the pragmatic genre names as "deliberative" and "forensic" or (worse) as "political" and "legal" discourse. Nor is the distinction entirely a matter of form, though highly wrought, elegant, and rhythmic style is generally considered characteristic of epideictic. For example, the major epideictics of Isocrates—such as *Panegyricus, On the Peace, Areopagiticus*—are all political discourses presenting arguments on affairs of state, and indeed Isocrates refers to them as *logos politikos.* Likewise, Isocrates' account of his rhetorical and pedagogical philosophy in *Antidosis* is presented in the form of a courtroom defense (like the *Apology* of Socrates), but again it is an epideictic. Further, as Chaim Perelman has argued, even the courtroom speeches of Cicero, when written up and published in a "polished" version several months or years after the event, become epideictics even if they are faithful reproductions of the original performance.[13]

This may seem confusing, but the principle is basic. What distinguishes the *epideiktikon* and the *pragmatikon* in every instance is the nature of the audience and forum to which the discourse speaks, and the function of the discourse for that audience in that forum. As Aristotle recognizes (in *Rhetoric* 1.3 1358b), pragmatic discourse is presented before an audience of *kritai,* "judges" or "deciders," people who have been formally empowered to make rulings within a particular institutional setting—that is, not people who make judgments in the general sense of forming an opinion about something (*gnômê*), but people who actually determine the practical outcome of a contest or dispute by casting votes. Thus, "forensic" or what Aristotle calls "dikanic" discourse (*dikanikon*) consists of speeches concerning questions of justice (*dikê*), presented before a juror (*dikastês*) or assembly of jurymen (*dikastai*) in a court of law (*dikastêrion*). Likewise, "deliberative" or what Aristotle calls "symbouleutic" or "demegoric" discourse (*symbouleutikon; dêmêgorikon*) consists of speeches of counsel (*boulê*) for or against a particular initiative, presented before councilors (*boulêtai*) in a council-hall (*bouleutêrion*) or before a crowd of assemblymen (*ekklêsiastês*) in the public assembly (*ekklêsia*) or "demegore" (deme-agora: *dêmos,* the district or its people, and *agora,* meeting-place); the verb *symbouleuô* means "give advice"; *symboulos* means "advisor." The function of either dikanic or symbouleutic/demegoric discourse, in its particular setting, is to produce a specific kind of action (*praxis*), namely a vote that constitutes a formal judgment (*krisis*) by an institutionally empowered body of *kritai*: a decision of guilt and the assessment of a punishment (or an acquittal), the enactment (or rejection) of a law, or the enactment (or rejection) of a proposal. The production of such institutional transactions (*praxeis*) of the public business (*pragmateia*) is what defines a discourse as a *pragmatikon.*

There is a tendency, in modern thought, to define the *epideiktikon* in simple opposition to the *pragmatikon* by its lack of a pragmatic business function. To a certain extent this is accurate, though inadequate. One can say the defining characteristics of an *epideiktikon* are that it is presented in nonpragmatic settings, such as festivals, public ceremonies, or symposia, and that its audience does not have the role of a juror or councilor/assemblyman: at the end of the speech there is no vote and no verdict is formally enacted, no legislation put into law, no policy adopted. The audience simply applauds, disperses, and goes home (or, in the case of a published text, the audience stops reading, puts down the scroll, and goes on to the next thing). Thus the published texts of Cicero's courtroom speeches or Demosthenes' speeches to the Athenian assembly, having been removed from their original pragmatic forums and placed before a reader years, decades, or even centuries later, cease to be *pragmatika* and instead become *epideiktika:* they become, in effect, performances the reader "witnesses," as if in a theater—or performances the reader mimetically rehearses, if we take the usual assumption that reading in antiquity normally was reading aloud, in other words, oral interpretation.

But epideictic can be defined in more positive terms as well. As Aristotle notes (*Rhetoric* 1.3 1358b), the role of an epideictic's audience is to be not a *kritês* but a *theôros*, that is, one who is to make "observations" (*theôriai*) about what is praiseworthy, preferable, desirable or worthy of belief in the speaker's *logos*. (It is worth noting that *theôria* can also mean "speculation," and that *theôros* can also mean an "ambassador" sent to consult an oracle.) The role of the *theôros, in short, is not to make rulings but to form opinions about and in response to the discourse presented*.[14] Isocratean *logoi*—such as the argument of the *Panegyricus* for Panhellenic unification in a great crusade against the Persian empire or the defense in the *Antidosis* of his rhetorical and pedagogical philosophy—can in this sense best be understood as epideictic discourse that asks its audience to form opinions, or even to revise their existing beliefs and attitudes on a given topic. The same would hold for the histories of Thucydides, the dialogues of Plato, the poems of Sappho, the *Olympic Speech* of Gorgias, the *epitaphios* of Pericles, sophistic declamations and panegyrics, and the published orations of Demosthenes and Cicero as well. In every case the function of the epideictic in its nonpragmatic setting is a suasive "demonstration," display, or showing-forth (*epideixis*) of things, leading its audience of *theôroi* to contemplation (*theôria*) and insight and ultimately to the formation of opinions and desires on matters of philosophical, social, ethical, and cultural concern. In Cicero's *Defense of Milo*, as Chaim Perelman has pointed out, the reader knows that Milo was convicted and that Cicero did not actually deliver the speech (because he was intimidated by an audience packed with armed thugs), but is asked to consider whether Milo should have been convicted, what constitutes justice, what sort of person he was (and what sort his accusers were), what sort of person (and orator) Cicero was, what constitutes the admirable in politics and human conduct (and in oratory), and so forth.[15]

In this view, "epideictic" appears as that which shapes and cultivates the basic codes of value and belief by which a society or culture lives; it shapes the ideologies and imageries with which, and by which, the individual members of a community identify themselves; and, perhaps most significantly, it shapes the fundamental grounds, the "deep" commitments and presuppositions, that will underlie and ultimately determine decision and debate in particular pragmatic forums. As such, epideictic suasion is not limited to the reinforcement of existing beliefs and ideologies, or to merely ornamental displays of clever speech (though clearly it can serve such purposes as well). Epideictic can also work to challenge or transform conventional beliefs—plainly the purposes of Plato's dialogues, Isocrates' panegyrics, what remains of Gorgias's epideictics (particularly *Helen* and the surviving paraphrases of *On the Nonexistent*), and the sophistic or Protagorean practice of antilogy that is parodied in the "speech of Lysias" in Plato's *Phaedrus*. All such discourses, again, are "epideictic" according to the late-sophistic theory of Hermogenes of Tarsus, and according to the definition I am employing here. When conceived in positive terms and not simply in terms of lack, epideictic discourse reveals itself (as Perelman recognized) as the central and indeed fundamental mode of rhetoric in human culture.[16]

Conceived in positive terms, then, the distinction between the *epideiktikon* and the *pragmatikon* comes down to this: the *epideiktikon* is the rhetoric of belief and desire; the *pragmatikon* the rhetoric of practical civic business, a rhetoric that necessarily depends on and appeals to the beliefs/desires that epideictic cultivates. This relation is, as I will show more fully in chapter 4, recognized quite explicitly by Cicero. And it is, arguably, the relation that Hesiod describes between the rhetoric of *aoidos* and *basileus*. The forums for the poetic/epideictic eloquence of the *aoidos* in eighth- to sixth-century Greece are the formalized occasions provided by festivals and civic or religious ritual, the informal, symposiastic forums of male and female "clubs" (*hetaireiai* and *thiasoi*), and the paideutic forums of aristocratic education—in which, before the fifth century B.C., the central practice was the memorization and recitation of poetry—from which the good *basileus*, being well educated, derives the knowledge of *epea* that constitutes the store of "precedents" (or wisdom-lore) and the stylistic paradigms his eloquence depends on.[17] The forums for the pragmatic eloquence of the *basileus*, likewise, are the public assembly, or what Hesiod calls the *laoi agorêphi*, the "peoples in assembly" (or "in-agora") to settle a dispute (88–89), and (presumably) the other scenes of Zeus-like rulership, such as the embassies and councils Homer represents. In effect, Hesiod presents to us a picture of the primacy of epideictic rhetoric, which for Greek culture of the eighth century B.C. is virtually coextensive with the category of rhythmic discourse, of "poetry" or *epos*. In Hesiod's world, the *aoidos'* poetic/epideictic discourse is the mode of suasion that both establishes and mnemonically sustains the culturally authoritative codes of value and the paradigms of eloquence from which the pragmatic discourse of the *basileus* derives its "precedents," its language, and its power. The poetic/epideictic discourse of the *aoidos* is, in sum, what might be called the "primary" form of "rhetoric" in that world, while the pragmatic discourse of the *basileus* is an applied, "secondary" projection of that rhetoric into the particular forums and dispute occasions of civic life.

Epideictic and Pragmatic Discourse in "Traditional" Societies

While contemporary theory generally (and reasonably) looks at universalizing statements with suspicion, at this point I must pause to risk a reasonably well-founded generalization. For lest one think that I have put too much upon Hesiod's use of the word *epea*, let us reflect on the fact that what Hesiod describes is mostly consistent with what we know about the discourse practices of oral or "traditional" societies worldwide, both past and present. So here I shall briefly turn to modern ethnography—then back to Greece again.

In brief, what we know is this: Discourse that is performed in ritual, festal/ceremonial and paideutic settings in "traditional," oral-archaic societies is almost universally rhythmically structured, tropologically figured, and formulaically composed; and it is typically declaimed, chanted, or sung with stylized intonation and/or gestures. The rhythmic structuring of such discourse sometimes may take the form of what we recognize, in the archaic Greek context, as metered "verse" or *epea*, as in Solon's elegiacs, Pindar's or Sappho's song-measures, or Hesiod's hexameters. The more general and more fundamental principle, however, is that of prosodic repetition or "equivalence"—or what more recent, crosscultural studies of "oral poetry" and ritual language have generally termed "parallelism," "diphrasis," or "bipartite design."[18] Adopting the language of classical rhetorical theory, we might call this very basic rhythmic principle "isocolonic patterning" or "isocolonic doubling," insofar as *isokôlon* means "equivalent phrase," or phrases (*kôla*) of similar length and structure.

Whether such discourse ought to be described as "poetry" or "rhetoric" is largely moot, and indeed the question is probably misleading. Students of "poetry" or "rhetoric" in oral and archaic cultures are liable to apply such terms based on modern preconceptions about what is "poetic" or not. Thus what are seen as "lyrical" expressions of personal feeling, "epic" narratives, and "dramatic" mimesis will tend to be classified as "poetry," while argumentative, didactic/encyclopedic, political, and juridic discourse will be classified as "rhetoric," "oratory," or "prose." Or the distinction may be based on whether a discourse is sung (or chanted) or not or seems more "musical" or in some other way matches conventional ideas of poetic form. Some modern commentators have had difficulty accepting as "lyric poetry," and thus implicitly as "poetry" at all, the verses of such ancient elegists as Solon and Mimnermus, because they seem so much like "essays" on political and moral questions.[19] But, as Ruth Finnegan has pointed out, in her eminently sensible study of what she calls oral poetry, such distinctions are for the most part irrelevant when considering oral and archaic cultures.[20] By Finnegan's standards, any rhythmically structured discourse is indeed a "poem," as are Solon's elegies, Sappho's erotic lyrics and epithalamia, or Pindar's odes for victorious athletes. But to say so is not to preclude the fact that all these texts are also quite clearly "rhetoric" and play very definite suasory and sociopolitical roles and often are quite explicitly argumentative, as I will show in some detail in part III.

In general, the conventional poetry/rhetoric distinctions of the modern mind are more likely to confuse than to illuminate our understanding of oral and archaic discourse practices. We can gain a much more intelligible understanding by instead thinking broadly in terms of epideictic and pragmatic eloquence—as I have defined those terms here—and by considering the relationship between them.

The power of epideictic discourse in oral societies is difficult to overestimate. In the first place, because it is designed to be memorable and repeatable at significant, recurring occasions in a culture's pattern of experience, it is felt to be more "permanent" than the comparatively ephemeral language of everyday business talk. As Walter Ong has noted, such business talk has no means of being preserved in a nonliterate society and is thus "used up" as soon as its immediate, practical function has been performed.[21] The felt "permanence" and memorability of epideictic, by contrast, give it a cultural presence, or prominence, that the more ephemeral pragmatic genres lack. It abides through time, and in people's minds, repeating its "timeless" rhythmic words. Second, and perhaps most important, epideictic discourse carries great suasive power. This power derives, in part, from its felt authority as "permanent" or "timeless" discourse embodying ancient, ancestral wisdom. We might say, to speak in more contemporary terms, that the epideictic discourse of an oral or "traditional" society enunciates, or is felt to enunciate, that society's archival knowledge, its deep belief systems, its sacred postulates, its precedents and premises.

Beyond this ancestral/archival authority, moreover, and whether or not a given epideictic discourse enunciates and amplifies the memorious formulae of traditional wisdom, it exerts considerable suasory power sheerly by virtue of its rhythmic eloquence—what Gorgias (again) described as the hypnotic "witchcraft" of poetry and sacred incantations. Modern analyses have attributed this psychagogic power to the bodily and subliminal effects of acoustic rhythm and even tonal quality acting on the central nervous system and/or the sheer aesthetic pleasure and sense of "rightness" created by the skillful arousal, complication, and fulfillment of rhythmic and formal expectancies.[22] We thus have, in sum, a discourse that joins the subliminal and aesthetic suasion of its rhythmic "witchcraft" to the felt "timelessness/permanence" and ancestral/archival authority of "ancient wisdom" to generate, in the mind of its audience, a mood of numinous "truth" surrounding whatever is being said. As Roy Rapoport has put it, in his ethnological account of ritual, "[t]he unfalsifiable [sacred postulates] supported by the undeniable [the mood of numinousness generated by ritual discourse and procedure] yields the unquestionable, which transforms the dubious, the arbitrary, and the conventional into the correct, the necessary, and the natural."[23] Or, as Hesiod (*Theogony* 26–32) says the Muses said to him on Helicon, as they gave him the laurel wand of bardic authority and breathed into him a magic voice, "We know how to say many false things resembling the real [*etymos*, actuality/reality], / But we know how also, when we wish, to sing the truth [*alêthea*, truth as opposed to lies]" (27–28). He is, in effect, given the power both to utter truth and to make anything whatever seem believable.

From one point of view, the ancestral/archival authority and rhythmic psychagogy of oral/archaic epideictic can make it a deeply conservative, even oppressive social force.[24] One is hypnotized by the beautiful words repeating themselves forever, and constrained in thought by compositional principles that lend themselves more to the copious stacking-up of equivalent phrases than to reasoned inquiry. But to say this is to overstate the case. Audiences and human minds are not that passive, and always have the potential to differ or disagree. And in any culture there will be many kinds of epideictic, ranging from festal, symposiastic, paideutic, and ceremonial discourse to religious rituals, from rhythmic argumentation to repetitive, hypnotic chant, and with many degrees of formalization and flexibility. Moreover, as Ruth Finnegan has argued, "oral poets" are not in fact constrained simply to be the mouthpieces of traditional thought. They have a more dialogic relation with the societies and audiences for which they perform, play a wider range of social roles, and exhibit a greater degree of creative freedom than imagined by most conventional (and basically romantic) notions of "oral tradition" and "oral-formulaic" consciousness.[25] Even the discourse of religious ritual in "traditional" societies is not completely rigid or inescapably conservative. It tends to alternate between periods of conservatism and crises of belief that generate doctrinal disputation, revision, and revivalism, so that it functions as a medium for both the exercise and contestation of authority and social power.[26] In sum, then, the ancestral/archival authority and the rhythmic/psychagogic spell of epideictic discourse are not inherently insidious forms of authoritarian mind control but suasory means—illusionistic "witchcraft"—by which skillful speakers, chanters, and singers may promote traditional, untraditional, or even antitraditional values and beliefs.

While the language of pragmatic discourse in oral/archaic cultures tends to be more conversational, ephemeral, and "disposable" than that of epideictic, it is not sharply separable from it either. In the first place, there is pragmatic and pragmatic: the pragmatic discourse that occurs in casual, daily talk can be distinguished from the kind that occurs in formalized public forums.[27] The Melpa of Papua New Guinea, for example, distinguish between discussions of minor disputes or preliminary negotiations, which can take place inside people's houses, and the formal discussion and resolution of socially significant major disputes, which must take place outdoors, in a public or ceremonial space, and generally within the context of a *moka* (exchange) ritual. The Mursi of southwest Ethiopia, similarly, distinguish what they call *tirain*, or "chatting," from *methe*, a council meeting at which some public issue is to be settled. They also distinguish between a small group discussion that minimally qualifies as a *methe* and a big, formalized *methe* or "debate" attended by large numbers of people and accompanied by ritual performances.[28] The Iroquois, likewise, traditionally distinguish what they call talk "in the bushes"—the informal discussions and deal-cuttings that take place away from the council fire—from the speeches delivered in the ritualized, public setting of a tribal or intertribal council.[29] In general, what we can recognize as "civic oratory" in oral/archaic societies is characteristically framed within the formalized, ritualized setting of epideictic and may even model its forms and procedures on those of epideictic forums. The types and sequencing of speech events in Iroquois embassies, for example, traditionally were based on the ceremonial procedures of the Condolence Council (an intertribal ritual marking the death of a chief and installing a new one), which seems to have provided the basic paradigm for all Iroquois diplomacy.[30]

The language of formalized pragmatic discourse in oral/archaic cultures, moreover, is itself characteristically informed and structured by the relatively stable, authoritative paradigms of eloquence embodied in the memorious, memorable language of epideictic. For example, in the formalized oratory of Huli disputes (in Papua New Guinea), speakers employ what they call *pureremo*, epideictic formulae, to invoke general truths they wish to establish as the grounds of argument in a particular debate, or simply to speak impressively. Even the non-*pureremo* talk of a skillful Huli speaker will tend to exhibit (though more loosely) the isocolonic doubling, structural balance, and distinctive intonational contours of *pureremo*.[31] Likewise, Tshidi political oratory (in Botswana) incorporates two basic speech registers: a "formal" register for invoking basic ideals and values, and an "evaluative" register for discussing actual people and events. The "formal" (or epideictic) register relies on traditional formulae, metaphor, and indirect assertion, whereas the "evaluative" (or pragmatic) register relies on nonformulaic, direct, and explicit statement; both registers will be employed in any given speech.[32] In traditional societies such as these, fluency in epideictic discourse not only makes a speaker's argumentation more effective but also signifies knowledge and confers prestige. Like Hesiod's good *basileus*, speakers who demonstrate their mastery of epideictic codes and formulae typically are thought to be not only eloquent but especially wise, and often are accorded special titles. Among the Huli, for example, such a person is called a *manali*, "mana man," among the Malagasy a *tena ray aman-dreny*, "true wise elder," and among the Mursi a *jalabai*, an "orator."[33]

In sum, the pragmatic and epideictic discourse genres of oral/archaic cultures fall into a sort of spectrum, with the casual business talk of everyday life at one extreme, and the highly formalized song and chant of religious ritual at the other. Between these extremes, we find a heterogeneous collection of epideictic and formalized pragmatic genres, ranging from song and intoned or spoken "recitative" to oratorical declamation and plain speech—but a plain speech, if it is skilled, that will be punctuated and pervaded by sententious flights of wisdom-invoking eloquence, and often a general sense of rhythmic composition as well, derived from epideictic registers. Speakers and singers learn their eloquence and wisdom, and audiences learn what counts as eloquence and wisdom, from the models embodied and preserved in epideictic discourse. This is the characteristic pattern of oral or "traditional" societies worldwide, and of the archaic Greek world of the eighth century B.C. that Hesiod describes.

Can we see this pattern reflected in Homer, or in the very early Greek speaking practices that Homer represents? Modern readers tend to assume that, although all the speeches in Homer are rendered in hexameter verse, we are to imagine the speakers as always speaking "prose." But this assumption is grounded in no real evidence and simply reflects our sense of the normal in contemporary culture. Instead, it seems more likely that Homer's ever-sententious speakers do indeed reflect the pattern that Hesiod describes and that ethnologists observe in oral or "traditional" societies worldwide—and that they range between plain talk and epideictic registers.

Let us take one example. In the "embassy" scene of *Iliad* 9, after Achilles has refused Agamemnon's offer of gifts and reconciliation (as tendered by Odysseus) and all have been reduced to silent astonishment at the "roughness" of the young man's speech (*kraterôs apéeipein*, 9.431), old Phoenix—Achilles' tutor—attempts to intervene. Phoenix's job is to teach Achilles "to be a speaker of speeches and a doer of deeds" (*mythôn te rhêtêr emenai prêktêra te ergôn*, 9.443): as such, he figures as someone who knows and can model the art of princely eloquence. So how does he speak to Achilles? After a ceremonious, formal prologue in which he narrates the history of his friendship with young Achilles (and Achilles' father), he turns to his main argument:

> But Achilles, tame your great spirit! It does not befit you
> to have a pitiless heart. Even the gods themselves are flexible,
> and theirs is the greater excellence, honor, and power.
> *Indeed they are with sacrificial offerings and reverent vows*
> *and libations and rising fragrance turned from wrath by human*
> *supplications, when someone transgresses and does wrong.*
> *For prayers are the daughters of great Zeus,*
> *halting and wrinkled and of squinting eyes,*

and mindful are they after recklessness to go.
And recklessness is strong and swift of foot, so that all
she far outruns, and goes before everyone on earth
ensnaring humankind; and prayers thereafter make amends.
And he that reveres the daughters of Zeus when they be near,
him they greatly bless and hear him when he prays.
But should he refuse them and stubbornly disown them,
then to Zeus the son of Kronos do they go and make their prayers
that recklessness attend him, that he be ensnared and pay the penalty.
But Achilles, see to it that you too give honor to Zeus's daughters,
and attend them. (9.496–514)

In the lines that I have italicized, it seems clear that Phoenix is invoking traditional wisdom-lore, and indeed that he is "quoting" the sort of verse one might expect from a poem like Hesiod's *Works and Days*. The passage operates much like the
"formal" register of Tshidi oratory or like *pureremo* in Huli speech performances:
Phoenix's digression on "prayers" is an indirect parallel to and commentary on
Achilles' rejection of Agamemnon's effort at reconciliation—Agamemnon has
been "ensnared" by the "recklessness" (*atê*, folly/sin/guilt) that led him to wrong
Achilles and is now "supplicating" the hero by means of this embassy and the offer
of gifts that it conveys; Achilles' refusal is a rejection of "prayers" and makes him
liable to divinely sponsored punishment. Moreover, by this passage Phoenix invokes precisely the sort of "precedent," or general premise, that Hesiod says the
good *basileus* must "discern" and apply to the case in hand: and in the succeeding
passage, Phoenix applies it explicitly to the particular case of Achilles' dispute with
Agamemnon, exhorting him to receive the king's offers and the embassy more gra-
ciously. Phoenix follows this application by declaring that "until now no one could
blame your being angry," for "thus have we heard the fame of the men of old, / the
heroes" who became enraged yet still "by gifts were wont to be persuadable and by
words" (*dôrêtoi te pelonto pararrêtoi t' epéessi*, 9.523–526); and he then says he is reminded of one such story, which he proceeds to tell for the next seventy one lines
(9.529–599). The rest of the speech is a short, concluding exhortation to Achilles
to relent. Again, it seems most likely that, in Phoenix's telling of the tale, we are to
see a skillful speaker invoking poetic lore in a skillful recitation of *epea*, verses, to
invoke a "precedent" for determining the case in hand. Moreover, it seems likely
that we are to think of these materials as being woven skillfully into the general
texture of the speech, with the rest of Phoenix's speaking framed in a generally sententious, ceremonious, and rhythmic language.

There are many speeches in the *Iliad*, as in the *Odyssey*, representing a variety
of speaking situations: from the relatively formal speeches of the "embassy" scene,
or Agamemnon's harangue to the assembled army in *Iliad* 2 (or the speech of the
false "herald" in Agamemnon's dream) to Odysseus's conversations with his swine-
herd in the *Odyssey*. What is characteristic of them all, and especially the utterances of speakers said to speak well and to give good counsel, and especially in formal speaking situations, is that the speeches often are framed in a general
ceremoniousness and are (in varying degrees) punctuated with sententious, gnomic
sayings that invoke general truths or premises and that probably should be thought

of as poetic formulae derived from traditional epideictic registers. Skillful, "good" speakers weave such materials seamlessly together with "original," pragmatic utterance that applies to the immediate situation. In contrast, the least estimable character in the *Iliad* (and perhaps in all of Homer), the scruffy and worthless footsoldier Thersites, is introduced as *Thersitês ametroepês*—"Thersites of unmeasured words"— and is immediately described as having a mind full of "words (*epea*) both disorderly (*akosma*) and many," which he spouts, or spews, "not according to good order" (*ou kata kosmon;* 2.212–214). Thersites' *epea* are, in essence, indecent and inelegant expressions that constitute the contents of his mind and that simply issue from him haphazardly without artistic composition: badly formed, ignoble phrases put together badly, reflecting an ignoble, ignorant, wisdomless sensibility, an *êthos* that cannot command respect. Thersites, in effect, represents the opposite of the eloquence that Hesiod describes and Homer represents, the civic eloquence descended from poetic discourse, "the Muses' sacred gift to humankind."

So it is not true, that tale that says pragmatic discourse, or what can be seen as civic oratory, is the "primary" form of "rhetoric" in its "preconceptual" state, before it emerges into history as a named and theorized discipline, in Greece, in the fifth and fourth centuries B.C. The opposite can more persuasively be argued. In that archaic realm, epideictic or "poetic" discourse is the "primary" form of "rhetoric" on which pragmatic discourse, and especially formalized pragmatic, is dependent for the major sources of its power—the culturally authoritative paradigms of eloquence and wisdom on which it draws. Insofar, then, as we find Hesiod's account reliable or persuasive, and I think we should, he requires us to consider the epideictic roots of eloquence, and of what eventually would be called the "art of rhetoric," *rhêtorikê*.

The Emergence of *Poiêsis,* *Logos,* and *Rhêtorikê*

Thus far I have pursued an argument that "rhetoric" in its primitive, "preconceptual" state in "traditional" or archaic cultures, and in archaic Greek culture in particular, finds its "primary" embodiment in epideictic, or more specifically in the memorable, memorious eloquence of poetry. But I have not addressed what is the crucial moment, or the crucial passage, in most traditional histories of rhetoric. And that is the moment or passage in which both "poetry" and—most crucially of all—"rhetoric" appear and stand side by side as named and conceptualized discursive practices.

That moment is the fifth to fourth centuries B.C., the moment that for nearly every modern history of rhetoric culminates in Aristotle. But it has a long foreground too, in the profound changes that Greek culture undergoes in its transition from Hesiod's oral/archaic, eighth-century world to the beginnings of the classical period. Not all these changes will directly concern us here, but as they are the background to (and very much the enabling conditions for) both the conventional tale and the differing tale this chapter unfolds, at least some of the major developments need at least to be noted and kept in mind. Here we can make do with a quick, short list. First, the oral/archaic society ruled by the Hesiodic *basileus,* which was little more than a collection of agrarian villages, gives way to the more literate, more highly urbanized society of the classical *polis.* Second, the power of the *basileus* himself gives way to that of aristocratic oligarchies or, at Athens at least, to the citizens' assembly, the *ekklêsia.* Third, in the wake of (or as part of) the breakdown of traditional authority, traditional thought is put in question by the new, more skeptical and rationalistic philosophies of the pre-Socratics and the sophists. Finally, perhaps because of this new skepticism toward traditional belief and structures of authority, and perhaps also because of the sociopolitical changes underway, there is an increasing trend toward individualistic self-assertion (at least among those privileged enough to participate in politics or to come in contact with the new philosophies).[1] We can, either for purposes of argument or for the rather good reason that these developments probably really happened, take the general scenario they constitute as mostly factual. Nevertheless, even as fact, the scenario provides a not-very-constraining set of conditions that can enable different versions of the "very same" tale.

In the conventional tale, this scenario—featuring prominently the birth of democracy, rationality, and individualism—gives birth to "rhetoric," conceived as an art of civic argument that originates in history with the practice of the fifth-to-fourth-century *rhêtôr*, and especially the Athenian *rhêtôr*, debating proposals in the public assembly and arguing cases in the people's courts. In the conventional tale, this practice becomes conceptualized and named as *rhêtorikê* and is then what Aristotle decisively theorizes in the *Rhetoric*, thereby inaugurating the discipline that has played so central a role in most of the two thousand–plus years of Western education and that now comes down to us in English and speech departments. Clearly, both this tale and the scenario it is embedded in (or the particular interpretation and salience it gives to that scenario) sit well not only with a neo-Aristotelian cast of mind but also with a more or less Jeffersonian ideal of civil liberty. I personally have no desire to antagonize that ideal, essentially because I believe in it. Indeed its justly powerful appeal, functioning as the basis of what Kenneth Burke might call an "ingenuous and cunning identification,"[2] goes a long way to explain the enduring hold of the conventional tale. There is even a sense, as I will show, in which the tale is true. But a limited one.

The burden of this chapter is not, however, a refutation or deconstruction of the conventional tale. Rather, I will be most centrally concerned with the more difficult job of constructing a positive rather than a negative case: I will, that is, be tracing an alternative tale that arguably is just more true. Of course, it will not be wholly unlike the conventional one. As Plato's Socrates says in *Phaedrus*, as he sets out to produce a better version of the discourse that the sophist Lysias has produced, it would be impossible to treat the subject adequately without addressing many of the same topics and without, at certain points, saying very similar things (235–236). Moreover, both the alternative tale and the conventional tale necessarily rest on the same basic body of evidence, and both are committed to the same or similar democratic ideals. There will be many points of correspondence and agreement between both tales. Nevertheless, the alternative tale argues a nearly opposite claim.

The claim I will pursue, in essence, is that what comes to be called the art of rhetoric, *technê rhêtorikê*, in fact originates not from the pragmatic discourse of the fifth-to-fourth-century *rhêtôr* but from an expansion of the poetic/epideictic realm to include, first, various kinds of epideictic prose and, ultimately, epideictic imitations of pragmatic prose. That is, rather than seeing the "literaturization" of pragmatic discourse as a symptom of the decline or decadence of *technê rhêtorikê* (and, by implication, of "literary" or poetic discourse as well), my alternative tale projects a claim that a process of "literaturization" is what actually causes or produces the concept, and the conceptualization, of something called *technê rhêtorikê* in the first place.[3] And indeed, as with the princely and bardic eloquence that Hesiod describes, the art that emerges as *technê rhêtorikê* is largely grounded in, or centered on, the realm of epideictic. But by the fourth century this realm has been considerably ramified.

Perhaps the major and most obvious problem that this argument must confront is a matter of sheer etymology: does not the term *rhêtorikê* refer quite explicitly to the practical civic art of the *rhêtôr*? It does; but, as I will show, it also does not. My alternative tale will bring us to the answer that the term *rhêtorikê*, from the moment it enters Western discourse, is an equivocal term—a floating term—one that from the beginning is paradoxically invoked to name a discourse art that either cannot exist or, if it does exist, is different from and larger than the art its very name would seem to point to. And insofar as that art really does exist and can be studied as the object of a discipline, *rhêtorikê* is its name only by way of synechdoche, the name of a (conspicuous, distinctive) part representing the larger whole.

Before we turn to the emergence of the term *rhêtorikê*, however, we must first consider the longish foreground that prepares it. The central development in this foreground is the preclassical differentiation of epideictic discourse, between the eighth and fifth centuries, into *poiêsis* and *logos*—to which I now turn.

Poiêsis and Logos

By the fifth century, *poiêsis* and *poiêtês*, "poetry" and "poet," have displaced the archaic terms *aoidê* and *aoidos*, "song" and "singer," as the generic terms of choice for poetic/epideictic discourse and its practitioners.[4] As every poetry student has been told, the noun *poiêsis* and the verb from which it derives, *poieô*, have as their root sense the notion of "doing" or "making" or "fabricating" something, and can include the notion of "making up" an invented tale or a lie. Pindar, for example, uses the adjective *poiêtos* in this sense to tell how the crafty Hipployta devised a "false, invented speech" (*pseustan poiêton logon*) to deceive her husband into believing that the ever-virtuous Peleus had attempted to seduce her (*Nemean* 5.29). This sense of the word is what later permits Aristotle, in the *Poetics*, to define *poiêsis* as a mimetic art of constructing and representing a *mythos*, a story.

But Aristotle's position is eccentric, even if justified. The more prevalent meaning of *poiêsis* in Greek antiquity, quite simply, is the "doing" or making of verse.[5] This is what Gorgias recognizes, when he defines "all poetry" (*poiêsis apasa*) as "speech with meter" (*logos echonta metron*), or, to translate more literally, as "discourse having measure" (*Helen* 9). And this is what Aristotle implicitly confesses also, when he complains that "people" (*hoi anthrôpoi*) consider anything composed in meter to be "poetry," including Empedocles' scientific treatises in hexameters. Thus, as Aristotle grumbles, "people" call anyone who composes in dactylic hexameter an *epopoios*, "epic-maker," anyone who composes in iambics an *iambopoios*, "iambic-maker," and anyone who composes in elegiac meter an *elegeiopoios*, "elegy-maker," regardless of their subject-matter (*Poetics* 1 1447b). It is important to recognize that terms like "epic," "elegy," and "iambic" originally referred not to the heroic, threnodic, or satiric themes that came to be associated with these kinds of verse but to the form of the verse itself.[6]

Why the shift from *aoidê* to *poiêsis*, "song" to "poetry"? There probably can be no fully adequate explanation, but one important possibility is an evolution of the aoidic tradition itself between the eighth and fifth centuries.[7] This process has a double aspect. First, we find the dactylic hexameter of old-time Homeric and Hesiodic *epos* giving way to the metrical traditions of what twentieth-century nomenclature calls lyric poetry, namely *elegeia* (alternating lines of dactylic hexameter and pentameter), *iambos* (lines of iambic trimeter, or sometimes tetrameter), and *melos* (the varied meters and complex strophic forms of song poetry, such as Sappho's solo lyrics and Pindar's choral odes).[8] As it is sometimes suggested, the seventh- and sixth-century proliferation of iambic, elegiac, and melic lyric may have developed from archaic genres of occasional epideictic, such as the paean, the wedding song, the dirge, the dithyramb, the encomium, the invective, and so forth.[9] But it is significant that in this period the briefer, more occasional verse genres appear to become the chief modes for new and culturally significant poetic discourse and, as with Archilochus's iambics or Sappho's melics, are used as media for the expression of individual (and sometimes iconoclastic) opinion. As Bruno Gentili has suggested, the occasionality of such genres made them a "middle ground between tradition and innovation," a place where the mythic, timeless topoi of traditional *epos* could meet (or be confronted with) the evidence of personal experience and the changing sociopolitical realities of the *polis*, in a relatively open-ended engagement.[10]

Much the same could be said for the emergent tradition of dramatic poetry at Athens in the fifth century. Originating in choral performances of dithyrambic satyr songs, the drama developed as a form of state theater tied to the city's Dionysia festival, and as such became a venue for the dissemination of social and political as well as mythic thought, as we can see perhaps most clearly in Aeschylus's *Eumenides*, Sophocles' *Antigone*, or any of the comedies of Aristophanes. At the same time, fifth-century drama was also a reabsorption and transformation of the older and newer verse traditions that had preceded it, incorporating both melic verse (for the chorus) and iambic verse (for the actors' speeches), as well as plots, legends, and wisdom-lore drawn from archaic *epos*.[11] In sum, the elegiac, iambic, melic, and dramatic poets of the seventh to fifth centuries B.C. were what we might call the "modernists" of their time—appropriating, altering, and redefining the tradition they had received from ancient *aoidoi* like Hesiod and Homer and projecting that redefined tradition as a new poetry into the cultural debates and epideictic forums of the developing *polis*. The emergence of the terms *poiêsis* and *poiêtês*, then, may reflect in part the emergence of a modernism associated with lyric and dramatic verse in the seventh to fifth centuries B.C.[12]

The second major aspect of the seventh-to-fifth-century evolution of the old aoidic tradition is the differentiation of "song" into *melos*—"melodic" poetry meant actually to be sung with musical accompaniment—and nonmelic poetry meant to be performed in a recitative, "spoken" delivery.[13] By the fifth century, as can be seen in Plato's *Ion*, Homeric *epos* was no longer sung to the lyre but was declaimed by rhapsodes. Likewise, fifth-century iambics and elegiacs were also declaimed, though the older (seventh- and sixth-century) poems present themselves as being sung to the accompaniment of the lyre or the aulos (a clarinetlike reed-flute).[14] By the later fifth century, *melos* survived chiefly in dramatic poetry, where the choral interludes functioned much as in Pindaric or even Hesiodic song: the song of the chorus represented the archival, hieratic thought of the community, standing (and dancing) apart from the action while commenting on and judging its significance, while the *dramatis personae* of the action itself declaimed their more contingent, personal thought in iambic trimeter "speeches."[15] This differentiation into sung and "spoken" verse, along with the proliferation and complication of metric and strophic forms, may perhaps be seen as a continuing evolution of the metrical tradition, from primitive (and prehistoric) phrase-based song to metered song to metered speech, which in effect arises as an ultimate artifice.[16]

Whatever the aetiology of these developments may be, however, their upshot is reasonably clear. By the fifth century, the category of oral/archaic epideictic, which for Hesiod had been quite simply the domain of "song," had become an array of sung and "spoken" meters, modes, and strophic forms that could no longer be contained by the term *aoidê*. Nor could the term *aoidos* suffice for a class that included declaiming rhapsodes, actors, singers who composed their own songs, and those who composed for choral and theatrical performances. *Poiêsis* and *poiêtês*, then, emerged as the terms of choice for the artful invention of metered discourse of all kinds, for the artful discourse itself, and for its artificers.

But even if "poetry" had emerged as the name for an art-speech identified with metered discourse, metered discourse was no longer the whole of epideictic by the fifth century B.C.: philosophers, sophists, and historians had begun to produce an epideictic prose. The category of epideictic discourse had been ramified still further. We might attribute this development to the continued differentiation of poetic kinds: once "song" is expanded into "poetry," and poetry divided into the sung and the "spoken," the spoken in turn divides into the metered and the unmetered.[17] "Prose" thus emerges as unmetered "poetry," in other words a kind of free verse. That seems plausible, but certainly the overwhelming causal factor in this development is the advent of literacy in archaic Greece. This process seems to have begun sometime after the mid–eighth century B.C., and to have reached a kind of fulfillment by the end of the fifth century, when written textbooks became for the first time a basic medium of education.[18] I need not posit here the birth of a special literate consciousness with enhanced propensities for abstract thought and logical analysis, or even the transformation of an oral into a literate, book-based society. These popular notions from conventional orality-literacy theory do not really square with the known facts of archaic and even classical Greek culture, which remained fundamentally, profoundly oral, and continued to conduct its civic business and to disseminate important epideictic discourse primarily through face-to-face, speaker-audience transactions. The written text was, for that society, a script to be performed aloud, and was only a supplement to the living speech event and living memory—a memorandum or memorial.[19]

Yet that is the crucial fact. Written text took on the "timelessness" and permanence of metered poetry, and in principle and in fact could serve the same memorious functions.[20] The upshot of this development was a displacement of the traditional alignments and oppositions of epideictic and pragmatic, "permanent" and ephemeral, and verse and nonverse discourse. It was now possible for nonverse discourse, non-"poetry," to acquire the permanence of epideictic, and to become a kind of counterpart to verse, simply by virtue of being written down. The archaic Greek identification of epideictic discourse with "poetry" was undermined. Likewise, the mnemonic function of metered discourse was rendered obsolete, at least in principle, since any discourse deemed important now could be preserved as a written text, and could be stabilized in some canonic form. Thus, while the oral traditions of metered poetry remained quite strong, by the fifth century it was no longer strictly necessary for epideictic discourse to be composed in verse. However, since epideictic would continue for the most part to be orally performed and disseminated, and would still need to distinguish itself from pragmatic discourse as a wisdom-bearing eloquence equivalent to the old-time poetry, even a nonmetered epideictic "prose" would need to retain the memorability and the psychagogic power of verse.

These implications were realized in the work of the pre-Socratic philosophers, the historians, and the sophists. The pre-Socratic philosophers are the most obviously transitional. A number of early, sixth-century figures are said to have composed scientific or metaphysical treatises in prose—most notably Pherecydes of Syros, and the Milesian philosophers Thales, Anaximander, and Anaximenes—but virtually nothing survives aside from paraphrases and quotations by later writers who cannot be presumed to reproduce the original language. The one surviving fragment that may be genuine is a single "poetically worded" sentence from Anaximander, quoted and remarked upon eleven hundred years later in Simplicius's *Physics* (c. 550 A.D.).[21] Indeed, many of the early, sixth-to-fifth-century philosophers from whom we have any substantial number of surviving fragments, such as Xenophanes, Parmenides, and Empedocles, were in fact verse writers. These figures seem to have lived the careers of itinerant bards, traveling from town to town and "publishing" their scientific and metaphysical doctrines chiefly by means of public recitation, very much like Hesiodic lore-singers—but with the difference, of course, that they were proposing new and untraditional cosmologies.

The first prose-writing philosopher from whom we have a body of surviving fragments, a collection of about 130 sayings, is Heraclitus (c. 500 B.C.). As is often said, Heraclitus's style in these fragments seems to imitate the rhythmic "lilt" of poetic discourse and to rely on schemes of assonance, repetition, antithesis, and symmetry for its effect. These are also the chief stylistic characteristics, a generation later, of the philosophic prose of such figures of the middle to later fifth century as Zeno of Elea, Melissus, Anaxagoras, and Diogenes of Apollonia.[22] Like the verse of Xenophanes, Parmenides, or Empedocles, such prose was meant for public recitation and was meant to retain the psychagogic power and memorability of rhythmically "measured" epideictic verse. In the philosophic prose of the fifth-century pre-Socratics, then, we see the beginnings of a new kind of poetry, one that arises from a Hesiodic tradition of lore and wisdom discourse and that arises "dialectically" in opposition to (or in competition with) the older song tradition and its older wisdoms.[23]

Much the same is true for the fifth-century historians Herodotus and Thucydides, and for the sophists. By now it is a commonplace that both Herodotus and Thucydides were more or less consciously working in, or against the background of, the tradition of Homeric narrative. Like Homer, both weave the memories of deeds performed in great, epochal wars, bestowing fame (*kleos*) on the doers and praise and blame upon the deeds; and both rely on narrative structures (such as ring composition) that are characteristic of Homeric tale-telling. Herodotus' style in particular, as it is often said, is reminiscent of oral-formulaic poetry, and it seems likely that his *History* was meant for public recitation. This can be seen in his proëmium:[24]

Herodotus of Halicarnassus' history's recital this is, so that
neither will what comes from human beings
  with time become forgotten,
nor deeds great and wondrous
   whether by Greeks or by barbarians performed
    become unknown,
nor especially why they went to war with one another.

Hêrodotou Halikarnêsseos historiês apodexis hêde, hôs
mête ta genomena ex anthrôpôn
  tôi chronôi exitêla genêtai
mête erga megala te kai thômasta
  ta men Hellêsi ta de barbaroisi apodechthenta
   aklea genêtai,
ta te alla kai di'hên aitiên epolemêsan allêloisi.

Herodotus's book here speaks with the voice of a herald, announcing itself as an *apodexis* (*apodeixis* in classical Attic dialect), which in this context means a public presentation, demonstration, recitation, or performance. Its purpose is to prevent the "great and wondrous deeds" of which human beings are capable from becoming "forgotten" or "unknown" (*aklea*, literally "without fame"). In this memorious role, the book-voice speaks a monumental language that relies on the same kinds of schemes the pre-Socratics relied on—repetitions, parallelisms, oppositions (neither/nor, whether/or, etc.), and phrasings that echo and come near to metrical construction—to generate an overall rhythmic balance and a prosody strongly reminiscent of poetic discourse.

This is what we find, as well, in the epideictic speeches of the early sophists. A particularly good example, if an extreme one, is the surviving fragment of Gorgias's *epitaphios*, a memorial speech for the Athenian war dead (or a fictive imitation of one)—which, again, relies on oppositions, symmetries, balances, repetitions, echoes, and rhythmic phrasings to generate a strongly "poetic" prosody. Here is the fragment in its entirety:[25]

For what was absent in these men
 that should in men be present?
And what was present
 that should not be present?
Would that I could speak what I wish,
 and wish what I should,
avoiding divine displeasure,
 and evading human envy.

ti gar apên tois andrasi
 toutois hôn dei andrasi proseinai?
ti de kai prosên
 hôn ou dei proseinai?
eipein dynaimen ha boulomai,
 bouloimên d'ha dei,
lathôn men tên theian nemesin,
 phygôn de ton anthrôpinon phthonon.

For these attained
a godlike excellence,
 and also a human ethicality,
often defending reasonability
 to willful prejudging justice,
and often to law's exactness
 speech's straightness,

outoi gar ekektênto
entheon men tên aretên,
 anthrôpinon de to thnêton,
polla men de to praon epieikes
 tou authadous dikaiou prokrinontes,
polla de nomou akribeias
 logôn orthotêta,

this holding a most godlike	*touton nomizontes theiotaton*
and most universal law,	*kai koinotaton nomon,*
the duty when dutiful	*to deon en tôi deonti*
to speak and be still and do [and be],	*kai legein kai sigan kai poiein [kai eian],*
and cultivating two things surely needful,	*kai dissa askêsantes malista hôn dei,*
insight [and might],	*gnômên [kai rhômên],*
the one deliberating	*tên men bouleuontes*
and the other accomplishing,	*tên d'apotelountes,*
caring for those	*therapontes men tôn*
unjustly suffering,	*adikôs dystychountôn,*
and punishing those	*kolastai de tôn*
unjustly flourishing,	*adikôs eutychountôn,*
persistent	*authadeis*
toward the useful,	*pros to sympheron,*
gentle	*euorgêtoi*
toward the suitable,	*pros to prepon,*
by mindful judgment	*tôi phronimôi tês gnômês*
checking mindless [strength],	*pauontes to aphron [tês rhômês],*
proud	*hybristai*
among the proud,	*eis tous hybristas,*
moderate	*kosmioi*
among the moderate,	*eis tous kosmious,*
fearless	*aphoboi*
among the fearless,	*eis tous aphobous,*
terrifying	*deinoi*
amid the terrifying.	*en tois deinois.*
As witness they set up this trophy	*martyria de toutôn tropaia*
over their enemies,	*estêsanto tôn polemiôn,*
to God an honor,	*Dios men agalmata,*
and to themselves an ornament,	*heautôn de anathêmata,*
not inexperienced	*ouk apeiroi*
neither in natural valor	*oute emphytou areos*
nor lawful passion	*oute nomimôn erôtôn*
nor well-armed war	*oute enopliou eridos*
nor honorable peace,	*oute philokalou eirênês,*
at once reverent	*semnoi men*
to the gods by means of justice,	*pros tous theous tôi dikaiôi,*
as well as dutiful	*hosioi de*
to parents by means of care,	*pros tous tokeas têi therapeiai,*
as well as just	*dikaioi de*
to citizens by means of equity,	*pros tous astous tôi isôi,*
as well as loyal	*eusebeis de*
to friends by means of faith.	*pros tous philous têi pistei.*
So though they have died	*toigaroun auton apothanontôn*
our yearning does not die with them,	*ho pothos ou synapethanen,*
but immortal	*all' athanatos*
in bodies not immortal	*ouk en athanatois sômasi*
it lives though they do not.	*zê ou' zôntôn.*

To understand the power that Gorgias's eloquence actually did possess—for we know that its power was considerable—one must envision, and hear, this *epitaphios* being declaimed on a ritual occasion to a crowd of possibly several thousand people. Or, to take an approximate example of twentieth-century Gorgianics, one must think of (and see and hear) an epideictic orator like Jesse Jackson at the 1988 Democratic National Convention. Gorgias's *epitaphios* represents the sort of rhythmic, prosodically and conceptually figured discourse that Gorgias knew, from his own experience (and as Jackson knows from his), to wield considerable psychagogic power over audiences, a power comparable to that of Hesiod's magic voice.

It is often said that Gorgias, or the sophists as a group, invented poetic prose. But since there was no such thing as epideictic prose of any kind before the later sixth and early fifth centuries B.C., it is probably much more true to say that what was being invented was a kind of prose poetry, or indeed a kind of free verse, and that it was being invented not only by sophists but also by philosophers and historians. Because of writing's impact on the realm of epideictic, the requirements of meter had been loosened, and what developed was a mode of rhythmic discourse that relied on schemes—such as repetition, symmetry, opposition, and balance—that were in essence variations on the primitive, underlying principle of verse, namely isocolonic or parallelistic doubling. The prosodic units of composition, likewise, became the phrase and sentence (*kôlon* and *periodos*) as opposed to the metrical line and strophe. In effect, the pre-Socratic philosophers developed a prose (or free verse) equivalent to Hesiodic wisdom-poetry; the historians an equivalent to Homeric tale-poetry; and the sophists, in occasion-bound sorts of epideictic like the *epitaphios*, an equivalent to lyric poetry. By the later fifth and early fourth centuries, of course, epideictic prose became considerably more sophisticated, more elaborate, and indeed more obviously "written" and literary: the more forthrightly oral styles of Gorgias, Herodotus, and the pre-Socratics gave way to the complexities and subtleties of Isocrates, Thucydides, and Plato, who were (along with other fourth-century writers, such as Lysias and Demosthenes) to set the standards for Greek literary prose for centuries to come. Nevertheless, what these writers were producing with increased refinement and elaborateness was what their predecessors had produced: a rhythmic, epideictic prose built on fundamentally poetic principles of composition. In sum, the prose epideictic of the fifth and fourth centuries B.C. was a new kind of poetry, and was the embodiment of a new modernism, just as the lyric and dramatic verse of the seventh to fifth centuries had been.

To a certain degree, the writers of the fifth and fourth centuries themselves were able to recognize the new prose epideictic as a kind of poetry. Isocrates explicitly likens his own epideictic practice to poetry, and himself to Pindar (*Antidosis* 45–50, 166). Likewise, as we have seen already, Gorgias takes poetic "incantation" as a paradigm of all persuasive discourse, and thus presumably also as the model of what he himself is practicing (*Helen* 9–10); and Aristotle opines that Plato's dialogues may be an as yet nameless kind of poetry (*Poetics* 1 1447b). The ancient writer Aelian tells us that both Gorgias and the sophist Hippias declaimed "in purple clothes," as would a rhapsode (*Miscellaneous History* 12.32).[26] "Poetry," however, was fixed as the name for metered verse. The name that attached to epideictic prose, or to nonverse generally, was *logos*, "speech" or "discourse." Thus Pindar, for example, speaks (or sings) of both *aoidoi* and *logioi*, "singers" and "speakers," as memorializers of great deeds and bestowers of *kleos*, fame (Nemean 6. 28–30, 45–47); and Herodotus presents himself as a *logios* in the passage immediately following his proëmium (*Histories* 1.1.1).[27] But *logos*, in the general sense of "speech," could be a name for pragmatic discourse also—and, as "discourse," could be a name for reasoning or thought in general. By the end of the fifth century, then, the categories of *poiêsis* and *logos* did not align with those of epideictic and pragmatic discourse. Some epideictic was "poetry," and some belonged in the very general category of *logos*, along with all the forms of pragmatic discourse, reasoned thought, and argumentation.

In this context, as the epideictic realm elaborates from *poiêsis* into *logos*, the terms *rhêtôr*, "orator," and *technê rhêtorikê*, "art of rhetoric," begin to emerge in the late fifth and early fourth centuries B.C.

Sophistic Discourse Art: From *Logos* to *Rhêtoreia*

Traditionally, the "invention of rhetoric" is credited to the sophists of this period. The key figures are the so-called older sophists canonized in Hermann Diels and Walter Kranz's *Die Fragmente der Vorsokratiker*, most centrally Protagoras and Gorgias, and after them the somewhat younger Isocrates, who is not one of the Diels-Kranz "older sophists" but is clearly a culminating figure for sophistic.[28] The sophists are credited with having been the first to theorize and teach the principles and practices of suasive discourse, thereby raising it (or at least claiming to raise it) to the status of a disciplined "art" or methodology, a *technê*, as opposed to an *empeiria*, a "knack" or skill in some traditional practice that is simply picked up from experience or learned by imitation (the adjective *empeiros* means "experienced" or "practiced").[29] And yet, as recent scholarship has pointed out, the sophists of the fifth and early fourth centuries B.C. themselves never spoke of an "art of rhetoric" at all. The first attested uses of the terms *rhêtorikê* and *technê rhêtorikê* are in Plato's *Gorgias*, and indeed virtually all surviving uses of these terms before the late fourth century occur only in Plato and Aristotle. Moreover, the art the sophists taught and practiced was not "rhetoric," at least not in the narrow, etymological sense that I considered at the beginning of this chapter.[30]

Just who the sophists were and what they stood for is, in truth, a matter of some vagueness. As a number of scholars have pointed out, the list of persons called *sophistai* by one or another writer in antiquity is quite diverse and extends not only to figures we might recognize today as sophists, such as Protagoras, Gorgias, or Isocrates, but also to poets and philosophers—including Homer, Hesiod, Pythagoras, Socrates, and Plato—as well as an assortment of rhapsodes, musicians, physicians, seers, mythical beings like Orpheus, Prometheus, or the phoenix, and even Jesus Christ. There is, however, a very basic paradigm that holds this rather disparate cast of characters together. For the most part, and excluding the perhaps more whimsical inclusions, the basic *definiens* is a general perception of the "sophist" as a professional intellectual, a "wise man" or "sage," or the possessor, performer, and professor of some special skill (for *sophia* means both "wisdom" and "skill"). The sophist might, perhaps, even be a "wizard," if we think of Gorgias's links to conjuring, or of the sophist Apuleius defending himself (in his *Apologia*) on a charge of using witchcraft to win a rich widow's affections in the second century A.D. In general, the person identified as a *sophistês* was one who claimed or was seen to possess a *sophia* that conferred upon its owner some special power, and who typically made a career of putting this *sophia*'s power on display and offering or selling instruction in it.[31]

For the type of sophist linked to the rise of "rhetoric" we can be somewhat more specific. There is a mainstream notion of "sophist" and "sophistic" that is more or less linked to both rhetorical and philosophico-literary culture and that survives from the fourth century B.C. to the so-called Second Sophistic of the later Roman period. This notion is centered on "sophistic" as what we might call wisdomology, an art or science of "making wise" in the sense of cultivating one's intellect or *phronêsis*, and on the "sophist" as—at a minimum, and whatever else he may be—a maker and usually a performer of epideictic discourse.[32] At the center of this version of sophistic is a concern with the powers and possibilities of *logos*, meaning not only the *logos* of public speech, both epideictic and pragmatic, but also the *logos* of inward thought and reasoning. And indeed *logos* is the term the sophists of the fifth and fourth centuries B.C. almost invariably use to name what they teach and practice.

The reasons for this overpowering sophistic concern with *logos* are most evident in the surviving paraphrases of Gorgias's famous treatise *On the Nonexistent* (which, appropriately, no longer exists), and in his other chief remnants, the *Encomium of Helen* and the *Defense of Palamedes*. In *On the Nonexistent* (77–86), Gorgias argues the surprisingly modernistic thesis that the human mind can neither know nor communicate the true reality of things—if indeed there is any such truth to know—because, in essence, what the human mind can possibly know, believe, or communicate is only a mental representation constructed by means of *logos*, and because *logos* itself has at best a problematic relation to reality (since *logos*, existing in human speech and thought, is not the same thing as the reality it represents). In the *Helen* (8–11), similarly, Gorgias declares that *logos* is a "great potentate" that can "stop fear and banish grief and create joy and nurture pity" as well as shape the "opinion" (*doxa*) that is the soul's chief "counselor" (*symboulos*), the soul having no other source of knowledge. The importance of this point is most evident in Gorgias's statement, in an often overlooked passage, that things in reality do not have the nature we wish them to have, but the nature they actually do have (15)—so that the soul's *logos*-built *doxa* leads it into choices that have real consequences, including "slippery and insecure" successes (11) as well as failures that may be catastrophic and irreversible. This point is emphasized in the *Palamedes*, as Gorgias's Palamedes reminds his judges (as he defends himself on the capital charge of treason) that it is not possible to clearly know the truth of actions by means of *logos* (35) and that a mistaken judgment will nevertheless make them responsible for "a dreadful, godless, unjust, unlawful deed" (36).[33]

There is, in sum, no transcendental or stable truth to which the human mind has any reliable access. We have only our fluctuating, slippery, and uncertain human *logos* by which to interpret, judge, and act within a world of dangers, desires, and probabilities; and the practical consequences of our *logos*-built beliefs, even if they have no certain epistemic truth to rest on, are matters of life and death, pleasure and pain, honor and dishonor, beauty and ugliness. *Logos* is all we have, and our chances for joy depend on the skill and wisdom, the *sophia*, with which we handle it.

The sophist, then, is the possessor-professor-performer of a *sophia* that is grounded in the knowledge and mastery of *logos*, or of a variety of *logoi*, and that confers on its possessor an enhanced capacity for intelligent thought, wise judgment, good counsel, and persuasive speech in all matters of public and private concern. This mastery is what the sophist displays in public (or private, symposiastic) performances of epideictic: if accomplishment in discourse constitutes excellence of mind, then displays of such accomplishment are demonstrations of such excellence. Moreover, such demonstrations, beyond being simple displays or advertisements of the sophist's *sophia*, most significantly function as acts of suasion that make claims upon their listeners' (or readers') thought, and function too as memorable, pedagogic models of eloquence and argument for the sophist's students. In all this the sophist is a successor to, and indeed a new version of, the poet.

Consider, for example, Plato's *Protagoras*, which can be taken (with some caution) as a more or less reliable portrait of the reputed oldest of the sophists.[34] At the beginning of the dialogue we find Socrates' naive companion, the young Hippocrates, believing vaguely and according to popular opinion that a "sophist" is a "knower of wise things" and a "master" of "making awesome talk" (312c–d). Protagoras himself declares that "I admit that I am a sophist and educate people" (317b), claims that his students acquire *euboulia*, "good judgment" in both private and public affairs (318e–319a), and opines that a major part of education is "skill in words," especially "the sayings of the poets" (338e–339a). Protagoras puts his own *sophia* on display in the so-called "Great Speech" (320c–328d), which consists of a lengthy telling and subsequent explaining of a fable concerning the origins of political wisdom, a telling/explaining that Protagoras describes as a *mythos* followed by a *logos* (324d) and that Socrates describes (in his role as narrator of the dialogue) as a "great and fine *epideixis*" that leaves him feeling spellbound (328d). What is meant by skill in "the sayings of the poets" is made evident later in the dialogue, as Protagoras leads his entourage and Socrates into an interpretive/critical debate concerning the intent and truth-value of an argument in a poem by Simonides (339d–347c).

It is evident in these passages that Protagoras's sophistic art is very much a development from the old traditions of poetic discourse. Plato deliberately emphasizes this point by having the sophist identify his predecessors as Homer, Hesiod, Simonides, Orpheus, and Musaeus, as well as a number of athletic trainers, physicians, and music teachers, all of whom he says were "sophists" though they did not use the name (316d–e).[35] The point is further emphasized, moreover, in the comically portrayed relation between Protagoras and his students, which parallels that between a poet and his devotees in Plato's *Ion*. Just as the devotees are bound to the poet like a string of magnetized iron rings descending from a magnet (*Ion* 533d–534b, 535e–536d), so Protagoras's students trail behind him in double file, ambulating back and forth in Callias's courtyard, spellbound by the sophist's "voice like Orpheus" (*Protagoras* 315a–b)—as is Socrates himself when listening to the

Great Speech. (These images can be compared, as well, to that of the companies of souls following their respective gods in the heavenly procession in *Phaedrus* 246a–256d.) Protagoras is not only a descendant of Orpheus, Homer, Hesiod, Simonides, and other poets; he is also gifted with their magic voice and psychagogic power.

If Plato's image of Protagoras is fictive, we can see something like it in the actual career and writings of Isocrates. Isocrates was famed not only as a writer of philosophico-political epideictic *logoi*, which he himself compared to the productions of the poets, but also as the founder of a school famed widely for its production of eminent statesmen, orators, philosophers, historians, and poets too. Dionysius of Halicarnassus calls Isocrates, who was roughly contemporary with (and slightly older than) Plato, the most illustrious teacher of his time, and his school the "image of Athens" in the eyes of Greeks abroad (*Isocrates* 1). In fact, Isocrates' school would prove to be the dominant model of education in antiquity. What is offered at this school Isocrates calls both *logôn paideia*, "discourse education," and *philosophia*, by which he means the pursuit of practical wisdom in all public and private matters. This philosophic discourse education Isocrates defines as a mental gymnastic meant to cultivate, through the critical study and practice of various kinds of discourse, an enhanced *phronêsis* or "intelligence" that is manifest in speech as resourcefulness and artfulness but most especially and importantly as *euboulia*, "good judgment" or "good counsel." The cultivation of *phronêsis/euboulia* requires a *logôn paideia*, as Isocrates argues, because *logos* is not only the faculty by which we persuade others and conduct transactions but also that by which we deliberate matters in our own minds. Discourse is constitutive of intelligence and is its embodiment. As Isocrates declares, one's speaking is the "great sign" of one's *phronêsis*: discourse that is "true and lawful and just" is the "image" of a "good and trustworthy soul" (*Against the Sophists* 14–15; *Antidosis* 181–182, 255–257).[36]

There were, as we should remind ourselves, differences and even sharp disagreements between the specific teachings of individual sophists, as is obvious in Isocrates' effort in *Against the Sophists* to discredit his competitors and present himself as their very antithesis—or, for that matter, in Alcidamas's attack on Isocrates in *On the Sophists*.[37] As people with a professional interest in methods of argumentation and the critical examination of belief, as professional teachers in competition with each other for paying students, and as individuals with differing social and political commitments, the sophists were by trade and inclination a contentious, fractious lot. In general, however, and as the example of Plato's *Protagoras* suggests, sophistic pedagogy was largely centered on the study and imitation of epideictic "demonstration" texts, including both poetry and prose *logoi* as well as, and most centrally, *logoi* composed and performed by the sophist himself.[38] This is what we also see quite clearly at the beginning of Plato's *Phaedrus*, where the adolescent Phaedrus has just come from listening to the sophist Lysias declaim, and is bringing with him a manuscript copy of Lysias's speech in order to memorize and practice it. As Isocrates says in *Against the Sophists*, the student "must learn the kinds of discourse, and be trained in their uses," and to this end the teacher must not only explicate each kind "as exactly as possible so as to leave out nothing that can be taught" but must also "in himself provide such an example that those who have taken its pattern and are able to imitate will quickly show themselves more grown and more graceful in speech than others" (17–18).

The sophist himself, then, was to provide the living model on which the students would pattern themselves, if they were able. The relationship was roughly that of master and apprentice, sage and disciple, mentor and protégé. The epideictic performances of the master might take the form of pseudo-Hesiodic wisdom-lore, as with Protagoras's Great Speech, or some other form of "philosophical" epideictic, as with Isocrates' political panegyrics. Or, as with the productions of a sophist like Critias, they might take the form of lyric or dramatic poetry.[39] But these performances might also take the form of imitations of pragmatic discourse—either fanciful, as in Gorgias's *Palamedes*, or realistic, as in Antiphon's *Tetralogies*. Such fanciful and realistic imitations were, in essence, the beginnings of what were later known in the Roman-Hellenistic school tradition as declamation exercises, the making of bouleutic/advisory or dikanic/judicial speeches (*suasoriae* and *controversiae*) in imaginary practice cases.[40] The sophists' art of *logos*, again, comprised both epideictic and pragmatic discourse, both public speech and private thought.

Further, while the primary medium of the sophist's *epideixeis* (and of the students' own practice performances) was oral delivery, such texts could also be made available in written form. This was common practice in Greek (or at least Athenian) education by the end of the fifth century B.C. It is likely, in fact, that the so-called *technai* or arts written by some of the early sophists were not "handbooks" in the sense of a systematic discussion of techniques, such as we find in the *technê* tradition from Aristotle onward, but simply collections of sample texts illustrating different types of discourse or different ways of handling some particular part of a discourse. (For an explication of these texts and of their principles, one would have to go the sophist himself; such instruction would not come cheap.) A sophist's published "art" or *technê* would thus consist, in effect, of his collected writings, or a sampling of them.[41] Clearly, such collections could include not only out-and-out epideictics (such as wisdom-tracts, panegyrics, poems, etc.) and fictive imitations of pragmatic discourse, but also literary "reproductions" of actual *pragmatika*, or revised copies of the *pragmatika* that many sophists wrote as "speechwriters" (*logographoi*) for various clients. Texts of the latter type would include, in the late fifth and early fourth centuries B.C., the six extant *dikanika* (courtroom speeches) that Isocrates wrote early in his career, and the various *dikanika* and *demegorika* (parliamentary speeches) composed by Antiphon, some of which survive in varying states of completeness and fragmentation. It was this development—the inclusion of pragmatic discourse within the concept of *technê logôn*, and thus the publication of "artistic" pragmatic *logoi*, both fictive and real, as epideictic demonstration texts in written *technai*—that was chiefly responsible for giving the sophists' general discourse art the name *technê rhêtorikê*.

So how did the term emerge?

As I have noted, the word *rhêtôr* first comes into use as a disciplinary term in the fifth century B.C. The term undoubtedly has a long prehistory: the word *rhêtêr* occurs in the *Iliad*, where Phoenix describes himself as teaching Achilles to be a "speaker of speeches" (*mythôn rhêtêr*) and a "doer of deeds" (9.443). But in the fifth and fourth centuries *rhêtôr* denotes a particular civic function that most probably was created by the emergence of democracy at Athens, namely that of a citizen moving proposals or making speeches in a political assembly or court of law.[42] As Mogens Herman Hansen has noted, "[a] citizen was *rhêtôr* in so far as he mounted the *bêma* [platform] and addressed his fellow citizens to make a speech or move a proposal. As a mark of his official status he wore a wreath while addressing the people. When he descended the platform and took off the wreath he was no longer a *rhêtôr*, except that he could still be held responsible for the speech he had made or the proposal he had moved."[43]

In principle, as it appears, any citizen could assume the function of *rhêtôr*. In practice, however, only a few could read and write well enough, or were skillful enough in *logos*, to draw up a proposal, prepare a lengthy speech for an assembly, or risk the hazards of debates and lawsuits. Few, moreover, were willing to try, since the maker of what turned out to be a bad proposal or a failed suit could himself be put on trial and convicted, sometimes with severe (even fatal) consequences. In consequence, by the fourth century there emerged a small, elite class of more or less professional *rhêtores*: men who generally came from aristocratic or wealthy families, who had the requisite education and the confidence, who regularly spoke before the people in civic forums, and who were the dominant force in city politics. These leading citizens had a social role and status comparable to that of career politicians and lawyers today, and like them were regarded with mixed feelings of respect and distrust.[44] By the fourth century B.C., in sum, a *rhêtôr* was what we still think of as an "orator," namely a professional maker of speeches in civic forums.

But while the *rhêtores* most usually came from wealthy and powerful families, a person might also gain wealth, prestige, and power by becoming a *rhêtôr*. There were "gifts," bribes, and fees to be gained by representing the interests of wealthy patrons who themselves were unwilling to have their names attached to lawsuits or proposals that might backfire. The would-be *rhêtôr* of modest means could get a start by being someone else's front man—the term for which was "sycophant" (*sykophantês*)—and from there he might rise in the world, if he possessed the requisite speaking skill to start with. Moreover, even those with no desire to become *rhêtores* or *sykophantai* needed at least a minimal training in public speaking, simply to be able to protect their interests, or themselves, when hauled into court. (Under Athenian law, both accuser and defendant had to argue their cases in person before the court: one could hire a speechwriter, but one would still have to deliver the speech oneself.) The Athenians were litigious people, and bringing indictments or using the threat of indictment as a form of blackmail was a major occupation of the sycophants.[45]

There developed, in consequence, a fairly considerable market for an inexpensive "short course" in the basics of demegoric and dikanic discourse, and especially dikanic discourse. Such instruction was clearly the most novel and most distinctive aspect of sophistic teaching, and it was what drew the largest number of paying customers. The average sophist stood to make a good living by servicing this populous market. The earliest sophistic *technai* that we hear of, those produced in the fifth century by the somewhat shadowy figures Corax and Tisias (now completely lost), apparently were focused on a few basic methods of arguing a case before a court. The earliest sophistic handbook that still survives intact, the *Rhetoric to Alexander* of the late fourth century B.C. is devoted almost entirely to the major genres of civic speechmaking (which it calls *logos politikos*) and gives the overwhelming bulk of its attention to demegoric and dikanic discourse, with comparatively brief discussion of the kinds of epideictic speech a *rhêtôr* might make in a civic forum (eulogies and public denunciations) and an even briefer discussion of what the author calls *exetastikon* or "examination," which he treats not as a separate genre but as a general mode of disputation that appears in all types of public discourse. *Exetastikon*, apparently, is what survives in the *Rhetoric to Alexander* of a more generalized sophistic art of *logos*. Popular perception and popular demand were defining sophistic teaching largely and increasingly in terms of cheap, basic, specialized instruction in the civic speechmaking of the *rhêtôr*.

This perception and demand are satirized in Aristophanes' *Clouds*—in which the hapless bumpkin, Strepsiades, sends first himself and then his spendthrift son to study with the sophists in Socrates' *phrontisterion* or "thinkateria," where all sorts of abstruse (and silly) subjects are being studied, merely to learn how to win lawsuits so he can avoid paying his debts. Such a reductive notion of sophistic teaching, likewise, is what Isocrates chiefly singles out for abuse in his diatribe *Against the Sophists* (9–21) and from which he most wishes to distance his own *logôn paideia*. Isocrates complains that the sophists who cater to popular demand for lessons in pragmatic discourse (and especially in dikanic discourse) seek to "attract great numbers by the smallness of their fees and the largeness of their promises" (9) and by the badness of their teachings bring discredit on himself and all who teach a genuine art of *logos* (11). The teachers who narrowly focus on pragmatic discourse, Isocrates argues, promise to make their students into clever *rhêtores* but actually teach them nothing but "meddlesomeness and greed" (9, 20), offering not a true *logôn paidiea* that cultivates good judgment and inventive thought but only elementary formulae for particular types of speeches (9–13)—by which Isocrates may mean simplistic rules or precepts but most probably means *technai* consisting of ready-made, fill-in-the-blank set speeches for those who cannot afford their own logographers.

We can imagine that the product of such training might be able to stand up in court or the public assembly and, acting as another's mouthpiece (or simply speaking in self-defense), deliver a more or less adequate boilerplate speech with all the usual parts. But Isocrates argues in *Antidosis* (47–50), apparently with the sycophants in mind, that even the most skillful products of such training possess not an art but only an *empeiria* for the routines of particular types of public speaking, are incapable of the "higher" *logos* of philosophical epideictic (such as we see in Isocrates' Panhellenic political panegyrics or Protagoras's Great Speech) and are little more than self-serving, officious busybodies who soon are despised by all that have heard them speechify two or three times in court. On the contrary, Isocrates maintains, the products of a broadly philosophic *logôn paideia* do possess an art that enables them to master any form of discourse they may wish to undertake, and they gain increasing admiration not only for their eloquence, but also (and chiefly) for their intelligence and their genuine usefulness to the city.

At the end of the surviving text of *Against the Sophists* (21), Isocrates invokes the term *rhêtoreia*—"oratory"—to describe what is aimed at by the teachers of pragmatic speechmaking. This is the earliest known use of the term (c. 390 B.C.), and it makes only two other appearances in Isocrates' extant writings (*Panathenaicus* 2 and *To Philip* 26).[46] It may be an Isocratean coinage derived from the term *rhêtôr* or, as seems equally likely, a derivation that has begun to circulate in popular usage. In Isocrates' three surviving uses of it, *rhêtoreia* seems not to be a term that he is using systematically or with a definite technical meaning: it may suggest the characteristic discourse of the *rhêtôr* (in the sense of "oratory") or the act of orating (in the sense of "delivery") or perhaps even the general quality of the "rhetor-y" (in the sense of "eloquence" or impressiveness). Nevertheless, it is equally clear in *Against the Sophists* that Isocrates invokes the notion of *rhêtoreia* in opposition to what he calls *philosophia*, and as the negatively valued element of the pair. He says, "those who wish to submit themselves to the precepts of *philosophia* will be helped more quickly toward reasonability and decency of mind than toward *rhêtoreia*" (21). The opposition, again, is between a general discourse education that aims to cultivate an ethically responsible, well-reasoning, and articulate intelligence, and a newly popular but superficial training that aims only to cultivate a certain rhetor-esque fluency in a handful of civic speech genres. Isocrates, in sum, holds out for the broader tradition of sophistic *logôn technê*, a tradition that includes pragmatic *rhêtoreia*—or has recently come to include it—but that cannot be limited to it, if an art worthy of being taught is to remain.

To take a modern (if somewhat inexact) analogy for what was happening, it is as if the entire enterprise of the discipline of "English" were to become identified almost exclusively with the teaching of business and technical writing. The analogy, of course, is inexact insofar as the discipline of "English" is itself far more narrow than that of an Isocratean *logôn paideia*. To be more comparable, "English" would have to include, at the very least, and in addition to its traditional curriculum, the discipline of speech communication, plus certain aspects of philosophy and political science, and many other disciplines as well. But the analogy is also accurate in this respect: while the teaching of business and technical writing represents a small fraction of the total curriculum of English and can be seen as a (relatively) recent extension of English from its traditional concern with mainly epideictic/"literary" kinds of discourse into more pragmatic kinds, it is also true that teaching business and technical writing draws an enormous clientele and is often by far the most popular (or in-demand) thing an English department does. It is not unusual for the number of students enrolled in business and technical writing courses to rival or exceed the number enrolled in all of an English department's "literary" offerings put together—even if business and technical writing represent only a sliver of that department's curriculum. The demand for such courses is spurred by the fact that large numbers of students see them (quite correctly) as directly relevant to their future careers and thus directly relevant to their personal well-being—just as the Athenian citizen of the early fourth century B.C. could see training in *rhêtoreia* as directly relevant to his (and his family's) personal well-being, and even to his physical survival.

To continue this analogy, imagine that people were to begin thinking of "English" simply as training in business and technical writing, and imagine that there had begun to appear departments of "English" that taught virtually nothing but such courses. Imagine further that people had begun referring to "English" not as

"English" but as (perhaps) "business writing," or "practical writing," or simply as "writing" or, to use the most common (though wildly inadequate) cover term now in use, as "composition." And then imagine that this term shift were to be appropriated by an extremely influential philosopher—or a university president—and that, in the long run, it were to stick. All this imagining would make the analogy reasonably complete. For that is approximately what happens in Plato's invocation of, and in his famous attack on, the name and notion of an "art of rhetoric," *technê rhêtorikê*, and in Aristotle's subsequent effort to recuperate *technê rhêtorikê* as a philosophically respectable discipline. As I will show, these two philosophers invoke "rhetoric" to encode as a distinct discipline a narrowed version of sophistic teaching that is centered on and includes little more than a few genres of pragmatic speechmaking—and yet, at the same time, as a discipline that cannot exist independently of something like a full-fledged *logôn technê*. "Rhetoric" emerges, from the start, as an unstable and problematic term.

From *Rhêtoreia* to *Rhêtorikê*: Plato and Aristotle

At roughly the same time as Isocrates' invocation of the novel term *rhêtoreia*, and probably shortly after it (probably by less than a decade), the equally novel term *rhêtorikê* makes its first known appearance in Plato's *Gorgias* (c. 387–385 B.C.).[47] As Edward Schiappa has argued, there is a strong case for believing that *rhêtorikê* is a Platonic coinage: Plato's writing shows a distinct penchant for neologisms using the *-ikê* formation to indicate an "art of" something, such as *dialektikê*, "dialectic," the "art of" philosophical conversation (*dialexis*).[48] But, as with Isocrates' *rhêtoreia*, it is also possible that Plato is adopting, or adapting to his favorite formation, a term that has begun to surface in popular use. *Rhêtorikê* first appears in Socrates' remark that Polus (a student of Gorgias) "seems to have had more practice in what is called *rhêtorikê* than dialogue" (448d). The Greek that is rendered here as "what is called rhetoric," *tên kaloumenên rhêtorikên*, may have the meaning of "what may be called," to indicate that Socrates is introducing a neologism, but it may also have the sense of "what people call" or "so-called"; both are common Platonic usages. The latter possibility—"the so-called art of rhetoric"—seems viable for *Gorgias* 448d, since at this point Socrates does not appear to be laying down a premise. He is simply responding to Polus's windy nonanswer to the question of what art Gorgias teaches, and he does not define the term but appears to assume (or Plato appears to assume) that it is more or less familiar. In any case, what Socrates seems to mean by *rhêtorikê* at this point is something very like Isocrates' *rhêtoreia*, for Polus's response to the question never actually names or defines the art that Gorgias teaches but launches into what sounds like a canned set speech, studded with flashy Gorgianic figures, eulogizing Gorgias's teaching as "the noblest of the arts" (448c): he speaks not like a participant in a conversation but like a grandiloquent *rhêtôr* before a crowd.

Whether he has invented it or not, the term *rhêtorikê* serves Plato much as *rhêtoreia* serves Isocrates—polemically—with the difference that Plato uses *rhêtorikê* more systematically and uses it to favor his own particular version of philosophy. This is evident already in Socrates' response to Polus's speech, which implicitly sets the Socratic mode of dialogic inquiry in opposition to the rhetor's monologue and establishes the basic tension from which the rest of the *Gorgias* unfolds. As the dialogue progresses, Socrates elicits from Gorgias the declarations—which the real Gorgias almost certainly would not have made—that the *technê* of which he is a "master" (*epistêmôn*) and teacher is *rhêtorikê* (449a–d) and that *rhêtorikê* specifically is an art of *logos* whose end is to persuade "jurors (*dikastai*) in a law court (*dikastêrion*), senators (*bouleutai*) in a senate (*bouleutêrion*), assemblymen (*ekklêsiastai*) in an assembly (*ekklêsia*) and in all other gatherings, any political gathering whatsoever that may convene" (452e). In essence, Plato capitalizes on the popular identification of sophistic teaching with instruction in pragmatic discourse to present and put in question a version of sophistic that is reduced to merely a *technê rhêtorikê*, an "art of the rhetorical," an art of what *rhêtores* do.

What follows from this reduction is the famous attack on *rhêtorikê* as not an art but only an *empeiria* for "flattery," by which a *rhêtôr* with no knowledge of or interest in the truth can demagogically persuade an ignorant crowd on matters of justice and injustice, or anything else, and can even seem more knowledgeable than someone who really knows. Gorgias himself is shown to have an ethics of persuasion, declaring that a *rhêtôr* should use his persuasive power justly and deserves punishment when he does not; and indeed Gorgias asserts that he gives his students instruction in justice, if they need it, as well as in *rhêtorikê* itself (456c–457c; 459b–e). What this amounts to is a recognition that a training in "the art of the rhetorical" cannot stand alone but must be embedded in a broader and more philosophical kind of training, such as Isocrates' *logôn paideia* (or so we might infer)—or even better, from Plato's perspective, a training in Socratic inquiry. Through this recognition, which Socrates calls "splendid" (460a), Gorgias himself is in effect let off the hook by Plato.

But Gorgias's followers, Polus and Callicles, reveal themselves in their ensuing and increasingly bitter dispute with Socrates to be interested in *rhêtorikê* only as an instrument of domination. For Polus, the glory of "good rhetors" is that "they have the greatest power in the *polis*" and can "act like tyrants and put to death anyone they please, and confiscate property and banish anyone they've a mind to" (466a–c). Callicles finds nothing in this view to be apologized for, arguing that it is "natural justice" for the strong to lord it over the weak and that people like Socrates who dabble in philosophy rather than *rhêtorikê* are childish weaklings who can be "slapped in the face with impunity" or for that matter hauled into court and put to death "by any sort of wretched and lowly person" who might decide to prosecute them (482c–486d, 521c). Plato clearly means these ominous words as an allusion to the actual fate of Socrates, as virtually every commentator on the dialogue has noted. Polus and Callicles speak the dreams of the sycophants and represent the potential viciousness that comes of a *technê rhêtorikê* cut loose from the kind of discourse art that Plato would call *philosophia*.

Plato's opposition of *philosophia* (as he defines it) to *rhêtorikê* is handled much more deftly in the later *Phaedrus*. Much of the argument in this dialogue depends on a deliberate slippage, which runs throughout the text, between the terms *technê rhêtorikê* and *logôn technê*, between "rhetorical art" and the more general concept of an "art of discourse." Plato, in fact, explicitly makes an issue of the relation between these terms when Socrates puts to young and unsuspecting Phaedrus the loaded question "Now isn't *rhêtorikê*, taken as a whole, an art of leading the soul (*technê psychagôgia*) through words (*dia logôn*), not only in law courts and in other public assemblies but in private gatherings as well?" (261a). This question, in effect, makes of *rhêtorikê* an Isocratean or Protagorean art of *logos* that applies to all public and private discourse, and that deals (as Socrates' following remarks make clear) with any subject matter whatsoever. The youthful Phaedrus's answer is a revealing and naive reflection of the popular view: "[n]o, by Zeus, not that at all, but a *technê* of speaking and writing mainly in lawsuits, and of speaking too in public assemblies; and more than that I haven't heard" (261b).

For Phaedrus, *rhêtorikê* is purely and simply the art of the *rhêtôr*; that's what people say. Socrates responds to this by playfully asking Phaedrus if he knows the *technai* by "Nestor" (Gorgias), "Odysseus" (Thrasymachus or Theodorus), and "the Eleatic Palamedes" (Zeno)—the first two are identified by Phaedrus, and the third is meant to be quite transparent—and from these references Socrates develops the distinctly Gorgianic argument (from the *Helen*) that those who argue lawsuits or debate proposals in assemblies "contend in speech" (*antilegousin*) and "make opposites appear true," as do those engaged in philosophical disputation (261c–d). This leads to the conclusion that "the art of contention (*antilogikê*) is not confined to law courts and assemblies, but . . . if it's a *technê* at all it will be one and the same in all kinds of speaking" (261d).

Socrates' point is that *rhêtorikê* is not a distinct art but a specialized part of a more general art of *logos* that here goes under the name *antilogikê*—"antilogy" or disputation—a term that evokes not only the sophistic (and originally Protagorean) practice of arguing both sides of any given question but also Socratic dialectic.[49] As the dialogue proceeds, and on the basis of this argument, Socrates continues to shift back and forth (or to move Phaedrus back and forth) between the terms *technê rhêtorikê* and *logôn technê* as if they were interchangeable. This shifting is itself an illustration and demonstration of what Socrates calls the method of argumentative or suasory "deception," *apatê*—a Gorgianic term for persuasion (*Helen* 10)—which consists of "shifting by easy stages from point to point" on the basis of resemblances (*Phaedrus* 261e–262a). Once Phaedrus (and the reader) have accepted the identification of *technê rhêtorikê* with *logôn technê*, or the subordination of the rhetor's art to a more general art of discourse, Plato's Socrates can move to considering what a genuine *logôn technê* must consist of, and thence to the famous conclusion that it must include true knowledge of the subject matters under discussion and the ability to analyze them into their components, as well as knowledge of the different kinds of "souls" and of the methods of effectively speaking to each soul-type (277b–c).

As Socrates convinces Phaedrus, of course, the way to attain these kinds of knowledge is dialectical inquiry. From Socrates' term-conflating account of *technê logôn/rhêtorikê*, then, the argument can "shift by easy stages" to the further conclusions that the true practitioner of such a discourse art must also be a dialectician and that his truest name is not *rhêtôr* but "lover of wisdom," *philosophos*, "or something of that sort" (278d). The dialogue then closes with Socrates instructing Phaedrus to carry this revelation to the sophist Lysias (his teacher) "and the other composers of *logoi*, and to Homer and the other composers of poetry to be recited or sung, and to Solon and all who compose in writing political *logoi* under the name of laws" (278c), thus subsuming poetry, epideictic prose, and civic discourse (including speeches and written laws) under the single heading of—and as the main divisions of—discourse art. In the final lines, significantly, Socrates makes a prophetic gesture toward "my beloved Isocrates" (who at the dramatic date of the dialogue was young), for "in the man's thought there's something of *philosophia*" (279b). Plato is, in effect, citing the source of his basic argument.

In sum, Plato's attack on what he calls *technê rhêtorikê*, like Isocrates' attack on the teachers of *rhêtoreia*, is an attempt to counter a popular but narrowed version of sophistic education focused on basic training in the methods of a few civic speech genres. It is a training whose most notable products are not *rhêtores* of Periclean distinction nor even such distinguished writers and statesmen as issued from Isocrates' school but *sykophantai* with the motives and values of a Polus or a Callicles.[50] Plato's response to this development, like that of Isocrates, is to insist on situating the rhetor's civic practice within a larger, more general, and more philosophic discourse art, and thus within a broader discourse education whose goal is to cultivate an ethically responsible, articulate, and well-reasoning intelligence that is interested as much in political wisdom as in political domination. Plato's difference from Isocrates, of course, is that he does not consider any version of sophistic other than his own an adequate method of *philosophia* or an adequate grounding for the pragmatic art of *rhêtorikê*. Indeed it is likely that a major part of Plato's polemical intent is to cast even Isocrates' *logôn paideia*—the chief competitor to the training offered at the Academy—into the category of mere *technê rhêtorikê*, or at least to disqualify it as *philosophia*. Plato is using his distinguished elder's own argument against him.[51]

Plato's argument about rhetoric recurs, obliquely, in *The Sophist* (a later dialogue than *Phaedrus*). There, the sophist is classed among the *doxomimêtai*, "opinion imitators," who can impress the ignorant but have no real knowledge (267e). The *doxomimêtai*, in turn, fall into two types: one "who can dissemble in long speeches before a crowd" and another who "in private and in short speeches forces his interlocutor to contradict himself" (268b). The first is to be called a "public speaker" (*dêmologikos*) as opposed to the genuine "statesman" (*politikos*) whom he imitates, and the second is to be called "the absolutely real and actual sophist" as opposed to the one he imitates, namely the genuine *sophos*, the person who is truly wise—the Socratic or Platonic dialectician (268b–c). The false imitator of the "statesman" is, in essence, practicing a false version of *rhêtorikê* (though this term does not appear), one that corresponds to the vacuous pseudophilosophy of the sophist (as defined by Plato); whereas, implicitly, the genuine statesman would be practicing a genuinely philosophical version of *rhêtorikê* that corresponds to (Plato's) genuine dialectic. But Plato does not come out and say so. The matter is left standing at this point, and is in fact left to Aristotle.

Aristotle's *Rhetoric*, which alone of all fourth-century sources consistently and systematically uses Plato's term *rhêtorikê* as the name of the art in question, almost certainly had its origin in the discussions that took place at the Academy—and in the lectures that Aristotle himself delivered there, as an afternoon "extension course" on rhetoric, early in his own career.[52] What Aristotle theorizes is precisely the philosophically respectable, statesman's *rhêtorikê* that Plato gestures toward in *Phaedrus* and *The Sophist*. Rhetoric is, as Aristotle famously says in his opening sentence, the *antistrophos* or "counterpart" of dialectic (1.1 1354a); and its "finer" and "more statesmanlike" form is the demegoric discourse of political assemblies (1.1 1354b).[53]

Aristotle's rhetorical ideal is evident in his general (though not consistent) preference for the term *symbouleutikon* as a name for demegoric discourse (e.g., 1.3 1358b), and in his citing of the Areopagus as an example of a well-ordered court of law (1.1 1354a). *Symbouleutikon* suggests primarily the discourse of the *boulê*, the "senate" or council, which deliberated and prepared proposals before they were heard in the *ekklêsia*, the popular assembly, and which appointed the officers who presided over the *ekklêsia's* debates and voting procedures. The *boulê* had a membership of five hundred; the *ekklêsia* could be attended by any citizen, required six thousand participants for a quorum, and by 340 B.C. could accommodate 13,800. The Areopagus originally was a ruling council of aristocrats but was deprived of significant political power in the democratic reforms of 462–461 B.C., and in Aristotle's time was a high court whose duties were restricted mainly to homicide trials (but were expanded again in the 350s). Other cases, including petty lawsuits as well as major political trials, were heard in the more turbulent *dikasteria*, people's courts where large groups of ordinary citizens (hundreds, and possibly a thousand or more at any given trial) were chosen by lot to serve as *dikastai*, jurors.[54]

These preferences—political deliberation over lawsuits, *boulê* over *ekklêsia*, Areopagus over *dikasterion*—may or may not reflect aristocratic sympathies, but they do point to an ideal of rational deliberation carried on in relatively small and dignified assemblies where emotional appeals are kept to a minimum, argumentation is focused on the presentation and interpretation of factual evidence, and comparatively strict standards of relevance and validity can be enforced. What Aristotle prefers, in short, are deliberative assemblies whose discourse can approach the condition of dialectic in a philosophical symposium. This is the Aristotelian ideal speech situation.[55] But Aristotle is enough of a realist to recognize that rhetoric and dialectic are not and cannot be identical. Thus, as he says, skill in the syllogistic argumentation of dialectic will also confer skill in what he calls the enthymematic argumentation of rhetoric, but only when the would-be rhetor understands the differences: for example, enthymematic argument is typically presented not in small-group conversation among disinterested experts but in continuous speech before crowds of persons who may not be able to follow a complex line of reasoning, and whose interests, moods, and passions may considerably affect their judgment (*Rhetoric* 1.1 1355a, 1.2 1357a, 2.1 1377b–1378a).

Aristotle's effort, then, is to describe the civic discourse of *rhêtorikê* as a distinct disciplinary practice that is distinguished from yet related to dialectical *philosophia*. The latter aims at discovering general truths and is practiced mainly in small-group dialogue; the former aims at discovering what is probably wise in particular, contingent situations that present alternative possibilities, and is practiced mainly in continuous monologue addressing large and heterogeneous audiences (1.2 1355b, 1357a). In this way rhetoric and dialectic are distinct. But *rhêtorikê* is also a "counterpart of dialectic" and as such is subsumed within a more philosophical art of *logos* and located (somewhat as with Isocrates) within the general domain of political and ethical philosophy (1.2 1356a).

This dual effort produces an enormously powerful and illuminating account of informal reasoning and argument—to which I will return in chapter 6—but it also produces ambiguities and tensions. As an empirical describer of real world discourse practices, Aristotle focuses on the specific speech genres practiced by the actual *rhêtôr* and dealt with in the narrowly pragmatic *technai:* symbouleutic (or demegoric) speeches delivered in political assemblies, dikanic speeches delivered in courts of law, and civic epideictics (speeches of praise or blame) delivered on ceremonial occasions. However, as the theorizer of a somewhat idealized model of philosophical rhetoric, Aristotle also turns his three rhetorical genres into abstract universal types. Thus symbouleutic discourse, for example, is treated not only as the type(s) of speech presented before political assemblies, but also as discourse that is concerned with the future, dealing with the probable advantages and disadvantages of a proposed course of action. Dikanic discourse, likewise, is treated not only as the type(s) of speech presented before law courts, but also as discourse that is concerned with the past, dealing with the justice or injustice of deeds that have been performed. And epideictic discourse is not only the type(s) of speech presented in non-pragmatic ceremonial settings, but is also discourse concerned with the present, dealing with the honorable and the dishonorable in personal character and action (1.3 1358b). This all too tidy classification scheme obscures the historically and socially determined specificity of the speech genres Aristotle is describing, and tends to make of them a set of timeless paradigms with only an approximate correspondence to actual speaking practices.[56]

It would be silly to say that Aristotle's setting up of timeless paradigms is wrong. After all, as Aristotle says, the function of an "art" is not to theorize about particular instances but about general principles (1.2 1356b–1357a), principles the skilled practitioner can then apply creatively and differently in different circumstances. One can argue, moreover, that the dominant purpose of the *Rhetoric* is not to neutrally describe and teach contemporary practices, which, from Aristotle's perspective as from Plato's, are liable to corruption and viciousness. Aristotle's purpose, rather, is to elaborate a reconceptualized, corrective image of *rhêtorikê* in order to promote a more intellectually and ethically responsible civic discourse.[57]

But the only way that Aristotle's taxonomy can be made to work, and in truth the way it usually has been made to work, is by simply disengaging the situational forum-and-function aspect of the definitions from the universalizing time-and-subject aspect, and by treating the three rhetorical genres as general argumentative modes defined by the kinds of questions they deal with, modes that occur at least potentially (and for the most part actually) in both epideictic and pragmatic discourse. But when "rhetoric" has been defined as a "counterpart of dialectic," a general art of reasoning and argument dealing with questions of advantage, honor, and justice in any kind of discourse—which brings us back to Plato's equivocation between *technê rhêtorikê* and *logôn technê*—there is no longer any need to identify "rhetoric" exclusively or narrowly with the characteristic genres of the professional *rhêtôr*. That this is so is at least tacitly recognized throughout the *Rhetoric*, perhaps most notably in Aristotle's pronounced habit of citing examples drawn from poetry as well as (though much less frequently) historical and philosophic writings, in addition to examples from the kinds of civic oratory he is ostensibly concerned with. Indeed, the poets and the other nonorators whom Aristotle cites provide the *Rhetoric* not only with examples of style and structure (in book 3) but also with examples of both general topoi and specific lines of argument for symbouleutic, epideictic, and dikanic arguments (e.g., 1.6–15, 2.19–24, and elsewhere). In Aristotle's treatment of it, as in Plato's, "rhetoric" cannot be detached from a more general art of *logos,* and indeed the "art" of rhetoric cannot be contained within the relatively narrow range of civic genres its very name implies.

In sum, both Plato and Aristotle invoke or appropriate the term *rhêtorikê* as the name for a distinct disciplinary practice that can be differentiated from philosophy—and from poetry and history as well—and that can at least potentially become a *technê* whose principles may be theorized and taught as a form of knowledge. Plato invokes *rhêtorikê* mainly to critique the narrowly pragmatic *technai* that popular demand has brought into existence, and the sycophantic rhetorical practices those *technai* all too easily serve, whereas Aristotle responds to that critique by reconstructing a philosophically respectable and ethically responsible version of *rhêtorikê.* In doing so, however, both adopt the fundamentally (or originally) Isocratean position that a genuine "art" of *rhêtorikê* cannot exist apart from, or must be embedded in, a broadly "philosophic," *wisdom-loving* discourse art and education, though they differ from Isocrates (and to some degree from each other) on what counts as "philosophic."

In effect, and despite their differences, Isocrates, Plato, and Aristotle all agree with Hesiod, or at least with Hesiod's account of eloquence. The discourse of the truly eloquent and truly sage *rhêtôr,* like that of Hesiod's eloquent and good *basileus*—discourse that is truly "the Muses' sacred gift to humankind" because it fosters justice, peace, and good judgment in civic and private life—arises from a *logôn technê* whose preeminent paradigms of eloquence and wisdom are embodied in the proliferating, much-ramified realm of epideictic, a realm that by the fourth century B.C. has come to include not only the (now rather antique) genres of sung and spoken poetry, but also the "modern" prose genres of history, philosophy, sophistic *epideixeis* on all sorts of topics, philosophicosophistic disputation and dialectic, declamatory imitations of pragmatic discourse, and literary imitations of actual *pragmatika.* It is this general recognition of the deeper, broader sources of the truly good and eloquent rhetor's art, coupled with the proliferating variousness of epideictic, that makes *rhêtorikê* from the start an equivocal, paradoxical term. From the moment it enters Western thought, *rhêtorikê* is invoked as the name for a specialized art of pragmatic discourse *that cannot exist* in and of itself, an art that cannot be centered or narrowly contained within the pragmatic realm, if it is to produce anything worth desiring. *Rhêtorikê* from the beginning is the misname of an art that keeps resolving itself back into, or that simply becomes, or that always was, something like an Isocratean *logôn technê.*

Or *rhêtorikê* is invoked as the synechdochic name for such an art, marking the larger and more general whole by what has become, in the fourth century B.C., its most novel and most distinctive aspect. In this particular sense, the conventional tale is true: the name and notion of an "art of rhetoric" arises from the fourth-century formation of the rhetor's practice as a conceptualized *technê*. But, as the argument of this chapter has suggested, the truth of that tale is limited. Only the *name* arises from the rhetor's practice, not the "art" itself, or at least not the whole art or the art's foundations. The deeper truth, or the truer tale whose outlines I have traced, is that the discourse art that acquires the misname or the synechdochic name of "rhetoric" originates from the expansion and ramification of the archaic poetic/epideictic domain from sung to spoken verse, then to the "prose poetry" of *logos*, and thence to the domain of *logos* generally—a process that is powerfully driven by the advent of literacy in Greek culture and the consequent displacement of memorious song by scripted prose—proceeding finally to the ultimate inclusion of declamatory and "literary" versions of the rhetor's discourse within an epideictic-centered *logôn technê*. What this tale suggests is that the process of "literaturization," far from being a symptom of "rhetoric" in decadence or decline, is in fact a major cause of its emergence.

What have we come to, then? By the mid–fourth century B.C., the general domain of discourse is mapped out somewhat asymmetrically, and is marked by terms that have varying degrees of specificity and (in-)stability. On one hand, there is a demarcation between *poiêsis*, a fairly fixed term specifically meaning versified or sung discourse, and *logos*, meaning "discourse" in a very general sense that includes public, spoken or written prose of all varieties as well as private, reasoned thought. On the other hand, there is also a demarcation between the general category of *logos* and the category of *rhêtoreia* or *rhêtorikê*, which in its narrowest sense refers to the pragmatic oratory of the professional *rhêtôr*. There thus appears to be a separating out of "poetry" and "rhetoric" from the general domain of "discourse" as distinct discursive practices, or as the practices of distinct groups of professionals. But, as we have seen, the terms of this demarcation are not stable. *Logos*, meaning "discourse" in general, can (and does) subsume poetic discourse as one of its varieties; "poetry" is both differentiated from *logos* (in the sense of "song" as opposed to "speech") and part of it; and epideictic *logos* is to some degree explicitly recognized as a newer form of poetry. And *rhêtorikê*, as the equivocal misname or synechdoche for the art of *logos* in a broad or general sense, thus implicitly subsumes all forms of *logos*—including both poetic *logos* and inward thought, as well as all varieties of "prose"—as part of its domain. Thus the suasive eloquence of "poetry" is at once a subset of the general art of "rhetoric" and at the same time is its ancient ancestor. Further, insofar as epideictic is the "primary" or central form of rhetoric, and poetry is the original and ultimate form of epideictic (or is understood as such), poetry is also the original and ultimate form of rhetoric. These implications, while mostly tacit in the tumbling, unstable terms of fourth-century thought, become, as I will show, explicit in the rhetorical tradition of later antiquity.

PART II

"RHETORIC" IN
LATER ANTIQUITY
A Short Revisionist History

3

Hellenistic Rhetoric

It's common to think of rhetoric as falling into decadence and decline in later antiquity, under Hellenistic kings and Roman emperors. And yet this period culminates in what has been called the "Greek renaissance" of the first to third centuries A.D., a "grand baroque age" of astonishing cultural vitality in which rhetoric, rhetoricians, and rhetorical literature seem highly prominent, prolific, and influential—the period that Philostratus called the Second Sophistic.[1] How is this "decline"?

Certainly, if one starts from the traditional presumption that "rhetoric" is originally, primarily, essentially an art of pragmatic oratory whose paradigmatic scenes are the civil forums of a democratic polity, then it would seem that "rhetoric's" fortunes must logically rise and fall with those of democracy. This presumption (abetted by others, such as a romantic-modernist antithesis between the practical and the aesthetic) defines an a priori plot that will structure, organize, and suppress, perhaps even produce, historical particulars according to its own internal logic, whether or not that logic is actually grounded in the particulars it organizes and suppresses. What results is a repeating tale of (brief) fluorescence and (lengthy) decay, in which "rhetoric" twice rises and falls. In rough outline, the traditional tale goes somewhat as follows.

Greek rhetoric reaches its acme in the fourth century B.C., in Athens, and most notably in Aristotle (for theory) and Demosthenes (for practice), both of whom die in 322 B.C. Demosthenes dies a martyr to democracy, in a doomed struggle against the imperial ambitions of Philip of Macedon and Alexander the Great: having led a failed rebellion against the conquering Macedonians, the great *rhêtôr* escapes to the sanctuary of Poseidon on the island of Kalauria (modern Poros) and there commits suicide in the sacred enclosure by chewing the poisoned tip of his pen while his Macedonian pursuers wait outside.[2] With the defeat of Athens and the subjugation of the Greek city-states to Macedonian hegemony, with Alexander's conquest and creation of a vast Hellenized empire, with the breakup of that empire after Alexander's death into the successor kingdoms of Egypt, "Asia," and Macedonia/Greece, and with the centers of political, cultural, and economic power shifting to such cities as Alexandria and Pergamon, the great moment of Greek (or Athenian) democracy fades away. And so, in the traditional tale, the great moment of Greek rhetoric fades away too. Presumably rendered insignificant in a world of autocratic potentates, rhetoric becomes (according to this tale) mainly an art of high-cultural display, an empty formalism, a school-bred exercise in bellettristic aestheticism for an elite and increasingly academic literary culture. "Asianism," a florid style "more reminiscent of Gorgias than of the Attic orators of Athens,"[3] comes into vogue. At the same time, with the emergence of the great libraries and intellectual centers at Alexandria and Pergamon, and with the development of an increasingly learned and sophisticated literary scholarship, the theory of rhetoric undergoes considerable elaboration and refinement in the Hellenistic schools—producing by the middle of the second century B.C. the standard version of what we still recognize today as "classical rhetoric"—though these developments, according to this tale, chiefly serve the interests of scholastic pedantry and bellettristic criticism.[4]

The story then repeats itself. The great age of Roman rhetoric belongs (the story says) to the period of the later republic, beginning sometime in the second century B.C., when the expansion of the Roman state has brought it into contact with the Hellenistic world, and when Greek rhetoricians and rhetoric schools begin to appear at Rome.[5] This age of Greek-inspired, republican eloquence then culminates in the brilliant civil oratory (and rhetorical theory) of Cicero. Parallel to Demosthenes, Cicero dies in 43 B.C. defending the doomed republic—he is murdered by Antony's thugs, and a spike put through his tongue—amid the turmoil and civil war that by 29 B.C. would produce the emperor Augustus. Augustus, in essence, takes on the role of a Hellenistic king, a *basileus*, as do all subsequent Roman emperors. Thus, with the civil forum subjected to imperial authority, there comes once more (by logical necessity, in this tale) the decline of rhetoric into secondary, "literaturized," epideictic forms, and the complementary corruption of poetic discourse by rhetoricality. We subsequently pass to the Second Sophistic, the general Hellenization of Roman literary culture, and the continuing elaboration of rhetoric as literary theory in the schools, as the virile virtues of the Romans gradually rot away.

But, as in the preceding chapters, there is a somewhat different—and more probable—tale that we can tell. In this chapter and the next, I shall reconsider the fate of "rhetoric" in the Hellenistic and Roman worlds.

Developments in the Hellenistic Period

It is often said that not a great deal is known about rhetoric in the Hellenistic period—the span of about three centuries that is conventionally dated from Alexander's death in 323 B.C. to the Roman conquest of Greece in 146 B.C., or to the crowning of the emperor Augustus in 29 B.C., at which point nearly all the Greek-speaking world in the eastern Mediterranean, North Africa, and Asia Minor had come under Roman rule. The Hellenistic world continued to exist for many centuries within the Roman Empire, and parts of it survived as the Byzantine Empire up to the fifteenth century. But from the Hellenistic "period" itself we have no surviving examples of civic oratory, compared to the relative wealth of examples from fourth-century Athens.[6] We do, however, hear of famous Hellenistic orators, such as the sophist Hegesias of Magnesia, the supposed paragon of "Asianist" style, who flourished around 250 B.C.; and we have reports of speeches delivered on significant occasions, particularly those in Polybius's history of the Roman conquest. Further, numerous papyrus fragments from Hellenistic Egypt and stone inscriptions from other parts of the Hellenistic world provide us with examples of schoolroom declamation exercises, documentation of judicial and legislative proceedings, and fragments of legal codes.[7]

We do not have many examples of rhetoric manuals or treatises on rhetoric of the Hellenistic period, either, although we do know that rhetorical theory underwent considerable development, as did Hellenistic literary theory generally. There appears to have been a tendency to multiply terms, and to subdivide rhetoric (or instruction in it) into constituent "parts"—the parts of rhetoric, the genres of rhetoric, the parts of an oration, the types of style, and so forth—and to analyze each, with increasing refinement and elaboration, into systematically organized collections of highly specific, identifiable methods and techniques. The major contributors to these developments are generally considered to be Theophrastus, who in 323 B.C. succeeded Aristotle as head of the Peripatetic school, and Hermagoras of Temnos, a sophist who flourished around 150 B.C. Theophrastus extended and developed Aristotelian theory, making probably his most distinctive contributions to stylistics. In particular, he is thought to have developed what became the classical notions of the "four virtues" of style (purity/correctness, clarity, appropriateness, ornamentation/figuration) and of the "three styles" or stylistic types (the low/plain, the middle/figured, and the grand/forceful); to have developed a fuller account of prose rhythm than Aristotle had provided; and to have developed an influential theory of delivery (which Aristotle had not provided at all). Hermagoras's most significant contribution to what became "classical" rhetoric was stasis theory, in essence a system for locating the type of question at issue and selecting the appropriate topics of argument invention for any given case. Hermagoras appears as well to have formalized what became the traditional division of rhetoric into its five "parts" (invention, arrangement, style, memory, delivery). The Stoics also taught rhetoric, and from Stoic *grammatikê*—literary analysis and exegesis—there developed what became the classical taxonomy of tropes and figures in rhetoric manuals (and style handbooks) from the Roman period onward. The other philosophical schools, which were more typically hostile to *rhêtorikê*, appear to have made no major contributions to its theory, although by the end of the Hellenistic period the Academics and Epicureans seem to have included some more or less derivative version of rhetorical instruction in their repertoire. We hear, for example, of the Academic Philo of Larissa among the youthful Cicero's rhetorical preceptors (*Tusculan Disputations* 2.9, *Brutus* 306), as well as Epicureans, Stoics, and the Rhodian sophist Apollonius Molon. The Epicurean philosopher Philodemus of Gadara, one of Cicero's contemporaries and a teacher of Virgil (and himself a writer of erotic verse), wrote lengthy, multivolume treatises on rhetoric and poetics, substantial fragments of which still survive.[8]

But, despite all this activity, virtually nothing remains of the primary sources on rhetoric from the Hellenistic period itself. We have none of Theophrastus's writings on rhetoric or poetics (with the exception of his *Characters*), none either from the Stoics or the other philosophical schools, and nothing at all of Hermagoras. The only genuinely Hellenistic treatise that still survives is *On Style* (*Peri Hermēneias*), a work ascribed by tradition since the first century B.C. to the statesman-scholar Demetrius of Phaleron—a student of Theophrastus, and for a time the governor of Athens (317–307 B.C.) under the Macedonian king Cassander, before becoming an advisor to Ptolemy Soter (king of Egypt 323–282 B.C.) and helping to establish the library of Alexandria. Though modern scholarship doubts the traditional ascription of *On Style* to "the Phalerean" and the dating is problematic, it does appear to have been written by someone named Demetrius probably sometime around 275 B.C., and to reflect Theophrastian or Peripatetic theory.[9]

Aside from *On Style*, the main surviving representatives of Hellenistic rhetorical instruction are three texts that frame the period. The first of these is the *Rhetoric to Alexander* (*Rhêtorikê pros Alexandron*), a manual of *politikos logos* of the late fourth century B.C. that is generally ascribed to the sophist Anaximenes of Lampsakos, who reputedly was one of Alexander's tutors and companions. The *Rhetoric to Alexander* generally is understood as a redaction of fourth-century sophistic teaching but, as I will show, it also can be read as an early Hellenistic document. Our other two surviving representatives, at the other end of the Hellenistic period, are a pair of Roman rhetoric manuals produced in the early first century B.C.: the *Rhetorica ad Herennium* (*Rhetoric to Herennius*), by an unknown author, perhaps a certain Cornificius, who for centuries was misidentified as Cicero; and Cicero's genuine but youthful and incomplete *De Inventione* (*On Invention*). Both texts are considered to be for the most part writeups of their authors' school lessons—Cicero was at most nineteen years old when he composed *De Inventione*—and both are thought to reflect the state of mainstream Hellenistic rhetorical instruction at the end of the second century B.C.[10]

The absence of preserved Hellenistic oratorical texts and the highly technical, formalistic character of the manuals that survive, combined with the presumptions that underlie traditional histories of rhetoric, have contributed greatly to the view that "rhetoric," meaning pragmatic oratory, fell into desuetude under the Hellenistic kings and was reduced to little more than an art of schoolroom declamation exercises and sophistical displays, while the rhetorical teachings of the schools themselves became increasingly pedantic and bellettristic. This view, however, is not particularly credible, and the reverse may very well be true. In the first place, arguments from silence or from absent evidence are dubious when one considers the vagaries of preservation (and nonpreservation) of ancient texts. The fact that we do not possess Hellenistic oratorical texts does not mean there were none worth preserving. Hegesias, for example, seems to have been widely talked about, and according to Dionysius of Halicarnassus he left behind a "large volume of writing" (*On Composition* 18); and he clearly was important enough for Dionysius to single him out for criticism.[11] And the speeches reported in Polybius's history of the Roman conquest, speeches delivered in embassies and assemblies, clearly were instances of skilled pragmatic rhetoric responding to, and shaping, momentous political occasions. Further, we have reasons to believe that, in general, there was no significant diminution in the opportunities for pragmatic rhetoric, or for the practicing *rhêtôr*, in the Hellenistic period.

Let me dwell on this point awhile.

In the Hellenistic period, Hellenic cities—Greek colonies—were established as far east as present-day Afghanistan. Transplanted Greeks and Hellenized non-Greeks formed a political and cultural elite that was layered over indigenous subject populations, such as Egyptians in the Nile valley or the various "Asian" peoples of the former Persian empire. Though Alexander's empire had fractured into the domains of Egypt, "Asia," and Macedonia/Greece, together these comprised a cosmopolitan social-cultural sphere, the so-called *oikoumenê*, in which a Greek (or Hellenized non-Greek) could travel about with relative freedom. There were ample opportunities, within this world, for the enterprising, Greek-speaking, Greek-educated male to seek his fortune. We hear, for example, of a certain Aetolian named Skopas who was turned out of office at home (in present-day Turkey, or "Asia") and so set out to try his luck at Alexandria, becoming within three years the *stratêgos* or "general" of the army of King Ptolemy V. It was a world in which Greek colonials became extraordinarily conscious of their Greekness, in which Greekness and the Greek *paideia* were prerequisites for membership in the sociopolitical elite, and in which a prosperous, educated Greek (or Hellenized non-Greek) could rise to wealth and power by selling his services abroad. Even if he did not rise to the top, like Skopas, he still could reach a position of local importance in one or another city.[12]

As far as we know, the Greek cities of the Hellenistic world normally were equipped with the traditional organs of Greek politics: a *boulê* or council, an *ekklêsia* or people's assembly, and *dikasteria* or courts of law, as well as various other kinds of traditional magisterial bodies (in differing variations). Such organs are attested for virtually all Hellenistic cities for which we have surviving records. We know, moreover, that Alexander gave all the seventy cities he founded at least the outward forms of a democratic constitution and that the Greek cities he considered loyal allies were granted *eleutheria kai autonomia*, "freedom and self-rule," a status that was partly fictional but that also did confer a genuine degree of sovereignty.[13] Ultimately, of course, the courts and assemblies of all Greek cities in a Hellenistic kingdom were under the king's authority, and they were not fully representative either, insofar as participation was limited to Greek and Hellenized citizens, who actually may have been a minority in their city (as at Alexandria). But this does not mean that a Hellenistic city's political bodies were merely ornamental or without real function. In general, a Hellenistic monarch stood as the guarantor of justice and the ultimate tribunal or "supreme court" for both the Greek and non-Greek populations under his authority, hearing complaints, appeals, and petitions, arbitrating disputes between cities, and issuing edicts in matters that involved powerful interests or that had more than local implications. Otherwise, however, Hellenistic kings normally did not interfere in their cities' local affairs or laws. Even when they did interfere, the kings themselves were likely to preserve at least a formal respect for democratic institutions, or for the principles and procedures of legality and justice—a respect on which their legitimacy depended—by having their decrees enacted into law, or "ratified," by city assemblies. The cities of the Hellenistic world, in sum, were able to exercise a substantial measure of autonomy over their local affairs, legislate for themselves in most matters, and judge the cases that came up in their local courts. And certainly the Greeks never ceased to be litigious people: there would have been no shortage of lawsuits and disputes between private persons or of appeals to the king's tribunals. There was plenty of work for the practicing *rhêtôr*.[14]

But the most significant forums for pragmatic rhetoric, or those in which it exercised most power in a Hellenistic kingdom, would have been those provided by the royal bureaucracy. At its highest level, this typically included the king's *synedrion* or "council," which was composed of the monarch's appointed administrators and advisors, who bore the official title of *philoi*, "friends." This was a Macedonian institution that passed from Alexander to his successors, though the original Macedonian term was not *philoi* but *hetairoi*, "comrades." The *philoi* of a Hellenistic king typically were drawn from all over the Greek-speaking world, were chosen for their ability, and were ranked according to their closeness to the monarch (the king's actual, personal friends and close relations were likely to be called by some other title, such as *syngênes* or "kinsman," which placed them both outside and above the official hierarchy of *philoi*). The kings frequently called meetings of their *synedrion* to consult, receive guidance, or obtain approval on questions of policy, administrative matters, and important judicial decisions. These were not necessarily rubber-stamp assemblies. A king would often need the counsel of his *philoi* on particular matters beyond his personal expertise, or would need to test their reactions to a decision or policy that he was contemplating, especially when powerful interests were at stake. A *synedrion* provided genuine occasions for symbouleutic and dikanic discourse. Beyond their roles as councilors and jurists in the *synedrion*, moreover, the *philoi* performed a variety of bureaucratic, political, and judicial functions, such as management of the royal archives and the treasury, handling correspondence, receiving ambassadors, hearing petitions and appeals that did not require the monarch's personal attention, acting as presiding officers in the courts and assemblies of the royal capital, and serving in ambassadorships, military commands, and provincial governorships. Moreover, the *philoi* serving as provincial governors held tribunals of their own, thus acting as a higher court above the local courts, or as a proxy for the king's tribunal. Like the king, the governors had their staffs of local administrators and advisors, *philoi* of the *philoi*, most of whom were drawn from the citizen body under the governor's authority. A governor's *philoi* could include both ethnic Greeks and Hellenized non-Greeks.[15]

There was, in sum, a hierarchy of civil forums in a Hellenistic kingdom where the Greek-speaking, Greek-educated, skilled *rhêtôr* could transact power and win a reputation—from the local courts and assemblies of individual cities to the tribunals of the governors and their magistrates, to the king's tribunal and (for a chosen few) the royal *synedrion* itself. Clearly, within this more or less pyramidal hierarchy the local courts and assemblies possessed a lower degree of political prestige and power, while providing the greatest number of opportunities for pragmatic rhetoric, or for starting an oratorical career. But rhetorical skill, persuasive eloquence, was an essential skill in any of a Hellenistic kingdom's civil and bureaucratic forums. And there were significant rewards for the successful. A local *rhêtôr* who won distinction and made friendships among (or did favors for) the powerful might gain appointment to the local governor's administration, or might be chosen by his fellow-citizens to go as an ambassador to the king's tribunal, and from such positions and with good fortune he might gain entry to the circles of the *philoi*. (Or, like Skopas of Aetolia, he could offer his services abroad.) This was a world in which pragmatic rhetoric was hardly dead. It was, as well, a world of political patronage, in which the ambitions of rhetorically skillful *sykophantai* could fulfill themselves spectacularly. The person skilled in eloquence and argument, and trained moreover in the methods of dikanic and demegoric/symbouleutic discourse, enjoyed considerable opportunity—whatever his motives might be—and the person who lacked such training was at a considerable social and political disadvantage. It thus comes as no surprise that rhetorical training remained central to the Hellenistic ideal of *enkyklios paideia*, the "rounded education," and that rhetoricians prospered in the Hellenistic world.[16] Far from being merely a genteel ornament providing a veneer of "Hellenism," rhetorical training was directly relevant to the practical needs of public and private life, and was particularly relevant to personal ambition.

It is in this context, then, that we should view the known developments in Hellenistic rhetoric. And what is most evident is that, while "rhetoric" continues to be understood in more or less Isocratean terms as (or as part of) a general art of eloquence and argument, an epideictic-centered *logôn technê* that applies to any sort of discourse and that finds its practical application in the civil forums of a Hellenistic kingdom, it also continues to be understood, more narrowly and probably more popularly, as an "art" consisting chiefly of basic, practical instruction in the methods of dikanic and demegoric discourse. It is this narrower view, and the rhetorical practice it supports, that seems predominant in the Hellenistic period. Or so it appears in the main surviving representatives of Hellenistic rhetorical instruction, to which I now turn: the *Rhetoric to Alexander*, the Theophrastian discourse art embodied in Demetrius's *On Style*, and the Hermagorean rhetoric reflected in the *Rhetorica ad Herennium* and Cicero's *De Inventione*.

The *Rhetoric to Alexander*

In the introductory "letter" that prefaces this text, the writer—presumably (though not necessarily) Anaximenes of Lampsakos—pretends to be Aristotle lecturing the young Alexander on the benefits of "holding fast" to what he calls *logôn philosophia*, the "philosophy of discourse" (1421a), though what he specifically offers in his opening sentence is a manual of *tas methodous tôn politikôn logôn*, "the methods of political discourse" (1420a). (This "letter from Aristotle" was, of course, the basis for the long misidentification of the *Rhetoric to Alexander* as an Aristotelian text, and thus its preservation as part of the Aristotelian canon.) It is worth noting that neither the "letter" nor the subsequent text describes what it is teaching as *rhêtorikê*, the art of the *rhêtôr*, except in the title, which is almost certainly some later copyist's addition. The probability that Anaximenes/"Aristotle's" teaching derives from a more generalized *logôn technê* but is also oriented toward a clientele interested in learning pragmatic rhetoric, is suggested partly by what we know about Anaximenes himself: that he was a sophist, that he was from Asia (Lampsakos was on the western coast of present-day Turkey), that he accompanied Alexander on his Asian campaign, and that he wrote histories (of Philip, Alexander, and Greece) as well as treatises on rhetoric and poetry, in addition to being a speechwriter and a practicing orator in both political debates and lawsuits. Dionysius of Halicarnassus describes him as "wishing to be foursquare," an all-round virtuoso, "in all the types of discourse" (*Isaeus* 19). Anaximenes, in short, appears to have taught and practiced a sophistic discourse art that included both epideictic/"literary" and pragmatic/"oratorical" genres.[17] But the probability is suggested chiefly by the suasory moves of the text itself.

In his opening "letter," Anaximenes/"Aristotle" tries to persuade young "Alexander" that it is "kingly" for him to "hold fast" to the "philosophy of discourse" and specifically "the methods of political discourse" for several reasons. The prime reason, he says, is that in "nations under kingly leadership," matters are decided with reference not to law but to *logos*, "discourse/reason" (1420a). This is a reference, it would seem, to the *logos* of the royal tribunals and the *synedrion,* over which the royal *logos* is the ultimate rule, though it is still susceptible to the persuasive force of other *logoi* presented by the speakers there. Here we must recognize that in a Hellenistic kingdom, where each city retained its own laws and constitution, and where the royal edict-law was for the most part a collection of ad hoc judgments and pronouncements made in response to particular petitions or emergent problems, there neither was nor could have been any uniform or systematic legal code. Litigants and petitioners in royal tribunals would have been arguing from differing, inconsistent, and at times incompatible legal precedents and precepts derived from their local traditions. It was thus inevitable that *logos* rather than *nomos* ("law" or custom-law) would be the arbiter of disputes in such a forum. What counted as "justice" was virtually to be determined anew each time. Anaximenes' second main reason for "holding fast" to the "philosophy of discourse" follows from the first, and is notably Isocratean: he says that the use of *logos* rather than bestial force to regulate both private and public life is quintessentially human, fundamentally "noble" (*agathos*), and universally praised, and therefore is something a good *basileus* should excel at (1420a–b)—an argument as old and authoritative as the tradition Hesiod gives voice to in his "Hymn to the Muses." Thus "Alexander" should "resolve to know the mother-city itself of good deliberation" (1420b) and recognize that "educated discourse" (*logos meta paideias*) is the *hegemôn* or "guide" of life, just as "the general is the preserver of the army" (1421a).

These sentiments sound much like a short, two-drachma version of the standard Isocratean or sophistic encomium of *logôn paideia,* "discourse education." But they are dropped at the letter's end. Our teacher declares abruptly that "these and similar things" may be "set aside" *kata ton hyparchonta kairon,* "at the present time" (or, more literally, "under the emergent circumstances") and then he turns to another line of talk. In a brief passage, he acknowledges that he has been commanded "not to allow this book to come into the possession of anyone else whatever"; he excoriates "the so-called Parian sophists" for selling the plagiarized teachings of others; and then he exhorts young "Alexander" not to let "these discourses" fall into anyone else's hands lest they become corrupted (1421a). No modern reader thinks it likely that Anaximenes—or whoever may have added this "letter from Aristotle" to the text—has written these remarks for Alexander. A papyrus fragment of the *Rhetoric to Alexander* dating to the first half of the third century B.C. has been discovered in Egypt, suggesting that the text was widely disseminated, probably in rhetoric schools, within twenty five to seventy five years after Alexander's death.[18] This book is, or was, a popular textbook, and it seems that the letter-writer is making an appeal to the practical ambitions of his actual or potential readership. Here are revealed, as the (probably youthful) reader is asked to imagine, the secret "methods of political discourse" that Aristotle once upon a time taught Alexander. Here is revealed the insider's art of speaking in a king's *synedrion*. What we see in this "letter" from Anaximenes/"Aristotle," then, is a sophist addressing a *logôn technê* to an audience or clientele consisting mainly of ambitious young men or boys (and their parents) of sufficient wealth to pay for lessons at the sophist's school or to buy a copy of the textbook (which would have been expensive), an audience/clientele that dreams of entering the political elite and wants to learn how to speak in the civil forums of a Hellenistic kingdom.[19]

Accordingly, what we find in the *Rhetoric to Alexander* proper is a manual that shows its derivation from a broader sophistic *logôn technê* but that is adapted to the satisfaction of its customers' desires. Of the *Rhetoric to Alexander*'s thirty eight chapters, the middle twenty three—comprising, however, only about one-third of the text—are devoted to a succinct overview of general principles of argument and style, principles that look for the most part to be derived from earlier, fourth-century sophistic teachings.[20] This core material is framed and overwhelmed by an explicit focus on pragmatic discourse. Thus the first chapter introduces the kinds of *politikos logos* "we shall employ" in *koinai dêmêgoriai*, "common assemblies," in *symbolaia dikaiologiai*, "legal arguments about contracts," and in *idiai homiliai*, "private discussions" (1421b). These kinds are demegoric speeches of exhortation and dissuasion (*protreptikon/aprotreptikon*), epideictic speeches of encomium and invective (*enkômiastikon/psektikon*), and dikanic speeches of accusation and defense (*kategorikon/apologêtikon*)—plus *exetastikon*, "examination," a general, floating mode of disputation that may function independently or with the other types.

What Anaximenes/"Aristotle" seems to have in mind, on one hand, are the local courts and assemblies, the sorts of places where (for example) one would argue lawsuits over contracts, though clearly exhortation/dissuasion, eulogy/vituperation, and accusation/defense could happen in royal councils and tribunals also. On the other hand, however, the prominent inclusion of "private discussions" and "exetastic" disputation among the scenes and types of *politikos logos* suggests a turn toward the rhetoric of consultation and debate in gatherings of *philoi*, and probably represents the *Rhetoric to Alexander*'s extension of traditional, fourth-century sophistic teachings to include the discursive practices of Hellenistic royal bureaucracies. Indeed, Anaximenes eventually notes that all the types of *politikos logos* can be used in combination with each other as well as separately (5 1427b), suggesting that he is thinking of their application in relatively fluid, unstructured speaking situations.

This impression is heightened as one proceeds through the text. The first five chapters are devoted to the topics of demegoric, epideictic, dikanic, and exetastic discourse (two chapters for demegoric, one each for the rest). From exetastic, the discussion opens to the book's twenty three short chapters on general principles of argument and style. These include the various "tropes of proof," *tropoi tôn pisteôn* (in chapters 6–21), and various techniques for speaking with *asteia*, "urbanity" (in chapters 22–28). The principles of *asteia*—speaking as briefly or copiously as needed, joining words euphoniously, framing "twofold statements" by various *schê-mata*, maintaining clarity, and creating balanced phrases with various kinds of antithesis and parallelism—point toward a more or less Isocratean style, or perhaps even a Gorgianic or "Asianist" style (though "Asianism" is a later concept). In effect, the *Rhetoric to Alexander's* core principles of argument and style appear to be part of a general sophistic art of argument and disputation, of which "urbanely" spoken exetastic discourse in "private discussions" is the underlying general model. But the emphasis throughout is on the practical application of this art to civic discourse, particularly that of city courts and "common assemblies," as well as the more "private" conferrings of a governor's or king's administrators. Of all the examples used in these middle chapters, only one is drawn from nonpragmatic or "literary" discourse: a passage from Euripides' *Philoctetes*, illustrating "anticipation" of an opponent's arguments (18 1433b).

These core chapters are followed, in turn, by nine relatively bulky chapters devoted to the actual, part-by-part procedures of demegoric, epideictic, dikanic, and exetastic speeches (six chapters for demegoric, one each for the rest), with advice concerning the appropriate topics and methods of introductions, narratives, proofs, refutations, recapitulations, and conclusions. From the discussion of exetastic speeches there follows a curious, miscellaneous-looking final chapter, which reviews the procedures for speaking and writing "most artistically" in "private and public contests" and in "discussions with others" (38 1445b) and adds some advice for living honorably. This material may sound like a turn from civic oratory to sophistical competitions and debates in private houses and public theaters, but it sounds still more like a turn toward discussion and deliberation in gatherings of councilors, or toward argument and disputation in royal tribunals. As Anaximenes/"Aristotle" says, to be persuasive in these "contests" one must maintain one's reputation—by keeping one's agreements, keeping the same friends "all through your life," and staying constant in one's habits and principles—and one must present one's arguments rapidly, clearly, and distinctly (1445b–1446a). These virtues would be relatively unimportant for a sophistical entertainment, where in fact copious elaboration was the name of the game, and where the sophist could adopt a fictive identity (although, of course, a reputation for good character would be important for a sophist hoping to attract students). But reputation and perspicuity together would count hugely in a *synedrion* or some other administrative council, where personal relationships among the *philoi* and the king (or governor) constitute the power structure and where one would not expect the *philoi* to be putting on extended oratorical displays. These virtues would count as well in a tribunal, where a speaker might present a petition or an appeal before the monarch or a single magistrate, or before a gathering of magistrates: busy officials lacking the time to listen to lengthy speeches and with whom one's personal standing and reputation would be crucial.

Anaximenes' final chapter, then, is offering advice not so much for sophistical brilliance in public and private *epideixeis*, but more for effective, impressive speech and writing in the administrative forums of a royal bureaucracy. ("Writing" would here include the drafting of letters and petitions to the king, and the formulation and drafting of responses and decrees for the king's signature by his *philoi*, as well as, implicitly, the writing of speeches for various occasions.) Notably, the chapter ends with an "appendix" of miscellaneous bits of political wisdom and advice, which seem to constitute a sort of primer for the would-be participant in affairs of state— such as (to take a semirandom sampling), "we shall establish relations of friendship with people with manners like our own . . . we should form alliances with the most just and the very powerful . . . as to financial provisions, the best thing is to derive funds from our own revenues or estates, second best from a tax on property, and third from contributions of bodily service from the poor, weapons from artisans, and money from the rich . . . services are always rendered for the sake of profit or honor or pleasure, or from fear," and so forth (1446b). This "appendix" is generally regarded as a spurious, later addition by an unknown hand. It shows, however, that its unknown writer well understood what kind of student and what kinds of purposes the *Rhetoric to Alexander* was meant to serve.

In sum, what we find in the *Rhetoric to Alexander* appears to be an appropriation of the teachings of an earlier sophistic *logôn technê*—visible chiefly in the encomium of *logôn philosophia*, the "core" principles of argument and style, and the discussion of exetastic discourse—but a *technê* reduced and adapted to the interests of a socially ambitious clientele that wants primarily, and perhaps only, to learn the methods of civil and bureaucratic *politikos logos* practiced by the political elite in a Hellenistic kingdom.

Theophrastus, Demetrius, and the Hellenistic Elaboration of Stylistics

If there is a "literaturizing" or bellettristic turn in Hellenistic rhetoric, it would seem to make its clearest appearance not in the sophistic or even "Asianist" tradition that Anaximenes may be seen to represent (or prefigure), but in the Peripatetic, Aristotelian-Theophrastian tradition embodied in Demetrius's *On Style*. Demetrius begins, from his opening sentence, by taking *poiêsis*, "poetry," as the paradigm for the analysis of prose style, noting that "[a]s *poiêsis* is divided by measures, such as the hemistich, the hexameter, and so forth, so likewise is *logos* articulated and divided by what are called *kôla*," or clauses (1). For Demetrius, as for virtually all later stylistic rhetoric, the *kôlon* in *logos* corresponds to the *metron* or line of verse, so that he generally analyzes the rhythmic structure of *kôla* in terms of poetic meters while noting that good prose rhythm is looser and more varied than that of poetry itself (118). Further, not only the discussion of prose rhythm but also the whole succeeding discussion of the "types of style," which occupies the remainder of the text, are illustrated with examples drawn primarily from epideictic literature, including poets (chiefly Homer, Sappho, and Aristophanes), historians (chiefly Xenophon and Thucydides), and philosophers (chiefly Plato and Aristotle), as well as figures that Demetrius identifies as orators (chiefly Demosthenes and Isocrates). Demetrius's examples do include such Hellenistic writers as the poets Menander, Philemon, and Sotades, the Cynic philosopher Crates, and the historian Cleitarchus, but for the most part he selects from the Hellenistic period's emergent canon of "classic" figures from the fourth century B.C. and earlier.

In all of this, Demetrius clearly is following the precedent of Aristotle's account of style in the *Rhetoric*, and presumably Theophrastus's elaboration of that account as well. According to Quintilian, Theophrastus considered the reading of poetry (which, in the ancient context, implicitly means or includes the reading of it out loud) to be "of the greatest benefit" to an orator, not only because it provided intellectual stimulation and recreation, but also and perhaps chiefly because it provided stylistic models (*Institutio* 10.1.27).

But does *On Style* embody a rhetoric infected with a "literary," bellettrizing turn? We need to keep in mind, first of all, what sort of book Demetrius has produced. *On Style* is, in the tradition of Theophrastus, an expanded treatment of one aspect of discursive art. Among the many books by Theophrastus mentioned in Diogenes Laertius's *Lives of the Philosophers* we find not only a general *Art of Rhetoric* (*Technê Rhêtorikê*), but also a multivolume treatise *On Kinds of Rhetorical Arts*, and individual (and sometimes multivolume) treatises with such titles as *Rhetorical Precepts, Starting-Points or Controversies, Polemics or The Theory of Eristic Discourses, On Invention, On Example, On Enthymemes, Epicheiremes, On the Maxim, On Nontechnical Proofs, On Judicial Speeches, On Counsel, On Praise, On Slander, Introductions, On Statement and Narration, On Style,* and *On Delivery*—as well as treatises on poetry, metrics, comedy, characters, and the ludicrous. Theophrastus also wrote more than twenty books of "theses," propositions on general topics that were probably meant to be the basis of school exercises in declamation and debate, and a *Collection of Arguments*.[21] With Theophrastus, parts or segments of Aristotle's *Rhetoric* receive expanded, book-length treatment, so that the three books of the *Rhetoric* become an entire bookshelf. Indeed, Theophrastus produced a virtual library, perhaps 225 books in all, on logic, physics, metaphysics, theology, mathematics, psychology, human physiology, zoology, botany, ethics, religion, politics, and music, as well as poetics and rhetoric.[22] Demetrius's *On Style* is to be seen as part of, and related to, such a Theophrastian organon—and as part of the broad *paideia* that such an organon supports.

On Style, moreover, is an expanded part not of "rhetoric" in the narrow sense, but of a more general *logôn technê*. In his introductory discussion, for example, Demetrius divides the kinds of prose composition into *historikê, dialogikê,* and *rhêtorikê* (19): the historical, the dialogical (as in philosophical dialogues), and the oratorical. These three categories appear to comprise, for Demetrius, the whole domain of discursive art outside of poetry. Notably, Demetrius follows Platonic, Aristotelian, and presumably Theophrastian precedent in using the word *rhêtorikê* to name the pragmatic discourse that Anaximenes calls *logos politikos*, but for Demetrius *rhêtorikê* does not denote the whole discursive art that he is teaching; rather, it denotes only one of the constituent genres of that art. But Demetrius never has practical or civic applications far from view. Near the end of the treatise, for example, there is a famous discussion of stylistic methods useful for writing letters *kai polesin . . . kai basileusin*, "both to cities . . . and to kings" (234), and for addressing advice or censure to a despot or "some other powerful (*biaiôn*) person" (289), as well as to "peoples" (*dêmoi*) that are "great and mighty" (*megaloi kai ischyroi*; 294).

It is worth noting here that *biaiôn*, or its root form *bia*, denotes "force" or "power" in the sense of physical compulsion and characteristically stands in opposition to the term *nomos*, "law" (or custom-law, communal agreement). Thus, just as the *Rhetoric to Alexander's* introductory "letter" is concerned with making *logos* rather than violence the means of arbitrating justice in tribunals where *nomos* does not apply, Demetrius likewise is concerned with methods of deploying *logos* to resolve issues with persons and communities who are *biaiôn*. He clearly is offering instruction that is useful and indeed essential for the functionary in a royal bureaucracy, or for a person presenting a petition or bringing an appeal before a king—or before any tribunal or forum where the power relations are unequal.

What we see in Demetrius, then, is probably not a "literaturized" or bellettristic rhetoric that has declined from its practical civic functions to decorative display. *On Style* is part of a broadly conceived, Theophrastian *logôn technê* that includes a wide variety of discourse genres and requires a broad *logôn paideia*, one that is centered on the models of eloquence and wisdom embodied in the major genres of epideictic discourse (poetry, history, and philosophy, as well as encomiastic and panegyric speeches) and that is meant to be applied to the scenes and occasions of spoken and written pragmatic discourse in a Hellenistic kingdom. Demetrius differs from Anaximenes in more fully representing what Anaximenes calls *logôn philosophia*, whereas Anaximenes is more narrowly focused on quick, concise instruction in the pragmatic genres of what he calls *politikos logos* and Demetrius calls by the Platonic-Aristotelian term *rhêtorikê*. The discourse art and discourse education that Demetrius represents, like that of Theophrastus, Aristotle, and Isocrates before him, is meant to cultivate not only basic competence in the methods of a few types of civic discourse, but also a sophisticated, articulate, and even eloquent critical intelligence endowed with an enhanced *phronêsis* for deliberation and decision in high councils. (It is significant, in this connection, that tradition since the first century B.C. has identified the Demetrius of *On Style* with the statesman-scholar Demetrius of Phaleron, even if that identification is incorrect.)

Given these observations, it seems reasonable to argue that the proliferating, oft-remarked-on Hellenistic (and subsequently Roman) concern with matters of style and delivery, which seems to begin in earnest with Theophrastus's and Demetrius's treatises on the subject, probably should not be thought of as reflecting a decadent bellettrism or academicism. The increasing refinement of stylistic analysis probably does reflect an increasingly *literate* and scholarly mode of analysis, and the emergence of an advanced literacy based on a growing corpus of written texts available for study by a cultural elite, as at the library of Alexandria, or in the philosophical schools of Athens; there was an enormous expansion in "literature" of all kinds.[23] But stylistic refinement also, and more crucially, reflects a shift in the nature of the speaker-audience relation. As students of Hellenistic literacy and literature have noted, in this period the written text acquires unprecedented dominance as a primary medium of important public discourse, and the experience of reading begins to displace the experience of hearing (or witnessing a performance) as the characteristic mode of participation for an audience. Alexandrian writers begin to drop the fiction of "speaking" or "singing" to an audience of hearers and frequently refer to their discourse with metaphors of textuality rather than orality. Addressing their readers as readers, they present a self-consciously erudite, writerly text that assumes a well-read audience and stands in complex relation to the canonized texts of past tradition.[24] For the bureaucrat as for the poet, the written word becomes a medium of suasion and communication in which a cultured, carefully modeled, and finely nuanced style becomes not only possible but also indispensable, insofar as he writes for an educated, cultured readership (for the most part composed of other bureaucrats) capable of fine-grained interpretation, appreciation, and critique. To fail to address the capacities and knowledges of such an audience is to not persuade.

But the Theophrastian or Hellenistic elaboration of stylistics cannot be seen simply as an effect of advanced literacy or cultural refinement within the sociopolitical elite. Arguably, its major motives must include a recognition of the practical truth in Demosthenes' famous statement that the three most important things in public speaking are delivery, delivery, and delivery—a statement that (as Athanasius reports) was echoed by Theophrastus in his own treatise *On Delivery*.[25] Closely related to this view, or behind it, is Gorgias's recognition of the druglike, suasive force of style in spoken discourse. In civic oratory, the actual articulation of the speaker's argument, its physical, moment-by-moment embodiment as a specific linguistic and semiotic texture in the tonal contours and phrasal rhythms of the speaker's voice, combined with his bodily presence and his gesturing before the audience, counts for much and sometimes for everything. Moreover, as Quintilian would later point out, it is not enough for the practical orator to write, memorize, and deliver a stylistically well-made discourse, like an actor performing a script. Rather, the practical orator who speaks in the public forum has to be responsive to the contingencies of an unstable, sometimes turbulent speaking situation where opponents or judges may respond and interrupt, where unforeseen topics of debate may suddenly emerge, and where an audience or even a crowd of onlookers may heckle and cheer—and where, moreover, one may be distracted by the general, extraneous noise of the surroundings. Like Hesiod's eloquent *basileus*, the skilled *rhêtôr* must be able to improvise persuasive, cogently argued, and stylistically well-turned discourse *ex tempore*.[26]

Such improvising required considerable inventional agility, or what Quintilian called *facilitas*, and its cultivation was necessarily a major goal in training the would-be practical *rhêtôr*. This necessity explains the Hellenistic period's as well as the Roman period's increasingly refined analysis and criticism of style in rhetoric manuals, as well as its broader tendency to analyze the "parts" of rhetoric, or of discourse art in general, into systematized collections of techniques. For even if (as it is often said) the stylistic richness of the greatest rhetors exceeded the descriptive powers of the rhetoricians, and if the rhetoricians' stylistic theories were for the most part backward-looking accounts of styles produced without the aid of their instruction, nevertheless it was also true that any particular style or stylistic move that a rhetorician could identify and describe could be observed, imitated, practiced, and acquired by the well-disciplined trainee of less than Demosthenic genius.[27] Just as a musical trainee could practice finger exercises and particular sequences, runs and trills that later could be recombined in musical performances or musical invention, so too the would-be civic orator could practice and acquire a ready repertoire of styles and figures that eventually would enable copious, fluent, and appropriate stylistic improvisation in public forums. Moreover, because of the advancing literacy of the sociopolitical elite in the Hellenistic period, and because of the enhanced capacities for stylistic analysis and training such literacy afforded, it seems likely that there would have been an escalation also in the stylistic fluency and copiousness of the trained *rhêtôr*, and with it an escalation in what audiences expected and responded to as well—eventually producing the florid excess that would be labeled Asianism, as the back-to-the-classics "Atticist" reaction of the first century B.C. set in.

My point, then, is that this escalating cycle of stylistic and technical facility in the Hellenistic period was the product neither of hyperaesthetic or academic bellettrism nor of a public speaking degenerating into sideshows. That cycle, rather, was most probably a product of the practical necessities faced by the *rhêtôr* in civic and bureaucratic forums. To be unable to speak in a style as *asteios* or "urbane" as one's opponent, while speaking before an audience of judges or councilors accustomed to stylistic virtuosity, would be to seem by contrast inarticulate, uneducated, and possibly stupid, a bumpkin, and thus to be unable to persuade. Likewise, it seems probable that the increasing refinement of stylistic analysis in this period was the product not of pedantry or of taste-mongering, but of the need for practical instruction in the resources for effective improvisational speech. It is therefore no surprise that by the first century B.C. *Rhetorica Ad Herennium*—a redaction of Hellenistic rhetoric devoted wholly to instruction in the methods of pragmatic discourse, and especially dikanic discourse—we find the entire fourth book (of four) devoted to a more or less Theophrastian classification and analysis of style types and stylistic principles, with the subsequent and by far the greatest part of the discussion devoted to an illustrated catalogue of over one hundred kinds of tropes and figures. The writer declares in his opening remarks to "Herennius" (and to the student who will use his book), "it is true that copious speaking and commodious discourse bear not a little fruit, if governed by right understanding and a strict discipline of the mind" (1.1.1). In this he is speaking directly to the interests, ambitions, and real-world needs of the would-be lawyer-politician-orators of Rome, who form his student readership and clientele.[28]

Hermagoras, the *Ad Herennium*, and *De Inventione*

Much of what I have said thus far can probably be said as well about Hermagorean rhetoric, or about Hermagoras's *logôn technê*, which he taught probably sometime in the middle of the second century B.C., and which we find appropriated (along with other sources) by the *Ad Herennium* and Cicero's *De Inventione* in the early first century B.C. It seems likely that Hermagoras taught a more general discourse art that is reduced, in the Roman treatises (and possibly in the Greek sources they derive from), to a more narrowly defined art of pragmatic rhetoric. Or so we might conjecture. Since none of Hermagoras's own writings have survived, we do not know even whether he called the discourse art he taught *rhêtorikê*, though he might have. The Skeptic philosopher Sextus Empiricus, writing in Greek sometime around 200 A.D., identifies Hermagoras as a teacher of *rhêtorikê* (*Against Rhetors* 62), though he is writing at a distance of at least three centuries and is hostile. Cicero's *De Inventione*, which is closer in time and friendlier (though critical), likewise identifies Hermagoras as a teacher of *rhetorica*, "the orator's art," but also declares him more truly a "philosopher" (1.6.8). This equivocation is significant.

What we do know is that, according to Sextus Empiricus, Hermagoras defined the goal of the discourse art he taught as "settling the proposed *politikon zêtêma*"— the political question or public issue—"as persuasively as possible" (*Against Rhetors* 62). This is the basic definition taken, with some variation, by the *Ad Herennium*: "[t]he orator's duty is to be able to speak on those matters that custom and law have constituted for civil use, and to bring his audience to agreement as far as possible" (1.2.2). Cicero's *De Inventione*, likewise, defines "rhetoric" as an art belonging to "civil science" and having the goal of speaking "in a manner suited to persuade an audience" (1.5.6). These definitions, and especially the Roman versions, suggest a "rhetoric" focused largely on pragmatic discourse. But Hermagoras's *technê* of "settling political questions" by means of *logos* was probably much broader.

Hermagoras divided "political questions" into two broad kinds, "theses" (*theseis*) and "hypotheses" (*hypotheseis*), which Cicero translates as *quaestionae* and *causae*, "propositions" and "cases" (*De Inventione* 1.6.8).[29] Theses/propositions were general issues for debate that, as Quintilian would later describe them, did not involve specific "persons, times, places, and the like." Hypotheses/cases, in contrast, were issues for debate involving such particulars (*Institutio* 3.5.5–7). The hypothesis/case, in other words, is a particular instantiation of a thesis/proposition within a specific set of social, legal, political, and historical circumstances. It is the sort of issue that one might argue in a court of law or political assembly. (This is Cicero's basic point in *De Oratore* 2.31.) The thesis/proposition, when taken alone as a general issue, is a topic for philosophical disputation or an *epideixis* of some kind or for a debating exercise in school.

Hermagoras's "rhetoric," in other words, seems to have resembled an Isocratean *logôn technê*, encompassing epideictic genres that "settle" general issues in political, moral, and legal philosophy, as well as the more pragmatic genres that "settle" the practical applications or instantiations of those issues in particular, real-world cases. It seems to have been, moreover, to some degree like a Theophrastian *logôn technê*, insofar as both Hermagoras and Theophrastus included the debating of "theses" as a significant part of their *paideia*. But there were differences as well. The focus implicit in Hermagoras's definition of his art as a *technê* of settling "political questions" suggests an Isocratean lack of interest in the metaphysical speculations of the philosophic schools. Further, the very terminology of *thesis* and *hypothesis*, though not specifically Hermagorean in itself, may suggest an orientation toward the practical. Insofar as *thesis* literally means "position" or "seat" (even in modern Greek, one can buy a ticket for a *thesis* in a train), and insofar as *hypothesis* means "under-position" or "foundation," the implication seems to be that "theses" must rest on, be grounded in, or arise from the practical, real-world situations of "hypotheses." Such an empiricist approach to the particular and actual as foundational for the general was, of course, not only sophistic but also Aristotelian and probably Theophrastian as well. But it seems likely that Hermagoras's Isocratean interest in "political questions" carried the sophistic tendency further, toward a more pronounced interest in "settling" by means of persuasive discourse the disputes and issues that arose in actual social or civic life, and in approaching general questions in political or ethical philosophy by way of the specific cases of *hypotheseis* (which students could treat in declamation exercises).

Hermagoras's stasis system was a systematic method for identifying the crucial point of controversy—*stasis* basically means position, faction, or discord—and thus for discovering the most appropriate and persuasive arguments available in a dispute.[30] As it is commonly understood today, the system included or was divided into "rational" questions, *logika zêtêmata*, and "legal" questions, *nomika zêtêmata*. This division, however, is actually Quintilian's (*Institutio* 3.6), and Quintilian clearly is working out his own view based on a synthesis of later sources. We do know that under the *logika zêtêmata* there were four main stases: *stochasmos* or "conjectural," dealing with questions of fact and probability; *horos* or "definitional," dealing with the name that should be applied to the agreed-on facts/probabilities in question; *symbebêkos* or *poiotês*, "circumstantial" or "qualitative," dealing with contingencies and considerations that affect the judgment or evaluation of the agreed-on, named/defined facts/probabilities; and *metalêpsis* or "translative," dealing with questions of the appropriate venue for judging the facts or the qualifications of the persons involved in the debate. The "legal" questions, the *nomika zêtêmata*, were (according to Quintilian, *Institutio* 3.6.60–61) five in number and dealt with the letter of the law; its intent; its rational applicability to cases not directly covered; ambiguous laws; and conflicting laws. All of these major stases, both "rational" and "legal," were subdivided further into complex sets of inventional topics, providing a more or less exhaustive inventory of possibilities.

Clearly, this was a system especially suited for, and seemingly based on, dikanic discourse. But again, there is reason to believe that it was actually meant as a general system that applied to all possible kinds of "political" theses and hypotheses. In *De Inventione* (1.9.12), Cicero notes with evident confusion that Hermagoras subdivided the "qualitative" stasis into four kinds of issues, which Cicero calls *deliberativum, demonstrativum, iuridicalem, negotialem:* that is, "deliberative" or symbouleutic issues of advantage and disadvantage; "demonstrative" or epideictic issues of praise and blame; "juridical" or dikanic issues of justice and injustice; and the still poorly understood "negotiative" issues, which may have included questions of feasibility or questions of legal interpretation. If so, the "legal questions" were connected to the "negotiative" substasis and thus actually belonged to the "qualitative" stasis in Hermagoras's system. This is, in fact, where Cicero places them (1.11.14). In the later, summative work of Hermogenes of Tarsus (c. 200 A.D.), the *nomika zêtêmata* likewise appear as part of the "qualitative" stasis, alongside the *logika zêtêmata*, which in turn include the dikanic and symbouleutic stases.[31] It would appear that Hermagoras, like Aristotle (and probably Theophrastus), treated the so-called "kinds of rhetoric" as argument genres or types of issues that might appear in any sort of discourse, and that he organized their topics under the "qualitative" stasis because they constituted the chief modalities of evaluation and judgment available for all "political questions."

In effect, Hermagoras provided a system of menus from which the discourse-maker in any kind of discourse could select as needed to invent arguments.[32] But the advantages of such a system for the practical orator improvising on his feet are apparent, as are the reasons why it would be popular with students of pragmatic and especially dikanic disputation. In the higher tribunals of a Hellenistic kingdom, as we have seen, *logos* or "discourse" rather than *nomos* or "law" was necessarily the chief determinant of what would count as "justice" in any given case, insofar as there was no systematic legal code or uniform set of legal procedures available. Hermagorean stasis theory, then, provided the *rhêtôr*, and the local courts and higher tribunals of a Hellenistic kingdom also, with the nearest thing to a systematic method for debating and resolving questions of justice in the absence of a determinate, authoritative code of jurisprudence. Hermagoras' *logôn technê*, while offering (probably) a general system of argument-invention, had a particular utility for the person intending to argue dikanic cases.[33]

The nineteen-year-old Cicero's problem with Hermagoras's system, or with what he has heard about it from his teachers, stems from his own assumption that it is intended purely for dikanic argument. Thus he declares, with all the pedantic fussiness of a brilliant schoolboy catching some philosopher in a theoretical contradiction, that Hermagoras has committed "no middling error" by including the major genres of speeches under a subhead of one of those same genres (1.9.12). But young Cicero has gotten it wrong. If Hermagoras's four "rational questions," the *logika zêtêmata*, are understood to constitute a general system for all argumentation whatsoever on any kind of "political question" or "public issue" that may occur in any kind of discourse, Cicero's objection disappears.

But that, of course, is not how Hermagoras is understood, or his stasis system appropriated, in either *De Inventione* or the *Ad Herennium*. In both texts, as in Anaximenes' *Rhetoric to Alexander*, a more generalized *logôn technê* has been trimmed down and rearranged to suit the purposes of an audience or clientele that is interested mainly in learning the basic methods of pragmatic discourse, and overwhelmingly those of lawsuits. The *Ad Herennium* devotes the first two of its four books to the methods of "juridic" speeches, with the third book devoted to "deliberative" and "demonstrative" speeches, and the fourth book to style. Likewise, 66 of the 117 chapters of *De Inventione* are devoted to juridic argument, with another 42 devoted to the parts of an oration, a mere eight to the topics of deliberative and demonstrative speeches, and one to the book's conclusion. In neither book, moreover, is the treatment of deliberative and demonstrative argument organized around a genuine stasis system. What we find, instead, is a listing of topics not much different from the pre-Hermagorean listings offered by Anaximenes. In sum, it appears that Hermagoras's teachings, or parts of them, have been taken over chiefly as offering a serviceable method for dikanic/juridic speeches.

Both young Cicero and Cornificius strike the conventional pose of a no-nonsense Roman impatient with Greek foolishness and manifest an interest only in those parts of Hellenistic rhetoric useful for the would-be lawyer-politician. Cicero, for example, censures Hermagoras for including the debate of philosophical *theseis* in his *technê*, since "everyone easily understands that these are remote from the business of an orator" (*De Inventione* 1.6.8), an opinion that the grown-up Cicero will reverse. Likewise, Cornificius says at the outset of the *Ad Herennium* that he will omit the "irrelevant notions" that "inane Greek writers" have discussed merely to make the art "seem difficult" (1.1.1). In the *Ad Herennium's* fourth book, moreover, he opens his treatment of style with a lengthy, seven-chapter criticism (4.1–7) of "the Greeks" for using examples drawn from orators, poets, historians, and other writers. As he says, the Greeks wish merely to parade their learning but instead reveal their inability to practice what they teach, and do not themselves dare "to come forth into the *stadium rhetoricae*" (4.3.4–5)—a criticism Cicero similarly levels at Hermagoras (*De Inventione* 1.6.8)—and further, as Cornificius says, it is difficult to develop a clear conception of the art from a "vast and diffuse" collection of literary examples such as the foolish Greeks assemble (4.2.3, 4.4.7). And so, for these reasons (as he claims), he proudly has produced his own stylistic examples in book 4, thereby demonstrating his Roman superiority to the Greeks in this most Greek of arts (though he has not produced his own examples in books 1–3). Virtually all his produced examples belong to the realm of pragmatic discourse. He does at one point say that periodic sentences should be arranged "in such a way as to approximate a poetic rhythm" (4.32.44), which is clearly a reflection of Hellenistic teaching, as is everything else he says, but he presents no poetry to illustrate the principles of rhythm. Elsewhere in the *Ad Herennium* (books 1–3) we do find some examples drawn from poetry, but these chiefly have to do with the predominantly literary subject matter of the traditional declamation exercises used in Greek and Roman schools. The few passages of actual poetry that are cited mostly illustrate *faults* that an orator should avoid.

However, despite their single-minded focus on pragmatic discourse and their gestures of contempt for Greekishness, both young Cicero and Cornificius—like Anaximenes in the *Rhetoric to Alexander*—preserve at least some traces of a broader notion of the discourse art they so reductively describe. These traces are most noticeable, or most revealing, in the largely conventional remarks that open and close both treatises. In the *Ad Herennium*, Cornificius opens by declaring to his friend and blood relative Herennius (a relation echoing that of *philos* and *syngênes* in Hellenistic political hierarchies) that he has taken time out from his busy "private affairs" and his leisure-time study of *philosophia* to write *de ratione dicendi*, "on the method [or theory] of speaking," and then he commends Herennius for wishing "to learn rhetoric," *cognoscere rhetoricam*, because of the usefulness and value of "copious speaking and commodious discourse governed by right understanding and a strict discipline of the mind" (1.1.1). There is thus an implicit equivocation, in which the "theory of speaking" appears briefly as a department or subdiscipline within the general "study of philosophy" and as a discipline of the mind, and is then renamed with the Greek term "rhetoric." These remarks appear to reflect a Hellenistic (or Hermagorean) presentation of *rhêtorikê* as a general *logôn technê*, a presentation that has filtered through to Cornificius from his teachers, but also one that is immediately dismissed—in his very next sentence—when he declares that he will omit the "irrelevant notions" that "inane Greek writers" have included.

This self-contradictory movement is repeated in the *Ad Herennium*'s closing remarks, as Cornificius exhorts Herennius to join him in constant "study and exercise," declaring that

> [W]e exercise together willingly because of our friendship, which blood-relationship has originated, and the study of philosophy [*philosophiae ratio*] has further strengthened; and we are not inconfident, because we have progressed somewhat

and there are other, better things we seek much more intently in this life, so that, even if we shall not have attained in speaking [*in dicendo*] what we desire, only a little of the most perfect life shall have been missed; and we have in mind the path that we should follow, because in these books no precept of rhetoric [*nihil rhetoricae praeceptionis*] has been passed over. (4.56.69)

This odd passage reinvokes, on one hand, the notion that the study of "speaking," which again is subsequently named as "rhetoric," is both part of and conducive to the philosophic life, the life that pursues, it seems, "better things" than those of an orator's career. Indeed, "rhetoric" provides "the path to follow" toward "the most perfect life," even for those who do not become accomplished speakers. And yet the art of "rhetoric" here consists wholly of the principles and methods of pragmatic discourse, and especially the principles and methods of arguing lawsuits, as outlined in the four books of the *Ad Herennium*. Such comments may reflect some version of Hermagorean (or even Isocratean) pragmatism, defining *philosophia* as an art of "settling political questions" in the disputation of *hypotheseis* and *theseis*: an art that is to be "studied and exercised" through the practice cases of declamation (with their fictive and literary contexts) and in other kinds of literary composition. But it seems more likely that Cornificius's remarks are the product of a simple confusion, the echoing of conventional sophistic praises of *logôn technê* from his teachers, and here applied as platitudes—without much recognition of incongruity—to a deliberately, rigorously limited version of the art, one meant chiefly for politically ambitious, well-to-do young Romans whose immediate goal is, in fact, to launch themselves in a lawyer-politician's career.

Cicero's *De Inventione* likewise echoes (and echoes more fully) a broader conception of rhetoric as *logôn technê*, before falling into similar inconsistency. Young Cicero devotes his first four chapters to a full-blown, Isocratean encomium of *eloquentia* as a faculty that, when combined with "wisdom," *sapientia*, has made possible the creation of civil life regulated by communally accepted principles of justice rather than by violence (1.1.1–5). He says:

[i]ndeed to me it seems that a wisdom [*sapientia*] neither mute nor poor of speech [*dicendi*] could have turned people from accustomed ways and converted them to different ways of life. Now surely, when cities had been established, how should they have learned to keep faith and uphold justice and willingly render service to others and not only take up labors for the sake of the common good, but even to think they should sacrifice their life—which ultimately could be done—unless by eloquence people had been able to make persuasive what their reason had invented? Certainly no one not aroused by a discourse [*oratione*] both weighty and entrancing [*gravis ac suavis*], who might be the most powerful of men, would have wished to yield to justice without compulsion, so that among those he could dominate, he permitted himself to be made their equal and by his own will desisted from a most agreeable custom, one that by then had acquired the force of a natural right by reason of long standing. (1.2.3)

Cicero's opening encomium invokes not "rhetoric" in the narrow sense of practical civic oratory, and in fact does not invoke the post-Isocratean word "rhetoric" at all. That term will not appear until chapter 5, where the *technê* proper starts, and

Cicero begins to recite his more or less Hermagorean lessons, while invoking Aristotle's restriction of "rhetoric" to the three genres of practical civic oratory—despite (says Cicero) the claims of sophists who, like Gorgias, have given "rhetoric" unlimited application (1.5.7). The opening encomium, however, invokes just such an unlimited art of persuasively spoken wisdom, one whose function is not only to win lawsuits or accomplish legislation or bestow civic honors but to shape culture.

Moreover, Cicero's Isocratean encomium sets a more strictly limited or narrowed art of pragmatic discourse in opposition to this larger, culture-shaping eloquence as its perverted double. As he says, "I consider wisdom without eloquence of little use to civil communities, but eloquence without wisdom is often quite harmful and never of use at all" (1.1.1). This idea leads to a tale of eloquence's and of Rome's corruption.

> When a certain complaisance, virtue's depraved imitation, without consideration of moral duty had acquired a copiousness of speech [*copia dicendi*], then malice abetted by talent became accustomed to corrupting cities and ruining people's lives. . . . [While in earlier times] the greatest affairs were managed by the most eminent men, there were others, I think, not unskillful persons, who would enter into the petty disputes of private citizens. As people became accustomed in such controversies often to stand with falsehood against the truth, frequency of speaking [*dicendi*] gave them audacity. . . . And so, as one might often seem equal to anyone in speaking [*in dicendo*] and sometimes even superior, he that had acquired an eloquence [*eloquentiam*] while neglecting the study of wisdom [*sapientiae*] altogether came to seem to the multitude and to himself worthy to govern the republic. (1.2.3–1.3.4)

And thus, as Cicero says, with such "rash and audacious persons" dominating politics, the republic was brought to many "shipwrecks," and *eloquentia* fell into such disrepute that "persons of the greatest talent" gave it up in favor of more honorable and more "secluded" studies (1.3.4). The conclusion of Cicero's encomium is that one ought still to study *eloquentia*, and join it with *sapientia*, in order to protect the common welfare from "great evil" (1.4.5). But what is significant about his tale of eloquence's decline into corruption, malfeasance, and disrepute is that, aside from its resonance with the violent turmoil of the Roman republic in Cicero's time and its revelation of his fairly admirable (and ultimately tragic) young ambitions, the tale quite faithfully replicates Isocrates' distrust of a *rhêtoreia* disconnected from *philosophia*, and especially the *rhêtoreia* practiced in "the petty disputes of private citizens"—private lawsuits—even though this is the very art that all the rest of *De Inventione*, with its pose of Roman disdain for Greek frivolities, is overwhelmingly about.

The "Old and Philosophic Rhetoric" in Eclipse

I will return to Cicero. For now, however, my point is that it hardly seems believable to say that "rhetoric" declined, in the Hellenistic period, from a pristine art of civic oratory to merely an art of bellettristic, academic formalisms. Rather, it seems more reasonable to say that "rhetoric" continued in good health, but as an equivocal identity in two, or more, main versions. In one of these, from Isocrates and Aristotle through to Theophrastus and Demetrius, and probably Hermagoras as well, "rhetoric" either is, or is part of, a general and more or less philosophic *logôn technê* whose goal is the production of eloquent, well-deliberated wisdom in any form of discourse—a *technê* that requires a *logôn paideia* centered on the study and practice of the major epideictic genres (poetry, history, philosophy, panegyric, and declamation), that addresses various kinds of *theseis* and *hypotheseis,* and that applies pragmatically to the discourse and epistolography of civil and bureaucratic forums. In the Peripatetic tradition that Demetrius represents, the name of this pragmatic application is *rhêtorikê,* whereas for Hermagoras and the sophistic tradition *rhêtorikê* seems to have been a more generalized or even (as Cicero suggests) "unlimited" term with roughly the same meaning as the older terms *logôn technê* or *logôn philosophia.*

In other philosophic schools, *rhêtorikê* seems chiefly to have meant an epideictic-centered art of suasive eloquence. The Epicurean philosopher Philodemus of Gadara of the early first century B.C., for example, maintained in his treatise *On Rhetoric* (*Peri Rhêtorikês*) that there was no art of *empraktos rhêtorikê,* "practical rhetoric" and that the only genuine art of rhetoric was *sophistikê rhêtorikê,* which he claimed that Epicurus and his follower Metrodorus had defined as an art of *epideixis* or "panegyric" (*panêgyrikê*) and which Philodemus seems to have considered chiefly an art of composing well-made *logoi* that are "most forceful," "beautiful," "persuasive," and "not without charm"—*logoi* that exert a psychagogic power over listeners (*psychagôgia*). In *On Poems* (*Peri Poiêmatôn*), Philodemus ascribes precisely the same effect to poetry. Interestingly, for Philodemus's version of Epicureanism, "[i]t is not at all the case . . . that the *rhêtôr* is simply a *politikos,* nor is the *rhêtôr* wholly a *politikos* either, not even in the narrower sense of the word among the ancients by which all who spoke amid the people [*en dêmôi*] were called *rhêtôr.*" This argument effectively strips the term *rhêtôr* of the particular meaning it had held in the fifth-century Athenian assembly. *Rhêtorikê* and politics are not identical. Philodemus did, however, also recognize that "rhetoric" as an art of sophistic eloquence still could be (and was) projected into politics, and when combined with political experience and knowledge was able to produce a political rhetor of exceptional skill and power. Ultimately, insofar as we can judge from what remains of Philodemus's text, he seems to have wanted to combine this power with philosophy as well, in order to render it intellectually and morally responsible.[34]

Similarly, in the traditional Stoic account of eloquence that surfaces in Strabo's *Geography* (c. 17 A.D.), we find *rhêtorikê* defined broadly as "wisdom applied to words" (1.2.5), that is, an art of articulating *phronêsis,* "wisdom/intelligence," with an eloquence comparable to and indeed derived from that of poetry. As he subsequently says, what distinguishes *rhêtorikos logos* from ordinary *logos* is a *phrasis* or "style" that is *kataskeuasmenos,* "well-turned," and that is both an "imitation of the poetic" and a descendant of it. "For *poiêtikê* that was well-turned came first into the midst of things and was esteemed; then came the imitators [*mimoumenoi*], loosening the meter but otherwise preserving the poetic qualities [*ta poiêtika*], writers like Kadmos, Pherekydes, and Hekataios.[35] . . . The fount and origin of *phrasis* that is well-turned and of *rhêtorikê* is the poetic" (1.2.6).[35] Interestingly, Strabo categorizes both poetry and rhetoric as forms of *logos,* and as the "metrical" and "prosaic" forms of "excellent" *logos* respectively (1.2.6). *Poiêtikê,* for its part, is defined for Strabo by "the ancients" as "a kind of first philosophy" that effects both "soul-guiding" (*Psychagôgia*) and "instruction" (*didaskalia*) by means of "pleasure" (*hêdonê*), so that, as he says, "Our school [the Stoics] . . . declared that only the wise man may be a poet" (1.2.3). Here, as with Philodemus, the term *rhêtorikê* does not signify an art identified primarily with pragmatic discourse. Instead, *rhêtorikê* signifies a more general art of copious and suasive eloquence that in principle includes all forms of *logos*, or at least all forms of prose *logos*. For the Stoic tradition, *rhêtorikos logos* is quite simply an "excellent" and "flowing" psychagogic eloquence by which the judgments of *phronêsis* may be given powerful expression, an eloquence that both derives from and resembles in "loosened" ways the "well-turned" *logos* of *poiêtikê*, and that accomplishes comparable effects.

Philodemus and Strabo both postdate the Hellenistic period proper (though not by much); but none of these ideas originates with them. The use of the term *psychagôgia* to name the persuasive effects accomplished by the "well-turned" eloquence of poetry goes back at least to the Alexandrian critics of the middle to later third century B.C., such as Eratosthenes of Cyrene, who became head of the Library of Alexandria in 246 B.C., and his contemporary Neoptolemus of Parium, whose now lost treatise on poetry was a major source for Horace's *Ars Poetica*.[36] And, of course, the use of *psychagôgia* to name the persuasive effects of rhetoric goes back at least to Plato's *Phaedrus* (261a). Likewise, the notion of *poiêtikê* as both the source and model of "well-turned" prose style clearly has an antecedent in Demetrius's *On Style* and is traceable back to Theophrastus and Aristotle, and further back as well to Gorgias's account of the "witchcraft" and druglike power of poetry and rhythmic prose (*Helen* 8–14). Some later Hellenistic version of this notion is reflected in the introductory description in the *Ad Herennium* of *rhetorica* as an art of *copia dicendi*, as well as the (probably) Stoic-derived account of figuration it incorporates. Finally, Philodemus's attribution to Epicurus of his account of "rhetoric" as the psychagogic *technê* of sophistic *epideixis* places that account at the end of the fourth century B.C., or at the beginning of the third—Epicurus taught at Athens from 306 to his death in 270—at a time when rhetorical practices in that city would hardly have been different from the time of Aristotle. (Dinarchus, the last of the canonic Ten Attic Orators, was still alive when Epicurus set up his school and would have been in active practice when Epicurus was a student; Demetrius of Phaleron was also active at that time.) And, of course, the obvious antecedent and model for Philodemus' Epicurean account of "rhetoric" is Isocrates's panegyric-centered *logôn technê*.[37]

In both philosophic and sophistic schools, then, there was a persisting conception of "rhetoric" as (or as part of) a general art of suasive eloquence and wisdom, and a persisting *logôn paideia* whose products would not be *rhêtores* in the narrow sense but statesmen, writers, and thinkers able to exercise good judgment and to speak with power in any sort of discourse. Among the known students of Theophrastus, for example, we find not only the statesman-scholar Demetrius of Phaleron and the orator Dinarchus, but also the comic poet Menander (the founder of the so-called New Comedy), as well as seventeen other writers and philosophers; there is also the perhaps apocryphal tradition that Demosthenes had "visited Theophrastus' door." At the end of the Hellenistic period, we find the great historian Polybius, who seems to have been influenced chiefly by Peripatetic and Stoic teachings, active in politics as a statesman/ambassador of the Achaean League. In 155 B.C., Carneades the Academic, Critolaus the Peripatetic, and the Stoic Diogenes of Babylon—the heads of their respective schools—were sent by the Athenians as ambassadors to the Roman senate "on business of supreme importance" (Cicero, *De Oratore* 2.37.155), and while there they delivered not only speeches to the senate, but also public and highly sophistic *epideixeis*: on different days, Carneades both praised and dispraised justice. The Romans regarded them as both philosophers and rhetoricians, and Polybius described their speeches as exemplifying the Theophrastian three styles (Carneades the grand, Critolaus the middle, Diogenes the plain). And at Rome in the middle of the second century B.C., we find Diogenes and his fellow Stoic Panaetius, with Polybius, the principal educators of the eminent statesmen-orators, poets, and writers of the so-called Scipionic circle.[38]

We should not forget, either, the documented tendencies of at least some sophists, such as Anaximenes of Lampsakos or Hegesias of Magnesia, to be wide-ranging intellectuals and writers, composing histories as well as other kinds of treatises, while also being all-round, virtuoso performers of panegyric, declamation, and what Philodemus calls *empraktos rhêtorikê*. Moreover, as Graham Anderson recently has argued, we see this range of activities and interests persisting also in a number of Greek sophists active toward the end of the Roman republic, such as Hybreas the Elder of Mylasa and Potamon of Mytilene, figures who "serve to confirm the existence of several generations" of predecessors who were similarly versatile. At the court of Cleopatra, we find the sophist Philostratus the Egyptian, whom Plutarch describes as an accomplished extempore speaker and agile courtier who "styled himself a philosopher" and who studied philosophy and literature with the queen. It is apparent that this Philostratus embodied an already well-established, recognizable sophistic type.[39]

But, as the surviving *technai* suggest, there was another and more dominant version of "rhetoric" in the Hellenistic period. From the early Hellenistic *Rhetoric to Alexander* to the late Hellenistic, post-Hermagorean instruction offered in the *Rhetorica ad Herennium* and Cicero's *De Inventione*, we find that a more generalized *logôn technê* has been reduced to practical instruction in the methods of civic oratory, and chiefly (in the Roman texts) the methods of arguing lawsuits, though some trace of the original derivation is preserved.

What happened to "rhetoric" in the Hellenistic period is pithily summed up for us, albeit with hyperbole, by Dionysius of Halicarnassus. Dionysius, residing and writing in Augustan Rome sometime between 30 and 8 B.C., begins his essay *On the Ancient Orators* (*Peri tôn Archaiôn Rhêtorôn*) with a tale that echoes Cicero's.

> In the time before our own, the old and philosophic rhetoric [*archaia kai philosophos rhêtorikê*] was so abused and endured such terrible mistreatment that it fell into decline; after Alexander of Macedon's final breath it gradually withered away, and by our generation had come to seem almost extinct. Another stole past the guards and took its place, intolerably shameless and theatrical, and comprehending nothing either of philosophy or of any other liberal training [*eleutherios paideuma*], escaping notice and misleading the ignorance of the masses, it came to enjoy not only greater wealth, luxury and splendor than the other, but also the honors and high offices of cities, which rightfully belong to the philosophic, and it was wholly vul-

gar and importunate, and finally made Greece resemble the households of the prof-
ligate and evil-starred. For just as in these there sits the freeborn, sensible wife
[*eleuthera kai sôphrôn gametê*] with no authority over her domain, while a senseless
harlot [*aphrôn hetaira*] brings ruin upon her life and claims control of the whole estate, casting filth upon her and putting her in terror, so too in every city and even
among the well-educated (for this was the utmost evil of them all) the ancient and
indigenous Attic muse was dishonored and deprived of her possessions, while the
new arrival, some Mysian or Phrygian or Carian trash [*kakon*] just recently come
from some Asian pit [*barathron*], claimed the right to rule over Greek cities and
drove her rival from the commons, the unlearned driving out the philosophic and
the crazed the sensible. (1)

This tale—with its histrionic account of the "old, philosophic rhetoric" as a
wifely, sensible "Attic muse" displaced and dispossessed by an Asiatic *hetaira* (a female "companion" of the husband, a mistress/prostitute)—has typically been read
as an expression of the "Atticist" reaction against the supposed stylistic excess and
poor taste of "Asianism." But more is at stake than taste. While the bad prostitute-
rhetoric is indeed identified with "Asia" and the good, wifely one with what is
"Attic," the constitutive opposition is between what Dionysius subsequently calls
the "ancient, sensible rhetoric" (*archaia kai sôphrôn rhêtorikê*) and a "new and mindless" (*nea kai anoêtos*) counterpart that has usurped its civic place (2). The old, good
rhetoric is identified with the well-born citizen who is *eleutheros*, "free," who is
given *eleutherios paideuma*, "liberal education" (literally "the freeborn person's education"), and who is or should be *eupaideutos*, "well-educated." The other is "unlearned" (*amathês*), "senseless" (*aphrôn*), "crazed" (*mainomenê*), not to mention
"mindless," and is metaphorically and hyperbolically identified with ignoble and
lowborn "trash," *to kakon* (literally "the bad"), such as prostitutes and criminals.
Being thrown from a precipice into a deep cleft or "pit," a *barathron*, was a form of
execution. But this *hetaira* rhetoric is also seen as having been quite effective and
successful at seducing crowds, enriching its practitioners, capturing positions of political importance, and dominating politics in "every city" of the Hellenistic world.
What Dionysius describes, in sum, is the triumph of a nonphilosophic, narrowly
educated, technically skillful, "shameless" and sycophantic rhetoric for hire, with
the concomitant eclipse of an "older," broader ideal of public discourse art and
discourse education such as Isocrates, Aristotle, or Theophrastus might have approved. The consequence, for Dionysius as for Cicero, has been a decline in the intellectual and ethical quality of what Dionysius calls *politikos logos* (1) and thus also
a decline in the prudent management of civic affairs.

As the obvious class prejudice in Dionysius's metaphor suggests, moreover,
he associates this new, triumphant kako-rhetoric with ambitious, opportunistic
arrivistes "just recently come" from outside or below the traditional ruling orders:
outsiders with sufficient wealth to pay for a sophist's lessons and who hope to advance themselves by means of an orator's career, or a sycophant's career. This is, in
essence, the sort of audience we chiefly find addressed in the *technai* this chapter has
surveyed—an audience that seems to have provided a ready, steady, and lucrative
market for practical instruction in the methods of resourceful argument and urbane
style. Philodemus of Gadara complains:

[Our students] are led astray by sophists and pay them money merely to get the reputation for political ability. . . . Epicurus says, whenever they listen to [the sophists'] displays and panegyrics, and are beguiled [psychagôgêthôsi] . . . they give no heed to whether [the speech] is advantageous or disadvantageous, or even true or false, but being beguiled [psychagôgoumenoi] by the sound and the periods, parisoses and antitheses and homoioteleuta, [they] think that if they could talk like that they would succeed in assembly and court. . . . That is why they spend money on sophists.[40]

This complaint resonates with Isocrates' early-fourth-century grouse about students flocking to cut-rate sophists who promise to teach the techniques of rhêtoreia. Since Epicurus flourished in the late fourth and early third century, the citation of him implies that the phenomenon that he, Philodemus, and Isocrates all complain about has more or less continued unabated from the classical period right through the Hellenistic period and into the Roman period as well.

If, then, we are to say that rhetoric "declined" in the Hellenistic period, it appears to have been a "decline" not from a pristine art of practical civic discourse into bellettristic hyperaesthesia or tedious scholasticism. Rather, if there was any "decline" at all, it appears actually to have been the rise and dominance of a version of rhêtorikê disconnected from a larger logôn technê and focused on practical instruction in the "art" or technique of effective pragmatic discourse—an instruction that became increasingly sophisticated, and with time increasingly standardized—and the rise as well of the civic discursive practice that such an art supports, namely the sycophantic, "mindless" hetaira rhetoric that Dionysius caricatures, or the "rash and audacious," technically skilled and philosophically vapid speech that Cicero portrays as eloquence's evil twin.

4

"Rhetoric" from Cicero to the Second Sophistic

Here I continue the tale begun in the preceding chapter. As I noted there, the traditional tale of rhetoric's rise and fall repeats itself, first at Athens in the fifth to fourth centuries B.C., and then at Rome in the late republic, producing a narrative in which rhetoric enjoys two brief moments of florescence, followed by much longer periods of "decline." The argument here, however, is that in the Roman period after Cicero, just as in the Hellenistic period, there is no "decline of rhetoric" in any meaningful sense. And indeed we might argue that, under the Roman emperors, what we find is actually a triumph of the Ciceronian ideal—not, however, the Ciceronian ideal as propagated by Quintilian and identified with the oratorical practices of the late republic, but the Ciceronian ideal as understood from an Isocratean or sophistic perspective, and as advanced by Cicero himself.

"They Shattered the Republic": Cicero's Isocrateanism

As we have seen, both young Cicero and Dionysius of Halicarnassus do speak of rhetoric as having suffered a "decline"; but a significant feature of these tales is that they both include the period of the late Roman republic—the very period that traditional histories regard as Roman rhetoric's great moment of florescence. The grown-up Cicero, moreover, gives this tale a second rendition at the outset of his major treatise on rhetoric, the "Aristotelian" dialogue *De Oratore*, completed in 55 B.C. when he was fifty-one years old.[1]

> Indeed should I wish to use examples from our state [*civitatis*], as well as others, I could cite more harm in public affairs, than benefit, produced by persons of surpassing eloquence: but, putting the rest aside, of all that seem so to me, excepting, Crassus, you [and Antonius], the most eloquent that I have heard were Tiberius and Gaius Sempronius [Gracchus], whose father, a person of wisdom and gravity, but noway eloquent, was many a time, and especially when censor, the republic's salvation. And by no abundance [*copia*] of well-wrought speech [*orationis*], but by a nod and a word, did he transfer the freedmen into the city tribes; and had he not done this, we would have long since lost the republic which, at present, we scarcely

retain. But truly his fluent [*diserti*] sons, equipped in every way for speaking [*ad dicendum*] by both nature and instruction, when they had inherited a state that was flourishing because of their father's counsels as well as ancestral arms, then by means of that eloquence that, according to you, is the splendid governess of civil communities [*civitatum*], they shattered the republic. (1.9.38)

The speaker of these lines is the elderly Quintus Mucius Scaevola the augur, the most eminent jurisconsult of his time; the dialogue is set in 91 B.C., when Cicero was fifteen or sixteen years old and Scaevola was eighty. Scaevola's lines are spoken to the famed orators Lucius Licinius Crassus and Marcus Antonius, the dialogue's principal speakers. Crassus has commenced a discussion of rhetoric that will occupy the company for two days, by delivering an Isocratean encomium of artful, persuasive "speech" as that which establishes and sustains civil communities. According to Crassus, "the perfect orator's guidance and wisdom" (*perfecti oratoris moderatione et sapienta*) ensures "the safety of the greatest number of private citizens and of the whole republic" (1.8.30–34). Scaevola's objection to this notion establishes the opening issue for the subsequent debate.

Crassus is of course the dialogue's protagonist and is generally seen as Cicero's mouthpiece. And one can reply to Scaevola—as Crassus does—that his objection is a common argument advanced by those who deny to rhetoric "all learning and knowledge of greater things" and keep its scope confined to "law courts and little meetings [*in iudicia et coniunculas*], as if in some pounding-mill" (1.11.46; *coniunculas* is a diminutive form of the gerund for *coniungo*, "bring together" or "form a contract"). But neither Scaevola nor Antonius are mere foils for Crassus. All three of these figures were not only eminent persons but were also close friends of Cicero's family and were Cicero's personal mentors in his youth (*De Oratore* 2.1.3).[2] These are people whom Cicero respects, admires, and even loves, and within the dialogue they represent positions that are not simply to be dismissed.

There is a further resonance to Scaevola's remark, moreover, in that he, Crassus, and Antonius, as well as nearly all of the dialogue's minor speakers, are to die within four years. Crassus will be dead within a week. Only Scaevola will die peacefully. The rest will be victims of the late republic's turmoil—which had begun, as Scaevola declares, with Tiberius and Gaius Gracchus, who were tribunes of the people in 133 and 122–121 B.C. respectively.

Let us consider this point awhile. The Gracchi threatened the hegemony of the Roman senatorial class by proposing a series of reforms. These included expanded political participation for the "equestrian" class (*equites*, originally the Roman cavalry but in Cicero's time wealthy landowners and businessmen), the social rank just below the senators; the redistribution of land from agricultural estates to alleviate Rome's urban poverty; and extension of Roman citizenship to Rome's Italian "allies" (subject cities). We should not, however, imagine that the Gracchi were protosocialists. At that time Rome had acquired already an empire, comprising not only Italy but nearly all of the northern Mediterranean basin and a part of North Africa (the former Carthage), with vast exploitable wealth. This new empire and its wealth were controlled by a city council, the Roman senate (or *curia*), which was in turn controlled by the city's "best" few hundred families, the *boni*, who constituted the senatorial class—though their decisions, and their election to positions of authority, depended also on the vote of those (carefully manipulated) groups of citizens who qualified for membership in the popular assembly. Within this mostly oligarchic system, political power depended on patron-client relationships: the patron with the greatest number of clients controlled the greatest number of votes when standing for election to high office.

The Gracchan reforms, then, probably were motivated less by notions of social justice than by desires to expand their clientele. The Gracchi themselves were members of the senatorial class and had every interest in maintaining and enhancing their position. (Later politicians who would present themselves as *populares* or "leaders of the people" typically were from senatorial families that had suffered eclipse in the scramble for position.) Likewise, the purpose of agrarian redistribution was not economic justice but expansion of the numbers available for military service. There was a minimum property requirement, and the growing destitution of Rome's common citizens meant that fewer and fewer were qualified, at the very moment when the needs of empire called for ever larger military forces. Soldiers, moreover, typically became the clients of their generals. The Gracchan reforms, in short, were self-serving moves in a game of power politics, and they exacerbated tensions. In 133, Tiberius Gracchus and three hundred of his supporters were clubbed to death, at a meeting of the citizens' assembly, by a crowd consisting of angry senators and their clients. In 121, Gaius Gracchus was similarly beaten to death, and three thousand of his supporters were subsequently put on trial and executed. These events irreparably polarized Roman politics and set in motion the series of convulsions and civil wars that brought the republic to an end.

De Oratore is set on the eve of one such convulsion: the ruinous Social War of 91–87 B.C.—the revolt of Rome's Italian allies (*socii*)—and its violent aftermath. In 91 B.C., Marcus Livius Drusus, a son of one of the principal opponents of the Gracchi, was elected to the tribunate and thereupon proposed enfranchisement of the Italians, as part of a program of compromise reforms. Again, this move was probably Drusus's bid to expand his power base. He explicitly portrayed himself as patron of the Italians, and elicited from them an oath that they would be his clients, while using strong-arm tactics (including violent street gangs) against Rome's urban voters. During the bitter debates that followed from Drusus's proposal, and just a few days after the dramatic date of *De Oratore*, Crassus delivered in the senate what Cicero calls his "swan song" speech, in support of a motion by Drusus to censure the consul Philippus. It is doubtful that Crassus supported Drusus's reforms, but he was outraged by Philippus's having attacked the senate in a speech before the assembly. A vehement oratorical duel ensued, with Philippus attempting to enforce a punitive measure against Crassus, and Crassus attempting to put through (apparently successfully) the motion of censure against Philippus. Crassus, who was forty-nine at the time, so strained himself that, as Cicero says, "while speaking he felt a severe pain in his side, followed by profuse sweating . . . after which with trembling and fever he went back home, and within a week he died of pleurisy." (Though Cicero calls it pleurisy, the symptoms described suggest a heart attack.) Afterward, young Cicero and his brother Quintus revisited the senate-house to gaze at the spot where Crassus had spoken his last oration (*De Oratore* 3.2.6).

Ultimately, Drusus's proposed reforms were all rejected by the senate, and Drusus was murdered (in the house that Cicero some decades later would purchase for himself, on the Palatine hill near the forum). The killing of Drusus provoked the four-year Social War, which ended with Rome victorious yet granting citizenship to the Italian cities after all, in various degrees of limitation depending on their loyalty. This war produced, in turn, the power struggle between the generals Marius and Sulla, and continued civil warfare through the eighties, leading to Sulla's dictatorship in 81 B.C.. In 87, during Marius's short-lived reign of terror with the consul Cinna, Antonius was proscribed and murdered; later, during Sulla's proscriptions (in 81), over ten thousand were put to death and their severed heads displayed in the forum. Of all the speakers in De Oratore, only Cotta would survive these proscriptions. In his introduction to the third book of De Oratore, Cicero describes their deaths in lurid terms as part of a bloodbath in which the republic itself had died (3.1–3).[3]

Thus, although from a Roman perspective Scaevola's retort to Crassus can be dismissed (as Crassus dismisses it) as Greek inanity, it also has portentous resonance with the political events in which the dialogue is embedded, and carries the weight of Scaevola's personal authority. Moreover, Scaevola's contrast between the elder Gracchus and his "fluent" sons marks the arrival and subsequent effect of Greek rhetorical instruction at Rome. Let us consider this point too. Roman contacts with Greek culture developed between the fourth and second centuries B.C., as the Roman state expanded into the Hellenistic world.[4] We first hear of Greek rhetoricians (as well as grammarians and philosophers) teaching at Rome during the lifetime of Cato the Elder, who served as consul in 195 B.C. and censor in 184. Cato was acquainted with Greek literature and rhetoric but thought it not worth detailed study and considered the Isocratean paideia a waste of time. For Cato, the point of education for patricians destined to the senate was practical sensibility and moral probity rather than brilliance in speech and argument. Thus, in Cato's famous dicta, the orator was "a good man skilled in speaking" (vir bonus dicendi peritus) for whom the fundamental rule was "seize the subject, the words will follow" (rem tene, verba sequentur). Speaking well was a function of knowing well and thinking prudently, and the authority of what was said would arise from the speaker's dignitas, while the speaking "skill" itself was mostly a matter of practical experience and not of art. (The adjective peritus can also mean "experienced" or "practiced," and is thus closer to the Greek empeiria than to technê.) In 161, we hear of the senate advising the praetor Pomponius to banish Greek philosophers and rhetoricians from the city. We first hear of Latin rhetorical instruction in 92 B.C., during the consulship of Crassus, when he issued a decree of disapproval with the censor Ahenobarbus.[5] (In De Oratore 3.24.93–95, Cicero's Crassus offers a rationale for the decree: he was opposed not to the spread of rhetorical instruction in Latin per se but to the reductive, corrupt version of Greek rhetoric being taught by the Latin rhetoricians of that time.)

The elder Gracchus was consul in 177 and 163 and censor in 169; he thus belongs to the generation in which the study of Greek rhetoric first began to establish itself at Rome. He seems, in fact, to have learned Greek, for in the Brutus Cicero says that he composed and delivered an oration in Greek "before the Rhodians," presumably as an ambassador, and was "weighty (*gravem*) and even eloquent at that time" (79). But the key feature here is the elder Gracchus's *gravitas:* his eloquence is an epiphenomenon of weighty thought delivered straightforwardly, by a person of dignity and substance; such eloquence may consist simply of "a nod and a word." For Cicero's Scaevola, the elder Gracchus illustrates the truth that civil institutions are founded and protected not "by fluent, elaborate speaking" (*disertis et ornate dicentibus*) but "by wise, courageous men" (*sapientibus et fortibus viris; De Oratore* 1.8.36–37). The elder Gracchus thus belongs, with Cato, to an older tradition of Roman oratory and Roman education—to which an acquaintance with Greek culture has been added, as a sort of veneer. The younger Gracchi, by contrast, are endowed with all the skills of artful, elaborate speech that "nature and instruction" can provide, and the instruction is altogether Greek. As Cicero notes in the *Brutus*, the younger Gracchi, through "the diligence of their mother Cornelia," were trained from boyhood in Greek letters and were "furnished always with carefully chosen Greek tutors," such as Diophanes of Mytilene, "the most skillful speaker of Greece at that time" (104, 125–126). Thus, in this account, the sons are more eloquent than the father but less wise: unlike the father, who successfully resolved an issue of citizenship rights and was able to "preserve the republic," the sons speak brilliantly but advance imprudent, self-serving proposals that only deepen the existing class conflict and generate violent reaction. Implied in Scaevola's retort to Crassus, then, is an argument not only that the arrival of Greek rhetoric (and its Latin appropriation) has caused a "decline" in Roman oratory—yielding public discourse that is not *gravis* or *sapiens* but merely *disertus, ornatus, copiosus, politus* (skillful/fluent, elaborate, copious, polished)—but also that, because it has produced such discourse, this reduced and Latinized Greek rhetoric has contributed not to the construction and maintenance of civil community, but to the sowing and intensification of civil discord and the ultimate unraveling of the Roman state.

How much does Cicero mean for this argument to be believed—and how much should we believe it? Surely Scaevola's case is overstated, or is stated as strongly as possible, to define a controversy for debate. But Scaevola's case is not without merit either.

Consider judicial rhetoric, which at Rome was crucial both to the political life of the republic and to political careers, and was seen as the orator's chief and most distinctive occupation. An important means of defeating a political opponent was to prosecute and convict him of crimes in office—or of any crimes—or to prosecute and convict his clients, thereby undermining his support. Moreover, a would-be politician acquired important clients chiefly by representing their interests in the courts, and indeed the most common way to begin a political career was by conducting a political prosecution or (less commonly) a defense; one's choice of whom to prosecute or defend was typically seen as a declaration of affiliation.[6] Cicero's own entry into politics was his defense of Roscius in 80 B.C., at the age of twenty-six. (It was not his first case, but his first politically important case.) One Chrysogonus, a favorite freedman and henchman of Sulla, had engineered the murder of Roscius's well-to-do father and then had had the man's name added posthumously to the proscription lists as an enemy of the state. The elder Roscius's property accordingly was confiscated and sold at auction, and Chrysogonus arranged to have it sold to himself and his associates (some of whom were relatives of Roscius) at an absurdly low price. Finally, to silence Roscius the son and rightful heir, Chrysogonus charged him with his father's murder. Roscius's family had important friends among the nobility, but most orators were too afraid of Sulla to undertake the defense, and so it came to the then obscure Cicero. Cicero's deft handling of the case won Roscius's acquittal and squelched Chrysogonus, while carefully absolving Sulla from blame (the great man was too busy with important things to know what all his underlings were doing, and could not be held responsible for their crimes). With this success Cicero won fame and influential clients and launched the career that eventually took him to the consulship in 63 B.C..[7]

A Roman trial in the latter years of the republic, and especially a political trial, was an uncertain affair in which the legal basis of the case was likely to be vague and even could become irrelevant. In the first place, there was no systematically organized body of statute law and there were no established canons of juristic interpretation. Beyond the archaic and largely outmoded Twelve Tables (composed c. 451 B.C.), what counted as "the law" consisted principally of a welter of decisions made in previous cases, and being "expert" (*peritus*) in the law meant knowing the history of these decisions and the tradition they constituted. This expertise generally was the property not of orators but of jurisconsults (*iuris consulti*) like Scaevola, who did not practice in the courts but specialized in giving legal opinions and writing contracts. There was, moreover, no systematic method of acquiring this expertise. There were no law schools as such, no comprehensive treatises on the law, no organized collections of documents recording court decisions. Rather, a legal education such as Cicero received consisted of sitting in attendance at a jurisconsult's sessions, which typically were held in the jurisconsult's home or in the forum, usually with an audience present. One simply listened to the jurisconsult formulate replies, *responsa*, to particular questions put to him by persons seeking his assistance. These *responsa* would consist, in essence, of identification, interpretation, and application of the relevant legal precedents for the case in hand. Thus, though orators could acquire at least a working knowledge of Roman law, many or most had relatively little. Juries might have even less, or none at all. In order to establish the legal basis for a case, then, orators typically relied on written *responsa* from respected jurisconsults, whose opinions stood as expert testimony (*De Oratore* 1.57.242, 58.250). But these opinions were just that—opinions—and differing opinions in favor of both sides of a case could always be produced. Jurisconsultative *responsa*, then, had no definitive legal status, and in a law court their probative force as statements of the law could be and often were disputed. As Cicero's Antonius observes in *De Oratore* (1.56.237–239, 57.241–242), cases in which the law was "settled," or undisputable, never went to trial; and in those that did go to trial, the legal basis always would be in dispute, so that it was not the law but the orator's eloquence that decided the final outcome.[8]

Thus, while Roman republican law was chaotic and knowledge of it hard to get, and while this law was only a weak determinant of the outcome of a trial, Greek rhetoric offered the would-be Roman orator and politician—just as it did to the Hellenistic *rhêtôr*—a systematic method of arguing judicial issues with persuasive cogency and eloquence, as well as a systematic training in that method, for cases in which *logos* rather than *nomos* would decide. It seems likely, moreover, that the predominant version of Greek rhetorical instruction that took hold at Rome during the second and early first centuries B.C., and particularly the version that took hold in Latin rhetorical instruction, was the kind we see embodied in the *Ad Herennium* and *De Inventione:* Hermagorean stasis rhetoric adapted chiefly for judicial argument, and supplemented with stylistic training. As Cicero remarks in the *Brutus,* "the precepts of Hermagoras" provided "arguments, like spears equipped with straps for skirmishers to throw, ready-prepared and suitable to every kind of case" (271). The pragmatic Romans, typically impatient with Greek philosophizing and mainly interested in practical advantage, were most likely to be drawn to the narrower versions of Greek rhetoric—those that Cicero's Crassus describes as limiting rhetoric to "law courts and little meetings, as if in some pounding-mill" and excluding from the orator's art "all learning and knowledge of greater things."[9] As Antonius declares in the second book of *De Oratore,* "not one of our men studies eloquence save to shine forth in the forum; whereas among the Greeks the most eloquent men, aloof from forensic cases, apply themselves not only to other distinguished matters but especially to writing histories" (2.13.55). The more narrowly pragmatic Roman version of rhetoric is what Antonius defends in the first book of *De Oratore* (or pretends to, for the sake of debate): a rhetoric in which the orator's specific function is to produce "words pleasing to the listener, and ideas fitted to convince as far as possible in forensic as well as public causes," supplemented by "voice, delivery, and a certain charm" (1.49.213). For this, the would-be orator has little need for extensive learning or deep studies, and no need even for knowledge of the law. The orator's art needs only natural ability and at most a basic training in the methods of effective courthouse eloquence; the rest is practice and experience. And that is all.

Historians of Roman law tend to portray the effects of such rhetoric in the late republic as ranging from bad to catastrophic. According to Bruce W. Frier, for example, the version of Greek rhetoric that took hold at Rome provided a "relativistic framework" of endless argumentative positioning and counter positioning—the essence of sophistic antilogy—but "had only marginal room for the notion of an uncontested positive law" and "tended . . . to expand the room for controversy . . . [and thus] to pry apart any notion of legal fixity." The consequence of this progressive undetermining of an already vague and chaotic body of law, as Frier argues, was "a sort of legal entropy, in which the outcome of lawsuits became increasingly unpredictable and 'lawless,'" so that a trial in the late republic could become "a fundamentally irrational proceeding."[10] Richard A. Bauman presents an equally dismal picture of "a legal system in chaos," dominated by not law but orators and overwhelmed with a "bloated mass of controversial points which threatened to swamp the carefully nurtured consensus which was the *ius non controversum,*" the established law. In the last years of the republic, as Bauman says, few knew or could determine or agree what the law really was or what it meant in any given case; many persons presenting themselves as jurisconsults were incompetents or frauds; deception in legal matters had become "almost a national sport"; and many magistrates and jurymen were willing simply to ignore the law whenever it suited them to do so, even if the law was relatively clear.[11] Thus Antonius declares that an orator need not know the law, and thus Crassus and Scaevola both complain that many and even most orators in their time not only are completely ignorant of the law but frequently do not even care what it is (*De Oratore* 1.10.40, 1.36–40).

Something of this situation can be seen in Cicero's *Pro Caecina*, the last judicial speech of his career, in which the centerpiece is a passionate defense of the very notion of civil law. Caecina had inherited a parcel of land from his wife's estate. His claim was disputed by one Aebutius, who seized the property and hired a gang of armed men to prevent Caecina from entering. Caecina sued for restitution of his property. The basis of the suit was a well-known edict that required such restitution for a person driven out by force from property that he legally possessed. Aebutius's basic argument (or that of his advocate, Gaius Calpurnius Piso) was that Caecina was not entitled to restitution because he had not been "driven out" from property that he "possessed": he had been driven *away* and thus had never "possessed" the property at all, since he had not entered or occupied it; and he had not been driven away "by force" since he had not actually been struck by the armed men who threatened and chased him; and furthermore he could not inherit the property because he was from Volaterre, an allied city with reduced citizenship status. Cicero's argument for Caecina was, in brief, that Volaterreans were in fact entitled to inherit land as Roman citizens (it's fairly clear that Piso's argument on this point was merely an evocation of Roman prejudice against the "foreigner"), that Caecina's legal ownership of the property had been recognized already in various transactions, and that Piso's wrangling with the words of the edict was a manifest distortion of its intent as recognized by all of the most reliable jurisconsults. The interpretation of this edict was the crucial part of the case, and Piso's reply, it appears, was that the opinions of the jurisconsults—and thus the whole tradition of the edict's meaning and application—should not be taken into account. Cicero's response consists of a declaration that he is "amazed to see it maintained in trials, and not infrequently by ingenious men, that neither should the jurisconsults be followed nor should the law prevail in every case" (24.67), followed by a grand-style encomium of law: "O splendid thing and worthy of your protection, gentlemen! For what is civil law? What neither favor can bend, nor power break, nor wealth corrupt" (26.73), and so forth. Cicero probably won, but the seeming absurdity of Piso's argument should not persuade us that Cicero won easily. *Pro Caecina* was delivered on the third hearing of the case, which had deadlocked on two previous occasions. Had Cicero's services not been retained for the third hearing, or had he delivered a weaker speech, Piso and Aebutius may well have prevailed. In the *Brutus*, Cicero describes Piso as "an orator of steady and ample speech, by no means slow in invention, but yet by facial expression and dissimulation"—that is, by his manner of delivery—"he seemed even more intelligent than he was" (239); he was a formidable opponent.

It seems reasonable, in sum, to argue that Scaevola's retort to Crassus at the outset of *De Oratore* embodies a case that has some merit, even if Scaevola has overstated it. The art of "eloquence" cultivated by the limited version of Greek rhetoric that became predominant in the Hellenistic period and at Rome in the second and first centuries b.c.—the version we find in the *Ad Herennium*—could just as easily be, and probably was, more often a weapon of civil discord than a "splendid governess of civil community," more often a tool of factional strife and irresponsible power politics than an instrument of wise deliberation, more often a corrosive to the rule of law than an art of justice. Surely the Roman republic came unglued not because of a corrosive rhetoric alone, but because of its intractable, and growing, social and economic problems.[12] Nevertheless it clearly can be argued that the version of rhetoric that flourished in the late republic worked chiefly not to solve but to exacerbate those problems.

The late republic, in Cicero's eyes, is not a period of great rhetoric, or even good rhetoric, although there may have been some "men of surpassing eloquence" and some ingenious (if sleazy) orators like Piso. A central point of Cicero's historical survey of Roman orators in the *Brutus*—in addition to its obvious suggestion that Cicero is himself the best of the lot—is his assertion that "I wish for you to see that of the whole collection of those who have ventured to speak before the multitudes, few deserve to be remembered, and indeed all who have won a name have not been many" (69.244). In the *Orator,* Cicero's last treatise on rhetoric (written in 46 B.C.), he declares that the "perfect orator" he wishes to describe "perhaps has never existed" (2.7). And in *De Oratore,* likewise, a repeated point is that Crassus's "perfect orator" whose eloquence both constructs and protects the civil community is an ideal and that great orators who even approximate this ideal have been extremely rare. Indeed, Cicero declares that in all the generations of Roman orators one can scarcely find even a "tolerable" orator at any given time (1.2.6–5.19; 1.26.118). All of this should certainly be taken with several grains of salt, but neither can it be dismissed.

The point is that *De Oratore* is Cicero's assertion of a rhetorical philosophy that *opposes* the prevailing instruction and the prevailing practices at Rome in the late republic. What he asserts is a syncretic version of the "old and philosophic rhetoric" that Dionysius of Halicarnassus will describe—about three decades after Cicero—as having suffered eclipse in the Hellenistic age. What this rhetorical philosophy consists of is a mixture chiefly of Isocratean and Aristotelian perspectives, although there clearly are Academic and Stoic influences as well: as Cicero declares in a letter of 54 B.C., the three books of *De Oratore* "disagree with the commonly held precepts, and embrace the rhetorical theories of all the ancients, both Aristotelian and Isocratean" (*Ad Familiares* 1.9.23), suggesting that his theory derives not only from these two figures, but also from their successors in the sophistic and Peripatetic traditions, particularly Theophrastus.[13] But, as Michael Leff has argued, Cicero's approach appears to be most fundamentally Isocratean: the dialogue presents an expansive notion of rhetoric as an unbounded art of eloquence and practical philosophy, a *logôn technê,* ranging across all genres of epideictic and pragmatic discourse and across all fields of human inquiry (but especially those related to politics and ethics) and functioning as a culture-shaping art that both constructs and preserves the possibilities of civil community. This Isocrateanism is held in "ironic" or dialectical balance, as Leff argues, with a more systematically preceptive, Aristotelian/-Peripatetic approach to "rhetoric" as the discourse art embodied in the genres of practical civic discourse, and especially judicial discourse, which Cicero and his speakers, in typically Roman fashion, consider the "most difficult" and crowning genre in which the whole art is subsumed.[14]

Crucial to the rhetorical philosophy that Antonius and Crassus are shown to agree on (from the second book onward) is the more or less Isocratean notion that the greatest eloquence is impossible without a wide-ranging *logôn paideia* that is both "philosophic" and literary: a discourse education that includes the study of poetry, panegyric, and history, as well as the philosophical debate of general "theses" and declamations on particular, fictive cases or "hypotheses," is the necessary preparation and foundation for the "perfect orator's" pragmatic eloquence in lawcourts and assemblies. Antonius declares in his discussion of invention that those "professors" are foolish who divide the "modes of discourse" according to "two kinds of issues," *duo genera causarum*—the *universa genera* that are deliberated without reference to specific persons or occasions, and the "other" kinds that are bounded by such particulars. For, Antonius argues, general and specific issues are never separable in practice: "all controversies" ultimately turn upon the *universa genera causarum* which underlie them, and indeed, "there is in fact no case" in which "the thing to be decided turns upon the personalities involved and not upon consideration of the general principles that are themselves in question" (2.31.133–135). For Antonius, this means that the infinitude of particular cases can methodically be reduced to the limited number of general issues that underlie them, so that the well-trained orator must have a full supply of *loci communes*, "commonplaces," for speaking on each type of general issue. For these, Antonius turns to the Aristotelian/Peripatetic "art" of topical invention (*topikê*; 2.36–40; Cicero gives this art a fuller and more systematic exposition in his *Topica*). Moreover, the orator must be able to elaborate and amplify such *loci* with impressive style and with suitable pathetic force, a point that Antonius discusses at some length (2.41–53). Later, when discussing *dispositio*, Antonius notes that the audience's emotions should be roused not only in the peroration and exordium, but also in any other part of a speech by means of opportune "digressions," and that the best opportunities for emotively resonant, moving digressions will arise from cases that involve "weighty" *loci* (2.77.311–313). That is, the orator must find moments for waxing eloquent and passionate on the general principles and issues embodied in the specific case, and the "weightier" those principles and issues are, the greater will be his opportunities for emotively powerful "digressions" rich with amplification and embellishment.

These ideas are developed further by Crassus. Crassus declares that "[t]he crowning glory of eloquence is to amplify the matter with ornamentation" (*summa laus eloquentiae est amplificare rem ornando*; 3.26.104), particularly when waxing eloquent on the *loci* mentioned by Antonius, in order to move and persuade an audience (3.27.104–5). For this the orator especially needs the *loci* of "laudation and censure" (*laudandi et vituperandi*) – or in other words the *loci* of the *universa genera* concerning "virtue, duty, equity and good, and dignity, utility, honor, ignominy, reward and punishment, and the like"—for "nothing is more suited to the heightening and amplification of an oration" (3.27.105–108). Crassus then discusses the argumentation of such general issues for several chapters (3.28–31), showing that they also fall within the Hermagorean system of stases, and noting that, with respect to the argumentation of *hypotheseis* or actual cases, "The most ornate orations are . . . those that range most widely and turn aside from the particular dispute to an unfolding of the general issue's significance" (3.30.120). This is, of course, precisely what Cicero himself does in many of his own orations, such as *Pro Caecina* with its grand encomium of law, or *Pro Archia Poeta* (a defense of the Greek poet Archias's claim to Roman citizenship), which consists chiefly of an encomium of poetry and also an encomium of Archias himself as a noble poet. Cicero's argument for Archias is, in brief, that Archias does indeed have legal title to Roman citizenship, although the documents recording it have been lost (a point that is disposed of very quickly), and that in any case he *should* have Roman citizenship because of the value of poetry in general and because of the value of Archias's poetry in particular to Rome (points that are expanded on considerably).

So Crassus argues, in books 3 and 1 of *De Oratore* (e.g., 1.15–16, 34; 3.31–35), that the "perfect orator" must be well acquainted with the argumentative *loci* of the general issues involved in any particular dispute, and indeed must be acquainted with all fields of knowledge, but especially those pertaining to "life and conduct" (*vitam atque mores;* 1.15.68–69), so that a rhetorical education must include a philosophico-literary education. Significantly, Crassus also includes legal studies in such an education, and offers a fairly lengthy discussion (1.36–46) of what an "art" of law would need to include, were it to exist. (Cicero, of course, more fully takes up the topics of ethical-political-legal philosophy in such dialogues as *De Re Publica, De Legibus, De Officiis,* and the *Tusculan Disputations.*) Finally, the point is emphatically made— through Catulus's response to Crassus (3.32), and through Crassus's reply (3.33–35) as well as other speeches in the dialogue (e.g., Crassus's thumbnail history of the divergence of rhetoric and philosophy after Plato, 3.14–21)—that what Crassus advocates resembles the old sophistic *paideia,* or the Isocratean *paideia,* which after Plato and Aristotle had been displaced (as Crassus says) into the more specialized subfields of the philosophic schools, leaving to "rhetoric" only the techniques of practical oratory in courts and assemblies.

But for Cicero's Crassus, rhetoric is more than philosophy, and indeed is the crown of philosophy, because unlike the philosopher the rhetor must also have the poet's powers of evocative and moving expression, or even greater powers. As Crassus puts it in a famous passage,

> [i]ndeed the poet is closely related to the orator, somewhat more restricted in rhythm, yet more free in his license with words, and surely in many kinds of ornamentation his partner and almost peer; and certainly in one respect almost the same, as he neither circumscribes his bounds nor limits his authority, which would permit him less to range with such power and abundance where he will. (1.16.70–71)

Again in book 3, he says that poets are *proxima cognatio cum oratoribus,* "next of kin with orators" (3.7.27). Both orator and poet claim the right to exercise their powers of eloquence across the whole domain of possible thought, and the stylistic differences between them are matters of degree and not of kind. Thus Crassus considers the pen "the best and most eminent producer and teacher of speech" (*dicendi;* 1.33.150) and recommends a full course of literary studies for the would-be orator, conspicuously including the study and translation of poetry as well as other composition exercises (1.33–34; 3.49). Significantly, when Crassus in the dialogue's final chapters (3.37–61) offers a lengthy discussion of the principles of style and delivery for flights of "ornate," moving eloquence, the examples are drawn overwhelmingly from poetry. Moreover, when he is discussing prose rhythm (3.44–51), he offers an account based on comparisons with poetic meters (and with music), such as we find in Demetrius's *On Style*, while invoking Peripatetic theory (Aristotle and Theophrastus both are mentioned). At the same time, Crassus offers the strikingly Gorgianic (and possibly Theophrastian) observation that "[n]othing is so cognate with our feelings as rhythms and sounding words, by which we are excited and inflamed and soothed and mellowed and often brought to mirth and melancholy," while adding that "the supreme power" of rhythmic words is "more suitable to poetry and song" (3.50.197).[15]

Cicero gives this account a more extensive treatment in his last treatise on rhetoric, the *Orator*, which rehearses the rhetorical philosophy presented in *De Oratore* and is devoted overwhelmingly to style. Nearly half the treatise is devoted specifically to prosody (thirty three of seventy six chapters), and indeed Cicero claims to have written "more about rhythmic speech than anyone before us" (67.226), a claim that may be sustainable if "anyone" is limited to Latin writers or analyses of Latin prose rhythm. But clearly Cicero is working from Greek sources, and like them he relies on a fundamentally poetic analysis of prose rhythm as composed of metrically structured periods, clauses, and phrases, which he says the Greeks call *periodoi*, *kôla*, and *kommata* (56.204, 62.211) and which, as compositional units, are the orator's equivalent of the poet's lines. He repeats the Stoic doctrine that poetry is the original and most distinctive form of rhythmic composition, adding that "there are no rhythms outside those of poetry" (56.188), that lyric poetry comes nearest to the orator's prose—for "when the singing is stripped away, almost naked speech remains" (55.183)—and that prose and poetry differ only by the arrangement of their feet, prose having greater freedom (67.227). Finally, Cicero's analysis of rhythm in the *Orator* is grounded on the premise that rhythm is "that which suits the measures of the ear" (20.67) and is based on intuitive, even instinctual capacities for response (see also *De Oratore* 3.50). In a striking illustration of this premise, Cicero provides a close analysis of a short passage from a speech delivered by one Gaius Carbo in the people's assembly, notes that the terminal ditrochee of the final phrase elicited "such a shout from the crowd that it was marvelous," and argues that this response was produced by the rhythm (*Orator* 63.213–215). Poetry, in sum, remains for Cicero as for Demetrius (and other Greeks) the paradigm example of rhythmic prosody, while rhythmic prosody is understood as central to the psychagogic power of discourse and as crucial to an eloquence that aims at passional response. It's worth noting here that Cicero was himself one of the more accomplished poets of his generation, though his poetic achievement was soon eclipsed by the great Augustans.[16]

We know, of course, that in his later years Cicero was faulted by his "Atticist," plain-style contemporaries for the expansive, "Asiatic" style of his orations. The *Brutus* and *Orator* have commonly been read as (among other things) Cicero's response to criticism.[17] But within the text of *De Oratore*, he seems already well aware that his stylistic theory (like his general rhetorical philosophy) runs counter to the predominant Roman practices and teachings. In book 3, Crassus remarks that the stylistic principles he professes are "not conveyed in the common training" (the *vulgari disciplina*), and are not part of what Catulus describes as the "everyday standard exercises" at Rome (3.49.188). Likewise, despite the fact that Cicero's

Crassus and Cicero's own practice emphasize the centrality of epideictic *loci* (and the general questions epideictic argues) to passional, persuasive eloquence in law-courts and assemblies, Cicero's Antonius nevertheless observes that, although the genres of "laudation" are many and widely practiced among the Greeks, they are little practiced and less studied at Rome, so that Roman rhetoricians have scarcely bothered to discuss them. The main epideictic genres practiced by Roman orators, he says, are either laudations delivered in the forum, which consist of "a brief, bare, and unadorned testimonial," or simple epitaphs composed for funeral gatherings where magniloquent displays would be unseemly (2.84.341).[18]

What sort of rhetoric is Cicero proposing? Clearly, Cicero retains the conventional Roman republican attitude that judicial rhetoric is the crown and summation of the orator's civic art, his most distinctive practice. Yet the rhetorical philosophy embodied in *De Oratore* implicitly presses toward a different kind of practice also, indeed the sort of practice Cicero began from in his younger years (as a publishing poet) and returned to in his later years (as a writer of dialogues). As we have seen, Cicero's "perfect orator" is one who knows the discourse of philosophy—though he need not follow the school philosophers into their abstruser speculations, which he, like Isocrates, considers useless, and he is more likely to focus on questions of moral and civic wisdom. But what chiefly distinguishes this "perfect orator" from the philosopher is his possession of a virtually poetic stylistic power. According to Crassus, the philosopher qua philosopher possesses only wisdom, *sapientia*, while the genuine orator possesses *sapientia* and *eloquentia* together, so that the orator can speak before a public gathering on any subject the philosopher may speak on, but better and more persuasively; and persons called "philosophers" who speak with eloquence in public performance are, in fact, orators (3.35.142–143). As Cicero's audience would certainly have recognized, this is the same line of argument that Plato's Gorgias takes (*Gorgias* 456b–c). What seems to be implied, then, is an image of the "perfect orator" that looks remarkably like a sophist, albeit a Romanized one whose chief practical ambition and public glory is to exercise his skills in law courts and assemblies, but nevertheless a sophist whose major sources of emotive eloquence and power derive from epideictic registers: from poetry, from philosophic dialogue and dialectic, from history, from panegyric. In sum, despite his typically Roman laudation of judicial speech as rhetoric's crowning genre, there is an undercurrent in Cicero's argument suggesting that epideictic discourse is the realm of highest eloquence—where the rhetor can engage most fully with grand conceptions, and can approximate most nearly the "supreme" poetic power of rhythmic eloquence, while performing upon the stage of public, civic *mores*. It may seem unlikely that Cicero would intend this implication, but it is, in effect, the drift of the Greek tradition he appropriates and champions.

Oddly, it is the triumph of this tradition in the next few centuries, under the Roman emperors, that traditional histories regard as a "decline of rhetoric."

Rhetoric under the Roman Emperors

Much of the traditional image of "rhetoric in decline" seems to be reflected in the following anecdote from Philostratus's *Lives of the Sophists*. Here we find an Asiatic sophist of the mid–second century, Alexander Peloplaton ("Clay-Plato"), on an embassy for Seleucia (present-day Silifke, in southern Turkey) to the emperor Antoninus Pius (r. 138–161 A.D.):[19]

> Thinking that the emperor [*basileus*] was inattentive to him, Alexander raised his voice in imprecation and said, "Pay attention to me, Caesar!" Whereupon the ruler [*autokratôr*], exasperated with him for using so presumptuous an address, said "I am paying attention, and I know you well. For you," he said, "are the one who is always arranging his hair and cleaning his teeth and polishing his nails and smelling of perfume." (1.5.571)

Philostratus says there had been "slanders" circulating about this sophist, to the effect that he was using cosmetics to make himself look younger—although, apparently, he had only recently "reached manhood" (1.5.570)—so it seems that Alexander was the victim of false rumors, and was facing an emperor who considered him personally repulsive even before he spoke. (Philostratus also says that Alexander, like his mother, was exceptionally good-looking.) Nonetheless the anecdote may seem to represent the traditional image of a decadent, degenerate rhetoric "in decline": the image, that is, of the perfumed sophist prancing in finery before an absolute, imperial authority.

The crudely gendered nature of this image, in which "decadence/degeneracy" is figured as "effeminacy," is obvious enough. But Philostratus's story also has some noteworthy aspects that the traditional image tends to elide: first, that Alexander Peloplaton is indeed speaking as an ambassador, on behalf of a large, important city, and that real political business is being conducted; second, that Philostratus's chapter on this sophist (1.5.570–76) describes him as performing several important embassies on behalf of various cities during his career, as well as eventually serving as Marcus Aurelius's imperial secretary for Greek correspondence (*ab epistulis Graecis*); third, that, as the nickname "Peloplaton" or "Clay-Plato" suggests, Alexander represents a version of sophistic that portrays itself as "philosophical"; and fourth, that Philostratus portrays this sophist as a widely respected intellectual and literary figure with extraordinary skill in public declamation, a figure who can attract large audiences. Alexander's unlucky encounter with Antoninus Pius is not a paradigmatic scene and is preserved by Philostratus precisely because it is unusual. It is worth noting, too, that Alexander does indeed presume that he can scold the emperor. His presumption is miscalculation only because the emperor's attitude toward him has been poisoned by malicious rumors.

Philostratus gives us other anecdotes as well. For example (2.32.625–627), Heliodorus "the Arab" had been "elected" (*echeirotonêthê*) as "advocate" (*prodikos*) by the Celtic tribes of his home community in Gaul—the verb *cheirotoneô*, "elect," signifies a show of hands—and he had been sent with a colleague on an embassy to the emperor Caracalla (r. 198–217 A.D.). But when his colleague had fallen ill, Heliodorus was called in suddenly and forced to plead his case alone without an adequate preparation, or without the materials his colleague would have brought. Heliodorus protested, but as Philostratus says, the official who summoned him was a *hybristês*, a "violent person," who dragged the sophist unceremoniously by his beard into the courtroom.

> But when [Heliodorus] had come in he boldly looked at the *basileus* and asked for his speaking-time, and skillfully managed his appeal, saying, "It will seem strange to you, greatest ruler [*megiste autokrator*], for someone to nullify his own suit by pleading it alone, without commands [to do so]." (2.32.626)

Philostratus does not give us the rest of Heliodorus's speech, but Caracalla was so impressed that he granted Heliodorus's suit and immediately bestowed on him and all his descendants the status of equestrian rank, and furthermore appointed him as head of "the most important of the public advocates under the Romans" (the advocates of the treasury),[20] because he was "suited for lawcourts and cases at law." Heliodorus returned the favor by offering to declaim impromptu on whatever theme the emperor proposed, which turned out to be "Demosthenes, Having Broken down before Philip, Is Accused of Cowardice" (32.626; this scene appears to have been witnessed personally by Philostratus).

In another anecdote preserved by Philostratus, the great sophist Aelius Aristides, upon the destruction of Smyrna (today's Izmir) by an earthquake (c. 178 A.D.), immediately composed a prose "monody" and letter to the emperor Marcus Aurelius, in full Asiatic style, lamenting the destruction and requesting funds and assistance to rebuild the city. Philostratus says:

> [h]e lamented in such a way to Marcus that, not only did the *basileus* groan often at other places in the monody, but also, coming upon "the west-winds blow through desolation," the *basileus* shed tears upon the pages, and in accord with Aristides' urgings he consented to rebuild the city. (2.9.582)[21]

We probably must think of Marcus Aurelius as reading this letter aloud, or having it read to him, and in the process being moved to weep before his advisors. The emperor had spent time in Smyrna, and the letter skillfully invokes his memories of the once-great city's beauties—offering a virtual walking tour of its vistas, its architecture, its harbor, its markets, its temples, its bustling streets, and so forth, as the emperor once saw them—while dwelling on their utter disappearance and exhorting Marcus to the noble task of city-building. (As Aristides' subsequent Smyrnaean orations suggest, the task was completed in about two years.)[22]

Philostratus offers a great many other anecdotes as well, but these brief episodes from the careers of Aelius Aristides, Heliodorus "the Arab," and Alexander Peloplaton may be sufficient to suggest a general picture of what "rhetoric" had come to by the late second century A.D., and indeed for the rest of antiquity. The sophist's Isocratean, "philosophic" art of *logos* seems everywhere dominant, and, while centered on the epideictic-literary genres and especially the practices of panegyric and declamation, it continues also to perform pragmatic functions, and can yet exert real power within the Roman state.[23]

One way to describe the government of the Roman Empire would be to say, as Fergus Millar has, "[t]he Roman Empire had no Government"—that is, no "body of persons formally elected or appointed who had the responsibility for effective decisions," nor any "representative body, duly elected, to which the 'Government' might have been responsible, nor any sovereign assembly or list of voters."[24] But there was an administration. The Roman Empire was governed personally by the emperor, with the assistance of an entourage of "friends" (*amici*) or "companions" (*comites*), from wherever he happened to reside, whether he was at home, or touring the provinces, or on a military campaign. The senate and most of the political institutions and offices of the republic continued formally to exist, but all decision-making power was ultimately vested in the emperor. The senate became an advisory body, but it was chiefly called on to support or confirm imperial decisions, and it seems to have become mostly ceremonial in function by the third century; it retained, however, some role in the formulation of private law and acquired the function of sitting as a court for certain kinds of cases (i.e., trials of members of the senatorial class). Virtually all appointments to magistracies, governorships, and other posts in the Roman administration came eventually to be matters of imperial patronage rather than popular or senatorial election, while the admission of "new men" to the senatorial class itself, and to the equestrian class also, likewise became matters of imperial benefaction. There was no real constitutional restriction on the emperor's authority and no particular civic edifice that was the "official" place of business for the imperial administration. The emperor in essence ran the empire from his house—the *palatium*, so named for its original location on the Palatine hill, but later the name for the imperial residence wherever it happened to be—or from his camp when on campaign. So far as we know, an emperor's typical work-day (when he was not engaged in warfare) appears to have consisted of a morning spent reviewing reports and correspondence, consulting with his *amici* and hearing various petitions and appeals, followed by an afternoon siesta period devoted to exercise, bathing, lunch, sleep and relaxation, possibly some left-over business in the late afternoon and evening, possibly some cultivated conversation in Greek or Latin, and a late evening dinner with his household. This leisured rhythm, with its treatment of political affairs as patron-client business conducted in face-to-face transactions chiefly during the morning *salutationes* in a reception hall at the patron's residence, was in essence a continuation of the Roman upper-class lifestyle.[25]

Despite the evolution of the emperor's role within the fiction that he was "first citizen" (*princeps*) among his fellow senators and commander-in-chief (*imperator*) of the Roman military, in reality his role evolved according to the model of the Hellenistic *basileus*—indeed, that was what his Greek subjects called him. Like a Hellenistic *basileus* with his *synedrion* of *philoi* (or *hetairoi*), the emperor ruled with the advice of his *consilium* or "council" of *amici* (or *comites*) and with the assistance of various secretaries and officials (such as the *ab epistulis*), usually of equestrian rank, who handled official correspondence, acted as jurisconsults, and so forth. By the third century, this more or less informal entourage evolved into the *comitatus*, the imperial central administration: the *consilium* became the "consistory" or council of state (*consistorium*), supported by various subordinate secretariats and by the emperor's domestic and military personnel; and the term *comes*, "companion," became an official title (from which we derive the word "count," or French *comte*). The *comitatus* traveled with the emperor wherever he went, and, since its total personnel (including support staff) would have numbered in the thousands, in transit it would have stretched for miles, carrying with it boxes of imperial records, the emperor's treasury, and even a mint. The *consilium/consistorium*, like a Hellenistic *synedrion*, was a genuine deliberative body with both political and juridic functions; and while its role was in principle advisory and all decisions ultimately were matters of imperial discretion, some decisions would be delegated to lower officials and re-solved without the emperor's direct involvement. By the fourth or fifth century the *consistorium* seems to have become a largely ceremonial institution, like the senate, and to have been displaced by an informal inner council which was, in effect, a re-instantiation of the original gathering of *amici*.[26]

Like the central administration, the provincial administration of the Roman Empire was an evolving structure that developed over time, but in general we can say that, like a Hellenistic *basileus* dispatching *philoi* as governors, ambassadors, and magistrates to the *poleis* of his kingdom, the Roman emperor ruled the provinces of his empire through appointed governors, legates, and various kinds of magistrates (such as tax collectors) empowered to act as his representatives—or through client kings, who retained their titles and privileges while functioning as Roman gover-nors. Like Hellenistic governors, each Roman governor (and to some extent each magistrate) performed his functions with the assistance of his own council of *amici* (and a staff), some of whom the governor/magistrate would bring with him and some of whom would be recruited from the local elites within the province. A gov-ernor/magistrate and his entourage thus constituted a provincial version, and an ex-tension, of the imperial *comitatus: amici* of the *amici*, *philoi* of the *philoi*. Governors and other magistrates generally resided in and ruled from a designated provincial capital, while the other cities of a province retained their local administrative struc-tures and for the most part exercised jurisdiction in their own affairs. There were, moreover, various provincial councils representing "leagues" of cities and profes-sional societies (such as the synods of athletes and performers), which looked after their particular concerns and sent embassies to governors and emperors alike to rep-resent their special interests.

In the far-flung Roman Empire, with its relatively slow communications and the prohibitive difficulties and the costs of sending delegates or bringing lawsuits to the emperors or even the provincial governors and magistrates, with its fairly casual (by modern standards) administrative structures, and with emperors and governors who tended to limit civic business to meetings with advisors, petitioners, and liti-gants during the morning hours, it was not really possible for all the business of the state to come before the central administration. A degree of local autonomy was unavoidable. The Roman Empire's proclivity for local governance was not, how-ever, a matter of *laissez faire*. Through legislative interventions by the emperors and provincial governors, Rome promoted city constitutions favorable to Roman-style oligarchy, both in existing, well-established cities (such as those of the Hellenistic east) and in new colonies. Thus in a Greek *polis* the ruling body typically would be the city council (the *boulê*) rather than the popular assembly (the *ekklêsia*), and council membership typically would be the prerogative of the local "curial" elite, as with membership in the senate (*curia*) at Rome. This was not a completely closed system, as the prerequisite for council membership was typically service as a city magistrate, and city magistrates were elected by citizen assemblies–although (to limit this apparent opening) the composition of such assemblies, and the list of can-didates, could be determined and controlled by city councils, much as the citizens' assembly in the Roman republic had been controlled by senatorial supervision.

The Roman governors thus ruled with the cooperation of their cities' elites, and it was from these elites that local worthies were recruited into the Roman administration, both provincial and central, as Heliodorus was recruited by Caracalla to head the advocates of the treasury, and as Alexander Peloplaton was made *ab epistulis* by Marcus Aurelius. Provincial leaders recruited into the Roman administration acquired equestrian rank Roman citizenship and could become eligible for promotion to senatorial rank, the chief qualification being wealth. By the later empire, we hear of members of the Roman senate, and even consuls, who had originated from provincial cities—so, of course, had many emperors as well—and certainly provincials made up a good part of the emperor's entourage. This pattern of symbiotic relationship between imperial administration, local elites, and city governments continued through to the Roman Empire's end.[27]

In sum, the Roman Empire came to resemble a greatly ramified version of the older Hellenistic kingdoms. The "loss of liberty" that is often associated with the republic's end was not so much a loss of liberty per se, nor even a "decline of democracy" (since the Roman republic had really been an oligarchy), but a shift of political hegemony: away from Rome's old, republican nobility, and in the long run away from the city of Rome itself, and toward a cosmopolitan network of elites participating in a system of imperial administration that combined autocracy with oligarchy and left much to local jurisdiction. Within this world, as within the older Hellenistic world, there remained considerable occasion for pragmatic as well as epideictic rhetoric, and considerable opportunity for the skilled, well-educated (and typically well-born) practitioner of discursive art—in local courts and councils; in embassies, petitions, letters, appeals, and lawsuits brought before a governor's or magistrate's or emperor's tribunal; in the councils of the governors, magistrates, and emperors with their advisors; and in the various forms and forums of declamation, panegyric, history, philosophy, and poetry, whether in private recitation or public performance in large assemblies. A person skilled in the discourse of such fora could rise to eminence and gain admission to the outer and inner circles of imperial *amici*. Rhetorical skill was expected, moreover, in the emperors and their representatives: skilled speech and reasoning, and the *paideia* that went with it, was essential to their perceived legitimacy, and to the policies and decisions they enunciated. An emperor who could not compose and effectively deliver his own speeches, such as Nero, was likely to be despised.[28] Finally, as Peter Brown has argued, the rhetorical *paideia* provided the empire's international elite with a common culture, and a common discourse, that not only consituted the chief available grounds of identification and cooperation, but also (and for that reason) gave the rhetorically skilled, well-educated provincial a means of countering and to some extent reducing the inequities of power when dealing with imperial authority.[29] Authorities whose local credibility and effectiveness depended greatly on their ability to represent the ideals of *paideia* had to be, in turn, responsive to an *eloquentia* that persuasively embodied it. A display of such responsiveness is what we see, at least in part, in Caracalla's exchange with Heliodorus.

It is probably true, however, that the usual forums for pragmatic rhetoric in the Roman Empire provided limited opportunity for great eloquence, or for Ciceronian expansiveness. Local courts and councils generally were confined to relatively petty matters, which would have left little opening for grand "digressions" on the fundamental principles at stake, unless an orator wished to wax absurd. What are the grand principles involved in a lawsuit over damaged caused to one's property by rainwater draining from a neighbor's rooftiles? As Quintilian says, "[i]n most private cases concerning loans, leasing and hiring and interdicts, what place is there for speech that raises itself above the measure?" (*Institutio* 4.2.61). In the discussions of an emperor or imperial official with his advisors, elaborate, extended speeches would have been inappropriate—the literary dialogue, with its conversational style, would have been a more appropriate model than the speeches of Demosthenes or Cicero—and the *Rhetoric to Alexander's* advice to present one's arguments concisely would have been most relevant. It is significant, in this connection, that the use of epigrammatic *sententiae* to pithily, emphatically, and memorably sum up one's major points of argument became a distinctive feature of first-century (A.D.) Latin rhetoric. Moreover, most of the business brought before the emperor and his representatives consisted of correspondence: letters, petitions, and appeals (*libelli*) on legal or administrative matters, typically delivered by an emissary with some oral presentation. The emperor (or the magistrate in charge) would generally consult with his *amici* on the issues posed by the letter-writer's request and dictate a brief, official reply (a "rescript") to be drafted for his signature by an *ab epistulis*, or an even briefer note (a "subscript") at the bottom of the original letter. Volumes of such correspondence were very probably handled by the secretaries themselves, with the emperor's (or magistrate's) role amounting to little more than adding his signature.[30] Such correspondence undoubtedly was essential to the governance of the empire, and its smooth functioning required a cultured written style (as well as rhetorical skill on the part of emissaries), but it normally would have been a routine bureaucratic discourse. At times it could indeed be powerfully persuasive, and in special circumstances highly eloquent, as in Aelius Aristides' monody/letter to Marcus Aurelius concerning the Smyrna earthquake. But the best surviving example of "normal" administrative correspondence in the Roman Empire is probably that between Pliny the Younger and the emperor Trajan, when Pliny was governor of Bithynia, around 110 A.D.; it is, in general, brief, straightforward, and businesslike.[31]

There may have been opportunities for grand eloquence in the more important embassies and lawsuits brought before imperial tribunals, or in the more serious cases brought before the courts, but procedural constraints often would have limited the possibilities. Because of the press of business and the limited time available, speakers normally were given fixed amounts of time within which to present their case. When Philostratus, for example, says that Heliodorus asked for his speaking-time after being dragged into Caracalla's court, the actual term used is *kairos hydatos*, "portion (or moment) of water," a conventional metaphor for a time allotment measured by water-clock. The time permitted could vary, depending on the seriousness of the business, and usually could be negotiated with the judge. As George Kennedy has noted, Pliny the Younger mentions being given seven hours to speak in a major trial before the centumviral ("hundred-man") court, a fact that Pliny considers remarkable (*Letters* 4.16). In 100 A.D., likewise, Pliny prosecuted Marius Priscus (an ex-governor of Africa) for extortion, in a trial held before the senate with the emperor Trajan present: the trial went on for three days, with Pliny himself speaking for about five hours on the first day, and his colleagues (including Tacitus) speaking on the second and third days (*Letters* 2.11). For Pliny these trials were reminiscent of the days of Cicero. But water-clocks measured time in twenty-minute increments, and in ordinary cases the speakers were likely to be given forty minutes or less, and sometimes as little as ten minutes (*Letters* 6.2).[32]

In addition to having generally strict limits placed on their speaking-time, speakers could expect to be interrupted and interrogated by the magistrate in charge. The fourth-century sophist Libanius, for example, in an embassy to the emperor Julian on behalf of Antioch in 338 A.D., pleads with the emperor not to be angry with him (for Julian was then displeased with Antioch) and begs the emperor not to interrupt him or engage him in debate (*Oration* 15.14). In Tacitus's *Dialogus de Oratoribus*—composed near the end of the first century, and set dramatically in about 75 A.D.—the chief speaker, Maternus, observes that "most cases" are heard in "recitation halls and record offices" (*auditoria et tabularia*), in which the "judge" (*iudex*) frequently will ask the advocate to come to the point and will interrupt him with questions, and even will make him stop so that evidence and testimony may be taken, while the whole proceeding goes forward in an atmosphere of "solitude" with just a few people present (*Dialogus* 39). Similarly, Quintilian says "the judge hurries toward what is most important" and hurries the advocate along as well, either with gentle reminders or with sharp insistence, depending on the judge's rank and mood (*Institutio* 4.5.10). The situation sharply contrasts with the large juries, teeming audiences, and virtual absence of restriction on the orator in Cicero's great orations. The scenes presented by Libanius, Tacitus, and Quintilian reflect what was ever more typically the norm of imperial Roman courts, in which the magistrate in charge, from the emperor down to the *iudex* in a *tabularium*, controlled the hearing and conducted it as an inquiry, while the advocate's job was to present concisely stated arguments and information on the specific points the magistrate wished to consider and pass judgment on.[33] These were conditions under which a speaker could seldom launch himself on a flood tide of rhythmic, psychagogic eloquence, and if he tried he could expect to be reprimanded, recalled to the immediate task at hand, and required to stick to the point and not waste time—much as in courts today.

One can argue that such restrictions, even if they did restrain the possibilities for eloquence, actually constituted an improvement in practical civic discourse, and juridic discourse in particular, for they can be seen as part of a movement towards the jurisprudence based on law that Cicero calls for in *Pro Caecina*. As historians of Roman government and law have noted, the emperor stood, like a Hellenistic *basileus*, as the virtual "supreme court" and guarantor of justice for his empire. Indeed, his primary and overwhelming function when not engaged in warfare was judicial, and even when on campaign the emperors still devoted large amounts of time to the judicial business brought before them by their subjects and subordinates. The emperor, of course, possessed an absolute power that could express itself as arbitrary, brutal force; to speak before the emperor was to speak as well before his ever-present guards and soldiers, a spectacle and sign of immanent violence that many speakers found unnerving (a fact that makes Heliodorus's boldness all the more significant).[34] But the perceived legitimacy of an emperor's regime, and the loyalty of

his subordinates and subjects, depended greatly on his image as the chief embodiment and guardian of law, at least as that was understood by the various elites that
constituted and subserved the imperial administration—but also as it was understood by common citizens and subject populations who retained and sometimes exercised the power of riot and insurrection, as well as milder forms of disobedience,
including public demonstration and passive noncooperation. Emperors who failed
to persuasively maintain the image of themselves as just could expect to meet (and
often did) a sudden, violent death.

Thus, in dealing with the constant stream of legal appeals and petitions from
their subjects, and with an equally constant stream of queries on legal questions
from provincial governors and magistrates, the emperors generally were careful to
base their judgments on advice from jurisconsults, who usually were appointed as
equestrian rank secretaries. From Augustus's principate onward, juristic scholarship
evolved as a function of imperial administration, as the jurisconsultative secretaries
gradually built up organized archives of imperial edicts, rescripts, and subscripts,
which could stand as the history of legal precedents and interpretations on which
every new decision would be based. Out of this imperially sponsored scholarship
emerged the first true law schools of the Western world, schools meant specifically
for the training of professional jurists. The earliest we know of were the schools of
Aetius Capito and Antistius Labeo, under Augustus, and these were followed in
subsequent centuries by many others, and not only at Rome: Beirut, for example,
became a center of legal studies in the later empire. Eventually, this developing
tradition of legal scholarship produced the great third-century juristic treatises of
Papinian, Ulpian, and Paulus and the comprehensive codexes of Roman law—the
Hermogenean and Gregorian codes (c. 295), the Theodosian Code (c. 438), and
finally Justinian's Digest and Code (c. 533–534)—which were to provide the foundation for all subsequent Western legal traditions.[35]

By modern standards, of course, the "classical" Roman law that developed
under imperial patronage was less than admirable. It explicitly encoded different
treatment for the rich and poor (*honestiores* and *humiliores*), prescribing severer punishments to the poor than to the rich for the same crimes. Moreover, commoners
usually could not afford the expense of taking a case to the imperial courts, or to the
emperor himself, so that a rich man almost always could defeat a poor man simply
by going to a higher (and more distant) court than his opponent could afford—
winning, in effect, by forfeit. Moreover, as the second-century writer Apuleius complains in *The Golden Ass* (10.33), Roman judges (and provincial governors and
magistrates in particular) remained susceptible to bribes, just as they had been
under the republic. The rich could therefore violate the legal rights of commoners
with near impunity, unless a member of the upper classes chose to prosecute, as
Pliny did with Priscius.[36]

Nevertheless, despite its failures and inequities, the jurisprudence that developed under the Roman emperors was still a considerable advance over the "lawless"
adversary trials of the late republic, which, after all, had given the common citizen
no better chance against an upper-class opponent and had made everything depend
on what amounted to a speech contest held before a jury but without a judge (in the
sense of a professional jurist) or any definitive legal code to regulate the process.

The Roman Empire's jurisprudence evolved increasingly comprehensive, rationally coherent legal codes and canons of interpretation as the basis for legal judgment, placing the judge and the law, and not the unrestricted orator, at the center and in control of the legal process. For litigants of equal social rank the system could work fairly well. It is hard to think of this development as a "decline." Historians of law most commonly regard it as a great achievement.

The major survival of the all-out political trials of the late republic was the *maiestas* or "treason" trial, which became a prominent feature of political life in the first century A.D. and persisted in varying degrees thereafter. *Maiestas* literally meant "dignity" or "majesty," and the *crimen maiestatis* might include any behavior construed as offensive, injurious, or in some way hostile to the state or the emperor, from defacing an image to plotting a rebellion to crimes of "immorality" that could be deemed to threaten the social order. It was a capital offense. Tacitus reports a case in which an equestrian noble was accused and convicted on a charge that he had assisted the adulteries of members of the imperial household and had spoken about a dream that seemed to foretell the death of the emperor (*Annals* 11.4). The *lex maiestatis*, which was itself a survival from the late republic (it had first been established c. 100 B.C.), provided that whoever could successfully accuse and prosecute someone on *maiestas* charges would be granted the civil status and part of the confiscated estate of their victim. The persons who brought such accusations were known as *delatores*, "informers" (or, in Greek, as *sykophantai*). Probably the law had been intended to encourage patriotic initiative and vigilance from all citizens; but under the emperors and in the practices of *delatores* it became an instrument of a particularly vicious sycophancy. Ambitious persons of relatively modest origins could (and did) rise to wealth and high position by destroying rich, high-ranking citizens and claiming the rewards; persons of high rank could use *maiestas* charges to destroy their rivals and enemies; and emperors could use the help of *delatores* to eliminate anyone they distrusted or found inconvenient, and to enrich the treasury, as well as to terrorize any possible opposition (especially from the senatorial class).[37] Unsurprisingly, the emperors who made most use of *maiestas* trials, such as Nero and Domitian, were also the most unpopular.

Maiestas trials were generally held before the Roman senate, as the defendants were usually of senatorial rank, and often with the emperor present. But some were held without the senate: Tacitus reports the case of Valerius Asiaticus, a former consul, who was tried before the emperor Claudius in a bedroom (*Annals* 11.2). Whether held before the emperor or senate, the procedure and outcome of *maiestas* trials seem to have been neither constrained by law nor very predictable. As in the old republican courts, conviction or acquittal seems to have depended chiefly on the relative success of adversarial speeches made in accusation and defense, and on the emperor's or senate's moods. Kennedy describes the typical *delator* as paying "little attention to argumentation and less to style"[38] and as doing little more than pouring out a torrent of alarming accusations, but the more prominent *delatores* seem to have been skilled orators. Domitius Afer, the teacher of Quintilian, was a well-known *delator*—Tacitus describes him as originating from "modest rank" and being "quick to shine by means of any crime" (*Annals* 4.52)—but Quintilian regards him as the greatest speaker of his day (*Institutio* 5.7.7, 10.1.118, 12.11.3). In his letters, Pliny the Younger portrays Aquilius Regulus, a famous and particularly vicious *delator* who prospered under Nero and Domitian, as inviting guests to hear a public recitation of the speech that he had made in a successful prosecution: though Pliny had a low opinion of Regulus's talents, evidently Regulus himself devoted thought to the composition, revision, and publication of his speeches, as Cicero had done before him, and indeed he held up Cicero as an ideal to be imitated (*Letters* 1.5, 4.7).

The cases of Regulus and Afer are instructive, for they suggest that the relatively "lawless" *maiestas* trials, as the main survival of the high-stakes political trials of the late republic, also may have been the chief scene in which the late republican image of the orator as courtroom hero could persist for the Roman mind. Indeed, as Michael Winterbottom notes, "the outstanding fact about first-century [Roman] oratory is that the only orators to achieve any prominence or influence *by means of their oratory* are the *delatores*."[39] Cicero's Catilinarian orations, the so-called "invectives"—and especially the first oration, in which Cicero accuses Catilina before the senate of plotting insurrection—could well have been a model for *delatores*, and for the vehement style that Kennedy describes. It is significant that Quintilian, when he rehearses the Ciceronian argument that "all cases stand upon general questions," draws his first example from a *maiestas* case, and his next from Cicero's defense of Milo (*Institutio* 10.5.13). It appears that for Quintilian these are the kinds of cases that involve great issues. In the *Annals*, Tacitus puts an eloquent defense of freedom of speech in the mouth of a victim of a *maiestas* prosecution (*Annals* 4.34–35). Although this speech is probably Tacitus's invention, clearly such a speech is an imaginative possibility for him and for his audience, as for Quintilian as well. A *maiestas* trial could be an occasion of high drama.

Aside, then, from *maiestas* trials—and aside from other high-stakes trials of upper-class citizens, such as Pliny's prosecution of Priscus, and aside from embassies or letters on important provincial issues—the major forums for culturally and politically significant high eloquence were those of epideictic discourse: history, philosophy, poetry, panegyric, and declamation. These were the genres that, as Cicero's *De Oratore* suggests, gave the practitioner of "rhetoric" the greatest scope to engage with resonant "general questions" relating to moral and civic life and that also gave the rhetor greatest scope to exercise high eloquence without restriction (or with less restriction). These were the genres in which the rhetor could most fully play the role of an Isocratean orator practicing a *logôn technê* meant to cultivate the possibilities of civil community. Further, the genres of epideictic discourse gave the skilled performer access to large audiences in public recitation. According to Cicero's Antonius in *De Oratore*, "since the orator's greatest stage appears to be that of a public meeting (*contio*), naturally we are summoned to the more ornate kind of speaking (*ad ornatius dicendi genus*), for a multitude has such a power that, no more than a flutist can play without a flute, neither can an orator be eloquent without a listening throng (*sine multitudine audiente*)" (2.83.338–339).

By *contio*, of course, Antonius means a "public meeting" of the citizens' assembly, which he says provides a better occasion for fully developed eloquence than even the senate (2.82.333–334); he is discussing what he calls *suasiones*, "advisory" or "suasive" speeches, though he also says that these and *laudationes*, "epideictic" or "panegyric" speeches, have more or less the same rules (2.81.333). Under the Roman emperors, however, the city of Rome's assembly had limited functions: it continued to meet as an electoral body until the third century, but only to ritually acclaim the candidate list presented to it by the central administration.[40] (Such meetings could, however, become occasions for demonstrations on other matters.) Local assemblies in the provinces may have had more substantial decision-making functions, and certainly the city councils did, in the matters that came under their governance. But the "listening throngs" available in every city of the Roman Empire were chiefly those that gathered, usually in theaters, to hear the famed sophists and itinerant speakers of the day declaim—or the "throngs" embodied in the less immediate but more extensive audiences of literary works.

It seems difficult to say that, in these circumstances, there was any meaningful "decline of rhetoric." One could just as well say, instead, that in a world in which rhetoric and rhetorical education were very much alive, we find the rise to dominance of an Isocratean rhetoric and rhetorical *paideia*, such as Cicero had called for and had asserted against the prevailing rhetoric of his time. From the point of view of an Isocratean or "philosophical" sophistic tradition, one could just as well argue—as did Philostratus, when he invoked the notion of a "second sophistic" (*Lives of the Sophists* 481)—that a great revival was underway.

Quintilian, Tacitus, and the Talk of Decline

Not everyone was happy with this change of circumstance, and especially not, it seems, at Rome. As every history of rhetoric at this point notes, we do find some complaints about a "decline of eloquence" in documents surviving from this period, most of them from roughly the first century of the principate. The best known instances are found in what is now the opening scene of Petronius's *Satyricon*, the preface to the elder Seneca's *Controversiae*, the last surviving chapter of *On the Sublime* by "Longinus," Quintilian's *Institutio Oratoria*—and its references to his now lost *De Causis Corruptae Eloquentiae*—and Tacitus's *Dialogus de Oratoribus*, which presents itself as prompted by the topic and offers a complex counterstatement that I presently will consider.

The complainers typically declare, without proof, that there has been a falling-off from the greatness of yesteryear, and then reflect on the possible causes. Some, such as "Longinus," briefly entertain and then dismiss the question whether changes in political conditions have caused the supposed decline, while the dominant explanations focus on ideas of moral corruption, the decadence of rhetorical education, and the practice of declamation in the schools. It is likely, as George Kennedy has argued, that such complaints were simply an expression of the traditionalist, classicizing mentality that seems pervasive in ancient Greco-Roman thought: the present tends always to be viewed as a falling-off from a better time. Or, as Graham Anderson has suggested, at least some of the complaints may have been expressions of Roman resentment at the growing preeminence of Greek literary culture.[41] Either way, it is questionable whether such complaints can be taken as factual description.

It is probably significant (as Kennedy notes) that as early as the *Satyricon* (c. 60

A.D.) the notion of "decline" appears to be satirized already as hackneyed common-place. Petronius's two speakers in the scene in question—the young, hapless Encolpius and the (Greek) rhetorician Agamemnon—declaim against the corruption of the rhetoric schools in general and declamation in particular, while standing in the portico of a rhetoric school in which Agamemnon has just been declaiming; Agamemnon then offers to take on Encolpius as a student (1–5). Their performance looks more than anything like empty posturing, as if it is merely yet another exercise, or coy play, as the speakers reel off the usual *topoi* with appropriate flourishes and figures. Encolpius's speech includes a denunciation of "Asianism" that echoes the diatribe of Dionysius of Halicarnassus' against the decline of "philosophic" rhetoric, a diatribe that for Petronius's audience already was more than sixty years old. (It may have been older still for Dionysius). Similarly, Agamemnon's speech includes a denunciation of corrupted modern youth, as well as an encomium in comically fractured verse of a "Ciceronian" (or traditionally sophistic) ideal of broadly literary education and high moral purpose. Agamemnon is, of course, trying to seduce Encolpius and later will bring him to the lengthy spectacle of excess at Trimalchio's feast (26–78). It seems likely that such speeches were, and had been for some time, part of the standard moralizing fare dished up by rhetoricians for memorization and recitation by schoolboys. Notably, Agamemnon doesn't bother to hear the end of Encolpius's speech but interrupts him; and Encolpius, despite an effort to "diligently listen," drifts away in search of his boyfriend Ascyltos while Agamemnon is still declaiming on the proper education of an *eloquentiae magister*, seemingly without noticing that his audience has disappeared.

In the elder Seneca's *Controversiae* (c. 38 A.D.), composed roughly two decades before Petronius's *Satyricon*, the notion of "decline" appears as part of an exhortation to his sons to study hard. Seneca says he will recall the great declaimers of his younger days, the near contemporaries of Cicero, to hold them up as models for study and imitation—although, as he says, "the imitation always falls short of the reality" (1.pr.6)—and as a measure for the sons to judge their generation's lassitude. The young, as Seneca declares, are more devoted to vice and luxury than to manly virtue and strict discipline; none can measure up to Cato's "good man skilled in speaking" (1.pr.8–10). The point, for Seneca's sons, is that they must rise above their slack contemporaries and apply themselves (to their declamation exercises) with diligence. In the concluding chapters of the younger Seneca's *Naturales Quaestiones* (c. 62 A.D.) a similar speech appears, this time as part of a Stoic thesis that "[g]reat things come forth slowly, especially if effort lags": we are told, with suitable amplification and examples, that the philosophical pursuit of knowledge is neglected because of the vice and luxury of the times; but "if youth applied itself soberly [to philosophy], if the elders taught it and the young learned it," great strides could be made (7.31–32). This speech, set within the catechistic, question-and-answer format of the *Naturales Quaestiones*, is again an exhortation to the virtues of hard study and has very much the flavor of a schoolroom set piece.

With the Senecas, in sum, the discourse of "decline" appears to be bound up with a pedagogical rhetoric of shame and exhortation that is probably traditional and that certainly goes back at least to Isocrates. For Isocrates likewise says that no one can achieve true eloquence without hard discipline and good character (as well as talent) and likewise denounces the depravity of the times, the viciousness and vapidity of contemporary civic discourse, the dissipation of even the most promising young men—who are more devoted to drinking, gambling, and flute-girls than to study—and the foolishness of those who claim to teach an art of *rhêtoreia* but themselves write speeches that are worse than those of the uneducated (*Against the Sophists* 9–10, 17–18, 21; *Antidosis* 164, 183–188, 201, 274–290).

A mixture of literary classicism and pedagogical moralism seems prominent as well in the sophistical tradition represented by the doubtfully dated (first to third century) "Longinus."[42] "Longinus" says the highest eloquence is that which stands the test of time—a standard that inherently discounts the present—and he counsels imitation of the thoughts of ancient authors as a method of invention (*On the Sublime* 7.4, 13.2–4). He also considers what he calls the "craze for new ideas" a source of faults (5.1). It is noteworthy that his discussion of "decline" actually concludes a discussion of stylistic faults, and is a transition to a (now lost) discussion of emotion, framed as a response to "a philosopher's" question why "our age" produces many "natures" that are "highly persuasive and political, both shrewd and versatile, and certainly rich in pleasing discourse" but seldom any whose conceptions are truly "most lofty" and "surpassingly grand" (*hypselos, hypermegethos*; 44.1). The "philosopher" speculates that the loss of democracy or "freedom" (i.e., for Greek cities) may be the cause (44.2–5). Lofty conceptions are, of course, for "Longinus" the first requirement of the highest eloquence (8.1), and so the lack of a morally great nature capable of such conception leads to skillful, even impressive discourse that yet falls short of the heights (5.1). But his response to the "philosopher" is skeptical: "It is easy," he says, "and characteristically human always to be finding fault with things as they are" (44.6). He then argues that the cause of subloftiness is not the loss of democracy, or "the world's peace" under imperial Roman rule; the cause, rather, is the incessant pursuit of wealth and luxury, with its attendant vices (44.6–12). But the very fact that "Longinus" has written his treatise shows that he considers genuine loftiness still possible, if rare, even in his own time; he really is less concerned with notions of "decline" than with enforcing a lesson about what enables or prevents achievement of the highest eloquence. Students are to study hard and imitate the greats, and must be earnestly high-minded, if they hope to measure up.

From Quintilian's *Institutio Oratoria* (c. 95 A.D.)—and probably from his now lost *De Causis Corruptae Eloquentiae*—we have the major argument that the "causes of corrupted eloquence" have chiefly to do with declamation in the schools.[43] Quintilian does of course consider declamation exercises useful, both for boys in school and for established, mature practitioners, but only when the declamations realistically resemble the speeches of the forum, or more specifically the courts (*Institutio* 10.5.14). For Quintilian, declamation exercises ideally should not be based on fictitious or mythological themes (like most Greek declamation) but on real cases. Declaimers should train themselves for battle "just as we see gladiators do" (10.5.20). But, Quintilian complains (e.g., 2.10), the often melodramatic declamation themes that were popular—such as The Pirate Chief's Daughter, The Father Dragged from a Graveyard by a Debauchee, The Man Who Was Raped in Women's Clothes, The Partly Fatal Potion, The Tyrannicide the Pirates Let Go, The Prostitute Priestess, The Hero without Hands, The Disinherited Nephew, The Five-Year-Old Who Testified against The Agent, The Madman Who Married His Daughter to a Slave, The Madman Who Let His Son Have His Wife, The Slave Crucified for Refusing to Give His Master Poison, The Parricide Who Kept His Brother Prisoner, The Vestal Virgin's Verse, The Crippled Beggars, Flaminius Executes a Convict at Dinner, and so forth—frequently had little relation to the cases one typically would argue in actual practice and were generally based on fictitious, fanciful, archaic, or outmoded Greek laws with little relation to actual Roman law (although they probably were fun for sixteen-year-old boys).[44] Further, declamation had become in many schools an end in itself, with teachers building reputations and attracting students through public performances. The result, for Quintilian, was often a self-indulgent, affected, overwrought performance art that was, in essence, a poetic form that could be highly entertaining and impressive but (in Quintilian's opinion) had little connection to the skills required for practical success in courts of law (5.12.17–23, 8.pr.23–33).

How should one judge Quintilian's complaint? To a certain extent, it resembles Isocrates' attacks on his inferior competitors (e.g., in *Against the Sophists*) as composers of speeches that would be ridiculous if actually delivered in real courts or councils. Quintilian's complaint can likewise be seen as part of an effort to establish or maintain his own preeminence as Rome's foremost rhetorician. The rhetoric of agonistic competition ("I teach the true art, my competitors a false one") was common among the teachers of antiquity, and almost every rhetorical treatise pauses somewhere to point out the inferiority of competitors or previous writers on the subject, while advancing its own (usually fairly commonplace) views. Quintilian, having been appointed by Vespasian (c. 71 A.D.) to the first imperially sponsored chair of rhetoric at Rome, certainly would have been skillful at such rhetoric and after his appointment would have been well positioned to engage in it—if not required to do so by potential challenges—with great authority. Throughout the *Institutio*, Quintilian tends to play the role of a *iudex* conducting a hearing, as he sorts through the positions of previous writers on various points of theory and then pronounces his opinion. Quintilian's criticisms of "corrupted" declamation, then, may simply be his personal, magisterial rendition of what had long been part of the rhetoric teacher's standard repertoire.

Further, there seems to be little evidence that the "unreal" declamations practiced in the schools were ineffective training. Seneca the elder does not seem to have thought they were, though he does deride particular declaimers for handling their themes foolishly, or for being "stupid," or for being schoolhouse orators incapable of facing the struggles of actual cases in the courts. But many of the declaimers he recalls were active, successful orators and politicians in the early principate, and he describes them as "gladiators" even when dealing with the most melodramatic themes. As Patrick Sinclair has argued, declamation in the principate provided a game by which, in part, orators won status in the intensely competitive Roman political elite. Moreover, the focus of declamation in this period was on the invention and deployment of memorable, penetrating, epigrammatic *sententiae*, which did in fact serve as a crucial weapon of "rhetorical attack" (and defense and counterattack) in actual political life and in the courts, as well as the full-earnest combats of *maiestas* trials. Michael Winterbottom, likewise, has argued that the fictive nature of declamation themes (and the laws they were based on) were actually much more suitable than "real" cases to the full development of the rhetorical skills required for effective, real-world practice, precisely because they permitted an unrestrained attention to and experimentation with the possibilities of argument and style.[45] And finally, many of the stock declamation themes—with their disinherited sons, abused daughters, abandoned parents, betrayed and loyal spouses, murderous stepmothers, rich men and poor men, slaves and masters, tyrants and tyrannicides, informers and traitors, pirates and rebels—involved deeper social issues that were potentially significant, even as they exercised the verbal skills essential for political survival and advancement in the Roman elite. Brigandage and piracy, the resorts of the economically desperate, were very real problems in the Roman Empire, as was the danger of insurrection; and family struggles over inheritances and the like did find their way into the courts. Nontrivial questions were at stake in such stock themes as "Cicero Deliberates Whether to Burn His Writings, Antony Having Promised to Spare Him If He Does So"[46] or in "Demosthenes, Having Broken down before Philip, Is Accused of Cowardice," which Caracalla proposed to Heliodorus.

Quintilian's objection to "corrupted" declamation may have been prompted by the late-first-century vogue for the younger Seneca.[47] As Quintilian says at *Institutio* 10.1.125–127, in his earlier work—presumably *De Causis Corruptae Eloquentiae*—he "condemned" Seneca because "I was attempting to recall a corrupted speaking . . . back to stricter principles of judgment," and because at that time Seneca's writings were "generally the only thing in every adolescent's hands" and were being widely imitated. In the *Institutio* Quintilian's judgment is more balanced. He grants that the younger Seneca has "many great virtues," that he deals with "almost all matters of study" in speeches, poetry (including tragedies), letters, dialogues, and other philosophical writings, and that his writings contain "many brilliant *sententiae*, and indeed much that is morally worthwhile to read"; but he is also "in expression [*in eloquendo*] mostly corrupt, as well as exceedingly pernicious [*perniciosissima*] insofar as his vices are abundant in attractions" (10.1.128–129). Quintilian's response to Senecanism is revealing. On one hand, Seneca clearly figures as a paragon of what Quintilian considers affected, artificial style, while the range of his output suggests a wide-ranging, philosophico-literary *logôn technê* centered on the epideictic genres: Seneca represents an eloquence that reflects the resurgent Isocrateanism of the sophists, and that Quintilian generally censures as unsuitable for the forum and objects to in "corrupted" declamation. On the other hand, Seneca was in fact a successful (if sometimes duplicitous) practical orator and politician in the dangerous world of Caligula, Claudius, and Nero, eventually serving for the early part of Nero's reign as a speechwriter and member of the emperor's *consilium*, and exercising a mostly beneficial if temporary influence on Nero's policies. (In 65, however, three years after his retirement, Seneca was implicated in a conspiracy and was ordered by Nero to commit suicide, which he did in the grand Roman manner: gathering his family, he opened his veins and died while discoursing on philosophy.)[48]

It could be argued that Seneca's wide-ranging discursive art represents a truly Ciceronian *paideia*. But Seneca (or Senecanism) differs from the more old-

fashioned, late republican image of Cicero favored by Quintilian and by the generation of Quintilian's teachers—the generation of the elder Seneca, the *delator* Aquilius Regulus, and the *delator* Domitius Afer. Regulus, as we have seen already, is described by Pliny as taking Cicero for his model, and it seems likely that Afer,
Quintilian's mentor, did likewise. The elder Seneca nostalgically invokes Cicero's
"living voice," describes his "genius" as "Rome's sole possession equal to its empire"
(*Controversiae* 1.pr.11), and clearly regards him as the ultimate model that a
declaimer could hope to imitate. According to Quintilian, similarly,

> [i]t was not without good reason that [Cicero] was said by his contemporaries to be
> sovereign in legal proceedings, and that truly for posterity "Cicero" has come to be
> the name not of a man but of eloquence itself. Let us therefore fix our eyes on this,
> let this be our principal pattern, and let him know he has advanced himself, who-
> ever shall admire Cicero intensely. (*Institutio* 10.1.112)

It is a commonplace that Quintilian's *Institutio Oratoria* promotes a Ciceronian
ideal. But, as this passage suggests, what Quintilian invokes in truth is a limited version of that ideal. The student is exhorted to fix his eyes upon the image of Cicero
"sovereign in legal proceedings," the late republican courtroom hero embodied in
Cicero's judicial speeches, rather than the more capacious figure promoted in *De
Oratore* and embodied in the full range of Cicero's writings.

It is true, of course, that Quintilian does censure the "ignorance" fostered by
rhetoricians whose instruction consists of little more than declamation exercises
with little attention to theory (2.10.3, 2.11). For Quintilian, declamation is properly a capstone exercise in which the student can synthesize and practice all the
principles he has learned. And it is true, as well, that Quintilian's recommended
paideia does resemble Cicero's, for it includes the study of history, philosophy, and
poetry as well as oratory, the debate of general "theses" as well as particular "hypotheses," and various literary exercises. And at times his "perfect orator" appears
to be something more than a courthouse advocate. In book 12, for example, Quintilian describes the "perfect orator" as a widely educated person whose abilities "will
shine forth more clearly in greater things," when "the counsels of the senate are to
be directed" and "erring public opinion is to be guided to better things"
(12.1.25–26). In the preface to book 1, similarly, Quintilian describes the goal of
the training he prescribes as "the man truly civil and suited to the administration of
both public and private matters, who is able to direct the state by means of his
counsels, lay foundations by means of legislation, [and] correct wrongdoing by
means of legal judgments" (1.pr.9). The person portrayed in such passages could
well be a member of an emperor's *comitatus*.

But the overwhelming impression of the *Institutio Oratoria* is that Quintilian's
orator-in-training is preparing to serve the state and emperor primarily through
judicial oratory, and especially through what Quintilian regularly figures as the
"gladiatorial" combats of the courts. Insofar as this figure is a Catonian "good man
skilled in speaking," he should not pursue the career of a *delator*, which Quintilian
says "is next to highway robbery" (1.pr.9, 12.1.1–3, 12.7.3). But, as Quintilian also
says, the person who brings accusations "to drive out internal pests" is "comparable
with the fatherland's defenders"; those who have been "leaders of the state" have

not refused this part of their duty, and "even young men of illustrious rank" are thought to give the state a "pledge" of their patriotic devotion, and proof of their own good character, by "accusing bad citizens" (12.7.3). The obvious model here, of course, is Cicero, whom Quintilian immediately cites along with several other figures from the old republic (12.7.4). Insofar as the greatest example of Cicero "driving out internal pests" is his series of orations against the Catilinarian conspiracy, Quintilian's illustrious young men would seem in fact to be directed toward *maiestas* trials as the scene of their highest aspirations—or (to take a less sinister view) to high-stakes trials like Pliny's prosecution of Priscius, though these appear to have been uncommon. (Virtually any serious crime by high-ranking citizens could in principle be viewed as injurious to the state and emperor, and therefore could be tried as *maiestas*.)

The key distinction is that, unlike the worst *delator*, Quintilian's good orator will not accuse and prosecute "bad citizens" for pay or with the hope of collecting a reward, though it is reasonable for him to take pecuniary gifts of "gratitude" from his clients, enough to meet his needs (12.7.8–12). Rather, says Quintilian, the orator should undertake cases out of a sense of public duty, or—and this is more likely—at the behest of "the noble" (the *optimi*)when they need his help, for "these the good man will have as his closest friends." He should refrain from serving the great against the humble but especially from serving "lessers" against those of higher rank, which Quintilian says is worse (12.7.5–6). To be fair to Quintilian, he also says that a "good man" will generally prefer defense to accusation, and will generally come to the aid of his noble clients as their defender, though he should never knowingly defend injustice (12.7.1, 6–7).[49] But this is quite an ethical tangle. And there are others, for Quintilian also says that a good man *will* sometimes knowingly defend the guilty, or will "defend what is untrue," when circumstances or "the public interest" require that he do so (2.17.36, 12.1.34–40). Likewise, since judges are not always enlightened, the orator sometimes must deliberately deceive them (2.17.28, 6.2.5, 12.10.53) or intimidate them with veiled threats, for which Quintilian describes two methods (4.1.20–22). Elsewhere, Quintilian discusses the handling of witnesses who promise to give false testimony, and double-agent witnesses hired by one side to deliberately sabotage the other (5.7.12–14).

In such passages, and indeed throughout most of the *Institutio Oratoria*, Quintilian's "good man skilled in speaking" appears to be mainly a courthouse battler whose stock in trade will be private lawsuits over contracts, inheritances, and the like—an orator whose greatest eloquence will be employed in service of the emperor's regime and the nobility to prosecute "bad citizens" and defend "the noblest," whose highest aspiration is to rise to "greater things" with an appointment to the imperial administration, and whose duties will require that he lie when necessary to protect the interests of the state. These were natural enough ambitions for the rich young men of Rome. But the sort of career that is implied suggests a "rhetoric" more narrow and more ethically compromised than that of Cicero's Isocrateanism.

While Quintilian does make gestures toward the ideal of an Isocratean rhetoric (e.g., 12.2.9), and while his prescribed curriculum does resemble (and invoke) the Ciceronian *paideia*, Quintilian himself exhibits a limited interest in such things.[50] In addition to teaching adolescent boys, Quintilian also practiced in the courts and probably engaged in public declamation also, but, unlike Cicero, he produced no treatises or dialogues on ethical, legal, and political philosophy, no poetry, and nothing like *De Oratore*, with the possible exception of the *De Causis Corruptae Eloquentiae*. Likewise, in the *Institutio Oratoria* the philosophico-literary aspects of Quintilian's curriculum are given a relatively marginal or supplemental function. Literary study, for example, is for the most part confined in the conventional Roman manner to elementary education, the "grammatical" curriculum, before the boy is sent to the rhetorician (at about fourteen years of age); likewise, panegyric speeches, the debate of general "theses," and other philosophico-literary exercises are treated as belonging to either the final stages of this elementary education or the introductory stages of rhetorical education (2.1–4). For Quintilian such studies are essential as "foundations" for rhetorical study (1.4.5), but in books 3–11 of the *Institutio*—roughly 80 percent of the whole treatise—the rhetorical education itself is focused overwhelmingly on the methods of judicial discourse. The only explicit discussions of epideictic and deliberative discourse occur in book 3, with about one chapter devoted to each, as Quintilian elaborates the standard account of the three genres of public speaking (3.4–9). For the rest of the treatise, Quintilian more or less assumes that the student is training for the courts and is practicing realistic judicial declamations (*controversiae*). Philosophico-literary reading does make reappearances in books 10 and 12, but chiefly as an embellishment. In book 10, the reading of literature serves mainly to develop a cultured style; and in book 12, the importance of legal study and the value of examples drawn from literature are invoked, but hardly elaborated on, for two very short chapters (12.3–4), the second of which consists of a single, one-hundred-word paragraph. Quintilian, in sum, is closer to Cicero's Antonius than to Cicero's Crassus or to Cicero himself. For as Antonius says, he devotes his leisure time to reading historians, some philosophers, and few poets, so that his speech (*oratio*) takes on a "color" from their discourse, just as his face gets tanned from walking in the sun; but he otherwise pays their writings no serious attention (*De Oratore* 2.14.59–61).

To all the talk of "decline" and "corrupted eloquence" that seems to have been circulating in this period, Tacitus's *Dialogus de Oratoribus*, composed perhaps around 97 A.D., offers a significant reply. The *Dialogus* has, of course, traditionally been read as yet another comment on the decline of eloquence in imperial Rome and as a kind of milestone marking the close of Roman rhetoric's great age.[51] All such views, however, tend to presume precisely what the *Dialogus* puts in question, namely that pragmatic speech is the "primary" form of rhetoric and that there is indeed a "decline" for Tacitus to be discussing. But the *Dialogus* is a counterstatement.

The *Dialogus* does begin, of course, from the notion of decline—from the very first sentence. Tacitus, however, presents that topic not as a thesis but as a question from his addressee.

> Often you have asked me, Justus Fabius, how, when in former ages so many eminent, brilliant, glorious orators flourished, our generation is so deficient that we scarcely retain even the word "orator" to praise the roundly eloquent; indeed, we thus designate only the ancients, calling our contemporaries pleaders [*causidici*], advocates [*advocati*], counselors [*patroni*], or whatever, rather than orators. (1.1)

Clearly, Fabius's complaint is by this time a conventional gesture, a commonplace pose, that Tacitus and his readers would have encountered many times before.

But what are we to think of Fabius's complaint? Tacitus defers his own opinion with a *recusatio* (1.2–4): "so great a question," he says (and not without some irony), is beyond him; he will instead present a conversation that he listened to "when quite a youth" among the orator-turned-poet Curiatus Maternus, the orators Marcus Aper and Vipstanus Messalla, and the orator-turned-historian Julius Secundus (the one speaker in the dialogue whose career path closely resembles that of Tacitus, and who remains almost entirely silent from beginning to end). The dramatic date is around 75 A.D., the sixth year of Vespasian's reign (17.3).[52] The dialogue's *dramatis personae* are introduced as figures "of our time" and as "eminent men" of "subtle thought" and "weighty utterance," indeed as "celebrated lights of our forum" (2.1), descriptions that in themselves may cast ironic light on the notion of decline. Tacitus completes his introduction to the dialogue by emphasizing that there was a division of opinion and that "there was one who took the opposite position also, and, much vexing and abusing the old order of things, preferred the eloquence of our time above the genius of antiquity" (1.4). What follows, then, is a divided dialogue in which the speakers disagree about not only why but also whether there has been a decline at all.

To presume that this debate straightforwardly expresses Tacitus's opinions may be to take inadequate account of its own rhetorical complexities. It has commonly been said, for example, that "Tacitus complains" that declamation perverted the training given in the rhetoric schools.[53] In fact, it is not Tacitus who so complains but the character Vipstanus Messalla, who figures as the dialogue's main exponent of a conservative, Quintilianic ideal. How should we assess Messalla's position, and the rhetorical force of his argument, within the context of the dialogue (and its cultural situation) as a whole? Messalla is not one of the dialogue's chief agonists— these are Aper and Maternus—but a supporting character. His criticism of schoolroom declamation echoes the familiar commonplaces satirized already by Petronius, but it most strongly resembles Quintilian, and may well be derived from Quintilian's *De Causis Corruptae Eloquentiae* or from public knowledge of Quintilian's lectures. The *Institutio Oratoria*, completed in about 95, may or may not have been available to Tacitus when he was composing the *Dialogus;* but according to Quintilian (*Institutio* 1.pr.7), around 90 there already were two unauthorized books of his lectures in circulation, and it seems likely that Tacitus would at least have been aware of them and the *De Causis*.[54] Messalla's Quintilianism is, moreover, rendered suspicious by the likelihood that Tacitus despised Quintilian for his complicity with the repressive regime of Domitian and his links to *delatores* like Domitius Afer.[55] Messalla himself appears in Tacitus's *Histories* as the half-brother and defender of the vicious and bitterly hated *delator* Aquilius Regulus, who prospered under Nero by destroying senatorial families and seizing their property. Tacitus illustrates Regulus's brutality by adding the detail (from the speech of Regulus's accuser, Curtius Montanus) that "after the murder of Galba, Regulus had given money to Piso's assassin and had torn Piso's head with his teeth" (*Histories* 4.42). This is what Messalla has defended. So much for Quintilian's good man speaking well.

But the central confrontation in the dialogue is that between Marcus Aper and Curiatus Maternus. The dialogue opens at Maternus's house, the day after a recital of his "Cato," a politically dangerous tragedy. Aper and Secundus enter (with, sup-posedly, young Tacitus in tow) to find Maternus calmly revising his seditious manu-script for publication, and planning a "Thyestes" that will say whatever his "Cato" has left unsaid. After Secundus expresses some alarm at these intentions, Aper as-sails Maternus for abandoning the forum for "Greekling" poetizing. Maternus rises to the defense, and replies that he is now practicing "eloquence in its more sacred and august form" (4.2). At this point the debate is joined, with Secundus more or less retiring to the sidelines.

Aper's first speech (5.3–10.8) is an argument for the superiority of oratory to poetry, and of the forum to the lecture hall and stage, in the pursuit of practical advantage.

> If advantage is to be the rule of all we choose to do in life, what is better than to exercise an art that always provides a weapon to protect your friends, to help strangers, to deliver those in jeopardy, and to put fear and trembling truly into ene-mies and enviers, while you yourself feel safe within a fortress of inexhaustible strength and even grandeur? (5.5)

Aper's argument, overall, is centered on the use of pragmatic rhetoric as a po-litical and social climbing tool. The orator wields tremendous power and can rise in the world and enrich himself, because all who need his services, including the noble and well-born, beat a path to his door (5.5–8.8). The poet, however, earns little profit from his labors and moreover must "run around asking people to consent to come and listen" (9.3). On one hand, this argument demonstrates (indirectly) the point that practical civic rhetoric still played a vital role in Roman society under the principate, especially in the courts. But on the other hand it also resonates trou-blingly with Callicles' embrace of power, in Plato's *Gorgias*, as the highest good—and so it is no surprise that Aper's chief examples of "the divine authority and celes-tial power" of eloquence (8.2) are the *delatores* Eprius Marcellus and Vibius Crispus, intriguers who rose from humble origins to the imperial circle through more or less criminal careers (though Marcellus was later implicated in a plot against the em-peror and forced to kill himself).[56] These sinister references clearly undercut the validity of Aper's argument. Further, they provide a persuasive basis for what will be Maternus's refutation and rejection of what he calls "the gain-getting, bloodthirsty eloquence now in use" (12.2), largely on the rather Socratic grounds (echoing the *Gorgias* again) that orators like Crispus and Marcellus in truth are slaves of the forces that control the forum and live in a state of perpetual anxiety that is hardly to be desired (13.4–6).

The center of Maternus's self-defense, however, is a return to his original claim that poetry is eloquence, or rhetoric, "in its more sacred and august form." "Here is eloquence's origin, here the penetralium"; poetry is the form in which rhetoric first entered human society as an art of panegyric praise and blame (12.2–4). At the heart of this argument, clearly, is the by now familiar and ancient topos that goes back at least to Hesiod and that resonates through the sophistic/Isocratean and philosophical traditions down to the Second Sophistic: namely, that the best and wisest eloquence descends, as a gift of the Muses, from poetry and the general do-main of epideictic to the practical civic orator. Furthermore, as Maternus suggests, this kind of discourse can itself exert a power and win a fame comparable to that of Aper's orator:

> By reciting tragedies I first put myself on the way to fame, when in Nero's reign I broke the power of Vatinius, that abomination and profanation of even sacred studies, and today if I have any reputation and renown the greater glory belongs to my poems than to my speeches. (11.2)

Of Vatinius, Tacitus tells us in the *Annals* that he was "one of the foulest prodigies" of Nero's court and that through "continual accusation" he acquired "such influence, such wealth, and such power of injury that even among scoundrels he was preeminent" (15.34). So the poet, acting as epideictic rhetor, can "break the power" of monsters like Vatinius and can exert a pervasive influence on the discourse of the town—for as Aper himself has recognized, a controversial poetry like that of Maternus is the sort of thing that "brings forth immoderate approval" (or "assent," *adsensus*) and "in the lecture hall is highly praised and soon is talked about by all" (10.7).

To this point in the *Dialogus*, the argument has been between the more or less sophistic (and Greek) tradition that Maternus represents and the purely pragmatic (and traditionally Roman) one that Aper represents, or that the *delatores* represent, over the question of what is the best sort of rhetoric to practice. There has been no real discussion of "decline," though Maternus clearly is disillusioned with the viciousness of *delatores*. Justus Fabius's question has so far undergone prolonged deferral. But now Messalla joins the conversation, bringing his Quintilianic discourse with him (14.1–15.3). We already know about Messalla. Here we need only note that his function at this point is mainly to change the subject and to provoke Aper to defend the moderns.

Notably, the heart of this defense draws from a topic Aper has conceded already to Maternus, that "all eloquence in all its parts is sacred and venerable" (10.4). Now he says to Messalla that "the forms and types of speaking change with the times," that "eloquence has more than one face," and that not all change is for the worse (18.2–4). These premises ground an argument that the rhetoric of "ancients" like Cicero no longer serves the practical orator. As Aper says, the orator now must seek "novel and exquisite eloquence" and even "poetic ornament" so as not to bore fastidious, well-read, sophisticated judges—magistrates who settle issues on their own authority, "not granting [the speaker] time, but setting limits, nor patiently waiting while the orator talks through his business, and furthermore often recalling him from some digression and declaring themselves in a hurry," and becoming offended, moreover, if there's nothing in the arguments and figures employed to pique their interest (19.5; 20.1, 5). Cicero could not get anywhere with such judges; the moderns meet a more difficult standard. Aper's argument undercuts Maternus's earlier evocation of poetry as the primordial form of rhetoric as well as Massalla's preference for the ancients. But Aper's argument opens the door as well to an inference that poetic/epideictic eloquence is what the times now require, and that, because of the constraints he labors under, the practical orator has something less than the "celestial power" that Aper wants to claim. This is the door that Maternus walks through in his final speech.

But Maternus now cedes the discussion to Messalla, declaring that not even Aper really considers orators like Crispus and Marcellus equal to the ancients (i.e., Cicero), and asking Messalla not to eulogize the ancients but to set out "the reasons why we have so much receded from their eloquence" (24.1–2). This Messalla fails to do. Instead, Messalla produces a series of mostly irrelevant, standard diatribes on the inferiority of modern eloquence, on the proper education of an ideal *eloquentiae magister,* and on the corruptness of schoolhouse declamation. Maternus must repeatedly interrupt, reminding Messalla that he is off the point and asking him to start again. Messalla's performance is nearly as mechanical as that of Petronius's declaiming clowns. But he does raise one important (if overly familiar) argument: that the "admirable eloquence" of a Cicero "abundantly flows forth" from "much erudition and many arts and a knowledge of all things" and that "the orator's function and activity is not . . . confined within narrow boundaries" (30.4–5). This line of thought, of course, is straight from Cicero, and ultimately from Isocrates; and the reader is asked implicitly to judge that, of the dialogue's three main speakers, it is Maternus who best embodies such an ideal.

Messalla's diatribe trails off into what is now a gap in the existing text, a missing part of unknown but probably not great length (a few pages at most). When the text resumes we find Maternus speaking, apparently having taken over from Messalla, and delivering his long last speech. The key to Maternus's argument is the notion of constraint. The modern orator, he claims, has no less capacity for eloquence than Cicero (41.5) but is confined (as Aper has recognized) within narrow boundaries, normally speaking on relatively minor issues before impatient magistrates in desolate petty courts with fairly strict rules of procedure, and even wearing clothes (advocate's robes) that restrict his movement (37–39). But for Maternus this is not a reason for complaint. The late republic's orators may have had greater scope for eloquence because they spoke in tumultuous, all-out trials and senatorial debates where momentous power struggles were transacted, but they also "tore the republic apart" (36.4). Indeed, as Maternus describes it (36–37), the rhetorical world of Cicero and his contemporaries was not so different from that of the *delatores*—a gladiatorial world in which eloquence functioned mainly as a weapon in the war of all against all for position, power, and prestige and found its greatest expression in high-stakes political prosecutions. We are asked implicitly to see the *delatores* as the true inheritors of that world. It is a world that, as Maternus repeatedly suggests, we should not wish for (37.5, 40.2), one that needs to be constrained. But great eloquence cannot happen under such constraint. Eloquence needs large issues, and, as Maternus argues, a large audience as well: "orators need applause to do their work, and what I call a theater" (39.4). This suggestion points us back again to epideictic, or to Maternus's controversialist poetry, which does indeed have an audience and a theater, can address large issues, can win widespread applause and be talked about all over town, and is not "confined within narrow boundaries."

This is not to say that either Tacitus or Maternus endorses the imperial system. A reading of *Agricola,* the *Annals,* and the *Histories* makes it apparent that Tacitus does not. But his criticisms are directed chiefly at imperial abuses of autocratic power, the craven collusion of the senatorial order in its own subjection— through the endless scramble for preferment, privilege, and profit in imperial administration—and the crude, amoral careerism of *delatores*.[57] It is less clear, and less probable, that Tacitus objects to strictly regulated court procedures, or to the evolution of Roman law. Again, his chief objection seems to be against *maiestas* trials, in other words, the place where that regulation fails (or has never been established). Thus, the oft-remarked irony of Maternus's peroration may be less stable than at first appears. He says:

> [i]f there somehow could be found a state where no one did wrong, the orator would be as useless amid the innocent as a physician amid the healthy. For just as the healer's art is little used and little advanced among those peoples that enjoy the most robust health and wholesome bodies, so the orator's standing is reduced and his glory unrecognized where people have good *mores* and are prepared to obey their rules. For what need is there for lengthy declarations in the senate, when the best people quickly reach agreement? Or for many speeches in popular assemblies, when it is not the ignorant many who deliberate about affairs of state, but the wisest one of all? Or for undertaking prosecutions, when wrongs are done so rarely and so trivially? Or for invidious and immoderate defenses, when the clemency of understanding goes to meet with those on trial? (41.3–5)

As Maternus goes on to conclude, Cicero's great speeches were the product of the turbulent, destructive conditions of his time. Cicero was a great rhetor enmeshed in a vicious world, one engrossed by the corruption and violence that ended the republic, that made the principate inevitable, and that survived in the practices of *delatores*. Under similar conditions, Maternus's best contemporaries would also play the grand Ciceronian role, just as now they show measure and moderation; but the orator cannot enjoy both "great fame and great repose" at the same time, and he should "enjoy the blessings of his time without disparaging another" (41.5). Great practical rhetoric is called forth by times of crisis, and especially by civil strife, but who would not prefer to live in times of peace and good government? The speakers then exchange embraces, joke that they will "denounce" each other, and depart in friendship.

This whole passage hinges on Maternus's *if*: he is describing a sort of hypothetical, Platonic utopia, the regime of the perfectly wise and just in a well-governed state ruled by a philosopher-king (the "wisest one of all"), a regime in perfect harmony with well-educated citizens of good morality who never commit more than trivial offenses against each other. When taken as a hypothetical premise that defines the basic terms and oppositions of Maternus's argument, this utopian image can be understood as *true:* it is *true* that *if* such a state existed, *then* there would be little need for the Ciceronian courthouse hero that Quintilian and Messalla yearn for, and that *if* the perfectly Hobbesian opposite of that state existed, *then* such an orator's role and social importance would correspondingly be maximized. Reality, of course, will always fall somewhere between, and the orator will always have a role, though (depending on conditions) the oratorical genres practiced by Cicero may cease to be the major media for eloquence and may be superseded by other discursive genres with greater cultural or political significance and less constraint, such as epideictic literature. We may judge Maternus's utopian image as a damning contrast to the realities of Roman imperial politics, in which the ruling classes were in fact frequently devoted to nothing but a Hobbesian struggle of all against all for personal profit and advantage. Or we may judge Maternus's peroration, like Pliny's *Panegyricus* to Trajan in 100—nearly contemporary with the composition date of the *Dialogus*—as not only a seeming (though perhaps ironic and insincere) praise of the imperial regime, but also an articulation of the measure by which the regime is to be judged.

It is significant that the framework of this image is largely juridical. On one hand, it responds to Aper's and Messala's (and Quintilian's) traditionally Roman concept of courthouse argument as rhetoric's central and crowning genre. On the other hand, it also reflects what was in fact the emperor's main role as virtual chief justice of the empire. In Maternus's account, it is because people "do wrong," and to the degree that they do it, that "declarations," deliberations, and prosecutions are required. This framing seems to reflect a situation in which orators are speaking chiefly to correct injustices and in which the senate, popular assemblies, and the emperor are chiefly functioning as courts—or as review boards in which the chief business is, if not judicial decisions, then edicts and replies to queries, appeals, petitions, and embassies from provincial officials and associations. To the degree that judgments given in this juridic and administrative realm accord persuasively with what is understood as *sapientia*, to the degree that the emperor as "chief justice" (or perhaps chief arbiter) persuasively functions as the "wisest" person at the top of the bureaucracy, to the degree that magistrates persuasively bring to those on trial "the clemency of understanding" in genuine jurisprudence, and to the degree that this whole system persuasively renders what is understood as "justice," a particular emperor's administration will approach Maternus's utopian ideal and will in his terms be *to that degree* successful. At the same time, the more an emperor's administration is successful in these terms, the less will be the *judicial orator's* opportunity to play grand roles. In a well and justly ruled and peaceful empire, there will be relatively few political trials and possibly no *maiestas* trials at all. The judicial orator still has an important civic role to play, but his chief work will be in the lower courts, arguing cases at private law concerning such things as interdicts, broken contracts, disputed inheritances, petty thefts and damages to property, and so forth: scenes in which Messalla's and Quintilian's Ciceronian hero will be, as Aper says, out of place.

But we may also judge Maternus's peroration—in its dramatic as well as historical context—as an expression of some hopefulness. The dramatic date, as we recall, is the sixth year of Vespasian's ten-year reign. Vespasian's reign had been preceded by the catastrophic years of Nero (54–68), under whom the *delatores* flourished, and after Nero's death the civil strife of the "year of four emperors" in 69: first Galba, Otho, and Vitellius, each of whom died violently, and finally Vespasian, who proved to be one of the most effective administrators in Roman history (and who died a natural death, after ten years in power).[58] In its dramatic context, then, Maternus's evocation of the emperor as "the wisest one of all," and of times of "great repose" as preferable to civil strife, is not entirely facetious or unreasonable, nor is it mere flattery. At the midpoint of Vespasian's reign, Maternus plausibly can engage in such encomiastic gestures. The irony here is that Vespasian's reign was followed (after the brief two years of Titus, who died somewhat mysteriously) by the oppressive and increasingly tyrannical regime of Domitian (81–96), under whom *maiestas* trials again became a major element in Roman politics. Domitian was murdered in 96, and here the uncertain date of the *Dialogus* is tantalizing. If Tacitus did write it in 97, it would have been during the brief, transational reign of Nerva, who peacefully ceded power to Trajan. If later (e.g., in 98, or sometime after 100, as some have argued),[59] it would have been written early in Trajan's reign (98–117). Trajan was a far better emperor than even Vespasian, and indeed was one of the most popular and most successful of all the Roman emperors, for which he was given the title *Optimus Princeps*, Best Ruler.[60] It may be, then, that in Maternus's peroration Tacitus is also looking with some hope toward Trajan, or at least toward better things after Domitian's violent demise (as he does, e.g., in *Agricola* 3, also composed in 97–98).

The point is that Maternus's argument—and finally Tacitus's argument as well—amounts to a refutation of the traditional Roman (and Quintilianic) ideal of judicial oratory, and perhaps pragmatic discourse generally, as the crown of the arts of discourse and the medium of greatest eloquence. The kind of rhetoric at which Cicero excelled so brilliantly was a product of the dysfunctional sociopolitical conditions of the late republic, which are not to be wished for; and indeed according to Cicero himself that kind of rhetoric (as well as the conditions that produced it) contributed to the republic's violent demise. Under imperial administration, the old, republican image of the orator no longer has much relevance, except possibly in *maiestas* trials (or the occasional senatorial prosecution); but in a well-governed state such trials would be unusual and would be subject to jurisprudential restraint. Otherwise, the judicial orator's main venues are the petty courts, which seldom provide an opportunity for Ciceronian grandiloquence, although they do require (as Aper suggests) a polished, sophisticated discourse studded with apt *sententiae*. Or the orator may play administrative roles, in which, again, skilled deliberation and sophisticated speech will be required but not grand eloquence. And the more justly and well ruled the empire is, the more true that will be.

Tacitus's argument, then, is that not "eloquence" or "rhetoric" has "declined" or been restrained, but only a *late republican, "gladiatorial" version of rhetoric centered on judicial oratory*—and that the restraint of such rhetoric (by the rule of law) may in fact be a good thing. Still, as Aper and Maternus have agreed, "all eloquence in all its parts is sacred and venerable" and must be suited to its times. Thus the polished but sublofty eloquence of the petty courts is not to be dismissed, nor is any other form of practical civic discourse in the various administrative and judicial forums of the Roman Empire, although the "bloodthirsty, gain-getting eloquence" of *delatores* is to be rejected on moral grounds. But the chief media for eloquence on culturally resonant questions of justice, honor, and advantage are the epideictic genres of poetry, philosophy, history, panegyric, and declamation. These are the media through which a cultural consensus might be cultivated, a civil community constructed and maintained—or something like what Jürgen Habermas might call a public sphere. For Maternus this means writing, performing, and publishing tragedies on politically charged subjects, and debating philosophical theses with his friends (for that is what the speakers of the *Dialogus* are doing).[61] For Tacitus, it means writing his *Histories* and *Annals* of imperial politics from Tiberius through Domitian, the *Agricola* (an encomiastic biography of his father-in-law, showing that "there can be great men even under bad emperors"), and his geographical treatise

Germania, as well as the *Dialogus de Oratoribus*, though he would also participate in the prosecution of Priscius in 100 A.D. None of Tacitus's argument, finally, amounts to a rejection of the Ciceronian ideal, though it does reject a conservative, Quintilianic version of it.[62] As the oft-remarked Ciceronian style and form of the *Dialogus* itself attest, Tacitus certainly wishes to identify with Cicero, but it is the Isocratean, philosophico-literary Cicero of *De Oratore* and other dialogues that is evoked, not simply Cicero the practical civic orator. This is, in effect, the version of "rhetoric" that Tacitus affirms—and that we find resurgent in the thought of such representative sophistic figures as Dionysius of Halicarnassus, Aelius Aristides, Hermogenes of Tarsus, and "Longinus," to whom I now turn.

Ideas of Rhetoric: Dionysius, Aristides, Hermogenes, and "Longinus"

In *On the Ancient Orators*, which Dionysius of Halicarnassus composed just two or three decades after Cicero's death, we hear not only that the "old and philosophic rhetoric" has been in eclipse from "Alexander of Macedon's final breath" to "our own generation" (1), but also that this rhetoric now "has been restored to the rightful place of honor it formerly held, receiving its due, while the new and mindless one has been restrained from enjoying fame it does not deserve and from feasting on others' goods" (2). Dionysius declares "the cause and origin of this great change" to be the good effects of Roman administration, which has placed the management of public affairs, he says, in the hands of intelligent, well-qualified persons and "has compelled the mindless to be sensible" (3). In consequence, he says, both Greeks and Romans recently have produced "many histories that are equally worthwhile . . . and many accomplished *logoi politikoi* and philosophical compositions that are by no means contemptible . . . as well as many other fine treatises" (3).

All of this, like Dionysius's description of the "old and philosophic rhetoric" as an Attic muse/housewife and its "mindless" nemesis as an Asiatic prostitute/criminal, is surely more than a little hyperbolic, and the praise of Roman administration can easily be read as mere flattery for the audience of cultured, upper-class Romans that Dionysius (who is living at Rome) most probably is writing for. Likewise, his tale of restoration seems a little premature, when one considers the continuation of a rhetoric that "feasts on others' goods" in the practices of *delatores*, especially in the next hundred years or so. Nevertheless, this tale of restoration also does reflect a striking recognition of the changed conditions for rhetoric under Roman administration, even as it makes a case for a resurgent Isocrateanism, or for conceiving "rhetoric"—as Cicero does in *De Oratore* and in *Orator*—as a broad, philosophico-literary discourse art that is oriented fundamentally toward "political" questions of justice, ethics, and the desirable in public and private life and that never forgets its practical applications in civic discourse (or what Dionysius in traditional sophistic fashion calls *politikos logos*) but is centered in the domain of epideictic.

Of Dionysius's writings, we still possess seven essays in rhetorical criticism (on Lysias, Isocrates, Isaeus, Demosthenes, Dinarchus, and Thucydides, and the introductory essay *On the Ancient Orators*), three letters on rhetorical-critical topics, the famous treatise *On the Composition of Words* (*Peri Syntheseôs Onomatôn*, often translated as *On Literary Composition*), and a major work of history, *Roman Antiquities*; but we know that he also produced a treatise *On Imitation*, of which some fragments remain, as well as a treatise *For Political Philosophy* and other critical essays (e.g., on Hyperides and Aeschines) that have completely disappeared (see *Thucydides* 1–2, *Letter to Pompeius* 3–6, and *On the Ancient Orators* 4). These writings bespeak an advanced Isocratean *paideia* devoted, on one hand, to historical and political-philosophical inquiry, and, on the other, to detailed critical study and imitation of exemplary practitioners of discursive art, as opposed to (or in addition to) the narrowly practical *paideia* that Cicero's Crassus dismisses as not worthless but elementary and insufficient. Like Cicero's later treatises, moreover, or like the Hellenistic philosophical-rhetorical tradition represented by Demetrius's *On Style*, Dionysius's extant critical essays and *On Composition* reveal a prominent interest in stylistic criticism and a persistent relating of practical civic eloquence to its sources and models in the eloquence of poetic, philosophic, and historical discourse. Notably, Dionysius argues that Demosthenes' civic eloquence is best of all because it combines, in a varied synthesis, the virtues of such precursors as the lyric poets, Isocrates, Thucydides, and Plato—and because that eloquence achieves in its consummate artfulness a rhythmic prosody resembling verse (*Demosthenes* 1–8, 14, 40, 50, *Thucydides* 52–55).

Indeed, according to Dionysius, Demosthenes' written *logoi*—epideictic reproductions of *pragmatika*, which Dionysius treats as carefully crafted works of literature—"are like the mightiest (*kratistos*) poems and lyrics . . . and especially his demegoric speeches against Philip and his dikanic speeches in public trials" (*On Composition* 25). It is worth noting that "mightiest," *kratistos*, suggests not simply literary quality but also the persuasive, psychagogic power that Gorgias long before attributed to rhythmic *logos*. Dionysius backs his claim with painstaking metrical analyses of passages from Demosthenes' orations—analyses reminiscent of Cicero's *Orator*—showing that, while Demosthenes' prose is not (and should not be) strictly "in" verse, it combines poetic meters to generate a broadly rhythmic, quasi-lyrical effect with an emotive and aesthetic force comparable to that of song (*On Composition* 11, 25; *Demosthenes* 22).[63] Moreover, as Dionysius goes on to maintain, there is a convergence between the prose art of *rhêtores* like Demosthenes and Isocrates and the lyric art of *melopoioi* like Pindar and Simonides. The lyric poets, as he says, differ from epic (hexameter) poets, who must break up the monotonous rhythm of their single meter by composing in clauses and periods of varied length and construction. The *melopoioi*, by contrast, not only can vary the length and shape of their periods and clauses, but also can compose in "polymetric" strophes, using "many meters and rhythms in a single period," thereby producing a subtle, varied prosody "greatly resembling speeches" (*On Composition* 26). The great lyric poets, in sum, move toward a free-verse eloquence comparable to that of oratorical and literary prose, while the most powerful prose writers and orators produce an eloquence like that of "the mightiest poems and lyrics."

While Dionysius's proclamation of "the old and philosophic rhetoric's" renaissance may have been premature, or hyperbolic, it nevertheless is clear that his notion of *rhêtorikê* as a general *logôn technê* centered in epideictic and applicable to pragmatic discourse was indeed to be the dominant, enduring view in the Roman world. We see it, for example, about one and a half centuries later (c. 146 A.D.) in Aelius Aristides' discourse *Against Plato Concerning Rhetoric* (*Pros Platona Peri Rhêtorikês*), an extended apologia—in the manner of Isocrates' *Antidosis*—in reply to Plato's *Gorgias*.[64] Like Dionysius and Isocrates before him, Aristides defines *rhêtorikê* as a general *logôn technê* (15–16) that originates, as he says, as a *phylaktêrion dikaiousês* or "safeguard of justice" from the wish to make persuasion by means of *logos* prevail over brute force (210–211) and to provide a check to tyranny (312). It is worth noting that, in Hellenistic Jewish usage, *phylaktêrion* could also mean an "amulet," a protective charm consisting of strips of parchment covered with inscriptions from the Laws. So defined, *rhêtorikê* is "nothing other than intelligence (*phronêsis*) that has acquired discursive power (*logôn dynamin*), so that one not only can discover for himself what is best but also can persuade others" (302). As such, it is "a kind of *philosophia*" (305) whose *ergon* or "product" is "to think rightly," *phronein orthôs*, and to persuade others to think (and do) rightly in private life and public action (392). This line of thought leads Aristides to declare that the genuine *rhêtorikê* and the true *rhêtôr* appear not only in public speech before the people but in any manifestation of eloquent and virtuous wisdom whatsoever, even in solitude (429–430). With Aristides, in short, the term *rhêtorikê* signifies an Isocratean discourse art that includes all forms of public and private discourse: this art is grounded in a broad, philosophico-literary *paideia* centered on questions of justice, ethics, and civic wisdom, and it aims to cultivate an articulate, eloquent, well-reasoning, and honorable sensibility capable of effective intervention in the thought and action of others.

To think of rhetoric as an "amulet" that safeguards justice, or that protects the bearer (and his community) against injustice, on one hand suggests the practical applications of rhetoric as intercessive discourse in petitions, embassies, letters, private consultations, and so forth, as well as dikanic argument in courts of law—and Aristides makes much of Plato's attempted interventions in the politics of Syracuse. On the other hand, Aristides' account of rhetoric also portrays it as a discursive practice and *paideia* that restrains the practitioner from *doing* as well as suffering injustice, while serving to cultivate the possibilities of civil community. As such, it both precedes and follows (as well as enters) the practical speech of judicial and political/administrative forums. As Aristides says, in his version of the myth of rhetoric's beginnings, "[w]hen rhetoric had come among humankind from the Gods [being sent by Zeus, via Hermes, at the instigation of Prometheus], humankind were enabled to escape the savage way of life among the animals, stopping the cycle of strife of all against all, and they discovered the origin of community" (398). From this "discovery" proceeds the establishment of communal agreements, which make possible the foundation of laws and civil institutions (398–399), which in turn make possible the practices of pragmatic rhetoric in political/administrative and judicial forums.

But, as Aristides adds,

> while the art of legislation is done with once it has established laws, and that of jurisprudence busies itself no more after the vote [of acquittal or conviction], yet like some sleepless guard [rhetoric] never ends its watch; it was joined with those

arts from the beginning, both guiding and teaching, and even now it treats all things anew, making proposals, going on embassies, forever shaping present circumstances. (401)

Rhetoric, that is, continually constructs and reconstructs the larger sphere of discourse within which specific acts of legislation and jurisprudence (decrees and judgments) have occurred and will occur. It not only leads to the production of laws and institutions through the cultivation of communal assent, and thence to the production of specific judgments in specific forums which enact and enforce the laws, but it also continues to cultivate the shared agreements on which the laws depend, as well as to instigate and shape the processes through which existing laws, policies, and civil institutions will be altered. As such *rhêtorikê* is the "guide" and "teacher" of legislation and jurisprudence and is necessarily "joined" with them "from the beginning" of civil society but is not identical with them or limited to their sphere. It is, rather, their condition of possibility.

In making these arguments, Aristides raises two significant points. The first is based on a direct quotation of the Hesiod passage with which this book began (*Theogony* 81–104). According to Hesiod, says Aristides, the Muses and Kalliope in particular bestow on a Zeus-beloved king the gift of *rhêtorikê*, thereby making him both wise and able to guide others to right decision and action. Hesiod thus "testifies" that rhetoric is "the councilor of kingship" and that "the title of wise and also of speaking well apply to one and the same person" (391–392)—an argument that, in passing, tacitly establishes Hesiod's good king as the model for Roman emperors and administrators to live up to and implies that *responsiveness to rhetoric*, as opposed to the rule of mere force, is essential to legitimate governance even in a monarchy. With Aristides as with Hesiod, *rhêtorikê* descends as an art of eloquent wisdom from the by now ancient realm of the poetic Muses, whom Aristides whimsically calls "the old ladies" (394), and this art confers the deliberative and discursive capabilities that enable good rulership and civic justice.

The second point seems, at first, to turn the matter around. In poetry as in all other forms of *logos*, says Aristides, the greatest, most distinguished and most famed is that which "comes nearest to *rhêtorikê*" (427–428). This point may be seen to illustrate the ever-equivocal nature of the term *rhêtorikê* in antiquity, signifying both a general art of wisdom-speaking eloquence (which includes poetry) and, more specifically, an art of prose *logoi* to which the greatest, most powerful poems approximate. But what is reflected here is the genealogy that Aristides like Dionysius inherits from Hellenistic thought: *rhêtorikê* originates, with the "old ladies," in the older (and by Aristides' time truly antique) traditions of poetic discourse, and afterward evolves into the "modern" practices of epideictic and pragmatic prose, which gradually take over the functions of the old poetic genres. Aristides was among other things a distinguished composer of prose hymns—which seems to have been his major innovation—as well as prose versions of other "lyric" genres, such as his *Monody for Smyrna*. (The "other things" include, in addition to his famous letter to Marcus Aurelius, symbouleutic speeches to city assemblies, dikanic speeches in lawsuits, panegyrics, literary *logoi* on rhetoric and other subjects, addresses to individuals, declamations, poems, dedicatory verses, and the curious *Sacred Tales*, an account of 130 dreams during his extended, twenty five-year illness and eventual cure by the god Asclepius.)[65]

In the proëmium of his oration *On Sarapis* (1–14), delivered in 142 A.D., Aristides prefaces his praise of the Egyptian god with a defense of prose hymns as at least equal or superior to hymns composed in verse, which he portrays as an old-fashioned, outmoded practice.[66] While Aristides here takes the apparently unusual position that verse composition did not "precede" the use of prose (8), his basic argument is that prose discourse should be acceptable to the gods because it is natural, whereas verse is a form of artifice added to natural speech. Further, Aristides' defense of prose hymns actually goes on to maintain that artful prose displays a more intricate, complex use of "measure" that pervades every aspect of its discourse, from its prosody to the "measures" of its reasoning (9–12). Artistic *logos* (or what Strabo calls "excellent" *logos*) thus displays an artifice that is far more advanced and subtle than that of poetry yet still imitates "natural" speech. In this it is like, but better than, the speeches of the characters in Attic drama, or the "mightiest" lyric poems.

What Aristides' position in *Against Plato* 427–428 amounts to, then, is an argument that the greatest poetry is "great" precisely because it embodies and prefigures the very same art of rhetoric that is embodied, but more fully and with greater sophistication, in the best of its oratorical and written prose descendants. By virtue of this art and to the degree that they possess it, both prose and poetry can be wise and powerfully persuasive and can have the power to be culturally and politically significant. The only real difference Aristides recognizes between the rhetoric of poetry and prose is that the poets can add to the force of their sometimes weak and unpersuasive inventions the psychagogic power of rhythmic song and incantation, which gives them license for freewheeling fabulation (*Sarapis* 1–4, 13). This view, of course, is hardly new with Aristides, and goes back at least to Gorgias (*Helen* 8–10) and Isocrates (*Evagoras* 9–11) and indeed to Hesiod—as well as to Cicero's notions of poetic and philosophic discourse as the main sources of high eloquence and of the poet as the orator's nearest kin.

We find essentially the same view taken in the stylistic theory of Aelius Aristides' contemporary, the short-lived prodigy Hermogenes of Tarsus (c. 161–184 A.D.), who was to be the last great rhetorical theorist of antiquity and the chief authority for Byzantine rhetoric up to the fifteenth century. Hermogenes first gained a Mozartish fame as a boy declaimer—Marcus Aurelius came to hear him, in 176, when Hermogenes was fifteen (Philostratus, *Lives* 2.7.577)—but his chief achievement was to write a series of rhetorical treatises before his death at about age twenty three.[67] None of Hermogenes' declamations are now extant, if they were ever published, and his known canon consists of a collection of *Progymnasmata* (elementary composition exercises) and a treatise *On the Method of Forcefulness* (*Peri Methodou Deinotêtos*), which have not survived (the existing texts are spurious), as well as three surviving texts that appear to be genuine: a more or less Hermagorean treatise *On Stases* (*Peri Staseôn*), a four-volume treatise *On Invention* (*Peri Heureseôs*), and a two-volume treatise *On Types of Style* (*Peri Ideôn*). Hermogenes also hints at studies of individual authors (*On Types* 1.1.214–215), though these apparently were never produced. This canon of surviving and missing texts clearly forms an unfinished encyclopedic project, or an incomplete pedagogical sequence, consisting of progymnasmata, stasis theory, invention (including discussion of the parts of an oration), style, "forcefulness" (the ultimate type of style), and study/criticism of particular writers, in all of which the student is generally presumed to be preparing for declamation or composition exercises. Of Hermogenes' treatises, *On Stases* and *On Types of Style* received the most attention from later commentators, were central to Byzantine rhetorical theory, and were studied in the Renaissance as well. *On Types of Style* was especially influential for Renaissance stylistic theory and today is generally regarded as Hermogenes' most important work.[68]

In *On Types of Style*, Hermogenes identifies and describes seven major stylistic "types" (*ideai*), which are seen to inform the eloquence of every kind of discourse. The seven types are clarity (*saphênia*), dignity/grandeur (*axiôma kai megethos*), elegance/beauty (*epimelia kai kallos*), vigor (*gorgotês*), character (*êthos*), sincerity (*alêthia*), and forcefulness (*deinotês*). The style of any given piece of discourse will—if it is good—feature some combination of these types, while the ultimate stylistic type, *deinotês*, arises from the apt combination and opportune use of all the other types (2.9.369, 378).[69] Demosthenes is, inevitably, the chief exemplar of *deinotês*, though poets (especially Homer), philosophers (especially Plato), historians (especially Herodotus and Thucydides), and the canonic Attic orators are discussed as well. Many of the stylistic types, moreover, include a number of subtypes from which they (like *deinotês*) may be variably composed: clarity, for example, includes purity and distinctness; grandeur includes solemnity, asperity, vehemence, brilliance, climax, and abundance/fullness; character includes simplicity, pleasantness, pungency/sharpness, and reasonableness; and so forth. Hermogenes' types and subtypes give him, in all, twenty stylistic *ideai*, each of which is given a systematic, detailed analysis that considers the "thought" (*ennoia*) appropriate to it; the "method" (*methodos*) by which it is constituted in figures of thought; and its characteristic style, whose constituents are diction (*lexis*), figures of speech (*schemata*), clauses (*kola*), composition (*synthêkê*, word-arrangement), cadence (*anapausis*), and rhythm (*rhythmos*). As Cecil Wooten has noted, this analysis derives from the stylistic tradition of Theophrastus, Demetrius, Dionysius, and Cicero (as well as a second-century treatise falsely attributed to Aelius Aristides and possibly by Basilicus of Nicomedia), but Hermogenes' theory is considerably more sophisticated and effectively replaces all that has preceded it.[70]

In the last three chapters of the treatise (2.10–12), Hermogenes makes distinctions between the genres of *politikos logos* and their respective styles and representatives. The basic categories are, of course, the traditional ones—dikanic, symbouleutic, and "panegyric" (epideictic)—while panegyric explicitly includes not only epideictic speeches but also philosophy, history, and poetry. According to Hermogenes, "[a]ll poetry is certainly panegyric, and is the most panegyric of all discourse. . . . If someone says that poetry is panegyric in meter, I shall not dispute it" (2.10.389). Further, in the final two chapters Hermogenes distinguishes between what he calls "pure" *politikos logos* and "pure" panegyric. This distinction is somewhat confusing, though it appears that by "pure panegyric" Hermogenes means strictly literary discourses as opposed to panegyric speeches meant to be delivered on public occasions, or to panegyric passages employed in dikanic and symbouleutic/demegoric speeches (i.e., what Cicero calls "digressions"). Thus "pure panegyric" is represented by writers who rank below Plato and Homer, such as Xenophon (who wrote both dialogues and histories), Aeschines the Socratic, Nicostratus (a sophist-philosopher), the historians Herodotus and Thucydides, and all the poets (2.12.404–412). The panegyrics of Lysias and Isocrates, however, are explicitly excluded from this category, on the grounds that they have "some measure of the panegyrical, but probably no more than a symbouleutic or dikanic discourse would admit" (2.12.408). "Pure" *politikos logos* is represented by the canonic Attic orators who rank below Demosthenes (2.11.395–403). Demosthenes, Plato, and Homer are not "pure" representatives of either category because, in essence, they represent *deinotês* within their respective genres and thus transcend the limits of the "pure political" and the "pure panegyric" styles in prose and verse. (The term translated here as "pure," *haplôs*, literally means "simply": the simply political, the simply panegyrical.)

Hermogenes, in sum, subdivides the realm of "rhetoric," or what he calls *politikos logos*, into "pure political" and "pure panegyric" discourse, categories that correspond roughly though not exactly to practical oratory and epideictic literature: the "pure political" subdivides into dikanic, symbouleutic/demegoric, and what might be called "practical" panegyric, meaning epideictic speeches for various kinds of ceremonial occasions; the "pure panegyric" subdivides into philosophy, history, and poetry, while poetry is "the most panegyric of all." Declamations and literary versions of pragmatic speeches are not specifically mentioned, but presumably these would fall into the "panegyric" category as well. Isocrates' *Antidosis* and Aelius Aristides' *Against Plato Concerning Rhetoric*, which are literary imitations of dikanic orations, might be classed as either "practical" panegyric or as "philosophy" under the heading of "pure" panegyric. This general division between practical and panegyric rhetoric reflects such earlier categorizations as Philodemus of Gadara's distinction between *empraktos rhêtorikê* and *sophistikê rhêtorikê* and Aristotle's recognition of two basic types of audiences—the *kritai* or "judges" who must decide a dikanic or symbouleutic issue and the *theôroi* or "observers" whose role is to reflect on and evaluate an epideictic discourse. Hermogenes, in short, gives explicit recognition to the epideictic/practical distinction that is implicit in ancient Greek thought at least from Hesiod onward and that we find recognized much later by Hermogenes' fifth-century commentator Syrianus in his deployment of the terms *to epideiktikon* and *to pragmatikon*.

Like Cicero and others, Hermogenes takes the epideictic/panegyric registers as the chief source and model for high eloquence in practical oratory, although, as he and all other theorists recognize, in symbouleutic and especially dikanic speech the most pronounced features of panegyric and poetic styles are generally to be toned down. In symbouleutic discourse, for example, Hermogenes says that the styles that produce grandeur (*megethos*) should predominate, with passages of forcefulness (*deinotês*), while dikanic speech requires chiefly a style that produces character (*êthos*) but also admits the specific type of grandeur produced by abundance (*peribolê*). All practical oratory, moreover, requires also the style of beauty (*kallos*), especially in passages of carefully reasoned argumentation (2.10.381–387). Clarity (*saphênia*) and vigor (*gorgotês*), of course, are always required for practical civic speech, and the best style in any kind of discourse will resort to any and all of the types of style as the circumstances and the speaker's purposes require. For practical civic speech the speaker needs a style that, while maintaining the clarity and vigor needed for effective communication and establishing a suitable *êthos* for the speaker, achieves impressiveness and strong persuasiveness through passages or moments of grandeur, beauty, and forcefulness—perhaps, for example, in the deployment of arresting *sententiae* to punctuate the speaker's arguments, or (depending on what the situation may permit) more extended flights of eloquence on resonant general themes.

While Hermogenes is not so explicit as Cicero in calling such passages "digressions," it appears—especially in the cases of grandeur and forcefulness—that he generally does think of them as digressive amplification on a topic. Concerning the grandeur produced by "abundance," for example, he says that it arises whenever one "adds" something extra to the "thought" of one's argument or steps aside from what the audience expects: one might, for example, enlarge on the "genus" to which a particular "species" belongs, as when Demosthenes in *On the Crown* (242) says: "[a] wicked thing, O men of Athens, an informer [*sykophantês*] is ever a wicked thing, and a cunning rogue by nature is this little man," and so forth (*On Types* 1.11.278–279). Likewise "solemnity," another subtype of grandeur, arises from "thoughts" concerning the gods; or "divine things" such as the nature and laws of the universe; or "divine things" in human affairs such as mortality and immortality, justice and law; or things that are "great and glorious" in human affairs such as the battle of Marathon (1.5.242–246). These clearly are topics for philosophical, historical, poetic, and panegyric discourses, and they would enter into practical dikanic and symbouleutic speech, as Cicero suggests, as digressions on grand themes. Other subtypes, such as asperity, vehemence, brilliance, and climax, while not overtly or necessarily digressive, involve the expression of angers, passions, or noble sentiments which serve to punctuate a speech with moments of memorable emotion and are especially suitable (though Hermogenes does not say this explicitly) to epigrammatic flourishes and barbs. Finally, the style of *deinotês*, while it arises generally from an apt combination and application of all the other types, arises especially from "thoughts" that are "paradoxical, profound, forcible, and altogether cunningly contrived" (2.9.373–374), in other words, from striking thoughts given striking expression, most especially in the diction, figures, and rhythms appropriate to solemnity, florescence, brilliance, and abundance (2.9.375). Thus *deinotês*, as well, appears to belong essentially to particular passages or flourishes that may "interrupt" the otherwise expected progress of a speech to wax eloquent, passionate, and powerfully persuasive (with the right stylistic turn for that specific moment) on some grand, memorable, impressive, astonishing, or conclusive idea.

The stylistic types that Hermogenes associates with interruptive or digressive flights of higher eloquence in practical discourse are, as well, the definitive types of panegyric. As he says, the "finest panegyric style," of which the best example (at least in prose) is that of Plato, arises from "all the types productive of grandeur, except asperity and vehemence" (2.10.387). Of the key subtypes of grandeur—solemnity and abundance—we have seen already that both arise from the kinds of topics by which a speaker may enlarge on the general principles involved in the specific case, and especially on those topics associated with philosophical, historical, poetic, and other panegyric discourse. Of solemnity, we learn that its prosody requires predominantly dactylic, anapestic, and paeonic rhythms, and sometimes iambics, spondaics, and epitrites (1.6.251–254). These are the rhythms chiefly of epic and the statelier kinds of lyric poetry, and it is significant that Hermogenes illustrates "solemn" rhythm almost entirely with examples from the *Iliad*, with the exception of one anonymous verse in iambics (possibly from the poet Sotades)[71] and a short phrase and a sentence from Demosthenes. Abundance may employ any type of rhythm, though it generally will rely on figures of accumulation, enumeration, and repetition with masked or delayed parallelism (1.11.287–295), in other words, the techniques of enlarged and elaborately spun-out sentences, such as one finds in the writings of Isocrates and Thucydides; such constructions are characteristic also of the grander passages of Demosthenes and Cicero (though with greater force). Of "beauty" (*kallos*), which Hermogenes says is best for passages of careful reasoning, we learn that its style requires balanced, parallelistic constructions such as one finds in the panegyrics of Isocrates and more moderately in the speeches of Demosthenes, as well as rhythms that produce a very nearly metrical effect, though solemn or "stately" rhythms should be avoided (1.12.299–310).

Hermogenes' modeling of prose rhythm on poetic meters is not limited, however, to panegyric or the panegyrical passages in practical orations. A central concern in *On Types*, as in Dionysius' *On Composition*, Demetrius' *On Style*, and Cicero's *Orator*, is "the extent to which it is possible to apply rhythm to prose without making a song out of it," and Hermogenes acknowledges the Gorgianic point that "rhythm," even without "articulate speech" (as in instrumental music), can be an exceptionally powerful means of moving a listener's mind (1.1.222–23). Thus, in his account of every stylistic type, Hermogenes analyzes its characteristic rhythms in terms of the meters composing its periods and cola. We learn, for example, not only that a writer or speaker intending a "solemn" effect should aim chiefly at dactylic, anapestic, and paeonic rhythms, but also that "purity," which is a subtype of clarity, requires a predominant use of iambics and trochaics while permitting some of the "less conversational" measures as the means of interrupting and avoiding an overly metrical effect (1.2.232–233). This distinction and relationship between the rhythms/meters of the more panegyric and the plainer passages of an oration corresponds roughly to that between the metrics of the choral odes and the "speeches" by the characters in Attic drama. Hermogenes' general point, like that of Dionysius and Cicero, and like that of Aristotle and Demetrius long before him, is that prose rhythm in general should be metrical "but not strictly metrical like that of poetry" (1.2.234); prose eloquence should break up its meters and employ mixed meters to generate a broadly rhythmic, quasi-lyrical effect. The eloquence of a powerfully persuasive practical oration, then, will need to maintain clarity, vigor, *êthos*, and sincerity as the basic constituents of its style, will need to maintain a general, quasi-lyrical rhythmicality based mainly on iambics, and will need to frame its reasoning in the well-wrought, well-balanced, and nearly metrical style of elegance/beauty, while punctuating its arguments with flights or flashes of high-flown, sententious eloquence derived primarily from epideictic/panegyric registers.

Hermogenes, then, like Dionysius of Halicarnassus and Aelius Aristides, embodies the predominant, persistent tendency in later antiquity to view the realm of rhetoric as centered on the epideictic/panegyric genres and to base the prosody of nonpoetic *logoi* on poetic models, while considering poetry the "most panegyric" rhetoric of all. That tendency seems not to be a matter simply of a "literaturization" and reduction of rhetoric to aesthetics. Rather, as we see in the sophists' recognition of the psychagogic power of rhythm and songlike prosody, or in the more or less Ciceronian recognition of the panegyric sources of the *topoi* for grand eloquence, the tendency seems to be more probably a matter of describing the rhetor's most powerful sources of persuasion. Hermogenes, Dionysius, and Aristides all describe "rhetoric" as a philosophico-literary art of eloquence that clearly will exercise itself most fully as a medium of ideological suasion and contestation in the genres of epideictic speech and literature but that also will apply to intercessive, dikanic, and symbouleutic discourse in the civil and administrative forums of the Roman world, from the emperor's *consilium* down to the courts of provincial governors and local magistrates.

This basic orientation toward describing the rhetor's major sources of persuasive power is especially evident in the famous treatise of "Longinus" *On the Sublime*. Because of the fad for "sublimity" that surrounded the rediscovery of "Longinus" in the eighteenth century, *On the Sublime* has largely been identified, and translated, as a protoromantic literary treatise devoted to the expression of imaginative "genius."[72] However, the explicit concern of "Longinus" is with a *technê* that is, as he says, useful "for political men" (1.2), and though he frequently and indeed constantly refers to poetry and other forms of epideictic literature, his ultimate point of reference is always the *rhêtôr*, and especially the ideal kind of *rhêtôr* embodied in the written speeches of Demosthenes. This *rhêtôr* does not have "genius" in the romantic (or the modern) sense but has what "Longinus" calls *megalophyes*, "greatness of nature," or *megalophrosynê*, "greatness of mind" (9.1). His concern, moreover, is not really with "sublimity" at all, at least not in a romantic sense, but with what is most usually known as the "grand" or "high" style—or, possibly, with what Hermogenes calls *deinotês*. "Longinus" has written a highly specialized rhetorical treatise focused wholly on the principles and techniques of a single type of highly persuasive style.

The term in "Longinus" that has traditionally (since the eighteenth century) been translated as "sublimity" or "the sublime" is *hypsos*, which means something like "height" or loftiness, or in metaphorical uses "top," summit, or crown. With "Longinus" it means something like "the heights" of eloquence or "the lofty"—so that the title traditionally attached to this treatise, *Peri Hypsous*, might better be translated as *On Loftiness*. He first says this about it:

> What makes elevation and prominence in *logoi* is the lofty [*hypsê*], and with the greatest of poets and history writers also this alone has given them preeminence and wrapped them in ageless fame. For not into persuasion [*peithô*] but into transports are listeners carried by the marvelous; and altogether does the wondrous overwhelm the persuasive [*tou pithanou*] and over the graceful prevail, and indeed while the persuasive [*to pithanon*] does determine many things with us, these [marvelous, wondrous, lofty *logoi*] bring to bear a majesty [*dynasteian*] and irresistable force that altogether masters every listener. (1.3–4)

What *Peri Hypsous* has in mind is clearly the "sublimity" or loftiness not of an entire discourse but of those "marvelous, wondrous" passages within a discourse—*logoi* in the sense of "words" or "sayings," or of apostrophic, epigrammatic declarations—that give memorable elevation and prominence to what is said at a particular moment and that exert an overwhelming psychagogic power. This soul-moving power is set in contrast to *peithô*, the weaker "persuasion" that is produced by "the persuasive" (*to pithanon*) and "the graceful," by which the treatise seems basically to mean the rational assent produced by well-knit, well-spoken argumentation, or what Hermogenes calls the "beauty" of careful reasoning embodied in a well-balanced, nearly metrical style.

But the persuasive/graceful and the lofty are not really placed in opposition. As "Longinus" goes on to say (in the next sentence), the lofty stands forth as an opportune or "timely" (*kairiôs*) flash of eloquence, striking "like a thunderbolt" and thus revealing in a single, compact stroke the *rhêtôr*'s Zeus-like power, while his "skill at invention and the arrangement and marshaling of facts" do not appear in one or two places only but are evident throughout his discourse (1.4). Argumentation is long, and is the substance of the discourse, working gradually toward assent; the lofty is brief and sudden, working all at once within an opportune moment. On these terms one cannot write a discourse that is wholly, unremittingly lofty, and to foolishly try would be to produce merely what "Longinus" censures as bathetic histrionics (3–4). We are to think of a master rhetor who can weave a well-made argument that is generally *pithanon*, "persuasive" in the sense of "reasonable," as well as "graceful" in Hermogenes' sense of "elegance/beauty"—but a master rhetor who can also at opportune moments rise to loftiness and enthrall his audience completely. The very reasonable position of "Longinus" is that such a rhetor will always be superior to those of moderate skill who never rise above the rational, graceful, well-knit argumentation of *pithanos logos*.

What *Peri Hypsous* is concerned with, then, is a specialized *technê* of loftiness, a version of the "grand style," one that presupposes the larger, more complete *logôn technê* in which it is embedded. And insofar as its evocation of the *dynasteia*, "majesty," of loftiness echoes Gorgias's famous statement that *logos* is a *dynastês megas*, a "great lord" (*Helen* 8), it seems clear that "Longinus" is developing a basically Gorgianic theory of stylistic suasion, one that looks to poetic "speech having measure" and "sacred incantations" (*Helen* 9–10) as an ultimate paradigm of psychogogic eloquence. Thus it is not surprising that "Longinus," while recognizing that loftiness is grounded in the conceptual and emotive power of grand ideas (*On the Sublime* 8.1), notes also that grand ideas can be borrowed from literary sources (7.2–5, 13.2–4) and chiefly focuses his *technê* on the stylistic means—figures, diction, and rhythmic composition—by which such ideas are made fully lofty and (thus) utterly enthralling, while taking his illustrations mainly from poetic discourse.

The Gorgianic aspect of this theory is particularly evident when the discussion turns to rhythmic composition (39–41). The account "Longinus" offers is much more brief than that of Dionysius, Demetrius, Hermogenes, or Cicero, and indeed "Longinus" tells us that he has written two treatises of his own on the subject and is here just summarizing (39.1–2). But like his predecessors he relies on a metrical analysis of prose rhythm, and like them is concerned with what he calls the overall "music" or *harmonia* that arises from the skillful composition (*synthesis*) of periods and clauses. To emphasize the importance of the subject, moreover, he declares that he "need add only this, that not only for persuasion and pleasure is *harmonia* natural to people, but [it] is also for grand utterance [*megalêgoria*] and for *pathos* a wondrous instrument" (39.1). He then illustrates the point by citing flute music and harp music, which induce "certain emotions" in their listeners and carry them away with "corybanitc" (divine) frenzies, while creating a rhythmic movement to which their bodies involuntarily respond (39.2); but the *harmonia* of *logos*, he adds, is more deeply embedded in human nature and therefore has an even greater power, for *logos* is composed not only of sound but of ideas and appeals not only to the ear but also to the soul, so that its *harmonia* generates in listeners a complex cognitive-emotive state and thereby "altogether rules over our thought" (39.3).

"Longinus" takes a more extreme position than Dionysius, Demetrius, Hermogenes, Aristides, or Cicero but not a fundamentally different one. Like them, he embodies a version of what had come to be the predominant view of "rhetoric" in later antiquity. In that view, "poetry" is distinguished from all other forms of *logos* as "*logos* having meter" but, with all the other forms, belongs to the general domain of "rhetoric." "Rhetoric" originally may have taken its name from the pragmatic forum, and indeed it always looks to the pragmatic forum as its ultimate point of application, but by the second century A.D. "rhetoric" is understood as an Isocratean *logôn technê* resting on the philosophico-literary *paideia* that both Isocrates and Cicero had advocated. "Poetry" stands to "rhetoric" as one of its major divisions, and as the eldest form of epideictic eloquence, along with the newer "free verse" forms of historical, philosophical, panegyric, and declamatory *logoi*, which are descended from Homeric narrative, Hesiodic wisdom-lore, and the varieties of lyric praise and blame. Epideictic rhetoric (in its manifold forms) stands to pragmatic rhetoric (in its manifold forms) as the domain of enduring, memorable models of eloquent wisdom. As such, "poetry" stands to "rhetoric" also as an ultimate paradigm of rhythmic and stylistic suasion—so that, as Aristides says, the greatest poetry is that which most resembles rhetoric (by having its discursive power), and the greatest rhetoric is that which most resembles poetry (by having its stylistic power).

Rhetoric as *Phylaktêrion*: Apuleius's *Apologia* (*De Magia*)

Sometime around 158 A.D. the famed Latin sophist Apuleius of Madaura defended himself on a charge of witchcraft before the proconsul of Africa, his *consilium* of advisors, and a large audience, in Sabrata—today's Zowara, Libya, now a dusty little town but then a large, prosperous port city sixty miles west of Tripoli, or what then was called Oea. Or so it appears from Apuleius's *Apologia*, also known as *De Magia*, which is generally thought to be the only surviving text of a judicial oration from the Roman imperial period. The text, however, is odd in several ways. First of all, it runs to more than twenty thousand words, more than one hundred pages in the Teubner edition of the Latin text, and it takes about four hours to deliver,[73] which seems rather long for an age in which busy magistrates normally put strict limits on an orator's speaking time. An important case involving a well-known person might, of course, be given more time, and witchcraft was a capital crime; but from Apuleius's speech it appears that the charges brought against him were almost patently absurd, even in a world that believed in and feared the magic arts. Further, Apuleius speaks in his own defense, which is characteristic of Greek but not Roman judicial procedure, while his accusers employ advocates in the usual Roman way. This oddity, however, may simply reflect provincial conditions: there was considerable Hellenistic influence in Roman Africa. But Apuleius's defense is almost comical at points. His first major argument, for example, begins with a little poem he has written on tooth powder and continues with an encomium on the benefits of brushing one's teeth, complete with an informative digression on how crocodiles' teeth are cleaned by birds (6–8). Finally, and perhaps most significantly, the rhetorical situation embodied in the text suggests a convoluted soap opera plot worthy of the most fanciful declamation exercise: The Sophist Accused of Charming a Rich Widow by Witchcraft.

It is possible that there was indeed such a trial, and that the *Apologia* represents a speech that Apuleius actually delivered. Augustine is our chief authority for believing that Apuleius actually was put on trial (*City of God* 8.19, *Letters* 138.19), but he is writing more than two centuries after the fact, and his only source of evidence appears to be the *Apologia* itself. Moreover, he appears to conflate the *Apologia* with another and presumably different case, in which Apuleius undertook a lawsuit against a number of citizens of Oea who had opposed the erection of a statue in his honor. Augustine's references to the trial, however, do show that to an intelligent, well-educated person in late antiquity (and indeed to a rhetorician) the *Apologia* was plausible as a real judicial speech. So the text at least possibly represents a trial that actually took place. But, as a literary version of a judicial speech, the *Apologia* probably has been extensively rewritten and expanded (as was Pliny's *Panegyricus* for Trajan) and it equally probably may be a total fabrication, that is, a literary declamation functioning as a pamphlet on a philosophical issue, much like Isocrates' *Antidosis* and Aelius Aristides' *Against Plato Concerning Rhetoric*. Or it may be a satirical broadside against those who had opposed the statue in Oea. In sum, the *Apologia* may be understood—whatever its origins may be—as a literary representation and defense of the philosopher-sophist's art and way of life, rendered as a persuasively versimilar imitation of a judicial speech.

Apuleius, a Latin product of the Second Sophistic, is at once a representative and extraordinary figure. The son of a wealthy, curial-rank family of Madaura—the ruins lie near today's Mdaurusch, in eastern Algeria—Apuleius was educated at Carthage and Athens, traveled widely, and spent time at Rome before returning to north Africa. He was fluent in Punic (his probable native language) and Greek as well as Latin, and his *paideia* was extremely wide-ranging even for a "philosophical" sophist of this time. His rhetorical practice was likewise highly varied. In addition to the *Apologia*, his extant writings include: *The Golden Ass*, the only complete surviving Latin prose romance, the work for which he is most famous; the *Florida*, a collection of excerpts from various panegyric speeches; a number of "philosophic" discourses (or public lectures) including *On the God of Socrates*, *Asclepius*, *On Plato*, and *On the Universe*; and a short handbook on logic called *Peri Hermêneias*.[74] We also know, chiefly from what Apuleius says in his extant writings (e.g., *Florida* 9, 17, and 20) and from references by other writers, that he produced dialogues, histories, poems, hymns, music, satires, a collection of love stories, another prose romance entitled *Hermagoras*, a translation of Plato's *Phaedo*, and discourses on mathematics, music, astronomy, medicine, botany, and zoology.[75] Some scholars have assumed that Apuleius must have been a superficial dabbler in all these fields of learning, but analysts of the logical theory in *Peri Hermêneias* regard it as embodying some genuine (if modest) advances over classical Aristotelian/Peripatetic and Stoic logic.[76] Apuleius generally presented himself as a Platonist, and he was one of Augustine's chief sources of information on Platonic doctrines. (*City of God* 8.14–22, for example, is chiefly devoted to refuting the Platonic theory of demonic intervention as described in Apuleius's *God of Socrates*.) Finally, we know not only that Apuleius undertook at least one lawsuit, and may have appeared in law courts on other occasions as well, but also that in later life he served as *sacerdos provinciae*, "provincial priest" of the imperial cult at Carthage, and undertook civic benefactions including the sponsorship of public games (Augustine, *Letters* 138.19; Apuleius, *Florida* 18).[77] But his career, as with most of the great sophists of this period, was based primarily on philosophico-literary performances in epideictic speech and writing. He was, in sum, one of the leading intellectual and literary figures of his time.

The melodramatic plot embodied in the *Apologia*—its *hypothesis*—is almost too convoluted to describe in less than several paragraphs or even pages; in baldest terms it might be put as follows. While traveling home from Alexandria to Madaura, Apuleius falls ill at Oea and is forced to spend some time there convalescing. He is taken in by a friend from his student days, one Pontianus, who persuades Apuleius to stay for several months at his home under the care of his widowed mother, Pudentilla, who is just over forty years old. Pontianus has ulterior motives. Pudentilla has for years been putting off remarriage to her brother-in-law (an unpleasant old man), which has been imposed on her as a requirement for inheriting her husband's rather large estate; but now the old man has finally died, leaving her free to do as she wishes. Pontianus wants Apuleius to marry Pudentilla: this will keep the estate in good hands. Apuleius resists, then thinks it over, then gradually warms to Pudentilla's virtues. (She is an educated woman, fully literate in Greek as well as Latin.) He courts her; he proposes; she consents; they marry.[78] This marriage enrages the brother-in-law's surviving brother (Aemilianus) and Pontianus's father-in-law (Rufinus), who both had hoped to get control of the estate. Eventually they turn Pontianus and his younger brother (Pudens) against Apuleius, by persuading them that Apuleius plans to do them out of their inheritance. Apuleius proves to Pontianus that his inheritance is safe, and they reconcile, but Pontianus not long after dies of a sudden illness. Pudens remains under Aemilianus's control, and gets hold of Pudentilla's letters, including one in which she declares (in Greek) that Apuleius is "a magician, and I have been bewitched to love him." Aemilianus, Rufinus, and Pudens then spread through the town the charges that Apuleius has murdered Pontianus and has practiced witchcraft. Apuleius challenges them to bring their charges into court and appeals to the proconsul, who orders a trial. The in-laws suddenly drop the murder charge, but they press ahead with the charge of magic, entering the indictment in Pudens' name with Aemilianus acting as chief advocate (with a team of hired advocates to help him). About five days later they go to trial in the proconsular court at Sabrata.

It is evident that this plot revolves around a lurid family drama turning on the struggle for control of an inheritance—as in many declamation exercises—and that, allegorically, it can be seen to represent the seduction of "Rome" (Pudentilla and her estate) by Hellenized, sophistic culture (Apuleius). (Compare Dionysius of Halicarnassus' allegorical use of a somewhat different family drama to represent the displacement of "philosophic" by "mindless" rhetoric in the Hellenistic period.) Further, this plot embodies a number of culturally significant oppositions. On one hand, for example, it pits what Tacitus calls "bloodthirsty, gain-getting eloquence," or the rhetoric that Dionysius portrays as a usurping whore, against the eloquence of what Apuleius calls *philosophia*. Aemilianus, Pudens, and Rufinus are attempting to remove Apuleius from the estate they wish to control by having him judicially put to death: their action is exactly parallel to that of *delatores*. On the other hand, the *Apologia* pits the crass, uncultured, provincial Roman against the cosmopolitan, cultured, Hellenized sophist, the man of *paideia*. As Apuleius says to the proconsul in his opening remarks, he feels especially confident and "congratulates" himself because "I am privileged to have the means and opportunity with you as my judge of clearing away the accusations of the ignorant against philosophy and of defending myself" (1). As Augustine's report of the business about the disputed statue suggests, or likewise Apuleius's own remarks at the beginning of *Florida* 9 (as well as *Apologia* 67), the cosmopolite sophist was not everywhere popular and sometimes encountered hostility and suspicion from those who took no interest in *paideia* and who resented his public prominence.[79]

Such attitudes form most of the basis for the indictment against Apuleius. At least half of the "evidence" adduced against him, aside from Pudentilla's letter and the putative evidence of witchcraft itself, consists of charges that appeal to conventional Roman prejudice toward "foreigners" and Greekified sophisticates. Apuleius is "a philosopher of elegant appearance," is "most eloquent in both Greek and Latin," and has long hair (4); he uses and encourages his friends to use a scented toothpowder to brush their teeth (6); he has written amatory poems to boys (9); he carries a mirror with himself at all times (13); he has few material possessions, lives like a poor man, keeps few or no slaves, and has actually given some slaves their freedom (17–18); he comes from Numidia and is half Numidian (24); so why would a woman like Pudentilla fall in love with such a man, except through sorcery? (27).[80] Most of the evidence for the witchcraft charge itself appeals to prejudice as well. Apuleius has been seeking out rare kinds of fish with strange names (27, 29); a boy had an epileptic fit in Apuleius's presence (27, 42); Apuleius keeps in his room a small cult object wrapped in a handkerchief (27, 53); a house that Apuleius once occupied was found, several months later, to have smoke stains and bird feathers in it (57); Apuleius has had a craftsman make for him a signet of rare wood, depicting a grotesque figure that he calls in Greek his *basileus*, his "king" (61); finally, Pudentilla has called him a "magician" (*magos*) in one of her letters (66, 82). What most of this "evidence" boils down to is a set of assertions that Apuleius is *effeminate* and *strange* from the viewpoint of provincial, stolid Romans like Aemilianus. As James Tatum has put it, Apuleius's enemies portray him as a "degenerate fop" who worships unfamiliar gods and whose behavior doesn't suit their notions of normality, and who is therefore likely to be practicing the witch's art—casting spells and concocting drugs (for Pudentilla) or poisons (for Pontianus).[81] As Apuleius says in his opening remarks, "Aemilianus's advocates have spewed with their hired loquacity many attacks against me personally, and against the philosopher generally the customary things one hears from ignoramuses" (3).

As legal argument, most of the "evidence" adduced against Apuleius is plainly ridiculous, and Apuleius makes numerous remarks about its silliness—noting at one point (the one concerning tooth powder), for example, that the audience could scarcely restrain its laughter at Aemilianus's charges (7). Elsewhere he praises the proconsul's ability to sit with a straight face through the accusers' buffoonish speeches (35) or remarks upon his astuteness at posing questions that expose the "evidence's" irrelevance (48). Indeed, from the proconsul comes what Tacitus's Maternus calls *clementia cognoscentis*, the "clemency of understanding" of a learned judge who knows the laws and understands the principles of jurisprudence. Aemilianus, in contrast, is portrayed throughout as a bumbling, ignorant, grasping "rustic" (60) with no real notion how to "accuse a philosopher" (17) nor even to conduct a proper prosecution. From Apuleius's presentation of the case, it is difficult not to suspect that the charges brought against him were so obviously foolish that the proconsul called a trial simply for the opportunity to hear and see the famed sophist perform, while permitting him to clear his name and publicly humiliate his false accusers.

Accordingly, with nearly every charge in the indictment Apuleius makes his refutation an occasion not only for the drubbing of Aemilianus and his coconspirators, but also for numerous panegyrical digressions on assorted topics of philosophical or literary interest. Apuleius offers to his judge (and the reader) a varied feast of entertaining bits of erudition, and to his accusers a set of lessons in the things they should have known but don't. For example, on the charge of being an elegant and eloquent long-tressed philosopher, beyond dismissing it with an ironic "What a crime!" Apuleius discusses the famous good looks of both Pythagoras and Zeno, while presenting himself as a haggard scholar with faded complexion and tangled hair (4). The tooth powder charge produces, in addition to a poem he sent with a gift of the powder to a friend, a little talk on personal and moral hygiene—with its account of how crocodiles clean their teeth, and an aside to note that Aemilianus doesn't even wash his feet—while the amatory poems to boys occasion both a poetry recital and a disquisition on morality in erotic verse and the distinction between the speaking figure in a poem and the author behind it, with references to poems by Plato and the emperor Hadrian, which of course Aemilianus has never read or even heard of (6–13). Concerning the mirror, Apuleius offers a lecture on its uses as an instrument of self-examination and meditation, noting that Socrates urged his followers to study their self-reflection and that Demosthenes trained himself before a mirror; this leads to further digression on some interesting problems in optics connected with mirrors, which Apuleius has been studying, with references to Epicurus and Archimedes (13–16). The charge of having few possessions leads to an account of indifference to wealth and luxury as a requisite of the philosophic life, again studded with references to many philosophers and philosophic schools (17–23), while the slur on Apuleius's origins receives a brief homily on the topic that character matters more than birthplace, as well as an encomiastic passage on the honorable status of Madaura and the civic standing of his family there (24).

Concerning the actual charge of witchcraft, Apuleius begins with an etymological derivation of the word *magos* from the Persian word for "priest," a note on Zoroastrianism and the education of Persian princes, and a quick review of the many distinguished philosophers accused of "magic" by the ignorant (25–27). Apuleius's accusers are not too clear, it seems, about what "magic" is, or indeed about the meanings of the other key terms in their indictment. Then, noting that the shortness of the accusation-speeches has left "plenty of water" on the water-clock—Apuleius at this point already has been speaking for more than an hour—he now proposes to discuss the specific charges, *si uidetur*, "if it may be permitted" (28). This locution suggests, again, that there is virtually no need to continue unless the preconsul and "all of this great crowd" (28) would like to hear Apuleius go on, which he does. On the matter of the fish, then, Apuleius points out at length, with references to Virgil, Homer, Pythagoras, and others, that nowhere in literature is there any mention of fish being used for magical purposes, or for the production of drugs or poisons, nor do the *names* of fish (such as "sea-skull") have any relation to their natures or uses, as Aemilianus seems to think; Apuleius then explains that he has been collecting and dissecting rare fish for scientific purposes, in hopes of extending the zoological researchers of Aristotle and others, which are briefly discussed (29–41). The matter of the epileptic fit produces, on one hand, a lecture on the uses of witnesses and testimony, and, on the other, a lengthy medical digression on the nature of epilepsy as discussed by Plato, Aristotle, and Theophrastus (42–52). The mysterious cult object wrapped in a handkerchief occasions more derision of Aemilianus (who does not even know what it is, although the proconsul does), further discussion of relevant versus irrelevant kinds of evidence, and some general remarks on religious mysteries and initiations (53–56). The smoke and bird feather business is refuted simply as a lie, a fanciful tale sold to a credulous, hapless Aemilianus by a well-known reprobate who has not even shown up at the trial, a point that leads to more instruction on legally valid evidence and testimony (57–60). The seal with a grotesque figure turns out to be, in fact, an image of Mercury (Hermes, the patron deity of rhetoric, and thus Apuleius's *basileus*) and occasions more digression on the nature of religious mysteries, with references to Plato's *Phaedrus* and *Laws* (61–65).

Finally, turning to Pudentilla's letters, Apuleius provides an extended narrative of their courtship and marriage, a careful reading of the "magician" letter, and an object lesson on the principles of textual interpretation—for the "magician" sentence has been taken out of context, and when read within the context of the whole declares the opposite of what Apuleius's accusers claim (66–102). The key sentence, of which just a fragment has been presented by the prosecution, is from a letter in which Pudentilla chides Pontianus for turning against her. The full sentence says, in Greek, with scolding irony, "[a]nd now that our malicious accusers are misleading you, suddenly Apuleius has become a magician, and I have been bewitched to love him" (83).[82] With simply the reading out of the complete letter to the proconsul, then, the accusers' case has utterly collapsed; indeed, there seems to have been no case at all.

All this is coupled with an indictment of Aemilianus and his associates' debased morality and their crudely avaricious motives, which are linked to their lack of interest in *paideia*. Apuleius says, for example, that Pudentilla's impressionable younger son Pudens has ceased to go to school since falling under Aemilianus's self-interested control. He now spends his time in debauchery "with the very worst young men, amid whores and winecups" or hanging about the gladiatorial schools, where he knows everyone. Having forgotten all his lessons, he now speaks nothing but Punic, knows only a few stray words of Greek picked up from his mother, and can barely speak Latin (28, 98–99). Pudens is Aemilianus's creature, the distinctive product of his un-*paideia*; ignorant, illiterate or semiliterate, the slave of his grossest appetites, weakminded, morally vacuous. Aemilianus himself is only slightly better. He can just barely read Pudentilla's literate Greek, and he has submitted in evidence an obviously forged, grammatically barbarous (and indecent) love letter to Pudentilla that he claims is from Apuleius, although the Greek is so bad that Apuleius could not possibly have written it (87).

Whatever the true origins of the *Apologia* may have been, it is clear that, as a literary declamation, the text invites its Roman reader to identify with Apuleius and (perhaps more important) with the learned proconsul, Claudius Maximus, while regarding as an object of derision not only Aemilianus, Pudens, and the other accusers, but also the sort of culture and the sort of rhetorical practice they represent—for theirs is a narrow, conservative, provincial version of Roman culture, productive of an *êthos* interested only in practical advantage in the crassest sense, motivated chiefly by avarice, and indifferent, suspicious, or actively hostile toward the kind of culture that Apuleius represents. Likewise, as I have noted, theirs is the "bloodthirsty, gain-getting," and "gladiatorial" rhetoric that defines the world of *delatores*: the philosophically vapid, ethically indifferent, power-seeking kako-rhetoric that Cicero describes as eloquence's evil twin and that Dionysius portrays as a corrupting force in the "house" or polis where communal life transpires. In the *Apologia*, such culture and such kako-rhetoric are portrayed as the source and instrument of injustice.

Apuleius, in contrast, embodies a rhetoric and *paideia* that function (in Aelius Aristides' terms) as a *phylaktêrion dikaiousês*, a "safeguard" or "amulet" of justice, as he thwarts the designs of his false accusers, wards off the injustices they would inflict on him and Pudentilla, and renders them as objects of the judge's, the audience's, and the reader's scorn. But, as the action embodied in the *Apologia* suggests, the "amulet's" protective magic is efficacious only when those endowed with juridic and social power themselves are steeped in the sophist's culture and can appreciate its values, including the values of political philosophy and jurisprudence. This is clearly the case with the proconsul Maximus, whom Apuleius repeatedly refers to and addresses as a learned and accomplished man, a distinguished scholar, a philosopher, an astute jurist and fair judge, a religious initiate, and so forth (e.g., 11, 19, 36, 47, 48, 64, 91, 103). Moreover, Maximus is presumed throughout to be familiar with, and to enjoy discussion of, the varied literature and fields of knowledge that Apuleius digresses into. It is this shared *paideia*, then, that enables Apuleius's discursive art to gain the "clemency of understanding" and to receive fair justice from his judge according to law. Apuleius's gestures toward Maximus's learning are thus not merely conventional efforts to conciliate or flatter a powerful authority (though they are that too), but—

through the text's function as a literary declamation—they also are expressions of a cultural and ethical solidarity the reader is asked to share. As Apuleius at one point says,

> [s]ee, Maximus, what a tumult they have raised, now that I have mentioned a few magicians by name! What shall I do with such rubes, such savages? Shall I demonstrate in reply that I have come across all these and very many other names in public libraries while reading the most distinguished writers? . . . Or, which is much better, relying on your learning, Maximus, and your perfect erudition, shall I disdain to give these clods and dullards a response to such things? Indeed that's what I'd like to do. (91)

The Roman reader in such passages, included in effect as a member of the audience thronging the proconsular court at Sabrata, is called on to adopt the position of the proconsul Maximus *and thus to be addressed by and responsive to* the sophist's discourse, while judging Apuleius (and all that he represents) and his accusers (and all that they represent) as Maximus presumably would do. More important, perhaps, the reader is asked to affirm, at least implicitly, a rhetoric founded on a broad, Isocratean *paideia* as that which sustains and makes possible civil culture, and indeed to affirm that Roman civil culture should be guided and informed by the sort of *paideia* that both Apuleius and Maximus embody. If the *Apologia* may be considered allegorically, we can say that it argues to its reader/"judge" that it is good for Pudentilla/"Rome" to be remarried to Apuleius/"philosophy," good for the affairs of her estate to be guided by the *êthos* and the discursive practices (in writing, speech and thought) that such "philosophy" makes possible, good for Roman authority (or the reader/"judge" himself) to be well educated and responsive to the sophist's art of wisdom-speaking eloquence, and good for the other "Rome" and "rhetoric" embodied in Aemilianus, Pudens, Rufinus, and their associates to be restrained.

In its incarnation as a literary declamation, then, Apuleius's *Apologia* belongs to a series of "defenses of rhetoric" that begins at least with Isocrates' *Antidosis* and that embodies the more or less Isocratean philosophy we find resurgent in such documents as Cicero's *De Oratore*, Dionysius of Halicarnassus' *On the Ancient Orators*, Tacitus's *Dialogus de Oratoribus*, and Aelius Aristides' *Against Plato Concerning Rhetoric*. As such, the *Apologia* both continues and embodies a tradition that for Apuleius is already more than five hundred years old, while it figures forth, in a paradigmatic scene, what is and what will be the place of rhetoric in the Roman world for the rest of antiquity and in the Byzantine world as well for another thousand years. That is, it figures forth precisely what Peter Brown describes as the relationship between sophistic rhetoric's *paideia* and the civic culture of the far-flung administrative networks that constituted the Roman state into the fourth and fifth centuries—a relationship, moreover, that provided the basis for the transformation of the Roman world from pagan to Christian and Byzantine culture, as the sort of Christian orator described in Augustine's *De Doctrina Christiana* came gradually to occupy what long had been the sophist's socio-political and cultural position.[83]

Here I must break off this tale. Suffice it to say, for now, that the conventional modern view that rhetoric "declined" in later antiquity seems improbable. As I noted at the outset of chapter 3, this view derives from assumptions that "rhetoric" is chiefly or primarily an art of practical speechmaking in courts and assemblies and that its fortunes must necessarily rise and fall with those of democratic institutions. The consequence of these assumptions is a narrative in which, rather oddly, "rhetoric" is seen to reach its apex only for two brief moments roughly corresponding to the lifetimes of Demosthenes and Cicero and to be more or less "in decline" for all the rest of antiquity—that is, for about seven of the ten centuries between the emergence of sophistic "rhetoric" and the beginnings of the Middle Ages—or indeed to be "in decline" for all the rest of time, with brief resurgences in the Renaissance, the Enlightenment, and the twentieth century.

But, as we have seen, practical rhetoric seems to have had no shortage of work in either the Hellenistic or Roman period, and demand for instruction in it seems never to have lessened. Certainly there were courts and trials and councils and deliberations and embassies and petitions and appeals and public ceremonies, and so on, as well as poems and panegyrics and histories and treatises and dialogues and declamations and literary imitations of *pragmatika*, and so on, through all this time in both the Hellenistic and Roman worlds. All we can say, perhaps, is that "rhetoric" took on different forms and roles with changes in political, economic, and social conditions and that the predominant pragmatic genres of Periclean Athens or late republican Rome may have become less politically important, or may have become less central media for culturally significant high eloquence, although (as "Longinus," Tacitus, and others suggest) the various kinds of pragmatic rhetoric certainly continued to be practiced with skill and sophistication by the best-trained, best-educated orators in courts and councils. We can also say that, with the evolution of Roman jurisprudence and its concomitant restraints on judicial procedure, the practice of juridic/dikanic discourse actually may have been improved.

Furthermore, if "rhetoric" is conceived in broad, Isocratean/sophistic terms as a general *logôn technê* that applies not only to pragmatic discourse but to all varieties of writing, speech, and thought and that is centered on the epideictic genres of poetry, history, philosophy, panegyric, and declamation—for indeed this was the persistent and finally prevailing view from early to late antiquity—then we can just as well and just as persuasively say that "rhetoric" *revived, flourished, enjoyed a great renaissance.* From Hesiod onward, the art of suasive, psychagogic, wisdom-speaking eloquence that passes from archaic poetry to sophistry, that comes in time to be called "rhetoric," and that we find embodied still in later sophistic theory persistently finds its major venues for culturally significant persuasion, as well as the models and sources for the practical orator's "applied" discursive art, in the domain of epideictic. For Hesiod, that domain is more or less identical with "song" or poetry (in the sense of rhythmically "measured" or versified *logos*); but from the presocratic philosophers, historians, and sophists onward, it proliferates into the varied kinds of spoken and written epideictic prose—histories and prose romances, dialogues and treatises, lectures and panegyrics, declamations and literary imitations of *pragmatika*, "hymns" and "monodies," and so forth—that, with the more traditional forms of poetry, continue to constitute the rhetorical *paideia*. Poetry, in turn, comes to be understood in ancient thought as the elder art of eloquence from which all "rhetoric" has descended and as the original form of "rhetoric" itself. This was, in sum, the persistent, enduring view for more than a thousand years.

By way of conclusion, let me consider one further line of argument. It seems reasonable to say that for "rhetoric," in this tradition, the key political term was not "democracy" but "justice," or (in Greek) *dikê*. By "justice" here is meant not only jurisprudence or judgment according to law within the context of a trial but, more broadly, judgment of what is "right," or fair, or appropriate, according to communally accepted codes of valuation and belief applied within a particular set of circumstances. The basic or "primitive" meaning of the term *dikê* was *what is right or fitting*, or *judgment* of such things; and by extension it came to mean as well a proceeding to determine legal rights or the justice rendered as the outcome of a trial. The adjective *dikaios*, "just," originally meant *observant of custom, well-ordered, civilized, observant of duty, righteous, decent, equal, well-balanced, fair, normal, real*, even *true* in the sense of *rightly, really, truly, having reason*. One could say, to express agreement with an opinion, "you speak justly." The noun *dikaiosynê* meant *righteousness*, or *justice* in the sense of "just-ness," and also *fulfillment of law* in the decision of a juror. The verb *dikaioô* meant *set right, deem right, claim as a right, do right to someone*, as well as *prove, test*, and *justify*, and eventually *give justice* in a legal proceeding. *Dikê*, as a concept for political or social thought, was primarily not a legal but a moral category that had to do with determining and "doing the right thing" in a given situation.

It seems clear that *dikê* and the range of terms and meanings associated with it were central to both Greek political thought and Greek notions of rhetoric or *logôn technê* from the beginning. Significantly, Plato portrays Protagoras as claiming that to be human is to have a sense of *dikaiosynê*, and that a civil community or *polis* cannot exist unless "all citizens" have such a sense in common, as well as *sôphrosynê*, temperance/sensibleness, and *to hosion*, respect for the holy: together these things constitute civic virtue (*Protagoras* 323b–c, 324d–325a). Thus, when Protagoras claims that the capacity for *euboulia* or "good deliberation" that he cultivates in students will make them better citizens as well as persons (318d–319a), he is also claiming—as Plato's Socrates recognizes (319a)—to teach a *politikê technê* founded on a developed capacity for making judgments about and acting in accordance with *dikaiosynê/sophrosynê/to hoison*, or in other words for action informed by good deliberation about the just, the right, the fair, the sensible, and the proper, in all facets of public and private life. Likewise, Plato portrays Gorgias as claiming to teach an art of persuasion that is concerned with *ha dikaia te kai adika*, "the just and unjust," not only in law courts but also in council halls and citizens' assemblies, and in "all other gatherings, any political gathering that may occur" (*Gorgias* 452d, 454b). According to such a view, all deliberations in all "political" (or public) forums are concerned, in some sense, with judging the "right" response to different kinds of situations: some will call for juridical determinations, some for policy decrees, some for intellectual, moral, and/or aesthetic evaluation, and so forth. Isocrates, like his sophistic predecessors, maintains that the capacity to establish judgments "concerning things just and unjust and shameful and good" by means of *logos* is what makes civil existence and indeed human existence possible (*Nicocles* 6–7); accordingly, the cultivation of developed discursive powers that can intelligently shape and effectively intervene in such judgments is the purpose of what he calls *logôn technê, logôn paideia,* or *philosophia.*[84] Isocrates' characteristic, formulaic phrase for good eloquence is *alêthês kai nomimos kai dikaios,* "true and lawful and just" (*Nicocles* 7; *Antidosis* 255–256); and while he denies the possibility of "an art that can implant *sophrosynê* and *dikaiosynê* in those of evil nature," he also maintains, like Protagoras, that in most people these virtues are never wholly absent and that those who desire to "speak well" can improve their intellectual and moral nature through the study and practice of a *logôn technê* focused on politically significant themes (*Against the Sophists* 21; *Antidosis* 274–275).

While Plato's intention is, of course, to put such sophistic claims in doubt, it is also true that the political philosophies of both Plato and Aristotle share the Protagorean (and Isocratean) assumption that a commonly accepted sense of "justice" or "the right" is a basic requirement for the existence and survival of civil communities. As David Cohen has put it, in Aristotelian and Platonic political thought "an essential element of what makes a polis a polis is the common capacity for moral judgment together with the political institutionalization of that judgment" in laws and in the various magistracies, delibrative bodies, and other agencies (including forms of education) that transact the public business and that arbitrate between competing interests.[85] Thus, as Aristotle declares in the *Politics,* the human being as "a political animal" (1.1.9.1253a) is "the best of all animals when completed" through the formation of communities, but is also "the worst of all . . . the most profane and brutal" when "divided from law and justice," from *nomos* and *dikê.* "*Dikaiosynê,*" he says, "is political, for *dikê* is an ordering of the political community, *dikê* being judgment about the just" (1.1.12.1253a). For both Plato and Aristotle, then, as well as for the sophists they are responding to, *dikê* is the fundamental, essential principle of politics, the principle that a successful polity must embody and protect, and without which it cannot exist.

A crucial motive for this line of thought is the problem of *stasis,* a term that in its political use (and before it becomes a technical term of rhetoric) means *faction, strife, feud,* or even *civil war.* As Cohen shows, political *stasis* was a very real, recurring problem for the agonistic culture of ancient Greek communities, just as it would be for the Roman world.[86] The breakdown or failure of shared persuasions regarding *dikê/dikaiosynê* within a community (or, for that matter, between communities) would mean, in essence, the irresolvability of *stasis* by means of *logos,* hence the degeneration of *stasis* into brutality, that is, into the rule of *bia,* coercive physical force, or a pandemic of *hubris,* violence/outrage, sometimes ending in an utterly catastrophic cycle of savagery and revenge—or what Hesiod calls *metatropa erga,* "turnabout works" (*Theogony* 89). Central to Cohen's discussion is Thucydides' account (3.81–3) of the degeneration of *stasis* into general feuding and wanton atrocity at Corcyra, early in the Peloponnesian War, as a paradigm that was to be repeated and exceeded in other Greek cities. Thucydides himself is worth quoting at some length:[87]

> Death in every form ensued, and whatever horrors are wont to be perpetrated at such times all happened then—aye, and even worse. For father slew son, men were dragged from the temples and slain near them, and some were even walled up in the temple of Dionysius and perished there. To such excesses of savagery did the

revolution [*stasis*] go; and it seemed the more savage, because it was among the first that occurred [in the Peloponnesian War]; for afterwards practically the whole Hellenic world was convulsed. . . . The cause of all these evils was the desire to rule which greed and ambition inspire, and also, from them, that ardor which belongs to men who once have become engaged in factious rivalry. For those who emerged as party leaders in the several cities . . . while they pretended to be devoted to the common weal, in reality made it their prize; striving in every way to get the better of each other they dared the most awful deeds, and sought revenges still more awful, not pursuing these within the bounds of justice [*tou dikaiou*] and the public weal. . . . And citizens who belonged to neither party were continually destroyed by both, either because they would not make common cause with them, or through mere jealousy that they should survive. (3.81.5–3.82.1, 3.82.8)

The recurrence of such events, and the continuing potential for their repetition—along with the excesses of injustice and misjudgment to which the Athenian democracy itself was prone, its susceptibility to demagoguery and sycophancy, its imperialistic dreams, and the oligarchic coups that periodically disrupted it—form the background for the beginnings of Greek political philosophy.

A conception of "rhetoric," then, as a culture-shaping art of *logos* (in all its epideictic and pragmatic forms) that serves the purposes of cultivating and maintaining intelligent public judgment about what counts as *dikê* or "the right" in different situations—the conception that descends from Isocrates to such later figures as Aelius Aristides and Apuleius—may be understood at least in part as a response to the problem of *stasis*. (And indeed the emergence of *stasis* as a central term in rhetorical theory from Hermagoras to Hermogenes seems especially significant in this light.) But such a conception of rhetoric nevertheless leaves open-ended the question of what will count as *dikê*, or of what will count as social justice in the distribution of powers, privileges, duties, and restrictions to the different sectors of a polity.

In this regard, the writings of Isocrates are instructive. As is well known, Isocrates writes in praise of both monarchy and democracy in different texts, while tending also toward a preference for the limited democracy embodied in the constitution of Solon (see, e.g., *Nicocles* 14–26; *Areopagiticus* 15–27, 60–70; *Panathenaicus* 130–147; and *On the Peace* 63–64, 75–79, 122–145). Much depends on whom Isocrates is writing to and what his purposes are, though it is worth noting that his chief defense of monarchy, in *Nicocles*, is written as Nicocles' address to his own subjects on the justice of his kingship. To the Athenians Isocrates praises democracy in his own voice, while criticizing the excesses of the radical democracy that developed after Pericles. The point is that, with Isocrates, the particular type of polity is less important than the ability of any given polity to maintain *dikê* and to serve—and to keep in balance—the interests of its citizens, including the sometimes conflicting interests of the wealthier elites and common citizens. As he says in *To Nicocles*, while advising the young monarch on the duties of kingship,

[c]are for the multitude, and be doing everything to rule agreeably to them, knowing that of oligarchies as well as other polities those endure the longest that best serve the populace. And you will lead the people rightly [*kalôs*] if you neither permit them to commit outrage [*hubrizein*] nor suffer them to be outraged

[hubrizomenon] but consider how the best may have their honors while the rest in no way shall be wronged [adikêsontai]; for these are the first and greatest elements of good government. (15–16)

Or, as he says in *Panathenaicus*,

I for my part hold the types of polity to be three only—the oligarchic, the democratic, and the monarchic—and that of the peoples under them, all that are accustomed to place in charge of their offices and other business the citizens who are most competent and who shall best and most justly [arista kai dikaiotata] govern affairs, such peoples will in any type of polity whatsoever manage well [kalôs], both among themselves and with others. (*Panathenaicus* 132–133)

Good government, in short, is "good" not to the degree that it is democratic but to the degree that it is intelligent and competent and just. Such government will not plunge the *polis* into carnivals of bloodshed by exacerbating *stasis* either among its citizens or with neighboring *poleis*.[88] Isocrates is more a political pragmatist than an ideologue with a fixed commitment to any one type of polity, and it seems reasonable to say that this is true as well for the sophistic tradition that he inherits and that descends from him.

We might, however, also argue that in Isocratean *philosophia*, and in the notion of "rhetoric" that it informs, there is at least an implicit (and sometimes explicit) orientation toward the democratic, insofar as a persuasively "just" and competent government must be "agreeable to the multitude" or must derive its legitimacy from popular consensus, if it is to rule successfully, and it must provide itself with both the means and capacity for intelligent deliberation and persuasive utterance about "the right" whenever judgments must be made. In *To Nicocles*, Isocrates launches his account of what practices a monarch should aspire to and avoid with this observation:

What educates those in private life consists of many things: first and foremost is the necessity not to be extravagant but to take thought [bouleuesthai] about their livelihood each day; next the laws under which they happen to conduct their civic lives; further, the freedom of speech [parrhesia] openly permitted to friends to rebuke and to enemies to attack each other's faults; and in addition to these things, some of the poets of previous generations have left behind suggestions that are needful for living; so that from all these things it is probable that they will be improved. For kings [tyrranois], however, there are no such advantages. (2–4)

Isocrates' advice is that Nicocles must therefore seek to provide himself with such an education, and that since he lacks the "advantages" that discipline the private citizen he must ensure that his own training and self-discipline are exceptionally rigorous. He should develop his capacities for good deliberation through the training and practice of *logôn paideia*, associating "with the wisest" (*tois phronimôtatois*) who can instruct him and becoming familiar with the discourses of "the renowned poets and sophists" in order to equip himself to be "a judge (*kritês*) of the lesser and a competitor of the greater" in speech and thought (12–13; see also 38–53). To rule acceptably to the populace, he should study the laws of different states, seeking for his own polity "laws altogether just and expedient and consistent with each other," and in the resolution of disputes his judgments should be likewise just, expedient, and consistent, exhibiting neither favoritism nor caprice (17–18); moreover, he should observe the traditional requirements of religion, conducting his life in the ways that are "the most good and just" and most acceptable to the gods (20). Finally, and most important, in choosing advisors and subordinate officials he must surround himself not with flatterers but carefully must identify and employ those persons of good judgment who are willing to censure his mistakes, giving them complete *parrhesia*, "freedom of speech" (27–28).

Isocrates thus holds that, for a monarch to rule successfully and justly, he must artificially construct for himself and even improve on the social conditions that "educate" and inform the thought of the private citizen who lives as part of a community. And so, implicitly, for those who govern in any other type of polity. Isocrates, of course, elsewhere maintains that monarchies or despotisms are the most likely to fail—to find themselves embroiled inescapably in unjust violence and intrigue (*On the Peace* 111–113)—and he maintains also that "even badly constituted democracies are the cause of fewer misfortunes" than oligarchies, while democracies "that are well constituted are more just, more open and impartial, and more pleasing to their subjects" than any other kind of government (*Areopagiticus* 70). In sum, the well-constituted, well-run democracy embodies the form of government to which all other polities must aspire, and which they must imitate, in order to rule effectively, wisely, and with *dikê*: that is, to maintain intelligent deliberation and decision adequately grounded in acceptable public understandings of "the right."

We might then argue that, for Isocrates and for the sophistic tradition that descends from him, "rhetoric" or *logôn technê* is, on one hand, politically pragmatic rather than idealist and therefore willing to work within and through the circumstances of any type of polity whatsoever. But, on the other hand, we might argue too that "rhetoric," in this tradition and in its role as a *phylaktêrion* or "amulet" of justice, also functions as an at least implicitly democratizing discourse art that mediates between the sovereign power and public judgment. Insofar as the sovereign power even in autocracy must emulate or imitate to some degree the conditions of democracy, it must make itself responsive in adequate measure to public judgment of "the right," must make itself available and open to argumentation, and must equip itself to judge and practice intelligent, responsible deliberation—so that it must also, in sum and in consequence, submit itself to the discursive arts that constitute the general realm of "rhetoric," and it must furthermore be willing to be persuaded. Further, insofar as "rhetoric's" major, culture-shaping role in this tradition is to disseminate public, popular discourse concerning "the right" in various matters of cultural, ethical, political, or philosophical concern—chiefly by way of epideictic, not only through "literature" (meaning written texts in libraries and in circulation) but also through public performances and recitations in theaters, schools, symposia, festivals, and other settings—"rhetoric" also shapes and sustains the prevailing modes of public judgment to which the sovereign power must be responsive, and itself embodies that judgment to the sovereign power. The image of the sophist on embassy to an emperor is especially apt. If all these things can more or less reasonably be said, we might argue too that "rhetoric" is, or was, at least implicitly the medium in which the possibility of democracy stood embodied, or existed in virtuality, even when no actual democracy was available.

To put it another way, we might argue that rhetoric (as defined by this tradition) is not made possible by democracy, but democracy by rhetoric.

To say so may, perhaps, be much too optimistic. Certainly, rhetoric in antiquity seldom operated in a formally democratic world, or one that we would recognize today as truly democratic. Certainly, ancient political thought had few or no models of a really successful democracy to work from. The classical Athenian democracy, while in many ways admirable, was unstable and susceptible to *stasis*, committed gross injustices, and at times was catastrophically imprudent, as Thucydides and Tacitus understood all too well. The Roman republic was in essence a modified oligarchy that, as Cicero recognized in *De Re Publica*, included some limited forms of democratic referendum to satisfy the crowd of common citizens while reserving real decision-making power for the nobility—and thus it was closer to (though not the same as) the sort of limited democracy that Isocrates preferred—but, whatever its virtues may have been, the Roman republic ended in violent turmoil, and it ultimately failed. The Roman imperial state, while hardly admirable from our contemporary point of view, arguably was in some ways an improvement over the late republic and may well have been inevitable, in its time, as the only feasible means of governing the multiethnic, largely Hellenized, far-flung empire the Romans had acquired. On the basis of such recognitions we might say that democracy as we conceive it was in "decline" or in eclipse for most or all of antiquity, or that it never flourished. But we cannot really say the same for rhetoric.

Perhaps, in sum, we can say this much: through long centuries of social inequity, gladiatorial power politics tending toward brute force, and Hellenistic and Roman imperial autocracies supported by ever more extensive administrative networks, what rhetoric did, in its function as a general, culture-shaping *logôn technê* grounded in a broad *paideia*, and in its function as a *phylaktêrion dikaiousês*, was to maintain the conditions of possibility for a never quite emergent concept of democracy. On one hand, rhetoric maintained the image of *logos* (in writing, speech, and thought) as opposed to force as the best and most legitimate means of deciding all matters of dispute, and as the chief criterion for defining a just regime. On the other hand, through its culture-shaping, psychagogic functions in the varieties of epideictic discourse and through *paideia*, rhetoric cultivated the general, cultural consenses on which civil institutions and a public discourse might be based. Admittedly, *rhêtorikê* was generally the privilege of rich, well-educated elites, was often the willing servant of established power, and in the pragmatic genres operated mainly within the givens of prevailing ideologies. But this was not always or necessarily so. At the heart of the sophistic/Isocratean tradition also lie the practices that are variously known as antilogy, "making the lesser argument the greater," arguing both (or multiple) sides of a question, and what the *Rhetoric to Alexander* called *exetasis*: the skeptical "examination" of fissures, contradictions, and inconsistencies in any discourse, in order to refute it, argue its opposite, or to open an alternative position.[89]

In general, what "rhetoric" in this tradition promoted and maintained was an image of possibility—one that might be summed up, or emblemized, by the stereotypical, fictive city that provides the setting of Greek declamation exercises even in late antiquity, and that D.A. Russell has described as "Sophistopolis": the *polis* where a generally well-educated, cosmopolitan populace enjoys a vibrant cultural life, lives under a democratic constitution, and adjudicates all differences of opinion, all questions of ethics, justice and policy, by means of argumentation and discussion in conversations, council chambers, courts, and the theaters and other venues where sophists declaim and poets sing on varied themes.[90]

PART III

RHETORICAL POETICS
Argumentation in Archaic Lyric

5

Theognis' Octopus

On Poetry as Rhetorical Transaction

Consider these scattered verses from the *Theognidea:*

> Demonax, much is heavy for you to bear; for you don't know how
>   to do what's not according to your will. (1085–1086)

> Will, turn toward all friends a many-colored *êthos*,
>   joining with whatever temper each one has.
> Have the temper of the convoluted octopus, which takes on
>   the look of the rock it is in converse with;
> now be in accord with this, and then be of a different hue.
>   Skillfulness is better than inflexibility. (213–218)

> Hearken to me, child, and discipline your wits; I'll tell
>   a tale not unpersuasive nor uncharming to your heart;
> but set your mind to gather what I say; there's no necessity
>   to do what's not according to your will. (1235–1238)

Consider as well this fragment from Evenus, preserved as a quotation in Aristotle's *Nicomachean Ethics* (7.10.4. 1152a):

> I say practice is long-lasting, friend, and moreover
> with humankind it finally comes to be their nature.

Theognis, as it happens, is one of the "poets of previous generations" whom Isocrates recommends to Nicocles as offering "suggestions that are needful for living" (*To Nicocles* 3, 43). Here, however, we might consider these verses from Theognis and Evenus as an embodiment, on one hand, of a fundamentally rhetorical understanding of the poetic that persisted and generally prevailed from early to late antiquity and, indeed, into the early modern period. On the other hand, these verses embody not only a recognition of the cultural place of poetry as an instrument of *paideia*, but also an intimation of the potential for a rhetorically diminished poetics, and hence for a rhetorically limited poetic practice, which this placement has at times entailed, and not least in the century that now has run its course.

In the argument that unfolds from here, my chief concern will be to construct an understanding of a rhetorical poetics that is derivable from ancient thought and practice: archaic lyric practice in particular, as chiefly (though not exclusively) exemplified by Pindar, Alcaeus, Sappho, and Solon, as well as by Theognis. The motivations for this focus (and this choice of examples) will, I hope, become sufficiently apparent as the discussion proceeds. But the basic motives are these: first, as I will argue more fully in chapter 6, what we loosely call lyric poetry—meaning, in essence, a relatively short poem that typically can be understood as a single "speech"—is arguably the most basic, most fundamental of all poetic genres. Lyric, then, might be taken as a convenient synecdoche for "poetic" discourse generally. Second, in archaic lyric we find embodied a poetic practice that predates the conceptualization of both "poetry" and "rhetoric" in the fifth to fourth century B.C.; it belongs to the Hesiodic realm of "eloquence" that I considered at the outset of this book and that is arguably characteristic of all "traditional" societies worldwide. Archaic lyric embodies a longstanding, mostly tacit, traditional understanding of "poetic" discourse in Hellenic culture that is not yet informed by disciplinary or "philosophic" efforts to systematically theorize its nature and proper function, such as we find in Aristotle's *Poetics*, or to provide principles of critical judgment that may shape the expectations of cultured audiences. Third, archaic lyric embodies a discursive practice that is clearly the nearest relation to, and indeed the precursor for, the epideictic or panegyric practices of the later "rhetorical" tradition, and especially the sophistic tradition. Fourth, as a fundamentally *rhetorical* practice, archaic lyric embodies a paradigm in which "poetry" may function (and did function) as culturally and politically significant civic discourse, that is, as an epideictic argumentation that can effectively shape communal judgments about *dikē*, or what is "right" in various kinds of circumstances, and so can effectively intervene in, intensify, or modify prevailing ideological commitments or value-hierarchies. And, fifth and finally, archaic lyric presents us with a paradigm for "poetry" that modern thought has generally found difficult to accept, or even perceive, and that in consequence has generally been unavailable as a guiding paradigm for what we tend to think of now as "advanced" or "literary," high-cultural poetic practice.

An explicitly rhetorical understanding of archaic lyric as a culturally significant and powerful epideictic practice, and as a synecdochic representative for the possibilities of "poetry" in general, then, is the major focus of part III. In part IV I sketch a sort of genealogy for the rhetorically diminished poetics we inherit and perforce must work with, or through, or out of, in our time.

But to Theognis.

Theognis, the Megarian elegist traditionally ascribed to the mid–sixth century B.C., is one of the few archaic lyric poets from whom we have a substantial body of surviving poetry, the nearly fourteen hundred lines of the *Theognidea*. This body of poetry, as we now have it, is a collection of epigrammatic verses—meant to be recited or sung, in varying selections and sequences, by the drinkers at symposia—with additions by other poets (including Evenus) up to about the end of the fifth century B.C., and some reorganization and re-editing by persons unknown.[1] The edition that we now have appears to be a Byzantine production of around 900 A.D., and is divided into two books, the second consisting of erotic verses, although there probably was no such grouping in the original.[2] The *Theognidea* thus embody a composite speaker, a variegated *êthos* of many hues, a "Theognis" based on the original poet yet produced by several hands, who speaks refracted through a mosaic of disassembled, reassembled, and recombinable bits. Such construction of an author figure as, in essence, a fictive role or subject position perhaps based on an original poet yet subsequently occupied and elaborated by later poets and performers—such as the Homeridae, or the followers of Archilochus or Sappho—seems to have been a common practice in the archaic period.[3] Hereafter, then, I invoke Theognis, without quotation marks, as the name of this composite author figure.

The political context in which the Theognidean voice developed is significant. From the seventh to the fifth centuries Megara was an important city on the western frontier of Attica and a sometime rival of the Athenians for power. Like pre-Solonic Athens, the city had an oligarchic constitution that seems to have included some role for a citizens' assembly. As in many Greek *poleis* in the archaic period, there were continuing political tensions and outbreaks of civil *stasis*, outbreaks which at Megara produced the tyranny of Theagenes (c. 630), a period of radical and apparently unstable democracy (c. 560), and finally the restoration of oligarchy.[4] As James McGlew has recently pointed out, tyrants in the archaic period typically emerged as pro-popular defenders of the *dêmos* against the excesses and injustices of an oligarchic ruling class (much like the revolutionary Great Leader of today who seizes absolute power and rules autocratically in the name of "the people"); in this sense, tyrants represented the same kinds of forces that eventually produced the move toward democracy, at Athens, in the sixth to fifth centuries.[5] During the Peloponnesian War, the tensions at Megara degenerated again into violent *stasis*, leading to the conviction and execution of the popular leaders— a conviction apparently ratified by the Megarian assembly—followed by the establishment of what Thucydides calls an extreme yet long-enduring oligarchy (c. 424 B.C.; Thucydides 4.66–67, 74). As the war progressed the Megarian oligarchs sided stubbornly with Sparta's Peloponnesian League against Athens, thereby exposing their city to protracted Athenian hostilities, which eventually reduced Megara to permanent insignificance. Centuries later, Pausanias would remark that "not even the emperor Hadrian could make the Megarians thrive" (Pausanias 1.36.3; 1.40.3); and indeed Megara would never amount to much again.[6] Megara's story, like that of Corcyra, is one of political failure.

Readers often have taken the *Theognidea* to reflect an oligarchic or "elite" class consciousness, but, as the verses just quoted suggest, Theognis's attitudes are variable and complex, and—much like his near contemporary, Solon—he is as critical of the city's oppressively corrupt, self-serving, hubristic rulers as he is disdainful of what he elsewhere calls the "the empty-minded populace . . . the despot-loving populace" of Megara (*dêmos keneophronos*; *dêmos philodespotos*; 847–850).[7] He most typically invokes a middle course, the "straight path" between factional extremes:

> Kyrnos, this city labors, and I fear she may bring forth a man
>   the corrector of our wicked *hubris*.
> For though the citizens are still sensible, their leaders

are preparing to fall into much wickedness. (39–42)
I go by the path as straight as a ruler, swerving
  to neither side; my thought must all be fitting.
I'll govern my homeland, the shining city, neither turned
  toward the populace nor persuaded by unjust men. (945–948)

The phrase translated here as "a man / the corrector"—*andra/euthyntêra*, a locution that signifies greater dignity than plain "corrector"—invokes the possibility
of a tyrant, a single man who will take it upon himself to seize power, settle accounts, and punish the misdeeds of the former "leaders" (*hêgemones*) whose rule has
been "unjust" (*adikos*). *Euthyntêra*, "corrector," derives from *euthyna*, which was the
name for the audit performed at the end of a magistrate's term of office: if the audit
turned up irregularities or malfeasance, the ex-magistrate would be subject to some
penalty. The word "sensible," *saophrones* (or *sôphrones*, the "standard" form in classical Attic Greek), suggests that the "citizens" (or "townsmen," *astoi*) collectively
possess the *sôphrosynê* or "sensibility" by which both the "wickedness" (*kakotês*) of
the "leaders" and the account-settling of the "corrector" will be judged. The speaker
in the *Theognidea* is indeed to be seen as part of a cultured elite, but also as someone
who, like Solon, attempts to voice *sôphrosynê-dikaiosynê*, a reasonable sense of justice, in the midst of a political situation fraught with real potential for destructive
stasis, or a collapse into tyranny and revenge.

But back to the verses I started from. Let me begin with their terms of argument. The Demonax addressed in verses 1085–1086 may be a real person—we
don't know who—but it seems likely that the name embodies a type. *Dêmônax* is
compounded from *dêmos* (district, people) and the Homeric word *wanax*, "lord" or
"master." *Dêmônax* thus means "deme-lord" or "lord of the people," and suggests the
type of an old-fashioned aristocrat whose traditional, archaic code of honor, like
that of the Homeric heroes (with the possible exception of Odysseus), renders him
inflexible, *atropos*, and thus unable to cope especially well with the shifting social
relations and increasingly complex politics of the *polis* of the seventh to fifth century. Much is "heavy" for Demonax to bear these days.

What Demonax lacks is the "skillfulness," the *sophia*, that Theognis invokes for
himself in verses 213–218: the ability to be like the octopus—the *polypous*, or *polypos* (in poetic diction)—which can alter itself to meet its circumstances, and which
is the very opposite of *atropia*. Indeed the name *polypous*, which can also mean
"polyp" in the sense of an amorphous growth, suggests the octopus's power to
change not only its color but even its shape, as it passes through narrow crevices
and passages in rocks where bonier, stiffer creatures would get stuck. Lacking, then,
the octopus's *sophia*, Demonax does not "know how" (*epistêi*) to adjust his "will" to
changing situations or to discipline his "will" to present a variegated, "many-
colored *êthos*" adapted to the "tempers" of his interlocutors. Note that "many-
colored," *poikilon*, can also be rendered (in different contexts) as "dappled, embroi-
dered, in-wrought, intricate, adorned, diversified, changeful, various, subtle, differing"; note as well that "tempers," *orgai*, can also be rendered as "angers, passions,
moods, dispositions." The word translated as "will" in these verses, *thymos*, more
generally signifies "heart" as the seat of emotions, desires and intentionalities, or
even "soul" or "spirit" as the source of animate energies. As "spirit" or "spirited-

ness," moreover, *thymos* can signify "anger" or "passion." The word I translate as "heart," *kardia,* signifies the physical organ but also, metaphorically, the seat of emotional response (with its bodily concomitants).

We have, in sum, a set of overlapping terms that adumbrate notions of emotionality, intentionality, and ethical performance. Demonax's problem is his lack of a *sophia* sufficient to discipline his *thymos* and his consequent lack of a range of performative possibilities, his *atropia*—and very probably, as a result, a propensity for displays of imperious, overbearing *hubris,* which, as we have seen, Theognis elsewhere treats as the major source of injustice, turmoil, and factional strife in the politics of Megara. Or we might say that Demonax's *thymos* is itself insufficiently skilled, insufficiently trained in a *sophia* that would enable him to *desire and intend* a greater range of performative possibilities in his relations with persons of differing "tempers." He has a limited emotional and ethical repertoire. He needs a *poikilon êthos,* or indeed a *poikilos thymos.*[8]

As Bruno Gentili has pointed out, Theognis's octopus can be seen, on one hand, as an emblem of a code of savoir faire for the noble who needs to exercise "adroitness" in the management of his public life and, on the other hand, as an emblem of the sixth-century poet's relations with different audiences, including the "friends" and patrons with whom he associates and for whom he performs.[9] Either way, the octopus signifies what we can call the rhetoricity of both the poet's and the noble's need to adapt their discourse and their self-presentation to the exigencies, opportunities, and limits afforded by the situations in which they must present themselves.[10] In this way, the poet's own skill at such rhetorical adaptation can itself be understood as a model of the *sophia* required for the ruling elites within the *polis*—just as, in Hesiod's "Hymn to the Muses," the epideictic discourse of the poet is seen to provide the stable, rehearsable paradigms of eloquence and wisdom for the public speech of the *basileus* whose persuasive utterance resolves disputes with "straight justice" before they can degenerate into cycles of vendetta.[11] The octopus-like, rhetorical *sophia* that Theognis both invokes for himself as poet and models for his audience of upper-class Megarians is, moreover, more than just a matter of superficial social skill (though it includes that). It is also, and crucially, a matter of profound political necessity, because it implies a principle of answerability that can enable the negotiation of competing interests within the *polis,* both elite and popular, according to some mutually acceptable accounting of *dikê,* "the right" (which, of course, may itself become an object of negotiation or dispute). That is, the octopus's rhetorical *sophia* provides a principle that can prevent an *agôn* of competing interests from hardening into factional polemics and degenerating into civil strife and bloodshed, with hubristic *atropia* the ruling ethic on all sides. Theognis's verse, addressed to his noble audience while evoking the "straight path" of justice between factional extremes, attempts to speak as the voice of this *sophia.*

This rhetorical *sophia,* and the principle of answerability it implies, also includes a recognition that the role of the poet's audience is to *judge,* not simply to have an aesthetic experience, and not simply to understand what the poet means—though the aesthetic experience is part of what will make the poet's discourse persuasive and is part of what the audience's judgment will respond to, and though an intelligent judgment must proceed from an understanding of the poet's probable meaning and intentions. We see this in Theognis's "Hearken to me, child" (verses 1235–1238), which presents a model both of the rhetorical situation for poetic performance and of poetry's paideutic function as a means of cultivating in the young the *poikilon êthos* required for an adequate civic life. The person addressed will be presented with a "telling," a *mythos* (a word that can mean, and does mean in this context, a speech or a piece of exhortation or advice); and the telling is to be at once *charis*, "charming," and *peithê*, "persuasive" to the listener's heart.[12] But the person addressed is also to make an effort to understand or "gather in mind" what the poet says and is not to do anything with which his own *thymos* does not agree: his assent or being-persuaded, in short, is not to be forced. Rather, it is to be a willing agreement based on careful assessment of the poet's charmingly persuasive telling, or in other words a response that has been mediated by some thought-taking. The function of the poet's telling is to persuade the listener's heart; the role of the listener is to exercise his judgment.[13]

The verses of "Hearken to me, child" occur at the beginning of the second book of the *Theognidea*, into which an ancient editor has segregated the collection's erotic epigrams.[14] As the foregoing argument suggests, however, there is more to this and similar poems than a pederastic proposition. That is, the vocative gesture toward the beloved *pais* or "child" (*ô pai*, "o child") can be understood as a conventionalized hailing of the Theognidean addressee, or of the audience of the poetry, while it invokes as a model for the poet-audience relationship the paideutic, homoerotic friendship widely practiced in aristocratic Greek culture, in which an older male acted as both lover and mentor to a younger.[15] It certainly seems likely that the *pais* or "child" of the *Theognidea* is a generalized version of Theognis's central addressee, the younger friend generally identified as Kyrnos Polypaides—so that, when verses of the *Theognidea* were sung at symposiastic gatherings, the singer whose turn it was adopted the position of Theognis, while the group of drinking-companions who constituted his audience were cast into the role of Kyrnos Polypaides and were addressed as "child," whatever their ages and whatever their actual relation to the singer may have been. (Even in modern demotic Greek, persons commonly will address adult friends as well as casual acquaintances as *paidiá*, "children"; likewise, *paidiá* is a common term of address to the audience in traditional Greek folk music.)

It is worth noting, further, that the notions of persuasion, love, courtship, and seduction often are closely linked in archaic Greek poetry. For example, in Pindar's ninth Pythian ode the centaur Chiron tells Apollo—as Apollo contemplates the beauties of the maiden Cyrene—"Secret are the keys of wise Persuasion [*sophas Peithous*] to the shrine of love" (39), meaning the bridal bed, thus figuring "wise Persuasion" as a goddess and keeper of the mysteries of courtship and seduction. Or, as Pindar says in his fifth Nemean, describing Hippolyta's efforts to seduce the ever-virtuous Peleus, "often with all her *thymos* / she entreated him with her persuasions," though he refused the proposed adultery (31–32).[16] Likewise, in Sappho's invocatory poem to Aphrodite, she calls on the goddess to be her ally or "fellow-fighter" (*symmachos*) in "persuading" a beloved to reciprocate; the verb, again, is *peithô*.[17] Concerning the *Theognidea*, then, we can say that the poet-audience relation is figured and conceived, through the speaker-addressee relationship between Theognis and his young friend Kyrnos, as one of courtship, seduction, or persuasion, with the speaker presenting himself as a would-be lover and mentor to the listener and offering ethical, rhetorical, and political wisdom in the form of elegiac, gnomic utterance.

But who is Kyrnos Polypaides? Again it seems likely that Kyrnos is a type, especially in his function as an addressee figure for symposiasts reciting or singing bits of the *Theognidea* to each other over their wine-cups. According to Gregory Nagy,[18] *Polypaidês* or "son of *Poly-paos*" derives from the verb *paomai*, "acquire," so that *Poly-paos* means something like "He-who-has-acquired-much," or someone who has acquired excessive wealth—or who has devoted himself primarily to such acquisition *by any means*, rather than the nobler virtues of *dikaiosynê/sôphrosynê*—suggesting that Kyrnos is the generic son of the generic rich man who has gotten his wealth unjustly. At the same time, there is also a noun, *paos*, which means a kinsman by marriage. Kyrnos may be the son of a rich but ignoble in-law or, as a generic type (and as his name implies), he may be the "son" of many such kinsmen. As for the name *Kyrnos*, there is on one hand a proper noun, *Kyrnos*, which is Homer's name for Corsica, and from which derives the word *kyrnios*, meaning both "Corsican" and "robber"; apparently, to call someone a "Corsican" in Homer's world was to call him a bandit. On the other hand (and as Nagy points out) there is also a common noun *kyrnos*, which means "bastard."

So Theognis's beloved younger friend and mentee Kyrnos Polypaides, the person addressed as "child" in the *Theognidea*, appears very possibly to be a generalized type whose name means something like "Bastard-robber son of Has-much," or "Bastard-robber son of Many-kinsmen-by-marriage," possibly both at once. One of Theognis's more prominent concerns is the debasement of Megara's ruling class through the practice of marrying for money: as he says in verses 183–192, the *agathoi*, the "good" or high born, are willing to marry the *kakoi*, the "bad" or base-born, as long as the *kakoi* are rich enough to give them *chrêmata polla*, "many possessions" or "much money." Thus for Theognis "wealth" (*ploutos*) has "mixed up" (*emeixe*) and polluted the "tribe" (*genos*) of citizens (*astoi*), "mingling the better with the base" (*misgetai esthla kakois*). Kyrnos, then, is the "bastard" or "mixed" product of such a union. Theognis himself, as his name implies, is *theo-genos*, "divinely bred" (or of the "godly tribe"). Kyrnos, in sum, emerges as a generic figure for a "son" of Megara's robber barons, who so often have ruled so badly: the offspring of inflexible, non-*poikilos*, willful, greedy, hubristic elites, and at the same time an in-law to the more "godly" tribe that Theognis represents. Meanwhile, the name *Polypaos* rings punningly (if by impossible etymology) with *polypos*, or *polypous*, the octopus: godly, *agathos* Theognis would have the debased, bastard-robber son of *Polypaos* become more like the *polypous*, acquiring the *poikilon êthos* and the rhetorico-political *sophia* and *dikaiosynê/sôphrosynê* that Theognis himself embodies (or claims to embody).

The paideutic relationship between Theognis and his listener is a recurrent and central topic of the *Theognidea*, beginning from the invocatory poem to Kyrnos:

> But I shall counsel you with good intentions, concerning the very thing,
>> Kyrnos, that I learned of good men when still a boy.
> Be wise, and acquire neither honors nor accomplishments nor riches
>> on account of unjust or shameful deeds.

So know these things: do not converse with wicked
    men, but ever be among the good;
and beside them drink and eat, and with them
    sit and give delight, whose power is great.
For from good men you'll learn good things; but if with the wicked
    you associate, you'll lose even what sense you have.(27–35)

Or, as Theognis elsewhere says:

[t]o be a guest at a banquet and to sit beside a good
    man who knows all wisdom is advantageous;
hear him whenever he says a wise thing, so that you may learn
    and possessing that profit go back home. (563–566)

Never be persuaded by the words of worthless people
    to quit the friend you have and join another;
often they'll say vain things against you before me,
    and against me before you; don't listen to them. (1238a-1240)

O child, you are by nature fair in form, but placed
    upon your head is a mighty crown of ignorances;
for in your mind you have the *êthos* of a quick-wheeling kite
    persuaded by the words of other men. (1259–1262)

What is at issue in these and similar verses elsewhere in Theognis is Kyrnos's need to learn to discriminate between better and worse would-be companions and to choose those who model the *sophia* required to conduct oneself well and justly in private and public life.[19] It is possible to read "good men" and "bad men" in these verses as nobles and commoners, but it seems more likely that Kyrnos is to choose among better and worse nobles—the sort of people who bear power in the city and whose "banquets" are important places to be seen. (The power of the good is "great," perhaps, not only because they are wealthy and wield authority but also because their wisdom is conducive to a sustainable civic life, whereas the scheming of "unjust men" is not.)[20]

Kyrnos, then, is to choose among competing bids for companionship and membership within different cliques of the Megarian elite; Theognis is competing with other voices in an *agôn* of persuasion. This choice of companions is, of course, what is at issue as well in the "Speech of Lysias" in Plato's *Phaedrus*: Whom should a well-bred adolescent choose for his lover-friend and mentor? Just as the youthful and inexperienced Phaedrus in that dialogue is rather easily turned round and round, persuaded by every speech that he is presented with, Theognis's addressee (at least in 1259–1262) is likewise easily persuaded by "other men" to shift allegiances: he has not the *poikilon êthos* of the *polypous* but rather the simple, flittering *êthos* of a bird (the kite) that is pushed about by every change of breeze. (The *polypous*, by contrast, may change its shape and color, but it holds its place and goes where it chooses.) And insofar as Kyrnos lacks the rhetorical skill to judge persuasions, or to adapt himself to audiences and to speak persuasively while not surrendering his judgment easily, he can be manipulated by those who would exploit him for their own self-interest, corrupting him with false persuasions and imprudent counsels, and finally causing him to lose "even what sense" he may have had.

How then will Kyrnos Polypaides acquire the judgment to discriminate between good and bad persuasions, or between better and worse companions—between those from whom he can acquire a civic *sophia* and those from whom he will acquire its opposite? Or how will he acquire the politically and rhetorically skillful *poikilon êthos* of the *polypous*? Theognis has no simple answer to this problem, because there truly is none available. In a passage of the *Theognidea* that Aristotle cites near the end of the *Nicomachean Ethics* (10.9.3 1179b), the difficulty is explicitly recognized:

> To beget and breed a man is easier than to put good sense
>   in him; no one has ever contrived anything
> that has made the senseless sensible and the wicked good.
>   And if to the children of Asclepius god had given this thing,
> to cure the most wicked and blinded wits of men,
>   they would have carried off wages many and great;
> and if thought could be made and put into men,
>   never would a good father's son grow bad,
> being persuaded by sensible *mythoi*. But by teaching
>   never will you make the bad man good. (429–438)

As pessimistic as this poem may seem, its basic argument—which Isocrates invokes, in both *Against the Sophists* (21) and *Antidosis* (274–275)—is probably to be tempered with the further presumptions that Isocrates makes the starting point of his *paideia*: that few are wholly bad, and that those who can admire a wisdom-speaking eloquence, and especially those who wish to acquire and practice it, are capable of developing their sense of *sôphrosynê-dikaiosynê* as part of a rhetorical *sophia*. So young Kyrnos is ignorant, foolish, and corruptible, but he is also improvable. One perhaps cannot implant in him the virtues of *dikaiosynê* and *sôphrosynê* by means of "teaching," *didaskalia*, meaning direct instruction through the narration of *mythoi*, "tellings," that embody good advice.[21] But one can cultivate and enhance such virtues, insofar as they exist in him at all, through the exercise of judgment and discursive skill in suasory encounters, and thus through the rehearsal of acts of conscious ethical positioning and deliberated choice. If Kyrnos cannot be taught, his *thymos* still can be persuaded, and the persuasions of his *thymos* may become part of his ethical repertoire.

This observation brings us back to the verses of Evenus cited at the outset of this chapter, which with Theognis's recognition of the problems of a narrative *didaskalia* appear to have been crucial to the Aristotelian notion of ethical development. As Evenus suggests, and as Aristotle more explicitly theorizes, *êthos* is a matter of acquired predispositions to judge, respond, choose, and act in certain ways: that is, a matter of the "habits," *hexeis*, of emotionality and intentionality that constitute a person's repertoire for ethical preference and performance.[22] These predispositions or "habits" are acquired by means of *rehearsal*. Thus, as Evenus says, "practice" or *meletê* is "long-lasting," *polychroniê*, and "with humankind it finally comes to be their nature." *Meletê*, "practice" in the sense of "exercise" or "rehearsal," can also be translated as "care" or "attention" paid to something (even anxious care); in the Greek rhetorical tradition, it also becomes the name for declamation exercises.[23] It thus implies "rehearsal" with careful, conscious attention paid to what one is doing. The word *polychroniê* suggests on one hand something already long-existing, well-established, ancient, and on the other something that produces enduring effects. The effect of *meletê*, as Evenus suggests and Aristotle agrees, is the cultivation of an acquired "nature," *physis*, or indeed a *thymos* or "heart" endowed with potentialities for emotions, intentions, and behaviors that will seem "natural" or intuitive to the person acting but that also may be consciously, deliberately invoked and performed—or examined.

This is not to say that one can just "put on" a character, like choosing a costume from a rack. As Judith Butler has argued, things are not so simple. I am, however, suggesting that both Theognis and Evenus have in mind something like what Butler describes as the "sedimented effect of a reiterative or ritual practice."[24] While Butler's attention is focused on the simultaneous constraint and instability of "naturalized" norms of behavior and identity in modern culture, and on the potential for disruption and contestation that the instability of those (or any) norms makes possible, my attention here—or Theognis's attention—is focused on the cultivation of a *poikilon êthos* or *poikilos thymos* endowed or "sedimented" with a range of performative possibilities that *all* seem "natural" but that are also available for deliberate inspection and selection. Theognis's *pais* is not to do, and perhaps cannot do, what is not "according to" his *thymos*. The point is to render his *thymos* capable of "according" by "nature" with a range of ethical possibilities and thus of being "flexible," *tropikos*, and "skillful," *sophos*, in its responses to the "tempers" of others.

Meletê, in sum, is the means of cultivating *êthos*: the *poikilon êthos* of the *polypous*, or the *atropon êthos* of a Demonax, or even the "quick-wheeling *êthos*" of a foolish young man "crowned with ignorances" and misguided and manipulated by the persuasions of bad companions. It all depends on whom one associates with, what one is persuaded by, and the acts of judgment one rehearses.

In Theognis, then, we find embodied a number of traditional assumptions about the nature and function of poetic discourse, both as a rhetorical transaction and as an instrument of ethical *paideia*. Insofar as the poetic transaction is presumed to be (and figured as) a rhetorical encounter—in which the speaker, as a competitor in an *agôn* with other voices, attempts to persuade/seduce his addressee to choose and keep him as a companion, mentor, and ethical model—it is also presumed that the role of the audience is to exercise its powers of judgment and response, in choosing to be persuaded or not persuaded to become a "companion" of Theognis, or to be persuaded or not persuaded by his counsels.[25] Or if the audience does not step directly into the role of addressee, and in effect adopts the third party position of another "banqueter" who witnesses Theognis's efforts to persuade and counsel his beloved but ignoble *pais*, the audience's role as judger is then to judge the quality of the persuasion Theognis offers, that is, to judge whether a young man (or an adolescent) ought to be persuaded to accept the guidance and companionship of such a person. Either way, the ethical effect is similar. As the audience rehearses its acts of judgment in response to the poetry, and insofar as it judges Theognis admirable and persuasive, it rehearses also various acts of assent that constitute a will to identify with the poet's *êthos* or, more precisely, with the shifting, complex, varied ethical positions figured forth in the poet's self-embodiment in his poetry. The audience's acts of judgment may consist, on one hand, of the actual process of performing the poetry, as the drinkers at a symposium take their turns reciting or singing verses, and reciting or singing further verses in reply, in which case they rehearse their identification with Theognis's *êthos* or a specific aspect of it by means of a ritualistic, bodily reenactment of the Theognidean utterance. (One may, of course, also perform the poetry ironically, sarcastically, insincerely, or uncomprehendingly, in which case one will be rehearsing different judgments and different ethical positions.) On the other hand, the symposiasts' acts of judgment may consist also of the somewhat more distanced activity of voicing opinions about the poetry, or about particular verses, or about the oral interpretation given them by a singer; but in this case they will still be giving bodily performance to one or another mode of assent or disagreement.

The presumption here, as in Evenus and Aristotle, is that the inviting and shaping of such responses in a rhetorical encounter necessarily will be more powerful as an instrument of ethical *paideia* than a simple, didactic recitation of principles and precepts, because the audience's act of assent or being persuaded—or, for that matter, an act of dissent or being unpersuaded—is also an act of willed preference, the formulation of an intentionality, the rehearsal of an ethical position. As Theognis says to his beloved *pais*, "there's no necessity to do what's not according to your *thymos*": insofar as the poetic transaction is understood as a rhetorical encounter, the *pais*, the addressee, and the audience of the poetry are conceived of as free to withhold assent (or to be ironic, etc.). But if the poet's persuasion has been truly successful, one's *thymos* in the act of being persuaded accords with what has been proposed, and one's assent, admiration, or identification is willingly performed. In such a case, the *thymos*-felt intentionality or preference that one practices through multiple rehearsals of one's being persuaded is on the way to becoming part of one's naturalized ethical repertoire.

The persistence into the classical period of the traditional, archaic assumption that the poetic transaction is a rhetorical encounter in which the poet's role is to persuade and the audience's role is to judge is reflected in Plato's *Protagoras* (339–347), as the discussion turns to critique and defense of arguments presented in a poem by Simonides. Doesn't Simonides contradict himself? Is the poem sage or foolish, and are the claims it makes (about the difficulties of becoming and being a good man) to be believed? Do they make sense in the context for which Simonides composed? And so forth. These issues then lead, in the subsequent discussion between Protagoras and Socrates, to arguments about the teachability of virtue. It is clear that all the speakers in the dialogue regard such talk as embodying the normal sort of response to poetic discourse; no one is surprised by it, it needs no justification, and indeed it embodies what Protagoras means when he voices the evidently unexceptional belief—it passes without remark or challenge—that "the greatest part of a man's *paideia* is to be capable concerning verses [*peri epôn deinon*]; that is, to be able to gather which of the sayings of the poets have been rightly done and which have not, and to know how to distinguish them and to give a reason when questioned" (338e–339a). Knowing how to read (or listen to) poetry means knowing how to judge the claims and the persuasions that it offers. The conventionality of such a notion is suggested in the dialogue not only by the complete absence of any objection or need for explanation, but also by Plato's portrayal of Protagoras as an inheritor of the older poetic tradition (with which Protagoras is made to identify himself explicitly, at 316d–e) and, perhaps most significant, by Socrates' effort to dismiss the whole discussion of Simonides as rather commonplace. This is the sort of talk one hears, he says, "at the drinking-parties of vulgar, common people"; the really refined, the intellectual avant-garde, should not waste time discussing poetry but should engage in dialectic (347c–348a). It seems clear that Socrates' fairly snooty attitude in this passage is eccentric for its time (as well as insulting to his interlocutors); and it certainly carried little weight with subsequent generations. As the elephantine, fifteen-volume collection of table-talk in Athenaeus's third-century (A.D.) *Deipnosophistai* or *Dinner-sophists* indicates, the recital and discussion of poetry would remain a central element of cultured partying for centuries to come. Poetry saturates all aspects of the sophists' table-talk for all fifteen volumes (and especially book 15); indeed, as Athenaeus's sophists note (15.696a–697b), even Aristotle composed and sang drinking songs in the dining hall of the Peripatetic school.

But if the discussion of Simonides in *Protagoras* reflects a traditional and fundamentally rhetorical understanding of poetic discourse as a suasory transaction—and if the audience's exercise of judgment in response to that transaction constitutes an important form of ethical *paideia* based on the ritualized rehearsal of willed acts of choice, preference, assent, or identification—that discussion also points to the ways in which the rhetoricality of poetry and its effectiveness as a medium of ethical persuasion also could be undercut in a paideutic setting. Poetry's rhetoricality could be undercut, that is, by its social institutionalization as a school subject, a medium of instruction for adolescent boys up to about the age of fourteen, in what was to become the part of the standard curriculum known as "grammar," *grammatikê*. The goals of *grammatikê* were, at the simplest level, the cultivation of alphabetic literacy and, at more advanced levels, the cultivation of grammatically "pure" Greek (or Latin, in the Roman world) and the correct reading and understanding of the poets and other canonic authors. Quite simply, the placement of poetic discourse in such a setting tended to diminish its character as a rhetorical transaction and to remove the possibility of a genuine exercise of judgment and thus also to reduce the possibility of the student's being genuinely persuaded (or not), because it tended to shift the emphasis to *correct performance* and *correct understanding*: the student was required to memorize and properly recite the poetry and to know the proper meaning of the poet's words, while the determination of what was correct or not would necessarily rest with the teacher, the *didaskalos* in the role of *grammatistês*, whose authority commonly was backed by the threat of corporal punishment. Unlike Theognis's *pais*, the student of the *grammatistês* would perform as instructed, under compulsion (or reward if he was good), whether his *thymos* was in accord or not.

Further, even without such compulsion, the "grammatical" orientation toward correct interpretation tended to shift the question of persuasion, and thus the suasory character of poetic discourse, into the background. In Plato's *Protagoras*, much of the discussion of Simonides does in fact revolve around the hermeneutic or exegetical question of just what Simonides' statements mean, or even what particular words mean in the context of his verses. This hermeneutical, philological sort of operation is, of course, necessarily a step on the way to judgment in a rhetorical encounter: one must determine an agreed-on version of the "facts" in any given case before advancing arguments and making judgments about those facts; one must reach a perception of what a poem says and what persuasions it advances before one can assent (or not) to those persuasions. Indeed the grammarian Dionysius Thrax, in the earliest surviving *technê grammatikê* (composed perhaps in the second or first century B.C.), lists the "critical assessment of poems" as the final and "noblest part" of the grammatical enterprise.[26] But in the same passage Thrax also defines *grammatikê* as "the practical study of the normal usages of poets and prose writers." Other than its one-sentence mention of critical assessment, Thrax's *technê* is concerned entirely with correct reading, grammatical parsing, and the explanation of obscure words; almost the whole text is given over to discussion of the parts of speech, and the topic of "critical assessment" is left wholly unaddressed—unless "critical assessment" means grammatical parsing, and so forth.

In the "grammatical" curriculum, the hermeneutic/philological enterprise was central, and it would become increasingly so in later antiquity as the "classic" texts of the school canon—and Homer in particular, who already was ancient literature by Plato's time—became increasingly remote, antique, and difficult for the students who had to read them.[27] Imagine that the English curriculum in all American junior high schools was centered on a requirement that every student read, memorize, and recite hundreds or even thousands of lines of Chaucer in the original Middle English, with correct pronunciation and perfect understanding of every line. The students' engagement with the poetry, their role as "audience," could hardly come to more than an effort simply to understand what it says and to recite it properly. For schoolboys reading Homer in antiquity the situation was comparable; by late antiquity the other canonic poets, though perhaps more linguistically accessible than Homer, still would have seemed remote. Some students might, of course, come to enjoy for its own sake the activity of puzzling out and learning to recite old poetry, and might take pleasure in being rewarded by the teacher for getting it right, and might desire the social distinction of outdoing their peers at a cultured game as well as the social-class distinction of possessing the cultural capital that such games required. But these are not the kinds of ethical rehearsal that a rhetorical transaction calls for. In the world of "grammar," it was possible for an encounter with the rhetoricity of poetry, and for the kind of judgment that such an encounter calls for, to be indefinitely deferred.

Still, at least two factors would have worked to sustain the rhetoricality of the poetic encounter. First, it was always possible that a schoolboy in antiquity, being the product of a culture and a *paideia* for which rhetoric was the paradigmatic discursive art, not only would understand Theognis, Homer, and other poets but would further understand them as offering persuasion. And he might, at some point, either in school or later in life, experience the poets and poems that he had been required to learn (or some of them) as movingly persuasive to his *thymos*, and eventually might come to love them and be ethically shaped by them. Or, rather, in the act of responding to them he might shape himself *against* the pressure of their persuasion, in both the rehearsal of his being persuaded and the rehearsal of his being unpersuaded, in the various scenes of ritual recitation and memorious recollection. Second, insofar as poetry continued to be a viable form of public discourse, on one hand performed in civic rituals, theaters, symposia, and other kinds of social gatherings, and on the other hand circulated in written texts beyond the confines of the school, it still could meet with audiences who were free to encounter it as a rhetorical transaction offering persuasion and calling them to acts of judgment and assent (or dissent).

It is arguable that such conditions held through most or all of antiquity. As we have seen already, poetry continued to be understood as the original and eldest form of rhetoric. And it is arguable as well that, insofar as poetry continued to be understood as rhetoric and continued to circulate in a public sphere beyond the confines of *grammatikê*, it still could be a culturally, ethically, and politically significant form of epideictic discourse. As Tacitus's speakers note in the *Dialogus de Oratoribus*, a controversial poetry such as Maternus writes may quickly become the talk of the town, and may have real political effects. But, to the degree that poetry also underwent a radical "literaturization"—that is, to the degree that it became chiefly an object for the exercise of *grammatikê* within a scholastic setting and had decreasing function as a public discourse beyond the school—both the perception of its rhetoricality and its rhetorical possibilities would tend to be diminished, even if a number of canonic poems retained a certain cultural authority deriving from their status as cultural capital defining social rank. And one can argue too that in certain respects this was (and has been) poetry's fate, as it gave way (and has given way) to various kinds of wisdom-speaking epideictic eloquence in prose.

Finally—to return to Theognis—it must be said that though Theognis has found his readers and lovers over the roughly twenty-five centuries since the *Theognidea* were composed, enough to make him one of the very few archaic poets from whom we still have a substantial body of surviving work, he seems not to have been especially successful in Megara. As he says in his invocatory poem to Kyrnos Polypaides,

> Kyrnos, let the seal of my skillfulness be placed
> > upon these lines, and never shall they be stolen unawares,
> nor shall anyone substitute baseness for their good company,
> > but everyone shall say, "These are the verses of Theognis
> the Megarian, famous among all people,"
> > though I cannot yet satisfy all my townsmen;
> and it's no wonder, Polypaides, for not even Zeus
> > pleases all whether he sends or withholds the rain. (19–26)

Or, as he elsewhere complains,

> I cannot judge the mind of my townsmen, whatever they think,
> > for I please them neither by doing well nor badly.
> And many find fault with me, both the bad and the good alike,
> > but to imitate me not one of the fools is able. (367–370)

"The fools," *tôn asophôn*, suggests both lack of wisdom and lack of skill. Elsewhere, Theognis appears to have suffered betrayal by his friends, the loss of his property, and exile as the consequence of political intrigue (811–814, 831–832 1209–1210). It appears that there were not enough octopi in Megara—or not enough citizens in whom Theognis could successfully cultivate a *poikilon êthos*, a rhetorical *sophia*, or a reasonable sense of justice—and that the city was more or less ungovernable except by rigid and imperious authority. The true reasons for Theognis's failure with his fellow citizens are, of course, unknowable. But one can guess. It may, on one hand, have to do with a stubborn, hubristic *atropia* too rigid to be amenable to persuasion: perhaps Theognis's Megarian audiences were incapable of identifying with, assenting to, or responding to anything not already identical with themselves. On the other hand, however, Theognis's failure also may have to do with the rhetorical limits of his own poetic practice, or the limits of epigrammatic verse, or the limits of the fragmented, tessellated kind of discourse gathered in the *Theognidea*, as aesthetically interesting as it may be. This is a topic to which I will return.

6

Lyric Enthymemes

As Bruno Gentili and others have noted, the ancient world's conception of poetry entails a number of assumptions that generally have been foreign, even antithetical, to modern thought. These include a presumption that poetry is public discourse and that, as such, it is most distinctly or primarily something to be performed in social or civic spaces—such as community festivals, male or female "clubs" with their political and ritual functions, or banquets and symposia—and that, like oratory, poetry is therefore also deeply embedded in the psychology and the performance conditions of an oral, speaker-audience transaction that is best understood as a rhetorical encounter.[1] Even private reading or reading in libraries, insofar as it was conventionally understood and practiced as reading aloud with appropriate intonation (or in other words, oral interpretation), was at base a practice of mimetically recreating or approximating the performance, and the situation of performance, embodied in a poetic text. Further, as we have seen already with Theognis, the presumption that poetry is rhetorical public discourse entails assumptions that it offers persuasion, that the audience's role is to exercise its judgment in response, that this exercise involves the adoption and rehearsal of ethical positions, and that, in consequence, poetry may have direct and indirect effects on social and civic life through the shaping of communally shared judgments and ethical commitments with regard to both particular and general kinds of questions (or what would come to be called hypotheses and theses).

Here I wish to pursue these assumptions further. My starting points are these: first, the basic, widespread, persistent notion of poetic discourse as a type (the oldest and original type) of epideictic rhetoric, which implies that it is also, by definition, a type of argumentation; second, Aristotle's famous notion of the enthymeme as the "body of persuasion" and the central, architectonic principle of all rhetorical argument (*Rhetoric* 1.1 1354a, 1355a);[2] third, Isocrates' description of both poetry and panegyric oratory as "seeking to employ enthymemes" (*Antidosis* 47); finally, the description by Dionysius of Halicarnassus of the best orations as "like the mightiest poems and lyrics" and of the best lyric poems as like orations (*On Composition* 25–26), a notion echoed in Aelius Aristides' assertion that the best poetry is that which "comes nearest to *rhêtorikê*" (*Against Plato* 427–428), with *rhêtorikê* defined as an art of eloquently reasoned argument. Taken together, these ideas suggest a rhetorical poetics that is centered primarily on what we might call lyric genres, that regards a poem as a kind of (sung or chanted) epideictic oratory offering enthymematic argumentation, and that can extend to "nonlyric" genres (i.e., Homeric narrative, Hesiodic lore-poetry, and drama) by regarding them as elaborated oratorical-suasory-enthymematic performances. But, of course, both "lyric" and "enthymeme" are problematic, anachronistic terms when applied to early Greek poetry, and I will need to spend some time defining them for the purposes of this discussion.

"Lyric"

As is well known, "lyric" or *melos* originated as a term of Alexandrian criticism, in the Hellenistic period, to refer in a broadly categorical way to poetry sung (or pretending to be sung) to the lyre. Alexandrian critics applied the term, retroactively, to earlier song-poetry such as that of Sappho or Pindar, though not to all poetry that we might call lyric now, such as iambic, elegiac, and hexameter verse, which had come by the fifth century B.C. to be delivered in a "spoken" recitative.[3] At the same time, in modern thought "lyric" is typically conceived as a poetry that projects a complex, interiorized, private, individualized subjectivity—the so-called lyric self—most typically through the shifting moods of a lyric sequence, such as Petrarch's *Rime Sparse* or Whitman's *Song of Myself* and its twentieth-century avatars. Placing these views in conjunction, Paul Allen Miller has argued recently that even archaic Greek melic poetry cannot really be considered "lyric," despite the Alexandrian critics' backward projection of the term, precisely because of archaic poetry's public, epideictic nature. Genuinely "lyric" poetry, as Miller argues, begins with *literary lyric*, the book of poems deliberately composed as a sequence, where the speaker or author figure in the poetry is not so much a public voice—not a ritual role through which the poet/singer engages with and celebrates/embodies some communal code of values in oral performances—but a private, unique, individualized identity that arises from the relationships between the projected moods and situations of the poems themselves: a textually adumbrated character embedded not in the mythic paradigms of ritual but in the story of a private, personal life. Thus, according to this view, the first true "lyric" begins to emerge only with the great Alexandrian poets of the Hellenistic period or with such Latin poets as Catullus, Horace, and Propertius, at the end of the republic and the beginning of the principate, even though (ironically or paradoxically) these poets composed chiefly in the very meters that the Alexandrians had not considered "lyric": hexameters, elegiacs, iambics.[4]

I will deploy the term "lyric" here differently. That is, "lyric" will be understood in the terms derived, as just discussed, from rhetorical thought and from Dionysius in particular: a relatively short poem that is comparable in scope to, and typically can be delivered as, a single "speech" within a particular occasion. A "lyric" is, in effect, a versified or sung oration, a variety of epideictic discourse. (Choral lyric, however, may create possibilities for antiphonal or "dialogic" double-voicing within a single discourse, as in, for example, some of the surviving fragments of Alcman's maiden-songs). From this point of view, "lyric" is a somewhat broader category than the Alexandrian critics may have been willing to recognize: Archilochus is as "lyrical" as Sappho, Theognis, or Pindar, or for that matter Callimachus or Catullus, whether or not the poetry is meant to be declaimed or sung. Likewise, some types of archaic hexameter poetry, such as the "Hymn to the Muses" that commences Hesiod's *Theogony* or the so-called Homeric epigrams, would also qualify. But this view does agree with the Alexandrians, *pace* Miller, in recognizing that archaic melic verse, in its function as public epideictic, is indeed "lyric." The limitation of Miller's argument is that, in essence, it overemphasizes the differences between the later, literary lyric and its archaic predecessors while underemphasizing the deeper continuities that Hellenistic and Roman writers recognized: on one hand, the fact that literary lyric could and did function also as public, epideictic discourse, even if it operated somewhat differently; and on the other, the fact that the public, epideictic character of archaic lyric does not preclude the projection of its author figure as a complex, varied, *poikilon êthos*, and likewise does not preclude the presentation of distinctive, possibly counterconsensual arguments and attitudes—making the weaker, culturally marginalized case the stronger. Indeed, it is hard to see that such arguments would be precluded in a culture that valued agonistic competition as much as archaic, classical, and postclassical Greek culture did.[5]

The argument that archaic lyric does not, or cannot, project the complex subjectivity that emerges from a literary lyric sequence, or can only project its author figure as a conventionalized type, rests on little evidence. With the exceptions of Theognis, Bacchylides, and Pindar, archaic lyric poetry survives only in scattered, battered fragments, with hardly a complete poem anywhere. What would the projected character of "Sappho" be, if we had all of the nine (and possibly more) books of poetry attributed to her by the Byzantine compendium known as the *Suda* and not just a handful of mostly incomplete poems supplemented with a basketful of stray verses, phrases, and single words scavenged from quotations in later writers and scraps of papyri? Or what would be the character of Archilochus, of whom we have even less? (Or Myrtis, Charixena, and others, of whom we have nothing at all?) Further, where we have a surviving collection or at least a substantial part of one, such as the *Theognidea*, we do indeed find a complex author figure who seems to speak from within a particular, individualized life that is inferrable from the collection as a whole, even if that life is purely a fiction or the reader's illusion: Theognis seems to have been involved at some point in the ruling of Megara, to have suffered betrayal, to have been exiled, to have lost his property, to have had an on-and-off relationship with his young friend Kyrnos, and (perhaps) to have endured and overcome his misfortunes, living out his life in a somewhat embittered state of resignation while continuing to value just conduct (as he defines it, at least) above the self-interested, amoral pursuit of wealth. The four books of Pindar's victory odes, likewise, project an individualized public figure with complex personal and political relationships with the patrons and cities for whom he performs, so that it has been possible for critics to reconstruct (however naively or fallaciously) a biography from the poems. Indeed, the poetry collections that were beginning to emerge by the fifth century B.C. and the later, more definitive editions of archaic verse produced by Hellenistic scholarship would have been among the chief models for later poets who self-consciously composed their books of lyric poetry *as literary imitations of those collections*.

And we have no reason to suppose that the author figures projected in the later, literary poetry are not equally fictive types or, for that matter, that the archaic poets are not equally "real." Admittedly, the literary lyric sequence may not be set against the background of traditional myth or ritual, as may be the case with at least some archaic poetry. As Miller argues, for example, Archilochus may possibly be playing the role (and indeed "Archilochus" may be the name) of a traditional "trickster" hero belonging to a *mythos* similar to that of Odysseus and connected to festal, carnivalesque, "wolf-dance" performances.[6] Archilochus is not, in short, an "individual" breaking free from the shadowy, prehistoric mists of "Homeric" folk consciousness.[7] But the notion of "individual consciousness" or "lyric subjectivity" that Miller denies to Archilochus but awards to later poets is itself problematic and probably cannot survive the postmodern critique of individual subjectivity. In truth, the image of Archilochus as a "voice" embedded in (and produced by) social practices and functions actually separates him very little from later Hellenistic and Roman poets, or for that matter modern poets, even when they romantically imagine themselves as pristine individualities: the specific practices and functions may change, but the social embeddedness does not, while the social embeddedness does not preclude a measure of individual subjectivity or agency. Further, while it does seem reasonable to think that a literary sequence can adumbrate a more consciously constructed "plot" than may be found in a simple collection of archaic poems, it nevertheless is arguable that the later, literary lyrics are set against equally conventionalized though less obviously "mythological" backgrounds, namely, the representative character types and stereotyped scenarios of the Hellenistic and Roman lifeworlds, such as we find portrayed in Theophrastus's *Characters*, Menandrian comedy, Theocritus's idylls, Herodas's mimes, Horace's satires, declamation exercises, and so forth.[8]

Consider Propertius's four books of elegies. The poems can offer a running commentary on Propertius's troubled love affair with Cynthia without actually telling or needing to tell the story of that affair directly, precisely because it fits a recognizable story type for upper-class Augustan society (while it is also set against the background of Augustan marriage laws, patriotic propaganda, concerns about contemporary *mores*, and so forth): the young man entrapped in erotic obsession by a sophisticated, educated, married, older woman who consorts with lovers of her choice. That general story type, with the cultural issues it puts in play, is what the elegies are about; and it provides the context that renders the specific, discontinuous episodes of different elegies both intelligible and meaningful for their intended audience. We might compare the archaic, sixth-century elegies of Solon (or what remains of them). Solon may cast himself in the conventionalized roles of Hesiodic wisdom-singer and city "mediator" and may draw on traditional myth and epic lore, but his elegies comment on contemporary political events in Athens (including his reforms of the Athenian constitution), events that are presumed to be familiar to the audience and so are not explicitly described.[9] Both Solon's and Propertius' elegies, in sum, operate in similar ways, by projecting their author figure as a conventionalized hero type embedded in a reasonably familiar background story on which he comments, though in Propertius's case the background story may have been more deliberately, artificially, artistically contrived.[10]

Further, even if archaic lyric poets do speak (or sing) in conventionalized roles and as the public voices of traditional thought, this does not mean that they cannot voice novel or counterhegemonic views. Indeed, given the agonistic character of ancient Greek culture, the voicing of novel views seems likely. Consider the tradition of poetic *agôn* represented, for example, by the legend of the "contest between Homer and Hesiod," which dates back at least to the late fifth century B.C. (and is probably older), by the tale of the poetess Corinna defeating young Pindar (five times) in a contest at Thebes, or by the mature Pindar's characteristic boast to be, like the victorious athletes he celebrates, "preeminent for skill among all Hellenes" (*Olympian* 1.116).[11] The "skill" that Pindar vaunts is, of course, *sophia*, or wisdom-skill, and should be taken to include the poet's whole art of wisdom-speaking eloquence. (His athletes are, by contrast, preeminent in *aretê*, excellence/virtue/nobility, so that Pindar can stand beside them as their equal and cochampion in differing but parallel achievements.) Notably, the extant version of "the contest between Homer and Hesiod" represents it as, in essence, a contest of inventive wit, in which the contestants win applause for saying admirable as well as clever things, and in which Hesiod finally wins by being judged to voice the better wisdom. Likewise, as we have seen, Theognis represents the poet's discourse as participating in a contest of persuasions and, of course, in his invocatory poem he declares that "the seal of my skillfulness" upon his verses will make them impossible to steal because "everyone" will be able to recognize that they are his (19–22) while he elsewhere declares himself inimitable by *asophoi* (370).

The tradition of poetic *agôn* suggests, in short, that poets needed to distinguish themselves not only by the aesthetic or formal excellence of their verse but also by virtue of saying something both admirable and distinctive. Why else would traditions of rhapsodic reperformance and preservation develop around particular poets' names?[12] Of course, a need for competitive distinction does not require absolute novelty. As Isocrates at one point says, the best and most difficult epideictic and poetic discourse is that which gives tried and true wisdoms original and freshly persuasive utterance (*To Nicocles* 41). But poetic *agôn* does not preclude, either, the arguing of unconventional positions. For as Isocrates' teacher Gorgias says, "[t]o tell the knowing what they know is to seem right, but it brings no delight" (*Helen* 5).

The lyric poets of the archaic period are contemporary with the "Greek enlightenment," of the seventh to fifth century, the waning influence of traditional, aristocratic ideologies and myths, and the sociopolitical transformations and tensions of the Greek *poleis*. It seems likely that there would have been an audience for poetry that articulated unconventional or countertraditional positions, or "minority" positions that ran counter to traditionally dominant values or beliefs—especially though not necessarily in comic, satiric, or invective poetry—while at the same time a poetry that voiced old-fashioned, aristocratic preferences could not have been uncontroversial in such a context and would have found itself obliged to engage in a contest of persuasions. (One thinks, again, of the legend of comedic drama's origins under the Megarian democracy, and of Theognis's efforts to maintain a traditional, aristocratic commitment to the virtues of *diakaiosynê/sôphrosynê*.) Indeed, it seems likely that a poetry capable of putting at least some beliefs in tension, or of articulating strikingly distinctive *and persuasive* ethical, philosophical, or political positions, would have been highly valued. It seems unlikely, then, that an agonistic poetry produced in such a culture would have been unable to engage in ideological contestation, or would have been constrained merely to "telling the knowing what they know," with no alternative to reconfirming its audiences' traditional presumptions.[13]

Thus, when Sappho argues (fr. 16) that "whatsoever one loves" is "the most beautiful thing on the dark earth" and is preferable to the martial splendor of marching armies, fleets of ships, and hosts of cavalry, it is a mistake to presume that she merely voices a traditional value or one associated with an aristocratic women's cult of Aphrodite, even if precedents can be found for it in Homer. For Sappho is indeed arguing against the dominant *hierarchy of values* of archaic Greek aristocracies. She provides, that is, a striking countervoice to the still normative *êthos* of the warrior-aristocrat, and, insofar as she speaks as a public figure, she does so for an audience that extends beyond the limits of her immediate circle; and certainly her poems were widely circulated and admired, among male audiences as well as female.[14] Likewise, when Archilochus speaks of abandoning his shield on the battlefield as preferable to being killed (fr. 6)—a declaration that apparently shocked the Spartans into banning him (according to Plutarch's *Spartan Institutions*)—he not only is fulfilling the comic-satiric role of a conventional trickster hero but also is voicing a counterperspective to the preeminent (if weakening) value-hierarchy of his time.[15] Or again, when Pindar disagrees with and revises conventional versions of the myths that he appropriates (e.g., *Olympian* 1) or defends his version of a myth against the possible offense that he may have given to an audience (e.g., *Nemean* 7), he clearly is not just passing on the lore that he inherits from tradition but is reshaping it for the purposes of a specific moment. And certainly Solon's elegies, in particular those that are cited in Aristotle's *Athenian Constitution*, are defending innovative, sometimes controversial policies and are making a case for genuine political change, even when they call on traditional lore *as grounds for that case*. In such moments of agonistic difference or reversal or revision (or simply of ludic gaming) it seems more reasonable to infer that the poets may really be doing something original and striking, that they are offering memorably distinctive, eloquently presented ethical positions and value-schemes, and that their persuasiveness in doing so is one of the chief reasons for their being preserved in subsequent tradition.[16]

To say this is not at all to reassert the now outmoded, overly romantic view that in archaic lyric poetry we somehow see an emergent, unprecedented individuality breaking free from the folkconsciousness (the ideological prison-house) of a shadowy, prehistoric "Homeric age."[17] Indeed, considered as an expression of agonistic competition, the seeming individualism of archaic lyric may well be deeply and fully traditional. It is Hesiod, after all, who declares in the poem of *Works and Days* that there is a "good Strife" (*agathê Eris*) as well as a bad one, the good kind inspiring people to excel each other in honorable competition—potter with potter, carpenter with carpenter, beggar with beggar, and poet with poet (*aoidos aoidôi*)— whereas the bad kind leads people only to injustice, outrage (*hubris*), violence, war, and general catastrophe (11–26, 214–247). And even this topic is presented agonistically: "[s]urely there is not one kind of Strife, but upon earth / there are two" (11–12). Hesiod seems to be countering the assertion of some opponent, or a general notion that might otherwise be believed, such as an indiscriminate belief that strife is strife, that all's fair in love and war, and so forth. And, of course, Hesiod is opposing this notion in the also-agonistic context of admonishing his ostensible addressee, his bad brother Perses ("Despoiler"), with whom he has been engaged in a lawsuit over their inheritance (27–41). It is not necessary to maintain that the explicit, articulated notion of "two kinds of Strife" is novel with Hesiod, though it might be. The key point is that Hesiod frames all of *Works and Days* within an *agôn* of opposed positions: two Strifes against one, good Strife against bad Strife, Hesiod against Perses, and Hesiod's catalog of instructions for honorable living (which takes up the body of the poem) against the corrupt, unjust behavior of Perses and the "bribe-eating lords" (38–39) who have judged the inheritance dispute with less than straight judgments. The tale of Perses' lawsuit and the "bribe-eating lords" is, it seems, for Hesiod's audience an all too familiar background story that *Works and Days* need only invoke without describing in detail. Being so framed, *Works and Days* is itself an enactment of "good Strife," deriving much of its interest from the dramatic tension between the ethical position that Hesiod represents and the bad but dominant (or at least widespread) social practices he both explicitly and implicitly condemns. This agonistic framing, moreover, places Hesiod's audience in the role of not simply listening to the catalog of advice but of embracing (or rejecting) it in the act of judging and choosing between opposed positions, an act that becomes a ritual rehearsal on repeated hearings of the poem.

In Homer too there are moments that suggest the potential in archaic and even prehistoric Greek culture for agonistic disputation to be enjoyed for its own sake and to be ritualized. Here let me take just three highly famous examples from the *Iliad:* the shield of Achilles, Agamemnon's harangue to the assembled army, and Achilles' speech to the embassy. Homer's famous description of the shield of Achilles, with its many scenes of archaic *polis* life, features prominently a crowd gathered in a market-place (an *agora*) to hear a dispute between two men over the reparations owed for a killing (*Iliad* 18.490–508). This scene is the earliest extant description of a Greek trial, and it has been cited as evidence for the existence of judicial procedures even in Homer's time, or before, though the procedures described are fairly primitive and do not much resemble those of the classical Athenian courts.[18] The case is being judged by "elders" (*gerontes*) seated "on the polished stones in the sacred circle" with a prize of "two talents of gold" placed before them in the center, presumably by the litigants, to be awarded to the one who gives the best verdict (the "polished stones" are probably altars or rostra of some kind, perhaps in the form of seats or benches, though they may be simple blocks). It appears that the elders are supposed to act more like arbitrators than like judges, as we think of judges now: the litigants present their versions of the case, and then each elder proposes his "judgment" (*dikê*) in turn; the one who proposes the "straightest judgment" (*dikên ithyntata*), or perhaps the judgment most acceptable as "fair" to both litigants, will take the prize. Thus both the litigants and the judges are placed in competition with their counterparts.

What is the crowd doing? They are not a jury but are certainly engaged, much like a crowd at an athletic event—or a poetry contest—"shouting in applause" (as Homer says) in favor of one or another litigant and being "kept back" by heralds. Indeed the litigants are described as "declaring [their cases] to the people" (*dêmôi piphauskôn*), although the elders will propose the judgments. Homer does not say whether the crowd's shouting affects the speeches of the litigants, or the judgments proposed by the elders, or the choice of the winning judgment. But it seems fairly likely that fervent, enthusiastic rooting for one or another speech would have some influence.

The key point here, however, is that this scene of formalized public disputation is presented not only as a significant and indeed a central part of public life but, more important, as public entertainment, in which the gathered crowd both has and exercises through "shouting applause" a keen appreciation for competing arguments and sallies of eloquence and in which the participants (and especially the elders) can win prestige as well as cash for the quality of their performances. Moreover, it is important to note as well that this trial scene is, in effect, part of Homer's portrait of the good life in peace and prosperity, for there are two "fair cities" depicted on the shield. The first, where the trial is taking place, is also a place of wedding-feasts and celebration, "brides from out their chambers under torchlight / led through town, calling forth much bridal song, / the young men whirled in dances, and amid them all / the flutes and lyres sounding" (18.492–495).[19] The other city is besieged, "on the walls dear wives and also little children / placed on guard, with the elderly men," while the rest of the able-bodied male population makes a desperate attempt to break the siege line, meeting "Strife and Uproar . . . and deadly Fate" in battle (18.509–540). The siege, moreover, is a scene of unresolved dissensions: the besiegers cannot agree whether they should sack the town or treat for half the city's treasure, while the besieged citizens will make no deal at all. There is no possibility of arbitration, no settlement short of bloodshed. Though both of the *poleis* portrayed on Achilles' shield are "fair" or good (*kala*), and though we probably are meant to think of the besieged citizens as conducting themselves admirably in adversity, clearly the contrast between the two scenes of peace and war provides a precedent for Hesiod's more explicit account of good and bad Strifes. To live in a peaceful town with time and wealth and leisure for festivities, and to go the marketplace and dicker, make deals, talk, and watch a trial, is a good thing.

My second example, from *Iliad* 2, is a curious episode in which Agamemnon, having been sent a false dream by Zeus promising victory, assembles his troops for battle. Agamemnon's plan for this assembly, as he tells his fellow lords in council, is that "first I myself will test [the troops] in speech, as is customary": that is, as he says, "I'll propose to flee with the many-benched ships; you hold [the troops] back with words [*epéessin*] from this side and from that" (2.73–76). Agamemnon's "test," in short, consists of a ritual failure-speech that all his fellow lords are meant to ritually disagree with in counterspeeches. The lords, in effect, will play a role analogous to that of elders at a trial, with the army in the role of clamoring crowd (with, again, heralds keeping the assembled multitude in order). Apparently the whole procedure is a ritualized version of agonistic disputation, meant to rouse the troops to battle by provoking them to join their lords in shouting down the proposal to give up.[20] Agamemnon's speech clearly is designed to elicit such rejection, or to provide cues for counterspeeches. He dwells on the Greeks' overwhelming numerical superiority to the Trojans, while complaining that Zeus has not been quick to deliver the victory that once was promised and that the Trojans' allies "hinder me" (2.110–140); this is easily refuted reasoning. But Agamemnon has miscalculated, and the ritual goes awry. Rather than shout down his proposal, and before the lords have a chance to speak against it, the war-weary troops (who already have been fighting for nine years) agree enthusiastically and head for the ships. To save the situation, Athena must intervene by calling Odysseus to exercise his cleverness, which he does by first humiliating the scruffy footsoldier Thersites (who has been hurling invective at Agamemnon) and then by making an extended counterspeech to Agamemnon's proposal, exhorting the troops to fight (2.155–332).

The dramatic interest of this episode, it seems, is meant to lie partly in its comic deflation of Agamemnon's kingly dignity but, more important (at least for my purposes here), in the fact that an intended ritual of agonistic disputation misfires and becomes a genuine *agôn* with an uncertain outcome. Ironically, this genuine *agôn* produces even more effectively the same result the "customary' ritual was meant to generate. The troops, even more fully caught up in the process of judging and choosing, and having been persuaded by Odysseus, enthusiastically return to camp to prepare for the next day's battle (which, by Zeus's design, goes badly for them). Much like the trial scene on Achilles' shield, then, this episode suggests that formal, even ritualized procedures of agonistic disputation were deeply woven into the fabric of Greek culture from an early time and that Homer's audience enjoyed the kinds of drama that such scenes could generate.

This brings us, third and finally, to the embassy scene in *Iliad* 9, in which Odysseus and the other heroes attempt to persuade Achilles to patch up his quarrel with Agamemnon and return to the war; this is, of course, one of the great cruxes of the poem. The key point here is not that the episode provides examples of highly skilled practical speechmaking from a very early time (as indeed it does). Rather, the point is that, in his rejection of the embassy, Achilles argues not only that Agamemnon has offended his honor too deeply for amends to be possible, but also that a long life at home without glory is preferable to the early death and eternal fame that prophecy has foretold for him if he rejoins the fight (9.308–429). It is hard to believe that Homer's listeners would not have found this latter line of reasoning paradoxical, especially since it comes from Achilles, and especially if we take the usual assumption that Homer, like the bard Demodocus in the *Odyssey*, mainly performed for noble patrons. And indeed Homer portrays Achilles' audience as shocked and stunned to silence (temporarily) by the young man's speech. Achilles' argument, like the more extreme (and from the Spartan point of view craven) argument of Archilochus for abandoning his shield, explicitly reverses the normative ethic of the warrior-aristocrat, who may well believe that nothing is finer than to win undying fame with a glorious death in battle. Further, within its particular context, Achilles' speech has a certain reasonability, at least for the audience of the poem. Achilles knows, after all, that he is fated to die young in battle against the Trojans if he joins the fight and that he must in consequence forego the pleasures of marriage (and of a rich man's life) that, as he says, are awaiting him at home. Given such knowledge, he reasonably can feel that Agamemnon's hubristic treatment of him has been too galling to be borne or forgiven. (The fact that young, unmarried Achilles refers to Briseis, the war captive that Agamemnon has stolen from him, as his "wife," suggests how much the things he must sacrifice for glory do matter to him.)

Homer's audience, then, is presented with a strikingly (even vehemently) well put yet paradoxical argument that, on one hand, agonistically challenges a dominant value-scheme and that, on the other hand, is fairly persuasive within its context, thereby calling for a complex exercise of judgment. Is Achilles just rationalizing what might otherwise be seen as cowardice, or as a young noble's excessive sensitivity to insult? Is his argument valid or persuasive only within a certain very specific context? Or is it persuasive in a broader sense? Isn't the peaceful city on Achilles' shield, after all, an image of the good life? It is hard, of course, to imagine that Homer's audiences would have thought it better for Achilles not to win his deathless fame and die, for otherwise (from their point of view) there would have been no *Iliad*. But at the same time, it is also hard to imagine that those audiences would not have found Achilles' argument provocative, insofar as it opened an agonistic moment in which, at least temporarily, a conventional and very powerful value-scheme could be put in question. (Perhaps Achilles' argument is meant to function, rather like Agamemnon's speech, as a way of bringing the poem's audience finally to reaffirm what the speech itself appears to deny; nevertheless, it is effective only insofar as the audience experiences it as an occasion for an actual exercise of judgment, that is, as a counterintuitive but paradoxically persuasive argument that cannot simply be dismissed.) For an audience that has experienced this encounter with Achilles' argument, the ethical significance and pathetic force of his eventual choice to join the war and die, of his desecration of Hector's corpse, of his final scene of reconciliation with king Priam, and of his reasons for doing what he does, are considerably amplified. As Socrates' youthful companion in the *Protagoras* (Hippocrates) might say, Achilles both says and does "awesome" (*deinos*) things, and the sayings make the doings yet more awesome. Encounters with opposing *logoi* are a major source of the power and pleasure of Homer's poetry. It's a good thing to go downtown to the marketplace, or to some banquet or festivity, and hear some interesting disputation, or to have some poet's psychagogic eloquence carry one's mind into unusual positions and provoke one into thought.

I have dwelt on Hesiod and Homer to underscore a basic point about archaic lyric, or about the cultural backgrounds of archaic lyric. While we need not attribute to this early poetry a romantic individualism or construe it as countercultural *Ideologiekritik*, we still can understand it as participating in a deeply traditional penchant for, and enjoyment of, agonistic competition and disputation. While the poets may, on one hand, identify themselves with largely traditional beliefs and may even be quite conservative (as, for example, Pindar is generally thought to be), they also, on the other hand, participate in public competition with contemporaries and with past poetic tradition, which impels them to stake out distinctive ethical positions in distinctive ways—and to do so persuasively—in a poetry that is understood as a rhetorical transaction that asks its audience to make judgments.[21] Such competitive differing does not require the poet to take up wholly original or countercultural positions or to explicitly reject or overturn traditional beliefs, but it opens the door to such possibilities.

When we consider this penchant for agonistic competition from a rhetorical perspective, it is clear that it need not and indeed *cannot* require that poets place themselves in utter opposition to the dominant value-schemes of their culture, or the audiences they perform for. Rather, as every rhetorician knows, all that is possible is to question a particular position, assert an attitude, rearrange a value-hierarchy, or make the case for a minority position (that is, "make the weaker case stronger") by means of connecting the "new" or unconventional position (or hierarchy) to an existing set of values and beliefs that the intended audience already considers authoritative. To the degree that the audience's adherence to that preexisting scheme can be intensified and transferred to the "new" position, the "new" position is correspondingly validated and made persuasive.[22] While archaic lyric predates the emergence of "rhetoric" as a discipline and thus belongs to a period that has no developed argumentation theory, the basic claim of argumentation theory (as I have rather reductively outlined it) is that it describes what is *necessarily* the case in any suasory transaction, or in any effective argumentational practice, whether or not the participants have an explicit conceptualization of it. The evidence from Homer that Greek culture sustained formalized argumentation practices and disputing rituals from an early time suggests that the participants would certainly have had some awareness of the necessities of argument, even without a developed theoretical discourse, and that those who were the most successful probably were quite astute.

The rhetor's necessity, in short, is to work within or through the presuppositional sets that both rhetor and audience can share, or that the rhetor is willing to concede, in order to win the audience's assent to the rhetor's particular claims—and to what is new and distinctive in the rhetor's discourse. This inescapable situation does not necessarily produce a mere reiteration of conventional beliefs (or "ideologies") because no body of conventional beliefs is ever (or can ever be) fully coherent, internally consistent, or systematic. Any culture's conventional values and beliefs, and value-hierarchies, are inevitably heterogeneous because they are the sedimented products of tradition, the happenstance products of a history and of cultural forces that no one person can ever fully perceive or control. It is always the case that at least some values/beliefs or hierarchies will be at least potentially in tension or conflict with at least some others, *especially in specific situations that bring those conflicts into high relief*. It is always possible to promote, demote, refute, problematize, satirize, rearrange, revise, revalidate (and so on) one established set of values by means of appeal to some other established set or, by the same means, to promote an unconventional or novel set. This is, in essence, how Archilochus justifies the otherwise shocking act of abandoning his shield, how Sappho demotes the traditionally favored notion that martial splendor is "the most beautiful thing on the dark earth," how Solon argues for his innovative laws, and how Pindar frames the terms of praise for athletes and their cities.[23]

The broad notion of "lyric" with which I am working, then, is not based strictly on either the Alexandrian genre classification from which the name originates or the modern conception of "lyric" as the expression of an individualized, textually constructed, private subjectivity, though it shares some affinities with each. As I have said, I am adopting the name of "lyric" for an epideictic "speech" composed in verse and meant typically to be performed in ritual, festal, symposiastic, or paideutic settings. "Lyric" in this sense may be distinguished on one hand from the more comprehensive or compendious "epic" modes of Homeric narrative or Hesiodic wisdom-poetry and on the other hand from the developed forms of drama that emerged in Attic tragedy and comedy, insofar as "lyric" as a "speech" is embedded in a particular situation or *type of situation* in a larger story. That "story" may be a familiar legend, a historical episode, or the more generalized "mythology" that constitutes a culture's understanding of its patterns of experience and the "chronic" or recurrent issues and occasions that emerge within that pattern. Neither Theognis nor Propertius tell the entire story in which a specific poem is embedded, nor do they offer anything resembling the "encyclopedic" compendiousness of poems like Hesiod's *Works and Days* or the *Theogony* (though the *Theognidea*, taken as a whole, may be thought of as constituting the pieces or the *topoi* from which an encyclopedic wisdom-poem could potentially be fashioned by an especially skillful master singer).[24] But any one of Theognis's or Propertius's poems can be conceived as a "speech" delivered either within or in response to a particular situation (or type of situation) framed in a larger story (or story type). Similarly, within a compendious "epic" poem there will be "speeches" or "songs" that can be taken independently as "lyrics," such as, perhaps most obviously, the "Hymn to the Muses" that commences Hesiod's *Theogony*, or the address to "Perses" at the beginning of *Works and Days*, as well as the speeches delivered by characters in Homeric narratives. Likewise, within a drama there will be set speeches by characters and choral interludes that may be taken independently as "lyric" poems, though they always are embedded in particular situations that lend them exigence, and within larger plots that amplify their resonance and significance.

But if "lyric" can be understood as embedded in a particular moment within a larger, tacit or explicit framing narrative, it also can be understood as a primal poetic mode from which both narrative/encyclopedic "epic" and dramatic poetry may develop as elaborations, or amplifications, of the basic epideictic speech act. "Lyric," in short, can be regarded as the most fundamental, most protean type of poetic discourse. This is more or less the view that Aristotle takes in *Poetics* 4: poetry has its origins, as he suggests, in "extemporaneous" or improvisational performances of invectives, hymns, encomia, dithyrambs, phallic songs, and so forth, from which evolve the more elaborate or extended genres of epic, tragedy, and comedy—and from which evolve also, as I suggested in chapter 2, the various genres of epideictic prose. As Georges Dumézil argued in a comparative study published in 1943, as Berkeley Peabody has more recently argued (in 1975), and as Paul Allen Miller has argued also, Aristotle's speculative genealogy may in fact describe a general pattern in Indo-European poetic traditions, in which the most basic forms are epideictic, "lyric" songs of praise and blame that serve social-regulatory functions. As Peabody puts it,

[s]o far as we can tell, narrative subject matter, which dominates epic as we know it, was not a fundamental concern in the early stages of oral traditions. . . . [The

early Sanskrit Gathas and Vedas, for example] consist in large part of hymns, magic formulas, prayers, curses, incantations, and the like. Within the span of recorded tradition, one can see narrative entering Indian hymns as gloss, developing into episodic passages, and gradually increasing in relative importance until the enormous classical Sanskrit epics like the *Mahabharata* appear. . . . [T]here is material in the Greek tradition that suggests a similar prehistory.[25]

As Eric Havelock has pointed out, there are problems with this argument, most of which arise from the fact that all the available evidence—meaning preserved texts—by definition postdates the prehistoric, nonliterate period in which the proposed evolution is said to have occurred.[26] Nevertheless, we still can regard this argument as describing a generally probable tendency in the generation of poetic forms. The point is that "lyric," conceived in its most general terms as an epideictic "speech" in verse or song, will provide opportunities for *expansion* or *amplification* of particular topics, either by way of illustrative narratives or by catalogic enumerations. Such expansion can yield an extended "lyric" or epideictic song that consists primarily of narrative (e.g., the Homeric *Hymn to Demeter*), or one that consists primarily of a list; and an extreme or hypertrophied development of such expansion, as well as the recombining of what originally were independent lyric songs, can yield an *Iliad* or a poem like *Works and Days*. Likewise, the proliferation of speakers and the expansion of dialogue in choral song-dance performance yields what we recognize as "drama."

But whatever form the expansion or elaboration of solo or choral lyric takes, it is important to remember that the hypertorphied narrative or catalogic epic, or the drama, still operates within the background frame of epideictic argumentation of some kind. As Peabody suggests, the persistence of such a frame is fairly evident in the opening song of *Works and Days* (1–292), with its admonitory "speech" to Perses (and its apostrophes to "bribe-eating lords") presenting the basic argument, which the subsequent catalog of instructions on how to live honorably both extends and amplifies; and indeed even the "speech" itself is expanded with narrative digressions on the myth of Pandora, the myth of the five generations of humankind, and the allegory of the hawk and nightingale. In the *Iliad*, the argumentative or "lyric" frame is less apparent, and we might describe it as being "atrophied" in proportion to the hypertrophy of the poem's narrative dimension, though we can also regard the argumentative dimension as persisting still in the direct "speech" and commentary of the authorial figure ("Homer"), in the speeches of various characters, and in the deeper, more tacit presuppositional networks shared by poet and audience, all of which together shape the hierarchies of value by which the audience is asked to judge the "facts" or "doings," the *pragmata*, that form the poem's subject matter (namely, the "wrath of Achilles" and the events that follow from it).[27] Further, as Achilles' speech to the embassy suggests, in an extended "epic" the frame argument can be played out against competing or contrasting arguments and so can be destabilized, complicated, and remodeled, as the poem progresses.[28]

It may be, of course, that posing a question whether story (narration) or argument (discursus) is more "fundamental" can only lead us to a chicken-or-the-egg problem that we ought not try to solve. Perhaps the most that we can say is that there will be places in an argument, or in a "speech" or "lyric," where stories/narratives will arise—most notably, for classical rhetoric, in the *narratio* section of the standard oration, though story/narrative can arise anywhere for purposes of amplification and even for proof—and there will be places in a story/narrative where argument/discursus (or "speeches") will arise, as the narrator and/or characters comment on their situations, deliver their rationales for one or another choice of action, debate with one another, reflect on the way of the world, apostrophize, and so forth. The crucial point, for present purposes, is that we cannot confidently presume that storytelling is the fundamental poetic mode, especially since we must always ask *for what purposes the story is being told, and in response to what occasions;* and we must consider as at least arguable the proposition that "lyric" epideictic argumentation is the most basic, most protean mode of poetic discourse from which all other poetic genres will derive (and have derived).

Another line of argument that bears on this question derives from Earl Miner's work in comparative poetics. Taking into account "Asian" (chiefly Chinese and Japanese, but also Indian and Arabic) and "Western" traditions, and dividing literary genres into the broad categories of lyric, narrative/epic, and drama, Miner presents a claim that lyric is "the most pristine, most basic" type, and offers two chief lines of evidence. First, not all cultures have a well-developed tradition of epic or dramatic poetry, but all (or all that we know about) do have a well-developed lyric tradition. Second, with the exception of the Western tradition in poetics that derives from Aristotle, all other "foundational" traditions have taken lyric as the paradigmatic mode. By a "foundational" tradition in poetics, Miner means one that stems from an originative, influential statement, like Aristotle's *Poetics* or Ki no Tsurayaki's preface to the *Kokinshu,* and that tends to define "the nature and conditions of literature" in terms of the originative statement's "esteemed genre." The "esteemed genre" then comes to provide the basic paradigm in terms of which all other poetic (or "literary") genres are subsequently theorized: dramatistic *mimesis* for the Aristotelian tradition in the West (as filtered, I would add, through the late medieval and Renaissance reception and conflation of the *Poetics* with Horace's *Ars Poetica*); lyricism for the Japanese tradition that derives from Ki no Tsurayaki; and so on for all the non-Western traditions that Miner studies.[29]

While this line of argument is provocative and useful, it has certain limitations. It fails to acknowledge, for example, that Aristotle does recognize lyric as the protean poetic genre (even as he privileges *mimêsis* as the definiens of "poetry"). Further—and most problematically—Miner tends to retain a Western, romantico-modernist notion of "lyricism" as the expression of personal feeling or subjectivity. Such a notion makes it difficult to account for the apparent ease with which, as Miner recognizes, the lyric-centered poetics of east Asia could absorb and accommodate what he calls "factual" writing (such as history) as a category of the literary[30] or, for that matter, the equal ease with which Western antiquity could likewise accommodate the "factual" discourses of history, philosophy, and oratory (both epideictic and pragmatic) alongside "poetry" in a single discursive art and could regard the written/published versions of the speeches of Demosthenes as "literature" comparable to the lyrics of Simonides (as Dionysius of Halicarnassus does). Notably, Miner settles on Horace's lyricism as the most capacious orientation to poetics,[31] though Horace cannot be accounted for by a notion of lyric as affective-expressive discourse *simply*. The *Ars Poetica* everywhere is concerned with the judgment-making role of the audience, with the poet's need to be persuasive, and with the functions of poetic discourse as a means of eliciting and shaping moral preferences, while Horace's actual lyric practice is deeply engaged in the politics of Augustan Rome.[32] In sum, Miner proposes lines of evidence for believing that "lyric" is *universally* the most protean, most basic mode of "poetic" or epideictic discursive art, but this claim can most intelligibly be held if we can escape the limits of a romantico-modernist notion of "lyricism" as "the expression of feeling" and reconceive it in broader terms as epideictic argument in verse or song.

In what follows, then, I will be working with such a notion. From the point of view of a rhetorical poetics, "lyric" as the song/verse equivalent of (and archaic prototype for) an epideictic "speech" can be understood, on one hand, as the most protean of all poetic modes and, on the other hand, as the closest link between the poetic and oratorical traditions in antiquity. But what it means to say that lyric poetry—and by extension any poetry—offers epideictic argumentation, and so (as Isocrates said) "seeks to employ enthymemes," remains to be considered.

"Enthymeme"

The idea that poetry in general and lyric poetry in particular "makes arguments" has typically been foreign, even counterintuitive, for Western literary-critical thought for most of the twentieth century. What we might call the mainstream modern view has been that, while poems may "contain" ideas, or thought, or "themes," or may be "informed" by certain intellectual or philosophical perspectives (including the latest postmodern theory), such things are merely there, contained, as useful and sometimes even interesting but finally dispensable accessories and props, *because the essential business of a lyric is to dramatize or express a state of feeling or subjectivity*. As Jonathan Culler has noted, this idea that lyric is the "dramatized experience of a consciousness" *rather than* an argument of some kind has so completely saturated modern literary culture that we can scarcely question it or think our way around it or beyond it.[33] As Culler also notes, this idea certainly can be questioned, and there have been some notable challenges to it from mid-century onward, but for the most part it has held its hegemonic status.[34] Thus, to take a fairly typical example, one critic begins a 1977 book on lyric by flatly declaring that it presents "an image of the poet's thought as it moves" through an intensely felt experience and is essentially dramatistic and expressive *rather than* discursive, argumentative, or suasory, even if it *seems* (to the reader) to be offering an argument that intends to create, intensify, or change beliefs and attitudes in its audience.[35] This statement is laid down simply as an axiom, with virtually no recognition of a possible disagreement (or of actual dissenting voices) and no sense of any need to present a justification (and none is presented). More recently, in a 1988 criticism of what he considers the tired, conventionalized romanticism of most contemporary American poetry, Charles Altieri reasserts the notions that the essential role of lyric is *not* to argue for particular beliefs, that "rhetoric" and "ideology" are forms of "duplicitous" false consciousness and that lyric poems present "acts of mind," in other words, embody a state of subjectivity.[36] Even the more radical poetics generally associated with what has been called language poetry in the 1980s and 1990s, and most prominently represented in the essays of Charles Bernstein, tends generally—even as it makes gestures toward a view of poetry as "political"—to retain a more or less traditional romantico-modernist suspicion of what Bernstein calls "argument," "rhetoric," and "rationalistic expository unity" as forms of socially constructed false consciousness. Bernstein thus tends to project a basic understanding of "poetic" or lyric discourse as in essence "a private act in a public place" that serves to represent or embody "thinking" liberated from the shackles of discursive reason *rather than* to present an argument for the reader's judgment.[37]

The major problems with all such thinking are that, on one hand, it tends to presuppose an extraordinarily narrow conception of "argument" as something like formal syllogistic or "scientific" reasoning and that, on the other hand, it leaves itself without any means of accounting for how a poetic practice—especially one that wants to be politically or culturally significant—can embody "thought" or "feeling" or a mode of subjectivity *persuasively* or can have a real effect on the beliefs and values of an audience that is not already predisposed to think or feel exactly as the poet does and that is free to differ or disagree.[38] Thus, for example, Charles Bernstein (whose words I have just been quoting) tends to conceive "argument" in terms of an "exposition" that appeals "to the logic of validity" as defined by "an eighteenth-century ideal of reasoning," which he rejects, while trying to "imagine a writing that would provoke philosophic insight . . . whose appeal would not be to the validity of argument but to the ontological truthfulness of its meanings."[39] This seems to imply a rhetoric in which the poet's audience is simply to recognize, as in a Platonic unforgetting, the "ontological truthfulness" of what the poet says by a direct recognition not mediated by any argumentational process. This is a rhetoric that can only tell the knowing what they know already, or remind them, or reinforce their commitment to the already known by re-presenting it in new and varied forms: a rhetoric that, in short, cannot in fact provoke any real "insight" whatsoever. Arguably, such a rhetoric can only serve the purposes of a kind of identity politics, in which poet and audience resonate together in their already shared commitments and in so doing intensify those commitments for each other, while having no means (if this is the only rhetoric at their disposal) to speak effectively and persuasively to those outside the closed circle of their communion. Such a rhetoric lacks the *sophia*, and the *poikilon êthos*, of Theognis's imaginary citizen-ocuptus and works chiefly to promote a balkanized politics of faction that is ultimately debilitating.[40]

My claim then, is that the ancient notion of "enthymeme" (*enthymêma*) as the distinctively "rhetorical" form of argument and reasoning, or as what Aristotle called the body of persuasion (*sôma tês pisteôs*; *Rhetoric* 1.1 1354a), provides a more adequate means of accounting for lyric argumentation. Before I can pursue this claim, however, there are two immediate problems to address. The first derives from Aristotle's famous dicta that the enthymeme is a "kind of syllogism" or a "rhetorical syllogism" and that rhetoric is a "counterpart" of dialectic (*Rhetoric* 1.1 1355a, 1.2 1356b, 1.1 1354a). Starting from these statements, modern interpretation has tended to define the enthymeme as an informal, elliptical syllogism based on probable rather than certain premises and on tacit assumptions shared by the audience and rhetor; or as "Toulmin argument"; or as a general mode of intuitive reasoning that is representable in syllogistic or Toulminian terms.[41] As Lawrence Green has demonstrated, this line of interpretation is hardly new, and is based on an ages-old misreading of Aristotle—one that probably derives originally from Stoic logic, and has been perpetuated through medieval and Renaissance receptions of ancient (both Stoic and Peripatetic) logical theory—in which Aristotle's "enthymeme" is persistently reduced to a "truncated" or "imperfect" syllogism despite the fact that there is no reliable warrant in Aristotle for such a reduction.[42] This line of interpretation does, however, have certain advantages. Chief among them is its recognition that the enthymeme, as an elliptical form of argumentation depending on shared assumptions, involves a dialogic, cocreative relationship between the audience and rhetor, in which the audience engages in a kind of "self-persuasion" by completing or constructing for itself the tacit, elided aspects of the enthymeme.[43]

The chief limitation of this line of thought, however, is that the very concepts of "rhetorical syllogism" and of rhetoric as a "counterpart of dialectic" tend to subsume the notion of "enthymeme" to that of "syllogism" and thus to "logic," or to what "syllogism" and "logic" have generally meant in modern, Western culture. The problem here is that, if one assumes that "syllogism" means formalized, propositional reasoning, such as Aristotle outlines in his logical treatises, or such as one encounters in elementary logic textbooks, or such as Bernstein associates with "an eighteenth-century ideal of reasoning," then the "enthymeme," even when conceived as elliptical, probabilistic argumentation, becomes assimilated to a fairly rigid notion of "syllogistic" form. That is, it tends to be presupposed that a "valid" enthymeme, however informal or elliptical its reasoning may be, still can be restated in proper syllogistic form. While *some* (even most) enthymemes may be so restatable, it is difficult to see how, even for Aristotle, such a limited construct could be conceived as the central principle of all rhetorical art or could account for all real-world argumentational procedures and especially those that operate in lyric poems, since it seems to leave little room for the affective dimensions of argumentation, or for argumentational procedures that cannot be resolved into straightforwardly "syllogistic" (or even Toulminesque) representations. Such difficulties go far to explain why modern efforts to theorize the enthymeme as a truncated, probabilistic "syllogism" generally have had little impact on the actual teaching of practical argumentation in modern times. It is not simply that the enthymeme so conceived falls victim to a modern or postmodern logic phobia; the problem is that it seems, and really is, too rigid and too narrow to be practically useful. A rhetor who attempted to conduct a real-world argument as if it were a simple, straightforward matter of "logically" laying out syllogisms, even probabilistic and elliptical ones, would be a fool—or a grinding bore. This is, after all, Cicero's point about Stoic orators (*De Oratore* 2.38.157–159; 3.21.78–79).

The modern tendency to subsume the "enthymeme" to "syllogism," even in some nonformal sense, takes inadequate account of what *syllogismos* means in ancient Greek apart from or before the technical, specialized significance it acquired in Aristotelian and subsequent logical theory. Plato, for example, appears to have used the term *syllogismos* to mean simply a putting-together of observed facts, an adding-up of things (*Cratylus* 412a).[44] Similarly, Isocrates in *Against the Sophists* (7–8) uses the verb *syllogizomai*, "syllogize," in reference to the way that ordinary, "private persons" (*idiôtai*) intuitively derive an inference or judgment from a bundle of observations. This intuitive, everyday "syllogizing" is, moreover, set in opposition to what Isocrates calls "eristics" (from *eris*, "strife"), the logic-chopping verbal combat of professional dialecticians who claim to have an exact science, or method, for producing true knowledge. Even Aristotle, at the beginning of the *Topics*, adopts a casual, informal definition of the "syllogism" as a *logos*, a "discourse," in which "certain things having been laid down, other things necessarily derive from them" (1.1 100a). At this point he seems to be drawing on a commonly received conception, one that would be familiar for the audience of an introductory lecture. In the same passage, moreover, dialectical syllogizing is defined as reasoning from *doxa*, "generally received opinions," or more specifically as reasoning from *doxa* granted or accepted by one's interlocutors, one's audience (1.1 100b).

My point is that the nontechnical meaning of "syllogism" in ancient Greek seems to be nothing more than ordinary, informal reasoning and inference and that, in the context of discussion and debate, this meaning includes informal (as well as formal) reasoning/inference from probable assumptions or received opinions granted by one's audience. If, then, "syllogism" can be used in such a sense with reference to everyday thought and discourse, why use "enthymeme" to name the same thing? By carelessly invoking "enthymeme" as "the rhetorical syllogism," one may make a distinction without a difference.

As I hope to suggest, however, the notion of "enthymeme" does mark a difference. As Green has argued, Aristotle's grand premise that rhetoric is an *antistrophos* of dialectic (*Rhetoric* 1.1 1354a) has, over the centuries, been the locus of interpretive controversies all too easily masked by the conveniently vague compromise used in most English translations, namely that rhetoric is a "counterpart" of dialectic. "Counterpart" suggests a loose equivalence, a loose analogy. *Antistrophos*, however, means something more specific (and more difficult to pinpoint): perhaps, as Green suggests, "a reciprocal and rule-governed transformation."[45] Rhetoric and dialectic are indeed related to each other, as are the enthymeme and syllogism, but the relation is one of systematic difference as well as similarity. The enthymeme, in short, is to the syllogism (or to "Toulmin logic," for that matter) as rhetoric is to dialectic: not merely its "counterpart," its loose equivalent, but its *antistrophos*, its differing sister. The nature of this difference will presently be my concern.

But there still remains a second major problem to address: the term "enthymeme" may seem anachronistic when applied to archaic poetry. Isocrates does, of course, use the term in reference to the way that both poems and panegyric oratory "seek to employ enthymemes"; but one might object that Isocrates himself is speaking anachronistically. "Enthymeme" is not attested as a rhetorical term before the fourth-century writings of Isocrates and Aristotle. However, it is probable that "enthymeme" was circulating more widely in a pre-Aristotelian, sophistic discourse that is no longer fully available to us and as a nontechnical term in common use.[46] The word is first attested in the fifth century, in Sophocles' *Oedipus at Colonus*, as a name for a piece of heartfelt reasoning (292, 1200); the related adjective *enthymios*, meaning "taken to heart" (or "enthymized," from *en* and *thymos*, "in heart"), occurs as early as Homer (*Odyssey* 13.421); the verb *thymoô*, "make angry" or "impassion," and its noun derivative *to thymoumenon*, "passion," occur in such fifth-century writers as Herodotus and the tragedians; and the verb *enthymeomai*, "lay to heart, ponder, consider, form a plan, infer, conclude, be concerned or angry at," likewise occurs (in various inflected forms) in the fifth-century historians Herodotus, Thucydides, and Xenophon.[47] Thus, although the word *enthymêma* is not attested before Sophocles, it may well have been in circulation for some time as a name for something pondered "in the heart" and stirring the *pathê*. It seems unlikely that Sophocles is coining a neologism or invoking a specialized, technical term.

The crucial point, however, is that "enthymeme" functions, even when it emerges as a technical term in rhetoric, as a name for an argumentational practice that is prior to and independent of the name itself: that is, it names what arguers (or effective arguers) always do and always have done whether or not they have any distinct conceptualization of what they are doing. As Aristotle says at the outset of the *Rhetoric*,

> [a]ll at some point attempt to critique or uphold an argument, or to defend them-
> selves or accuse. Now most people do these things either randomly or through fa-
> miliar customs out of habit. But since both ways are possible, it is clear that they
> can be reduced to method; for as to how some succeed by means of habit and oth-
> ers from chance, it is possible to observe [*theôrein*] the cause, and all would agree
> that such observation is the work of a *technê*. (1.1 1354a)

Some people succeed by accident, and others by virtue of customary, habitual-ized practices that they themselves do not conceptualize: people succeed without knowing why. Aristotle's point, then, is that the "random," "customary," and un-conceptualized argumentational practices of "most people"—or at least those that tend to be successful—embody general ways of doing that can be theorized and made usable as the basis of a more deliberate discursive art. For Aristotle, the en-thymeme is the rhetorical "way" par excellence and is observable in the argumenta-tional practices of the many orators, prose writers, and poets (including lyric poets) who have come before him and are cited in the *Rhetoric*. The "enthymeme" is not a "device" that has been "invented" by rhetoricians, or by Aristotle, any more than "metaphor" is; it is an everyday discursive practice, an existing feature of human be-havior, that rhetoricians can attempt to name and describe.

So what is an enthymeme? Just what "enthymeme" means to Aristotle, and to Isocrates and the other sophists from whom he has appropriated the term, has al-ways been a matter of conjecture and controversy.[48] For though Aristotle very clearly considers skill in enthymemes to be the heart of skill in rhetoric, the skill to which all other aspects of the art are prosthetic "accessories," (*prosthêkai; Rhetoric* 1.1 1354a), and despite his occasional references to the enthymeme as the "rhetori-cal syllogism," he seems to nowhere offer a sustained discussion of just what an "en-thymeme" is. As William Grimaldi has suggested, it may be that Aristotle is presup-posing a sophistic or a generally circulating notion of "enthymeme" that is already familiar to his audience and is in effect offering the entire *Rhetoric* as an explication, clarification, and emendation of that notion: that is, just as Aristotle in the *Topics* takes the everyday meaning of "syllogism" and refines it as a technical term of art, so likewise does he do with "enthymeme" in the *Rhetoric*.[49] If this is so, then we can best understand what "enthymeme" means by first considering the generally circulating and sophistic notions that Aristotle presupposes and leaves largely tacit in the *Rhetoric* and by then considering what he adds. My purpose, however, is not so much to reconstruct "what Aristotle must have meant" as it is to construct a broader, more general notion of "enthymeme" for which both Aristotelian and non-Aristotelian perspectives offer lines of description. Once we have arrived at a workable general definition, then, we can return to the question of what it means to talk about poetic or lyric enthymemes.

If *enthymêma* was already circulating in everyday discourse by the fifth century, when Sophocles used it to mean a piece of heartfelt reasoning in *Oedipus at Colonus,* it clearly was linked semantically to the family of terms that included *enthymios* and *enthymeomai* and that ultimately derived from *thymos,* meaning "heart" or "mind" or "spirit" as the seat of emotion, thought, wish, desire, intentionality, or will. In one's *thymos* one considers things, draws inferences, becomes impassioned, forms desires, has intentions, and makes plans. The Homeric *Hymn to Demeter* describes the goddess's *thymos* as "grieved" at the loss of Persephone (56); Pindar tells us that Hippolyta tried to persuade Peleus "with all her *thymos*" (*Nemean* 5.31); Hesiod advises Perses to "lay up these things in your *thymos*" (*Works and Days* 27); Solon concludes an elegy by declaring "this my *thymos* bids me teach the Athenians" (fr. 4.31); and so forth. In such archaic uses, *thymos* as "heart" is understood as both a principle or place of interpretation and a source of emotional response, urge, and intentionality.

Aristotle typically associates both *thymos* and *epithymia,* "desire," with the "nonrational" (*alogon*), emotive part of the psyche, which he nevertheless considers to "partake of *logos*" in the sense that it has a "hearkening and obeying" (*peithesthai kai akouein*) capacity for interpretive understanding and response (*On the Soul* 3.9 432a; *Problems* 28 949b; *Eudemian Ethics* 2.1 1219b).[50] That is, depending on what perceptions are present to the psyche, and depending on the predominant cognitive frames within which those perceptions are interpreted, the "nonrational" part of the psyche, or the *thymos,* recognizes the significance or salience of those interpreted percepts and mobilizes emotions, desires, intentionalities, and behavioral scenarios (as well as bodily arousal for physical action) in response. Moreover, the specific emotions, desires, intentionalities, and bodily states mobilized by the *thymos* largely determine the predominant cognitive frames and behavioral scenarios within which the psyche's subsequent perceptions will be interpreted and responded to. For example, in Aristotle's analysis of "anger" (*orgê*)—which he defines as the desire for a conspicuous revenge for a conspicuous insult, accompanied by "blood boiling around the heart"—one must be presented with a "painful" perception that someone has done an "insult" to oneself and must foresee the possibility and means of a satisfactory retaliation in order to formulate a will to punish and project a specific behavioral scenario or plan, an intentionality, for exacting one's revenge (*On the Soul* 1.1 403a–b; *Rhetoric* 1.11 1370a and 2.2 1378a–b). Likewise, a person already in an "angry" mood, either because of some perceived offense or because of some irascible predisposition arising form physiological causes or the effects of drugs, will be quick to interpret things as "insults" calling for retaliation. "Anger," then, is a specific mode of intentionality that arises quasi-syllogistically as a "conclusion" from a conjunction of perceptions and interpretive frames *including physiological states* that act like "premises," defining and identifying what constitutes an "insult," what constitutes a "revenge," what constitutes the behavior of "an angry person," and so forth. And so with every other emotion, mood, or desire (see *Nichomachean Ethics* 7.3 1147a; *Movement of Animals* 8 701a–702b; and *Problems* 30 953a–b, 955a).[51] It is this "in-thymatic" kind of rationality that makes it possible for one to judge whether a person's emotional responses to a given situation are "reasonable" (or simply intelligible) or not *under the circumstances*, and that makes emotional response at least potentially amenable to persuasion.

In sum, the complex notion of *thymos* embodies and makes available, on one hand, a concept of "heartfelt" interpretation, inference, and emotional response endowed with a sort of rationality that operates quasi-syllogistically from heterogeneous "premises" present to the psyche and, on the other hand, a concept of intentionality as an emotive state that both arises from and shapes a person's "thymatic logic." The point is that this "logic" cannot be reduced to or restated as a formal syllogism—at least not in a fully satisfactory way—because it is not strictly propositional and may include among its "premises" such things as sense perceptions, mental imagery, memories, cognitive schemata, deepset beliefs and values (ideologies), bodily states, the aesthetic effects of things like music or drugs, and existing emotional predispositions (the "habits" of response that Aristotle considers to constitute *êthos*),[52] as well as explicit propositions or "ideas" overtly present to the psyche. Moreover, as Aristotle notes in *Movement of Animals* (8 702b), the operation of such diverse "premises" depends on no linear, propositional sequencing but is "simultaneous and quick" (*hana kai tachy*) and may not be especially accessible to consciousness. The heterogeneous materials in consciousness (both tacit and explicit) act as a conjoined bundle, while the "conclusion" arising from them is primarily not a proposition or "thought" but an action or a will to act in a certain way. This will to act may, of course, be accompanied or supplemented by some consciously formulated, verbalized thought or declaration that names what is being felt ("I'm angry and will punish so-and-so in such-and-such a way, because he has done *x* to me"); and it may be "scripted" by cognitive schemata or scenarios already inscribed in the psyche for acting out certain intentionalities (e.g., "anger"); but the "conclusion" as *a physically embodied will to act* can take place without any conscious, propositional formulation of itself.

The basic notion of *enthymêma*, then, as an "in-thymatic" argument appears to involve notions not only of intuitive inference-making (which the term *syllogismos* covers) but also notions of affective force and passional response.[53] Or so it would seem, at least, in common usage. This is evident in Sophocles' two uses of the word in *Oedipus at Colonus*: "[t]o be frightened, old man, by the *enthymêmata* from you / is greatly necessary; for in grave words / they have been given" (Chorus to Oedipus, 292–294); "[f]or you do not have trivial *enthymêmata*, / with your blinded eyes bereft of wholeness" (Antigone to Oedipus, 1200–1201). In the latter instance, Antigone is speaking of the reasons that Oedipus has—the entire story that lies behind his blinded eyes—to reconsider his unwillingness to receive his son; Oedipus replies that he is "overcome" by Antigone's pleading and will do as she asks, "but your pleasure is my grief" (1204–1206). Indeed, Oedipus's "blinded eyes," and all that is attached to them in his memory, and the emotions these things generate in his considerations, *are* the *enthymêmata* that move and persuade him. In the former passage, the Chorus (of Athenians) is referring to the reasons that *they* have been given by Oedipus to fear the consequences of impiety if they refuse him sanctuary. In both cases, the word *enthymêmata* refers to emotively charged reasons *felt by an audience* for responding in a certain way, reasons placed or evoked "in" their *thymos* by what a speaker has said or presented to them. Or, to put it another way, *enthymêma* seems to mean, with Sophocles, a judgment-motivating argument *as perceived, interpreted, and emotively appreciated*: not only, or not simply, an argument stated by a speaker but rather the argument that transpires "in" the listener's heart in response to the speaker's words.

In sophistic, pre-Aristotelian theory, so far as we can reconstruct it—our chief sources being Isocrates and Anaximenes' *Rhetoric to Alexander*—the notion of *enthymêma* seems more closely linked with, or to include, *presentational* and inventional concerns: the means by which enthymemes can most effectively be generated "in" a listener's *thymos*.[54] That is, in sophistic theorizing "enthymeme" becomes conceived as a figure of discourse, or a discursive procedure, meant to produce what might be called an "enthymematic moment" in an audience's experience of a rhetor's discourse. (This would seem to make reasonably good sense, insofar as the function of a *logôn technê* is to theorize principles in order to develop more or less consciously controllable, tactical procedures by which a rhetor can attempt to guide with some effectiveness in the inference-making and emotional responses of an audience.)

In all of Isocrates' five attested uses of the word *enthymêma*, the notion of "enthymeme" is closely linked to concerns with style, and linked as well to notions of *kairos* or "the opportune" in any given discursive situation. In *Evagoras* (10), for example, where the term "enthymeme" occurs twice, Isocrates says that panegyric orators have more difficult work than poets, because the orator must use "only the words in public use" and enthymemes based on "the facts themselves," whereas poets can fabulate and use exotic diction and can make up for weak "diction and enthymemes" with the psychagogic spell exerted by the "rhythms and symmetries" of verse. In *Panathenaicus* (2), he boasts of having composed Panhellenic panegyrics "filled with many enthymemes, and with not a few antitheses and parisoses and the other figures of brilliance in *rhêtoreia*, and compelling the listeners to remark and shout applause." In *Against the Sophists* (16–17), he portrays the ability "to see what *kairos* demands, and speak a discourse wholly wrought with fitting enthymemes and words both rhythmic and musical" as the essence of rhetorical skill. And in *Antidosis* (46–47), he argues that panegyric oratory is more akin to poetry than speeches made in law courts because both poems and panegyrics "set forth facts in a diction more poetic and more varied (*poiêtikôteros kai poikilôteros*) and seek to employ enthymemes more weighty and more original, and moreover they furnish the whole discourse with figures more remarkable and more numerous." In *Panegyricus* (9–10), similarly, he uses an inflected form of the related word *enthymeomai* to say that the ability to "to have considered" (*enthymêthênai*) what is fitting to each case, and so to use the appropriate topics of argument "according to *kairos*" and "in words well arranged," is the special characteristic of "those of good intelligence." In Isocrates, no mention of the enthymeme or enthymeme-making is ever far from a reference to stylistic matters—indeed, they invariably occur together in the same sentence—

while notions of *kairos* and what we might call kairotic inventiveness are typically in near proximity.

Beyond the general tenor of these usages, however, Isocrates will not provide a systematic or explicit account of enthymematic argument. In general he denies the possibility or even the usefulness of exact knowledge about such things and does not consider rhetoric reducible to *technê*, or at least not the sort of *technê* that consists of simple rules and prescriptions such as one might find in elementary grammar (*Against the Sophists* 12). For a more explicit, methodical account, we must turn to Anaximenes' *Rhetoric to Alexander,* where we find the fullest surviving presentation of an early sophistic notion of "enthymeme"—one that is generally taken both to precede and follow Aristotle's *Rhetoric* and that, with a long survival in Hellenistic and Roman treatises and Byzantine commentaries, appears to be the dominant tradition in antiquity.[55] According to Anaximenes, enthymemes are composed from "oppositions" or contradictions "not only in words or in actions . . . but also in anything else." And they are invented, he says, by inspecting an opponent's discourse or an action for anything that is contradictory either with itself or with "the principles of justice, law, expediency, honor, feasibility, facility, or probability" or with "the character of the speaker or the usual course of events." The speaker is then to make his own case by showing that his words or actions are "exactly contrary to those that are unjust, unlawful, and inexpedient, and to the usual conduct of bad men, in brief to whatever is deemed evil" and by phrasing the enthymemes that embody these oppositions as briefly and as economically as possible (10.1430a). One can argue that this is what both Antigone and Oedipus do, in Sophocles, when making enthymemes. In both cases, the speaker urges the audience to take a specific course of action (Oedipus should receive his son; the Athenians should give Oedipus sanctuary) by setting it in opposition to an alternative course of action (Oedipus wishes to reject his son; the Athenians wish to deny sanctuary). This opposed alternative is placed in contradiction with the demands of piety, justice, human compassion, and prudence (since impious, blasphemous, and unjust actions can bring fearful retribution from the gods) as well as the audience's own past history and behavior (the story behind Oedipus's blinded eyes, Athenian traditions), and so forth. Such value-laden, emotively significant oppositions *and the compactness and forcefulness of their presentation* are the major sources of an enthymeme's persuasive power.

Anaximenes expands this account by noting that one generates and deploys enthymemes by following the methods of what he calls "exetastic" discourse (*to exetastikon*), or "examination" (*exetasis*). Exetastic discourse, as Anaximenes describes it, consists of an "exhibition" of inconsistencies or contradictions in someone's intentions, deeds, or words (5 1427b) and can be used either alone or in combination with any other kind of public discourse (37 1445a). The actual deployment of an exetasis in a practical oration is to go as follows: first, one introduces "plausible pretexts" for proceeding to an examination; then, one examines the actions, words, or intentions in question, exposing the contradictions into which they fall. Finally, as Anaximenes advises, "when you have carefully examined everything and have amplified your points, conclude by giving a concise repetition, recalling what you have said to your hearer's memory" (37 1445a–b). For Anaximenes, then, it would appear that an enthymeme is, or is like, the argumentational cap that finishes an exetastic movement: a concise, emphatic statement of an emotionally charged opposition—one that serves not only to draw conclusions (in the sense of rational inferences) but also to project a stance or attitude toward the subject under discussion and to motivate the audience to identify with that stance.[56] That is, the audience is to feel not simply that the speaker's claims are true or probable but to feel as well that both speaker and claims are good and admirable and the very opposite of what is false, bad, undesirable, and detestable. The exetastic movement functions as a buildup that prepares what we might call the "enthymematic turn," or the enthymematic cap, which the speaker presents in a compact, emphatic declaration.

Like Isocrates, Anaximenes appears to link stylistic with enthymematic concerns. Only seven of the thirty-eight chapters in the *Rhetoric to Alexander* are directly concerned with style, or with what Anaximenes calls the sources of "urbanity" (*asteia*), but, significantly, he begins the discussion with reference to the enthymeme: "[u]rbanity is achieved in this way—you state half an enthymeme, so that the audience may understand the other half for themselves" (22 1434a). Moreover, of the ten sources of "urbanity" that Anaximenes discusses, seven seem highly relevant to the concise, emphatic statement of emotionally charged oppositions: brevity; adapting "the ethos of the words" to that of the audience; methods of framing "twofold statements"; clarity; antithesis; and parallelisms of structure and sound. Moreover, while the other three sources of "urbanity" do not seem clearly related to the statement of brief, emphatic enthymemes—these are "lengthening" (by creating and multiplying divisions within a topic and dwelling on each); speaking at moderate length; and "composition" (the choice and arrangement of words)—they do seem relevant to the buildup of an exetastic movement and may perhaps also be seen as variant strategies for the statement of elaborated enthymemes, such as one may find in the complex, Henry-Jamesian periods of Isocrates. Anaximenes' discussion of style, in sum, seems mainly (though certainly not exclusively) concerned with ways of effectively stating or presenting enthymemes: that is, with methods for enhancing an enthymeme's prominence and memorability, or what Claim Perelman would call its "presence," in its audience's mind.[57]

There are, however, important differences between Anaximenes and Isocrates, and a failure to note them will commit one to an excessively narrow concept of the enthymeme. Anaximenes, after all, is the kind of sophist that Isocrates most detests: one who considers rhetoric reducible to recipe-like instructions (and who has therefore written a how-to manual) and who, moreover, focuses his teachings chiefly on the methods of arguing lawsuits. This emphasis is what explains the rather prosecutorial, inquisitorial nature that Anaximenes gives to both the enthymeme and exetastic discourse: he sounds very much like the eristical, combative kind of sophist, always "on the watch for contradictions," whom Isocrates takes to task (*Against the Sophists* 19–20; *Antidosis* 47–50). For Isocrates, as we have seen, enthymemes are used not only in the oratorical combats of the law courts or public assemblies, and not only in eristic disputation, but also in poetry and in what he calls the "philosophical," panegyric kinds of discourse that he himself practices and teaches; and he considers the enthymemes employed in these genres "more weighty and more original." It is difficult to see how one could generate panegyric and poetic enthymemes *exclusively* by indicting the flaws and inconsistencies of an opponent—although this is, in fact, a traditional epideictic strategy (as in Hesiod's address to Perses in *Works and Days*) and is used in several of Isocrates' panegyrics (as in *Against the Sophists,* or his framing of *Antidosis* as a "defense," or his critique of Athenian politics in *Areopagiticus,* and so forth). But Isocrates' notion of the enthymeme and his practice of enthymematic argument both have wider possibilities.

For example: in what is perhaps the most famous passage of the *Panegyricus,* one can see Isocrates exploiting oppositions in a noninquisitorial way to motivate identification, or what Chaim Perelman might call "adherence," with his concluding stance.[58]

> Athens . . . has honored eloquence, which all desire in the wisely skilled; for she realized that by this alone we are unique among all creatures, and that because of this advantage we have surpassed them altogether; and she saw that in other pursuits fortune is so capricious that often the wise fail and the foolish succeed, whereas words possessing both beauty and art are not the fool's but are truly the work of an intelligent soul, and in this respect the wise and the ignorant most completely differ from each other; and she knew, furthermore, that whether men have been liberally educated from the start is shown not in their courage or wealth or such advantages, but is most certainly made manifest in speech, which is of all such signs the surest proof of culture in everyone, and that those who use discourse well are not only influential among their friends but also are truly held in high esteem by others. *And so far has our city outpaced all others in thought and speech that her students have become the teachers of the rest, so that the word "Hellenes" suggests no longer a race but a way of thought, and the title "Hellenes" applies to those who share our culture rather than those who share a common blood.* (48–50; my emphasis)

In this enthymeme of great persuasive force and enormous cultural power, Isocrates presents the vision that will define the Greek ideal of *paideia* for centuries to come. This enthymeme's power derives not only from a quais-syllogistic marshaling of evidence to justify a conclusion: the claim that Athens has become the "school" of all Greece because it has most honored eloquence is, in truth, weakly supported here, though earlier passages do give it some evidential ground. Rather, much of this enthymeme's power lies in its use of emotively significant oppositions (human/animal, wise/foolish, cultured/ignorant, achievement/luck, and so forth), defining eloquence as the distinguishing feature of human-ness and the distinctive sign of an accomplished and wise intelligence, in order to motivate the audience's admiration and desire—the wish that Athens should indeed be the school of Greece—a desire that, if it is evoked, will drive *or simply be* adherence with Isocrates' vision of a cosmopolitan cultural identity defined by ways of thought (the distinctly human, the discursively constructed) rather than by blood (the animal and accidental). The Athenian *paideia* as Isocrates defines it is a good thing, and should define "Hellenic" identity, for the reasons embodied in the network of emotively significant, evaluative oppositions that his argument has mobilized. This enthymeme, in turn, is meant to motivate audience adherence with his larger theme, his call for Panhellenic unification under Athenian leadership in a campaign against the Persian empire.

In considering the differences between Anaximenes and Isocrates, moreover, we should recall Isocrates' emphasis on the kairotic aspect of enthymemes, and to this add his notion that the best enthymemes will be what he calls *apotomos*, "abrupt" (*Evagoras* 10–11). "Abruptness" may signify, from one point of view, simply the compact, emphatic quality that Anaximenes prescribes for enthymemes, or the idea that in public speaking enthymemes should be plain-spoken and to the point. But the adjective *apotomos* and the verb *apotemnô* from which it derives have other kinds of significance including "cut off" or "sever," and in the adjective a sense of precipitousness, or metaphorically of surprise, as in the feeling of coming suddenly upon a vertiginous drop, a dizzying vista. What this suggests is that, as opposed to Anaximenes' somewhat mechanistic picture of an exetastic movement grinding out an inquisitorial "examination" that is then pithily summed up with an enthymeme, for Isocrates the best and most effective enthymemes will in some sense come as a surprise—or with a sudden, dramatic sense of opening prospects—and will seem to stand apart from or go beyond what precedes them. That is, the best enthymemes will not be fully predictable, will not follow as inevitable conclusions necessitated by the "premises" preceding them (as in formal syllogistic reasoning), though the audience must perceive them as reasonably derived from the materials of an "exetastic" buildup. The best enthymemes will seize the *kairos* of the moment to move the audience to a decisive recognition that is, or seems, "weighty and original" while at the same time "cutting off" or shifting into the background other possible recognitions that may be latent in the buildup.

This is what we see, again, in the passage from Isocrates' *Panegyricus*. The culminating stance of that passage, while motivated and made persuasive by the preceding exetasis, does not inevitably follow from it and certainly does not summarize it. Isocrates might, for example, turn to blaming Athens' catastrophic defeat in the Peloponnesian War on failure to "honor eloquence" and on a consequent descent to politics characterized by hubris, arrogance, brutal force, and bad deliberation. Such a turn would not serve his purposes in the *Panegyricus*, but it is made possible by his exetastic buildup; and it is pushed into the background by what his *presented* enthymeme foregrounds. (In the following passage, he does in fact confront this latent, alternative line of inference by denying that he has praised Athens' cultural achievement for lack of "grounds for praising her conduct in war" [51].) Isocrates' enthymematic turn, in sum, is meant to strike its audience as a brilliant, inspirational, impressive, and persuasive stroke of insight, a decisive stance-projection that brings suddenly into focus and gives memorable presence to a specific line of inference and attitude made possible by the *kairos*, "opportunity," of its moment—a *kairos* artfully prepared by the preceding exetasis and exploited with deliberate skill—while shifting other possibilities to the margins of attention or leaving them undeveloped. The enthymeme that Isocrates presents is indeed *apotomos*.

Between Anaximenes and Isocrates, then, we can derive a picture of a sophistic, pre- (or non-) Aristotelian notion of the enthymeme, a notion that will subsequently be pervasive in Hellenistic rhetorical tradition. On one hand, in the common or nontechnical usage embodied in Sophocles, "enthymeme" suggests a heartfelt, "enthymized," emotively significant piece of reasoning *as presented to and felt by an audience*. On the other hand, in a more specifically technical sense, an "enthymeme" is a strategic, kairotic, argumentational turn that exploits a cluster of emotively resonant, value-laden representations and systems of oppositions made "present" (usually) by an exetastic buildup, in order to generate in its audience a passional identification with a particular stance. It ideally will seem to be an "abrupt," decisive stroke of insight *that caps or punctuates the discourse to that point*. To be most effective, moreover, this enthymematic turn or "cap" will exploit a range of stylistic schemes—figures, rhythms, and so forth—in order to intensify its impact and enhance its presence, impressiveness, and memorability in the audience's psyche. As such, the enthymematic turn is the rhetorical move par excellence for guiding an audience's inference-making and attitude formation in a particular direction.

From this perspective, it is not difficult to understand why the ability "to see what *kairos* demands, and speak a discourse wholly wrought with fitting enthymemes and words both rhythmic and musical" figures so prominently in Isocrates' account of discursive skill and why, after Isocrates, the enthymeme would figure so prominently as a key concept in Aristotle's account of rhetoric (and at the same time one that he can assume is familiar to his audience). For if the function of rhetoric is to guide an audience toward a particular recognition, stance, preference, emotional response, judgment, or choice of actions—and this is what Aristotle understands the function of rhetoric to be (1.2 1357a; 2.18 1391b)—then the setting-up and deployment of impressive enthymemes is indeed the essence and sum of what an effective rhetor does. All else is, as Aristotle says, "accessory" to enthymeming.

Aristotle's appropriation (and reconfiguration) of the term *enthymêma* must, I think, be considered to presuppose all that has preceded it in common and sophistic usage. It is significant, for example, that the types of so-called common premises (or *koina*) for enthymematic invention discussed in *Rhetoric* 2.19—the possible and impossible, past fact and future fact, and largeness and smallness (of goods and evils)—are largely matters of opposition or contrast. It is significant, too, that the famous catalogue of twenty-eight enthymematic *topoi* in 2.23 begins with argument from "opposites," which therefore seems to stand, like "anger" for the catalogue of *pathê* in 2.2–11, as a sort of paradigm for the rest. While not all the remaining twenty-seven *topoi* are clearly matters of opposition or contrast, most of them are (seventeen by my count). Even those that are not obviously matters of exploiting oppositions tend to be illustrated with examples that do just that, as in topic 5, "looking at the time" (from Iphicrates against Harmodius): "[i]f, before accomplishing anything, I asked to be honored with a statue if I succeeded, you would have granted it. Will you not grant it now when I have succeeded? Do not then make a promise in anticipation but refuse it in realization!" (2.23 1397b).

All of this is reasonably consistent with the picture we get from Anaximenes and Isocrates. The same is true for Aristotle's observations that the normal language of enthymemes is compact, antithetical utterance (2.24 1401a) and that opposites stand out more clearly when juxtaposed (3.17 1418b); or for his discussion of the advantages of periodic style, rhythm, antitheses, metaphors, and "bringing-before-the-eyes" for enthymemes (3.9–10); or for his advice that the proof section of a speech should not consist of a continuous string of enthymemes but rather the enthymemes should be "mixed in" (3.17 1418a). As Thomas Conley has observed, these kinds of remarks suggest that Aristotle is thinking of enthymemes as "nicely turned sentences or [elenchic, rhetorical] questions raised at climactic points."[59] Further, as William Grimaldi has suggested, Aristotle's inclusion of *pathos* and *êthos* among the enthymematic sources of persuasion in *Rhetoric* 2.2–17 suggests that, like Anaximenes, Isocrates, and Sophocles, he considers enthymemes to be "something more than an act of . . . reason" and to carry affective force.[60]

There is, of course, some question—and a history of disagreement—as to whether Aristotle considers all "rhetorical" argumentation enthymematic. The crucial locus for this question is *Rhetoric* 1.2.8 (1356a–b). Aristotle has just said (in 1.2.3–6 1356a) that "there are three kinds of *pisteis* provided by means of discourse," namely those arising from the *êthos* of the speaker, from the speaker's *logos* or "speech" itself, and from the *pathos* of the audience. Now (at 1.2.8) he says:

> [o]f those [proofs] through demonstration [*dia tou deiknynai*] or apparent demonstration, just as in dialectic there is induction [*epagôgê*] and the syllogism and apparent syllogism, so it is likewise here [in rhetoric]; for the example is an induction, the enthymeme a syllogism, and the apparent ehthymeme an apparent syllogism. All produce proofs [*pisteis*] through demonstration [*dia tou deiknynai*] by stating [*legontes*] either examples or enthymemes, and in no other way besides these.

Here it would seem that Aristotle is confining the enthymeme to "demonstration" by means of *logos*—or what modern thought has confusedly come to call the logical appeal as distinct from the emotional or ethical appeal—and indeed it seems that Aristotle is making the enthymeme merely one of two types of such appeal. Enthymemes and examples seem now to be the two types of "logical appeals," corresponding to the induction and the (deductive) syllogism in dialectic logic, and with "apparent" (invalid, logically faulty) enthymemes corresponding to the "apparent syllogisms" of dialectic. Or so this passage has commonly been read.

But there are other ways to read it. First of all, note that Aristotle elsewhere treats "induction" (*epagôgê*) as one of the twenty-eight *topoi* for the invention of enthymemes (2.23.11 1398a–b).[61] So the "example" (*paradeigma*), as rhetorical "induction," turns out to be another form of enthymematic argument, or an element of it, rather than a "nonenthymematic" form of proof. Similarly, as William Grimaldi and others have pointed out,[62] at the beginning of *Rhetoric* 2 Aristotle introduces his discussion of emotion and character by saying that, just as he has "drawn up" (in book 1) a list of the "propositions" (*protaseis*) from which enthymemes are generated in symbouleutic, epideictic, and dikanic discourse, so now "we shall do likewise with these [emotions] and shall analyze them in the aforesaid manner." In other words, *pisteis* arising from *pathos* and *êthos* function enthymematically, just as do the "proofs through demonstration" produced by the speaker's statements. Overtly presented, demonstrative proofs may take the form of *enthymematic figures* or *examples*, by which Aristotle seems to have in mind the direct presentation of discursive, quasi-syllogistic reasoning ("do this because . . .") and the narration of exemplary cases ("shall we do this? remember the case of *x*"), as well as the presentation of "inartistic" evidence (such as testimony, documents, or confessions). But all the *pisteis* operate enthymematically.

There is a distinction to be made between "enthymeme" as a general principle of reasoning and argument and "enthymeme" as a formal, stylistic feature, a presented "figure of thought," such as Anaximenes generally seems to have in mind. Aristotle's point appears to be that "enthymeme" in the former sense comprises all the *pisteis* used in rhetoric; "enthymeme" in the latter sense is what the sophistic handbook writers generally describe, *though they generally fail to explain what makes an "enthymeme" (in the latter sense) enthymematic.* This is, in essence, Aristotle's criticism of earlier *technê* writers (1.1.3 1354a; 1.1.9 1354b): they focus, he says, mostly on "accessory" matters, such as methods for handling the different parts of speech, or specific techniques for emotional appeals, while ignoring "the artistic sources of persuasion . . . that is, how something comes to be enthymematic." This is also why he says (at 1.2.7 1365a) that

> [s]ince the *pisteis* are from these [three sources, namely *êthos*, *pathos*, and *logos*], it is apparent that they are to be understood by the person capable of syllogizing [*tou syllogisasthai dynamenou*] and theorizing [*theôrêsai*] concerning characters [*êthê*] and the virtues and, thirdly, concerning the *pathê*—what each of the emotions is and what its nature, and from what things it arises and how.

That is, all the kinds of rhetorical *pisteis*, in all of the figures through which they might appear in discourse, are enthymematic and so are to be understood by the person capable of analyzing the rational, inferential processes by which they operate in the human psyche. A person who understands how "syllogizing" (in the sense of everyday inference) works can also analyze the enthymematic workings of the *pisteis*; likewise, a person clever at "syllogizing" (in Aristotle's more technical sense) will also be clever at turning enthymemes—as long as he remembers that he is not engaged in dialectical disputation (and knows the difference).

It is true, of course, that Aristotle also says that enthymemes should not be used when one is trying to arouse pathos or project ethos, in which he seems to differ from his sophistic predecessors. One can, however, resolve the seeming contradiction by noting that it is the exetastic buildup, and the resources of amplification and narration available to such a buildup, that will generate an affective charge that an enthymematic "cap" can then exploit. One might also note, as George Kennedy does in his translation of the *Rhetoric*, that Aristotle does in fact give examples of emotional appeals that take the form of enthymemes.[63] My own view is that the *pathê* do function enthymematically, both in their arousal and in their subsequent function as *pisteis* or "sources of persuasion" for further enthymemes—and Aristotle seems to recognize this, though at certain points he also seems to wish to minimize or contain the emotional dimension of rhetoric by subordinating it to discursive reason or by making it more similar to dialectic or by regulating the forums in which it appears.[64] Aristotle's statement about avoiding enthymemes when drumming up emotion can be understood in light of his other observation that a discourse should not, or cannot, consist of a continuous string of enthymemes—that is, a continuous string of conclusion-drawing, stance-projecting "caps" without any intervening matter (i.e., without a preparatory exetasis for each "cap"). Aristotle does not directly say so, but clearly such an "all-caps" discourse would sound more like a tightly reasoned string of syllogisms, or like the tediously logical proceedings of Stoic orators (as Cicero describes them), or, alternatively, like a bombastic torrent of groundless, arbitrary declarations and unjustified emotive posturings.

In sum, what Aristotle contributes to the notion of "enthymeme" is his focus on the enthymeme's underlying, in-thymatic rationality: his enormously productive recognition that, like a dialectical syllogism, an enthymeme also relies on a basic, intuitive capacity in human beings for deriving inferences and forming judgments (including the judgments embodied in emotional responses) from relationships between ideas—or, more precisely, from relationships between the various kinds of mental representations and physiological states that can act as "premises" within the psyche, in particular those that act with greatest force, energy, or "presence" at the moment of decision.[65] In other words, an appeal to emotion, or any other attempt at proof or persuasion, or any attempt to "cap" an argumentative passage with a striking declaration, can have no effect (or cannot have the desired effect) unless it functions enthymematically, and it cannot function enthymematically unless it is grounded in a "thymatic," quasi-syllogistic process of inference and interpretation that makes it seem intelligible, reasonable, and therefore persuasive *at that moment, within the circumstances*, to the rhetor's audience. Otherwise, the rhetor's attempt at an "enthymematic" gesture will *appear to the audience* as foolish, empty posturing, grandiloquent blather, or fake or inappropriate emoting, or simply bad reasoning, in which case the would-be enthymematic gesture will not in fact be an enthymeme at all. (Likewise, a seemingly persuasive enthymeme that is undone, refuted, or punctured by another rhetor's arguments becomes merely an "apparent enthymeme.")

As Demetrius *On Style* points out (1.30–33)—reflecting what is probably a later, Hellenistic version of Peripatetic theory—what makes an enthymeme an enthymeme is not its form but its rational coherence, the "thought" (*dianoia*) that constitutes its substance. Brilliantly pointed antithetical statements and periodic sentences may be good ways, he says, to state an enthymeme, but they do not, in and of themselves, an enthymeme make. Likewise, an enthymeme can be broken up and rearranged in various ways and still have its enthymematic force. The form of the enthymeme is not the enthymeme itself. The sophistic reply to this line of argument, however, is that it is also true that rational coherence or "reasonability" will not, in and of itself, be sufficient either: an enthymeme will generally not be perceivable, memorable, or energetically operative in an audience's consciousness, unless given specific form and so *made present and even memorable* by the rhetor's enthymematic gesture. And that is a crucial insight.

Aristotle's appropriation of the sophistic and everyday notions of "enthymeme" seems, then, to accept this insight while amending it with an added emphasis on the underlying, dialogic rationality that enthymematic argument shares with dialectic. The dialectical syllogism, in effect, stands as a kind of simplified analogy, an analytical heuristic, for explaining the more complex, affective rationality and persuasive force of enthymemes. Thus Aristotle can say that a person who is knowledgeable about the forms and methods of syllogistic argument will also have an understanding of enthymematic argument and can be skillful at it *when he understands the differences between enthymemes and logical syllogisms* (*Rhetoric* 1.1 1355a). It seems likely, of course, that Aristotle wishes to improve on the sophistic approach to rhetoric by cultivating a more technical, "artistic" approach to enthymematic practice that approximates (and incorporates) what for him are the more intellectually respectable methods of dialectic. But we need not go that far. As I have said, our purpose here is not to reconstruct a purely Aristotelian account of "enthymeme" but to develop a general notion of "enthymeme" for which both Aristotelian and non-Aristotelian approaches offer some lines of description.

One might, finally, put it this way: the syllogism, in Aristotle's technical sense, offers a kind of model, a pedagogic metaphor, for understanding enthymemes; but it is not the same thing, and eventually the metaphor must be dropped when one attempts to account for the full complexity of real-world enthymematic arguments. We are thus presented with a double perspective. An "enthymeme" is, on one hand, a complex, quasi-syllogistic structure of inference and affect that constitutes the substance and persuasive force of an argument *as perceived by an audience*. On the other hand, an "enthymeme" will typically and perhaps most forcefully appear *in discourse* as an emphatic, structural/stylistic turn that caps an exetasis, gives the inferential/affective substance a particular realization with a particular salience within a particular discursive moment, and thereby shapes its audience's perception of (and responses to) just what "the argument" is. Ultimately, the enthymeme is both these things at once and as such is the "body of persuasion."

So what does it mean to talk about enthymemes in poetry? Let me now turn to some examples.

7

A "Truest Paradigm for Western Lyric"

Pindar, Isthmian 3, *and* Olympian 1

I emphasize, again, that my purpose thus far has not been to reconstruct a specifically Aristotelian concept of "enthymeme." Rather, my point is that, between the perspectives offered by Sophocles' apparently common usage of the word *enthymêma*, the more technical, sophistic usage operative in Isocrates and Anaximenes, and Aristotle's reception and emendation of those usages, we can reconstruct a general notion of enthymematic argument—one that is less constricting than the conventional modern reception of "enthymeme" as "incomplete, truncated, probabilistic syllogism," with "syllogism" understood to mean the sort of thing that appears in logic textbooks. Indeed, the process of "in-thymatic" reasoning, on which enthymematic argument depends, is arguably more basic to human cognition than either the "syllogism" as defined by logic or the essentially propositional structures of practical reasoning described by Stephen Toulmin. Both can, in fact, be understood as specialized applications of a deeper, more basic enthymematic process. My claim, then, is that the notion of "enthymeme" that I have outlined here is broader, more flexible, and more capable of accounting for a wide variety of real-world argumentational practices, including poetic practices.

I emphasize, as well, that what follows in this and the next two chapters is meant to be illustrative and suggestive rather than exhaustive. My purpose is to sketch a general notion of enthymematic argument in ancient Greek poetry, with particular reference to "lyric" (as I am using that term) understood as a paradigmatic, protean poetic mode.

Isthmian 3

If one wishes to counter the pervasive modern resistance to the notion of "rhetorical" poetry, or to the notion of lyric argument in particular, Pindar may be the best of all possible places to start. Harold Bloom, for example, once declared that "[r]hetoric has always been unfitted to the study of poetry" because it "arose from the analysis of political and legal orations, which are absurd paradigms for lyric poems," while declaring also that Pindar's first Olympian ode is "still the truest

paradigm for Western lyric." As usual, no real argument is presented for these assertions; and Bloom completely overlooks the category of epideictic. But it is clear
that his assertions proceed, on one hand, from a fundamentally romantic presumption that "[l]yric celebrates the poetic self, despite every denial" and, on the other
hand, from a profound misunderstanding of "rhetoric" and of "rhetorical criticism"
as something that "treats a poem merely as a formal and linguistic structure."[1]
Rhetoric-as-formalism cannot engage with poetry as the sublime expression/
celebration of a (romantic, individual) poetic self that is enacted in the visionary
transgression or breaking-open of conventional linguistic and social forms, or so
Bloom assumes. I willingly will grant that Pindar's odes embody a "paradigm for
Western lyric," indeed perhaps the "truest" one, and possibly for any lyric whatsoever—at least in general terms—although it may be more circumspect to say that
Pindar represents a basic paradigm for lyric in antiquity. But whether one makes circumspect or sweeping claims for its centrality, Pindar's paradigm will not sustain
Bloom's claims about either lyric poetry or rhetoric.

Bloom's example is *Olympian* 1, but I will look first at *Isthmian* 3. I have chosen
this example not because it is a better poem—it isn't—but because it is short
enough to take in quickly. Arguably, it is equally representative of Pindar and of the
basic paradigm in question. This poem celebrates a certain Melissos of Thebes, who
has won the chariot race at the Nemean games, after having won the pankration (a
combination of boxing and wrestling) at the Isthmian games earlier that year; the
date is generally considered to be around 479 B.C. or shortly thereafter. Here is the
poem in full:

[strophe]
If any of men that are fortunate in glorious games
or strength of riches restrains dire excess in his heart,
he deserves embrace in townsmen's praises.
Zeus, great excellence to mortals comes
from you; longer lives the bliss of godfearing men, but with those of crooked heart
not equally does the blooming-time consort.
[antistrophe]
And for glorious deed's requital we must hymn the noble man,
and must in festal celebration with gentle graces raise him up.
And now it is for twice-victorious Melissos
his destiny toward sweet merriment to turn
his heart, for he was given crowns in Isthmia's glens, and in the deep-chested
lion's deep vale [at Nemea] he proclaimed Thebes
[epode]
by winning the chariot-race. Men's inborn
excellence he does not disgrace.
You surely know Kleonymos [Melissos's ancestor]
was famed of old for chariots;
and on his mother's side the partners in Labdakid wealth went their ways in striving at
  four-horse chariots.
But an age with its whirling days shall now and again bring utter change; the
  unwounded surely are the children of gods.

This is, admittedly, a rather bald translation. I have tried to render as directly as possible the line-by-line "contents" of the original within the bounds of English readability.[2] The point is that, when the poem stands thus in translation, stripped of the charm of Pindar's prosody, and of the (long lost) music and choreography through which it was originally performed by a dancing and singing chorus, what remains is recognizably a piece of epideictic oratory, composed for and performed within a ritual occasion.[3]

More specifically, *Isthmian* 3 like all of Pindar's "victory odes" (*epinikia*) has been commissioned and composed to be performed within the context of a public celebration for the victor, usually in his home city (Melissos's Thebes) after his return. The details of epinician performance are not well known, but the general shape of the victory celebration probably derived from the traditions of *nostos*, "homecoming," and *kômos*, a "revel" that included feasting, drinking, singing and dancing and that typically culminated in a torchlit parade of singing, dancing, inebriated revelers through the streets; the name and notion of *nostos/kômos* are frequently invoked in Pindar's odes. A traditional feature of the *kômos* was the arrival of the revelers at one or more houses, where they would stop and seek admission. This may have been the model for the scene of performance of an *epinikion*, as a sort of reception-song, at some point within the general framework of the celebration. Combining a number of scattered references from Pindar and other ancient sources, William J. Slater had offered a composite, hypothetical description:

> [A victory-ode] could be sung at any number of points during the ceremonies. Some may have been sung at the festival following the games as part of the celebration there. Most however are quite clearly set in the victor's homeland. He could return by ship or by land; he could be met outside the city by friends or garlanded officials and escorted inside to the sound of music by a flower-throwing crowd. A victor of 412 is said by Diodorus Siculus to have been escorted by 300 pairs of white horses. . . . The victory was formally celebrated at some point, perhaps in the agora; honours were decreed for the victor. The procession carrying the crown(s) [which the victor had been awarded at the games] then wound its way to a temple where they would dedicated, or to the victor's home, or both. Afterwards there was a public *hestiasis* [a "reception" feast] or a private symposium or both. Depending on the status of the victor, the ceremonies could be expanded to include wearing of white, public and private sacrifice, burning of incense and opening of temples.[4]

Or again, in another composite drawn from various representations in Pindar's odes:

> [t]he victor is accompanied by his friends [in the victory-procession]. . . . The *kômos* is said to come all the way from the place of victory to the home city, though this . . . is metaphorical. The chorus is dancing and is met by people throwing flowers. The victor is *komou despotês* ["lord of the revel"]. They are carrying the crown [*stephanophoria*] to a temple in procession; or they are singing before the victor's home. They seek reception. The victor is received by the city; the city receives the song; the city welcomes the victor and his comrades. . . . The song is in the evening and is followed by rejoicing in the streets all night long.[5]

As Slater notes, much of this can be metaphorical, and we seldom can be sure of the specific performance circumstances of any given *epinikion*. The point, however, is that the performance of an ode would have occured at some point within the general pattern of events that Slater describes and very possibly at the site where the victory-procession of the *kômos* arrived to be "received," whether at a public dancing space, a temple or some other sacred enclosure, or the victor's house, and just before the night-long reveling got underway.[6]

In the case of *Isthmian* 3, the received opinion is that it was probably composed and performed as a companion piece to *Isthmian* 4, a longer *epinikion* that celebrates Melissos's pankration victory: the two poems are metrically identical. This linkage explains why *Isthmian* 3, which actually deals with a Nemean victory, was classed by Pindar's ancient editors as an "Isthmian" ode. As for *Isthmian* 4, Eveline Krummen had argued that it probably was performed in the context of an annual Theban festival of Hercules and his sons, which was held outside the city walls, and which may have been connected with the mustering/initiation of young men into the city's army.[7] This would suggest, then, that we should think of *Isthmian* 3, insofar as it is linked to *Isthmian* 4, as being performed somewhere outside the walls of Thebes, in the midst of a victory-*kômos* combined with a public festival, at which a large portion of the citizen body would have been gathered. The key point here is that, as with Pindar's other *epinikia*, *Isthmian* 3 is part of a public, civic event, and as such is an instance of public, civic discourse addressed to a socially heterogeneous audience containing both nobles and common citizens.[8]

As an instance of civic discourse, and as epideictic rhetoric, the poem presents a more or less explicitly enthymematic argument. It works through an "exetasis," from its opening maxims (in the strophe) and its abbreviated narration of Melissos's achievements and ancestral history (in the antistrophe and epode) to an enthymematic cap or stance-declaration in the final line. At the simplest level of this argument, Melissos's double victory shows, or "proves," that he has the sort of straight, godfearing, noble heart in which the favor of Zeus may wax and blossom for a longer time, as it does not "with those of crooked heart." This latter phrase renders *plagiais phrenessin*, more literally "[with] slanting hearts" or "[with] slantwise purposes." *Phrēn*, which signifies the midriff region between the heart and abdomen, can like *thymos* be translated as "heart, spirit, mind, wits, purpose" and produces derivatives like *phronêsis* (prudence, practical wisdom) and *sôphrosynê* (sensibility, self-control). Melissos is presented, in effect, as a young man of "upright," well-centered, sensible ethicality. While some of Melissos's ancestors apparently have been affected for the worse by time's "whirling days," *kulindomenais hamerais* (a phrase that evokes something being tossed, tumbled, or rolled about), Melissos himself stands forth as one of "the unwounded," a worthy descendant of the famed Kleonymos who does not "disgrace" his "inborn excellence." Melissos appears, in short, as a man of manifest god-favored virtue whose rightful reward is "embrace in townsmen's praises." More precisely, he is *axios eulogiais astôn memichthai*, "worthy / in the eulogies / of [his] townsmen / to be joined together [with them] in hospitable relations." This attitude is then embodied, with an emphatic flourish, in the stance of the poem's enthymematic cap, which is a compressed, forceful, hyperbolic, and striking gesture of eulogistic praise: as one of "the unwounded," surely Melissos is the "child" or beloved *pais* of some god (*atrôtoi ge man paides theôn*).

But *Isthmian* 3 does more than argue why the "townsmen" of Thebes should "embrace" Melissos with praise and admiration, as they join in the *kômos*. As Leslie Kurke has shown, Pindar's *epinikia* are situated in and responsive to the same kinds of social and political strains that form the setting and central subject of Theognis's elegiacs.[9] Pindar's poems, composed perhaps about a half-century later than the Theognidean corpus, adroitly and persuasively negotiate the potentially violent, strife-producing tensions between aristocrats, who were the chief contestants in the great athletic festivals, and their nonaristocratic fellow-townsmen. Around this time the power of the traditional nobility in most *poleis* was being challenged and displaced, but not eliminated, by the emergence of a powerful "middling" class and by the consequent development of "middling," protodemocratic ideologies and institutions.[10] Indeed, the public performance of an *epinikion* was itself a newly emergent institution, originating perhaps in the latter half of the sixth century B.C., possibly with Simonides.[11] At the same time, the major Panhellenic athletic festivals represented a survival and transformation of archaic honor-competition—a symbolic replacement for aristocratic combat, which had been rendered obsolete by the closely packed marching formations of the phalanx (one of the major sources of "middling" ideology). Martial excellence had been (partially) replaced by athletic excellence, prowess for its own sake, as a source of aristocratic distinction and prestige.[12] According to Kurke, Pindar's *epinikia* typically respond to this complex political situation by maintaining the rights of aristocratic athletic victors to public honors, social prestige, and the "embrace" of their fellow-townsmen, while at the same time attempting to "modify and modernize" the behavior and attitudes of "a reluctant aristocracy" by *redefining the grounds of praise* in terms of communal, civic responsibility. Amid a komiastic celebration, the victor is reintegrated back into the complex sociality of the fifth-century *polis*, even as he stands exalted at the apex of (athletic) achievement.[13]

In *Isthmian* 3, we see this more complex argumentation represented in the following assertions: first, the "embrace" of praise (that is, being joined in friendly fellow feeling with one's townsmen) is owed to the "noble man" whose god-beloved excellence has made him "fortunate" in "strength of riches" or "glorious games," *but only if* he can "restrain dire excess in his heart." Since Pindar's opening location, "*if any* of men" (*ei tis andrôn*), singles out an inspecific "anyone" (*tis*) from a plural genitive (*andrôn*, "of men"), the clear suggestion is that *not everyone* who happens to be wealthy, powerful, accomplished, or successful in "glorious games" is equally worthy of his townsmen's "embrace." Pindar's "or," likewise, separates athletic success from "strength of riches," so that there is no inherent or necessary connection between inherited wealth/power and the sort of excellence that brings divinely sponsored good fortune in contests of excellence. Second, god-bestowed good fortune and "blooming" bliss will remain or "consort" longer with "godfearing" men but does not remain with those of "slanting heart" who fail to restrain their capacity for "dire excess." Third, time works "utter change" that sooner or later will "wound" or bring down the high, *unless* thay are specifically favored or sponsored by (are "children" of) some god—which can only happen, again, *if* they are "godfearing" and "upright" enough to "restrain dire excess" in their *phrên*. Thus, to keep their god-bestowed good fortune and their rights to civic privileges and honors, *and to have those rights endorsed by their fellow-townsmen*, they must possess an ethicality characterized by *phronêsis, sôphrosynê*, and piety (to *hosion*, or what Pindar here calls *hopis*, regard/reverence/awe for gods). This is what Pindar claims for the twice victorious Melissos.

Behind these assertions, tacitly, lie deeper mythic paradigms familar to Pindar's audience(s), paradigms of retribution visited on those who set themselves too high and thus incur godly wrath. And alongside those assertions, more explicitly, stand the briefly cited examples of the bygone "partners in Labdakid wealth" who "went their ways" or, somewhat less explicitly, the audience's own memories or knowledge of time-wrought change and falling fortunes. In this poem's more expansive companion piece, *Isthmian 4*, Pindar mentions (16–18) the recent death in battle of four members of Melissos's family. This has generally been regarded as a reference to the battle of Plataia (in 479 B.C.), in which the Thebans had fought on the Persian side against the allied Greeks, suffering defeat and heavy casualties. Pindar also mentions (22–23) a recent period of time, presumably subsequent to the battle, in which the "ancient fame for glorious deeds" of Melissos's house had "fallen asleep" though now it has reawakened with Melissos's victories. If Pindar is referring to Plataia, it is not something for a Theban to be proud of—from the Panhellenic perspective, it is a matter for shame—and the losses suffered could very well be seen as a sign and consequence of divine displeasure. Indeed, insofar as not only the Kleonymidai but all the traditional nobility of Thebes must bear responsibility for the failed policy of "Medising" (alliance with "Medes," the Persians), their ancestral rights to leadership and public honor in the city can be seen as questionable. The once proud Kleonymidai, standing as a synecdoche for the rest of the nobility of Thebes, have certainly not gone "unwounded" and have suffered an inglorious catastrophe.

What all this amounts to, in effect, is an admonitory enthymeme *delivered in the presence of the Theban people*, or at least a significant number of them, and directed toward Melissos and his family and by extension toward the nobility in general: a warning against "dire excess," or *hubris* in the sense of "wantonness, violence, insolence, lewdness, outrage, violation." (The Theban alliance with the invading Persians, in the hope of using Persian power as a lever for hegemony over the other Greek *poleis*, could certainly be seen as an act of *hubris* on the part of the aristocrats of Thebes.) In the phrase *aianê koron*, "dire excess," the noun *koros*, "excess," carries the more particular sense of an arrogance that arises from satiety, while the adjective *aianês* means not only "dire" but also "endless" and "wearisome." The phrase *aianê koron* thus means something like the "dire, endlessly wearisome arrogance" of the self-satisfied aristocrat who becomes encouraged, with a surfeit of wealth and honors, to set himself (or his clique) apart from and above the rest of the community while pursuing his own self-interested and unrestrained desires. Melissos, then, is presented, praised, and reintegrated into the social framework of his *polis* as a "noble man" whose excellence in wealth and physical prowess is to be measured, re-defined, and finally found honorable (or not) in terms of civic responsibility, or responsibility to the common laws of justice, reasonableness, and piety that govern the lives of fellow citizens. These are the terms of praise that Melissos must live up to if he is to retain the excellence that makes him "noble" and worthy of public honors—worthy to be received in *kômos* by his fellow-townsmen—and if he is to retain his place in the social and political fabric of fifth-century Thebes. And so for the rest of the nobility.

It would be too much to say that this admonitory enthymeme is the central argument of Pindar's poem. Pindar has, after all, been hired by the Kleonymidai to compose and probably to lead the performance of a public *epinikion* in praise of Melissos and their house, at a festive occasion not unlike a modern city's homecoming parade for a championship-winning team: Pindar has an obligation to his patrons and to the expectations inherent in the occasion.[14] Moreover, it is likely though not certain that the chorus itself, whether composed of boys, young men, or older men, was composed of persons from the most prominent Theban families.[15] To imagine that Pindar would then have composed an ode through which the chorus would publicly scold or wave a didactic finger at the Kleonymidai and by implication the rest of the Theban aristocracy, and in the midst of what was supposed to be a scene of "sweet merriment" for the victor, would be to imagine Pindar—who was himself a Theban—as extremely foolish, indeed as a rhetorical idiot.

That Pindar was not a rhetorical idiot, and that he fulfilled his commissions with great skill and satisfaction for the families and cities that hired him, is evidenced by the simple facts that they continued to hire him and that he was very highly paid. As Bruno Gentili notes, on one occasion the city of Athens paid Pindar ten thousand drachmas, and appointed him *proxenos* ("friend of the city," an honorary title with certain privileges attached), in exchange for a single dithyrambic ode. We also know that he was paid three thousand drachmas for *Nemean 5*, a victory ode in honor of Pytheas of Aegina. Gentili also notes, in comparison, that the famed sculptor Phidias was paid a salary of five thousand drachmas *per year* (for eight years) while he worked on the colossal gold and ivory statue of Athena for the Parthenon.[16] We know that Pindar, on at least one occasion, composed five Olympian odes in a single year[17] and that, of course, he received commissions not only for *epinikia* but for various kinds of poems, such as the dithyramb for Athens or paians or partheneia for religious or civic festivals. Pindar could well have earned as much as twenty thousand drachmas in a year, and possibly more. The typical wage of a skilled worker in Athens in the middle to late fifth century has been estimated at one to two and a half drachmas per day; from this we can infer that an ordinary citizen's annual income could have been under a thousand drachmas and perhaps as low as three hundred.[18] Pindar was, in short, a rich man whose poetry brought him an annual income possibly more than twenty times that of a common citizen and certainly more than even Phidias could command. The wealthy and powerful were willing and even eager to pay to be praised by Pindar, at extraordinarily high prices, and it appears that they were usually satisfied with what they got.[19]

But that observation does not reverse the argument I have outlined. The point, rather, is to reemphasize that an arguer's necessity is always to work through the "given" presuppositions circulating in and operant for the intended audience(s)—and through the constraints and opportunities afforded by the specific situation—in order to earn the audience's agreement or adherence with whatever is presented for its judgment. As Peter Rose has argued, Pindar clearly is a spokesman for aristocratic claims to "inborn excellence" and thus to rights of political and social privilege in an oligarchic state, although such claims are given important qualifications.[20] It is clear as well that the occasion and expectations for an *epinikion* set certain definite constraints within which Pindar must compose the discourse that the chorus will perform. But, given his apparent political conservatism, and given the demands of the situation, what is perhaps significant in Pindar is the recognition embodied in the poetry's very function that the nobleman's status is dependent on, and is to be approved in, the "embrace" of "townsmen's praises," by which he is received and reunited in friendly fellowship with the city. That is, the act of engaging in a rhetorical transaction that *argues for* such an "embrace" constitutes in itself an acknowledgment that the legitimacy of an oligarchic ruling class depends on some form of popular consent; such an acknowledgment is tacitly communicated even when the procedure of eliciting that consent is little more than an empty form. But in the turbulent world of fifth-century *polis* politics, those procedures cannot be and are not empty. Pindar is dealing in contested issues, through argumentation that addresses a mixed audience of commoners (in which I include the so-called middling, richer commoners) and nobles and that seeks to develop the complex, difficult grounds on which the noble may be found acceptable to the city as a whole. As Rose suggests, the epinician genre may well have been "an arena of ideological struggle" from its inception in the sixth century.[21]

How is our sense of Pindar's argumentation affected if we assume that the choral performers, the *choreutai*, were themselves members of the Theban nobility? It is easy, perhaps, to consider their performance of the ode, and thus the ode itself, as mere (but extremely well-done) political propaganda: the well-born choreuts, in praising Melissos, articulate before the Theban populace a code of ethics that serves to justify their class's hegemonic role as the city's "leaders."[22] Arguably, however (and as Rose recognizes, though for reasons other than mine), such inferences are too easy and too simple. To think rhetorically: the mere fact, after all, that a chorus of well-born boys or men publicly articulates and endorses a particular code of ethics does not, ipso facto, make that gesture credible or persuasive for their audience of fellow-townsmen. *The astoi* are not a lump of passive clay on which Pindar through the chorus inscribes aristocratic ideology, no matter how brilliantly or beautifully that inscribing may be done, and no matter how skillful the chorus's singing and dancing. If the audience can recognize a serious discrepancy between the projected *êthos* of the discourse and the actual, historically demonstrated *êthos* of the performers or their class or family—the known record of their behavior up to the present moment—the persuasiveness of their song and dance will necessarily be undermined or even utterly destroyed and will come across as just so much hot air and empty posturing to skeptical, resistant listeners. Indeed, if their performance is seen as empty posturing, the brilliance of the song itself may only intensify the audience's perception of insincerity, artificiality, dishonesty, and falsity. And the degree of distance between the choreuts' avowed and actually demonstrated ethics is something that an audience of fellow-*astoi* inevitably would measure with great acuity: indeed, as all readers of Pindar recognize, a central and recurring topic of his odes is the problem of resentful "envy," *phthonos*, directed against those who stand exalted above their fellow citizens.

Thus, the noble choreuts' performed articulation and endorsement of an ethic under which the "noble man" can be acceptable to the city is not a unilateral transaction. Rather, it enacts a sort of contract between the choreuts and the city. On one hand, the performers must be able to claim credibly that their social, political, civic conduct (or the conduct of their families or their class) really does measure up to their avowed ethic, at least most of the time, in order for their performed act of avowal to be believable. And for this reason well-known failures must be proleptically acknowledged and confronted in some way: this is why Pindar must include, in both *Isthmian* 3 and 4, references to the reverses that have befallen the Kleonymidai, and through such references also a coded acknowledgment of the Theban failure at Plataia (if the dating of the poem is correct). The performers enact an acknowledgment of failure: the nobility of the Kleonymidai had "fallen asleep," but now it has awakened in Melissos. On the other hand, by giving public, physically embodied avowal to the poem's projected ethic in the act of singing and dancing it before the *polis*, the performers also commit themselves to live up to it in future and be judged according to its terms.[23] As Eva Stehle has argued, in a choral performance of "community poetry"—such as an *epinikion*—the chorus must be able to speak credibly both *for* and *to* the community it addresses, if the performance is to achieve what she calls psychological efficacy (i.e., persuasiveness).[24] Whatever their social status, therefore, the choreuts must be able to present themselves, in the identity that they project, as a credible embodiment of a communal *êthos* with which their audience can identify or which it can at least find worthy of assent and can endow with authority: that is, the *êthos* of the *polis* and not of the nobility alone.[25] This means that the aristocratic ideology embodied in Pindar's odes, with its embedded qualifications and admonitions, is not and cannot be simply the nobility's justification of itself but is in effect a "bilateral," negotiated scheme of valuation that their fellow-townsmen really do (or can) recognize as persuasive, and according to which the traditional nobility really can be found acceptable (or not) in the world of fifth-century city politics.

We might ask, though we cannot finally know, whether or to what degree not only the citizen audience but also the aristocratic component of that audience and the well-born choreuts themselves would have been persuaded by the kind of argumentation that *Isthmian* 3 presents. Would the aristocratic listener have been persuaded to identify with the civic *êthos* embodied in and projected by the ode, and to what degree did the choreuts' own performance of the ode constitute an avowal of personally felt assent? Judging from the apparent fact that Pindar's *epinikia*, after their first performance, subsequently were widely diffused through reperformance in symposiastic settings, and since the symposium was chiefly an aristocratic venue, it is at least arguable and indeed quite likely that Pindar's odes generally were persuasive for aristocratic audiences. Further, we know that at least one ode was publicly inscribed in golden letters at a temple of Athena (in the city of Lindos, on Rhodes), and it is possible that something similar was done for the other odes as well. Pindar often uses language that portrays the ode being presented as an enduring object meant to outlast the moment of performance: in *Nemean* 5 for example, he (or the chorus) describes himself (itself) as setting up a "stele . . . whiter than Parian stone" from which "my voice" may be heard (ll. 81, 85–86).[26] In *Olympian* 1, the victor is said to be adorned "with folds of song," *hymnôn ptuchais*: the word *ptuchê*, "fold" or "leaf" or "layer," can also mean the folded boards of writing tablets, or by extension the painted boards on which public documents (such as Solon's laws) were preserved. Such locutions do suggest that at least some song texts were intended for public preservation and display. An ode preserved on stone or wood—or even a papyrus text dedicated to and stored in a temple or public building—would have been seen as a permanent possession and ornament of the city itself and not only of the person or family that had originally commissioned it. If this is so, it then seems reasonable to say that the argumentation of Pindar's odes probably did offer a "negotiated" scheme of civic ethics that both aristocrats and *astoi* could accept and even find desirable.

Remember, again, that Pindar's poetry is set in a world that offers virtually no example of a successfully functioning democracy and in a cultural situation fraught with possibilities for faction, polarization, and violent *stasis*—the sort of crisis that constantly troubled the Greek *poleis* in the archaic period. Such crises, if they produced any significant political change at all, most typically yielded not democracy but rule by tyrant, that is, the sort of autocratic "corrector" that Theognis fears Megara will "give birth" to. Tyranny, or dictatorship founded on a populist appeal to righting the wrongs of the former ruling class (who were likely to suffer banishment), was probably the chief political innovation of the seventh to fifth centuries.[27] It is not as if Pindar in the 470s has available to himself a fully fledged, coherent, democratic ideology that he can choose simply to embrace or reject. The most apparent choices in Pindar's world are between oligarchy, tyranny (or perhaps kingship), and the social chaos of bloody, factionalized feuding; and as I have observed already, the key term in this world for measuring the quality of any political regime is not "democracy" but "justice," *dikê*. Like Theognis, then, Pindar stands precariously balanced between the claims of oligarchy, justice, and the "despot-loving populace" (*Theognidea* 850), while attempting to effect a mutually acceptable accommodation between aristocrats and "townsmen" on the basis of a sharable sense of civic ethics. What is striking is that this accommodation is effected in the very gesture of praise itself, and in the *grounds of praise* mobilized in Pindar's enthymematic argumentation. Even if the gesture of praise itself is a conventional requirement of encomiastic discourse, the audience that is effectively persuaded to join that praise is also persuaded to commit itself to the enthymematic grounds on which the praise is founded. What is also striking is that, to judge from Pindar's clear status as the preeminent poet of his time, from the astonishing fees his clients were willing to pay to be praised by him in public, from the golden inscription at Lindos, and from his subsequent status in antiquity as the greatest of lyric poets, it seems that his enthymemes really were (and continued to be) powerfully persuasive.

Olympian 1

I now turn back to *Olympian* 1, Harold Bloom's "truest paradigm for Western lyric" and certainly one of the best examples of lyric argumentation in Pindar. It also may be Pindar's most fully representative poem, and it is arguably his best. As William

Mullen has noted, one of the speakers in Lucian's *The Dream or the Cock* calls *Olympian* 1 "the most splendid of all songs" (7) and appears to be citing a received opinion established centuries before by Hellenistic editors. *Olympian* 1 was placed first in the collection of Pindar's four books of *epinikia*, despite the fact that this violated the usual order, which was determined by type of event—in part because the Olympic games were the most prestigious of all (and thus occupied the first of the four books), in part because the victor being praised, Hieron of Syracuse, was a more important person than any other victor praised by Pindar, and in part because the ode itself was sufficiently dazzling to justify the rearrangement. *Olympian* 1 thus became, in effect, the overture and keynote to all of Pindar's odes.[28]

One of the most characteristic features of *Olympian* 1 and Pindar's poetry in general is the use of narrative expansions—extended passages of legendary or mythical material, or what have often and mistakenly been seen as gorgeous digressions—in order to amplify and intensify the grounds on which the poem develops its enthymemes.[29] In *Isthmian* 3, such expansions could have arisen, had Pindar added them, from the key topoi of the poem's argument: very probably a myth of god-bestowed good fortune being granted to or withdrawn from men of upright and "slanting" hearts; perhaps a myth connected also to the legend of Hercules, insofar as the poem was delivered in the context of a festival of Hercules and was about a Nemean victory (indeed, Pindar's glancing reference to the "deep-chested / lion's deep vale" alludes to the Hercules legend); perhaps a tale of the famed accomplishments of Kleonymos or the Kleonymidai; perhaps a tale about those who "went their ways" or the changes wrought by "whirling days." These sorts of expansions do, of course, occur in *Isthmian* 4.

The often dazzling and baroquely figured brilliance of the narrative "digressions" or amplifications in Pindar's poetry, the stunningly abrupt transitions by which they are often introduced, and the difficulty that modern readers sometimes have in reconstructing a myth's precise relevance to the particular occasion and overt purpose of an ode, as well as the complex stylistic and prosodic texture of his poetry in general, have created for many an impression of a "surplus" of meaning or aesthetic power, a "sublimity" in the romantic sense that goes beyond the poem's generic and situational requirements. Pindar seems, especially to readers of romantic inclination, to transcent the supposedly mere praise of athletic victors as he rises to the nobler heights of creative imagination. Thus Bloom, in praising *Olympian* 1 as paradigmatic lyric, and assuming that "[l]yric celebrates the poetic self, despite every denial," declares also that "[t]he first Olympic ode . . . overtly celebrates Hieron of Syracuse [for a horse-racing victory], yet the horse and rider more fully and implicitly celebrated are Pegasus and Pindar."[30]

Such an assertion could only have been made in either complete ignorance or blithe dismissal of the two decades of Pindaric scholarship that had preceded it; indeed none is recognized, and no evidence is offered for the claim. Note too that it asks us, once again, to imagine an extremely foolish, rhetorically and sociopolitically obtuse Pindar. Hieron, who had recently succeeded his brother Gelon as the *tyrannos* of Syracuse (but using the title of *basileus*), was at the time one of the most powerful and able rulers in the Hellenic world. In 480 B.C. the same year that the Athenians had won their spectacular, salvific naval victory over the Persians at

Salamis—perhaps even on the same day—Gelon and his brothers had won an almost equally spectacular victory over the Carthaginians at the battle of Himera, a battle in which Hieron fought and won an equal share of the fame and glory (Diodorus 11.51.1–2; Herodotus 7.165–167).[31] The Athenian victory of 480 at Salamis had been followed in 479 by the final defeat of the Persians at Plataia. The horse-race victory celebrated in *Olympian* 1 occurred in 476, the first Olympiad to be held after the great Greek victories, and two years after Hieron had inherited the rulership in Syracuse. At that Olympiad, in effect, the Hellenic world celebrated its double triumph over the Carthaginian and Persian threats from west and east respectively.[32] Hieron was a hero of Panhellenic "liberty," and his Olympic victory could only have redoubled and reconfirmed his already considerable prestige. Had *Olympian* 1 really celebrated "Pegasus and Pindar" more than Hieron and his horse (Pherenikos), even sneakily, it is hard to believe that the exceptionally capable, cultured, and ruthless Hieron would not have noticed and would not have been deeply offended. (On Hieron's ruthlessness, see Diodorus 11.48.3–49.4, 11.67.3–4.) Moreover, it is hard to believe that the audience who witnessed the performance would not have been offended either. Some part of Hieron's glory, after all, belonged to Syracuse as well. For its defeat of the Carthaginians the city could be seen, like Athens in Pindar's dithyramb, as a "bulwark" of Greek "freedom" (fr. 76, 77).[33] If Pindar really had praised himself above Hieron and the Syracusans, or if *Olympian* 1 had really been somehow more about himself or "the poetic self," such a presumptuous gesture would have seemed, at the very least, a gross violation of the ethics of guest-friendship and gift exchange within which every epinician transaction was conducted.[34] According to the conventions of that ethic, Pindar went to Syracuse as Hieron's guest; the *epinikion* he presented was his friendly gift to host and city; and Pindar's pay was Hieron's hospitable gift in recompense on behalf of himself, his house, and Syracuse.

Peter Rose has offered a more sophisticated and reasoned version of Bloom's argument. Rose says:

> [t]he nearest thing to subversive activity I attribute to Pindar is the self-consciousness of his affirmation that he alone as poet controls access to that realm of full gratification which might otherwise appear as the automatic consequence of inherited wealth, political power, and athletic success. . . . The inner logic of [a Pindaric *epinikion*] leads both to the fervent realization of aristocratic ideology in image, structure, argument, and to the transcendent negation of that ideology in its celebration and demonstration of the poet's mastery of access to a realm of being free of pain and guilt, full of sensuous gratification, and quite beyond the limited reality of the Greek ruling class. Indeed, it is in the end a moot point whether the net effect of the poem is more a celebration of their power or his.[35]

This is a much more careful formulation, grounded in an extended examination of *Pythian* 10. The argument is that the rhetorical effectivity of Pindar's aristocratic ideology is mitigated or "negated" by the poet's revelation, through his aesthetically dazzling poetic skill and his "deeply integrative imagination," of a "higher order of being" beyond the compartmentalizations and brutalities of the actual political order.[36] However, as we have already seen in *Isthmian* 3, the "inner logic" of

Pindar's poetry, its enthymematic argumentation, in fact portrays the "realm of full gratification" not as the "automatic consequence of inherited wealth, political power, and athletic success" but as the far from automatic reward of an excellence that includes an upright, sensible, and civically responsible ethicality, an excellence that deserves reward and praise only so long as it is maintained. Further, the notion that a poem like *Olympian* 1 might celebrate Pindar's aesthetic power more than Hieron's *aretê* leads us back, once again, to the problem of imagining Pindar as rhetorically and socially obtuse or Hieron as too dull to notice that he has been publicly slighted. Or, for that matter, we must imagine that all of his house, his entourage, the constantly-competitive poets, intellectuals, and artists gathered at his court, and rest of the assembled audience, were likewise imperceptive. Further, to say that the aesthetic experience offered by Pindar is "quite beyond the limited reality of the Greek ruling class" seems highly unpersuasive, since it is they who hire him and make the performance possible: Pindar is part of their reality. Finally, to recuperate the poem as a sumptuous aesthetic experience that operates somehow independently of its ideological or argumentative substance is, it seems to me, to fall back into a kind of formalism that empties and trivializes the poem, rendering it as little more than an object of luxury consumption for the rich, with Pindar presenting himself as chief purveyor. It makes more sense to consider the very real aesthetic power of Pindar's poetry as an aspect of its enthymematic argumentation—as one of the *pisteis* from which the poem's persuasiveness arises—and as part of its function as civic discourse.

But to the poem. *Olympian* 1 is generally believed to have been performed at Syracuse. Since Hieron was not actually the rider but the sponsor of the winning horse, as was usual in that type of competition, it seems probable that he did not personally attend the games. But Pindar's references to the topography of Olympia suggest that the poem *could* have been performed there, or that the poem fictively places itself and the scene of its *kômos* at the site of the victory. Pindar gestures toward the tomb of Pelops, whose myth the poem recounts, and the hill of Kronos— where he says he hopes he will *come back* someday to celebrate a yet "sweeter" victory, "finding the path of helpful words returned (*elthôn*) to the far-seen hill of Kronos" (109–111), which suggests that the celebration *now* is happening there. Likewise, the poem's famous opening line, "[b]est of all things is water,"[37] can be understood as a reference to the well-watered terrain of Olympia, which was (and is) situated at the confluence of the two rivers, the Alpheos and Kladeos, that formed its western and southern boundaries. In consequence Olympia featured (and still features) a lushness of greenery unusual for Greece and was considered especially beautiful in antiquity. There was also a connection between Olympia's waters and Syracuse: the Arethusa fountain at Syracuse, located in the older part of the city on the island of Ortygia, was fed by a freshwater spring that was believed, via hydrological fantasy, to originate from the Alpheos river.[38]

If *Olympian* 1 is spoken (or sung and danced) from a spot inside the sacred enclosure at Olympia—in front of the Syracusan treasury, or about one hundred yards west at the *prytaneion*, where the games' presiding magistrates resided and where the victors traditionally were feasted—the topographic features that Pindar gestures toward are all nearby and possibly in view. (The Syracusan treasury stood near the

western end of the row of the city treasuries on the north edge of the sacred enclosure; it occupied a point about halfway between the stadium, at the eastern end of
the enclosure, and the *prytaneion* at the western end; the city treasuries contained
ritual objects used by their delegations of *theoroi*, "ambassadors" to the games, and
possibly also some athletic equipment.) Indeed, if the poem is spoken from in front
of the Syracusan treasury, the audience is in effect placed in a patch of open ground
between the tombs of Pelops and his wife, Hippodameia (the central part of the
myth recounts how Pelops won her) and beside the altar of Zeus, with the hill of
Kronos directly in front of them, rising up behind the Syracusan and other treasuries. Or if the audience is facing the *prytaneion's* front porch, the "far-seen" hill of
Kronos may again be visible in the background and somewhat to the right, while
the Kladeos river is about one hundred yards away to the audience's left, on the far
side of a space that probably was occupied by a gymnasium. The extant gymnasium
remnant, which dates from the second century B.C. adjoins an older (fourth-
century) palaestra building, which had a water-channel running round all four of its
sides and entering from its northeast corner, almost directly opposite the *prytaneion*.
This fact suggests that even in Pindar's time this spot may have featured some sort
of fountain or watering-place for athletes: "best of all things is water."

But let us remain with the default assumption—that Hieron remained in Syracuse, and that the poem was performed there, during a victory-*kômos* held on the
return of the Syracusan delegation from Olympia—and assume as well that Pindar's
gestures toward the scene place the song's act of utterance, and its audience, fictively within the sacred enclosure of the games. Possible performance sites in Syracuse include Hieron's house, wherever that may have been; the Syracusan agora,
which now contains the large, sacrificial altar of Hieron II, dating from Hellenistic
times; or the sanctuary of Zeus, which lies beside the Cyane river about two miles
from the city proper; or possibly the fountain of Arethusa. This fountain stood (and
stands) near the water's edge, and if *Olympian* 1 was performed there the sea would
have been in view, and possibly the harbor where Syracuse's warships were kept: the
city at that time was becoming a major naval power.

The poem is composed of four twenty-nine-line traids (strophe, antistrophe,
epode) for a total of 116 lines, with Pindar's telling of the myth of Pelops extending
from the first epode to the first half of the fourth strophe, coming to rest at Pelops's
tomb, which is said to be "much-frequented with many visitors about the altar"
(93). This seventy-two-line telling is bracketed, at beginning and end, with references to the poem's occasion and Pindar's concluding gestures of praise. (If we remove the myth, what remains is a poem of about fourty-four lines). The opening
strophe and antistrophe begin from a priamel—an introductory *gradatio* that passes
through a series of possible subjects for praise before arriving at the focal topic—
invoking water as "best of all things," gold shining by firelight as the most splendid
manifestation of wealth, and the Olympic games as the greatest of athletic contests
and the best of all subjects for epinician song:

> but if to sing of games
> is your wish, my heart,
> look no further than the sun
> for any star by day warmly shining through the empty sky,

nor shall we proclaim a contest greater than Olympia;
from whence the much-remarked song disseminates itself
with poets' cunning, to celebrate
the son of Kronos [Zeus] as they come to the rich
and blessed hearth of Hieron (3–11)

These lines complete the first strophe. The song is portrayed, again, as originating from Olympia. "Poets' cunning," *sophôn mêtiessi*, suggests more specifically the *faculty of counsel* or wisdom (*mêtis*) which belongs to *sophoi*, the skillful/wise, and which is disseminated (*amphiballetai*, "thrown round") in the "much-remarked song" (*polyphatos hymnos*) of epinician poets. It is important that the song's wise counsels (or the *sophoi* bearing them) have now arrived at Hieron's "hearth" to celebrate *Zeus*, the god of kingship, whose shrine at Olympia was the central feature of the sacred enclosure—and whose sanctuary at Syracuse was large and important. The word rendered here as "come," *hikomenous*, more specifically means "arriving" or "approaching as a suppliant." And the word rendered as "hearth," *hestian*, can also mean "dwelling, altar, shrine," and is related to *hestiasis*, "reception feast," while the word "celebrate," *keladein* ("to hurrah"), evokes a sound resembling that of rushing water, or a crowd noise of mingled shouting, cheering, and singing. Where is Hieron's "hearth"? We have a conflated image: Hieron's dwelling-place, the scene of a *hestiasis*, and an altar or shrine of Zeus, perhaps somewhere near the sound or sight of water, where the victory-*kômos* has arrived to be received and where Pindar's *epinikion* is "spreading round" celebration and good counsel. Perhaps it is after sunset, as the gold shining by firelight suggests; or perhaps, as the reference to the sun suggests, it is sometime prior to sunset. We could be in either Syracuse or Olympia, or fictively in both at once.

The next lines (the first antistrophe) introduce Hieron and further redefine or complicate the scene:

. . . Hieron,
who tends the scepter of laws in sheep-rich
Sicily, culling the topmost part of every excellence,
and is glorified as well
in fine music,
such as we men play
often around the friendly table. But the Dorian lyre from its peg
take down, if any of Pisa's[39] and Pherenikos's grace
enthralled your mind to sweetest thoughts,
when beside Alpheos he sped. [11–20]

Hieron is here portrayed and greeted as a great *basileus* responsible for justice and as a patron of "music" or lyric poetry (*mousikê*)—he did in fact entertain a number of poets as his "guests" at court, including Simonides, Bacchylides, and Aeschylus, as well as Pindar—a fact for which Pindar later praises Hieron as equally "expert in fine things" and "sovereign in power" (104). Hieron is compared implicitly to the Hesiodic good *basileus*, who is "from Zeus" but also favored by the Muses. Notably, the description of Hieron as "tending" the laws of a country that is "sheep-rich" while culling the best of every "excellence" and the "finest" music, also portrays the king as shepherd: "finest," *aôtôi*, means "fine wool" and by extension "the best" of things. Hieron's "culling" is represented as sheep-shearing, something the king-"shepherd" is entitled to as long as he tends his "flocks" by maintaining the rule of justice. In effect, then, Pindar's poem comes as a suppliant to "celebrate the son of Kronos" at Hieron's hearth/altar/feast and has come to praise the godly image of a good *basileus* and good "shepherd" that may be seen—or not—reflected in the person and deeds of Hieron. Meanwhile, Pindar's reference to the "music" that "we men play / often around the friendly table" describes not so much the present scene of the *kômos* but the more private, symposiastic scenes of poetic performance at Hieron's court. However, with the song's gesture of "taking down" the Dorian lyre "from its peg" (where it hangs on the wall), the symposiastic context is also layered onto the broader scene and is conflated with a victory-*kômos* and *hestiasis* simultaneously taking place, fictively speaking, at both Syracuse and Olympia, at both house/hearth and shrine/altar, at both private banquet and public feast, and in both sacred enclosure and civic space.

Pindar, then, effects in his opening strophes—or attempts—a psychagogic "transport" of his audience into the layered scene he has invoked. Like Hesiod's bard or eloquent *basileus* he deflects the thinking of the listener, who may be well inebriated, from the quotidian present into a conflated and somewhat disorienting place and time that will provide the frame and context for the argument of the poem and the "counsels" it disseminates. This deflection then is taken one step further, in the next five lines, as Pindar briefly declares that Pherenikos's speed "beside Alpheos," which bordered the southern edge of the racecourse, has brought a victory to Heiron and made his fame shine "in Lydian Pelops's settlement abounding in good men" (24), meaning Olympia in particular, or more properly the territory surrounding it (Elis and Pisa) and more broadly the entire Peloponnese. This mention of the name of Pelops immediately produces (in the first epode) an abrupt transition to the myth:

> in Lydian Pelops's settlement abounding in good men;
> of him was enamored the mighty earth-upholder
> Poseidon, when from the purified cauldron Klotho took him
> equipped with a shoulder of gleaming ivory. (24–27)

This quick shift of scene, and the sudden emergence of Pelops from the cauldron *in the midst of the celebration*, must have been startling for Pindar's audience. As this audience would certainly have known, the scene that now is superimposed on the *kômos/hestiasis* is the feast to which Pelops's father Tantalos invited the gods and for which he killed and served up Pelops chopped in pieces in a stew. Discovering what had been done, the gods reconstituted Pelops, all but his shoulder (which Demeter unwittingly had eaten), necessitating a replacement shoulder made of ivory; and when Poseidon saw the devinely rebuilt Pelops resurrected from the stewpot, he fell in love. So the conflated scene has now been further modified. The "hearths" of Syracuse, Olympia, and Tantalos's house (on Mt. Sipylos, in Lydia) are superimposed, and placed in a conflated time that renders the victory being celebrated, the present moment, and the mythic past as simultaneous, so that Hieron and Pelops can themselves be superimposed and explicitly and implicitly compared.

Why Pelops? As William Mullen has remarked, the Pelops myth seems partly to have been a convenient solution to an inventional problem: "Hieron's status as a western colonial [i.e., as ruler of Syracuse] meant, among other things, that Pindar was unable . . . to come up with a mythical narrative and a choreographic realization that could draw into their design any heroic dead dwelling near the site of the performance or any sacred monuments of topography there."[40] Hieron wants an *epinikion* that will help to further glorify his Panhellenic reputation, but Syracuse—unlike the older cities of mainland Greece—has no authoritative, Panhellenic hero myth with which Hieron or his family can be linked. So Pindar chooses Pelops, the legendary first great king of the Peloponnese ("Pelops's island," the entire land mass of southern Greece), whose tomb is in the sacred enclosure at Olympia and whose myth is closely connected with the Olympic games: Pelops won both Hippodameia and his kingship by defeating and killing her father Oinomaos in a chariot race.[41] One benefit of choosing the Pelops myth, as we have seen, is that it enables Pindar to superimpose the more famous topographic features of Olympia on the performance scene at Syracuse, and, for purposes of symposiastic reperformance at later times and other places, it also enables Hieron to be framed within that famous topography, as if he stands crowned with the sacred olive wreath beside the tomb of Pelops. Further, Hieron and Pelops may be associated with each other insofar as their respective kingdoms both originated as colonial foundations: Pelops came to mainland Greece from Lydia, in what is now western Turkey. Both Pelops's family (the Pelopidai) and Hieron's family (the Deinomidai) can be seen as kingdom and dynasty founders. Moreover, from the Pelopidai descended such legendary kings as Atreus, Agamemnon, and Menelaos, a "fact" that may hint at a dynastic future for the Deinomidai. All this makes for suitably glorious comparison.

But clearly the most important feature of the Pelops myth, for Pindar's purposes, is Pelops's relation with Poseidon—it is the first thing Pindar mentions when Pelops is introduced. This relation makes Pelops, like Melissos in *Isthmian 3*, the beloved and indeed "unwounded" *pais* of a god, divinely sponsored in his undertakings; and so, by implication, is Hieron also. As Pindar says in his closing praises, "[a] god is minded to be your guardian, / Hieron, and to watch over your / concerns" (106–109). This notion is crucially amplified in the central portion of the myth. On the night before the race with Oinomaos, Pelops walks "beside the gray sea alone in darkness" (71) and calls on "the loud-thundering Good-Trident god" (72–74) to help him, invoking Poseidon's reciprocal obligation for love gifts given in the past (75–76) and pointing out that Oinomaos already has defeated and killed Hippodameia's thirteen previous suitors (76–81). Pelops then makes his central plea:

> the great adventure never takes hold of a strengthless man.
> Since everyone must die, why should anyone
> vainly sit in darkness stewing an anonymous old age,
> without a share of everything fine? But to me this contest
> will be offered; may you give the wished-for outcome. (81–85)

This is an admirably concise articulation of the heroic ethic on which the traditional aristocracies had staked their claims to honor and prestige. Poseidon, of course, is persuaded and gives Pelops what he needs—Poseidon's horses—to win the race and Hippodameia. The point would seem to be that Hieron, like Pelops, has dared and won great things: the high and dangerous "adventures" that present themselves only to heroic worthies and never to "strengthless men," trials of strength and ability that separate the god-favored chosen ones from the rest. The audience is to think not only of the sacred horse-race at Olympia but also of Hieron's role in the battle of Himera and his subsequent success in making Syracuse a dominant power in the western Mediterranean. As with Melissos's second athletic victory, Hieron's Olympic victory confirms the god-assisted status that has enabled him to dare and win preeminence; this status, in turn, confirms that Hieron has the sort of excellence that wins the love and favor of the gods.

Pindar, then, develops in Hieron's praise an enthymematic argument that resembles in general terms the argument for Melissos. But by retelling the myth of Pelops as an archetype with which the deeds of Hieron resonate, Pindar endows that argument with considerably greater power. When Pindar (or the chorus) delivers as an enthymematic cap the declaration that "[a] god is minded to be your guardian . . . and to watch over your concerns," it arrives—or is meant to arrive—with resounding and ample effect.

However, as mind-bending psychagogy, as amplification for argumentative topoi, and as a source of enthymematic "proof" or persuasion (*pistis*), Pindar's appropriation and retelling of the Pelops myth also bears with it an admonitory aspect, a conditionality that provides a scale of judgment against which Hieron's *êthos* can be measured. The Pelops myth has dark shadows. These include, on one hand, the "fact" (according to legend) that Pelops defeated Oinomaos and secured his kingdom not only through Poseidon's help but also through treachery and murder, and on the other hand, the tale of Tantalos's evil fate. Tantalos, as Pindar's audience well knew, was guilty of the presumptuousness and excess that bring retribution from the gods, and was condemmed to eternal torment. Different myths recounted different versions of his crimes, most of which involved some form of profaning the sacred or some attempt to deceive the gods; but clearly the key crime was the *hubris* and impiety of feeding his own son's flesh to his divine guests as a trick or test of their peerceptiveness. This topic of murder/outrage/treachery is thematized in the traditional myth of Pelops also. Pelops bribed Myrtilos, Oinomaos's charioteer, to sabotage Oinomaos's chariot by removing the pins that secured the wheels to the axles: the chariot collapsed, and Oinomaos became entangled in the reins and was dragged to death. (One version says that Hippodameia, in love with the noble-looking Pelops, did the bribing.) To conceal this crime Pelops murdered Myrtilos, for which the dying Myrtilos placed a curse on Pelops and all his descendants. This curse produced recurrent episodes of tragedy, including the fratricide of Pelops's favorite son by his brothers (whom Pelops then banished), and the grim history of the house of Atreus at Mycenae.[42] In sum, both Tantalos and Pelops themselves were guilty of acts of outrageous *hubris*, and from them descended a family history fraught with dynastic struggles, murder, violation, and sacrilege. These grimmer aspects of the Pelops myth may be applicable to Hieron. Two years after Himera, Hieron succeeded his brother Gelon, who seems to have died rather suddenly, through a vicious struggle with his brothers; and he consolidated Syracuse's power through subjugating the other Sicilian *poleis* (Diodorus 11.48.3–49.4). Indeed, Hieron's rule was eventually to distinguish itself not for mildness or for justice, for which Gelon had been admired, but for ruthlessness, greed treachery, and violence (Diodorus 11.67.3–4).[43]

Given the darker shadows and potential implications of the Pelops myth, then, Pindar's sudden invocation of Pelops and the cannibalistic feast of Tantalos—with Hieron looking on—may well have seemed more than startling to his audience. It may have been outright alarming. That Pindar recognizes the dangerous implications of the myth is evident in one of the more famous features of *Olympian* 1, namely his disagreement with the traditional tale. This disagreement is announced, with fanfare, immediately after the emergence of Pelops from the cauldron:

Klotho took him
equipped with a shoulder of gleaning ivory.
Marvels indeed are many, but somehow mortal speech passing the true account
beguiles with ornate lies in cunningly crafted tales.
And Grace, who fashions all soothing things for mortals,
bestows honor and often intends the unbelievable
to be believable;
but the days to come
are the wisest witnesses.
Fitting it is for a man to speak well about the gods; there is less cause for blame.
Son of Tantalos, of you, and against the earlier tales, I will declare . . . (26–36)

He will declare, that is, that he cannot believe that gods would eat human flesh. Pelops was not killed and eaten, even partially; rather, he was carried off to Mount Olympus by the love-smitten Poseidon, just as Ganymede was carried off by Zeus at another time, and envious neighbors explained the disappearance with a malicious tale about a cannibalistic feast (37–52). Pindar caps this revisionary passage with the declaration that "[p]rofitlessness has often been the lot of evil-sayers" (53), after which he recounts the fate of Tantalos as illustration (54–64).

Does Pindar have the authority to rewrite, by personal fiat, a well-known Panhellenic myth? Perhaps, but probably not. Moreover, Pindar's revision is rather problematic: If Pelops was not eaten, why does Pindar first present him as resurrected from the stewpot with an ivory shoulder?[44] Moreover, if no abomination was committed at the feast, why is Tantalos condemned to eternal torment? To a certain extent, perhaps, Pindar cannot avoid mentioning these things because they are familiar features of the myth—which underscores his inability to rewrite it—and because the ivory shoulder (probably a large bone of some kind) was a cult object exhibited at Olympia.[45] But why, again, invoke this myth at all? Pindar could, perhaps, have chosen the myth of Hercules, which also is connected to Olympia: Hercules held the first Olympic games, it was believed, by organizing a footrace among his brothers (Pausanias 5.7.6–7), probably in honor of Zeus and Hera, both of whom had shrines in the sacred enclosure; comparing Hieron to Hercules certainly would amplify his glory, *if* it could be done persuasively. Similarly, the myth of Alpheos and Arethusa might have been a possibility, especially since it linked Olympia with the founding of Syracuse, though it may not have had sufficiently grandiose implications.[46]

The Pelops myth may have had a more obvious connection to a horse-racing victory, though Pelops won a chariot-race, which is not quite the same thing. But it seems most reasonable to believe that Pindar has chosen this myth, and has chosen to engage in an elaborate, proleptic denial of its darker aspects, precisely because similar things already are being said about the ruthless Hieron. Hieron certainly had enemies and enviers who would have been more than willing to say about him the worst things that people were capable of believing about tyrants: consider Alcaeus's poetic invectives against Pittacus, the tyrant of Mytilene, whom later tradition would regard as a "sage." Pindar's denial of what he represents as malicious rumors about Tantalos and Pelops acknowledges the presence of what he denies and brings it emphatically into the foreground of attention. Insofar as Pindar's commission in *Olympian* 1 is to enhance Hieron's Panhellenic reputation, the darker tales about Hieron *that the audience already may know* are part of the rhetorical situation and must be confronted. Thus Pindar places emphasis on the power of rumor to generate "cunningly crafted" lies, on the power of poetry to enhance and disseminate such lies, on the potential danger and blame inherent in telling or disseminating falsehoods that offend the gods (and the powerful), and finally, on the notion that "the days to come / are the wisest witnesses." Pindar, in effect, leaves in place the possibility that the grimmer stories about both Pelops and Hieron may be true, while declaring that he cannot bring himself to believe them and that the wiser, safer course is to "speak well about" gods and legendary figures—the actual term is *daimonôn*, "spirits/demons," which has wider and more ambiguous application than *theôn*, "gods"—although in doing this, as Pindar explicitly suggests, he may be making the unbelievable seem believable, or the false true, or (to borrow the Protagorean slogan) the lesser argument the greater, just as the Muses do in Hesiod's *Theogony*. But while Pindar prefers to "speak well about" Pelops/Hieron and "stand back" (*aphistamai*, 52) from "evil-saying," the proof of truth or falsehood will be given in the "witnessing" of "days to come": that is, the truth or falsehood about the quality of Heiron's rule will be demonstrated in what he does from this day forward. But again, the "fact" that divine favor has granted Hieron an Olympic victory functions, like Melissos's second victory, as evidence that Hieron has maintained his *aretê*, at least up to the present moment, and that the bad tales told about him probably are malicious rumors.

In sum, Pindar's use of the Pelops myth enables him to confront and dispel the negative elements in Hieron's budding reputation as a ruthless tyrant—whether these elements are by 476 B.C. incipient or actual, rumor or thruth—while making a persuasive case for praise in the present moment. It also enables Pindar to present himself in agonistic relation to tradition, meeting it as an equal and contesting its claims and thus to enhance his own authority as a practitioner of wisdom-skill. But what is dispelled for the moment is not erased, and remains as an admonitory presence and a future possibility. As Pindar has suggested in the opening strophe of this ode, he has come with his song to "spread around" both praise and counsel *in honor of Zeus,* and thus in honor of the Hesiodic good *basileus* "from Zeus" that Hieron may or may not embody. Insofar as Pelops/Hieron fulfills that image, the praise is his. Insofar as he fails to meet the criterion and strays into hubristic excess like Tantalos and Pelops (and their descendants), his reputation must suffer the consequences. The praise, meanwhile, remains with Zeus, and with the good *basileus* in whom a Zeus-like image can be seen reflected. Pindar's praise for Hieron, in other words, invokes the criteria by which a ruler like Hieron will eventually be judged, when "the days to come" have done their "witnessing." These are the criteria by which Diodorus, writing some centuries later, will judge the reign of Hieron to have been vicious, violent, and ignoble.

All this is brought together in the final antistrophe and epode of the song. Having brought the myth to rest at Pelops's tomb, and having declared that an Olympic victor for the rest of his life enjoys a "honeyed happiness / as far as games go" (98–99), Pindar then concludes:

> [b]ut always the day-by-day goodness
> is the highest thing that comes to any man. My fate it is to crown
> that man [over there] with horseman's song
> in Aeolic measure.
> And I believe there is no
> guest-host, equally expert in fine things and also more sovereign in power,
> whom in our time we shall adorn with glorious folds of song.
> A god is minded to be your guardian,
> Hieron, and to watch over your
> concerns; and if he does not abandon you,
> a yet sweeter thing I hope
> to celebrate with swift chariot, finding the path of helpful words
> returned to the far-seen hill of Kronos. So for me
> the Muse keeps yet the mightiest missile in her power;
> men are great in one or another way. But the utmost fulfills itself
> in kings. Look no further beyond!
> Let it be yours to walk this time upon the heights, and mine likewise with victors
> to keep company, being far-famed for wisdom among all Hellenes. (99–116)

Pindar does several things in this conclusion. First of all, he combines in an enthymematic "cap" both the encomiastic and admonitory arguments embodied in the myth of Pelops, and endows them with the emotive resonances of that myth— resonances that would seem to range from wonder and exhilaration to terror and foreboding. Pindar's effort to momentarily hold in check the possibilities for terror/foreboding, insofar as it is persuasive, releases the audience into an intensified mood of wonder/exhilaration and celebration, and makes the gestures of praise that much more effective. At the same time, Pindar invokes the future, in which Hieron's patron god may or may not abandon him, and the possibility for another and yet greater occasion for praise *if Hieron can continue to maintain his kingly excellence*. The Muse's "mightiest missile" (or arrow) is waiting in reserve; the last word has not been said. Second, Pindar foregrounds in general terms the ultimate criteria for judging a person of Hieron's status when "the days to come" have testified: not Olympic victories, which confer a limited sort of happiness, but "the day-by-day goodness" required for a *basileus* who must maintain the rule of *dikê*; not preeminence as a warlord only but the tempering of "sovereign power" with knowledge of "fine things," by which Pindar means Hieron's relationship with poets or more generally with *sophoi*, bearers of discursive wisdom-skill, and the counsels they disseminate; and not the exercise of kingly power for self-aggrandizement or the pursuit of unlimited desire, but the restraint of hubristic excess by looking "no further beyond" what constitutes the greatness of a king. Third, as these criteria suggest, Pindar invokes as an essential of good rulership the bard-*basileus* relationship that Hesiod invokes in his "Hymn to the Muses": the best *basileus* is "from Zeus" and is also favored by the Muses; from the domain of poetic discourse the *basileus* derives the terms of thought and the paradigms of eloquence that constitute the wisdom-skill, the rhetorical *sophia*, by which he can effectively maintain the rule of *dikê* in civic life.

This is the point of Pindar's final lines: he and Hieron, bard and *basileus*, stand side by side "upon the heights" in kingly and poetic preeminence, in Hesiodic symbiosis, before the civic audience for which the poem has been designed. This is not a praising of "Pegasus and Pindar" more than "horse and rider"; kingly status, which is "from Zeus" (while poets are from Apollo and the Muses), is still the highest and grandest greatness in Pindar's world. But bard and *basileus* have a reciprocal relation. Because Pindar can claim to share the "heights" of preeminence with Hieron—each having contested and won the peak of excellence in his respective domain—the praise and counsel that he offers can be seen as a gift exchange between equals: best poet to best king. Because Pindar can claim this status, the gift is meaningful, and the arguments he offers have authority *for the poem's intended audience*, which in this case is not only Hieron and his entourage but also the Syracusan audience present for the poem's original performance at the victory celebration, and more generally the Panhellenic audiences to whom the poem will continue to speak its arguments, for years to come, in symposiastic reperformances or through preservation as a publicly displayed or circulated text. At the same time, Pindar has this status *because he is called on by Hieron* or more generally by the great and is thereby validated as a "preeminent" Panhellenic poet. To sing for Hieron is a poet's victory. King and poet place crowns on one another's heads, standing together by the house/hearth/altar in the sacred enclosure of Olympia/Syracuse, by the tomb of Pelops and the shrine of Zeus, at a reception-feast/symposium, perhaps near water and/or the sound of cheering and singing voices, as the *kômos* is received and the night-long revels get underway. Even the symposiast and symposiastic audience of some later time, through reperformance of the poem's speech act, are fictively transported back into the "folds" of this layered, conflated scene where Pindar's argument transpires.

If *Olympian* 1 and *Isthmian* 3 can be said to embody a "truest paradigm for Western lyric"—and I am willing to argue that they do—clearly we are speaking in very general terms. Not every poem is an *epinikion*. Most broadly, as I have been suggesting, the paradigm these poems embody is that of enthymematic, epideictic argument in sung or spoken verse that is understood to function as civic discourse, or what the sophists would come to call *politikos logos*, and that is therefore also understood to engage its audience in a suasory transaction calling for an act of judgment in response to the enthymemes presented in our through the poem. Such judgment need not and probably often will not take the form of conscious, rational calculation and decision. It can take the form of an emotive identification with the stance presented in an enthymematic cap, or some other emotional response, or some expression of that response in physically embodied behavior (such as dancing). And "the enthymemes presented in or through the poem" include not only the poem's explicitly presented arguments but also the "in-thymatic" structures of interpretive inference and affect mobilized in a listener's psyche in response to what the poem overtly says. Because it operates as an enthymematic suasory transaction, the argumentation presented in (or through) a lyric poem must ultimately ground its persuasiveness in schemes of belief and valuation that the audience can accept as credible, authoritative, and even true. If the poem's argumentation is to function powerfully, those schemes of valuation and belief must bear emotive significance and resonance as well. This means that the "ideological" or presuppositional substrate of rhetorically astute lyric poetry is always and necessarily determined by the audience and that rhetorically effective lyric argumentation necessarily must be to some degree a bilaterally negotiated construct. Poetry that fails to meet this condition with any given audience will fail to be persuasive (and, at an extreme, will be unintelligible). Thus Pindar's *epinikia* cannot simply be an imposition of aristocratic ideology on an unwilling or unwitting "middling" class.

At the same time, just as Pindar's argumentation works to support an accommodation between aristocrats and townsmen—by modifying the attitudes of a "reluctant aristocracy" while also persuading the *polis* to accept and value the modified, qualified version of civically or ethically responsible nobility presented in the poem—lyric poetry in general has the capability to mobilize resources to shape or modify the presuppositional grounds on which its enthymematic arguments depend. That is, audiences can be induced to commit themselves to altered or modified grounds of judgment, in the process of persuading them to commit to a particular "conclusion" in the form of a judgment/response regarding the poem's overt, focal issue(s). This principle underscores the rhetorical significance of Pindar's narrative amplifications and proleptic "digressions," which construct and amplify the argumentational topics that constitute the grounds on which the audience is asked to base its judgments/responses. It also underscores the rhetorical significance of the aesthetic and psychagogic effects exerted not only by those amplifications and "digressions" but also by the stylistic and prosodic texture of the poetry, by the dramatistic staging of the poem's speech act, by the (long lost) music and choreography to which it originally was set, and by the general spectacle of the performance in its komiastic scene. The "aesthetic appeal" or psychagogy arising from such sources must be counted as a *pistis* belonging to the more general category of *pathos,* and as part of the enthymematic *pisteis* available to lyric (or indeed any) poetry.

But, again, not all poems are *epinikia.* I will now consider some examples of less obviously public poetry.

8

Argumentation Indoors

Alcaeus and Sappho

Observe Alcaeus's nobility, brevity, and sweetness combined with forcefulness, and also his use of figures and his clarity, as far as that has not
been ruined by his dialect; and above all the *êthos* of his political poems.
Quite often if you were to strip away the meter, you would find political
rhêtoreia.

Dionysius of Halicarnassus, *On Imitation* 421s

And the [love] of the Lesbian [Sappho] . . . what else could it be but
this, the *technê erôtikê* of Socrates? . . . For what Alcibiades and
Charmides and Phaedrus were to him, this to the Lesbian were Gyrinna
and Atthis and Anactoria; and whatever to Socrates were his rival-artists
[*antitechnoi*] Prodicus and Gorgias and Thrasymachus and Protagoras, this
to Sappho were Gorgo and Andromeda; sometimes she censures them,
and sometimes she cross-examines and uses ironies just like those of
Socrates.

Maximus of Tyre, *Orations* 18.9

The first thing to say is that these statements cannot necessarily be taken as reliable, and indeed should be taken with many grains of salt. Alcaeus and Sappho
were active in the early sixth century B.C., about five and a half centuries before
Dionysius, and about seven centuries before Maximus.[1] Dionysius's reference to the
difficulty of reading Alcaeus's archaic dialect (Aeolic) is an index of that distance.
Both Dionysius and Maximus are, moreover, the inheritors of literary-biographical
traditions that all too often seem to have evolved as fanciful mixtures of fact and
fabulation, or as simple confusion, especially in the case of archaic poets about
whom there was little documented testimony—and this is perhaps most true for
Sappho.[2] Further, it might be argued that Dionysius and Maximus have projected
onto the poets a sophistic, rhetorical-critical interpretive frame that is anachronistic or that is, in Donald Russell's words, "fundamentally not equal to the task of ap-
praising" poetry.[3]

My argument in this chapter is, however, that Dionysius and Maximus probably have gotten it about right, even if there is a measure of the fanciful in what they say. Without a doubt their statements are fallible interpretive constructs rather than reports of documented fact or testimony; but we might also temper our skepticism by remembering that both of these writers certainly had access to more documents than we do now, including complete collections of the poets' poetry. The question, however, is to what degree their statements can be understood as reasonably persuasive metaphors, and that is the possibility I will pursue.

Both Alcaeus and Sappho can be thought to offer us a contrast to the more public kind of lyric represented by Pindar's *epinikia,* or by other kinds of choral and monodic song performed at city festivals, communal celebrations, or Panhellenic gatherings. Alcaeus very probably composed such poetry: Himerius mentions and paraphrases a *paian* to Apollo (*Orations* 48.10–11), "Menander Rhetor" mentions hymns to Hermes and Hephaestus (*On Epideictic* 149; see also Pausanias 7.20.4, 10.8.10), and there are extant fragments of hymns to Artemis, the Dioscuri, Athena, and Eros, as well as fragments of heroic narrative derived mainly from the Troy legend.[4] We know too that Sappho's repertoire included *epithalamia* performed at wedding celebrations—which could be regarded as a sort of female counterpart to *epinikia*—as well as songs to be performed at religious festivals by choruses of girls whom she had trained, or possibly by herself in solo performance. Fragments of some of these survive. But both Alcaeus and Sappho were and are most famed for what looks like "private" poetry, that is, poems that seem to have been meant for performance in symposiastic settings or small gatherings: Alcaeus's "stasiotic" (civil war) and other poems addressed to the *hetairoi,* "companions" that belonged to his faction in a losing struggle with Pittacus the tyrant-sage, and Sappho's erotic poems addressed to the women of her circle, whom she addressed likewise as *hetairai* in the sense of intimate "friends."[5]

However, the "private" or symposiastic lyrics of Alcaeus and Sappho also are embedded in the factionalized, turbulent society and politics of sixth-century Lesbos—Alcaeus's poetry quite obviously so, but Sappho's no less so. And when the poetry is viewed from this perspective, the rhetorical interpretive frames applied by Dionysius and Maximus acquire heuristic value and become much more intelligible and persuasive. For as Dionysius recognizes, Alcaeus's lyric poetry is indeed a form of *rhêtoreia,* "oratory," offering argument and exhortation on ethico-political themes for his *hetairoi.* As for Maximus, we should probably discount his portrayal of Sappho's "art of love" as "Socratic," if that suggests a strictly intellectual relationship and thereby masks the probable realities of her (and her companions') sexual practices. My focal interest here, however, is the other aspect of Maximus's portrait: Sappho as a sort of protosophistic figure. Maximus himself is probably best described as one of the "philosophical" sophists of the second century A.D. an itinerant performer who specializes in popular "talks" or "lectures" (*laliai; dialexeis*) on moral-philosophical themes and who (like Apuleius) likes to style himself a Platonist, though clearly his commitments are eclectic and nondoctrinaire.[6] In setting up an equivalence between the Sapphic and Socratic circles, Maximus portrays Socrates as a sophist who belongs to the same professional category as his "rival-artists" Protagoras and Gorgias and who practices an art of discursive *sophia* with a circle of companions and intimates; and so Sappho too. This discursive *sophia* is the medium and instrument of a *technê erôtikê*, revolving around questions of who to love, and what, and why, and how. It is, of course, a stretch to think of Sappho as a "sophist" simply; there were, after all, no such things as "sophists" in her time. Maximus's image of her can be taken only metaphorically. But it is also true, as Plato's portrait of Protagoras suggests, that the sophists were the successors of the poets, and that the circles that formed around archaic poets were the precursors of the circles that formed around the sophists.[7] In sum, the underlying model that Alcaeus and Sappho share, and that connects them (especially perhaps Sappho) to the sophists of the fifth and fourth centuries, is the deeply traditional cultural practice of symposiastic filiation and factional rivalry, such as we have seen already in the *Theognidea*.

To view Sappho through the metaphor of "sophist," and Alcaeus through the metaphor of "orator" on political themes, is to view both as performers of argumentation and exhortation—but also as performers who, in their more or less symposiastic settings, address themselves not to the more heterogeneous civic audience of Pindaric *epinikia* but chiefly to circles of insiders. This implies, at least in theory, an argumentation that can presuppose a greater degree of homogeneity, and thus a greater range of tacit assumables that can simply be invoked and need not be defended or negotiated. The performer, the poet, is under less pressure to construct the enthymematic grounds of judgment through the development and amplification of argumentative topoi. The performer/poet is *in principle* given greater license simply to "express" and artistically enhance particular modalities of judgment, particular attitudes, particular ethical positions, particular "feelings," with which the audience can be expected to identify already. The closed circle of the symposium, in sum, implies *or can be taken to imply* a setting for a version of lyric that more nearly corresponds to twentieth-century notions of "lyricality" as the dramatized expression of personal emotion, the rhetorical function of which is to reinforce or intensify the insider group's solidarity and adherence to their shared ethico-political and ideological commitments. As such, it would seem most suitable to a factionalized identity politics. But to say this is to speak in abstract principle only. Much depends, in the concrete instance of any particular act of poetic argumentation, on how much the circle is really "closed," on how permeable its boundaries really are, on the degree to which the topics of discourse are open to contestation, and on how much homogeneity can really be presupposed.

Let us take up Alcaeus first.

Alcaeus

As Anne Burnett has said, "Alcaeus sang for men whom he believed to be like himself, and his music was meant to ready them for action by reaffirming the unity and permanence of their common convictions."[8] In his performance of that role he has impressed most modern commentators as a political reactionary whose ideas and whose *êthos* cannot possibly be admired, though one can still appreciate the technical elegance and eloquence of his poetry. Denys Page's judgment of 1955 still seems definitive: "[w]e shall not judge that Mytilene lost a statesman of any good promise in one who struggled so long and so vainly against the stream of history. . . . All through his stormy life he had neither might nor right on his side. There is little to admire in the man except his poetry."[9]

There is no need to be greatly concerned here with the details of Alcaeus's life, sparse and fragmentary as they are, but a very brief outline will be useful.[10] Alcaeus, like Sappho, was a citizen of Mytilene, the chief city of Lesbos, a large island situated near what is now the western Turkish coast, adjacent to the Troad and the rich kingdom of Lydia. Mytilene was an important trading center through which the luxuries of Asia passed to the Greek West and especially to a Greek nobility increasingly concerned with refined consumption and sumptuous display. Alcaeus was a member of one of Mytilene's four aristocratic clans, one of which, the Penthilidai, had been the traditional rulers of the island up to the beginning of his adult life. The Penthilid rulers held the title of *basileus*, "king," but seem to have had more the function of a supreme magistrate who governed in conjunction with an oligarchic council of the noble families. The Lesbian nobles apparently were intensely proud, competitive, and given to factional tensions and feuds. The Penthilidai, in turn, appear to have been fairly brutal: Aristotle says "they went about striking people with clubs" (*Politics* 1311b).[11] By 620 B.C, the tensions between the Penthilidai and the other nobles had produced an uprising of at least one of the clans, and finally the killing of the last Penthilid king, possibly in revenge for raping the wife of a certain Smerdis.[12]

What followed was a period of violent *stasis* in which the noble houses struggled with one another for control, a period that more or less coincides with Alcaeus's (and Sappho's) adult life and poetic career. Perhaps a few years after the Penthilid collapse, the fighting was suspended temporarily through an alliance of some sort and the setting up of one Melanchros as tyrant. Around 612, however, Alcaeus and his brothers conspired with Pittacus—then a newly emergent but marginal figure among the Mytilenean nobility, and apparently of non-Lesbian descent—to assassinate Melanchros and restore the old political order, intending most probably to seize the former Penthilid position for themselves. Pittacus accomplished the assassination, but another tyrant, Myrsilos, emerged in the ensuing instability. Alcaeus's faction appears at this point to have sworn oaths with Pittacus to eliminate Myrsilos and restore the rights of "the people" (*damos*), which for Alcaeus most probably meant the landholding citizens under noble "leadership."[13] Pittacus, however, broke his oath and went over to Myrsilos, with whom he seems to have shared power while driving Alcaeus and his fellow-plotters into exile. After Myrsilos's death (c. 590) Pittacus became sole ruler of Mytilene and subsequently married a Penthilid, possibly to form an alliance to bolster his position against the revenge-minded families of Alcaeus and Melanchros. Aristotle says (*Politics* 1285a) that Pittacus was appointed *aisymnêtês*, "mediator" (or elected dictator) by the Mytilenean assembly to put an end to the depredations of the exiled factions "led by Antimenidas and Alcaeus the poet"; tradition says that he ruled as tyrant or *aisymnêtês* for ten years and voluntarily relinquished power. Alcaeus spent most of his adult life reviling Pittacus in poetry, calling him among other things an oath-breaker, a "gobbler" of the city, "Paunch," and the "base-born . . . tyrant of the gutless, ill-fated city" (fr. 70, 129, 348) and struggling fruitlessly to depose him and restore the old political order. Alcaeus seems to have suffered exile as many as three times, and may have spent time in Egypt, Thebes, and Sicily. In the end he may have been pardoned and permitted to return; he may have died fighting as a mercenary in a Lydian campaign.

Despite Alcaeus's hatred of him, Pittacus was in fact an astute, effective, and popular ruler, and was to acquire a quasi-Solonic reputation for being just—despite the fact that he had committed at least one murder on his way to power. Later tradition named him one of the "Seven Sages" of the Hellenic world. Once in power, he seems to have struck a protodemocratic accommodation between the *dêmos* and the traditional nobility, though (unlike Solon) he undertook no constitutional innovations.14 As Page has said, Alcaeus was on the wrong side of history. As a politician, he generally seems to stand for nothing but factional self-interest and vendetta, and nothing but the resistance of archaic aristocracy to the political and social changes that were underway between the seventh and fifth centuries B.C.

Alcaeus's stasiotic poetry is chiefly committed to reinforcing the solidarity of his faction and exhorting his *hetairoi* toward some course of action. This is perhaps most apparent in his so-called "ship of state" poems.15 Two fragments will illustrate the type:16

[fr. 208]
I do not understand the *stasis* of the winds:
for one wave rolls in from this side,
and another from that, and we in the middle
together with our black ship are carried
much distressed by the great winter storm;
for the bilge-water's about the mast-hold,
and all the sail is a tattered rag already,
with great gaping rents running down it,
and the anchors are slackening, and the [rudders]
   . . .

   . . .
with both feet holding fast . . .
in the coils; and this alone [saves]
me; the cargo [has fallen overboard]
   . . . above . . .
   . . .

[unreadable fragments of one more strophe]

[fr. 6]
This next wave comes on [like?] the preceding
[wind?], and it brings us much trouble
to bail the water, when it enters the ship's
   . . .

   . . .

   . . .
Let us shore up [the ship's sides] with all speed,
and into safe harbor we shall run;
and let not fainthearted fear take hold
[of any of us]; a great [ordeal] stands clearly forth.
Remember the previous [distress];

now let every man be proven steadfast.
And let us not disgrace [with unmanliness]
our noble fathers [lying] beneath the earth

. . .

. . .

[fragmentary phrases from four more strophes]:
from fathers . . . our *thymos* . . . is like . . . quick . . . let us not . . . *monarchia*
. . . let us not accept . . .

As D. A. Campbell notes, fragment 6 contains the first known occurrence of
the word *monarchia*, and the now illegible marginal comment on the papyrus shred
from which it comes contains the word "Myrsilos." Further, Heraclitus's comment
on fragment 208 (*Homeric Allegories* 5), which says that 208 is about "Myrsilos's
tyrannical conspiracy against the Mytileneans," is immediately followed by the first
words of fragment 6.[17] So these fragments appear to belong together—perhaps in
this order, though we cannot know—and both appear to belong to the period of
Myrsilos's tyranny. A papyrus fragment of a first-century A.D. commentary to a passage that is now completely illegible says, "in the first exile when Alcaeus's party,
having prepared a plot against Myrsilos . . . fled into Pyrrha to escape being subjected to justice."[18] This would seem to be the general context for 208 and 6.

While it is impossible to know exactly what was argued by the ruined poems
these battered remnants have been salvaged from, it is clear enough that 208 and 6
are allegorical (as Heraclitus says) and that the allegory serves a hortatory function.[19] Singing to his comrades in symposium, Alcaeus represents the political tur-
bulence of the Mytilenean *stasis* as a dangerous winter storm at sea. The storm may
also represent, more specifically, the latest reversal of fortune suffered by the failed
conspirators, who have been outmaneuvered, confused, and overwhelmed by forces
they cannot control. The ship in which Alcaeus and his faction ride—not really a
"ship of state" but just "our boat"—is beset by waves and wind that threaten to destroy it. The poet's exhortation to his *hetairoi* to shore up the ship and run for safe
haven would seem to indicate a flight into exile. The "next wave" that is coming on
in fragment 6 may be the tyranny of Myrsilos after that of Melanchros, or simply
the latest round of trouble that besets the defeated faction. The invocation of "our
fathers . . . beneath the earth" seems linked to notions of protecting one's patrimony, including the political privilege of a nobility that rules in council with a
basileus, and to notions of resisting the erosion or cancellation of those privileges
under what Alcaeus styles as *monarchia*, "one-man rule." Every man must do his
duty, hold his position, rouse his *thymos*, and meet the onslaught bravely.

The rhetorical function of this poetry clearly is to maintain the cohesion of the
faction as a political and fighting force, at a moment when it is threatened with defeat and disintegration—a crisis that apparently was chronic for Alcaeus and his coconspirators.[20] Pittacus's departure and switching of allegiance to Myrsilos, whether
it occurred before or after fragments 208 and 6, was a major instance of the kind of
rupture that had to be prevented if the group was to pursue its goals effectively. At
issue, then, is an ever-present question of solidarity: Alcaeus must exhort his comrades to stick together and to persist, even in exile, precisely because their ability to
continue doing that is in doubt.

The allegory functions as an enthymematic *pistis* by giving enhanced and memorable presence to a paradigmatic narrative that defines and evokes the proper "in-thymatic" response to the question at issue in the crisis situation that the poem is about. The allegory does this, in essence, by calling on the audience's tacit understanding of the emotive significance of the narrative and the proper or necessary ways of behaving in the scene that is described. Alcaeus's *hetairoi*, as the warrior-aristocrats of a maritime island-state, would be familiar with seafaring and with the meaning of a winter storm at sea; likewise, they would be familiar with the martial ethic of being "steadfast" in the face of danger. The ship-in-storm allegory thus fuses the audience's seafaring knowledge with its code of manly, soldierly behavior. The persuasive force of this allegorical fusion derives, in part, from the sheer evocativeness of amplified description, the accumulation of vivid details not all of which are strictly necessary to the argumentative import of the comparison. As in Pindar's mythical "digressions," Alcaeus's detailed rendering effects a psychagogic transport of the listener into the scene and lends it an enhanced emotive resonance. Insofar as Alcaeus's listener has experienced such storms, and insofar as the poem's descriptive psychagogy—enhanced by rhythmic prosody and musical performance—brings him to a well-realized visualization, it is likely to bring him also to rehearsal of a visceral, habitual response: he knows where to put his hands and feet, and what to do. Further, the language of the description has (or would have had, for Alcaeus's companions) clear resonances with Homer, Archilochus, and other poets who likewise had invoked "sea-storm" imagery as figures for war and political strife.[21] These resonances give authority to the poet's voice by way of a citational effect, and at the same time (and for the same reason) warrant his invocation of the sea-storm narrative as appropriate and reasonable in the present circumstance: this is how poetic *sophia* speaks and has spoken of such things.

That observation raises an important point. On one hand, the allegory may create a "surplus" of evocative effect through the accumulation of descriptive details that exceed the strictly comparative-analogical function that they may have as metaphor: to what, for example, does one refer the "gaping rents" in the tattered sail? Or the "coils," *bimblessi?* This odd word may mean "ropes," but also is etymologically related to *bimblinon* or *biblinon*, "made of *biblos*," meaning strips of papyrus fiber (from which ropes or twine might have been made). But *biblos* also can mean a roll of papyrus paper, a "book": in the midst of the storm, with waves washing over the deck, the speaker's feet (or the feet of the sail?) are somehow caught in bookish things, papyrus rolls, "and this alone saves me." On the other hand, however, even while it opens up such wayward and sometimes charming channels of suggestion, the allegory *and the psychagogic force of its descriptive rendering* also closes off major lines of thought that might otherwise be possible. Insofar as Alcaeus's listener is fully beguiled by the description, is fully caught up in imagining the scene and projecting himself into it, or plays out possibilities of meaning within its terms, it becomes difficult for him to conceive in any other terms the circumstances that the poem in actuality refers to. The listener's mind is filled with this particular scenario; all others are excluded. Suppose that Alcaeus had not chosen the ship-in-storm paradigm as the basis of his allegory—but instead, perhaps, the paradigm of army in distress, such as one sees often in the *Iliad*, or possibly an Odyssean tale of extricating oneself from a catastrophe by means of unheroic but clever stratagems (e.g., *Odyssey* 14's account of being defeated in battle by the Egyptians, begging for mercy from the Pharaoh, and afterward living a prosperous life in Egypt). What exhortations, and what judgments, are potentially warranted in such a scenario but excluded from the one that Alcaeus has employed?

Page, in his account of fragment 6, observes that there are obvious inconsistencies (from a realist point of view) between the ship-in-storm scenario and Alcaeus's exhortations to manly valor. Those exhortations, as Page argues, are more appropriate to "the soldier on the eve of battle, or the morrow of defeat, not the storm-tossed mariner," because the mariner has no choice. Unlike the soldier, he cannot retreat or surrender, cannot beg for mercy, cannot leave the boat, and can only weather the storm or drown. Page makes this argument to support the political-allegorical reading of this and other "ship of state" poems against a line of literalist interpretation that treats them simply as seafaring songs (so that one must imagine Alcaeus absurdly banging on his lyre and singing to his shipmates in the middle of a storm, while they contend with waves and wind and cargo washing overboard).[22] But Page's argument can be turned another way. The fusion of the storm scene with the battlefield-style exhortation is not only an index of the poem's allegorical intent but also a means of filtering and limiting the choices available to the listener's reasoning. By leading his audience to perceive the battlefield-style exhortation through the filter of the storm scene, Alcaeus removes all options but one. Like storm-beset sailors, Alcaeus argues, "we" have no possible option but to stick together and keep fighting. Surrender is not a possibility, nor suing for peace, nor "leaving the ship," since within the logic of the allegory all three are equivalent to certain death; tactical retreat to a "safe harbor" is permitted as a means of continuing the struggle and at the moment is the thing to do. Further, this option-reducing argument is reinforced by being fused with exhortations not to "disgrace with unmanliness our noble fathers lying beneath the earth." To give up the struggle or "leave the ship" is to lose one's manhood and one's claim to noble status also, as one sinks beneath the waves of political change brought on by Myrsilos. Within the terms of Alcaeus's aristocratic ideology, this is a fate worse than death. As long as Alcaeus's companions remain persuaded that the seafaring allegory is the appropriate means of representing and interpreting their circumstances and is the appropriate filter for the battlefield-style exhortation to continued struggle—as long as this scenario fills their minds and they cannot imagine other possibilities—their enthymematic reasoning will keep coming back to the same conclusions and the *stasis* will go on.

Alcaeus's *hetaireia*, his symposium-group, was probably a leaky boat in more than one way. As I have noted already, it was leaky in the sense that it was constantly in danger of defection and dissolution. But it was leaky also in the sense that, even as it cohered, its boundaries were permeable and could be crossed by arguments of different kinds. The group certainly would have been aware of discourses other than its own—discourses that offered the very kinds of arguments that Alcaeus's poems seem meant to counteract.

Moreover, Alcaeus's poems were surely meant to be performed more than once, and they had the potential to be reperformed in other contexts and to circulate beyond his immediate circle. From this perspective, Alcaeus's "ship of state" and other stasiotic poems can be seen as a rhetoric of justification meant for potentially sympathetic audiences elsewhere. Alcaeus presents the course of action that he and his *hetairoi* have taken as the properly noble and heroic thing for manly men to do in the face of tyranny. For this reason Quintilian can say, centuries later, that "Alcaeus deserves to be awarded the golden plectrum in the part of his work in which he attacks tyrants, and even now contributes much to morals" (*Institutio* 10.1.63). But even in Alcaeus's time we can imagine that at least some of his poems could have been circulated in Mytilene and would have served as political propaganda, including his poems reviling Pittacus, just as Archilochus's invective poems against Lycambes and his family would have circulated in Paros as they caught on and were reperformed in various symposium gatherings.[23] Alcaeus's stasiotic and "ship of state" poems, in short, could have served to rally any groups who felt themselves unjustly deprived of their entitlements or oppressed by those in power. What the poems (or the remnants of them that we have) do not address, however, is the question whether the oppressor-enemy reviled in the poetry is in fact unjust; this point generally seems to be taken for granted. Nor does Alcaeus's poetry do much to construct an argument, so far as one can tell, about what constitutes just or unjust governance. Aside from reviling Pittacus for being a traitor to the faction and for lacking the qualities that define aristocratic status—thus producing such insult-epithets as "base-born," *polis*-"gobbler," "Paunch," and so forth—the poetry that survives appears to offer no arguments at all about the actual quality of his (or for that matter Myrsilos's) rule.

Alcaeus, then, appears neither to have offered any strong argument to counter the opinions of those at Mytilene (and elsewhere) who thought that Pittacus's rule and his resolution of the *stasis* were just and wise; nor does Alcaeus appear to have attempted anything like bilateral accommodation. Whether his poems are meant only for the immediate circle of his *hetairoi* or for a more extended audience of like-minded aristocrats, he speaks primarily to those who can identify already with his sense of having been offended by a despicable regime, he demonizes the opposition, and he offers no counsel but an exhortation to fight on, as in this perhaps nearly complete poem (fr. 140) quoted by Athenaeus (*Deipnosophistai* 14.627a–b):

. . .

. . .

and the great hall gleams
with bronze, and for Ares all the ceiling is adorned
with shining helmets, down
over which nod white horsehair
plumes, for the heads of
men a glory; and bright bronze greaves
hang round and conceal
the pegs, defense against strong missiles,
and corselets of new linen
and hollow shields are thrown down on the floor;
by them are Chalchidean swords
and by them many belts and tunics also.

Of these there is no forgetting, since
we first and foremost have set ourselves upon this task.

Athenaeus, writing in the third century A.D., cites this poem in connection with a remark that "ancient" song-poetry could be an "incitement to bravery [*andreia*]," and adds that Alcaeus was "more warlike than is right" (14.626f–627a). Page's commentary notes Alcaeus's use of Homeric diction in his description of the weapons and armor—which are quite old-fashioned (e.g., bowl-shaped "hollow shields" and "Chalchidean swords" of bronze, not iron)—to invoke an archaic warrior ethic that is also not to be forgotten and that grounds the exhortation to the *hetaireia*'s warlike "task."[24] The *hetairoi* in symposium drink and sing, poetically surrounded by mythic fighting gear that seems to have been recently used and that is waiting to be taken up again by heroes as of old. The Homeric, mythic resonance endows the task at hand with an antique beauty and renders it a pleasant object of contemplation for the companionable men of Alcaeus's fighting band. Again, the "task" itself is taken as a given; the companions are sworn already and nothing remains but to fulfill the glorious work of honor.

Not all of Alcaeus's poems, of course, are stasiotic songs, and not all the stasiotic songs are devoted to that sort of exhortation. But in virtually every poem of which we have reasonably substantial fragments, Alcaeus, like Pindar, offers enthymematic arguments for his audience's judgment and response, and most typically amplifies the argumentative topics from which judgment is to be derived by means of mythico-narrative expansions. The *mythos* may be invoked, as in the previous fragments, as an allegorical screen through which to view and interpret present circumstances, or as a sort of proof by illustration or example, or both at once. Consider the following (fr. 38A).

Drink [and get drunk,] Melanippos, with me. Why suppose
[that when . . . eddying] Acheron's great ford
has been crossed you'll see the sun's pure light
[again]? Come, do not aim at such great things.
For indeed King Sisyphus Aeolus's son [supposed],
of all men being most thoughtful, [to master death?];
but even his cunning was ruled by fate, [and twice]
he passed over eddying Acheron, and a suffering
[was devised] for him to have by Kronos's son [the king, below][25]
the dark earth. Come, do not [hope for such a thing].
    . . . while we are young if ever [now it is right]
[to bear] whatever of these sufferings [the god may give].
    . . . the north [wind] . . .

The last, fragmentary phrase may actually be the beginning of another poem,[26] so it is possible that we have here a complete (though damaged) poem in twelve lines. It appears to belong to one of Alcaeus's periods of exile: he has "crossed over Acheron," and like the dead he cannot go back. But the immediate frame for the poet's speech act more nearly resembles the paideutic-erotic setting of the *Theognidea*. Alcaeus counsels young, impatient Melanippos ("Darkhorse") that now is not the time to attempt return: for now they should bear misfortune patiently and console each other over wine. If "the north wind" and the scattered words that appear to follow it in another fragment (38B) are in fact a continuation of this poem, we have some hint of what Alcaeus may be counseling Melanippos to do: ". . . the north [wind] . . . city . . . lyre . . . under the roof . . . share . . ."[27] The north wind suggests winter, a bad time for seafaring—or, metaphorically, for whatever action Melanippos might wish to undertake—and thus a time for sensible men to stay indoors and content themselves with shared companionship, wine, and song.

This poem invokes mythic narrative both as allegory and as proof by example. On one hand, by figuring exile as "crossing Acheron," or in other words as death, the poem constructs an allegorical interpretation of the present situation that, as in fragments 208 and 6, limits the possible range of responses. If one accepts the notion that one is "dead," at least for the moment, then there is no room for entertaining thoughts of "going back." On the other hand, the admonitory tale of Sisyphus functions as an example that further "proves" and reinforces the inadvisability of bucking unpropitious circumstance. And of course Sisyphus's famous punishment is itself a metaphor for futile undertakings. For Melanippos to attempt now to "return" would be a Sisyphean exercise in futility: not only would he not regain what he has lost, but he would lose everything absolutely and irretrievably and would spend the rest of his existence in misery. (Sisyphus was able to return from death, temporarily, not by a heroic overthrowing of the ruling powers but by a clever trick: he arranged for his wife to omit his funeral rites, then told the underworld gods he had to go back and reprimand her; once back, he stayed until death came round again. It was this ruse, an act of *hubris* against the gods, that brought on Sisyphus' eternal punishment.) If we are to understand Melanippos's situation via the Sisyphean fable, we might say that he has cast his lot with Alcaeus's faction, and so for him the die is cast; he must now ride out his appointed fate. To attempt a Sisyphean return—which would be, in effect, to attempt some scheme or to cut a deal for himself alone—would be to renege on his commitments and thus to attempt to outwit destiny, which is a punishable act of *hubris* as well as an act of disloyalty to the group, which in this particular metaphoric framework seems to occupy the position of an underworld power. So, even as Alcaeus invites young Melanippos to put aside his dreams of going home and to settle down (for the time being) with wine and song and friends in shelter from the storm, the subtext of his argument also contains a subtle threat: stay with us, even on this side of Acheron, and like a manly man accept what "the god may give" or die forever.

It seems reasonable to infer that Alcaeus is making this sort of argument because Melanippos, or someone like him, is in fact thinking of returning—one way or another. Even if Melanippos is a fictive addressee figure, Alcaeus's argument works to maintain solidarity and commitment to the group by casting Melanippos's wishes into the category of the unthinkable and by reinviting him into the companionship of the *hetaireia*. As in fragments 208 and 6, likewise, the persuasive force of this argument largely depends on the listener's willingness to accept the allegorical construction and the example-myth as authoritative interpretations of the situation. And that willingness largely depends, in turn, on Alcaeus's authority as a speaker/singer of traditional *sophia*, and on the aesthetic appeal and psychagogic power of the mythical material as Alcaeus renders it in song. As long as this material seems authoritative, seems more or less to fit the situation, and fills the listener's mind, it becomes difficult to think of the situation in other terms.

I will consider one other poem (fr. 42), which is badly damaged but possibly (though not certainly) complete.

> According to the tale, [because of] evil [deeds]
> bitter [pain once came] to Priam and his sons, [Helen,]
> from you, [and with fire Zeus destroyed]
> holy Ilium.
> Not so she that Aeacus's [noble] son,
> [inviting] all the blessed gods to the wedding,
> carried away from the [halls] of Nereus
> an elegant maiden
> to Chiron's house; [and he loosened the pure]
> maiden's girdle; and affection [bloomed]
> between Peleus and the best of Nereus's daughters,
> and within a year
> she bore a son, of demigods [the bravest,]
> a blessed driver of chestnut horses.
> But they perished for H[elen's] sake, [the Phrygians]
> and their city too.

This poem apparently puts in play two legends: that of the marriage of Peleus (Aeacus's son) and Thetis—producing their demigod son, Achilles—and that of the rape of Helen, which brought destruction to the "Phrygians" (the Trojans) and their city. Two "marriages" or couplings are in contrast: one sanctified, and legitimate, and the other not. By portraying Thetis as an "elegant maiden," *parthenon abran*, Alcaeus seems to place the sanctified-legitimate marriage within the framework of aristocratic guest-friendship and gift exchange. The adjective *abra* (or *habra* in the more "standard" Attic dialect) belongs to the family of words clustered around the name-notion of *habrosynê*, "luxury," a central preoccupation of sixth-century aristocracy.[28] To describe Thetis the bride as *abra*, "elegant," is in effect to define her as a refined, expensive delicacy and the marriage as an exchange of costly gift-goods cementing friendship between aristocratic houses (one of which, in this case, is actually a god's house). In contrast, the seduction and taking of Helen from her husband as stolen spoils is an act of *hubris* that violates the principles of such exchange, and so it brings divine retribution not only for the perpetrator but for his entire city.

Why is Alcaeus telling this tale? Page suggests that Alcaeus is offering an uncharacteristically moralistic argument about the differences between good and bad wives, a sort of didactic fable, perhaps in response to Stesichorus's famous (and vanished) poem of blame against Helen.[29] Burnett, on the other hand, has argued cogently that the poem is rather unlikely as a piece of moral didacticism and reads it instead as not about a comparison of wives or marriages but a reflection on the paradoxical waywardness of fate. The "good" marriage of Peleus and Thetis produces Achilles, who is in large measure responsible for the destruction of Troy, and dies there himself. In his view, all the characters in the Troy tale are caught in an unfolding tragic destiny that begins not only from the rape of Helen but also from a wedding attended and sanctioned by the gods: destruction has come as much from the good marriage as the bad by the inexorable working-out of destiny.[30] But this is to read the poem rather too much in a high new critical style, as if Alcaeus were Yeats, and it ignores the force of the final two lines as an enthymematic cap that lays admonitory emphasis on Troy's fate as punishment. And it is not Achilles the fallen hero that this poem invokes but Achilles the charioteer with his chestnut horses, Achilles the splendid warrior, Achilles the punisher.

It seems likely that this poem, even if complete, is part of some larger sequence (or a repertoire), the character of which can be surmised from another fragment (298) that also derives material from the Troy legend. This fragment, though longer than fragment 42, is clearly not complete. It consists of twenty-seven more or less legible lines (though the left-hand edge is damaged) followed by a scattering of words from the beginnings of nineteen other, mostly obliterated lines. Most of it narrates the rape of Cassandra within a precinct of Athena during the sack of Troy, and the consequences of Athena's anger. But the opening segment invokes the topos of "shaming" someone who commits injustice and declares that "we must put [a noose] around his neck and stone him [to death]." The explicit point of the narrative is that it would have been better for the Greeks to have punished the rapist (Locrian Ajax), because the unappeased anger of Athena led to the destruction of much of the Greek fleet in a storm during the return from Troy. Finally, among the one-word scraps the word "son of Hyrrhas," meaning Pittacus, appears in the fragment's penultimate line. The point would seem to be that Pittacus, like Ajax, deserves to be punished for some crime that he has committed, and that if the punishment is not exacted some divine vengeance is likely to fall on Mytilene. Burnett remarks upon this fragment that "[g]nomic argument is abandoned [after the first few lines] for pure lyric discourse" as "[r]hetoric gives way to narrative."[31] But surely the narrative, as in Alcaeus's other fragments, and as in Pindar, is an integral part of the poem's enthymematic argumentation and a major source of whatever persuasive, rhetorical power it may have.

Let us now step back to fragment 42. While it is impossible to know just what specific circumstance Alcaeus is arguing about in this poem, its focus on sanctioned and unsanctioned marriages and on the divine retribution visited on the latter makes it at least possible that what is at issue is Pittacus's marriage to a Penthilid.[32] If so, the point would seem to be that Pittacus—a person of foreign extraction marrying into the former ruling clan of the Mytilenean aristocracy, as part of a strategy to seize and consolidate tyrannical power—has entered into an unholy, unsanctified union that is likely to provoke divine anger and so bring disaster to the city. Underlying this argument, and warranting it, is a tacit assumption or set of assumptions to the general effect that, because Pittacus derives from "foreign" aristocracy and not from the traditional aristocratic clans of Mytilene, he therefore is an outsider with no right to marry in and for that matter no right to rule the city; since he has no right, his marriage to a Penthilid woman cannot be seen as occurring within a legitimate gift exchange framework, and therefore must be understood, along with his "gobbling" of the city, as a hubristic taking analogous to the rape of Helen (as well as, perhaps, the rape of Cassandra). If so, the Mytilenean nobles are *or should be* cast into the role of Homeric heroes at war with Troy. But this argument can have political effect, of course, only if Mytilenean audiences outside Alcaeus's circle are willing to make or accept such assumptions about Pittacus's marriage or to resent him from the start as an arriviste usurper.

In another fragment of identical strophic form (283), Alcaeus takes up the same general theme, focusing instead on the seduction of Helen and concluding again with reference to the destruction of the Trojans; the fragment may include a reference to Achilles' role in the slaughter. Page makes the point that "[t]he Lesbians had a more or less proprietary interest in the Homeric monuments of the Troad; and among the holiest of these was the tomb of Achilles."[33] The deeds of Achilles were, for Mytilenean nobles, a favorite patriotic theme. It is possible that Alcaeus composed and performed songs about Achilles and the Troy legend generally as a sort of miniaturized version of bardic storytelling and that his symposiastic audience(s) would have delighted simply in hearing these tales retold. But the evidence of fragment 298, on the rape of Cassandra, suggests otherwise. Rather, it appears that Alcaeus is invoking—and amplifying, in greater or lesser detail—the materials of traditional epic legend in the service of lyric argument. The legendary materials function as allegorical screens for interpreting present events, as exemplary "proofs" for gnomic generalizations, and as a source of psychagogy. Insofar as the materials are vested with authority as the discourse of traditional *sophia*, Alcaeus's interpretations of events are given some credibility, and insofar as the legends can preoccupy the listener's mind, preclude other interpretive frameworks, and generate an emotive charge, they lend Alcaeus's arguments a sense of inevitability and a measure of persuasive power. Achilles is being invoked, in fragments 42 and 283, not simply as a patriotic hero figure that Lesbian audiences like to hear about, but also as a resonant figure for the sort of punishment/revenge that Pittacus, and the city that accepts him, deserves.

Alcaeus's *hetaireia* was a leaky boat, and it seems likely that his poetry—in its effort to sustain his perpetually losing group as a coherent and committed fighting force in opposition to the tyranny at Mytilene—is meant both to counter discourses originating from outside the group and also to circulate beyond it, at least among potential allies who can share the poet's sense of resentment and dispossession. But it also is apparent from the poetry still available to us that, although Alcaeus does offer argumentation to the judgment of his audience(s), he is arguing primarily to his friends. While myth and allegory typically are invoked as interpretive frames for present circumstances, and indeed as a means of reducing options for interpreting the present, the reasoning that sustains belief in the appropriateness of the frame is for the most part just assumed. Alcaeus can, perhaps, persuade an audience beyond his own *hetaireia* to accept the frame through sheer hypnosis, or through the aesthetic charm of his song; but his effectiveness probably is limited chiefly to those who share already, to some significant degree, his assumptions about the ethical quality of his enemies. For those who do share Alcaeus's assumptions, and in effect already are members of his *hetaireia,* his use of allegory and myth will chiefly serve the purposes of intensifying those assumptions and the group's oppositional resolve. From this perspective, Alcaeus's argumentation seems more suitable to sustaining the politics of faction than to persuading those not already convinced of the justice of his cause. Thus his relative lack of effect on Mytilenean opinion, which seems to have preferred his enemies overwhelmingly, and his apparently continual frustration.[34]

But, to offer a brief last word in Alcaeus's favor, one might also say that his poetry could travel still beyond the bounds of his *hetaireia* and effect persuasion, in the sense that audiences removed in time (or place) from the original events could see the situations embodied in the poems as allegorical equivalents to their circumstances and could see in the stance(s) Alcaeus offers persuasive modalities of judgment and response. In such a case the poems then lose whatever character they may have had originally as practical political discourse: they in effect cease to be specifically about the situation in early-sixth-century Mytilene; "Pittacus" (or "Myrsilos") becomes simply the name of a general tyrant type; and "Alcaeus" becomes the voice of epideictic argumentation on the general theme of "resisting tyranny." An audience removed in time (or place) may be persuaded to identify with Alcaeus's response to his predicament or at least may feel the persuasive force of his argumentation, as well as appreciate the eloquence and aesthetic appeal with which he renders it. Or indeed the audience may feel, and be susceptible to, the psychagogic and persuasive force that *resides in* the poetry's aesthetic power. A person who feels stuck or stranded anywhere by adverse circumstance may, for example, find some consolation in the argument and stance of "Drink and get drunk, Melanippos, with me." It is worth remembering too that, although Alcaeus's notion of the *dêmos* (or *damos*, in his Aeolic dialect) is limited chiefly to his own class, nevertheless much of his argumentation is about preserving the political rights and institutions of a *dêmos*—however defined—against the encroachments of one-man rule. Such a stance can be abstracted away, in different historical moments and different performance contexts, and reapplied in the resinging or recital of Alcaic song. Any who feel themselves oppressed or violated by what appears to them as unjust tyranny may feel the force of Alcaeus's arguments, even in perpetual defeat and exile, for sustained resistance to an unacceptable regime. This would seem to be what Dionysius and Quintilian have seen.

Sappho

Alcaeus (fr. 130B) provides us with a path to Sappho.

> [Among the *agnus castus* trees?] . . . wretched, I
> live possessing a rustic's portion,
> longing to hear the assembly
> being summoned, Agesilaidas,
> and the council; what my father and father's father
> have grown old possessing among these
> citizens who do one another harm,
> from these things I have been cut off,
> exiled to the outer edges, and like Onomakles
> here alone I have settled in wolf-thickets
>   . . . [leaving?] the war; for *stasis*
> against . . . is [ignobly] taken back;
>   . . . to the precinct of the blessed gods

. . . treading upon dark earth
. . . meetings themselves I
dwell keeping my feet out of troubles,
where Lesbian women are judged for beauty
going to and fro in trailing robes, and all around rings
the wondrous echoing sound of the women's
sacred annual ululation
. . . from many [troubles] when will the gods
. . . the Olympians
. . .
. . .

This fragment is generally read as bitterly self-ironic. Driven out of Mytilene and forced to take refuge in what is probably the sanctuary of Hera, Zeus, and Dionysius—the oldest, largest, and most important shrine-complex on Lesbos . . . Alcaeus finds himself among elegant, elaborately dressed, aristocratic women who come and go, in what appears to be a beauty contest, during a women's festival that prominently features sacred "ululation," *ololygê*, a loud and joyous outcry or triumphal singing. Alcaeus, unable to retrieve his patrimony, skulks amid (or nearby) the ululating and parading women as his manhood and nobility suffer deep humiliation.[35]

Alcaeus's gloom aside, his poem provides a brief glimpse of women's culture on Lesbos, and of the sort of world in which Sappho and her circle moved. Indeed, if Alcaeus is describing a scene that he has witnessed, it is possible that Sappho, his contemporary, is actually there.

We really do not know much about women's culture or the contexts for women's poetry on Lesbos, but some cautious generalizations may be and have been based upon analogies with better-known practices elsewhere.[36] These include women's festivals like the Thesmophoria at Athens, and Alcman's maiden-songs at Sparta. At the Thesmophoria, a three-day festival in honor of Demeter *thesmophoros*—Demeter the law-giver or law-bearer—married citizen-women more or less took over and camped out in the city center. During this time they organized themselves in temporary civic structures resembling those in which the city's men participated, held assemblies, and elected *archousai* (female magistrates) to preside over the festivities, which seem to have included processions, singing/dancing, and feasting/celebrating, as well as the religious rites themselves, which were connected with fertility and childbirth (and involved the slaughter of pigs).

Margaret Williamson makes the point that, because Athenian law required that Thesmophorian women's activities be financed by their husbands, the political organization and ritual symbolism of the festival reflected the interests of the male elite, with leading roles played by the women of prominent families.[37] While this is probably true, and while one function of the Thesmophoria was very probably to regulate female sexuality—by having married citizen-women publicly signify their allegiance to the city's patriarchal code as a frame for their fertility—it is also worth noting that this and other women's festivals were an object of male fears about female sexual license. In Lysias's speech *On the Murder of Eratosthenes*, for example, the defendant (Euphiletus) mentions that his wife, having been seduced by Eratosthenes, used the Thesmophoria as a cover for intriguing with Eratosthenes' mother to prolong the adulterous affair (20). Whether or not this claim was true, it is evident that an audience of Athenian jurors could regard it as a possible scenario. Lucian's *Dialogues of Courtesans* (7.4) says that the celebrants at another women's festival, the Haloa, engaged in lewd joking and fantasies about adultery.[38] In other words, women's festivals were an object of male fears because they provided settings in which women were not in fact directly subject to their husbands' oversight; such festivals not only regulated women's sexuality and subjectivity but also gave their sexuality/subjectivity an opportunity to escape control. One might argue further that the requirement that husbands finance their wives' participation at the Thesmophoria was not only or even primarily an instrument of patriarchal regulation, since women did not control property anyway, but rather an instrument of compulsory permission: if a woman wished to attend, her husband legally could not prevent her by refusing to pay; and once she was there he could not determine what she did, or even know, since men were legally excluded from the proceedings.[39]

The point is that festivals like the Thesmophoria produced a number of contexts for women's public discourse, including poetic public discourse, addressed to audiences of women. This does not mean that Thesmophorian women would have been making speeches and producing civic song that addressed the public issues that exercised their husbands. As Eva Stehle points out, women generally were not authorized to make such commentary, at least not directly, and to do so would have been regarded as unseemly.[40] But it does mean that women had, in settings like the Thesmophoria, a forum to engage in discourse on the topics that mattered to them as women and as representatives of the city's ever-competitive leading households.

Our second parallel for Sappho's possible performance-contexts is Alcman's *partheneia*, or maiden-songs. These reflect the Spartan institution—described by Plutarch in *Lycurgus* (14)—of female initiation groups, *agelai*, in which unmarried girls received an education that included training in athletics and choral song. Such songs were performed naked at public ceremonies. (Spartan boy choruses and adult male choruses also performed naked at certain festivals.) The function of the training was, in essence, to prepare the girls for their civic role as wives, and the choral performance of a *partheneion* functioned in part to present nubile virgins to prospective marriage-partners. Plutarch says, however, that the girl choruses also engaged in praise and blame of young Spartan men, so that those who had been mocked were stung as if they had been formally reprimanded by the city magistrates. While presenting themselves as desirable marriage-partners, the girls of the chorus also presented themselves as the embodied voice of community morality.[41]

One particular fragment of Alcman (3) reveals significant aspects of the character of these female initiation groups and the way that they were viewed, in choral performance, by the city:

Olympian [Muses], fill my heart
[with desire for new] song
full; and I [wish] to hearken
to the voice [of girls]
singing a lovely song [to the heavens]

will scatter sweet [sleep] from my eyes
 . . . and leads me to go with the gathering
 . . . most [rapidly] I'll shake my yellow hair.
 . . . soft feet

[fifty lines missing]

with limb-loosening desire, more meltingly
than sleep or death she gazes;
and not a uselessly sweet [thing is] she.
Yet Astymeloisa requites me not at all,
[but] holding the garland
like a brilliant star
in the wide-spread heavens
or a golden shoot, or tender, bare
 . . .
 . . . she stepped with outstretched [feet;]
the hair-beautifying, moist charm of Kinyras[42]
sits [upon] her maiden tresses.
[Indeed] through the crowd Astymeloisa
[goes . . .] a darling to the people
 . . . chosen
 . . . I say;
 . . . for if only a silver
 . . .
 . . . I would see if she would likewise love me
if she came closer, taking my soft hand,
and I instantly became her suppliant.
And now . . . the deep-minded girl
 . . .
girl . . . me having
 . . . the girl
 . . . grace

[thirty unreadable lines]

This poem was composed to be delivered by a chorus of *parthenoi*, in (or in connection with) a procession: the singer says that her desire for maiden-song leads her to "go with the gathering," where—after the fifty-line lacuna—we find a girl named Astymeloisa "holding the garland" that signifies her as the chorus or dance leader, stepping along "with outstretched feet." The occasion may possibly be a festival of Hera, the Antheia.[43]

Obviously, this *partheneion* was composed not by the band of girls that performed it but by their male chorus trainer, Alcman; and that is one reason for the song's authority as the voice of community morality (though Alcman himself was a foreigner in Sparta). Nevertheless it shows us two important features of the maiden chorus and the girl initiation group that composed it. The first—which has been most frequently remarked on—is the open display of erotic attraction among the girls. This display has generally been taken as an analogue and precedent for the *gynaikerasteia* or "woman-love" expressed in Sappho's poetry, since the terms of erotic desire seem strikingly similar. This resemblance has also encouraged a line of interpretation that views Sappho as a chorus trainer and teacher of girls, presiding over an initiation group that bears a certain (though limited) resemblance to the Spartan *agelai,* in which a part of a young, unmarried woman's education involved the development of her sexuality and her capacity for sexual pleasure.[44] Like the love-relationships between the men and boys of a *hetaireia,* erotic relations between the members of such initiation groups were acceptable and were not deemed inconsistent with heterosexuality in marriage. Female homosexuality was, as Burnett says, "neither sanctioned nor prohibited by the community," in essence because it had no consequences that mattered to the patriarchal order.[45] The fact that Alcman has composed a song in which *parthenoi* declare erotic love for each other in choral performance at a civic event suggests that such desires are consistent with approved community morality. Indeed, insofar as the girls of Alcman's chorus also are presenting themselves as marriage candidates, their display of a developed capacity for erotic pleasure appears as part of their attractiveness to potential husbands: that Astymeloisa is not "uselessly sweet" is an important point. Something similar was likely true for Sappho's world as well. Lesbian women had a reputation in antiquity for uninhibited sexual proficiency; to "lesbianize" (*lesbiazein*) was to perform fellatio. On Lesbos as elsewhere in the Hellenic world, and perhaps especially on Lesbos, heterosexual and homosexual desires and practices were part of a single spectrum of "normal" sexuality for women as well as men and were not presumed to be mutually exclusive.[46] Sappho herself was not only a "woman-lover" but also, at the same time, a married woman and a mother, and she held a respectable position in society.

The second feature of Alcman's fragment—one that has less often been remarked on—is the characterization of the chorus leader, Astymeloisa, as going "through the crowd . . . a darling to the people" (*melêma damôi*). This expression has a distinct resonance, though it is expressed in somewhat different terms, with Hesiod's description of the eloquent *basileus* as likewise going "through the gathering, like a god admired with honeyed reverence, conspicuous amid the throng" (*Theogony* 91–92). The terminology does not exactly correspond, but there is no strong reason to expect that Alcman, working in a lyric idiom, would employ the dactylic hexameter formulae of Hesiodic epic. The name "Astymeloisa" means something like "City-darling" (or, more clumsily, "the beloved care of citizens"), and thus appears to be a type-name or title for the chorus leader, who has been "chosen" and projected into prominence most probably because of her performing skill and beauty, the very qualities that cause the chorus-singer to "melt" with "limb-loosening desire" and to make gestures of loving from afar.[47] Like the crowd that admires Hesiod's rhetor-prince "like a god," the chorus-singer hopes to make herself Astymeloisa's "suppliant" and so signifies a communal attitude toward what Astymeloisa, in her role as the city-beloved "Astymeloisa," embodies. The point is that, even if the girls of the chorus are performing an approved communal morality rather than their "own" subjectivity, and even if they are performing a song composed for them by Alcman, it is also true that a girl in Astymeloisa's position is cast into a significant public role and is endowed, while she performs, with a certain social prestige and power pertaining to that role. The song, in sum, projects the chorus-members and particularly the chorus leaders into an eloquence-performing "speaker-function" that is itself endowed with the sorts of attributes that Hesiod attaches to the Muse-beloved *basileus* and bard, even if those attributes cannot be attached to the girls themselves as girls in Spartan culture.[48]

But Lesbos was, of course, neither Athens nor Sparta. Neither the Athenian Thesmophoria nor Alcman's maiden-songs can be taken as precise models for the context(s) of Sappho's poetry. First of all, as Denys Page has remarked, upper-class Lesbian women seem to have enjoyed more freedom than their counterparts elsewhere. They were neither subjected as girls to the compulsory, state-sponsored training of the Spartan *agelai* nor were they, on marriage, sequestered within their husband's house (as at Athens). Though they were, as elsewhere, excluded from direct political participation, it seems that upper-class Lesbian women were able to appear and associate informally in public and to "mix" in male as well as female society. They were able also to form women's "clubs" or associations comparable to, though probably not the same as, the male *hetaireia*, and possibly based on the model of a *thiasos*, a religious fellowship. And they were likely to be well educated, though the education was most probably received informally through the medium of female associations, particularly those devoted to the Muses.[49]

Further, the chief women's festivals on Lesbos seem to have been less sharply focused on regulating women's reproductive powers. These festivals included the relatively informal Adonia, as well as more formal, state-sponsored rites in the great shrine of Hera-Zeus-Dionysus, where we find Alcaeus skulking in fragment 130B. As Page remarks, this cult center seems to have been founded originally as a shrine of Dionysus, with Hera and Zeus added later. Dionysus was an Asiatic import, transmitted to the Hellenic world from Lydia and Phrygia, and seems to have arrived in Lesbos at a very early date. The orgiastic Dionysian rite—concerned more with promoting than controlling vital energies (the force that through the green fuse drives the flower)—was primarily a women's festival and had offshoots in the rites of Artemis (Asiatic Cybele), which were also celebrated on Lesbos. At the shrine of Hera-Zeus-Dionysus, Hera was the preeminent deity, as she was for Aeolic Greek culture generally, while her association with Dionysus was unusual: it appears that the Lesbian-Aeolic cult and rites of Hera, which probably included the beauty contest described by Alcaeus, were grafted onto and combined with those of an older cult of Dionysus.[50]

The Adonia, centered on the Aphrodite-Adonis myth, also was an Asiatic import. According to Margaret Williamson, the symbolism of this festival, unlike that of the Thesmophoria or other women's festivals devoted to mother gods, was less focused on fertility/childbirth than on sexuality per se. Its activities seem to have featured "enjoyable and private merrymaking . . . in which women were released from the burden of being responsible for national fertility and simply got together, without a script, to have a good time"; in Attic comedy, we find men complaining about being kept awake all night or prevented from conducting normal business by women's noisemaking during the Adonia (Aristophanes, *Lysistrata* 387–398; Menander, *Girl from Samos* 43–44).[51] Festivals of Aphrodite-Adonis and Hera, as well as Dionysiac and Artemisian celebrations, would seem to have provided Lesbian women with occasions that had more to do with the affirmation than the disciplining of women's power as sexual beings.

These contexts—informal, symposiumlike women's gatherings and women's festivals, as well as wedding celebrations—provide the most likely settings for the performance of Sappho's poetry. An epigram in the *Greek Anthology* (9.189) describes her as leading the "Lesbian women" (*Lesbides*) in a dance procession to the shrine of Hera, holding a "golden lyre" and setting the tune; and among Sappho's surviving fragments are a hymn to Hera and legendary materials from the Troy-tale connected to the shrine (fr. 17, possibly 44).[52] It seems likely that Sappho would have played some role in the festival proceedings witnessed in Alcaeus's poem, either as a performer in her own right or as a trainer of girl choruses (or both). Ancient writers also credit her with hymns to Artemis (Philostratus, *Apollonius of Tyana* 1.30; "Menander Rhetor" 9.132), though virtually no trace of these remains.[53] And we have fragments of epithalamia that clearly are connected to wedding festivities. Aphrodite, however, is overwhelmingly the predominant deity in Sappho's extant poetry, while references to Adonis occur as well (e.g., fr. 96, 140[a], 168). It is possible that at least some part of Sappho's verse was intended for performance in women's gatherings during the Adonia, but by far the majority of what survives, and virtually all the poetry that has sustained her modern reputation, appears to be most suitable to symposiumlike gatherings by a circle of *hetairai*. These could have been social gatherings that took place during the Adonia or that simply met, without any particular festival-context, at various times and at some appropriate meeting-place: a house, most probably, or a shrine precinct suitable for a meeting of a female *thiasos* devoted to Aphrodite and the Muses.

At this point it is worth recalling Hesiod's phrase "conspicuous amid the throng," *meta de prepei agromenoisin*, since what is meant is a crowd of commoners gathered in a public meeting-space. "Throng" renders *agromenoisin*, a past (aorist) participle of the verb *ageiro*, "gather together," which is used by Homer to signify herded swine (*Odyssey* 16.3). Hesiod's rhetor-prince and Alcman's Astymeloisa both are made distinctive by virtue of a trained excellence and impressiveness—including the hint of cultured luxury in "the charm of Kinyras" (an imported, expensive, perfumed oil) on Astymeloisa's hair—that sets them apart from ordinary folk and that makes them powerfully attractive, widely admired, and effective in public. Concern with such distinction is pervasive in Sappho's extant poetry. In one of her more famous fragments (96), for example, a departed companion is said now to be "making herself conspicuous (*emprepetai*) among Lydian women" like the moon after sunset, or in other words, to be presenting herself impressively, outshining all the bright stars around her, even in the land of luxury where noble women are especially refined. In another fragment cited and partially paraphrased by Athenaeus (fr. 57), Sappho derides Andromeda, one of her competitors according to Maximus, by saying "[w]hat country girl [*agroiôtis*] enchants your mind . . . done up in country stuff [*agroiôtin stolan*] . . . not knowing how to raise her fineries above her ankles?" The word "done up," *epemmena*, suggests cookery and thus meniality; and "fineries," *ta brake*, is an ironic swipe at a commoner's hopelessly gauche, unstylish, and crucially underfunded effort at dressing up in clothes that she doesn't quite know how to wear. Sappho's point is the low, bumpkinesque quality of Andromeda's circle. Andromeda's *hetairai*, unlike Sappho's, are not "conspicuous amid the throng," much less among Lydian women. In the beauty contest described in Alcaeus's poem, the women who parade in trailing robes amid the ululation are most probably being judged not by men but by each other, while the "beauty" in question, *phua*, is a matter of bearing or "stature"; this is no Miss Lesbos contest. The women are competing with each other for preeminence in matters of cultured "conspicuousness," refinement, and impressive self-presentation.

It seems likely that Sappho played some role in training upper-class young women to be "conspicuous amid the throng"—not only in daily life but also, and most important, as performers of song in public and private contexts, as this was a sine qua non of aristocratic accomplishment—and this training probably took place through informal association at private gatherings. A papyrus fragment of a second-century (A.D.) commentary on Sappho's poetry says that "she in peace and quiet trained the noblest girls, not only those of local extraction but also those from Ionia" (fr. 214B). "In peace and quiet" translates *eph' hêsychias*, which could also be rendered as "at leisure," "in peacetime," or "in a quiet and sequestered place"; "the noblest girls" translates *ta arista*, which more precisely means "the best female persons" and thus could mean "women" also (though the verb "trained," *paideuousa*, suggests *paides*, girls, rather than *gynaikes*, mature women). The commentary's statement that Sappho's associates were not only local *arista* but also from other parts of Ionia is more or less corroborated by the Suda's much later testimony that her "students" (*mathêtriai*) included Anagora of Miletus, Gongyla of Colophon, and Eunika of Salamis (test. 2). Further, Philostratus's novel *Apollonius of Tyana*, which is roughly contemporary with the papyrus commentary, mentions a Damophyla from Pamphylia (a Greek settlement in what is now southwestern Turkey) "who is said to have associated with Sappho, and to have composed the hymns they sing to Artemis of Perge in both Aeolian and Pamphylian modes"; moreover, Damophyla "is said to have gathered girl associates (*parthenous homilêtrias*) and to have composed poems both erotic and hymnal, in Sappho's manner," while she "copied" (*parôidêtai*) her hymns to Artemis from those of Sappho (1.30; test. 21).

It would be a mistake to think of Sappho as the head of an official "school" for girls or as a priestess in charge of a *thiasos* (though she may have played some role in a cult of Aphrodite and the Muses); these once popular views, along with views of Sappho as a sort of archaic Greek geisha or musical prostitute, have long since been discredited. But is it less difficult to imagine her, as Maximus does, in a quasi- or protosophistic role: that is, as a person who has attracted or "gathered" to herself an informal circle or "salon" of friends, devotees, and apprenticelike followers by virtue of her *sophia*, wisdom-skill, in the cultivated arts that counted most for "conspicuousness" among aristocratic women in Mytilene and elsewhere—and who, by virtue of her reputation for such *sophia*, would be a mentor-figure with whom the "best" families might wish their daughters to associate. As such, Sappho would seem to be a precursor for such later figures as Aspasia and Diotima, who survive for us now mainly through caricatures and references in Plato, Plutarch, and elsewhere.[54] Further, the references to Sappho's "students" in the testimonia, and especially the non-Lesbian students, suggest a picture consistent with Gregory Nagy's account of archaic rhapsode societies such as the Homeridai (the "sons of Homer") or the followers of Archilochus.[55] As Nagy suggests, the chief means of poetic preservation and dissemination in the predominantly oral world of archaic Greece, and especially in the seventh to sixth centuries, was the reperformance and reembodiment of the "original" poet's voice by subsequent generations of followers: the Homeridai as reembodiers of "Homer" in the reperformance and indeed the recomposition of what we might call Homer-songs, and the followers of Archilochus as reperformers/recomposers of "Archilochus-songs," most typically (especially in later centuries) in symposiastic contexts. And so, it seems quite possible, with Sappho too.

The fact that Sappho's "students" seem to appear nowhere outside the ancient biographical notices suggests that they were, for the most part, learning to rhapsodically reperform "Sappho-songs," including hymns and epithalamia for festival occasions as well as erotic and other "private" songs for symposiumlike women's gatherings. Though we probably should not imagine anything as formal as a professionalized guild of "Sappho-singers" like the Homeridai, Philostratus's reference to Damophyla does suggest the existence of women who were Sapphic reperformers, some of whom may have become poets (that is, original composers rather than recomposers) as well as song teachers in their own right. Even if Philostratus' Damophyla is fictional (as she is generally thought to be), she clearly is presented as a probable fiction meant to be consistent with what Philostratus's audience knows about the world: it would seem that circles of "Sapphic" performers and followers existed, at least in some places, and at least in the time before the repertoire of Sappho-song was written down, collected, and organized into a definitive "edition" by Hellenistic scholars sometime between the third and first centuries B.C.[56]

Sappho's circle, then, would appear to have been an informal fellowship somewhat like a male *hetaireia* and in some ways resembling or prefiguring the sophistic circles of later centuries. It probably included both *parthenoi* who were there as "students" or followers of Sappho and married women, *gynaikes*, who were there as Sappho's associates and friends. And it probably was much more permeable, more "leaky," than Alcaeus's faction: probably not so much a "boat" but a fluctuating network.[57] First of all, the membership was more unstable and probably was in constant flux, as younger women joined the group and left again upon their marriages—some of them arriving, like Eunika, from as far away as Salamis, and some, like Anactoria, departing for Lydia (fr. 16, 96), depending on the arrangements their families made. Others who stayed in Mytilene may have remained in the fellowship beyond their marriages, and surely some did, but as with Alcaeus's *hetaireia* there would have been shifting allegiances and defections. One fragment excoriates a certain Mika for choosing "the friendship of Penthilid ladies," calls her an "evildoer," *kakotropê*, and says "I will not allow you" to join in the musical and other pleasures of the group (fr. 71); another faults Atthis for tiring of Sappho and "flying off" to Andromeda (fr. 131), despite the fact that "I loved you . . . once long ago" (fr. 49).

The reference to "Penthilid ladies" raises a second cause of the group's permeability. As Eva Stehle points out, women's groups in Mytilene probably "formed a system of political communication separate from, but interlacing with, men's symposium groups."[58] That is, like the quasi-political women's organizations in the Athenian Thesmophoria, women's groups in Mytilene probably reflected the factional alignments of their families, so that the discourse and rivalries of women's circles were traversed and affected by, and were part of, Mytilenean city politics. In one fragment, which Maximus cites as an example of Sappho's "Socratic" irony, she says "I wish the Polyanactids' daughter a very good day" (fr. 155); the conspicuous invocation of the family name, rather than the girl's own name, seems to indicate a basis for enmity. (Another badly damaged fragment [99] also seems to indicate hostility to the Polyanactids, though it is hard to tell.) Elsewhere, Sappho expresses concern for the shame that her brother's misadventures may bring upon "us" and expresses hopes that he will recover from his errors and become "a joy to his friends and a misery to his enemies" (fr. 5); what seems to be at stake is the relative standing and reputation of noble houses/factions jockeying for position and prestige.[59] Sappho distances herself, her family, and her circle from her brother's misdeeds and thereby reasserts her (and "our") respectability within the city. Finally, Sappho appears to have been exiled to Syracuse for a time (test. 5, fr. 98), perhaps the same time that Alcaeus was exiled to Pyrrha by Myrsilos (c. 605 B.C,), which suggests that she, her family, and her circle were implicated in the stasiotic struggles then going on in Mytilene. If Sappho suffered one or more periods of exile, it is likely that much of her circle would have been dispersed and that she would have had to reconstitute a circle from the society available to her; the fact that there was until Cicero's time a highly valued portrait statue of Sappho in the Syracusan prytaneion (Cicero, *Against Verres* 2.4.125–127; test. 24) suggests that she may have established a Syracusan following while there. Unlike Alcaeus's group, Sappho's circle was not so much held together as continually reconstituted.

A third and related cause of permeability is the fact that, though Sappho's poetry speaks primarily to the women of her fluctuating circle, or figures them as addressees, Sappho's confidantes do not constitute her only audience. This is so in part because of the "traversing" of women's circles by the concerns of city politics and in part because of the relatively greater freedom that Lesbian women enjoyed (compared, at least, with Athenian women) and the apparent tendency in Lesbian culture to separate men's and women's spheres less sharply. While men were excluded from the Athenian Thesmophoria, we find Alcaeus observing the women's doings at the festival of Hera; men did not participate, but apparently they were permitted to be there. The same was true for the Adonia. And it was probably true for other women's gatherings as well.[60] If "mixed" company was possible on Lesbos, then it is possible too that men could at least sometimes be present when Sappho performed her songs—as at the salonlike gatherings of Aspasia, at Athens, over a century later.[61] And in general, of course, the culture of Lesbian women was still enclosed within a dominant patriarchal order that never could be fully excluded from their discourse.

Beyond Sappho's immediate, primary audience of *hetairai* there was always a secondary audience of men. This was, moreover, an audience with which she clearly was successful, as witnessed most simply by the fact that male writers and scholars in antiquity compiled and edited Sappho's poems, and canonized her— even as they maligned and mythologized her—as a "tenth Muse" and one of the greatest of lyric poets. The fact that she was parodied in Attic comedy suggests that her poetry was, in fact, controversial or disturbing to conventional patriarchal culture: it pressed the boundaries of acceptability. The fact that she was canonized suggests her ability to persuasively maintain a controversial position, making "the weaker case stronger," within the wider realm of Hellenic culture. Sapphic imitations by such later poets as Catullus and Horace attest a tradition of male reading and reperformance of Sappho-songs, and we know that, even in Sappho's lifetime, her songs already were being performed by men at male symposia, and as far away as Athens. According to Aelian, Solon (who was Sappho's contemporary) heard his nephew sing a Sappho-song at a symposium and asked the boy to teach it to him; when asked the reason for this request, he replied "So that I may learn it and die" (as quoted by Stobaeus, *Anthology* 3.29.58; test. 10, tr. Campbell). Plutarch, writing in the late first or early second century A.D., nearly seven centuries after Solon, remarks on Sappho-songs that still were being sung at men's symposia (*Sympotic Questions* 622c, 711d).[62] Sappho's songs could travel well, and did, quite far beyond the boundaries of her circle.

By considering her songs as enthymematic arguments—insofar as we can observe this in some of her key fragments—we might approach an understanding of Sappho's power. We might begin with what is certainly the most famous fragment of them all, which "Longinus" quoted (and so preserved) as an illustration of "sublimity" (10.1–3).

[fr. 31]

He seems to me an equal to the gods,
that man who sits opposite you
and hearkens close to your sweet
speaking

and lovely laughing—truly it
makes my heart shake in my breast;
for when I see you briefly, I cannot
speak at all,

but my tongue is broken, a faint
fire quickly spreads beneath my flesh,
and I see nothing with my eyes, and my
ears roar,

and my sweat pours down, and a trembling
seizes me all over, and I'm more moist than
grass, and I seem to myself scarcely
short of dying.

But all is to be borne, since [even a pauper?][63] . . .

Eva Stehle has argued that this and other erotic poems of Sappho's cannot properly be placed in a symposiastic setting, in essence because its intensely personal address, and the implied closeness of speaker and addressee, would violate the basic symposiastic function of promoting or maintaining group solidarity. In consequence, Stehle argues, this poem (and others like it) could not have been intended for performance at a women's gathering and must have been given instead as a *written text* to an individual friend or lover—perhaps on the occasion of her departure—for her to perform for herself in privacy, thereby keeping Sappho "with" her even in separation. Sappho's erotic poetry thus embodies a then unprecedented use of writing to create and communicate a private, "lyric" subjectivity (in the romantico-modern sense), one that, because it is so intensely private, provides the addressee with a model of female identity that both escapes from and resists the traditional gender norms imposed by patriarchal public culture.[64]

Stehle's argument is provocative and ingenious, but I think it is unlikely. One reason for my doubt is the general lack of evidence that writing was used as a primary means of communication or medium for poetry in the late seventh and early sixth centuries. (The earliest surviving Greek alphabet inscription, the so-called Dipylon jar from Athens, dates to roughly the beginning of Sappho's lifetime.) There is, in the National Archaeological Museum in Athens, a piece of pottery that shows an image of Sappho sitting on a chair and reading a scroll while surrounded by female figures holding a lyre and a garland above her head; but it dates from the fifth century B.C., when written poetry-texts were becoming more common. Another pot from the early fifth century shows Sappho and Alcaeus together, both holding lyres. And the earliest known image of Sappho, dated to the early sixth century, shows her holding a lyre and striding forward as if leading a procession.[65] That image reflects how poets in general and Sappho in particular were understood. In short, the evidence that Sappho would have been likely to use writing as a primary medium of communication, or to compose poems as "letters" or gifts to individual friends, is weak.

Another consideration is that, on one hand, there is no strong reason to believe that what I deliberately have been calling symposium-*like* women's gatherings would have been precisely the same as men's symposia or would have served exactly the same purposes. Alcaeus's *hetaireia* was a tightly knit political faction with a relatively stable membership whose coherence as a fighting unit had to be sustained; Sappho's circle, with its fluctuating personnel, may have been more like a salon devoted to the pursuits and pleasures of cultivated women—or like a sophist's circle, with friends, associates, and students gathered round a master performer famed for wisdom-skill, *sophia*, in some art—or like the late-fifth-century "salons" of Aspasia and Diotima. Could fragment 31 not have been performed in such a setting, as an *epideixis* that mimetically embodies the speech of a lover to a beloved? Or an argument dramatistically presented through the figure of apostrophe?[66] Is it necessary to consider the poem as a "love letter" to an actual, specific person, especially when the addressee remains unnamed? (Consider the "speech of Lysias" in Plato's *Phaedrus*.) On the other hand, there is no strong reason, either, to believe that a poem like fragment 31 could not have been performed in symposiastic (as well as other) gatherings. Could Sappho not have composed this poem, and taught it to her friends and devotees, as part of a repertoire available for reperformance in symposia? Certainly one likely reason for the poem's dissemination and survival, over the centuries from Sappho to her Hellenistic editors and finally to "Longinus," would have been its continued popularity as part of such a repertoire. If the poem had really been meant as a "letter" or gift for a single, specific person, who would then perform it to herself in solitude, it is difficult to understand how it would have been disseminated and preserved. The fact that "Longinus" has not quoted the entire poem and has omitted at least its final strophe (though he "cites" the remainder by stating its opening phrase) indicates that he expects his reader to be familiar with it.

Consider this poem from the *Theognidea* (1299–1304):

Boy, how long will you flee from me? O, how I run after you
    and plead! I pray that there might be some limit
to your anger. Yet you with your raging, headstrong *thymos*
    flee, having the merciless *êthos* of a kite.
But stay with me, and give to me your favor. Not for long
    will you possess the gift of Aphrodite, the violet-crowned.

Clearly this poem is more emotionally restrained than Sappho's fragment 31. Theognis generally speaks with "manly" circumspection. But this poem also casts itself as a "personal" lover's declaration and complaint: like the speaker of Sappho's poem, or like Alcman's maiden-singer gesturing toward Astymeloisa, Theognis is overwhelmed by the force of Aphrodite embodied in the boy and is reduced to the status of a suppliant, or indeed of a "pauper" who must beg, while his passion goes unrequited (though for different reasons). As in Sappho's poem the beloved is unnamed, and figures as a stock addressee-figure. My point is that there is little question that Theognis's poem, even though it seems to be a private declaration, is meant for symposiastic reperformances. Why not Sappho's poem? The difference in emotional intensity cannot be taken as decisive evidence to the contrary. That difference may be the product simply of differential gender norms for both emotional experience and expression.

So what is happening in Sappho's famous fragment 31? It is important to keep in mind that the poem, as we have it, is incomplete: the fragment's final line is the beginning of what was at least one more strophe. What we have, in other words, is the amplification of a *topos* that served as the setup and as a source of persuasion for a now-missing enthymematic cap that cannot possibly be reconstructed (unless it turns up in an Egyptian papyrus-dump someday). Catullus 51, which is an imitation of this poem, clearly substitutes a different ending—"[i]dleness, Catullus, does you harm," and so forth—and so can be no help. The amplification reaches a cap of its own in the climactic declaration that "I seem to myself scarcely short of dying," but the *poem's* cap cannot be reconstructed precisely because an enthymematic "conclusion" does not follow by logical necessity from what precedes it, but functions as a selection and foregrounding of one among many inferential possibilities at a particular moment within a discourse, and derives persuasiveness not only from the overt discourse that has preceded it but also from the tacit presuppositional (ideological, cognitive, perceptual, etc.) frames brought to it by an audience. We do not know, and cannot know, specifically what argument Sappho meant this poem to make.

But it is obvious enough that it is an erotic poem, and evident that Sappho has amplified the general *topos* of "I'm overcome with love whenever I look at you" in order to invest the poem's closing stance (whatever it was) with persuasive force. This is, in effect, "Longinus's" point about the part of the poem that he has cited: Sappho's "excellence" and indeed her "sublimity" in this passage resides in her ability to portray *erôs* by selecting and combining the most outstanding *pathêmata* that accompany and constitute it, rendering it as not a single thing but a "congress of emotions" (*pathôn synodos;* 10.1, 3).[67] By rendering the general *topos* through a virtual narrative of the details constituting *erôs* "whenever I look at you," Sappho endows it with considerable presence and psychagogic power: her audience can project themselves into, and indeed are drawn into, an entire scenario that is both as-tonishing in its vividness and resonant with their own experiential knowledge. "Longinus" says, immediately after citing this passage, "are you not amazed?" and then remarks that "all such things occur with lovers" (10.1.3). It is striking too, and a demonstration of "Longinus's" point, that nearly all readers of this poem, espe-cially modern ones, have tended to regard it as a *cri de coeur*, a mimesis of the mo-ment of overwhelming passion itself, when Sappho is in fact *describing it*, with con-siderable self-control, as an "emotion recollected in tranquillity"—she is speaking now, in an apostrophe, of a speechless state that overcomes her "whenever I see you"[68]—though the description is indeed evocative and intensifies its effect through an accumulation of polysyndeta leading to the climactic declaration. Even "Longinus" gets caught up in this passage's extraordinary psychagogy and speaks as if Sappho is exhibiting rather than describing the "symptoms" of erotic love.

It is not entirely clear to us, however, just what the full scenario is. Where is the speaker, and to whom does she speak these lines? And who is the godlike man that sits opposite the beloved? There is a largely now-discredited history of interpre-tation that regards the poem as meant for a wedding celebration: the man is the beloved's husband, and Sappho—or the speaker in the poem, or the girl or woman who performs it—is (or pretends to be) stricken with grief, or jealousy, at the thought of separation from her beloved friend, or she is presenting her lovestruck wonder at the bride as a form of praise.[69] But there is no particular reason to sup-pose any of this; certainly "Longinus" does not suppose it. The woman and man may or may not be married, and the occasion at which they sit facing each other is not necessarily a wedding celebration and is not necessarily the occasion of the poem itself either. Perhaps Sappho has invoked an image of a typical dinner party in Mytilene. Probably the poem is meant to be performed at a women's gathering, or a "salon." Moreover, even if the woman and man in the poem are married, and if the woman is part of Sappho's circle, there is no particular reason to suppose that her husband displaces Sappho in her affections or that she is going away. Another, perhaps more credible line of interpretation regards the poem as a sort of hyberbolic compliment, not for a bride but for a friend or lover: "anyone who can look at you and hear your voice and not be swept away is more (or less) than human."

Anne Burnett fairly persuasively suggests that Sappho is, on one hand, appropri-ating and refashioning a traditional praise topic that can be found in Pindar and, on the other hand, responding to "one of the stock philosophical debates of her time," regarding the question of what man could claim (and when) to be like a god, the usual answers being he who experiences the bliss of the wedding day or he who has won an athletic victory. Sappho, then, shifts the debate by suggesting that it is not so much the fact of being married and thus possessing a beautiful wife that makes "that man" blessed enough to be "an equal to the gods" but the sheer fact of being near to and experiencing (without dying) the presence of a woman as conspicuously impres-sive as one of Sappho's dear companions.[70] Nevertheless, it is to "you," the woman, that Sappho directs her apostrophe, while "you" remains an inspecific person: she is, in effect, whoever it is that Sappho loves and is any and all of her *hetairai*.

One might pursue this line of thought a little further. The poem can be seen as setting up a contrast between two typical scenarios. In one, the otherwise unde-lineated "that man," a type, sits opposite "you," also a type, at some occasion: apparently calmly, perhaps blandly, he takes in the pleasures of her "sweet speaking and lovely laughing"; she is for him an ornament to the banquet, objectified in his gaze. In the other scenario, Sappho (or whoever speaks) is overwhelmed by *erôs* even at a glimpse of "you" or of the scene, and she fully feels the force of what Theognis calls "Aphrodite's gift" or indeed the embodiment of Aphrodite's power in the woman's presence. But this contrast is a bit too simple. What "that man" is "hearkening" to is the woman's *ady phôneisas*, which can be rendered as not only "sweet speaking" but also "sweet sounding" or vocalizing, a vocalizing that spills over into "lovely laughing," *gelaisas imeroen*, or more precisely a laughter that causes yearning and desire (*imeros*, or *himeros* in "standard" Attic dialect). So it is not simply that she says "sweet" things, but that she speaks "sweetly" with cultivated grace and skill, with a woman's *eloquence* that is pleasant and beguiling and that includes not only the speaking itself—though that is the focal point of attention—but also, probably, the impressiveness of her entire bodily self-presentation, her delivery, as she vocalizes. Further, "that man," though he may seem to be an impassive, godlike figure, is "hearkening," *hypakouei*, a verb that means not only "listen to" but also *be obedient, answer to, heed, accept, comply, give way, submit*. The verb *hypakouô* signifies the response of the ruled to those who rule them. Thus, while the man in this scene may be maintaining an outward demeanor of "manliness" or emotive self-control, what Sappho sees is a virtual theophany of Aphrodite manifested as persuasive power *in the woman's act of speaking*.

Sappho's described response to her glimpse of the woman's presence, or to the scene itself—the "it" of "it makes my heart shake" ambiguously refers to either—suggests that it is a glimpse of Aphrodite, or of a divine impressiveness and power, that she is responding to. The verb that I have rather lamely translated as "shake," *eptoaisen*—which others have rendered equally unsatisfactorily as "tremble," "flutter," or even "cower"[71]—derives from *petomai*, which means "fly" (as of birds and insects) and by extension *dart, rush, move quickly, make haste, be on the wing, flutter*. Since Sappho is speaking of the *kardia* in her breast, her "heart" as physical organ as well as seat of emotion, the general sense is of a suddenly quickened heartbeat, a palpitation, as well as a metaphorical suggestion that her heart "takes flight" in a sudden emotional rush. To say that "my heart flutters" seems, in English, too weak a phrase for what Sappho signifies. In another fragment, Sappho uses *eptoiase* to signify the excitation of desire in one of her companions, Abanthis, at the sight of Gongyla (fr. 22). More specifically, she says that "yearning," *pothos*, "once again flies round you [. . .] the lovely one [*tan kalan*]; for her dress [*katagôgis*] excited [*eptoaise*] you when you saw it, and I rejoice."[72] *Katagôgis* may signify not only a woman's dress but also anything that descends, trails down, wraps or winds around, provides enclosure, and is seductive; and "the lovely one" may signify either Gongyla or the glimpse of Aphrodite that she projects, and at which Sappho rejoices (Aphrodite, "the Cyprian," is mentioned two lines down, just as the fragment trails off in incoherent scattered words).[73]

Sappho says this in the context of "bidding" or instructing Abanthis to "sing of Gongyla," and it seems that what Sappho does in fragment 31 is precisely, or is a model for, what Abanthis is asked to do. Abanthis and Sappho celebrate the apparition of Aphrodite in a beloved, an apparition whose presence is known by its effects on a beholder, which are the effects enumerated in fragment 31. This enumeration on one hand makes persuasive Sappho's climactic declaration that the sudden, heart-shaking congress of *pathêmata* that she undergoes is a "near death" experience, an erotic swoon, and the persuasiveness of this declaration in turn enforces the inferential likelihood that the cause of what she feels is Aphrodite's briefly glimpsed apparition. Sappho's shaken, paralyzed speechlessness is very like the terrified response of queen Metaneira, in the Homeric *Hymn to Demeter*, to that goddess's sudden revelation of herself (she had been disguised): "[a]nd [Metaneira's] knees were straightway loosened, and for a long time she was speechless, and forgot to pick her darling child up from the ground" (281–283). In sum, Sappho's portrayal of her response as a "near death" experience also justifies her implicit claim that she has seen an apparition of divinity and so justifies in turn her explicit declaration that it takes an "equal to the gods" to closely gaze at and listen to "you." Indeed, by the end of the fragment, the person addressed as "you" may be Aphrodite as much as the nonspecific woman in the figured scene.

Fragments 31 and 22, then, both portray being stricken suddenly with *erôs* as the result of a briefly glimpsed virtual theophany of Aphrodite. Moreover, they portray this virtual theophany as effected through the *speech and clothing* of Sappho's conspicuous, impressive, cultivated friends: Gongyla's trailing dress and "your" sweet utterance and bodily presentation (or what rhetoric manuals would later call "delivery"). "Aphrodite," then, is figured as a persuasive/seductive effect that is produced by means of the cultured arts that Sappho and her companions practice—arts that include knowing how to sing, how to talk, how to walk, how to wear fine clothes, and in general how to present oneself as a woman, as well as how to experience love and pleasure. "Aphrodite" is not embodied in Andromeda's "country girl" who lacks the *sophia*, the know-how, that Sappho's companions share. Women who do possess it are endowed with an extraordinary and indeed holy power, and by virtue of its possession, moreover, they require extraordinary persons as their equals and companions. "That man" to whom "you" speaks in fragment 31, though he is not the focus of the poem, does figure as the sort of consort, or husband, that Sappho's friends deserve: his act of *hearkening*, his susceptibility to persuasion effected by means of art (as opposed to brute force) suggests that he too experiences, though perhaps less intensely, the manifestation of Aphrodite that so shakes Sappho's heart. This fact makes him praiseworthy, and indeed makes him "an equal to the gods," at least for the time.[74]

What I am suggesting is that fragment 31 is in some ways a poem about "rhetoric"—though that term does not exist in Sappho's world—or about "eloquence" figured as an art of *erôs*, a *technê erôtikê* of persuasion/seduction, embodied in the kind of women that Sappho loves and celebrates, and in the kind of speech act that Sappho's poem performs. Further, Sappho presents this art as constituting a realm of blessedness, in which "that man" and "you" take on the look of a quasi-divine couple: Aphrodite-Adonis, Hera-Zeus.

It is clear enough, I hope, how this poem addresses itself as an act of argumentation to the women of Sappho's ever-fluctuating circle—how it functions to persuade them of their power and significance as cultured women who can present themselves effectively, and how it affirms, like much of Sappho's poetry, the affections that tie them even more closely to each other and the culture they share than to the men they happen to be paired with (as elegant items of gift exchange in marriage contracts).[75] The "proof" for both assertions lies in Sappho's amplified account, her narrative, of the sudden *erôs* that overcomes her at the virtual theophany that occurs "whenever I see you briefly" sitting in conversation with "that man." But the poem also makes a case to men, and largely by the same means, for the kind of women and the kind of love that Sappho celebrates. Indeed, like Alcman's maiden-songs this poem makes a case to the wider community about what kinds of women are best and most desirable: "that man" is blessed whose companion or wife is the cultured, conspicuous, eloquent sort of woman who can inspire such love in Sappho. At the same time, moreover, it argues what kinds of men are best: namely, those able to value and "hearken" to the art of eloquence embodied in such women, and so to inhabit the blessed realm it constitutes. This is a significant argument, when one considers the political situation in Mytilene when Sappho first performed this song.

What is perhaps most striking about Sappho's argumentation is that, unlike Alcaeus, she does not (or does not always) invoke conventional *topoi* or mythic frames simply as authoritative filters for controlling an interpretation of the present, or as a means for placing present circumstance under the sign of a traditional *sophia* which itself remains beyond examination. Certainly Sappho does invoke traditional beliefs and mythic resonances. But, as we have seen in fragment 31, Sappho can, and at least sometimes does, appropriate and reconfigure conventional *topoi* in order to shift, or rearrange, traditional or prevailing value-hierarchies: that is, to assert the values of her women's circle within a space otherwise dominated by the patriarchal values of archaic Greek aristocracy, and so to make the lesser case greater.[76] Moreover, as Denys Page has noted, Sappho's language seems remarkably "independent of literary tradition . . . [and] close to the speech of every day."[77] One way to say this is that Sappho both appropriates tradition and marks, through the voice that she projects, her independence from it (or her dialectical relation with it) as a specific, individual woman—her capacity to differ. In Sappho's own "sweet speech," then, we hear not simply the repetition and invocation of tradition as a source of authority, but also the transformation of tradition in a woman's voice that apparently derives authority and persuasiveness from the vividness and psychagogic power of its own self-presentation and the argumentation that it offers.

Let us consider two more fragments— 16 and 1—which, after fragment 31, are the best known and certainly the most substantial examples of Sappho's poetry. In fragment 16, which possibly (though not certainly) contains a complete poem, we get what is perhaps the clearest view of Sappho's argumentative procedure.

> Some say a host of cavalry, others infantry
> and others ships upon the dark earth
> are most beautiful, but I say it is what-
> soever one loves;
>
> and one can easily make this understood
> by everyone, for the much admired
> beauty of humankind, Helen, her husband
> who was most noble

she put aside and sailed to Troy
and neither child nor loving parents
did she keep in mind, but was led astray
    . . . by [love?]

    . . . unharmed for . . .
    . . . lightly . . .
    . . . and has reminded me now of Anactoria
who is not here;

and I would rather see her lovely walk
and the bright glance of her face
than Lydian chariots and armored
marching troops.

    . . . impossible to happen
    . . . humankind . . . but pray to share

[nine lines missing]

unexpectedly.

It is possible that the fifth strophe, with its reference to "Lydian chariots and armored marching troops," is the end of the poem and that what follows are the paltry remnants of three strophes of another poem (parts of the first two lines and the twelfth line).[78] In any case, it is clear that the first five strophes do constitute a complete enthymematic argument.

One conspicuous feature of this argument is that it is explicitly confuting the very code of value that is invoked in Alcaeus's "hall of armor" poem, where indeed nothing is finer than the sight of military splendor and the call to martial heroism that it embodies. To a certain degree, Sappho's opening priamel may seem initially to destabilize the principles of judgment by which "some" have attempted to define the "finest thing." Insofar as the phrase "whatsoever one loves" implies that what makes something "finest" or "most beautiful" (*kallistos*) is not an inherent quality but the attitude by which it is perceived, what is introduced is not a fourth and trumping candidate for "finest thing" but a different and disruptively relativistic principle of definition. Anne Burnett argues that this opening parodically reduces conventional masculine modes of disputation, especially about such questions as "what is most beautiful," to absurdity.[79] But the sense of a parodic reduction or destabilization is fleeting at most, for Sappho's offering of "proofs"—the story of Helen and her own longing for Anactoria—quickly establishes *erôs* as the "finest thing" and indeed as a trumping term to the varieties of military splendor. "Whatsoever one loves" becomes the person one loves, or whatever it is about that person that inspires one's love. This is made clear by the poem's (or the fragment's) enthymematic cap: the sight of a beloved such as Anactoria *really is* "the most beautiful thing on earth" and preferable to the sight of "Lydian chariots and armored marching troops." So there is, after all, a principle of judgment. There is a quality that inheres in persons like Anactoria (or in the impressive way that they present themselves) that calls forth *erôs*, and this is the best and most beautiful thing there is, on earth, for human beings.

Sappho's use of the Helen tale as a "proof" that will "easily make this understood by everyone" is both conventional and revisionary. Conventionally, Helen functions as a familiar illustration of the notion that the force of *erôs*, the "madness" of love induced by Aphrodite, can overwhelm all other attachments and allegiances: Helen abandons her noble husband, violates her marriage oath, and so forth. But Helen also represents, conventionally, an image of sinfulness, both her own and that of Paris. With Alcaeus, the "rape" or theft of Helen constitutes a violation of the principles of guest-friendship and gift exchange, bringing a divinely sponsored punishment to Troy. With Sappho, however, such notions of guilt and retribution seem not to figure in at all. What is emphasized instead is Helen's *excellence*. Helen is the "much-admired beauty of humankind," *poly perskethoisa kallos anthrôpôn*, that is, the best of all women (and indeed of all human beings). It is because of this status, according to legend, that Aphrodite awards her as a prize to Paris—in exchange for judging Aphrodite the most beautiful of goddesses—and sets in motion the workings of fate that lead to the fall of Troy. But Troy's fate is not important here; it is not even mentioned. Rather, if we think of the war (and the fate of Troy) at all, the important point seems to be that both sides fought over Helen because of her status as the world's most excellent woman; and in the end Helen herself went home unharmed. That which inspires *erôs* is the ruling power, for the sake of which all else happens; and that thing is embodied superlatively in Helen, and (to some lesser degree) in Anactoria. It seems that what Sappho says about Helen and love would be true whether the Trojan war had taken place or not. (And indeed one could argue from this perspective that the cause of the war was not Helen's action but the will of men to regard her leaving as a theft of property requiring, as a point of honor, punishment of the "thief" and retrieval of the goods.)

Sappho, then, emphasizes elements of the Helen-tale that are not emphasized, for example, in Alcaeus, while deemphasizing or simply dropping elements that usually are more central. Further, another traditional feature of the myth is Helen's more or less passive victimhood: she is possessed by a mania visited on her by Aphrodite, and is raped or stolen by Paris. This is true even in Gorgias's *Helen*. There were also versions of the tale, as what is known about Stesichorus's famous lost palinode suggests, in which Helen was defended through the claim that she never went to Troy at all (but was spirited off instead to Egypt); but again she is essentially passive. In Sappho's version, however, Helen is the one who acts: she "puts aside" her husband and "sails" to Troy, and "forgets" her child and parents. Sappho does construe this as being "led astray," as she probably must: it would be difficult, in the early sixth century (as now), to argue that abandoning one's children or parents is a good thing. Still, the general sense of Sappho's presentation, as with Gorgias's *Helen* more than a century later, is that Helen's actions are justified and blameless even though they contravene traditional morality. Because she has glimpsed in Paris an *erôs*-inspiring vision sent by the goddess, the erotic mania that she feels *and that she acts on* is not only "heart-shaking" (as in fr. 31) and not only troubling to the usual order of things but also holy.

Sappho's appropriation of the Helen tale is revisionary both because she shifts its emphases and, more important, because she appropriates it in service of a larger claim that is, in fact, a challenge to the traditional ethic of the warrior-aristocrat (such as Alcaeus), for whom *erôs* appears chiefly as a symposiastic pastime to take up slack between rounds of fighting. As an apparently popular drinking-song of

Anacreon says, "[b]ring water, bring wine, dear boy, bring us flowery / garlands; have them brought, that I may box against Love." This is "Love" regarded as something to do when drunk, along with playing games like cottabus.[80] Sappho's version of the Helen tale is still sufficiently traditional to function with some authority as a "proof" for the counterclaim she offers to that ethic, while the counterclaim itself is not a complete rejection of it either (nor, realistically, could it be). Certainly the notion that a beloved is beautiful in one's eyes or that love compels people to do strange things or that one is "conquered" by "limb-loosening desire" would not have been startling and could have passed as more or less standard poetic sentiment at a symposium. Anacreon might say the same. And certainly Sappho's poem does grant that a host of cavalry, ships, or infantry *is* a splendid sight. But Sappho's claim that *erôs* or *the quality that calls it forth* is the highest and overruling value, the best of all things on earth, and better explicitly than martial splendor, proposes a reordering of Hellenic culture's normal (or predominant) value-hierarchy. The degree to which Sappho's version of the Helen tale (with its shifted emphases) still remains authoritatively "traditional" for her male and female audiences—the degree to which they can perceive it as a warranted interpretation of the myth—is also the degree to which it is effective as a source of persuasion for her larger, more disruptive claim, and "easily makes this understood by everyone."

This larger claim may not, however, be so "easily understood." For Sappho turns, after two lines that are mostly lost, to a second "proof," namely her longing for the absent Anactoria, which immediately becomes an enthymematic cap. Sappho's yearning replicates, in personal rather than mythic terms, the holy desire that made Helen "stray" with Paris. Both derive from the same source: the *erôs*-producing apparition of Aphrodite in a beloved. This is the heart-shaking glimpse that arises for Sappho from Anactoria's "bright-glancing" face and "lovely" (*eraton*) walk. (And probably from other qualities as well, since Anactoria generally is regarded as the departed companion of fragment 96, who shines like the moon amid the women of Lydia: it is worth noting that "bright," *lampros*, also signifies *splendid, radiant, distinct, brilliant, magnificent.*) Insofar as the audience's experiential knowledge enables them to identify with Sappho's yearning as something that they themselves have felt or (if not themselves) as something that people feel, this yearning functions as a "confirmation" of the version of the Helen tale that Sappho has invoked. It is not just a fabulous tale but something that really does happen, even now, in varying degrees of intensity; most people really do yearn more for absent lovers than for the sight of a marching army, as splendid as that may be; and a *magnificent* beauty like Helen's and like Anactoria's produces a yearning more intense than usual.[81] This reinforces the Helen tale as "proof" of Sappho's general contention. At the same time, the tale *as Sappho has configured it* reciprocally justifies her yearning for Anactoria as something more than "womanish" nostalgia and makes her enthymematic declaration that Anactoria would constitute a finer sight than "Lydian chariots and armored marching troops" something more than emotional caprice. The audience is asked, instead, to view that declaration as a warranted assertion of the fundamental truth of Sappho's general claim about what really matters most to human beings—a specific instantiation, in a specific person's life, of a deeper mythic paradigm that instantiates itself as well in her listeners' lives.

Sappho's argument, moreover, implicitly defines and warrants her yearning for Anactoria as a justified wish to "stray," and this may be the most ideologically disruptive aspect of the poem. If the mostly obliterated three strophes that followed Sappho's enthymematic declaration were a continuation of this poem, it seems possible that the phrase "impossible to happen" introduced a new line of argument about her blocked desire to "stray." Sappho has no realistic way to go to Lydia, and neither Anactoria nor Sappho occupies a social position that gives them the degree of agency available to men—neither has the material resources to play the role of Paris to the other's Helen. From this topic the argument may have turned (perhaps) to some concluding, consolatory hope that love or an excellence like Anactoria's might come again "unexpectedly." If this is what the poem did, Sappho's avowal of the limits placed on her as a woman would have defused (for male audiences) the dangerousness of Helen's example, while at the same time reasserting the validity of Sappho's desire and of her general contention about what is "most beautiful" and best. This is utter speculation, of course, but it is interesting to contemplate not only women's gatherings but also, and especially, men's symposia taking in an argument about the rightness of a woman's wish to wander through the world and finding it persuasive. Moreover, if we think back again to the *stasis* convulsing Mytilene in Sappho's lifetime, Alcaeus's "hall of armor poem" and his overwhelming concern with enforcing factional solidarity, and Pittacus's shift of allegiances, it is truly remarkable to think of this poem, with its demotion of martial ideals and its defense of "straying," being performed at gatherings of Lesbian women and men.

Fragment 1, while it is the only certainly complete poem by Sappho that survives, and is second in fame only to fragment 31, may in some ways be less typical of her usual argumentative procedure.

> Ornately throned immortal Aphrodite,
> wile-weaving child of Zeus, I beg you,
> do not with aches and sorrows overwhelm,
> lady, my heart,
>
> but come here, if ever and otherwhere
> when hearing this voice of mine from afar
> you acquiesced, and leaving your father's golden
> house you came
>
> in your harnessed chariot; and the beautiful
> quick sparrows brought you over the dark earth
> with thick-whirring wingbeats from bright-shining heaven
> through the middle sky,
>
> and quickly they arrived; and you, O blessed one,
> with a wide smile on your immortal face
> asked what I've suffered this time and why
> I'm calling this time,
>
> and what do I most wish would happen to me
> in my maddened heart; whom shall I persuade this time
> to bring you back in her affection? Who, O
> Sappho, does you wrong?

For if she flees, soon she will pursue;
and if she does not accept gifts, nevertheless she'll give;
and if she does not love, soon she will love
even against her will.

Come to me now, release me from hard
anxieties, and make fulfilled all that my
heart desires to be fulfilled; and you yourself
be my ally.

This poem seems less typical essentially because it takes the form of a cletic hymn—an invocation to a deity (whose name is adorned with suitable epithets), a reminder of past services, and a request. It probably was the first poem of the first book (of nine) in the canonic edition of Sappho's verse.[82] If so, one might guess that it was given this position by Hellenistic editors because they considered it a "prelude" to Sappho's *oeuvre*, like an invocation to the Muse in bardic poetry or like the invocational hymns that were chanted by rhapsodes at the beginning of a performance.[83] Editors, in short, may have seen this poem as invoking the central deity-muse and the central theme(s) of Sappho's poetry, as well as embodying her characteristic style and verseform (the "Sapphic stanza") while introducing her distinctive voice (and indeed her name, much as Theognis's invocatory poem introduces his name as a "seal" upon the *Theognidea*). Sappho's fragment 1 introduces and sets the stage for all her poetry.

Recent readings have tended to regard Sappho's use of the cletic hymn in fragment 1 as an instance of playful genre-bending—an instance of the tendency we have observed already to reconfigure traditional materials in the service of other purposes.[84] This poem appropriates and reconfigures traditional materials in other ways as well. But I would like to retain the idea that it could have functioned, in performance, as the proëmium or "prelude" to (some part of) the Sapphic repertoire and as a means of investing the poetry that followed with an additional dimension of persuasive power. For as such this poem is quite extraordinary.

What is most extraordinary about this poem is its management of voice, especially when we consider it as something to be performed, either by Sappho to her friends or by later performers of Sappho's poetry in women's (or men's) gatherings. I have deliberately omitted the quotation marks usually attached by translators to the speech of Aphrodite—from "whom shall I persuade this time" to "even against her will"—in part because there would have been no such punctuation to mark the shift of speaker in a performance and in part because an absence of such marking and the resultant potential for blurring the transition seems essential to the poem's effect. (There would have been, of course, no such punctuation in the ancient editions of Sappho's poetry; nor is there any in the standard modern editions of the Greek text.) While both Sappho and Aphrodite speak in the poem, one performer is performing all the lines; and this performer is not necessarily Sappho; and there is no sharp boundary between them. (Or the performer becomes all three at once.)[85]

In performance, the performer reembodies Sappho's voice, though it is not necessarily apparent that Sappho has been speaking until the fifth strophe, where she is addressed by name by Aphrodite. By this means Sappho's "signature" is placed on the performance, and Sappho is brought before the audience, or materialized, as the one who speaks: the song announces that the performer is "doing" and is indeed "becoming" Sappho for the duration (of this and all the poems that follow). At the same time, the poem narrates with charming digressiveness Aphrodite's hearkening to "this voice of mine from afar" and her travel by sparrow-drawn chariot down through the sky from heaven. But this narration, which ostensibly is reminding the goddess of her previous acquiescence to the speaker's requests, is delivered apostrophically (as indeed the whole poem is delivered) in second-person address as if the goddess is already present and as if her swift journey down from heaven is happening now, in the moment of speaking.[86] The psychagogic effectiveness of the description, insofar as it beguiles the audience to visualize the journey, makes it "present" for them even as it is narrated in past tense. This confusion or conflation of past and present is exploited and intensified in the speech the goddess delivers on arrival. The first part is delivered as indirect reported speech, in the speaker/performer's voice, with a shift into present tense—"and you . . . asked what I've suffered this time and why I'm calling this time, and what do I most wish would happen to me in my maddened heart"—while the second part, which begins in the middle of a line and is set off by not a period but a semicolon,[87] shifts abruptly to direct, present-tense address in the voice of Aphrodite herself: "whom shall I persuade this time to bring you back in her affection? Who, O Sappho, does you wrong?" What follows from this, as Aphrodite's voice continues, is a quasi-magical formula that constitutes the goddess's fulfillment of Sappho's request: "For if she flees, soon she will pursue," and so forth.

The effect *for the audience* is one of voices emerging from voices: from the performer emerges Sappho's voice, and from Sappho's voice emerges Aphrodite herself, who is now present and speaking in the poem *even though the speech is represented as having been spoken in the past.* Sappho, and through her the performer, suddenly has become the speaking goddess, and the audience receives an astonishing "glimpse" of the goddess in her presence.[88] Readers have remarked on the triple repetition of "this time" (*dêute*) in Aphrodite's speech (twice in Sappho's report of her utterance and once in her direct utterance) as marking a certain playful humor. The goddess seems to say, "what is it *now,* Sappho? What do you want *this time?*" as if in gentle, wide-smiling reproof of one who calls her just a little too often.[89] This may be so— for certainly playfulness is one of Aphrodite's attributes, and surely the seemingly familiar closeness between the goddess and Sappho is crucial to this poem's point— but the triple repetition of "this time" (which again sounds like a magic formula) also serves to emphasize that the event being narrated not only happens "then," in the past, but also "now" and always, in every instance of the "this time" in which the poem is performed. Aphrodite, then, is already present and speaking in the poem, in the "now" of the poem's utterance, and is already speaking the very things that Sappho is calling on her to come and speak. Thus, when Sappho's voice returns in the final strophe to ask the goddess to "make fulfilled all that my heart desires to be fulfilled" and to "be my ally," within the poem's act of utterance it *already has happened,* and the request already has been granted.[90]

In this way the poem acts as, or like, what speech-act theory calls a performative: it brings into existence the very state of affairs that it invokes—or at least creates a persuasive illusion of doing so.[91] Aphrodite is present in and through Sappho, who is present in and through the performer's reembodiment of her voice. Aphrodite is Sappho's (and the performer's) "ally" and familiar, and Sappho (and the performer) speak with an authority derived from, or backed by, this relationship. In sum, this poem establishes by way of its performative effect an implicit claim to bardlike authority.[92] This claim is made persuasive to the degree that the performative is persuasive; and the performative is persuasive to the degree that the "theophany" of the goddess in and through Sappho's voice achieves sufficient psychagogic, illusionistic power to beguile the listener's mind into acceptance. The fact that Sappho was regarded in antiquity as a "tenth Muse" and as the "female Homer" suggests that she was, in fact, fairly persuasive in this claim.

Other aspects of this poem's argumentation are worth remarking on. The first is Sappho's characterization of Aphrodite. The epithets that Sappho attaches to her name in the poem's opening invocation—*poikilothronos* ("ornately throned"), *athanata* ("immortal"), and *pai Dios doloploke* ("wile-weaving child of Zeus")— reflect traditional formulas but at the same time seem to be at least partly new inventions. These epithets on one hand stress the sorts of attributes one might expect, emphasizing Aphrodite's divine status and the *poikilos*, "ornate" beauty of her throne in Zeus's golden house. On the other hand, the epithets also stress her status as a goddess of subtlety and persuasion. *Poikilothronos*, as Page points out, "is not found elsewhere, and the idea expressed in it is not at all common in [ancient] literature"; and it has, as Page also notes, a punning resemblance to *poikilophronos*, which in fact occurs in some of the surviving manuscripts of this poem and which means "cunning" or "clever."[93] Like Theognis's *poikilos thymos*, it suggests a variegated, adaptable "heart"/sensibility (or *phrên*). *Doloploke*, an expression that Sappho may have coined, portrays Aphrodite as a girl "weaving" in her father's house—but she is weaving *dolos*, the basic meaning of which is "bait" and which extends to stratagems and clever contrivances for catching, beguiling, or deceiving something or someone.[94] Like Hesiod's Muses, who can confer on their poet (when they wish to) the power to make anything whatever seem believable, Aphrodite is thus invoked as a figure who presides over an art of "weaving" beguilement, seduction, persuasion. And indeed this is precisely what Sappho is asking for: as the goddess says, "whom shall I persuade [*peithô*] this time?" and so forth. This characterization of Aphrodite as *poikilo-thronos/phronos* and as *doloploke*, as a goddess of persuasion (whose throne is suitably "ornate"), folds back into the poem's performativity: insofar as Sappho successfully accomplishes her illusionistic effect, she demonstrates in herself the "wile-weaving" power of Aphrodite and signifies, once again, that her request for an "alliance" has already been fulfilled.

Second, Sappho's request for Aphrodite's help in love-persuasion, and for Aphrodite to become her "ally," *symmachos*—and Aphrodite's reply—portray that love persuasion as an agonistic contest. Someone "pursues" and someone "flees"; someone offers "gifts" and someone "accepts"; and someone "soon" is brought to love "even against her will." Likewise, at the beginning of the poem, Sappho asks not to be "overwhelmed" with "aches and sorrows": that is, to be not the one who loves unrequited but the one who is loved (and pursued and given gifts, etc.). Page duBois suggests that Sappho figures "love" within an "aristocratic drive for domination, in the agonistic arena of Greek social relations," as a struggle in which the successful lover dominates and a conquered beloved submits; and according to duBois, such a scenario cannot be assimilated to "some . . . vision of nonviolent eros" projected by an essentializing feminism.[95] To persuade another to love and give sexual favors is to be victorious; to fall in love is to be defeated or subjugated. *Symmachos* means "fellow fighter," and is a term with military resonance. Notably, the poem's enacted interchange between Aphrodite and Sappho resembles, and parallels, the scene in Pindar's *Olympian* 1 where Pelops calls on Poseidon and asks for assistance in the great, life-and-death contest that Pelops is about to face (in which he will "win" Hippodameia's hand in marriage). Sappho represents her love affair through the mythic typology of aristocratic combats and trials of excellence and casts herself in the role of the god-beloved hero. Once again, this self-portrayal both supports and is reciprocally justified by the persuasiveness of the poem's illusionistic and performative effects: insofar as Aphrodite's voice appears to emerge from (and merge back into) Sappho's, and insofar as her support as *symmachos* already has been granted, Sappho does indeed appear to be god-beloved and god-assisted.

Another way to put duBois's point is to say that Sappho's account of love as an *agôn* involving conquest and defeat appropriates traditional presuppositions (and representations) as part of the grounds of this poem's argument. There clearly is a resonance with, say, Anacreon's representation of himself as "boxing with Love"; in one fragment (346[2]), he says that he has been "boxing with a tough opponent" but now can raise his head again, and gives thanks that he has "escaped love's bonds completely, bonds made harsh by Aphrodite."[96] But duBois's characterization may oversimplify. For in asking Aphrodite to be her *symmachos* in persuasion, Sappho is indeed assuming that she herself will pursue, give gifts, and so forth, and that "success" or "victory" will consist of becoming in turn the one who is pursued, and so forth, and who finally, perhaps, consents to love—and so is "conquered" also (as she has been, say, by Anactoria). This scenario does presume a sort of reciprocity, insofar as lover and beloved in effect switch roles, trade places. Unlike Anacreon's love boxing, moreover, it does not necessarily involve the erotic conquest of an adolescent by an adult but may involve *erôs* between adult *gynaikes* who are social peers. And even in Anacreon, to "lose" a contest with "Love" does not always mean to be subjected in love to another. Sometimes, it simply means to fail to persuade, or to be rejected.

[fr. 358]

Once again with his purple ball
golden-haired Eros strikes me,
and with the girl in fancy sandals
    summons me to play;

but she, for she is from well-built
Lesbos, with my hair,
for it is white, finds fault,
    and opens toward someone else.

Old, drunk, white-haired Anacreon in this poem is a comically bested boxer of Love, having been "defeated" by a younger fellow symposiast in competition for the Lesbian girl's attentions; and she is "lesbianizing" the winner.[97] Anacreon's desire, the "summons" of Eros, has been aroused at sight of the girl but he cannot fulfill it.

Further, to equate persuasion with "domination" with *violence* as if all three terms were interchangeable is to blur some extremely important differences.[98] This is especially so when we are considering not an Anacreon fumbling after a flute-girl (or a prostitute) from Lesbos but Sappho contesting for love among girls and women who are, probably, her social equals. There is an immeasurable difference between "conquering" a social peer erotically (or in other ways) by persuading them (with gifts, speeches, and other overtures) and, say, putting a knife to someone's throat and demanding sex. Even to say that "if she does not love, soon she will love even against her will" does not imply violent subjection in the sense of physical coercion. "Even against her will" translates *kôuk etheloisa*, a participial phrase that also could be rendered as "even not intending [it]." The verb *thelô* signifies willing, wishing, or purposing some future event: this participial phrase suggests not so much forced compliance as the breaking down of resistance to the seductive/persuasive effect of the lover's self-presentation.[99] "She" does not (now) want/intend to be "in love" with Sappho (or perhaps anyone), but soon she will find that she is "in love" anyway, overwhelmed by the force of desire inspired in her by the persuasive effect of "Aphrodite" in Sappho's self-presentation, even while she still is thinking "I don't want/intend to be in love." The point is that her mind (or heart) will change and that she soon will, indeed, be pursuing Sappho though now she is indifferent.

What seems important here, however, is less the question whether Sapphic *erôs* is "dominative" or "reciprocal" (or something else) but rather Sappho's portrayal of female agency: woman as persuader and as "hero" in an erotic *agôn*, as the one who "conquers" rather than a passive object to be conquered, defined by male desires, or traded as an elegant object of gift exchange. Further, as suggested by duBois's recognition that Sappho's love scenario is embedded in "the agonistic arena of Greek social relations"—or as suggested also by Theognis's portrayal of his relation with Kyrnos (or his unspecified boy-addressees)—what is at stake is not only the satisfaction of Sappho's erotic desires but also a question of factional affiliation.[100] To love Sappho, to be persuaded to love her, is to become a member of her circle as opposed to some other, such as Andromeda's or that of the "Penthilid ladies." The women of Sappho's circle are, as her poetry claims, the best, the most accomplished, the most impressive, the most refined in their pursuit of luxuries and pleasures; and the men who sit "opposite" them, in the blessed realm their cultured discourse constitutes, are likewise excellent. And the women of Sappho's circle are the best *because* they are devoted to the cultivation of the Muses, the pursuit of refined pleasures, and "wile-weaving" persuasion, and so forth, as opposed to the "Penthilid ladies," whose clan has been most notable in Sappho's time for beating people with clubs and for provoking (possibly through an outrageous rape) a period of stasiotic bloodshed, and as opposed as well to the circle of Andromeda, who courts the favors of uncultured, unimpressive, and probably socially unequal "country girls." Sappho, in sum, portrays herself and the women of her fluctuating circle as engaged in a contest of persuasions, a contest that is embedded in and part of the factionalized sociopolitical competition of Mytilene.

In fragment 1, then, we find a quasi-bardic invocation in which Sappho calls on Aphrodite to assist her in a contest of persuasions—an erotic *agôn* with social and political implications—and argues indirectly, by way of a performative effect, that what she asks for already has been granted. The proof is the poem's illusionistic power, the psychagogic effectivity of Sappho's management of voice, as "Aphrodite" comes down from heaven and then emerges, abruptly, briefly, teasingly, playfully, and astonishingly, from within Sappho's speaking. And what fragment 1 announces, in a performance, is that the audience will now experience the persuasive, seductive force of Sappho's Aphroditean art. This lends considerable authority to her verse.

A corrective note is probably in order here. Certainly Sappho represents the interests of archaic aristocracy, and the emergent interests of aristocratic luxury-consumption and (competitive) display in the seventh and sixth centuries B.C. Sappho's disdain for Andromeda's "country girl" sums up that orientation. So does her straightforward remark in another fragment, where she mentions having grown too old to dance with young girls and concludes "but I love luxury [*egô de philemm' abrosynan*] . . . and for me this love [*eros*] has obtained the brilliance and beauty of the sun" (fr. 58; one could also read *abrosynan* here as "elegance").[101] It is clear that Sappho's sympathies are not democratic. Judging from her banishment at the same time that Alcaeus was banished, it seems likely that her family and her circle were out of sympathy with the Myrsilos-Pittacus faction and would have been unhappy with Pittacus's populist appeal as *aisymnêtês*, "elected dictator." One can guess what she thought of Pittacus's politically opportunistic marriage to a Penthilid woman. It is not impossible that Sappho and Alcaeus belonged to the same clan, or moved in overlapping circles.[102]

Even so, however, Sappho does speak as the voice of an ideological shift, asserting the values of *habrosynê* and of what Maximus calls her *technê erôtikê*—which is an art of persuasion, and an art that seems to be centered in the type of women's culture exemplified by her circle—over the older, more archaic, aristocratic (and patriarchal) ideal of martial valor that Alcaeus remains committed to. This is not a simple opposition, or a zero sum game or combat in which one set of values cancels and replaces the other; rather, it is a suasory reordering of the traditionally predominant value-hierarchy of Hellenic culture. The values that Alcaeus represents are not "rejected" but absorbed within and subordinated to those that Sappho represents, in a contest of persuasions regarding what is best and most desirable for human beings. It is worth noting that the values of Alcaeus are, in essence, precisely those that have brought on the *stasis* in Mytilene and that sustain it: although Alcaeus longs, on one hand, for the council and assembly where his ancestors were entitled to speak and wield political authority, on the other hand his politics, like those of the Penthilidai (apparently), ultimately reduce to brute force in service of the interests and entitlements of his faction. Alcaeus's aristocratic politics, in Mytilene as in other sixth-century Greek *poleis*, have come to catastrophe. Sappho pursues (women's) politics by other means and proposes as *superior* the *êthos* of her circle: an *êthos* in which *habrosynê*, cultivated excellence, or the thing that calls forth *erôs* in human beings, is the highest good; in which persuasion understood as an erotic *agôn* figures as the medium of social competition and the constitutive principle of a realm of blessedness; and in which cultivated, "conspicuous" women exercise a measure of agency as persuaders. Indeed, Sappho's argument demonstrates that Alcaeus's longing (and perhaps also his gloom as he skulks alongside the festival of Hera, listening to the women's ululation) is in effect a confession of the superiority of her position. In promoting a counterhegemonic scheme of values, in other words, "making the lesser case the greater," and in her role as the leader of a fluctuating circle of friends, lovers, associates, and students devoted to cultivating the poetic and other arts that constitute the excellence she celebrates, Sappho plays the protosophistic sort of role that Maximus assigns to her.

Both Alcaeus and Sappho, as I suggested at the outset of this chapter, can be understood as offering lyrical argumentation to an audience that consists primarily of the members of their circles, most typically through performances in symposia or symposiumlike gatherings: argumentation indoors, so to speak. As I also suggested, such a context implies a "closed" argumentative system, in which a great deal of homogeneity can in principle be presumed, so that the poet can simply "express" or dramatize ethical positions and modalities of judgment that the audience can be expected to agree with already. Such a situation, in fact, requires little more than a rhetoric of recapitulation, a means of reiterating, intensifying, and solidifying the group's shared attitudes and identity. But in both Alcaeus's and Sappho's case such a simplified image does not quite hold. Alcaeus's "boat" is leaky, his argumentation must meet counterdiscourses from both within and outside the group, and at least to some degree that argumentation is meant to be projected beyond the group as a rhetoric of justification. Sappho's circle is probably still more permeable, and her argumentation engages with, reappropriates and reconfigures, and contests—rather than simply invokes (as Alcaeus often seems to do)—what have traditionally been the dominant schemes of value in Lesbian and Hellenic culture. My point is that it is not the insulation of the "inside" group, or a privacy that supposedly enables the expression of an untrammeled "lyric subjectivity" freed from the pressures of community morality, that makes either Alcaeus's or Sappho's poetry a distinctive, significant cultural force. And this is so especially in the case of Sappho. It is not because her poems are private communications to her nearest and dearest friends that they are and have been so compelling to so many for so long. Rather, just the opposite is true: because they offer enthymematic argumentation that engages with the discourses of a wider audience "outside" her inner circle, Sappho's poems have traveled far.

9

Solon *Sophôtatos*

On Lyric Argument Maximal and Minimal

In Plato's *Timaeus*, Critias calls Solon "the wisest"—*ho sophôtatos*—of the Seven Sages, and recalls how in his boyhood an elder had praised Solon as the wisest of all men and the noblest of all poets (20d, 21c). Indeed, said the elder, if Solon had not spent so much time in politics he would have surpassed even Hesiod and Homer. In those days (says Critias) Solon's poems were still new and much in vogue, and all the boys were learning them for poetry recital contests at public festivals. Plato may, perhaps, intend for us to take these statements ironically, but it doesn't seem likely: Solon is being invoked as an authoritative source for the Atlantis myth. Either way, however, Critias's recollections show the degree to which Solon's poetry was in fact revered by his contemporaries, as well as by subsequent generations.

Solon makes a fitting cap to this account of argumentation in early lyric poetry for two main reasons. On one hand, as I will presently suggest, there is reason to apply to Solon as poet the honorific epithet *sophôtatos*, meaning both "most wise" and "most skillful." On the other hand, he falls into that category of elegiac poets that W. R. Johnson excludes from his otherwise explicitly rhetorical account of ancient lyric. Johnson says that such poets "seem rather impersonal for the most part, do not dramatize the situation of their discourse, and are less interested in imagining emotion than in constructing lapidary gnomes; they are closer to the essayist and the modern epigrammatists than to the lyric poet."[1] Johnson cannot account for Solon, or for that matter Theognis, because he still is working with a fundamentally romantico-modernist notion of "lyricism" as the dramatized expression of emotion; the rhetorical dimension of his account consists of a supplemental recognition that ancient lyric is often presented as addressed to a specific audience or addressee, so that the poem is a mimesis of a speech.[2] As such it may *include* some form of argumentation or deliberation, but insofar as it fails to dramatize emotion it falls short of lyricality as Johnson defines it. Johnson's account of "lyric" as "rhetorical" is not *rhetorical enough* to take in Solon or Theognis. As I will show, Solon "most skillfully" embodies a paradigm of "lyric" as epideictic argument in verse—the paradigm we have observed already in Pindar, Alcaeus, and Sappho—and is one of the nearest links to the *logôn technê* of the sophists and the later rhetorical tradition.

Before I take up Solon, however, it will be useful to turn back briefly to Theognis and the "epigrammatic" kind of lyric that he embodies.

Symposium and Epigram: "Insider" Argument Once More

As I noted in the preceding chapter, symposiastic poetry implies in principle a relatively closed, homogenous circle of "insiders" as the audience for poetic argument—so that the poet can presuppose a relatively high degree of like-mindedness and is, in consequence, under little pressure to construct the enthymematic grounds of persuasion. All that is required, in essence, is an effectively stated enthymematic cap, or the bare invocation of a topos; the poet can just "express" an attitude or judgment with which the audience is expected to agree already. The argument hardly need be argued. Or, it can be presented obliquely, elliptically. For the inside audience the grounds of judgment are obvious enough and "commonsensical" already. Under such circumstances what matters most is the stylistic elegance, charm, and memorability of the expression. The audience finds attitudes with which it identifies already being presented, mimed, "danced" (to use Kenneth Burke's expression), or given a distinctive turn, with striking and aesthetically pleasing eloquence, grace, and wit.

With Alcaeus and Sappho, as I also noted, this theoretical principle does not quite hold, or it holds only weakly, because their circles in varying degrees are unstable and "permeable" to competing discourses from "outside," so that both poets must (and do, to varying degrees) develop enthymematic argumentation to justify their stances. With epigrammatic and gnomic poetry, however, we seem to find a situation where the principle holds more strongly and lyric argument approaches its minimal condition. Consider these examples.

> 1. Inscription on an Attic grave marker, sixth century B.C.[3]
> O person who comes down the road, at heart desiring other things,
>   stand and feel pity, seeing Thrason's marker.

> 2. Theognidea 461–462
> Never set your mind upon impracticalities, nor be eager for
>   things from which there comes no accomplishment.

> 3. Athenian drinking song (Athenaeus 15.695)
> Under every stone a scorpion, my friend, conceals itself.
> Take care that he not sting you; all guile attends what is unseen.

> 4. Asclepiades (*Greek Anthology* 5.150)
> She promised to come at night to me, the infamous
>   Niko, and swore by solemn Demeter.
> She does not come, and the watch has passed. Did she mean
>   to falsely swear? Extinguish, boys, the light.

> 5. Meleager (*Greek Anthology* 5.152)
> Fly for me, mosquito, swift messenger, and on the ear's-rim
>   of Zenophila lighting whisper to it thus:

"Sleepless he awaits you; and you, forgetful of your lovers,
  sleep." *Eiya,* fly! Yes, song-lover, fly!
But softly speak, and do not waken her bed-companion
  and rouse the pain of jealousy because of me.
But if you bring the girl to me, I'll hood you with a lion-skin,
  mosquito, and give you a club to carry in your hand.[4]

6. On a statue of Sappho, in the gymnasium of Zeuxippos at Constantinople, c. 532
A.D. (*Greek Anthology* 2. 69–71)
  And the clear-sounding Pierian bee, Sappho
of Lesbos, was seated at rest; she seemed to be weaving
a well-hymned song, devoting her mind to the silent Muses.

7. Leontius Scholasticus, on a picture of the dancer Libania (*Greek Anthology* 16.288)
You have a name of frankincense [*libanos*], body of Graces, *êthos* of Persuasion,
  maiden, and Aphrodite's girdle flows from your waist.
And yet in the chorus-dance, like light Eros, you frolic,
  both by beauty and by art attracting all.

The first three of these epigrams belong to the sixth to fifth centuries B.C.—the third was known to Aristophanes (who parodies it)[5] and apparently still was popular in Athenaeus's time. The fourth and fifth are Hellenistic. The sixth is from a series of poems on the statues in the gymnasium of Zeuxippos, which burned down in 532 A.D.; and the seventh is from a compilation by Maximus Planudes, a Byzantine scholar of the twelfth or thirteenth century. To these examples we might add the poems of Anacreon that were cited in the preceding chapter or the Theognidean poems cited earlier. And many more besides. Between the various compilations that comprise the sixteen books of the *Greek Anthology,* and various other collections, a considerable volume of such poetry has been preserved, most of it from later antiquity and the Middle Ages. Neither my nor any other brief selection can possibly represent its full variety, but arguably the poems presented here are *reasonably* representative, at least for the purposes of this discussion. For I think a basic, two-part claim about the character of all such poetry *as argumentation* can reasonably be made.

The claim is this: First, each of these poems is, in essence, a dramatized expression of an attitude—and little else besides. In other words, each fulfills *precisely* Johnson's criterion of "lyricality," though he might consider only poems 4 and 5 (which explicitly frame themselves in a dramatic situation) as doing so. Second, the attitude that each poem offers, or calls for from the audience, is more or less conventional.

Poem 1, a grave inscription, is not meant to be recited at symposia, but it offers a model on which much epigrammatic poetry was based; from the Hellenistic period onward there was a vogue for literary imitations of epitaphs and other kinds of monumental inscriptions.[6] Poem 1 embodies a voice that speaks from the grave marker itself and offers to its audience (the "passerby") a declaration or gesture that sums up the situation and proposes the fitting attitude to take. Thrason is dead; we are to pity Thrason. Why? Well, we know (or are supposed to know) already: the mortality of human beings is pitiable. The inscription, in effect, reminds its audience of, and reinforces, the standard pieties and attitudes surrounding death. I do not wish to demean or diminish the cultural or human importance of such grave inscriptions or the potential effectiveness of their rhetoric. Within the fairly narrow range of conventionalized expression available to them, many do achieve what often strikes the modern viewer as extraordinary poignancy. My point, however, is that their basic function is to prompt a set of pious attitudes, a *pathos*, that the audience is predisposed to.[7] The inscription operates as an enthymematic cap to a body of discourses and stereotyped narratives already inscribed, by tradition, in the audience's heart.

Very similar things could be said about poems 2 and 3, both of which certainly were recited at symposia. Both offer gnomic nuggets of standard wisdom—don't waste effort on impracticalities; watch out for treachery—that might be applied as an enthymematic cap to sum up a situation. Poem 2 comes close to the position of Alcaeus's "drink, and get drunk with me," though it is far less developed; and in a symposium it might be invoked as a pithy response to the general kind of situation that Alcaeus is responding to. Likewise for poem 3: it might be invoked when the symposiast's friends are engaged in a business fraught with possibilities for betrayal (or have suffered it already). This poem does outline the minimal components of an enthymematic argument, offering in its first line a description of the situation (there are "scorpions" under "every rock") and in its second line a projection of the appropriate attitude to take ("watch out!"); but each component is left as a more or less bare *topos*. The key feature of both of these two poems, from a rhetorical point of view, is that the audience is expected to *get it* with virtually no additional argumentation supplied: the reasons that warrant the epigram as an apt, persuasive comment on the situation must already be apparent to the listener. We must know already, for example, who the "scorpions" under the "rocks" are; or we must know already that the business in question is impractical; and we must recognize already as authoritative, traditional wisdom the poem's briefly invoked response to the situation it briefly names.

Poems 4 and 5, literary productions of the Hellenistic era, frame themselves (as I have noted) more explicitly in a dramatic situation, are more developed, and indeed are by far the most sophisticated poems in this group. Both offer what is meant to be seen as an amusingly witty rendition of a basically conventional pose in response to a stereotypical situation: the "lover" lies awake at night, his "mistress" (a courtesan?) somewhere else, with someone else.[8] In poem 4 the lover wonders if he's been fooled, and strikes a pose of resignation; in poem 5 he treats his situation playfully, with wry and mildly self-ironic humor. Both are musing on the unreliability of the girls (or high-class prostitutes) that well-bred gentlemen play with and on the comedy of their own positions. We're in the realm of Anacreontic love-boxing, playing out its variations. Poems 6 and 7, which are much later and much inferior Byzantine productions, work similarly though with different kinds of effects. In poem 6 the speaker stands before a statue of Sappho and is properly bemused; the past-tense description suggests that the poem, and the series to which it belongs, could have been composed after the gymnasium of Zeuxippos had burned down, in which case the speaker's pose is recollective and nostalgic ("And there was Sappho, communing with the Muses," etc.). And in poem 7 Leontius Scholasticus offers a fulsome compliment to the dancing-girl Libania, or to her picture ("My, you're lovely, and you dance so well!"). None of these poems does much to argue *why* the speaker should respond as he does or to persuade its audience to accept or identify with the speaker's pose; nor does the poem really need to, since both the situation and the pose are more or less conventional—though the wittiness of the Hellenistic poems gives charm to what may be novel modifications of the standard repertoire of poses. Each of these seven epigrams offers a gesture that constitutes an *amplified enthymematic cap* to a situation or scene that is minimally described, a cap that rests on a framework of assumptions (about the situation-type and the attitudes/poses it permits) that is taken as already understood. In such cases, and in the Hellenistic poems most notably, the interest of the poem lies chiefly in the vivacity, charm, sophistication, and cleverness with which the gesture is carried off.

Epigrammatic poetry could be rhetorically effective, even powerful. It could be poignant, it could be trenchant, it could be charming, and it could be moving. Simonides' famous epigram for the tomb of the Spartans at Thermopylae is a case in point.

> O stranger, report to the Spartans that here
> we lie, obedient to their commands.[9]

Like the grave-marker verse for Thrason, this poem invokes an attitude already well established in its audience: the heroic self-sacrifice of the Spartans at Thermopylae was famous. At the same time, in its function as an enthymematic cap to an already understood discourse (or set of discourses), the poem invokes a particular aspect of that heroism and serves to render it even more admirable and stirring. What is emphasized is not so much the Spartans' well-known martial valor—which in the poem is understood—but their sense of civil duty, their keeping-true to their fellow citizens' "commands" (*rhêmata*). They have not died because a death in battle is the most glorious thing they can imagine (though they have achieved great glory); they have not died because they wanted to win a soldierly distinction (though they did); but they have died in order to keep their word, to keep their covenant with their fellow citizens, and to preserve Greek "freedom" from Persian domination (since that is what the covenant involved). Moreover, through the locution "here we lie" the epigram constructs the fallen heroes as speaking even now (via their grave marker) and as still fulfilling their duty in the present moment. The general effect is to endow the Spartans' self-sacrifice to civic and Panhellenic duty with a virtually transcendent, eternal nobility and to elicit from the audience a deeply felt sense of admiration. It seems to have worked. This epigram became a widely cited patriotic poem.

My point, however, is that as effective as such poetry can be, it operates by an inherently conservative rhetoric. The epigram operates as a free-standing enthymematic cap, an *elliptical argument*, that exploits what is taken to be already understood or given in the thinking of its audience. The epigram can call on powerfully felt beliefs and attitudes, on deeply resonant cultural presuppositions, on operant ideologies. It can elicit pathos, including anything from heart-piercing passion to states of mild amusement; and through prompting its audience to rehearse a range of attitudes it can intensify their ethical commitments. But it cannot elicit what is not already there. Because the highly elliptical, oblique argumentation of epigrammatic poetry has sharply limited means for building and reconfiguring the enthymematic grounds of persuasion, it has an equally limited potential for "making the lesser case greater" or for *successfully* holding out a counter position to prevailing ideologies. An epigrammatic poem that calls for an attitude or judgment that its audience does not already share will simply fail, insofar as it lacks the means to construct the grounds on which that attitude/judgment can persuasively be invoked. The audience that does not already recognize and identify with the poem's presumptions will probably find its overt gesture nonsensical, counterintuitive, foolish, wrong, or even offensive. For these reasons, epigrammatic poetry functions chiefly as a means of reaffirming— rather than troubling or modifying—an audience's value-hierarchies and its sense of self-identity. It is effective chiefly with an "insider" audience that shares already the presumptions and pieties it gives expression to.

Another feature of epigrammatic discourse, in its function as "insider" discourse, is that the basic poetic function of praise and recommendation—*ainos* (or *epainos*)—may shift toward "riddling" (*ainissomai*) or speaking in coded discourse (*ainigma* and *allêgoria*) meant to be significant to insiders and opaque to others. This is not a feature of epigrammatic discourse only but a potential of "insider" discourse and symposium poetry generally. Thus, when poem 3 above (the Athenian drinking song) warns its audience to watch out for "scorpions" under "rocks," the group for whom it is meant will recognize just who or what is being talked about, while those outside the group may not. This is what we see, as well, in Alcaeus's "ship of state" poems. While the argumentation of the poems is sufficiently developed (even in their fragmentary state) for us to recognize that they are allegorical, nevertheless we can only speculate about precisely what events Alcaeus was actually referring to, though this would have been quite clear to the members of his *hetaireia*. Here we should recall those modern readers who have read the poems naively as seafaring songs, completely missing their political dimension; such readers have effectively been excluded from Alcaeus's inner circle.

Likewise, in later reperformances in other times and places, the poems could have been used, like the "scorpion" song, as coded commentaries on particular events or situations that the performer's fellow-symposiasts would recognize. To take a Hellenistic example: as Plutarch reports (*Sympotic Questions* 9.1), a rhapsode performing at the wedding of king Ptolemy Philadelphus to his sister Arsinoë (c. 279 B.C.) began by quoting *Iliad* 18.356—"[b]ut Zeus spoke unto Hera, wife and sister"—as a pithy reply, from Homeric authority and divine precedent, to opinions that Ptolemy's marriage was "unnatural and unlawful." The line of Homer thus functioned as an epigram with pointed enthymematic force *for the audience present.* As Alan Cameron has argued,[10] its point would have been apparent to anyone at Philadelphus's court; and the rhapsode would not have needed to say more, since the audience present at the marriage, and Philadelphus in particular, would not only have grasped the point quickly but would have been predisposed to agree with its implied argument. (Of the same marriage, the poet Sotades—who seems to have specialized in insulting kings—had written: "Into an unholy hole his prick he's shoving"; Sotades was later murdered.)

An important rhetorical effect of "riddling" or coded discourse—*ainigma* and *allêgoria*—is that, insofar as the intended audience is to "get" what is unspoken, the poetry helps to intensify an exclusivist sense of inside/outside while reaffirming and intensifying the inside group's self-identification as a fellowship of like-minded comrades. Gregory Nagy has argued that such coded discourse is a characteristic of Theognidean poetry (or at least some of it): one component of poetic *sophia*, on the audience's part, is the ability to recognize the poet's indirect or tacit meaning.[11] This seems to be partly what is meant, for example, when Theognis counsels his beloved boy to "set your mind to gather what I say" (*Theognidea* 1237). There is more to what the poet says than what his words may outwardly seem to signify. Thus, when Theognis declares, in one poem, "[n]ever have I betrayed a loving and loyal comrade, / nor is there anything slavish in my soul" (529–530), we may read this as a straightforward, gnomic declaration of ethical principle, but for Theognis's immediate audience (or the audience of a Theognidean reperformer) it may have had a more specific, situationally determined significance: someone has betrayed the group, perhaps, and has proved himself "slavish" in doing so—perhaps because he has done someone else's dirty work or has been bribed to put aside his loyalties and has shown himself to be a sycophant. And so we pass the wine around and sing *You'll never see me doing such a thing*. But the allegorical and riddling possibilities in Theognis are sometimes taken further. Consider these examples.

> If you wish to wash me, from the top of my head unsullied
>   ever clear [or white][12] the water will flow;
> you will discover me for all business purposes like refined
>   gold, red to view when rubbed with the touchstone,
> the surface of my skin affected neither by dark rust
>   nor mould, and its bloom ever pure. (447–452)

> I am a good and prize-winning horse, but most wicked
>   is the man I bear, and to me this is most grievous;
> and often I've been about to burst through the bridle
>   and escape, casting aside my wicked rider. (257–260)

> Having snatched the fawn from its mother like a confident lion
>   with strong claws, the blood I have not drunk;
> having climbed the highest walls, the city I have not plundered;
>   having yoked the horses, the chariot I have not mounted;
> while acting I have not acted, and I have not achieved while achieving;
>   while doing I have not done; while finishing I have not finished. (949–954)

These poems equally may be political or erotic—they have been read both ways—and perhaps they are meant to be taken either way, depending on the situation they happen to be performed in. The first poem may be speaking of factional loyalties, with Theognis declaring himself a comrade "as good as gold"; or he may be presenting himself as an ever-ready lover. The second poem figures its speaker-horse as feminine (through the gendering of the adjectives "good" and "prize-wining" and the participle "casting aside")[13] and thereby resonates with a famous fragment of Anacreon (417) in which he addresses a courtesan as a "Thracian filly" and declares that he can "ride" her "round the turnpost of the racecourse." But horses are conventionally figured in the feminine in ancient Greek, and Theognis's poem could just as well be an allegory for a badly ruled city.[14] The third poem likewise resonates with another fragment of Anacreon (408) in which he seems to be comparing an attractive boy to a "newborn fawn" left away from its mother (and thus exposed to the lion's/Anacreon's pounce); but Theognis's poem could also refer to seizing yet not abusing power in the city, or to wielding that power ineffectually, or both. The truth is that no one now can say with certainty just what these poems originally were meant to be about.[15]

These observations suggest a possible reason for Theognis's relative ineffectuality with his fellow citizens in Megara. As I suggested at the close of chapter 5, Theognis's failure may have been caused, in part, by the stubborn, hubristic *atropia* of his fellow citizens—an ethical rigidity that rendered them more or less incapable of being persuaded, or unable to identify with anything not already identical with themselves. Despite the fact that Theognis has attempted (as he says) to walk a "straight line" between aristocrats and commoners and to speak as a voice for justice, the result has been that he has pleased almost no one, and "many find fault with me, both the bad and the good alike" (369). Megara may have been too factionalized, and its factions too hardened into their self-interested positions (like Alcaeus's faction in Lesbos), for anything but the politics of *stasis* and vendetta or for anything other than governance by harsh authority. However, as I also suggested, Theognis's failure may have had to do as well with the limits of his own rhetorical practice.

Despite the fact that Theognidean poetry bespeaks an understanding of poetic discourse as a rhetorical transaction—and despite the fact that Theognis evokes as an ethical and civic ideal the notion of a *poikilon êthos* or a "many-colored," variegated, and adaptable sensibility that keeps to the "straight line" between factional extremes and is *dikaios*, "just"—it is also true that his epigrammatic poetry generally has too limited an argumentative potential to do much more than invoke the counsels of a right-minded *sophia* for those who already are "right-minded" in Theognis's terms. There are, of course, some relatively well developed Theognidean poems, but these are relatively rare. For the most part Theognis's epigrammatic, symposiastic poetry lacks the rhetorical means sufficient to project his discourse *persuasively* beyond his inner circle to the wider audience of the *polis*. He talks to his friends, usually with eloquently pithy brevity, and sometimes in code, about the wisdom they have and others lack. And so we hear in several poems, or seem to, the exasperated complaints of a political poet who cannot quite connect with, or even fathom, the audiences he needs to persuade: as he says, "I cannot judge the mind of my townsmen, whatever they think" (367), and he ends by declaring them "fools" (370). Theognis himself was not *poikilos* enough.

Solon was more successful.

Talking to the Polis: Solon's Civic Elegies

Eva Stehle has suggested that Solon's poetry appropriates but also violates, or "abuses," the conventions of symposiastic poetry—projecting Solon not as a member of and voice for his *hetaireia* but as an isolated, "monumentalized" *egô* detached from every faction in the city and mediating between them.[16] Indeed, as Solon says in a famous fragment where he defends his policies during his archonship at Athens,[17]

> [a]nd I myself as in a frontier between two armies
> stood, a boundary-stone. (37)

Or again (in another fragment, possibly from the same poem):

> mixing up strength from every side
> I turned about like a wolf amid many hounds. (36.26–27)

Or again (in another poem):

> [a]nd I stood with a strong shield held between both sides,
>   permitting neither to triumph unrighteously. (5)[18]

In these striking images Solon certainly does appear as the partisan of no single faction—a marker in no man's land, a "lone wolf," a solitary figure.[19] He stands heroically between the factions or the "armies" of nobles and common citizens, holding them apart, preventing them from doing each other mutual harm, and balancing their competing claims. Stehle suggests that Solon's ability to present himself in such a way arises from the possibilities of writing, which, "because it disjoined speaker and audience, permitted a kind of self-representation in absence that could be forthright, unmindful of counterclaim," and enabled "representation of a self not defined through jostling for position within a group."[20] Solon may or may not have meant his poetry to circulate in manuscript or to be posted somewhere (on painted boards?). However, as with Sappho (and for similar reasons), I think the probability is slight. Virtually all poetry from early to late antiquity was intended originally for performance and was, like oratory, published in written or "book" form afterward.[21] More important, I think it unlikely that Solon's self-representation has been enabled by being insulated from "counterclaims" or agonistic "jostling for position within a group" or the larger community. This could be better said about Theognis; and that is Theognis's limitation. Rather, I think that in Solon's case the opposite is more probable. The distinctiveness of Solon's poetry arises precisely from the fact that it is meant to be projected beyond his inner circle of likeminded friends to the whole community, to engage with counterclaims, and to jostle for position. Solon's argumentation is meant to meet and persuade his audiences on every side. As Emily Katz Anhalt says, Solon "manipulates . . . poetic traditions" in order to "create poetry that will serve the needs of the *polis* as a whole."[22]

Only a little need be said about Solon's policies and his reforms of the Athenian constitution, in part because, beyond what Aristotle says about them in the *Athenian Constitution* (5–13) and beyond what Solon himself reveals in his surviving poetry, not a great deal is known.[23] As Aristotle says (5), Solon came to power during, and because of, a period of *stasis* (c. 594/593 B.C.). The increasing impoverishment of the lower classes and the practice of debt slavery had resulted in "the many being enslaved to the few," and the *dêmos* consequently rose against the nobles; the struggle that followed was both violent and prolonged. In this situation Solon was appointed to the double office of "mediator" and chief archon by common consent of the warring parties. It is worth noting that, according to Aristotle,

Solon became the mutually preferred person for this role after composing (and presumably performing) a poem that began "I mark, and pain afflicts my heart within / to see Ionia's eldest land be slain"[24] and went on to "do battle" for each side and finally exhorted both to end their "strife-love" or contentiousness (*philoneikia*). Plutarch (*Solon* 14.1–2) suggests that Solon was chosen because he was implicated in the factional interests of neither side—being of noble birth but not rich—and had already established a reputation for sagacity during the Athens-Megara conflict over Salamis. But the poem that Aristotle cites could well have been a motivating factor in the decision, insofar as it presented the already reputable Solon as a possible and willing arbiter and made a persuasive case for arbitration.

Once in power, Solon decreed the cancellation of debts, the *seisachtheia* or "shaking-off of burdens"; he also ended the practice of debt slavery and enacted a number of economic reforms that tended to improve conditions for the rural peasantry while also promoting manufacturing and commercial activity in the city. Indeed, as Solon boasts in fragment 36, he "freed" mortgaged land and repatriated impoverished citizens who had been forced or sold into foreign bondage—citizens whose speech was "no longer Attic"—while releasing those still in Attica from serfdom (fr. 36.8–15). At the same time, however, Solon resisted popular demands for a general redistribution of property, thereby protecting what the nobility would have seen as their legitimate rights.

Solon's constitutional reforms were a significant step in the direction of democracy. In essence, Solon ended the aristocrats' exclusive control of political power and expanded popular participation—while at the same time, again, balancing popular gains with concessions to noble interests. As Aristotle reports, Solon divided the citizenry into four "tribes" defined by annual income: five-hundred-measure-men, horsemen, teamsters, and laborers. He distributed political offices to each tribe in proportion to their assessment, and he made the offices elective. The highest offices were reserved for the five-hundred-measure-men, while laborers were permitted, for the first time, to serve on juries and participate in the general Assembly (the *Ekklêsia*). This arrangement meant that most of the highest offices would continue to be held, at least for awhile, by the traditional nobility. However, since tribe or class membership was now defined by income rather than by lineage, and since a person's status and tribe enrollment could change, it also meant that the highest offices were no longer a matter of hereditary privilege. In addition to the Assembly Solon created a Council (*Boulê*) of four hundred, with its membership divided equally among the tribes; and he redefined the Areopagus (the old aristocratic council) as "guardian of the laws." At the same time, he revised the austere legal code of Draco, generally making the punishments milder (with the exception of the punishment for murder). Aristotle thought the most democratic of Solon's reforms, beyond the repeal of debt slavery, were the right of anyone to prosecute on behalf of injured persons and the right of appeal to the popular jury courts. This last reform, as Aristotle says, was "the chief source of the multitude's power . . . for the people, being master of the vote, becomes master of the polity" (*Athenian Constitution* 9.1; see also Plutarch, *Solon* 18.2). That is, the right of appeal to jury courts made the rulings of magistrates subject to popular consent, as did the electoral procedures for civic offices. Solon's reforms established the grounds for the more radical reforms of Cleisthenes in 508 B.C., and the yet more radical reforms of Ephialtes, the so-called birth of democracy (the establishment of the people's Assembly, the *Ekklêsia*, as sovereign), in 462–461.

Considering these policies and reforms, it seems to me unlikely that Solon's textual self-representation as a "lone wolf" or "boundary-stone" or "shield-holder" or arbiter between aristocratic and popular factions was enabled by being insulated from contention. Rather, Solon's political activities—insofar as we know them—place him already at the center of contention and provide the basis for his self-representation in his poems. The poems are embedded in, and part of, his political activities. As Solon maintains in fragments 34 and 36, many on both sides of the *stasis* had thought that he would assume tyrannical powers to serve the interests of their faction and were angered when he did not. But acting as the servant of factional interests would have produced catastrophe.

> And laws alike for the lowly and high,
> arranging straight justice for everyone,
> I wrote. But if another man had seized the goad,
> someone bad in counsel and gain-loving too,
> he'd not have restrained the people; for had I purposed
> what was pleasing to the opposition then,
> and then again what the other side preferred,
> of many men this city would have been bereft. (36.18–25)

While both sides understood the *stasis* as a zero sum game in which "resolution" would mean the defeat and plundering of one side by the other (as Solon suggests in fr. 34), any policy that responded to such thinking could only intensify the conflict and provoke a bloodbath. Thus his only or best alternative, as Solon argues, was to write "laws alike for the lowly and high, arranging straight justice for everyone." This meant that he would necessarily place himself at odds with factions on both sides, disappointing and opposing nearly everyone's wishes to some degree, and fully satisfying no one, while attempting to strike a workable balance that would seem reasonably fair and sufficiently acceptable to most.[25] Thus he presents himself, in the two lines following the passage quoted here (fr. 36.26–27), as a "lone wolf" turning round and round, holding a pack of hounds at bay. Solon's self-representation is not an effect of textuality but a result of his politics and is not insulated from contention but is but fraught with controversy on all sides.

Further, the legend regarding Solon's early elegy *Salamis*—perhaps his first major entry into political poetry—suggests clearly that his poems were meant primarily for performance, including public performance, rather than manuscript circulation. *Salamis* was composed well before Solon's archonship, during the Athens-Megaa conflict over that island. According to Plutarch (*Solon* 8.1–3), the Athenians had wearied of the war, which had been long and costly, and had passed a decree quitting their claim to Salamis and forbidding anyone to renew it on pain of death. Solon subsequently pretended to have fallen into mental illness and had his family spread the story through the city, while secretly composing his elegy and preparing to perform it. When he was ready, he "suddenly" went into the agora, wearing a cap (which signified that he was ill); and when a crowd had gathered, "he mounted the herald's stone and in song went through the elegy," beginning from these lines:

> As a herald I have come from lovely Salamis,
> adopting a song of ordered words instead of speech. (fr. 1)

The elegy went on for a hundred lines. According to Diogenes Laertius (*Solon* 1.2.2), its climactic, stir-causing lines were these:

> Then may I be a man of Pholegandros or Sicinus
> instead of an Athenian, changing my country;
> for soon would this become the report among humankind:
> this man's an Athenian, one of the Salamis-abandoners. (fr. 2)

> Let's go to Salamis, to fight for the lovely island
> and to free ourselves from terrible disgrace. (fr. 3)

Plutarch says that, after this performance, "Solon's friends began to praise him," opinion shifted, the decree was repealed, the war was renewed, and Solon was put in command (*Solon* 8.3).[26]

This poem and the legend surrounding it are significant in at least three respects. First, while modern translations of Plutarch's account have tended to represent Solon as "writing" and "memorizing" *Salamis*,[27] what Plutarch actually says is that Solon "composed" or "put together" (*suntheis*) his elegy and "practiced" it (*meletêsas*) "in order to speak from memory" (*legein apo stomatos*, literally "to speak from the mouth"). Likewise, Plutarch describes Solon in performance as "going through the elegy in song" (*en ôidêi diexêlthe tên elegeian*). Plutarch's language reflects to some degree the presumptions of his own highly literate time, when poets and epideictic orators might write and memorize; the verb for "practice," *meletaô*, is also the root for *meletê*, the Greek term for declamation. But *meletê* was, of course, even in Plutarch's time a matter of oral performance in which extemporaneous improvisation, and not the mere recitation of a memorized text, was highly prized. "Composing" could also mean the putting-together, devising, or planning of an oral performance, a process that need not involve writing at all. And indeed Plutarch's description places overwhelming emphasis on such performance, and nowhere explicitly mentions writing. Solon is represented as "composing" not "writing" his elegy and as delivering it not by textual dissemination but by "singing" or reciting it, in the agora, as public utterance to an assembled and heterogeneous crowd.[28]

Second, the legend represents Solon as appropriating and reconfiguring a number of discursive conventions to achieve a speech act of considerable originality. The image of Solon in sick-man's cap rushing into the agora to sing/declaim his elegy has often been regarded as a dubious bit of mythification, on the assumption that his elegies, like elegiac verse generally, most likely would have been intended for performance at symposia. And indeed this is probably true for much of Solon's poetry (not all of which is political). But an essential feature of the tale is that, in Solon's specific circumstances, to perform *Salamis* in symposium with his friends would have been illegal. The fact that the poem was composed in elegiac meter cannot be taken as an index of its conformity to the usual genre conventions or performance conditions of elegy. By feigning madness, and by presenting his elegy as a poetic *mimesis* of a herald's discourse—while at the same time presenting it from the actual herald's stone (a sort of rostrum)—Solon found a way to circumvent and subvert the law. The poem was and was not a public declaration from the herald's stone; it was and was not the product of a disordered mind; it was and was not an elegy; and it was and was not an exhortation to fight for Salamis, though it *had the effect of an exhortation* if (and when) the audience found Solon's argument persuasive. Solon was, in effect, converting the normally private, insider discourse of symposiastic poetry to public theater, fusing the conventions of elegiac verse with those of bardic poetry, and conflating the conventions of epideictic/poetic performances (i.e., at public festivals by rhapsodes) with those of political decrees (by heralds). When one considers the theatrical stunts employed, for example, by Peisistratus to manipulate opinion and seize power, the legend of Solon's astonishing performance does not seem implausible.[29]

Third, in its appropriation and reconfiguring of elegiac/symposiastic discourse as public discourse, *Salamis*—with its hundred lines—seems probably to have offered a considerable amount of argumentative development. In the three fragments that have been preserved, all we have are the opening and what we might guess are the poem's chief (or most memorable) enthymematic caps. These stand alone, now, as epigrammatic flowers of eloquence, but it seems reasonable to suppose that the other ninety two lines would have been devoted to establishing and amplifying the grounds from which they derived persuasive force. This would be consistent with the poetry that still survives. As Emily Katz Anhalt has suggested, the most substantial fragments of Solon's major political elegies reveal an argumentative operation in which the poem introduces a topic, expands it in one or more ways (sometimes at substantial length), then introduces and expands a second topic arising (or following, etc.) from the first one, and so forth.[30] As I will presently show, moreover, each segment is also an enthymematic segment, while the sequence of segments establishes and accumulates a set of argumentative topics that provide, in turn, the basis for what might be called the poem's chief or climactic enthymemes, its culminating stance-figures and exhortations.

After *Salamis*, of course, Solon would not have delivered his political poems by pretending to be out of his head, rushing down to the agora wearing a sick-man's cap, and declaiming (or singing) from the herald's stone. The *Salamis* performance surely was a unique event. Even so, however, it reveals an intention to speak in public to the city. Anhalt argues that, while Theognis tends to regard the symposium as a microcosm of the *polis*, Solon finds this traditional, aristocratic conception inadequate and directly critiques it. A *polis* cannot sustain an adequate politics and is likely to disintegrate if citizens understand themselves only as members of particular insider groups or if citizens regard their particular group as the true and essential embodiment of the *dêmos* (as Theognis and Alcaeus seem to do).[31] If Anhalt's reading is persuasive—and I think it is—then it also seems likely that Solon recognized as well the rhetorical limitations of symposiastic insider discourse as a medium of political persuasion. While Solon's political poems after *Salamis* may have been performed first within a symposium, among his immediate associates and supporters, it seems likely that they also were meant to circulate to other groups (by

way of reperformances). But they also may have been designed for public, quasi-
bardic performances: Critias's boyhood memory of learning Solonic songs for poetry
recital contests at public festivals suggests that public recitation could well have
been the original and intended medium for Solon's major poems. It seems reasonable, in short, to believe that Solon adapted elegiac verse for public performances of
political epideictic. One effect of such performance may have been to reconfigure
the assembled audience as an expanded symposium-group, in which each audience
member would have been addressed as a "comrade" of not whatever faction he belonged to, but of the citizen body as a whole.

Let me briefly consider one major fragment (fr. 4).

> And our city will never perish by Zeus's decree
>   and the will of the blessed gods immortal;
> for so greathearted a guardian, she of the mighty father,
>   Pallas Athena holds her hands above us;
> but the citizens themselves, persuaded by money, are willing
>   to ruin this great city by their folly,
> and the people's leaders are of unjust mind, and are set
>   to suffer much pain for their great crimes;
> for they know neither to restrain their excess nor to govern
>   in peace the joys of their feasting
> . . .
>   and those persuaded to unjust deeds grow rich
> . . .
>   neither sacred property nor what is public
> sparing, by thievery they snatch what they can from one another,
>   not regarding the holy grounds of Justice,
> the silent one who knows what happens and what was before
>   and in time arrives to claim the penalty from all.
> Presently this comes to all the city, an inescapable wound,
>   and quickly it falls into wretched slavery,
> which wakens strife within the tribe and war from sleep,
>   which has destroyed the prime of many;
> for from those of ill-will quickly the much-loved town
>   is consumed in gatherings dear to wrongdoers.
> Among the populace this evil circulates; and of the poor
>   many come to some foreign country
> sold into bondage and bound in unseemly fetters
> . . .
> Thus the public evil comes to every house,
>   and the outer doors will no longer hold,
> and it leaps over the highest wall, and finds one out,
>   even if he should hide in his inmost room.
> This my heart bids me teach the Athenians,
>   that Lawlessness brings to the city the greatest evils;
> but Lawfulness makes all things balanced and well-ordered,
>   and often puts unjust men in shackles;
> rough things it polishes, it stops excess, outrage it effaces,
>   it withers the blooming flowers of sin,

it puts crooked judgments straight, and overweening deeds
  it tames; it stops the works of dissension
and stops the gall of grievous quarreling, and under it
  all human life is prudently in balance.

Anhalt has discussed the thematics of this thirty nine-line poem (or poem fragment) at length, and my shorter discussion is indebted to and will parallel hers in
several respects.[32] In particular Anhalt stresses Solon's resonance with traditional
poetic (Hesiodic, Homeric, and lyric) concerns "with the problem of consumption
and the requirement of society that it be regulated," as well as his (more original)
emphasis on the intellectual responsibility of citizens to recognize and take responsibility for the probable consequences of their actions.[33] What I wish to emphasize,
however, is the poem's function as an argumentative procedure.

The poem clearly operates as a series of enthymematic units. The opening segment offers a pair of enthymematic arguments, the first of which declares that the
city cannot "perish by Zeus's decree" or the will of the gods because it is under
Athena's protection. But this briefly stated enthymeme is immediately discarded, as
the poem moves to its central argument: while the gods will not destroy the city,
"the citizens themselves . . . are willing to ruin this great city by their folly." This
topic is introduced in lines 5–10 as a compressed enthymeme that most of the rest
of the poem will develop: the people are "willing to" wreck their city *because* they
are "persuaded by money"; and the "unjust mind" (*adikos noos*) of "the people's leaders" (*dêmou hêgemonôn*), meaning the nobility, has set them up "to suffer much pain
for their great crimes" (*hubrios megalês*). Everyone is devoted to the unlimited acquisition of wealth and spectacular consumption; their appetites and their symposia
run riot. Both the *dêmos* and the *hêgemones* are included in this condemnation; both
cooperate in the destruction of "our" city. The "we" that is invoked as this poem's
audience includes both groups and at the same time is distanced from them: "we"
will consider the failures of both the people and their leaders and the consequences
for "our" city. The audience is constituted, in effect, as a third body removed from
and comprehending both popular and noble factions: it occupies a "boundary" position much like Solon's.

Theognis might stop at this juncture, assuming that his friends (or anyone
worth talking to) will get the point.[34] But Solon continues. The next six lines
(11–16), which are interrupted by two lacunae, amplify the topic of "injustice as a
consequence of insatiability": because they are "persuaded by money" and are insa-
tiable, everyone in the city is "snatching" as much as possible from everyone else,
and even from "sacred property," heedless of the "holy grounds of Justice." "Justice"
thus is constituted as a spirit or *daimon* whose "grounds" (or sacred precincts) have
been violated. This amplification, and the first major unit of the poem, is then
capped with an admonitory evocation of Justice as a vengeful *daimon* who remembers and who comes to "claim the penalty." All of this resonates, on one hand, with
the Athenian audience's own recognition of actual conditions in the city and on
the other hand with such poetic precedents as Hesiod's account of the "bad Strife"
and civil corruption in *Works and Days*. Insofar as the audience can indeed recognize these resonances and find them apt—insofar as they really do seem to fit actual
conditions and to echo traditional wisdom-lore—Solon's argument acquires au-

thority and persuasiveness on this point. At the same time, by portraying Justice as a vengeful, penalty-claiming *daimon* who sees and remembers all, Solon further plays off traditional lore (regarding, e.g., the Furies) while emphasizing that Justice's revenge will "come" as an inexorable consequence of the citizens' behavior.

What follows, in the next major unit of the poem—from "[p]resently this comes to all the city" to "even if he should hide in his inmost room" (lines 17–29)—is in essence an amplification of the notion of "Justice claims her penalty," leading to another enthymematic cap. The amplification, again, resonates with the recent (or current) situation that Solon's audience has actually been experiencing: "all" (or much) of the city has fallen (or will fall presently) into "wretched slavery," and this has awakened "strife within the tribe" (*stasin emphylon*) and "sleeping war" (*polemon heudonta*); factions motivated by "ill-will" and vendetta are striving to "wrong" and damage each other, and to enrich themselves, at the city's general expense; and the poor have fallen into bondage. Solon's suggestion that "all" the city will eventually fall into "slavery" resonates, moreover, both with Hesiod's account of the misruled city and with general experience: cities weakened by internal dissension and a general neglect of justice fall into poverty and ruin and are easily defeated and enslaved (economically or militarily) by greater powers. The Athenian audience's ability to see this as a credible description of what actually has been happening lends additional persuasive force to the notion of "Justice claims her penalty" and to the *predictive* or consequential logic inherent in that notion. The audience is confronted with a mythic pattern, a paradigmatic event structure, that they can recognize as *happening now* and as leading inexorably toward a certain kind of outcome if left to run its course. The persuasiveness of this paradigm/scenario is then exploited by the unit's enthymematic cap, which explicitly invokes a "conclusion," namely that "the public evil" eventually comes "to every house" and no one can be insulated from it. Indeed, the image of someone attempting unsuccessfully to hide "even . . . in his inmost room" in an apparently large house with "high walls" and "outer doors" suggests a relatively prosperous and secure house in the city (as opposed to rural peasants reduced to serfdom). In this the audience may see, in a completion of the enthymeme that the opening of the poem invoked, the city's "leaders" suffering "great pain" as they become engulfed in the *stasis,* impoverishment, and general collapse of the city (or find their homes invaded by a popular mob that has successfully overthrown them or a tyrannical power that has chosen to dispossess them in the people's name). But the audience also may see a representation of themselves, or of every individual citizen still in a position to undertake civic action, as unable to evade the broader consequences of a narrowly conceived pursuit of self-interest. Insofar as this concluding image arises from a paradigmatic story that the Athenian audience can recognize as true, and as fitting their actual situation, it also carries an admonitory force that is truly frightening: the vision of a "public evil" leaping the wall and passing through the (probably bolted) outer door to find the once manly citizen cowering in his "inmost room" has a monstrous, nightmarish quality.

The last ten lines (30–39) are an amplified enthymematic cap to all that has gone before, as Solon turns to an apostrophic stance figure: "[t]his my heart bids me teach the Athenians," and so forth. "Lawlessness" or misrule (*dysnomia*) brings the city to "the greatest evils," but "Lawfulness" or good rule (*eunomia*) puts all things right. It is worth noting that this declaration almost perfectly fits Anaximenes' definition, in the *Rhetoric to Alexander*, of the *enthymêma* as an argument from opposites that has been prepared for by an *exetasis*, an "examination." Solon's enthymematic declaration is amplified with a short catalogue of *eunomia*'s good effects, a catalogue that is itself ordered as a *gradatio* leading up to a climactic cap (which Aristotle might call the enthymeme's "epilogue"): *eunomia* "stops the gall of grievous quarreling, and under it / all human life is prudently in balance."[35] While the modern reader may be tempted to regard this concluding enthymeme and its epilogue/cap as platitudinous, it very likely would not have been so for Solon's audience. The enthymeme derives salience and force from the enthymematic units that lead up to it and from the frightening alternative prospect that those units have developed; and what it proposes is not yet, in fact, an established notion in early-sixth-century Greece. The rule of law, as opposed to the rule of "the best" (or whichever elite faction could seize and hold power), would not really be the predominant ideal at Athens until the mid-fifth century.

What is evoked, in sum, is the ideal of a well-ordered *polis* under the regime of a balanced justice that is "suitable" or "fitting" for all—the opposite of the *polis* condemned by its citizens' "folly" to the inexorable process of mutual injustice, civil *stasis*, and eventual disintegration. The way out of the city's problems, then, is not for Solon (or anyone) to act as tyrant-champion for one faction or another, but to establish *eunomia*: a code of justice under which all factions in the city can pursue their purposes fairly and in reasonably prudent balance with each other. Solon can be understood as making a general case, at the level of broad principle, for his legal and constitutional reforms. He is making this argument not to one particular faction or symposium-group, but to the city as a whole; and to do that he is giving his argument relatively full and explicit development, building and amplifying the enthymematic grounds of judgment on which his ultimate exhortations rest.

Solon's immediate effects, perhaps, were transitory. After completing his reforms, he retired from his archonship and went traveling, ostensibly to let the Athenians work out for themselves the implications of his laws; within five years, according to Aristotle, the factional strife returned and ended with Peisistratus making himself the city's tyrant (in 561 B.C.; *Athenian Constitution* 13–15; see also Plutarch, *Solon* 29–31). Solon may well have felt that his political reforms had come to nothing. But Peisistratus also seems to have been a "moderate" tyrant: Aristotle says that his rule was "more constitutional than tyrannical" (*Athenian Constitution* 16.2). Plutarch, similarly, says that Peisistratus "honored" Solon and consulted with him, despite the fact that Solon originally had opposed him, and he continued to observe "most of Solon's laws" (*Solon* 31.1). If these accounts are right, it seems likely that Peisistratus's tyranny was mitigated by the political ideology that Solon had put in play. Eventually, after Peisistratus's less moderate sons were driven from power (in 510), the restoration and reforms of Cleisthenes (in 508) produced a constitution that was still more democratic than its Solonic predecessor (Aristotle, *Athenian Constitution* 21–22); and Ephialtes' constitution in 462–461 was more democratic still. Solon's constitution, then, did not last long, but the political ideology it embodied and that was propagated in his poems continued to be popular and persuasive. Indeed, as the boyhood memories of Plato's Critias and the evident continued popularity of Solon's poetry suggests—fragment 4, for example, has been preserved for us as a long quotation in Demosthenes' fourth-century speech *On the Embassy* (254), where it is invoked as an authoritative statement of political ethics—it may have been Solon's poems more than his laws that accomplished and sustained his long-term ideological effect on the Athenians.

It seems reasonable to say, in sum, that Solon succeeded where both Alcaeus and Theognis failed. While he put himself at odds with factions on all sides—though he must have had a core group of allies and supporters—he was also able to make a generally persuasive case *to the city* for what was, after all, a highly original and certainly controversial political innovation. He did so, much as Sappho did, by appropriating traditional wisdom-lore and existing poetic conventions and reconfiguring them for the purpose of justifying his position and his policies, and by developing an explicit, amplified enthymematic argumentation that could escape (to a considerable degree) the limitations of "insider" discourse in symposiastic poetry. Solon's poetry and politics cannot be called "subversive"—at least not in the sense of being relentlessly oppositional or countercultural—but at the same time it clearly is the case that Solon did indeed effectively and persuasively promote what was to be a decisive shift, and one for the better, in Athenian political ideology and social life. For this he can be called *sophôtatos*, "most skillful/wise."

Argument Maximal and Minimal

Here one might step back and take a longer view.

In archaic poetry—and especially lyric poetry—we find embodied a general paradigm of rhetorical, epideictic practice, which is to say a suasory, argumentative, enthymematic practice. When Isocrates suggests that lyric poets "seek to employ enthymemes," or when Aristotle cites lyric poets in the *Rhetoric* to illustrate lines of argumentation, or when the later rhetorical tradition considers poetry the eldest, original form of "rhetoric," or when Dionysius likens the best orations of Demosthenes to "the mightiest poems and lyrics," we can understand all this as something better than the quaint delusion or confusion that modern thought has often taken it to be. Rather, it reflects a sensible understanding of the actual nature of poetic practice and of archaic poetic practice in particular. The poet offers persuasion, and the audience exercises judgment, enacting and rehearsing in its responses particular modalities of ethical commitment or assent. From the lyric argumentation of such poets as Sappho, Solon, and Pindar there is, in truth, a fairly direct line to the panegyric prose of such sophists as Gorgias and Isocrates, and beyond them to such later figures as Apuleius and Aelius Aristides.

This general paradigm—of lyric (or poetic discourse generally) as enthymematic argument—is of course subject to many, potentially an infinite number of, specific variations. These will depend on the particular contexts in which the poetry is composed and meant to be performed, on generic conventions and audience expectations, on the particular suasory purposes that a poem is meant to fulfill, and so forth. But we can plot at least one modality of this variation along a scale of argumentative fullness. Enthymematic argument in lyric poetry may be given relatively explicit and full development, frequently by narrative or other amplifications of the argumentative topics (or minor enthymemes) on which the poem's ultimate stance-projection or "conclusion" is grounded. On one hand, insofar as lyric poetry is meant to be projected outward, beyond the relatively private enclosure of the symposium-group, it will tend to develop such explicit, amplified argumentation in order to engage with the various discourses and potential audiences circulating "outside," in public, civic space. On the other hand, insofar as a lyric poem is meant for an "inside" group whose homogeneity and agreement can be presumed, the argumentation may become elliptical or minimal. It may simply invoke and amplify what already is taken as authoritative wisdom. Or the poem's argumentation may be reduced to little more than a declaration or dramatized presentation of a stance, an enthymematic cap standing alone and virtually without an overt presentation of the grounds from which it derives persuasive force. In such a case, the successful poem will offer its audience an elegant, memorable, aesthetically satisfying representation of situations and attitudes with which they more or less identify already: the audience sees itself, or its values, reflected strikingly. The epigrammatic or minimal lyric poem, in essence, prompts an act of recognition combined with enjoyment of the skill (or memorability, wit, panache, etc.) with which the poem's enthymematic gesture is accomplished; and the enjoyment reconfirms the ideology on which the recognition is grounded as a "good thing."

Among the sources of enthymematic persuasion available to poetry are the sheerly aesthetic effects of such things as prosody, music, or style—what Kenneth Burke calls the "appeal of form"—as well as the effects of delivery, in the sense of performance and spectacle. When we read archaic poetry now, and especially when we read it in translation, some of these effects may be retrievable; but others, such as the effects of the music and choreography of Pindar's odes, are nearly or wholly lost. But, as Isocrates recognizes, in performance these features of poetic discourse, which we might sum up as *mousikê*, gave the poetry an additional and considerable dimension of psychagogic power (*Evagoras* 10–11), a power to beguile, to hypnotize, to carry off the listener's mind, as well as ways to convey attitude/stance by means of tone, rhythm, melody, bodily movement, gesture, costume, spectacle, and so forth. That is, *mousikê* could convey the attitude/stance that embodied the poem's enthymematic "conclusion," while at the same time psychagogically beguiling the listener's mind to sympathize (or, in Kenneth Burke's terms, to identify) with that "conclusion" or even to dance along with it, as at a victory *komos* where a Pindaric *epinikion* was being performed. A recognition of that kind of power is, of course, one of the chief bases for the Socratic or Platonic worry, in the *Republic*, about the corrupting effects of poetry on the souls of unguarded youths.

Both minimally and maximally developed lyric argument could be, can be, quite effective, quite charming, quite powerful. It does, however, seem that the more "minimal," elliptical rhetoric of insider discourse and of epigram will tend to serve inherently conservative purposes and to have a limited potential for projecting itself beyond the group whose sense of self it enacts, expresses, and reinforces, however beguilingly it does so. The rhetorical effectiveness of *mousikê*, with no other argumentative support, is limited. A charmingly refined, aesthetically appealing expression of attitudes that an audience finds repugnant or nonsensical remains, for them, just that: an elegant expression of repugnant, nonsensical attitudes. And the elegance of expression may then become, in itself, a sign of the speaker's ethical corruption in the unpersuaded audience's eyes. (Who would want or knowingly choose to say an ugly or stupid thing with wit and charm? Who would lovingly lavish fine words and melodic phrase on ignoble, foul, or foolish ideas? I do not mean here the expression of "bad" ideas by characters in a narrative or drama who are meant to be seen as ignoble, foolish, or mistaken—characters whose badness is eloquently revealed—but "bad" ideas, from the audience's point of view, asserted and affirmed directly by the poet, with no attempt at justification, in an elegantly composed, euphonious epigram.)

In contrast, a more explicitly developed, amplified, "maximal" enthymematic argumentation—especially to the degree that it appropriates and reconfigures (as opposed to merely citing or invoking) culturally authoritative wisdom-lore and ambient presuppositions and insofar as its persuasive force is then amplified by the aesthetic appeal of *mousikê*—has a greater potential for "making the lesser case greater," or for effectively promoting marginalized positions, or for promoting ideological or social change. This is what we see in the lyric practices of Pindar, Sappho, and Solon. A rhetoric of argumentative fullness will not *necessarily* have such effects, of course, but for the controversialist poet, or the poet who wants to do more than "tell the knowing what they know" already, it offers greater possibilities.

This rhetorical possibility seems to have been recognized, at least obliquely, by Isocrates. As he observes in *To Nicocles* (42–49), a poetry consisting largely of a euphonious recitation of worthy precepts, such as that of Theognis or even Hesiod, tends to have a relatively slight effect on people's actual thinking and behavior. Indeed, the worthiness and wisdom of the precepts will be apparent only to those who happen to be "wise" already. Most people, as Isocrates says, are too preoccupied with their personal appetites and desires to be amenable to didactic admonitions, or declarations like "Associate with good men, Kyrnos, and never seek unjust riches," unless they already are committed to them (and know what they mean). "How then," asks Isocrates, "shall one either recommend or teach or say anything useful to such people and yet please them?" (46). Isocrates' answer is that the poet or writer who wishes to be "pleasing to the many" must "not seek the most useful discourses, but the most mythical" (*tous mythodestatous*)—that is, not the most earnestly moralizing discourses but those that are most enriched with storytelling and most poetic—since "listeners are delighted by such things, as spectators are by games and contests" and by Homer and the tragedians (48).

Isocrates' point is not that one should "entertain" rather than "instruct," since his concern is how to "say anything useful" *effectively* to popular audiences. Nor is he recommending that one should turn simply to fabulation, narration, and drama (at least not exclusively), although it is worth noting that his two most distinguished students were the historian Theopompus and the tragedian/panegyricist Theodectes—and that Theodectes was to be the focal figure of Aristotle's *Theodectea* and a source of examples for enthymematic topics in the *Rhetoric*.[36] Nor is Isocrates suggesting poeticity as a sugar coating for the serious pill of doctrine, as the Stoics would do later. Isocrates elsewhere presents his own panegyric practice as superior to that of "Homer, Hesiod, and the other poets" and boasts that he can "silence those who chant their verses in the Lyceum and prate about them" (*Panathenaicus* 33).[37] Isocrates' panegyrics are closer in character to the poetry of Solon than to epic narrative or drama, and, as we have seen already, in the *Antidosis* he explicitly compares himself to Pindar. His arguments are amplified considerably, frequently with extended passages of narration, much of it historical. Likewise, his discourses are composed as extended dramatizations of himself as speaker and with an elaborately contrived (sometimes overcontrived) euphony. Isocrates' point would seem to be that an effective public epideictic, whether in verse or prose, must develop and intensify its enthymematic force by maximally amplifying its argumentation, perhaps chiefly with narrative excurses or "digressions," and by exploiting as well the dramatic possibilities and the aesthetic force of poetic utterance. The point is not that the poet (or rhetor) should "teach" and the audience should "learn" a string of elegantly stated precepts; nor that the poet (or rhetor) should merely entertain. The point, rather, is that the poet (or rhetor) should *persuade* and the audience should *respond*, from its *thymos*.

From the maximal development of enthymematic argument in lyric we can in principle proceed, as Aristotle suggests in *Poetics* 4 and as I argued in Chapter 6, to the extended narratives of what we now call epic poetry—such as we find in Homer, or Apollonius's *Argonautica*, or Virgil's *Aeneid*—or to the extended arguments and encyclopedic lore of philosophic epic, from such poets as Hesiod and Empedocles to Callimachus's *Aetia*, Aratus's *Phainomena*, or Lucretius's *De Rerum Natura*. Or we can proceed as well from the dramatistic potential inherent in the performance of public poetry, especially choral poetry, to the development of drama. In "epic" narrative and drama, what we in essence find is the elaboration of an argument in terms of a case, or what Hermagoras would come to call a *hypothesis*, which in turn provides a context for the staging of various lines of argument in different voices by different characters, as the poem enacts its own contest of persuasions.[38] This is what we likewise find in the literary lyric sequences of Hellenistic and especially Roman poets, insofar as these offer a similar kind of staging: a "case" embodied in the "story" (or stories) obliquely adumbrated by the poems themselves and about which the poems make various kinds of arguments from various positions in different circumstances.[39] Further, from the maximal lyric/poetic argument and its "epic" and "dramatic" elaborations, we also proceed, as I argued in chapter 2, to the varieties of epideictic prose: the epideictic or panegyric speech, the sophistic address, or the "prose hymn" (with Aelius Aristides); the philosophic dialogue, lecture, or treatise; the historical narrative; and the Hellenistic and later the Roman "novel," such as Petronius's *Satyricon*, Apuleius's *Golden Ass*, or Philostratus's *Life of Apollonius of Tyana*.[40] Indeed, in collections such as Apuleius's *Florida* (a compilation of "flowers of eloquence" or favorite passages from his speeches), and perhaps in the Senecan fad for *sententiae*, we find even something like a prose equivalent of epigrammatic poetry. In sum, if we can understand archaic poetry as an enthymematic argumentative practice—in both its "lyric" and its more elaborated "epic" and "dramatic" versions—then we also can understand the emergence of sophistic "rhetoric" and the varieties of epideictic and literary prose not as a sharp discontinuity, and not the displacement of "mythical" by "rational" thinking, but rather as a continuation and further evolution of the poetic tradition (and its methods of argument) into new stylistic registers. This is, in fact, the prevalent understanding in antiquity.

Folding this discussion back to the concerns with which I ended part II, one might ask to what extent archaic poetry, as a mode of epideictic rhetoric, could be said to constitute "conditions of possibility" (or a condition) for democracy. Obviously, archaic Greek poetry operates in a world in which democracy is scarcely thinkable: a world in which the most conceivable possibilities are kingship, oligarchy, tyranny, or *stasis* collapsing into bloody feud and civil war. Much archaic poetry, perhaps nearly all, speaks for the perceived interests, rights, or entitlements of endlessly competitive aristocratic cliques, while the varieties of "insider" poetry adopt a rhetoric that seems best suited to reaffirming and reinforcing the "inside" group's identity, its values and presumptions, its ideology. (The "inside" group can, of course, be as small as a group of friends at a symposium, or as large as "all Greeks," say, in contrast to barbarians.) And as with the later rhetorical tradition, the key political-moral term for archaic poetry is not "democracy" but *dikê*, "justice" or the "right," or equity or reciprocity, however such notions may be defined by poets as different as Alcaeus, Pindar, Sappho, Theognis, or Solon.[41]

But it is precisely at this point—where the poetry is perceived as a medium in which ideas of the just or fair may be negotiated, asserted, contested, argued *in a rhetorical encounter*—that the possibility of democracy becomes at least implicit, however faintly. Insofar as the poet's audience, like Theognis's *pais*, is understood not simply as an "understander" (or aesthetic appreciator) and not merely as the recipient of morally improving instruction but more fully as a judge whose agreement is to be earned and who is not compelled "to do what's not according to your *thymos*," the scene of the poetic encounter is marked by an equity that implies, or is, the minimal condition for a democratically constituted community. This implication is most apparent in the maximal versions of lyric argumentation and perhaps Solon's lyric argumentation in particular. Insofar as such poetry projects itself beyond its inner circle to an "outside" where its positions are contestable (or constitute a "lesser" discourse to prevailing ideologies and attitudes), and seeks to construct and make available the enthymematic grounds on which its positions may be judged persuasive, it projects as well a civic or public space where communal judgment is authoritative. Or one might say that it projects the implicit image of a community, and a mutually shared public domain, constituted through a process of persuasion and communal judgment enacted in a common discursive space. This is, of course, the root image in Isocrates' political mythology, which imagines the art and practice of eloquently reasoned discourse as the socially constructive agency through which human communities were formed and from which all civic institutions have derived (*Antidosis* 254); and it is the root image, as well, in Aelius Aristides' much later account of rhetoric as not only that which forms communities and civil institutions but also that which afterward maintains or modifies them, "making proposals, going on embassies, forever shaping present circumstances" (*Against Plato Concerning Rhetoric* 401). It is, in short, from the possibilities of a "maximal" lyric argumentation that rhetoric emerges as an art of public discourse oriented toward the formation and revision of communal consensus on questions of what is just, or honorable, or wise: an art in which the minimal conditions for democracy are implicitly embodied, in the conditions of the rhetorical encounter itself, even when real political conditions make democracy impossible, unavailable, or unimaginable.

Finally, one might ask whether or to what degree this notion of poetic discourse, or of lyric discourse in particular, was reflected in ancient poetic theory. As W. R. Johnson has argued, there seems to have been a general "absence" of lyric theory in antiquity, or at least no theory that truly grasped the nature of the great lyric poetry composed in the archaic period.[42] Johnson attributes this seeming dearth partly to a decline of lyric practice well before the emergence of any systematic theory of poetics, that is, before the *Poetics* of Aristotle. Johnson suggests that lyric, or at least archaic lyric, did not well fit the predominant categories of poetics from Aristotle onward. And when critical accounts of lyric did begin to emerge, in the Hellenistic period, these were largely products of not the rhetorical but the grammatical tradition: formalistic accounts of the "rules" or genre conventions for various types of poems that for the most part were no longer being practiced or that were no longer part of a live tradition, though they might be revived as erudite literary imitation. The result in later antiquity, according to this view, was all too often a literary lyric practice that amounted to little more than prosaic musings, occasional ephemera, letters, and whatnot tricked out in "mechanical verse and mechanical rhetoric," technically correct and even (at times) ingenious but largely devoid of the "passions and paradoxes of great lyric poetry"[43]—though such poets as Catullus, Horace, or Propertius would rekindle this highly mannered art and raise it to extraordinary brilliance and indeed to genuine rhetorical power.

But Johnson's is a fundamentally romantic view of lyric as the dramatized expression of emotion[44] and one that, as we have seen already, does not extend its perception of the rhetoricity of lyric far enough to account even for the full variety of archaic practices, or for Solon's practice in particular. And it is possible to argue that there was, in fact, always an account of lyric poetry available in antiquity. That account was rhetoric, as rhetoric was understood in the sophistic tradition that stretched from Isocrates to Dionysius of Halicarnassus, Aelius Aristides, Hermogenes of Tarsus, and "Longinus." As a general theory of persuasive discourse, rhetoric accounted quite well for lyric (or any other kind of) poetry as epideictic, enthymematic argument in verse. There is, of course, no explicit or systematic set of "rules" for writing poetry in the surviving rhetorical *technai*, such as we find for dikanic and demegoric/symbouleutic speeches (or for *controversiae* and *suasoriae* in declamation exercises). This omission of explicit rules for poetry is not surprising—just as it is not surprising that we find no rules either for histories (or philosophical dialogues, etc.), though these are also kinds of "rhetoric" according to Hermogenes and others. The *technai* were produced, in essence, for training sixteen-year-old would-be politicians in rules of thumb, or behavioral routines (like the reflexes of athletes), for the particular kinds of speech acts required for success in courts and councils. As the speakers in Tacitus's *Dialogus de Oratoribus* note, the world beats a path to the practical orator's door and can make him very rich (if he's any good, or at least competent), while to become a poet (or historian, etc.) is generally not the way to worldly wealth and power. There was, in short, no widespread market for handbooks on how to write poems or histories.

Yet it is clear that rhetoricians—at least those of the sophistic, Isocratean tradition—included poetry (and history, etc.) among their concerns and that at least some of their students became poets (or historians, etc.) rather than professional orators. There may well have been a discourse, in the schools, on the principles of persuasive eloquence in various kinds of literary or poetic epideictic. Indeed, Dionysius of Halicarnassus's discussion of historians in *On Imitation*, or the fragment of it preserved as a long quotation in his surviving *Letter to Pompeius*, suggests quite clearly that such discourse was in fact produced.[45] Further, as Cicero's Antonius argues in *De Oratore*, beyond providing a general theory of argumentation and persuasion, rhetoric had no need to give specific rules for writing histories or any other kind of epideictic/literary discourse (2.15–16). The fundamental "rules" of persuasive discourse were, in essence, sufficient and the same for every kind of epideictic rhetoric, and could be applied differentially and flexibly according to the needs of different genres and circumstances and according to the requirements of a particular subject matter and the writer's argumentative intentions; and describing the specific formal characteristics of different genres was the work not of rhetoric but of grammar. As Isocrates suggests in *Against the Sophists*, eloquence in panegyric or any other kind of discourse does not arise from the mechanical, formalistic application of rules and recipes such as one finds in handbooks (for which his metaphor is, precisely, the fixed, invariant rules of elementary grammar; 9–10). It seems unlikely, in short, that the rhetorical tradition that descended from Isocrates would have been interested in prescribing "rules" for particular types of poetic and epideictic discourse or in *technai* that embodied such rules.

I can, however, agree with Johnson in one important respect. In the tradition of poetics that more or less descends from Aristotle, there is a gradual occlusion of the fundamentally rhetorical notion of poetry as enthymematic argument offered to an audience in a suasory encounter. The result is a rhetorically diminished account of "poetry," and, insofar as (or whenever) this account determines actual poetic practices, it is likely to promote a rhetorically diminished poetry as well. This is, in essence, the poetics of the grammatical tradition—from which the poetics of the modern West descends.

THE FATE OF "POETRY"

10

Aristotelianism and Grammar

To speak of the "fate of poetry" is, from one point of view, too portentous. Certainly poetry continued to be written and performed, continued to play cultural, social, and political roles, and continued to be understood in rhetorical terms from early to late antiquity. There is, however, a well established agreement among classical scholars that poetry "declined," from the Second Sophistic onward, as the proliferating varieties of epideictic prose became the predominant and most lively media for significant epideictic discourse and original invention.[1] Such a view may reflect, in part, an inability like that of W. R. Johnson to view a poetry like Solon's as "poetic." However, it does seem true that little poetry of consequence was written in late antiquity—that is, after the third or fourth century—or little that can seriously be compared with what remains of Sappho, Solon, Pindar, or the great Hellenistic and Augustan poets. The poets of late antiquity (or those whose writings have survived) are often regarded as well-trained hacks, many of whom are little more than antiquarians or well-bred poetasters indulging in verse as a courtly hobby. The better poets do rise above mediocrity, but not very far: mostly they rework an exhausted body of conventional materials and forms, with laborious if ingenious pedantry. In short, poetry became for the most part a minor and often second-rate form of epideictic. Such is the standard view.

While we need not dispute this general scenario, the usual explanation for it—that poetry had become "rhetorical"—seems unlikely. Poetry *always was* "rhetorical," and always was composed according to whatever understandings of discursive art and suasive eloquence were available to poets and their audiences. Moreover, it is clear that even in the fourth century A.D. an epideictic literature pervasively informed by rhetoric could rise to greatness, as is plainly the case, for example, with Augustine. Likewise, traditional sophistic oratory continued to be vital, if rather baroque, and even enjoyed something of a renaissance in the fourth and fifth centuries, as paganism held its ground awhile against the Roman Empire's emergent and increasingly powerful Christian culture.[2] If late-antique poetry is mediocre, this is so not because the poetry is "rhetorical" but because it is mediocre rhetoric. Or because it is not *rhetorical enough*. The difference is not rhetoricality but inventional and persuasive power.

Poetry's fate, as I will argue here and in the next chapter, was to be conceptualized—chiefly in the Aristotelian and grammatical versions of poetics—in ways that obscured or diminished its rhetoricity or that constrained its rhetorical possibilities. And it was poetry's "fate," moreover, for this reduced and fundamentally *grammatical* conception to become the dominant version of poetics transmitted to the literary culture of the modern West. I will consider these claims in turn, beginning with Aristotle.

Aristotle's Double Vision

First, one should be fair to Aristotle. It is commonly recognized—and obvious, since he directly says so—that Aristotle sees the relevance of rhetoric to the "speeches" of the characters in a drama. Rhetoric provides the principles by which the characters may say "what is possible and fitting" in particular circumstances, as they express their "thought" (*dianoia*) in the form of arguments that "something is or is not" or "declarations of some general principle" (*katholou ti apophainontai; Poetics* 6.1450b, 19.1456a–b). This would include the choral interludes as well, since Aristotle says the chorus is properly "one of the actors" and integral to the play's action (18.1456a): a drama's choral odes are "speeches" by "characters" too.

One can argue, moreover, that Aristotle at least obliquely recognizes the basically rhetorical character of all poetic discourse. This is inferable from several things: the conjunction of his notion of rhetoric and *dianoia* with his hypothetical genealogy deriving all poetic genres from lyric encomia, hymns, and invectives (4.1448b–1449a); his suggestion that, apart from the use of meter and music, the *dynamis* or function of style is essentially the same in poetry and prose (6.1450b, 19.1456b); his requirement that a tragedy or an epic have a well-constructed plot, a *mythos* that proceeds according to "probability or necessity" (8–9 1451a–b); and his definition of the effects of poetry in general and tragedy in particular as the provocation of insight and the *katharsis* of emotion (4.1448b, 6.1449b). I will unpack the relationships between these notions briefly.

Aristotle's speculative genealogy for poetry may or may not, of course, reflect the actual evolution of poetic genres in Greek culture. All that matters here is that he thinks the lyric genres of encomium, hymn, and invective poetry are logically prior to the more extended, elaborate discourses of epic and drama—and thus figure as a "primitive" origin and essence for all poetry. The point is that, with Aristotle, the "first" or most basic kinds of poetry are in principle *speeches* embodying *dianoia*, differing from prose orations chiefly, or only, by virtue of their being composed in verse. We see this in the poem that, according to Athenaeus (*Deipnosophistai* 15.696a–697b), Aristotle himself composed and sang at the daily meal of the Peripatetic school. Athenaeus says it is a *skolion*, a drinking song, eulogizing Aristotle's deceased friend Hermeias of Atarneos.[3]

> Excellence laborious for mortal kind,
>   the loveliest prize in life,
> for your beauty's sake, maiden,
>   even to die is an enviable fate in Greece
> or to undergo hard unceasing toils;

upon the mind you cast such
    godlike fruit superior to gold
or parents or soft-eyed sleep.
And for your sake godly
    Hercules and Leda's sons
endured much in their toils
    to seek your power;
and from desiring you Achilles and
    Ajax went to Hades' house;
and for your dear beauty's sake Atarneos's
    nursling left the sunlight widowed.
Therefore is he storied for his deeds,
    and his immortality will be augmented by the Muses,
Memory's daughters,
    exalting the majesty of Zeus hospitable
    and the gift of steadfast friendship.

Athenaeus says that Aristotle was prosecuted on a charge that this song was a *paian* and therefore impious, since a *paian* could only be addressed to a god. So the song may be a sort of hymn as well, or at least could plausibly be taken as one, for if the charge had been utterly implausible there would have been no trial (the song's rhythm does have paianic features). Either way, the song exemplifies what Aristotle thinks is the most basic kind of poetry. It is, in effect, a versified speech embodying *dianoia* in the form of an enthymematic argument asserting "that something is or is not" or declaring "some generalization." Indeed, the song's enthymematic cap, following the "therefore," asserts that "something is" with respect to Hermeias (that he is worthy of remembrance and celebration in song) and rests on a general declaration (regarding the pursuit of excellence), which is amplified and "demonstrated" through an invocation of mythic examples. Aristotle is perhaps no great shakes as a poet, but the basic operation of his song is of a piece with what we have observed already in Alcaeus, Sappho, Pindar, and Solon. (And one should not forget that Aristotle was, in fact, admired in antiquity for his literary skill.) The art or *technê* that describes the principles of this song's argumentation is clearly rhetoric, as Aristotle understands it, supplemented by the principles of versification, music, and song performance.

If one considers Aristotle's remarks about *mythos* or "plot" in drama (and implicitly in epic) one can understand the *mythos* itself as an argument regarding the way things "probably" or "necessarily" would happen in a given set of circumstances and as what the *Rhetoric* calls an "example" or *paradeigma* that "inductively" demonstrates a general pattern in the way things are (*Rhetoric* 1.8 1356b). In the *Rhetoric*, Aristotle says a *paradeigma* may be a "comparison" (*parabolê*) based on fact—that is, a "parable" embodying a general principle that applies to the present case—or it may be an invented, fictional "fable" (*logos*) that likewise embodies a general principle, as in the Aesopic tales (2.20 1393a–1394a). In the *Poetics*, similarly, *mythoi* may be either "factual," in the sense of involving legendary but supposedly real events and persons, as Aristotle says is usual in tragedies; or *mythoi* may be completely fictional, as is usual in comedies (9 1451a–b). Both *mythos* and *paradeigma* become persuasive by virtue of a consequential logic, in which events and actions appear to unfold "according to probability or necessity" (9 1451a); and *mythoi* based on real events tend to be more persuasive, or to produce a stronger sense of probability, since "things that have occurred are manifestly possible" (9 1451b). It is by virtue, then, of achieving a persuasive appearance of probability/necessity that a poetic *mythos*, like the rhetorical *paradeigma*, both embodies and communicates general truths or principles, *ta katholou;* and it is by virtue of embodying *ta katholou* that poetry is, as Aristotle says, "more philosophical and more serious than history" (9 1451b). A poem's *mythos*, then, operates as a probabilistic argument concerning *ta katholou*, the general principles and patterns at work in human action and experience.[4]

A *mythos*, then, is a sort of "case" that demonstrates the way things are, or could be, in a particular set of circumstances. And thus it is not surprising that, in Hellenistic literary theory, Aristotle's term *mythos* was generally and rather quickly replaced by the term *hypothesis* as the name for the basic plot, or story, constituting the subject matter of a poem.[5] Indeed *mythos* may never have been the dominant term of choice. A terra-cotta lamp from the third century B.C., found in Athens, bears an image of three actors and the following inscription: *Mimologoi. Hypothesis Hekyra* ("Mime-actors. Plot: The Mother-in-Law").[6] Even in popular usage then, *hypothesis* was the going name for "plot" or "story" as little as a quarter-century after Aristotle's death, well before its emergence as a technical term in Alexandrian literary criticism. *Hypothesis* was, of course, also the Hellenistic rhetorical term for the particularized "case" of a declamation, involving specific persons, events, circumstances, and so forth, as opposed to a general proposition or *thesis:* for example, the case of the father who disowned his son for marrying a pirate chief's daughter (as in the elder Seneca's *Controversiae* 1.6, with several more circumstances added), as opposed to the question of when, in principle, a father may disown a son. The general *thesis* is instantiated in the specific *hypothesis*, as Cicero recognizes, just as *ta katholou* are instantiated in the Aristotelian *mythos*. A *mythos* as Aristotle understands it is, in sum, a *hypothesis*, and a poem about that *mythos/hypothesis*—whether narrative, dramatic, or lyric—constitutes a sort of declamation arguing an interpretation and a judgment of the case.

In the *Poetics*, the probable, persuasive presentation of a *mythos/hypothesis* is understood to have a twofold effect on its audience. On one hand the audience experiences the pleasure of noetic insight, insofar as it grasps the *katholou* or general principles and paradigms of human action exemplified or demonstrated in the *mythos*: people "enjoy seeing likenesses" because in doing so they "learn and infer what each thing is, for instance that 'this is that'" (4 1448b). An effective presentation of a *mythos* persuades and teaches its audience how things can and do happen in human life. On the other hand, the audience also experiences *pathos*—in tragedy, for example, a *katharsis* of pity and fear (6 1449b)—as a result of witnessing how the logic of events has brought the characters to the consequences that befall them. The emotional response is the enthymematic completion of the audience's cognitive experience and constitutes the ultimate act of judgment that the poem, as argument, is calling for; and the rehearsal of such judgments constitutes a sort of ethical training for the audience.[7] Thus Aristotle says at one point in the *Poetics* that the principles of rhetoric include not only the argumentative procedures and persuasive effects of speeches expressing *dianoia*, but also the production of "pity, terror, grandeur, or probability" by means of the "events" (*pragmasin*) comprising a tragic plot (19 1456a–b).

One can, in sum, argue that the *Poetics* presupposes a fundamentally rhetorical conception of poetic discourse, a presupposition that is nowhere directly argued—because it does not need to be, in Aristotle's world—but that is recoverable from the statements I have been examining. The principles that govern the persuasive, argumentative functions of poetry are discussed most fully in the *Rhetoric* and in the *Poetics* are supplemented with additional principles that pertain to poetry specifically (and most specifically to tragedy). The probabilistic argument embodied in the basic *mythos/hypothesis* of a poem can be amplified, and its effects intensified, by its exfoliation into episodes (and the arrangement of those episodes), characterization, speeches, and so forth and by the addition of rhythm, music, theatrical delivery, and spectacle. Viewed from this perspective, then, the *Poetics* offers an implicitly rhetorical account of poetry and cannot be fully understood without the *Rhetoric*.

The *Poetics*, however, has a double vision: while at least implicitly acknowledging the rhetorical, argumentative, suasory character of poetic discourse, Aristotle in other ways occludes it. This occlusion is the consequence of two well-known and closely related claims in the *Poetics*. One is Aristotle's insistence that versification *cannot* be the defining feature of "poetry"; the other is his focus on *mimêsis* as the definiens instead. These claims are, of course, responses to the Platonic critique of poetry in books 2, 3, and 10 of the *Republic*.[8] For Plato the most insidious features of poetry—and of tragedy most of all—are the psychagogic power of prosody and mimesis to generate irrational emotion and belief, and the inherent falseness of mimetic representations that merely offer semblances of semblances with no connection to real knowledge (*Republic* 10.595a–602b): poetry persuades the ignorant into false belief and foolish emotion through the psychagogic power of "meter, rhythm, and [musical] harmony . . . so great is the charm these things exert on them by nature" (601a–b). Plato is, in fact, worried about precisely what Gorgias celebrates: poetry, as "speech having meter," has a druglike power to induce emotion and belief (*Helen* 14). Or, as Gorgias elsewhere says in a fragment preserved in Plutarch, tragedy works a persuasive "deception" in the audience's soul by presenting "myth and suffering" in "marvelous sound and spectacle."[9] Plato is, moreover, worried about the ethical effects of poetry's charms in education, for the young not only are presented with psychagogically beguiling falsehoods, but through the traditional practice of poetry recitation they will rehearse and thus acquire the ethical habits of ignoble characters (2.376e–3.403c).[10] Aristotle evades the critique of "music and rhythm," or what he calls *melopoeia*, and makes the very things that Plato finds most suspicious, mimesis and drama, the heart of his defense.

Aristotle's response to the Platonic objection to rhythmic, musical psychagogy is basically dismissive. On one hand, he simply denies in his opening statements that meter (and, presumably, everything that goes with it in performance) is a defining or essential feature of "poetry" at all (*Poetics* 1 1447b). On the other hand, he downplays its persuasive power. As he rather surprisingly says at one point, even a bare statement of a well-conceived tragic plot should produce the tragic effect:

"[t]he *mythos* should have been constructed in such a way that even without seeing the tragedy performed the person who hears the events that occur will shiver with fear and feel pity as a result of what happens" (14 1453b). Meter, rhythm, and music may be instruments for enhancing this effect, as may spectacle, but they are supplementary and inessential. When Aristotle turns to matters of style in chapters 20–22, he has nothing whatever to say about meter or music or delivery, and only in chapter 24 (where he is discussing epic) does he pause to remark, in passing, that the "heroic" hexameter is "the most stately and dignified" of all meters and is suitable for epic, while iambics and tetrameters are "lively" and well suited to "dancing" and "action" (1460a). This suggests that meter and rhythm, far from having the sort of power attributed to them by Gorgias and Plato, simply set a framing mood, a ceremonious decor, that may or may not be appropriate to the story and the speech acts being performed. Similarly, in the *Rhetoric* "rhythm" is treated chiefly as an aid to clarity and memorability (3.9 1409b) or as a means of lending "urbanity" and dignity to speech, while its psychagogic power to move an audience's *thymos* goes largely (though not wholly) undiscussed. In general Aristotle seems not to grant the reputed power of rhythmic and melodic discourse.

As I have noted earlier, Aristotle's rejection of versification as the defining feature of poetic discourse is simply eccentric. From the fifth century through late antiquity "poetry" was in fact the name for versified, metered composition, whether sung or "spoken," while prose versions of originally poetic genres *never* were identified as "poems" (though they might be called "hymns" or "monodies," etc.). Metered rhythm, and the possibility of its being performed as song or declaimed in rhythmic recitative, was the definiens of "poetry" in ancient culture. Aristotle seems to recognize this in the *Rhetoric*, when he declares that oratory "should have rhythm, but not meter, for then it would be a poem" (3.8 1408b). Moreover, in the *Rhetoric* and the *Politics* Aristotle betrays a recognition that rhythmic, musical, and "emotive" prosody can have the very sort of power that Gorgias celebrates and Plato fears. In *Rhetoric* 3, for example, Aristotle says that "delivery" (*hypokrisis*) is a matter of "how voice should be used for each emotion" by modulating its loudness, tonal pitch, and rhythm (*megethos, harmonia, rhythmos*) and he recognizes that it has "great power" over audiences and frequently determines victory in both poetic and oratorical contests (3.1 1403b–1404a). Indeed, an "emotional" style tends to make audiences "sympathize" with the speaker and credit what he says, "even if he says nothing," because the speaker's prosody infects them with the same emotion— so that "many overwhelm their audiences by confusing them with noise" (3.7 1408a). Likewise, in *Politics* 8.7 Aristotle describes the emotional effects of music in fairly Gorgianic terms. He says that persons who happen to be susceptible to the type of emotion evoked in a piece of what he calls "cathartic" music will be "put into a state just as if receiving a medical treatment and *katharsis*," as when persons susceptible to religious *enthousiasmos* hear "enthusiastic," ecstatic music at a festival; indeed the same experience will come to "the compassionate and the timid and all other emotional people (*hoi pathetikoi*) generally, in the degree that falls to each," whenever they experience the appropriate type of music (1342a). The metaphor of "medical treatment and *katharsis*" here implies that music is indeed a drug, as Gorgias says, capable of generating an emotional state in the listener and effecting persuasion sheerly by means of rhythmic, harmonious "noise."[11] In the *Poetics*, however, this recognition is consigned to silence.

The catch, with Aristotle, is that the "cathartic" effects of prosody depend on the "depravity," *mochthêria*, of common audiences (*Rhetoric* 3.1 1404a). *Mochthêria* derives from the verb *mochtheô*, which means *to be weary with toil, to labor, to undergo hardships or execute painful tasks*. Aristotle has in mind, it seems, the blunted, lowbrow sensibilities of *hoi polloi*, "the many," the crowds of working-class citizens who fill the theaters and assembly places of Greek cities for poetic and oratorical performances. And thus he says the art of rhythmic, melodious delivery "seems vulgar, when rightly considered" and ideally would be unnecessary (3.1 1404a). Likewise, in *Politics* 8.7 Aristotle's point is that only "emotional types," *hoi pathetikoi*, are affected by "cathartic" music; those trained in proper self-control are less susceptible. For the better sort, then, poetry is to be experienced as a disembodied *logos* reduced to its propositional content.

This point is bound up—much as it is in Plato's *Republic*—with questions about the educational uses of *mousikê* and the ethical development of the young. As Aristotle declares, for example, banausics and thetes (craftsmen and laborers) respond emotionally to "distorted" music featuring high-strung, chromatically irregular melodies and discordant harmonies, because their souls have been "distorted from their natural dispositions" by their laborious occupations and low-class lives (*Politics* 8.7 1342a). Thus the well-born young should never be taught to play such music, lest through rehearsing its moods they distort their own souls into banausic and thetic vulgarity (1341b). Indeed most or all of the "cathartic" types of music should be excluded from education, just as most types of poetry are excluded in the *Republic*. Just as Plato will allow the young guardians-in-training to learn and practice only odes with dignified rhythms in praise of noble men, likewise Aristotle considers only the "ethical" types of music, *ta êthika*, suitable for the young to play, and in particular the Dorian mode, which is "most steady" and has a "manly character" (1342a–b).[12] Aristotle's quasi-paianic encomium of Hermeias is precisely this sort of song. (In the *Rhetoric*, Aristotle recommends paianic rhythm as a model for prose on the grounds that it has the "dignity" of epic hexameters without an obvious metricality; 3.8 1408b–1409a.) He does however say that all types of music may be *listened to*, for amusement and without harm, by those who are well educated.

The point is that, for Aristotle, a well-trained citizen who is not emotionally "depraved" and has a "steady and manly character" will be resistant to the "cathartic" effects of emotive music. He can hear and aesthetically appreciate, for example, the pitiable wailing of a tragic song, judging its appropriateness to the events in which it is embedded (and the character of the speaker, etc.), without actually being overwhelmed and persuaded into piteous feelings by the psychagogic force of the music itself. For such a person the prosodic and musical effects of verse can, in short, be nothing more than supplements to the *mythos* of a well-made poem, filling it out with greater or lesser degrees of satisfactoriness or propriety.

The corollary of Aristotle's dismissal of verse as an essential or even important feature of poetic discourse is that he fixates on *mimêsis*, the other great object of Platonic worry, and makes *it*, rather than meter or "song," the defining feature of all poetry. It seems unlikely that Aristotle can mean *mimêsis* in its most general sense, as "representation" (or even "interpretation"), since *mimêsis* in that sense is characteristic of any public discourse whatever, including political and legal oratory, and including as well the text you now are reading. Every discourse "represents" its subject matter in some way and "represents" its author and its author's attitudes and moods by various more or less dramatistic means, as Aristotle recognizes in the *Rhetoric* (1.2 1356a; 3.1 1403b–1404a; 3.7 1407b; 3.16 1417a). Every discourse performs, mimes, a mode of subjectivity. Aristotle cannot mean, either, *mimêsis* in the sense of "imitation" or fictive impersonation of speakers other than the author or performer. Obviously this happens in much poetry and certainly in a drama. But it happens in prose epideictic also, as in Gorgias's *Defense of Palamedes* (in which Palamedes is the speaker) or in the thousands of declamations performed in schools and public demonstrations by the sophists and their students or in any of the dialogues of Xenophon or Plato. No one ever called any of these things a "poem," though Aristotle does suggest in passing that "Socratic" dialogues and the prose mimes of Xenarchus and Sophron of Syracuse might be an as yet nameless kind of "poetry" (*Poetics* 1 1447b)—a throwaway remark that neither he nor anyone in antiquity ever took up afterward. Finally, it can be said that *mimêsis* as "imitation utterance" is characteristic even of "ghostwritten" practical orations by logographers such as Lysias, who composed in the voices of their clients, while many poets such as Solon seem to have composed a great many of their poems to speak *in propria persona* and in response to actual events. *Mimêsis* in the general senses of "representation" or "imitation" or "fictive utterance" cannot possibly mark a useful distinction between "poetic" and "nonpoetic" kinds of discourse or even between pragmatic and epideictic kinds.

Aristotle's notion of poetic *mimêsis* is much narrower. It boils down to "representation" of *stories* that embody the general truths of human experience. It is, of course, this definition that enables Aristotle to reclaim on more or less Platonic grounds a philosophical respectability for poetry, and especially the very kinds of poetry that Plato finds most objectionable, namely epic and drama.[13] Aristotle's argument in the *Poetics* is, among other things, a witty turning of the tables on his old professor.

But this specialized notion of *mimêsis* has problems too. As I have noted already, *mimêsis* as the representation of a *mythos/hypothesis* comes very close to the *Rhetoric's* notion of "example" or *paradeigma*. Examples "inductively" establish general statements which then combine, enthymematically, with other statements (tacit or explicit) to generate an attitude, inference, judgment, or conclusion of some kind. So for argumentation in practical oratory and in prose of nearly all descriptions. And so too, as we have seen, in archaic lyric and even in purely narrative art: the poetic fable is an elliptical form of argument, a *paradeigma* resting on a set of tacit premises that generate interpretation. Enclosing the narrated tale, the myth, we find an abstract discursive frame, an implicit enthymeme (or set of enthymemes). So *mimêsis* as the "representation" of *mythoi* embodying *ta katholou* does not seem convincing, either, as a means of distinguishing "poetic" from "nonpoetic" kinds of discourse.

One might speculate that Aristotle's *mythos* is a specialized type of *paradeigma* dealing only with human actions—whereas *paradeigma* proper, as a general device for rhetorical and philosophical disputation, is not so limited. Indeed this seems to be precisely what he means. But if this is so then poetry, as Gerald Else observes, is circumscribed within a limited range of subject matters and also within a limited part of the rhetorical spectrum, namely the illustrative or exemplary fable, or even the *allegorical* or symbolic fable, if one emphasizes the Platonic undertone of Aristotle's argument.[14]

That undertone is real and has certain consequences. For if the poetic fable is an allegorical representation of some general truth, then the noetic insight experienced by the audience is not so much an experience of being persuaded that the tale is probable (and fearful/pitiable, etc.) as an experience of *recognizing* the general truth it exemplifies. That is, in performing the pleasurable cognition that "this is that," the audience applies its preexisting knowledge to identify the story as an instance of a *katholou* that it knows already. This is in fact what Aristotle says, if one looks at his statement more closely.

> Learning things is pleasurable not only to philosophers but also to others likewise, though they share this pleasure less. This is why they enjoy seeing images, because what happens is that, as they observe, they learn and infer what each thing is, for instance that "this is that"; but if one should happen not to have seen the thing before, it will produce pleasure not as *mimêsis* but through its craftsmanship or its color or through some other such cause. (4 1448b)

The pleasure of "learning things," here, is the pleasure of *getting it*, the flash of recognition. And what is "learned" is not the general pattern that is represented; rather, one "learns" that the poem embodies or exemplifies that pattern. ("Ah: this is that.") Those who do not already know and so cannot perceive the underlying pattern in the *mythos*—those who do not *get it*—will merely be entertained by the spectacle, the music, the superficial appeal of the play's events, the technical skill of the performance, and so forth. And those who do perceive the underlying pattern, and who do experience the intellectual pleasure of *getting it*, will be *those who have seen that pattern before* and know it already. So the audience's noetic experience, if it happens at all, is more like a Platonic recollection.

This point holds as well for the audience's emotional responses. According to Aristotle, a person's state of character determines which emotions he or she is capable of feeling. In both the *Eudemian* and *Nichomachean Ethics*, "virtue" is an acquired predisposition or *hexis* ("habit") with respect to both actions and feelings: the person of good ethics is one who has acquired through training a set of predispositions to respond to certain "causes" or "premises" for emotion in certain ways, with certain feelings; the person of bad ethics has acquired a different set of *hexeis* and a different emotional responsiveness.[15] Moreover, as suggested by Aristotle's account of character types in *Rhetoric* 2.12–17, people's emotional predispositions vary not only according to the habits they have acquired through education and practice but according also to their age and social status.[16] And in *Politics* 8.7, as we have seen, different kinds of souls have different degrees of responsiveness to the mood-inducing powers of any given type of music, so that irascible types are quickly roused by angry music, and so forth, and banausics and thetes are stirred by the "distorted," high-pitched music that a well-bred aristocrat finds merely vulgar (but possibly amusing). What all this implies, in sum, is that different people are unequally responsive to the same "causes" or "premises" for emotion, or will not respond in the same way, or simply may have little or no capacity for the particular *pathos* that a rhetor or poet wishes to evoke. The person moved to the right measure of fear and pity by some tragic tale—and who can judge the poet's prosody and song as suitably dignified and pathetic—is the one who can *recognize already* the fearful, the pitiable, the dignified, and the proper. This person is reminded by the drama that "this is that" and is recalled to the right attunements of his soul.

Viewed from a Platonizing perspective, then, Aristotle's *Poetics* defines "poetry" as, in essence, mimetic representation of a tale of human action, a mimesis that is philosophically respectable because it allegorically figures forth or "represents" general truths and that (if it is well done) aligns those truths with an appropriate emotion, mood, or attitude that the well-bred observer may properly entertain. As such, poetry functions much as the *Phaedrus* says good writing should: as a *reminder* to the audience of what they know and feel already, as an occasion for the rehearsal of their existing attitudes and beliefs, and as a form of recreation. For, as Plato's Socrates declares,

> [the serious man will hold] that in written discourses on any subject much is necessarily playful, and that no discourse written in meter or without it has ever merited serious attention—including the rhapsodes' recitations, delivered for persuasion's sake [*peithous heneka*] without questioning or teaching—while the best of them have served to remind us of what we know. (*Phaedrus* 277e–278a)[17]

If this is the framework within which we interpret the *Poetics*, the role of the well-educated, "philosophically" inclined audience is largely a matter of hermeneutic insight and aesthetic judgment. The discerning spectator is to recognize whether the poem is the "better" sort or not, on the grounds of how satisfactorily or pleasingly it represents the "deeper" truths and values inscribed already in his *thymos*. To the degree that this is true, poetry would seem to be defined according to a model of symposiastic "insider" discourse.

An orientation toward hermeneutics and aesthetic judgment becomes most apparent in *Poetics* 25, which offers a very compressed discussion of the "Homeric problems" or criticisms raised against the *Iliad* and *Odyssey* by various Presocratics (problems Aristotle had addressed more fully in a now lost treatise). As Aristotle says, most of those objections are concerned with representations of impossibilities, illogicalities, and immoralities or with contradictions or technical infelicities in the representation itself (1461b).[18] There is no need to be concerned here with the details of his responses, other than to note the key one: namely, that "the standard of correctness is not the same between politics and poetry, nor between any other art and poetry" (1460b). It is less important whether a poet has represented things that are "correct" (in the sense of corresponding to truth) and more important whether he has "correctly" represented what he meant to represent. And indeed "with respect to poetry a persuasive impossibility is preferable to an unpersuasive possibility" (1461b), though Aristotle generally would prefer persuasive possibilities. The point is that he here sets up a more or less formal criterion of aesthetic judgment. The poet's *mimêsis* is good if, on its own terms, it effectively fulfills its purposes, and it is not to be judged with respect to external standards. A *mythos* may be full of absurdities and immoralities, but it still can be represented well and to good effect. So here the notion that a poetic *mythos* offers a probabilistic argument about "the way things are" seems to be discarded—insofar, at least, as the "surface" story need not correspond with real-world fact or notions of verisimilitude—while the notion that it offers a "philosophical" representation of *katholou* can be rescued only by separating the "surface" tale from the "deeper" truths that it conveys. The *Odyssey*, for example, can be read as fanciful fabulation, a fairy tale that nevertheless embodies some general truths and that fulfills the possibilities of its impossible, fictive premises effectively. Aristotle does not directly say this in *Poetics* 25, but it seems to be the implication of his argument. If so, the audience's role is on one hand hermeneutical, as it attempts to understand the poet's *mimêsis* on its own terms and to recognize its "deeper" meaning or significance; and on the other hand its role is aesthetical, as it attempts to judge how "correctly" or satisfactorily the poet has accomplished his formal intention: that is, how well he has represented what he meant to represent.

To the degree that this is true, the poet-audience transaction becomes less like a rhetorical encounter and more like the proffering of a formal object for refined appreciation. The Aristotelian audience still is judging, but they are not so much responding to the poet's persuasion as deciding what *katholou* the poem's *mimêsis* signifies and whether it is well done. This audience is, in short, performing what would be for most of antiquity the typical activities of advanced *grammatikê*, "grammar."

Aristotle's foregrounding of the mimetic representation of *mythoi* as the definiens of poetry has one other major consequence. This is the oft-remarked demotion or even elimination of "lyric"—both in its narrower sense as melic verse and in the wider sense I have been employing—from what was to be the classical poetics of the grammatical tradition.[19] If metered and/or musical composition is not the definiens of "poetry," then from Aristotle's point of view there is nothing left to distinguish lyric poetry from oratory. This holds true for both the "spoken" and sung varieties of lyric but especially for the "spoken," such as iambics and elegiacs, which by the Hellenistic period would largely take over the functions of the archaic song genres.[20] And so the *Rhetoric* cites lyric poets, including Archilochus, Alcaeus, Sappho, Simonides, and Pindar, to illustrate lines of (epideictic) argument and such argumentational tactics as "replying to an opponent" (*Rhetoric* 1.6 1363a; 1.7 1365a; 1.9 1367a, 1367b; 2.15 1391a; 2.24 1401a; 3.17 1418b), while the *Poetics* cites no lyric poet whatsoever. "Rhetoric" describes the art of speeches, both those that appear in prose and verse; lyric poems are versified speeches. Paradoxically, then, Aristotle on one hand posits lyric as the primal poetic mode, while on the other hand by means of his omissions and consignments he seems implicitly to deny that it is "poetry" at all, or is not essentially "poetic," insofar as it is not *mimêsis* in his terms.

For lyric discourse to be "poetry" in the terms of the *Poetics* (and under this interpretation), it must be reconceived as something other than epideictic argument. That is, its specifically "poetic" quality must inhere in its mimetic representation of an action, and indeed of a type of action embodying some *katholou*. What is implied is not so much a full-fledged story, for that would give us epic narrative or drama

proper. Rather, the Aristotelian lyric poem appears instead as a sort of *scene*, a crucial moment abstracted from an implied enclosing story, while the speaker's utterance is a sort of apostrophe. Such a lyric is in essence a minidrama, and its speaker a
more or less Theophrastian "character," a type, speaking either to an audience of
other characters included in the fictive scene or to himself or herself in soliloquy.
The lyric act must be an exemplary, paradigmatic act, showing how a certain type of
character would or should behave and feel in certain circumstances (for that is, in
general, what Aristotelian poetry must do); and the speaker's act of speaking, or the
embodiment of the speaker's thought and feeling as it moves and fluctuates, will
constitute the lyric "plot." This represented act of subjectivity, then, is to be understood in Aristotelian terms as the architectonic "origin," the *archê*, of the lyric
poem (*Poetics* 6 1450a).

What this line of thought produces is, in essence, the lyric of W. R. Johnson's
The Idea of Lyric, with its dramatized "situation of discourse"[21]—or indeed, and already (if only in principle), the "verbal icon" of mid–twentieth century high modernist criticism: the poem that is a dramatized complex of attitudes, an "expression
of emotion." Such a poetry may, of course, still include argumentation or the presentation of *dianoia* just as a drama might, and thus an Aristotelian reconfiguring of
lyric may still include such poets as Pindar or Sappho, though it may value them for
other things, such as their exemplary representation of particular modalities of
mood. But this reconfiguring will have trouble, as Johnson does, with understanding a poet like Solon as "poetic" at all. Crucially, within this framework *dianoia* now
is secondary, or tertiary (as it is in the *Poetics*), and is to be understood as a supplemental, even dispensable element that a lyric poem may or may not happen to contain. What matters now is the exemplary dramatism of a theatrically rendered act of
utterance projecting a paradigm of subjectivity, and the aesthetic interest of its representation, whatever might be said; or, if one emphasizes the Platonic undertone
again, what matters is the allegorical or "deep" significance of the speaker's dramatistically rendered act of subjectivity. Either way, within this view neither argumentation nor rhythmic prosody are the essentially poetic elements of lyric or of the
speeches in an epic or drama.

This reconstituted image of the lyric is, of course, theoretical only, and not
necessarily a description of actual poems—indeed, to a large degree it is not—
though it does bear some resemblance to the mime, that is, the one-scene minidrama or dramatic monologue, which was to become one of the most popular Hellenistic genres and by late antiquity would displace the full-fledged drama more or
less completely. (I would, however, argue that the mime is better understood
through the rhetorical framework of declamation than through an Aristotelian
poetic.) But whatever the actualities of mime may be, one can say that in the theoretical framework entailed by the *Poetics* the lyric has been substantially transformed. Although the "Aristotelian" lyric in this reconfiguring may be a counterpart to the "elder" lyric of archaic practice, it is also a rhetorically restricted
counterpart. Dramatic declaration framed within a fictive scene now substitutes for
the epideictic song presenting enthymematic argument in response to a significant
exigence in a culture's or community's pattern of experience. That is, the apostrophic lyric is now the theoretical paradigm for "lyric" generally: the short poem

neither narrative nor argumentative in itself but a self-expressive, emotive outburst uttered by a speaker with his or her back turned to the audience of the poem. That is, we produce something like the literary epigrams of Asclepiades and Meleager, which I considered in chapter 9 (though not the major lyric poetry of the Hellenistic period, such as Callimachus's hymns, or of the Augustan period either). Archaic lyric could, of course, be epigrammatic or apostrophic also, but not necessarily and not always or even usually. The point is that, under an Aristotelian poetic, a relatively open-ended range of rhetorical possibilities is exchanged for one selected type of lyric rhetoric, which becomes the paradigm of "lyric" generally.

One can argue that this rhetorically restricted paradigm for lyric is also, in principle, a paradigm for minor poetry. First of all, it is by definition subordinate to narrative (or to embodied narrative in drama): apostrophic, "lyrical" outbursts appear at certain junctures or pauses in a surrounding plot, whenever narrative time or progress breaks. The real poetic act and the intellectually substantial act, in this perspective, is the creation of the fable itself—so that epic, tragedy, and (eventually) prose fiction become the necessary major venues for "serious" and challenging fictive literature. The lyric, by comparison, becomes at least potentially definable as a sort of purple patch, an interlude, an elegant attitudinal display, for which the epigram may be the paradigmatic model. The displayed emotion of this interlude, moreover, is likely to be conventional: that is, what the context "should" produce, or would be expected to produce by the poet's audience. Otherwise, and insofar as the apostrophic, epigrammatic poem does not (or cannot) adopt the argumentational means required to justify its mimetically displayed attitude or state of subjectivity, the speaker's feelings run the risk of seeming to an "outside" audience unreasonable, foolish, offensive, or simply unintelligible.

These observations bring us to a second source of minorness for apostrophic lyric. Although it has indeed an argumentative dimension—insofar as it contains, embodies, or implies a structure of ideas constituting some sort of argument—it is nevertheless offers an elliptical or covert sort of argumentation, one in which the basic codes warranting the speaker's emotive gesture may go unmentioned, assumed, or unexamined.[22] The poem, in short, does not overtly *argue* the "argument" it tacitly presents, or it does so only minimally. Persuasiveness is therefore limited in principle to those already in agreement or in sympathy with the speaker's projected mood, and lyric invention is in principle constrained to "representation" of existing attitudes and values within the poet's intended audience. Any act of persuasion, of course, must ground itself somewhere in the beliefs and values of those it would address. The difference is that an overt rather than elliptical argument is able to make its premises explicit or to draw the audience's attention to premises that may have been overlooked (or not connected to the issue at hand in *this* particular way), or to question or revise the premises and presumptions the audience habitually brings into play. In this way an argument may create new grounds for new conclusions the reader/listener would not initially grant, and is not obliged to accept on credit, at least not in a relatively democratic situation. But such a possibility is not available to apostrophic, epigrammatic lyric. This is, in short, a poetry that generally cannot escape the rhetorical limitations of symposiastic insider discourse.

In sum, Aristotle offers a double vision, seeming both to recognize poetry's rhetoricality and to occlude (or limit) it. On one hand, poetry is epideictic argumentation in verse—an argumentation that can employ an open-ended range of rhetorical possibilities, all the possibilities available to prose, *plus* the possibilities afforded by rhythmic, musical prosody, and all that may go with it in performance. On the other hand, poetry is limited to mimetic representation of *mythoi* embodying human actions that exemplify (or allegorically signify) *katholou* to an audience that already knows them and that will engage in hermeneutic and aesthetic appreciation. Within this latter framework, poetry—whether the presentation of exemplary fables to those who know and can appreciate already what they signify or "lyrical," apostrophic, epigrammatic declarations for more or less the same kind of audience—seems relatively weak as a means of creating, changing, revising, or otherwise shaping potentially contestable beliefs within the larger community beyond the poet and the closed communion of his or her intimates. Insofar as the poet disagrees with the larger world outside, that world must cease to be the poet's audience. Or the audience the poet actually can engage diminishes to an inner circle of kindred souls, those who *get it* and agree already. Yet the shaping of communal, public agreement about the probable, the preferable, and the right is the very work by which an epideictic discourse establishes itself as major literature. For the poet who really works within this "Aristotelian" paradigm, such a possibility is in principle diminished or disallowed and is correspondingly ceded to the prose writers. "Poetry" (or poetic literature) is redefined as a cultured entertainment through which a well-bred audience finds pleasure in well-done reconfirmations of its values.

Grammatical Poetics: From Neoptolemus to "Plutarch" and Plutarch

Aristotle may or may not have intended the sorts of implications I have just drawn from the *Poetics*. Those implications are, however, largely borne out in the subsequent development of the grammatical tradition.

   Grammatikê, the "art of letters," seems to have become a formalized, distinct discipline sometime in the Hellenistic period. The Alexandrian scholar-critics of the third and second centuries B.C. clearly were engaged in a grammatical kind of enterprise, as were many of the Presocratic, sophistic, and philosophical poetry critics before them; but Dionysius Thrax's *Technê Grammatikê*, composed in the second or first century B.C., is the earliest surviving treatise that gives itself that name. By late antiquity *grammatikê*, or Latin *grammatica*, became a scholastic discipline of great prestige. In its developed forms it included, at the most elementary level, instruction in basic literacy, usually beginning from around age seven (this elementary teaching was sometimes referred to separately as "grammatistic," *grammatistikê*). But for *grammatikê* proper, the higher and chief concerns—and the chief pedagogical mission—were the correct interpretation and appreciation of canonic literary texts (especially Homer) and the cultivation of grammatically pure, grammatically refined speech and writing embodying a lettered, artificial dialect based on the canonic authors. Children of well-to-do parents generally began this instruction as soon as they could read and were old enough (as Quintilian says) to "leave the nursery" for formal schooling and typically continued until the age of about fourteen or fifteen, at which point rhetorical, philosophical, or other studies might begin.[23] *Grammatikê* was thus the gateway discipline to the "higher" studies for those who could afford them and wished to continue and in itself was an essential marker of upper-class cultivation. The person of *paideia* was at a minimum trained in *grammatikê*: steeped in what Martin Irvine calls the "cultural scripture" of canonic literature and trained in the dialect of lettered speech, he (or she) was endowed with a cultural capital that made him (or her) distinct from the vulgar crowd.[24] The often laborious and sometimes painful acquisition of this capital was invested, moreover, with notions of sacred and high attainment. As Robert Kaster notes, a grammarian of the first century A.D. declares on his tombstone that "I began the holy instruction . . . of wellborn children"; another declares himself devoted to the "study of sacred letters"; and the late antique grammarian Diomedes avows that the "toil" of grammatical study confers "the square-set soundness of speech and its polished brilliance produced by skill" that makes the possessor "as superior to the uneducated as they are to cattle."[25]

But if *grammatikê* did not emerge as a formal discipline until the later Hellenistic period, grammatical inquiry and instruction certainly had its origins much earlier, in the poetic/musical training of the preclassical *paideia*, in Presocratic inquiries into language and the traditional poetic heritage, and in the Platonic and Aristotelian responses to those inquiries. Plato's Protagoras declares that "the greatest part of a man's *paideia* is to be skillful with respect to verses (*deinon peri epôn*); that is, to be able to understand in the sayings of the poets what has been correctly done (*orthôs pepoiêtai*) and what has not" (*Protagoras* 338e–339a). As I noted in chapter 5, this statement could be understood to mean a rhetorical engagement, in which the educated, "skillful" person responds to the poet's suasion with an exercise of judgment; indeed this seems to be what Plato's Protagoras intends, as he launches his critique of a poem by Simonides. But in Plato's rendering of it, most of the subsequent discussion turns on questions of the *meaning* of certain statements and of particular words in Simonides' archaic usage (339a–347b). The "solution" and rescue of Simonides that Plato's Socrates arrives at, finally, amounts to a glossing of problematic expressions and the production of a paraphrase that renders the poem's meaning (or one part of it) as a statement that agrees with notions of moral truth that Socrates and his interlocutors can accept. Simonides, or the paraphrase that supplements and replaces him, is measured against and made to fit the truths determined already by "philosophy." If a fit can be established—if Simonides can be understood to anticipate the enlightened doctrines of current philosophy—he is "correct" and worthy of approbation. If not, not. This operation embodies a sort of paradigm for what would be the fundamental literary-critical enterprise of *grammatikê* from its emergence onward.

The literary theory transmitted by Aristotle's Peripatetic successors provided the starting points for what became the grammatical version of poetics.[26] We can see this in what is known of the lost poetics of Neoptolemus of Parium, an Alexandrian Peripatetic of the later part of the third century B.C., who has been credited as the chief theoretical source for Horace's *Ars Poetica*.[27] Neoptolemus divided poetic art, *poietikê*, into three aspects—*poiêma, poiêsis, poiêtês*, or poem, poesy, and poet—each of which provided a focus for criticism. Here the first two of these divisions, and the distinction between them, concern me most. (The third, if one can judge from Horace, had to do with the offices of the poet who undertakes *poiêma* and *poiêsis* in an act of *poiêtikê*.) *Poiêma* seems to have referred to the poem as a formal, stylistic object defined by versification and other features of poetic diction or poetic genre: anything composed in verse was a *poiêma*, a "poem," and could be measured against the formal standards of poetic diction and the rules (or conventions) of specific genres. *Poiêsis* referred to the *mythos/hypothesis* of the poem, or the process of inventing and arranging it as "plot" distributed into sequenced episodes: anything that represented a complete, unified story was an instance of *poiêsis*, "poesy" (or "poetic invention"), and could be measured against the appropriate standards of mythic probability, philosophic depth, and moral quality. As the first-century (b.c.) Stoic Posidonius would say, "[a] *poiêma* is . . . metrical or rhythmic diction (*lexis*) with a finish exceeding that of prose . . . but a *poiêsis* is a significant *poiêma* (*sêmantikon poiêma*) containing a *mimêsis* of things divine and human" (as quoted in Diogenes Laertius, *Lives* 7.60). Modern commentators often have reduced *poiêma-poiêsis* to a "form-content" distinction, which is reasonable but probably too simple. As Diogenes' formulation suggests, it was possible to have a *poiêma* without *poiêsis*, while *poiêsis* always was embodied as *poiêma*.[28] A poem without *poiêsis* still would have a "content" of some kind, though Neoptolemus might call it "nonpoetic." Poetic art in its fullest form, for Neoptolemus as for Aristotle, seems to involve the representation of a complete piece of "poesy," a unified and coherent tale that signifies general truths, in an epic or dramatic "poem."

Neoptolemus's distinction between *poiêma* and *poiêsis* reflects the double vision of Aristotle's *Poetics* and maps out the characteristic chief concerns of literary-critical *grammatikê* for centuries to come. Poetry is on one hand versified discourse, endowed with rhythmic (and prosodic-musical) effects and a psychagogic force—a stylistically mediated aesthetico-suasive power—not available to prose. On the other hand, poetry is the mimetic representation of fictive or legendary tales embodying *katholou*, or what Posidonius's Stoic formulation calls "things divine and human." *Poiêma* thus marks the focus for grammatical, philological investigations of poetic language and poetic form in Hellenistic and later scholarship: the glossing of rare and archaic "poetic words" (e.g., in Homer), the linguistic parsing of utterances and the analysis of syntactic forms, the classification of tropes and figures, the definition of "correct" pronunciation for the reading-performance of literary texts (and the invention of diacritical marks to guide pronunciation), the codification of the versification rules and genre characteristics of the various kinds of recorded poetry, the organization of a stable canon of "classic" texts and authors, the establishment of definitive editions, and so forth. *Poiêsis*, in contrast, marks what would become the focus of grammatical hermeneutics, especially in Stoic and (later) Neoplatonic criticism: the explication of the "things divine and human" signified in the fabulous myths and legends of Homer and other poets.[29] The Aristotelian (or Peripatetic) framework advanced by Neoptolemus, in sum, helped to codify the organization of grammatical poetics around philological-formal analysis and thematic-allegorical exegesis.

This double vision and double enterprise—and especially the hermeneutic enterprise—were linked to what still were, after centuries of discussion, urgent issues in Hellenistic philosophical debates about poetry. On one hand, there was the durable question whether poetry produced *psychagôgia* or *didaskalia:* that is, whether it accomplished an illusionistic beguilement for pleasure's sake only (as mere entertainment) or "taught lessons." On the other hand there was the closely related question whether, if poetry did "teach lessons," the lessons were false and morally harmful. Behind all this was the sort of thesis put by the anonymous author of the *Dissoi Logoi:* "the poets not for truth's sake but for people's pleasure make their poems" (*Dissoi Logoi* 3.17).[30] In the Hellenistic period, the Epicureans would take up a similar position, as would Neoptolemus's near contemporary Eratosthenes of Cyrene, the scholar-poet, critic, and geographer who became the head librarian at Alexandria in 246 B.C. If this position were correct there could be little justification, at least from a philosopher's point of view, for poetry's continuing central place in the grammatical *paideia* or indeed in any grownup's serious attention. This was why, as Plutarch says, the Epicureans thought the young should "flee from poetry and steer clear of it" (*How the Young Man Should Study Poetry* 15d). For poetry to remain a suitable part of the grammatical curriculum, or of grammatical investigation generally, it had to "teach lessons," and the "lessons" had to be defensible.

The basic grammatical solution was that of Neoptolemus, or of the Peripatetic line of thought he represented, which held that (good) poetry effected both *psychagôgia* and *didaskalia*. It accomplished *didaskalia* by means of *psychagôgia* or it accomplished *psychagôgia* for the sake of *didaskalia*—which is not quite the same thing, and the ambiguity is worth preserving. Poetry taught "lessons" while beguiling and pleasing with fabulous myths, marvelous illusions, and the charm of poetic language.[31] Or, in the still more influential Stoic reformulation of this notion, transmitted by Strabo and eventually picked up in Sidney's *Defense of Poetry*, "the poetic art (*tên poiêtikên*) is a kind of first philosophy, introducing us into life from childhood and teaching ethics, emotions, and actions with pleasure" (*Geography* 1.2.3). Both Neoptolemus and the Stoics stand behind Horace's famous dictum that poetry should be both *dulce* and *utile*, "pleasant" and "useful," entertaining and instructive (*Ars Poetica* 333–346). But such a formulation also could enforce, or encourage, a split between the psychagogic entertainment function of poetic discourse and its presumed didactic function. In a rhetorical poetics, the function of poetry is not so much to "teach lessons," in the sense of a preceptive didacticism, as to *persuade*, or to engage the audience in a suasory encounter; the ethical-paideutic effect lies in the audience's act of being persuaded or not being persuaded, its *responsiveness*. Pindar and Sappho do not "teach lessons"; they argue positions. This is a key distinction. In a grammatical poetics, in contrast, it becomes possible to consider the psychagogic function of poetic discourse not as the *source* or *cause* of persuasive and ethical effects but as a sort of entertainment invoked to make a poem's didacticism more pleasant and palatable or as a means of disguising "hard" philosophic abstractions in "easy" or "beguiling" metaphors: that is, it becomes an attractive wrapping for instruction, the sugar coating on the serious pill of doctrine, a pabulum suitable for those not ready for direct instruction or not capable of it. Thus, as Strabo says,

[n]o crowd of women, at least, nor any vulgar multitude can be brought round by
the philosopher's discourse, or be urged to reverence, piety, and faith, but supersti-
tious fear is needed also, and not without mythifications [*mythopoiías*] and tall tales
[*terateias*]. For thunderbolt, aegis, trident, torches, dragons, and magic javelins—
the weapons of the gods—are myths, and so is all the ancient theology. But these
things the founders of polities allowed, as bogeymen to frighten childish minds.
. . . But at long last the writing of history and now philosophy have come upon
the scene. Philosophy though is for the few, whereas poetry [*poiêtikê*] is more to the
public benefit and can fill theaters, especially Homer's poetry. (*Geography* 1.2.8)

In Strabo's Stoic formulation, "poetry" is equivalent to "myth" or Neoptolemus' "poesy," and myth/poesy is a means of representing theological and philosophic truths to children, women, and the "childish" common crowd; Homer is the
example par excellence. Grown-up, intelligent, well-educated men—the fit though
few—will graduate to philosophy.

The Stoic formulation was, in fact, decisive in the disciplinary formation of
grammatikê and of grammatical poetics in the Hellenistic and Roman periods.[32]
Stoic literary theory divided poetry into *lexis* and *logos*—corresponding roughly to
Neoptolemus's *poiêma* and *poiêsis* or simply to "style" and "content." As *lexis*, poetry
could be appreciated for its formal qualities, that is, for the technical excellence of
its diction, rhythm, figures, and so forth. As *logos*, it participated in the Stoics' universal *logos*, the divine reason immanent in nature and in human nature and potentially manifest in the *logos* of human utterance and inward thought. In this way poetic *logos* could reveal the truth of "things human and divine." Indeed the divine
logos could in principle speak itself through poetic *logos* independently of the poet's
knowledge or intention: deep truths could be manifest in *mythoi* whose poets had
no idea they were transmitting them, though in general the Stoic notion of the true
poet was the *sophos* or "sage" who coded his wisdom-lessons for popular dissemination in mythical tropes, mythical declensions. This notion of poetic *logos* encouraged, or underwrote, a tendency toward tropical interpretation that focused on
hyponoiai, the "under-thoughts" or "deeper meanings," immanent in the otherwise
unbelievable and sometimes immoral fabulations of the canonic, mostly archaic
poets who formed the core of the "cultural scripture," Homer (again) in particular.
Eventually the name and notion of *hyponoia* gave way to, or became, that of *allêgoria*, which by late antiquity would have a central place in Neoplatonic and Christian hermeneutics.[33] Plutarch, writing in the late first or early second century A.D.,
would remark that interpreters of Homeric myths converted them to what "used to
be called hyponoias but now are called allegories" (*How the Young Man Should Study
Poetry* 19e–f). Hyponoiac, allegorical reading consisted, in effect, of working back
through the mythical and tropical declensions of the poetic *logos* to the underlying
code, which only philosophical discourse could articulate and explicate.[34]

Plutarch notes the extremes that such reading practices could reach. He says:

[s]ome who force and twist [Homer's tales] by means of what used to be called hyponoias but now are called allegories say that Helios reveals Aphrodite debauched
beside Ares because the conjunction of the planet Venus with Mars portends adulterous births, and when the Sun returns in his course and comes upon them they
cannot be hid. And Hera's adornment of herself for Zeus and the charms con-

nected with her girdle these people would make a kind of purification of the air as it draws near the fiery element—as if the solutions were not given by the poet himself. (19f)

This kind of "forced," cosmic allegoresis went back at least to Metrodorus of Lampsakos, the fifth-century (B.C.) Homeric interpreter who, according to Tatian, "exceedingly goodheartedly reckoned everything by converting it into allegory." ("Goodheartedly" here, *euêthôs*, could also be translated as "simple-mindedly.") According to Hesychius and Philodemus, Metrodorus rendered the heroes of the *Iliad* as representations of natural or cosmic forces, and the gods as representations of human body parts: Agamemnon signified the aether, Achilles the sun, Helen the earth, Alexander the air, and Hector the moon, while Demeter signified the liver, Dionysus the spleen, Apollo the gall-bladder, and so forth.[35] One wonders what illuminating theories of heavenly and bodily phenomena Homer was thereby made the "teacher" of. While neither Plutarch nor the more enlightened versions of Stoic *grammatikê* were inclined to such extremes of allegorical fantasia, nevertheless by Plutarch's time—more than six centuries after Metrodorus—this kind of interpretation had a well-established tradition in grammatical hermeneutics and the grammatical *paideia*.[36]

What may be a typical result of this tradition appears in the *Essay on the Life and Poetry of Homer*, written by an otherwise unknown and probably quite average grammarian of the late second century A.D., who is known to us now as "Pseudo-Plutarch" (the text at some point was ascribed erroneously to Plutarch and preserved as part of the *Moralia*).[37] "Plutarch," who seems to be addressing himself to students, declares in his opening sentence that

[i]t is appropriate that Homer, who in time was among the first of poets and in power was the very first, is the first we read. In doing so we reap a great harvest in terms of diction, understanding, and experience of the world. (1)[38]

This "harvest" consists of an explication of all the forms of knowledge, all the "lessons," contained in Homer's poetry. These begin—after a brief biography of Homer and an overview of his poetry (1–6)—with sixty-seven pages on the grammatical technicalities of Homeric *lexis*: the heroic hexameter and the various dialects employed in Homer's verse (7–13); archaisms (14); tropes and schemes (15–40); figures involving syntactical shifts (41–64); figures of sense, such as prosopoieia, irony, and hyperbole (65–71); and types of style (72–73). Homer, in short, is found to exemplify nearly all the elements and virtues of distinguished literary language.

The remaining 145 pages of the *Essay*, or about two-thirds of its total bulk, are devoted to Homer's *logos*, which is found to contain all the major "types" (*eidê*) of artistic discourse—the "historical" (74–90), the "theoretical" (91–160), and the "political" (161–199)—plus the discourses of medicine, seercraft, tragedy and comedy, epigram, and painting (200–218).[39] Moreover, Homer's *logos* embodies as well a prescient awareness of virtually all the knowledges connected with each type of discourse. Thus, under "theoretical discourse" for example, Homer is found to anticipate or be the source of the various doctrines of natural philosophy, theology, psychology, and ethics propounded by Plato, the Peripatetics, and the Stoics, as well as Pythagorean mathematical and musical doctrines. Or, under "political discourse," Homer is shown to be the founder of rhetoric, law, statecraft, religious and familial customs, and the arts of warfare. And so forth. As "Plutarch" declares in his overview remarks,

> [e]ven in [Homer's] mythical or fabulous passages, if one considers carefully and not superficially the specific things he has said, it becomes clear that he was adept at every kind of wisdom and skill and provides the starting points and so to speak the seeds of all kinds of discourse and action for those who come after him, not only for the poets but for writers of prose as well, both historical and speculative. (6)

"Plutarch's" demonstrations of this claim frequently consist of the sort of "forced" interpretation that Plutarch himself dismisses. Thus, for example, as "Plutarch" is discussing Homer's cosmological knowledge, he says that

> [i]n the lines in which the poet says Hera, Zeus's sister, cohabits with him, he seems to be allegorizing [*allêgoreisthai*] as follows: that Hera [*Hêrê*] represents "mist" [*aêr*]—the damp substance—and so he says, "Hera spread deep mist / before them" [*Iliad* 21.6–7], and Zeus represents *aither*, the fiery, hot substance: "Zeus's portion was wide heaven in the *aither* and clouds" [*Iliad* 15.192]. (96)

Or, as "Plutarch" discusses Homer's psychological knowledge, the poet becomes a proto-Peripatetic.

> He likewise understood the causes of those things that are the consequences of the passionate part of the soul: he shows anger, which arises from pain, to be a sort of boiling of blood and of the spirit in it, as in these verses: "in a rage—his darkened mind was filled / with anger and his eyes gleamed like fire" [*Iliad* 1.103–104 and *Odyssey* 4.661–662]. With the word "anger" [*menos*], he seems to be designating the spirit and he believes that this is extended and bursts into flame when a person is angered. The spirit of those who are experiencing fear, on the contrary, is contracted and cool. (131)[40]

And this bit of knowledge about cool fear is found reflected in other lines from Homer, and so forth. Elsewhere, Homer's "historical" discourse is mined for its exemplification of the "circumstances" (of character, place, time, cause, instrument, deed, impact, and manner) typically dealt with in the advanced grammatical and beginning rhetorical composition exercises known as *progymnasmata* (74). As J. J. Keaney and Robert Lamberton remark in a note to their translation of this passage, "it is admittedly difficult to understand just how this classification contributes to the reader's understanding of Homer."[41] Indeed much the same could be said of "Plutarch's" overall approach. In general he contributes little to an understanding of Homer's poetry per se; indeed he frequently makes it *more difficult to understand*, while mining it for edifying "lessons" that derive from "philosophy" and can be tweezed out from, or shown to be reflected in, selected lines, passages, or phrases taken in isolation. Homer stands as a primer of all the forms of knowledge and all the branches of discursive art: a set of lessons in first philosophy.

What "Plutarch's" whole approach comes down to is stunningly revealed in the final two sentences of his *Essay*.

How then could we possibly not attribute every virtue to Homer, when those who have come after him have even found in his poetry all the things he did not think to include? Some use his poetry for divination, just like the oracles of god, while others put forth entirely different subjects and ideas and fit the verses to them, transposing them and stringing them together in new ways. (218)

Homer's poetry contains wisdoms that even he did not think of! The Homeric *logos* is a sort of rebus, an oracular object, in which the hyponoiac interpreter may "find," at deeper levels, all sorts of knowledges—or force the poetry to fit them—and then present them as "lessons" taught by Homer (or transmitted in his discourse). This procedure works to endow Homeric *logos* with a continuing and indeed ever-growing authority as the fount of all wisdoms; at the same time and by circular logic, it also endows the interpreter's confabulated "lessons" with the authority of a prophetic, all-knowing, Homeric *logos* through which the cosmic *logos* is whispering itself.

"Plutarch's" schoolmasterly Homer exegesis would remain the dominant version of grammatical hermeneutics into late antiquity, especially in Neoplatonic circles. As Robert Lamberton has noted, "[f]or readers such as Porphyry in the third century and Proclus in the fifth, the true subject of the *Iliad* and *Odyssey* was the fate of souls and the structure of the universe."[42] Homer had become, in effect, a cosmologist and theologian. What did schoolboys of perhaps ten to fourteen years of age think of the Homer thus presented to them or of the canonic poetry of the grammatical curriculum in general? The discourses of what were, after all, antique, archaic, and increasingly remote poets could hardly have appeared to them—under the grammatical regime—as offering rhetorical encounters calling for acts of judgment and response. Rather, the poetry would appear as a study object, an occasion for an arduous lesson that required two kinds of proper understanding. On one hand, the student was to appreciate the formal excellence and distinction of the poet's *lexis*. On the other hand, the student was to "get" the deeper lessons of the poet's poesy, his fabulation, his *logos*, lessons that in fact were accessible only to those who knew them already and could find them in the poem, saying "this is that." For the young student, then, the poetry set before him almost necessarily would appear to be an opaque, inscrutable object that could not mean what it seemed to say and that would have to wait for an interpretive authority, namely the schoolmaster, to explicate its formal virtues and unlock its deeper secrets with a performance of hyponoiac expertise. The student who failed to grasp the schoolmaster's explications of a poet's *lexis* and *logos* could look forward to a beating, while those who learned their lessons right acquired a type of cultural capital that conferred distinction and qualified the bearer for privileged social standing. Poetry thus presented its young student, or the well-born, well-trained product of grammatical education, with not a rhetorical but a disciplinary encounter, in which the object of the game was to demonstrate one's level of lettered cultivation and separateness from the vulgar crowd.

Here we might turn back briefly to Plutarch himself and regain our balance—somewhat. Placed beside "Plutarch's" *Essay*, Plutarch's essay on *How the Young Man Should Study Poetry* (*Pôs Dei Ton Neon Poiêmatôn Akouein*, more literally "how the young male should hearken to poems") seems eminently sensible. Addressing himself to a certain Marcus Sedatus, on the occasion that "my Soklaros and your Kleandros" (15a) are now old enough to be exposed to poetry, Plutarch discusses how the boys' experience can best be managed. On one hand, he recognizes and asserts on Homeric authority the rhetorical, suasive power of poetic discourse.

> For it seems it may be said not only of the Egyptians' land but also of poetry [*tês poiêtikês*] that it yields "drugs, and many are good when mixed and many baneful" to those that use them. "Therein are love and desire and friendly converse, / suasion that swiftly steals away the mind of even the wise." For its deceptiveness does not lay hold of altogether fatuous and mindless persons. (15c)[43]

Poetry has a suasive charm that affects especially those of lively intelligence and imagination. On the other hand, Plutarch's chief concern, like that of Plato and the philosophico-grammatical tradition generally, is how to render the boys immune to the friendly-speaking suasion of the poets and make the poetry yield true and morally beneficial lessons. And so, invoking the image of Odysseus lashed to the mast to hear to the Sirens, Plutarch suggests that he and Sedatus not "stop [the boys'] ears with wax" nor "force them to set sail in an Epicurean boat" that steers clear of everything poetic; instead "we shall guide and closely guard them, setting their judgment up against straight reason and bind it fast, that it not be carried off by delight toward what is harmful" (15d). What Plutarch proposes is in effect a double strategy, a defensive hermeneutic, by which the "drugs" of poetry will be "mixed" with another discourse—that of philosophy—to render them beneficial, or at least harmless, while at the same time the boys' judgment will be "bound fast" to standards of right reason so that they cannot be persuaded to admire what is improper. The goal, in sum, is to "use" poetry as a *prophilosophêteon*, an "introduction to philosophy" (15f–16a).

Plutarch's prophylaxis begins from an Aristotelian dismissal of and inattention to the charms of poetic *lexis*, combined with a focus on the dangers of poetic *logos*. For, as he says,

> neither meter nor figure nor stately diction nor timely metaphor nor melody and composition has so much allurement and charm as a tale well-woven of mythology . . . [and] we do not know of any *poiêsis* with neither fable nor falsehood. The verses of Empedocles and Parmenides, the *Antidotes* of Nicander, and the gnomologies of Theognis have borrowed from poetic art its meter and stateliness as a vehicle, that they may avoid prosiness. (16b, c–d).

Empedocles, Parmenides, Nicander, and Theognis have made *poiêmata* without *poiêsis* and therefore have not really made "poetry." Poetic *lexis* appears as merely a decor that gives a composition a certain ceremonious dignity, a certain finish that can make things go more pleasantly, and that can be admired, but that otherwise has little suasive or psychagogic force. Note that this view can more easily be taken when poetry has been textualized as "literature"—that is, removed from its original performance circumstances, stripped of its musical or song dimensions, and made an object of schoolroom study and recitation. Plutarch is speaking of poetry as it comes from the murmuring lips of teacher and students as they read it off the papyrus scroll before them, in a small room. In such a circumstance poetic *lexis* may endow the text with a certain elegance, an antique patina like the fine green rust on ancient bronzes; but apart from the aesthetic value this "patina" may have as a sign of tradition or cultural authority, the psychagogic force of poetic *lexis*, and of its prosody in particular, is greatly diminished. And if little attention is paid to prosody, if the schoolmaster and his boys murmur the script of poetry as if it were essentially no different from prose, the psychagogic power of its unheard music will evaporate.

As the charm of *lexis* disappears, or is dissipated, poetry is in essence reduced to *logos*, the "fable and falsehood" of the poet's poesy, which in its own right still can exert considerable psychagogic power. Plutarch's prophylaxis therefore seeks to lessen or nullify this power in two ways: first, by foregrounding poesy's fictionality to undercut its pathetic force; second, by explaining the *logos* of the text away or converting it into another *logos*. In the first of these operations, the boy is to be continually reminded that poetic fables—at least on the surface—have little concern with or connection to reality or truth. Thus,

> he that always remembers and keeps distinctly in mind poetry's sorcery in dealing with falsehood . . . will neither suffer dire effects nor be persuaded to vulgarity but will hold himself back when he fears Poseidon and is alarmed lest the god shatter the earth . . . and will cease to shed tears over the dead Achilles and Agamemnon in Hades. (16d–e)

The boy, in short, is to continually remind himself that "it's only a story" and is to maintain a Stoic *apathein* that renders him unresponsive (or minimally responsive) to the pathetic force of represented scenes. One might place this unresponsiveness next to Gorgias's famous claim—which Plutarch cites (15d)—that "he who is deceived [by poetic illusion] is wiser than the undeceived," in essence because he has chosen to yield himself to the full experience of the poet's suasion. Plutarch's boy, however, is to be rendered incapable of this experience.

With the boy now rendered immune or numb to the stylistic and mimetic sources of poetic suasion, Plutarch turns to the correct interpretation of poetic *logos*—especially those passages from which a boy might get the wrong ideas—as a source of beneficial lessons in protophilosophy. While Plutarch is dismissive of the "forced" allegoresis of interpreters like Metrodorus, "Plutarch," or the Neoplatonists, he nevertheless is equally concerned with finding "solutions," *lyseis*, to what seems improper or untrue. (The word *lysis*, it should be noted, can also mean a setting loose, a ransoming, an atonement, or a deliverance from guilt.) Plutarch's general preference is to let the "solution" be "given by the poet himself" whenever possible (19f), and he therefore focuses considerable attention on the ways that other statements given by the poet, either in the immediate context or anywhere else, can indicate the poet's true judgment of the apparently ignoble behavior of a character and so generate the proper lesson (e.g., 19–20). But this is not always sufficient. Sometimes one must rely on statements by other writers, when the poet himself has given no clues, in order to forestall misjudgment of bad characters (21); or one can provide glosses of the poet's language, or very close-grained syntactical analysis, to suggest that his words do not really mean what they seem to mean (22); or one simply can "amend" what must, after all, be acknowledged as not right (32).

And so forth. As the young reader is taught what is repugnant and noble in the poet's tales, the poetry becomes a set of edifying lessons in ethics, or provides occasions for such lessons. As Plutarch says,

> [b]y indicating these things to the young we shall not permit a tendency to develop vulgar habits of character but an admiration and preference for the better, if we promptly render blame for the one and praise for the other . . . [And] as the youth learns [gignôskôn] the good and vulgar characters and personages, let him attend to the sayings and actions which the poet assigns as suitable to each. (27d, 28f)

This looks, in some ways, like a rhetorical transaction, as the boy is taught to practice good judgment concerning base and noble characters. But, in fact, he is learning to say that "this is that." The judgments are provided from elsewhere—from the boy's guide in reading, the grammarian (or his father in the role of grammarian)—and the boy is then to regard the poet's character portrayals as exemplifications of good and bad types: "this is what a coward (or brave man, etc.) looks, acts, talks like."

Finally, these lessons are to be broadened into an introduction to various philosophical doctrines.

> Moreover, just as above by ranging the logoi and the maxims of esteemed and statesmanlike men against vulgar and noxious poiêmata we thought to get clear of and push back their persuasion [tên pistin], so whenever we find something urbane and useful in them, we ought to nurture and amplify it with proofs and testimonies from philosophers, giving them credit for the discovery. For it is right and helpful, and our faith [tês pisteôs] takes on an added strength and dignity, whenever what is spoken from the stage and sung to the lyre and studied in school agrees with the dogmas of Pythagoras and Plato, and the precepts of Chilon and Bias lead to the same opinions as those of our children's readings. (35f)

Poiêmata here can be read as either "poems" or passages in poems, insofar as poiêma means a piece of verse; the same poem may contain poiêmata that are both vulgar/noxious and urbane/useful, so that some are to be countered with better logoi and others are to be aligned with, and converted into, doctrines "discovered" and propounded by philosophers. Alternatively, some poems are just plain vulgar—such as, probably, most of the popular stuff performed in theaters in Plutarch's day—and must be rejected. The boy's instruction in proper reading will prepare him, beyond school, to rightly interpret and evaluate poetry when he does encounter it "spoken from the stage and sung to the lyre": he will judge the degree to which it fits what he knows is good and proper and urbane, according to the best authorities and the standards of right reason, while being largely unaffected by it.

Plutarch is a writer whom it is easy to admire, and his argument in *How the Young Man Should Study Poetry* does indeed seem reasonable in many ways, especially when placed alongside "Plutarch's" *Essay*. Certainly the judgment of young, adolescent boys is easily misled; and certainly their reading practices can benefit from guidance. It would hardly be desirable for an adolescent reading Homer's *Iliad* to think, for example, that everything Achilles does—such as desecrating Hector's corpse—is admirable just because Achilles is a hero. In many ways Plutarch sounds like a modern parent concerned about the potentially corrosive ethical effects of, say, television, movies, or music videos on his children, a parent looking for ways to guide "Soklaros's" experience of such things rather than simply banning them. Plutarch and son will attend to them together, or rather they will "listen to" poetic fabulations as they read, and discuss them, in order to model more sophisticated kinds of interpretation and moral evaluation. Nevertheless, the version of grammatical *paideia* that Plutarch thus invokes for "my Soklaros and your Kleandros" greatly diminishes both the rhetoricity of poetry and its significance as a mode of epideictic discourse, and it does so in two ways.

First, poetry is characterized as protophilosophy *for children*, and otherwise (as Strabo says) for "those of childish minds." Thus it is not a medium for the serious, intellectually substantial discourse of well-bred men, though they might invoke or quote the best known maxims of the traditional canonic poets, which they would have learned in their schoolboy days, as sources of sententious wisdom and as signs of their educated status. This kind of attitude may leave "the divine Homer" and other canonic poets in a privileged position—as the cultural patrimony of the ruling elites—but it also leaves little space for new poetic composition to be taken seriously. Beyond the schoolroom, it is either a vulgar, popularizing discourse or, conversely, a sort of gentlemen's recreation, as they relax their standards and indulge themselves at some convivial occasion, or pen some clever epigrams.

Second, while poetry's psychagogic, suasive, argumentative potential is recognized, it is also quarantined—or the boy is immunized against it—so that the poetic encounter *for the educated person* becomes less and less like a rhetorical encounter. Instead the well-bred product of *grammatikê* is trained to exercise a kind of distanced art appreciation, based on two kinds of assessment. On one hand he judges whether the poet's *logos* accords with the recognized truths of moral (as well as other kinds of) philosophy. On the other hand he judges how well the representation has been done, considering both the technical quality of the *mimêsis* itself and the stylistic "urbanity" or elegance of the *lexis*, the *poiêma*, through which it is presented. As Plutarch says at one point, as he speaks of the dreadful things sometimes portrayed by poets and painters (such as Orestes killing his mother or "the unchaste intercourse of women with men"),

> in these matters it is especially necessary that the youth be trained [*ethizesthai*] by being taught that we praise not the action which the *mimêsis* has portrayed, but the art [*technên*] if the theme has been fittingly represented [*memimêtai*]. (18b)

As with Aristotle, then, we are to approve the *art*, the *technê*, of the artwork or the poem before us. Has the artist portrayed Orestes' killing of his mother in a "fitting" way? Is the portrayal technically competent, and does it offer a suitable sort of "lesson"? And has the verse been skillfully turned out? It is worth noting that, in this passage, the "action" (*praxin*) that the *mimêsis* represents is not necessarily the same as its "theme," its *hypokeimenon* (that is, what is "put under" or "suggested").[44] The well-bred person is, in effect, to think of poetry as a popularizing yet oblique mode of moral-philosophical didacticism, a reminder "lesson" in things he or she knows already, done up in entertaining tropes and figures and decorated with meter and other flowers of poetic *lexis* with greater or lesser degrees of technical expertise. Insofar as this well-bred person is made the audience of poetic recitation—at, say, a banquet—it will most likely appear to him or her as an unserious matter, an entertainment, a cultured delicacy presented for amusement and appreciation.

Recall now that in the period that Plutarch and "Plutarch" bookend—from the late first or early second century to the late second—poetry seems to have been eclipsed decisively by epideictic prose.

Rhetorical Poetics Revisited: Horace's *Ars Poetica*, Dio Chrysostom, Hermogenes, and Menander Rhetor

The grammatical *paideia* did not, of course, straightforwardly determine or control poetic practices in later antiquity—or the responses of audiences, especially popular audiences, whose education and literacy were minimal. Nor did every person steeped in the grammatical *paideia* become its ideal product. The grammatical *paideia*, after all, was embedded in a profoundly rhetorical culture: grammar stood beside rhetoric, led into it, overlapped with it, and was conditioned by it. And poetry did, as I suggested at the outset of this chapter, continue to be understood rhetorically and practiced (outside of grammar schools) as a mode of epideictic discourse.

One of the most striking things about the poetics of the grammatical tradition, along with its occlusion of poetry's rhetoricality, is its seeming disconnection from the actual poetic practices of later antiquity, especially popular poetic practices (or what we know of them). While the grammatical tradition tended to emphasize the hyponoiac-allegorical interpretation of poetic fables, the overwhelming majority of the poetry actually produced, from hymns and encomia to panegyrical epics, drama, mime, and of course the epigram, was not allegorical at all. And while the grammatical tradition from Aristotle and Neoptolemus onward tended to emphasize the construction of a coherent, unified plot (embodying *katholou*), very little poetry from the Hellenistic period onward seems to have been especially concerned with such a unity.[45] The most common and enduring forms of epic were historical or mythological panegyric, and the "philosophical" (or "didactic"), encyclopedic epic. The historical or mythological panegyric was in essence an encomiastic chronicle of deeds, such as Claudian's *Against Rufinus, Against Eutropius, The War against Gildo,* and *The Gothic War,* or his panegyrics on the consulships of the emperor Honorius and the general Stilicho; or Quintus of Smyrna's *Posthomerica,* which filled in the events between the *Iliad* and *Odyssey;* or Nonnus of Panopolis's *Dionysiaca,* which recounted the god's exploits in India, in forty eight books. The encyclopedic, "philosophical" (or "didactic") epic in essence was a Hesiodic collection of wisdom-lore, as transmitted by such Hellenistic exemplars as Callimachus's *Aetia* or Aratus's *Phainomena:* late antique examples include Oppian's five-book *Halieutica,* about fishing; or Peisander of Laranda's encyclopedic sixty-book *Heroic Theogamies,* on the marriages and love affairs of the gods, the longest epic ever written in Greek. In either panegyric or Hesiodic epic, what one typically finds is a loosely strung together collection of episodes, descriptions, expositions, and speeches organized around some central topic. The basic frame for all such poetry, as well as for the shorter verse encomia, ekphrases (descriptions), hymns, and epigrams that constituted the "lyric" tradition in later antiquity, is epideictic rhetoric as described (for example) by the third-century treatise of Menander Rhetor.

As for drama, it is commonly recognized that from the Hellenistic period onward poets seem to have been more concerned with representing character types and *dianoia* than with inventing plots. Hellenistic and Roman dramatists tended to work with a repertoire of stock plots, and stock character types too, which would have been quite familiar to audiences and which supplied materials (and pretexts) for staging a variety of scenes and speeches. Moreover, while the Aristotelian thread in the grammatical tradition represents the classical Attic drama as the crowning paradigm of all poetic art, from the Hellenistic period onward both tragedy and comedy gradually gave way to mime and pantomime—or to variety shows including mime and pantomime performances, excerpts from old plays, sophistic declamations, musical numbers, and so forth—as the predominant and most enduring forms of public theater. (A mime was, in essence, a one-scene sketch involving speeches by two or three characters, or even a dramatic monologue, resembling an excerpt from a larger play. A pantomime was silent gesturing, or a sort of expressive dance, accompanied by music and/or a singing chorus.)[46] After the second century A.D. virtually no new comedies or tragedies were being produced, and by the fourth century no full-length dramas, old or new, were being acted on stage. Mime and pantomime would remain the most popular forms of dramatic poetry into the Byzantine period, until they were banned by an edict of Justinian in 524. Since we hear of them being banned again in 692, they probably continued to survive in popular tradition, perhaps away from centers of authority. Indeed it has been suggested that the *jongleur* tradition of the Middle Ages was a continuation of the mime.[47] These developments suggest that, for audiences, the chief interest in dramatic performances was seldom or never plot, at least not in the Aristotelian sense. A play or mime would have to have some sort of plot, some *hypothesis*, of course; and it would have to be reasonably intelligible. But the *hypothesis*, the "case," generally was familiar, even stereotyped, and was chiefly a context for the staging of episodes, or of *scenes* in which the characters could make various kinds of speeches, which probably formed the chief point of interest. It seems likely that, for most audiences, a play was in essence a sequence of mimes, while a mime in essence was a setting, or point of departure, for a declamation in "spoken" verse or song (or a dialogical or antilogistic exchange). The speech performance was the thing.

Despite its apparent disconnection from actual poetic practices, however, *grammatikê* did condition to some degree the rhetorical perception of poetic discourse and did condition to some degree the possibilities for poetry—or, at least, for a *literary poetry* directed to an educated, upper-class audience. *Grammatikê*, after all, did precede and overlap with rhetoric and did occupy an influential cultural position as the foundation and gateway to lettered learning. The conditioning worked both ways. I will conclude this chapter with four brief examples of this conditioning: most notably, Horace's *Ars Poetica*, which was to be the single most influential statement of "classical" poetics transmitted from antiquity to the Middle Ages and subsequent posterity; more briefly, Dio Chrysostom's "literary criticism" in *Oration* 52, the remarks of Hermogenes of Tarsus on poetry in *On Types of Style*, and Menander Rhetor's account of "hymns." These examples span a period from the first to the fourth centuries A.D.

That Horace's *Ars Poetica* views poetry rhetorically is, of course, a common-place. And it is obvious in several respects: Horace invokes a traditional myth of the first poets as the purveyors of a civilizing eloquence, like Isocrates' or Cicero's first orators (391–407); he emphasizes that poems "must have charm [*dulcia*] and lead the hearer's soul wherever they will" (99–100); he stresses the importance of presenting characters persuasively (153–178); he adopts from Neoptolemus the no-tion that poetry is more than merely psychagogic entertainment and must be both *dulce* and *utile*, offering moral judgments relevant to the hearer's life and to society at large (309–322, 333–346); he addresses writerly concerns with the processes of writing and revising (385–389, 438–452); and he is preoccupied throughout with the necessities of writing for reception by an audience. Like Cicero's oration *In Defense of the Poet Archias*, the *Ars Poetica* reflects what is probably a widespread, com-monplace view that poetry offers instructive portrayals and judgments of human character, persuading its audience to admire and emulate the noble, laugh at the ridiculous, disdain the base, and so forth. Horace says nothing at all about hy-ponoiac interpretation and indeed suggests that poets who claim to be inspired—to be channels for some sort of cosmic *logos*—either are pretentious fakes or crazy (295–304, 453–476). And of course Horace's own poetry is brilliantly rhetorical.[48] But there is another aspect to the *Ars Poetica*. Insofar as Neoptolemus or a tradition deriving from him is the chief theoretical source for the *Ars*, the *Ars* is also very much inflected by *grammatikê*. Horace inherits an Aristotelian (or Peripatetic) dou-ble vision.

As it has often been observed, the *Ars* is oddly disconnected from Horace's own poetic practice. While he does include a brief, thirteen-line overview of epic, elegy, iambic, and song-poetry (73–85), the *Ars* follows its Aristotelian and Neoptolemic model in being devoted chiefly to drama and (secondarily) to epic, the two genres that Horace never practiced. It is possible, and is often suggested, that Horace's aris-tocratic addressees, the Pisos—"O father and sons worthy of the father" (24)—are thinking of writing plays and have asked the famous poet for some advice. This is possible but not especially probable. There is little evidence that complete plays were being produced in Horace's time, and indeed it seems that mime shows (to which Cicero refers) already had become the predominant form of theater.[49] Fur-ther, even if Horace really is writing to would-be playwrights, it is unlikely that the aristocratic Pisos would plan to write for actual theatrical performances before mixed and vulgar crowds: that is, they will most likely be composing "literary" po-etry for recitation to genteel audiences in lecture halls and small gatherings or for private reading. Indeed, as Horace suggests, the serious poet should not aim at "what the buyer of nuts and roasted chickpeas might approve" and should aim in-stead at pleasing "those of knightly status, lineage, and substance," the people who reward the poet with "crowns," or prizes, gifts, and patronage (248–250). This ori-entation does, in fact, explain Horace's discussions of *choosing* discriminating people rather than flatterers to show one's compositions to, as well as his remarks on elicit-ing and accepting criticism, revising and repolishing, and waiting "nine years" be-fore publishing (385–390, 419–452); and it explains as well the general absence of remarks on spectacle and delivery. But it also makes curious his references to theater audiences and what "the public expects," and the presentation of events "on stage," and the uses of the chorus and styles of music (112–113, 153–157, 179–219).

It seems, in sum, that much of Horace's *Ars Poetica* focuses on types of poetry that neither he nor his addressees are likely to be practicing, essentially because he is reproducing the somewhat outmoded theoretical focus and backward gaze (to classical Attic drama, and to Homer) of Neoptolemus. He reels off a collection of familiar precepts from the grammatical tradition and "instructs" the Pisos (or the sons of the worthy father?) in the things that every well-bred Roman should have learned in grammar school. Thus we get, among other things, an Aristotelian-Neoptolemic requirement that a *poiêma* be a coherent, unified, self-consistent representation of a story (1–45, 119–152);[50] a quasi-Stoic requirement that the poet derive his subject matter from a knowledge of philosophy, or what Horace calls "the Socratic pages" (309–318); injunctions to follow the classic Greek models (268–274); and a miscellany of technical rules regarding proper diction (46–72), the subject matters appropriate to each type of verse (73–98), the characteristics appropriate to each type of character (153–178), the kinds of things that should not be shown on stage (179–188), the number of acts (five) and the number of actors (three) that a play must have (189–192), the proper functions of a chorus (193–201), the limits of taste in chorus music and satyr plays (202–250), metrically correct versification (251–268), and so forth.

In all this grammatical material, with its emphases on convention, correctness, and propriety, Horace is reflecting an awareness of the necessities of writing for a cultured audience whose sensibilities are steeped in the grammatical *paideia*: the necessities, that is, of writing poetry that will meet the test of what he calls "the well-pared fingernail" (294). The rules he enunciates are not, in fact, methods of invention or composition; they are standards for aristocratic aesthetic judgment, standards derived from grammar. Horace's recognition of the grammatical dimension of his audience's expectations is, of course, rhetorically astute. But it is almost impossible to believe that his own poetry could have been produced according to the rules enunciated in the *Ars Poetica*. Rather, all that a poet could produce, at best, would be a competent imitation of "classic" literature, suitable to meet the approval of well-bred gentlemen. Horace is not revealing to the Pisos the secrets of his own invention, or its rhetorical (argumentative, suasory) functions, or what it is that makes his poetry (or Virgil's, or Propertius's, etc.) something more than a good facsimile of the best Greek models, or what it is that makes his Hellenistic models, such as Callimachus, something more and other than facsimiles of the classic poetry that preceded them. Did Horace himself really wait "nine years" before "publishing" (that is, presenting in public) his poems? How could this have worked for his *Carmen Saeculare*, which was performed at the Secular Games of 17 B.C. by a chorus of boys and girls?[51] Or what of poems like *Odes* 4.2, which celebrates the return of Augustus' from Gaul in 16 B.C.? Waiting "nine years" would have made such a poem more than a little *akairios*, untimely. One may suspect, indeed, that the *Ars Poetica* works as a gentle, tongue-in-cheek satire on the ambitions of genteel amateurs—people whose ambitions are not so much rhetorical as grammatical, insofar as they want merely to produce "fine writing" as a sort of hobby—as he reviews *grammatica*'s rules of taste and counsels his addressees to keep their poems locked up at home.[52]

Horace's *Ars Poetica*, then, displays a sort of double vision—at once rhetorical and grammatical—similar to that of Aristotle (and probably of Neoptolemus). A poem on one hand is a rhetorical transaction, offering its audience a suasory encounter on matters of moral judgment; on the other hand, it is an aesthetic, literary object proffered for refined appreciation and approval.

Turning to Dio Chrysostom's *Oration* 52, we find an example of the sort of "grammaticalized" reading-performance that both Horace and Plutarch seem to have had in mind. Dio Chrysostom was a major sophist of the first to second centuries A.D. (c. 40–120), which made him Plutarch's contemporary. In *Oration* 52, which is a short, informal talk, he describes how he spent a day when he happened to be ill by reading and comparing three versions of the tragedy *Philoctetes* by Aeschylus, Euripides, and Sophocles (only Sophocles' version still survives). Dio's reading of the plays, as one would expect of a sophist, is in many ways informed by a fundamentally rhetorical orientation: he says that he played the role of *dikastês*, "judge" (4); he remarks, though rather casually and in passing, on how the choral odes and speeches (especially those of Euripides' Odysseus) are "most political and rhetorical" (11); he notes that Odysseus makes the drama more complex by creating "occasions for speeches" and being "most resourceful" in arguing opposites or turning "political enthymemes" (11, 13); and he offers impressionistic comments on the characteristics of each writer's eloquence, in a manner vaguely reminiscent of Dionysius of Halicarnassus.[53] But he offers no serious critique of the poems as rhetorical transactions, no sense of what issues were at stake when their poets composed them, and no sense of what still might be at stake for a reader of them now, other than questions of artistic excellence. The bulk of his commentary is really closer to an Aristotelian or Neoptolemic appreciation of *poiêsis* and *poiêma*. He comments chiefly on the probability and propriety of the poets' handling of plot and character (while explaining away a number of apparent inconsistencies), commends the "exhortations to virtue" included in many speeches (14), and praises each poet's stylistic skill. Dio praises not so much Odysseus's "political enthymemes" as the portrait of Odysseus as an orator: *this is that*. Dio does not so much enact a rhetorical encounter with the poems as represent an exercise in educated art appreciation. Moreover, what he appreciates is the sort of canonic, "classic" poetry that Horace would have the Pisos imitate, and he appreciates it in the proper ways. In sum, Dio's *Oration* 52 offers a display (or demonstration) of grammatically impeccable taste in canonic, *literary* poetry, while implicitly representing this poetry as a refined means of passing time when one is indisposed. Fine literature (from the shelves of Dio's personal library?) is part of the furniture of well-bred aristocratic leisure.[54]

About one century later (c. 180), Hermogenes of Tarsus—in his treatise *On Types of Style*—offers his brief account of poetry as one of the types of "pure" panegyric (or epideictic) rhetoric. Indeed, as I have noted earlier, he declares that "all poetry is panegyric and is, in fact, the most panegyric" of all artistic discourses and is in essence "panegyric in meter" (2.10.389).[55] In this he is recognizing poetry as *poiêma*. But he also recognizes poetry as *poiêsis*, fabulation: "all mythical thoughts (*mythikai ennoiai pasai*) are typical of poetry . . . [and] in general poetry indulges in marvelous stories that are impossible and unbelievable," as in Homer (2.10.390–

392). This two-part definition may be consistent with actual poetic practices in the later second century, insofar as the chief modes of public poetry, aside from mimes, were historical and mythical panegyrics performed at festivals or ceremonial occasions and were probably the types most likely to be produced by an epideictic orator. In considering all such poetry as panegyric rhetoric, and as a mode of public discourse, Hermogenes seems more cognizant of actual poetic practice than does "Plutarch," his contemporary.

However, Hermogenes' two-part definition also reflects the influence of *grammatikê*, not only because he thinks in terms of *poiêma* and *poiêsis*, or *lexis* and *logos*, but also because he seemingly conceives of poetry's *essential subject matter* as "impossible and unbelievable" fabulation. (In this he is not, in fact, consistent with contemporary practice.) At the same time, Hermogenes also affects something like an Aristotelian skepticism concerning the psychagogic power of "musical" rhythm. Although he recognizes the kinds of claims that, say, "Longinus" and (unnamed) musicians make concerning the power of rhythmic discourse and says he will not dispute them, he also takes the position that "rhythm does sometimes contribute a great deal to the production of one style rather than another, but not so much as the musicians say" (1.1.223). The distinctive stylistic feature of poetry, then, does not endow it with special persuasive power but simply "contributes to" one or another type of style, such as "solemnity" (1.5.251–254), which may also be achieved—and with considerably greater flexibility—in panegyric prose. Or perhaps it contributes simply to a "poetic" style, a style appropriate for old-style speaking framed in an imaginary, "Homeric" universe of tall tales. Thus, while Hermogenes' account of poetry recognizes it as a mode of epideictic rhetoric and is probably more consistent with actual practice than the poetics of "Plutarch's" *Essay*, it also is sufficiently inflected by *grammatikê* to carry a suggestion that poetry is *in essence* versified fabulation: a form of epideictic that is most typically confined within a particular type of (deeply traditional, mythological) subject matter and that employs verse as a decor that endows poetic speaking with a certain antique dignity, or a certain mood suitable to "Homeric" or "poetic" speaking.

Another hundred years or so later (c. 300) comes Menander Rhetor's treatise(s) on epideictic.[56] The only form of poetry that Menander includes is "hymns to the gods," of which he recognizes eight types: cletic (invocatory); apopemptic (farewell); "scientific" (cosmological); mythical (traditional tales about gods and heroes); genealogical (the births of gods); "fictitious" (invented myths, typically representing such things as Abundance or Poverty as demigods); precatory (requests); and deprecatory (requests that something be averted). Significantly, virtually all these types of hymns can also be done, he says, in prose. The only exceptions are apopemptic and "scientific" hymns. Apopemptic hymns are "very rare" and are performed only at certain (and very ancient) shrines—such as the shrines of Apollo at Delos and Miletus and the shrine of Artemis at Argos—when the god takes his or her seasonal departure (336). "Scientific" hymns (*physikoi*), which include the poetry of Empedocles and Parmenides, *may* be done in prose, as in Plato's *Phaedrus*, but generally are more suitable for poetry (336–337; it seems the allegory of the soul in Socrates' second speech is meant). Menander seems to think of "scientific" hymns as cosmological allegory, as when "we identify [Apollo] with the sun, and discuss the nature of the sun, or when

we identify Hera with air or Zeus with heat,"[57] behind which we can hear
Metrodorus, "Plutarch," and the Neoplatonists. Indeed, he says that such hymns
"should be carefully preserved and not published to the multitude . . . because they
look too unconvincing and ridiculous to the masses" (337), which suggests that he is
thinking of an esoteric, coded discourse requiring special interpretation. Likewise,
"mythical" hymns may include "some scientific doctrine concealed by allegory (*hyponoia*), as indeed occurs in most stories concerning the divine" (338). Here we are in
essence back to the grammatical reading of Homer and Hesiod. Menander, then, like
Hermogenes, treats poetry as a form of epideictic rhetoric, while seeming to identify
the poetic chiefly with mythological subject matter, indeed to associate it with the
most archaic, deeply traditional forms of myth and ritual. It is possible, of course, that
the other kinds of epideictic that he treats could also be done in verse, and some
kinds certainly were (for example, Claudian's panegyrics on the consulships of the
emperor Honorius, or his epithalamium for the emperor's marriage). But for Menander "poetry" seems most essentially to be a hymnic discourse dealing with traditional
mythology and mythic fabulation, and in this he appears to have been influenced by
the grammatical tradition. In short, "poetry" has been confined to a very narrow, very
old, and deeply conventionalized spectrum of epideictic discourse.

As the example of Claudian suggests, and as we should remind ourselves once
more, poetry did indeed continue to be understood and practiced as a medium of
epideictic rhetoric—for Claudian (c. 370–404), who lived and wrote in the last
years before the sack of Rome in 410 A.D., is in every way a rhetorical, indeed political poet.[58] In panegyrics meant probably to be performed at court, he heaps abuse
on the regime's defeated enemies and celebrates and magnifies its deeds. But, as the
grammatical inflection of even rhetorical poetics from Horace to Menander Rhetor
also suggests, the educated person's notion of "poetry," and thus the expectations
and responsiveness of aristocratic audiences, had also been disciplined in fairly re-
strictive ways. If "poetry" was not an old-fashioned indulgence in "impossible and
unbelievable" fables, if it was not a backward-looking evocation of an imaginary,
"Homeric" universe of myth and legend, if it was not a form of ritual or ceremonial
discourse for deeply traditional, religious occasions, what was it? Insofar as "poetry"
could simply be *poiêma,* meaning epideictic rhetoric composed in verse, then verse
as a "poetic" decor performed the rhetorical function of framing the discourse on one
hand in an atmosphere of literate refinement and, on the other hand, within an
evocation of an idealized, ancient, deeply traditional, "divine" and timeless realm of
mythic typologies—the realm of a changeless "eternal Rome"—a phantasmal realm
within which deeds and persons could be resonantly praised and blamed. Poetic
lexis, in short, could in itself perform the function that myth performs in a Pindaric
ode. Thus, while verse might not be necessary for panegyric, it could add a dimension of noble ornament suitable for the ritual praise of emperors and Roman heroes,
as well as for the reinforcement of cultural solidarity within an educated aristocracy.
And so the poet, such as Claudian, might lay on the ornament as thick as possible,
piling figure on figure, amplification on amplification, set piece on set piece, and
with metrical ingenuity, just as one might (and did, in late antiquity) adorn imperial robes with a heavy weight of cleverly woven golden thread and jewels. The result, for modern sensibilities, is an often tedious verboseness, a churning display of

technical virtuosity, and a sort of literary pedantry that sometimes astonish but ultimately wear the reader down. The result, in sum, is an inflated, mediocre rhetoric,
at least from our point of view.

Let me close with this: perhaps the most accomplished poet of late Latin antiquity was the fourth-century Gallo-Roman rhetorician and grammarian Ausonius
(310–393), Claudian's older contemporary. Ausonius's contemporaries deemed him
an equal to Virgil and Cicero. In his younger years he practiced in the law courts of
his native town, Bordeaux, before turning to a scholarly and literary career and winning some repute as a grammarian (or so he tells us in *Prefaces* 1.17–19). He wrote
chiefly verse encomia, such as *The Professors of Bordeaux*, a series of commemorative
eulogies on the distinguished grammarians and rhetoricians of that city's schools,
where he himself had taught for nearly thirty years. His reputation as a man of letters earned him an appointment in the 360s as tutor to the adolescent future emperor Gratian; and this appointment led eventually to the imperial *consilium* and to
the consulship in 379, where Ausonius seems to have had some real effects on legislation and policy.[59] Ausonius's best poem was probably *The Moselle*, a 483-line encomium to that river and the environs of Trier, the site of the imperial residence in
Gaul.

> Hail, great mother both of fruits and men, Moselle!
> Your glorious nobility, your youth trained for war,
> your eloquence rivaling Roman tongues adorns you. (381–383)

And so forth. The poem commemorates Ausonius's journey to Trier to take up his
post as imperial tutor. *The Moselle* can be understood as the sort of epideictic described by Menander Rhetor under the headings of how to praise countries and
cities or perhaps even under the heading of the "arrival speech," the *epibatêrios
logos*: it begins with a short narrative of Ausonius's journey to Trier and is amplified
with set pieces on the river and its region—including a famous *ekphrasis* or "description" of the river's fish –leading enthymematically to gestures of praise. (The *ekphrasis* was a school exercise, one of the traditional *progymnasmata*; for poetry the key
progymnasmata were description, character portrayal, and encomium.) Ausonius's
surviving works also include a prose oration of thanksgiving on the completion of
his consulship, addressed to the emperor (the *Actio Gratiarum*); a verse *ekphrasis* of a
painting (*Cupid Crucified*); poems on his personal life and relations (most notably
Ephemeris, a series of lyrics on his daily round); numerous letters in both prose and
verse; and numerous epigrams and various *jeux d'esprit* produced as literary games or
symposiastic entertainments. Of these the strangest is the *Cento Nuptialis* or "Wedding Patchwork Quilt," written on command for (and apparently to the tastes of)
the emperor Valentinian: a technical tour de force of more than 130 lines consisting entirely of patched-together lines and tags from Virgil, ending with an explicit,
pornographic description of "wedding night" sex (all composed, again, in Virgil's
words), followed by a prose disclaimer to the reader. Ausonius also wrote various didactic poems probably meant for his younger students, such as the *Eclogues*, on topics like The Good Man and How Many Days There Are in Each Month, or *The
Twelve Caesars*, a set of epigrams on the emperors described by Suetonius, giving a
neat, memorizable, recitable summary for each.

Ausonius, in short, was both rhetor and poet and was both rhetorician and grammarian. His poetry reflects the literary culture, the grammaticalized rhetorical poetics, and the grammaticalized, literary poetry of the educated upper classes in his day. He displays considerable technical virtuosity, but he is fundamentally conventional, deeply conservative, essentially pedantic, and often dull. He writes for the most part minor, ornamental epideictic: a poetry contained within the rhetoric of insider discourse, presenting his noble audience with an aesthetically pleasing representation of their image of aristocratic refinement and pious sentiment. Of him his recent editor, R. P. H. Green, has said, "[Ausonius' poetry] does not present a strong literary personality. Still less does it present the thoughts of a reflective mind like that of his contemporary Augustine. . . . He is, of course, no Cicero either." Similarly, the historian Michael Grant has said that Ausonius's "whole attitude is a complacent acceptance of things as they are, without a single new idea," at a time when the Roman world is in crisis and is soon to meet catastrophe, namely Alaric's sack of Rome and the subsequent dissolution of the western empire.[60]

But Ausonius himself has offered us the last word on his poetry, and on the literary poetry of late antiquity:

> I know that my poor poems are fated to be read with weariness, for that indeed is what they deserve. But some are recommended by their subject matter; and at other times the title alone incites the reader, so that by pleasantry the poetry persuades and renders him content to bear its insipidity. (Preface, *Parentalia*)

"With weariness," *fastidiose*, is a double-entendre, meaning both "with critical discrimination" and "with feelings of disgust" or nausea. Ausonius is writing elegant trifles for an exercise of taste, which soon becomes tiresome, while aiming merely to "persuade" the discriminating, literate reader to accept his trifling art. And he does so with great, even consummate skill. Such was the fate of "poetry" in late antiquity.

11

Toward Modernity

There remains a long and complex tale to tell, more than can be told in a single chapter, more perhaps than can be told in a single volume. Nevertheless I will attempt to sketch an outline here, by way of concluding. My claim, to put it in simplest terms, is that the dominant notions of "poetry" and "rhetoric" that modern culture has inherited—and its notions of "poetry" in particular—are largely products of the grammatical tradition in late antiquity. My sketch consists of a few brief stops in what is truly a long and highly complex itinerary. First, I'll consider a medieval Greek definition of "rhetoric" and Augustine's *De Doctrina Christiana*, which is probably the most crucial text in the transmission of rhetoric, or a notion of it, from late antiquity to the Middle Ages and subsequent posterity; then I'll consider Sidney's *Defense of Poetry*. I hope that, with readers' patience and charity, Augustine's and Sidney's texts can stand as a synecdoche for the larger history they represent.

The Grammaticalization of Rhetoric in the Middle Ages: Augustine's *De Doctrina Christiana*

Consider, first, these definitions:

> Let rhetoric then be a faculty of observing in each case the available means of persuasion. (Aristotle, *Rhetoric* 2.1.1355b)

> Rhetoric is an artistic faculty of persuasive discourse in public matters, having the goal of speaking well according to the possibilities. (Dionysius of Halicarnassus, fragment from *On Imitation*)[1]

> Definition of rhetoric: Rhetoric is an artistic faculty of persuasive discourse, *on account of building and other businesses and vulgar crafts*, in public matters, *by means of grammar and dialectic, the first of these being concerned with syllable quantity, pitch accent, breathings, and moods of words, and the other with everything*, having the goal of speaking well according to the possibilities. *This is taken from the goal, for the rhetor does not always persuade but now and then misses the mark; it nevertheless is needful to go over this begotten thing.* (From an anonymous synopsis of an epitome of the rhetoric of Hermogenes; my emphases)[2]

As we can see, from Aristotle to Dionysius—from classical Athens to Augustan Rome—there is a certain consistency despite differences in emphasis. Aristotle's famous definition makes rhetoric a "faculty" or *dynamis* for "observing," *theôrêsai*, the "available means of persuasion," *to endechomenon pithanon*, in each "case" or situation. "Available" translates *endechomenon*, which can mean both "allowable" and "possible," making rhetoric a faculty both of judging and generating enthymematic argumentation: the person who can recognize the "allowable/possible" grounds of persuasion in a given set of circumstances will be able to discover the best available enthymemes (what is possible?) and to evaluate the enthymemes actually presented (what is allowable?). Dionysius's more sophistic definition picks up some of Aristotle's terms, likewise making rhetoric a *dynamis* that operates "according to the possibilities," *kata to endechomenon*, in order to speak well, *eu legein*, or as well as the circumstances permit. Dionysius emphasizes also that rhetoric is a faculty "of persuasive discourse," *pithanou logou*, and that it is an "artistic" faculty, a *dynamis technikê*, or in other words a faculty that operates according to knowable principles and that can be cultivated by training. Dionysius may differ from Aristotle in seeing rhetoric as an Isocratean *logôn technê* not limited to the genres of practical oratory. In Isocratean rhetoric, matters of invention come under the *pragmatikos topos*, the "topic" of "subject matter"; and the phrase "in public matters," *en pragmati politikôi*, permits *politikôi* to be read as either "political" or "public" and *pragmati* as either "affairs" or "subject matters." The phrase thereby suggests political/public issues or themes that may be addressed in epideictic/panegyric discourses (such as Dionysius's history of early Rome) as well as practical orations.[3] Despite these differences of emphasis, however, both Aristotle's and Dionysius's definitions coincide in seeing rhetoric as an "artistically" developed faculty of mobile invention: that is, a capacity for generating well-made enthymematic argumentation from within the possibilities afforded by a particular set of circumstances at a given time.[4]

The third definition, composed probably sometime in the late Middle Ages (it appears in a thirteenth-century manuscript)—by an anonymous monk who is adding some "synoptic" commentary to an older, Byzantine epitome of Hermogenes—presents us with a significant transformation. On one hand, of course, it appears that nothing has changed. This commentator simply repeats verbatim Dionysius's definition, while adding glosses (the phrases I have italicized).[5] From this point of view, we may regard his definition as an index of the complete triumph of Isocratean rhetoric, or of the "philosophic" strand of sophistic rhetoric, transmitted via Dionysius and the tradition of Hermogenic commentary in Byzantine schools; and to some extent that is what it is. Indeed, even the gloss regarding "grammar" and "dialectic" as the instruments of rhetoric can be compared with Cicero's notion that the "perfect orator" needs both literary (or poetic) and philosophical training or with Isocratean notions of liberal education as the foundation for a "philosophic" *logôn technê*. "Rhetoric," as an art of wisdom-speaking eloquence, draws stylistic competence and interpretive skills from *grammatikê* and habits of agile reasoning from *dialektikê*. They thus appear as propaideutic, "basic" disciplines for advanced rhetorical training.

On the other hand, however, this monk's glosses also make of "rhetoric" something rather different; indeed they cause it virtually to disappear. In the first place, by glossing the "persuasive discourse" of "rhetoric" as something that occurs "on account of building and other businesses and vulgar crafts," he reasserts an Aristotelian restriction of rhetoric to the practical domain and furthermore sharply restricts the kinds of "public matters" that rhetoric pertains to. He seems to have in mind the relatively petty businesses of city councils or municipal administrators, who must, for example, supervise public works and deal with the "vulgar crafts," the *banausous technas,* involved in maintaining buildings, roads, and so forth: does the city basilica (now a church) need new tiles for its roof? How much will it cost, who should we hire? Though he says nothing about juridic/dikanic discourse, his vague reference to "other businesses" may also suggest private lawsuits over such matters as property rights and contracts or disputes between craftsmen (banausics) and customers, which a magistrate may have to judge and arbitrate. "Rhetoric," in short, seems to be given a narrow and generally mundane range of applications, while "dialectic" pertains to "everything" as the one, all-purpose art of reasoning. Moreover, the final gloss—which seems to be an explanation of the phrase "according to the possibilities"—seems to suggest a dismissive attitude toward rhetoric as a hit-or-miss sort of art, a mere "begotten thing" that one "nevertheless" needs to "go over" (i.e., in a synopsis), as if it is necessary to apologize for even bothering to discuss it. "Begotten thing" translates *pephykota,* or "what has arisen, sprung up, grown from nature" or "what has been born," and seems to characterize "rhetoric" as well as its uncertain outcomes as belonging to sublunary, carnal existence.

Further, this monk's glosses in effect *replace* rhetoric with grammar and dialectic. "Grammar," as he defines it, pertains to "syllable quantity, pitch accent, breathings, and moods of words": these are, in essence, matters for the *correct pronunciation,* or the correct reading, of standard literary Greek—indeed, they indicate phonetic features of the literary dialect that had mostly dropped out of vulgar spoken Greek. "Moods of words" is a compromise translation for *pathê logôn,* which could mean "styles of speech" and may suggest rhetorical notions of "types of style," figures of speech, and/or emotive utterance. Taxonomies of tropes and figures had, after all, long been part of the grammatical *paideia;* and Hermogenes's elaborate classification of stylistic *ideai* would remain central to Byzantine rhetoric to the end. However, in grammatical terminology the *"pathê* of words" could also mean modifications of word forms (as in declensional paradigms), or modifications in syntax, or passive constructions, or the use of diacritical marks (in addition to those used for pitch accent and vowel "breathings") to guide the correct reading and phrasing of written texts. Diacritics or grammatical modifications may well be what this monk means by *pathê logôn,* since all the other items in his list of grammatical concerns pertain to diacritics and pronunciation. He seems to consider the stylistic concerns of rhetoric to be identical with those of literacy training, and he in effect reduces the rhetorical functions of style to matters of grammatical correctness in the writing, reading, and pronunciation of literary Greek.

Similarly, he replaces rhetorical argumentation and invention with dialectic, which he says pertains to "everything." Even Aristotle, who makes rhetoric a "counterpart," *antistrophos,* of dialectic, does not go so far. Recall some important distinctions. While rhetorical argumentation is enthymematic, dialectical argumentation is syllogistic: that is, dialectic is a matter of propositional reasoning, according to formalized rules of correct inference, starting from authoritative or indubitable premises granted by an interlocutor. Rhetorical, enthymematic argument attempts to elicit the willing responses of an audience—one that remains free to be unpersuaded or to resist the invitation—and this is why the rhetor "does not always persuade." But dialectical argument *forces* the interlocutor to accept the conclusions drawn by logical necessity from the granted premises. Dialectic compels, while rhetoric persuades. This difference is, of course, the basis of the ancient metaphor of rhetoric as an "open hand" and dialectic as a "closed fist." Further, while the emotional responsiveness, experiential knowledges, and phronetic intuitions of an audience are integral to enthymematic reasoning and persuasion, they are mostly irrelevant to the logical necessities of syllogistic, propositional reasoning in dialectic. All that matters, again, is that one start from authoritative premises (recognized *katholou*) and proceed according to the rules of logical necessity, which can operate as an autonomous validity-machine, needing no one's cooperation. Once the interlocutor has supplied or acknowledged the starting premises, his participation in the unfolding syllogistic process is scarcely required, other than to grant the validity of the inferential rules invoked or to grant the additional premises invoked at each step along the way or (if he does attempt resistance) to engage in logic-chopping, eristical debate. However, an interlocutor who refuses to accept logically necessary conclusions derived from authoritative (or acknowledged) premises is, from a dialectical point of view, simply demonstrating that he needs correction, instruction, punishment, or ostracism.

This monk is no genius, and he seems confused. He certainly cannot be much of a rhetorician. For while his patched-together, heavily glossed definition of "rhetoric" has been appended to an epitome of Hermogenes' *On Stases*, it seems impossible that it could have been Hermogenes' definition. Our monk has transformed "rhetoric" by making it an art of correct dialectical reasoning, generated according to syllogistic rules of formal validity, presented in well-formed, grammatically correct literary Greek, on matters of mundane municipal business. The precepts of Hermogenes (especially those pertaining to stasis theory) are perhaps to be seen as supplements to the general rules of dialectical argumentation, to be applied in the sublunary, quotidian matters that "rhetoric" deals with. Otherwise, however, this monk seems not to recognize a difference between "rhetoric" and the dialectical and grammatical arts that, in his mind, constitute it. It seems we must imagine a rhetor or some sort of official in a city council or petty court, or in a piece of administrative correspondence, behaving as if he were conducting a scholastic exercise in logical disputation and demonstration, or perhaps a hermeneutic *explication de texte* (e.g., on the meaning and application of a law, or the proper interpretation of some event), in an educated, artificial language far removed from common speech. This image may or may not reflect the actual rhetorical practices of civil forums in, say, twelfth-century Constantinople—indeed it seems improbable—but it offers us an index of a widespread notion of "rhetoric" circulating in scholastic settings in the Middle Ages.

This monk is, in fact, reflecting a tendency that has its great inauguration in Augustine's *De Doctrina Christiana*, probably the single most influential text in the transmission of "rhetoric," or notions of it, from late antiquity to the Middle Ages. Indeed, it long has been a standard view that there is virtually no original

treatment of rhetoric, after Augustine's time, until the twelfth century.[6] The ancient rhetorical tradition did continue to be represented by a few texts that remained in circulation—chiefly, in the Latin West, Cicero's *De Inventione* and the
"Ciceronian" *Rhetoric to Herennius*, Horace's *Ars Poetica*, and fragments of Quintilian, and in the Greek East the Hermogenic corpus—and by the texts of the canonic
orators, especially Demosthenes (in the Greek east) and Cicero (in the Latin
West)—and by a continuous tradition of scholastic commentaries and synopses.
And within the commentary tradition there were, of course, various strands of interpretation that could interact in various, complex ways that have yet to be untan-
gled. But Augustine seems to have established, or prefigured, the dominant framework within which "rhetoric" would be appropriated and preserved as a school
subject by the literate elites of Christian Europe for most of the next millennium.

Most of the first three books of *De Doctrina Christiana* were written in 396–397,
not long after the emperor Theodosius's edict abolishing paganism (in 392); the
third and fourth books, the last of which deals most explicitly with rhetoric, were
completed in 427 (seventeen years after Alaric's sack of Rome). The text, which in
essence is a manual for homiletics based on scriptural exegesis, often has been described as salvaging rhetoric from among the pagan arts, adapting it for Christian
purposes, and making a crucially persuasive case for its continued utility and propriety in Christian culture—when that utility and propriety were very much in
doubt among Christian authorities.[7] Augustine himself, of course, had been a
teacher of grammar and rhetoric in North Africa, at Thagaste and Carthage, and
then at Milan, in the years before his conversion; and he appears to have been
a rhetor of consummate skill, both before and during his ministry. But, in *De
Doctrina*, Augustine "saves" rhetoric mainly by reducing it to the grammatico-
dialectic art of this late medieval Byzantine monk.

The first three books of *De Doctrina*, which are concerned with the correct interpretation of Scripture, have been described as offering a hermeneutic method
that takes its origins from the legal stases of juridic rhetoric, that is, from the stases
concerned with interpreting the letter and spirit of laws, ambiguous laws, and
conflicting laws; but it is probably more true to say that Augustine derives his
hermeneutics chiefly from *grammatica*.[8] Augustine announces in his preface that he
intends to provide "certain precepts for treating the Scriptures" (pr.1); and in the
opening sentence of book 1, he declares that the "treatment of Scripture" depends
upon two things, "a way of discovering those things which are to be understood,
and a way of teaching [*proferendi*] what we have learned" (1.1).[9] This may suggest a
homiletic rhetorical theory divided roughly into invention/judgment (as the creation and critique of interpretive arguments) and arrangement/style (for the presentation of those arguments), much as Isocratean rhetoric was divided into the *pragmatikos topos* and the *lektikos topos*. And to some extent that is what it is. However,
the speaker that Augustine has in mind is more like a *grammaticus* than like an
Isocratean or Ciceronian rhetor. For, as he also says in his preface, "he who explains
to listeners what he understands in the Scriptures is like a reader who pronounces
the words he knows, but he who teaches how the Scriptures are to be understood is
like a teacher who advises how the words are to be read." In this way, "he who receives the precepts" will thenceforth be able to interpret Scripture for himself, and

"may come to the hidden sense [*occultum sensum*] without any error, or at least will not fall into the absurdity of wicked meanings" (pr.9). In "teaching what he has learned," Augustine's scriptural explicator is not simply to declare his reading of the text but to demonstrate how the reading has been derived, so that his listeners will be put on the path of right interpretation and (like Plutarch's boy) will be made resistant to perverse, unorthodox understandings.[10] The initial emphasis, in short, is on the Christian speaker as one who *teaches* the proper way to read the "hidden meanings" of the Scriptures—a method of hyponoiac reading derived from the grammatical tradition of *ennarratio poetarum*, the "explication of the poets."

While teaching the listener how to "read for himself" may suggest a kind of liberation, in fact it implies a power relation in which the "teacher" as *grammaticus* speaks from a position of authority to an audience cast in the role of student-child, an audience whose proper task is not to judge (or offer counterarguments) but to correctly understand and accept the teaching. In this regard, Augustine's preface offers a remarkable and revealing declaration. Casting himself in the corporate "we," he notes that some "will condemn our work" (*reprehensuri . . . opus nostrum*) either because they do not understand it, or do not find it useful, or feel they can read the Scriptures well enough already for themselves. He then dismisses the first two of these three groups with what amounts to an ad hominem:

> to those who do not understand what we write, I say this: I am not to blame because they do not understand. In the same way, if they wished to see the old or new moon or some very small star which I was pointing to with my finger and they did not have keen enough sight even to see my finger, they should not on that account become angry with me. And those who have studied and learned these precepts and still do not understand the obscurities of the Holy Scriptures think that they can see my finger but not the heavenly bodies which it was intended to point out. But both of these groups should stop blaming me and ask God to give them vision. (pr.3)

For Augustine, such people are merely stupid and blind, and no amount of method, or pointing, or teaching, will help them. Concerning the third group, he argues (pr.4–9) that they should not be too proud to submit to instruction from other men, just as the apostle Paul was not too proud, and that, if they wish to teach their understanding they must, like a good *grammaticus*, teach the means by which it was arrived at—or refrain from speaking. That is, they must submit themselves to the discipline of an authoritative hermeneutic method meant to secure the production of valid, orthodox interpretation and to disqualify unsanctioned, aberrant readings. What all this amounts to, in effect, is an argument that those who fail to grasp or who reject Augustine's teachings in *De Doctrina* simply lack perception, or are morally flawed, or both. Their failure to be taught, or their resistance, demonstrates only their defect or perversity. They are bad students. They do not, in short, have a right to decline what is being offered: they must submit to correction and receive and accept the teaching or be dismissed as unredeemable. Significantly, none of these groups is addressed directly; they are cast in the third person, as if already removed from the corporate "we" that speaks and is spoken to, while the reader who joins the "we" steps into the circle of enlightenment.

Augustine begins book 1 by making a distinction between things and signs, and then devotes most of the rest of the book to a discussion of the "things" that Christian doctrine is concerned with—things to be loved in themselves (the Father, Son, and Holy Ghost) and secondary things (oneself and others, the material necessities of life, and various arts and crafts) to be loved and used for the sake of the higher goods. Book 1, in essence, lays out the basic Christian "lesson" that all correct interpretation must arrive at, or must be consistent with, in order to be valid. Augustine concludes:

> [w]hoever, therefore, thinks that he understands the divine Scriptures or any part of them so that it does not build the double love of God and of our neighbor does not understand it at all. Whoever finds a lesson there useful to the building of charity, even though he has not said what the author may be shown to have intended in that place, has not been deceived nor is he lying in any way. . . . However, if he is deceived in an interpretation which builds up charity, which is the end of the commandments, he is deceived in the same way as a man who leaves a road by mistake but passes through a field to the same place toward which the road itself leads. But he is to be corrected and shown that it is more useful not to leave the road, lest the habit of deviating force him to take a crossroad or a perverse way. (1.36.40, 41)

While Augustine does allow leeway for a range of possible interpretations that remain consistent with the fundamental Christian lesson, the parameters for correct interpretation are set from the start and predetermine the allowable possibilities. The proper lessons are to be discovered in the text by those who know already what they should find and how to find it: they know the destination and the road (or several possible roads) by which they will arrive. Further, Augustine invokes the hermeneutic principle that the hyponoiac/allegorical interpreters of Homer had long since established: the text embodies truths "divine and human" and teaches lessons that the original writer may not have intended, because those truths are immanent in the cosmic *logos* transmitted in the human *logos* of the text and are available to those equipped to recognize or construe them. As he at one point says, multiple readings of the same passage are permissible, even when the writer's original intention remains undiscoverable, as long as those readings remain consistent with Christian truth. This is so because "the Spirit of God, who worked through that author, undoubtedly foresaw that this meaning would occur to the reader or listener" (3.27.38). At the same time, however, the interpreter must follow valid hermeneutic procedures, lest his lucky intuitions tempt him into undisciplined, perverse interpretations later.

Books 2 and 3, then, are concerned with the methods of arriving properly at a proper and reasonable interpretation. This leads Augustine into a discussion of signs—natural or conventional, literal or figural, and known, unknown, or ambiguous—and the resources available for dealing with the hermeneutic problems raised by scriptural passages that seem obscure, ambiguous, or inconsistent with Christian teachings and morality. Such passages, says Augustine, have been covered with "a most dense mist" by God expressly to "conquer pride" and to make the lessons learned seem valuable, since what is easily gained is easily disdained; they

also reward the reader who reaches a correct solution, for "what is sought with difficulty is discovered with more pleasure" (2.6.7–8). This resembles Aristotle's notion
that metaphors and other forms of unusual speech are like "riddles" and give pleasure through the audience's act of hermeneutic insight (or recognition); but Aristotle also says this insight should arrive quickly (after a momentary disruption of ex-
pectation) or the pleasure will be destroyed, and in general he does not consider
unintelligible jargon aesthetically desirable (*Rhetoric* 3.2 1405b, 3.10 1410b, 3.11
1412a; *Poetics* 22). Augustine, however, considers the degree of pleasure to rise with
the degree of interpretive difficulty, at least for those who do succeed in finding a solution and are not simply defeated and chastened into deep humility by scriptural
impenetrability. And those who do succeed will not, in truth, be many.

As Augustine says, the resources required for solving the puzzles God has set include: subjection to God's will (2.7); a thorough familiarity with all the canonic
books of Scripture, meaning those most universally recognized by the best authorities, especially the Churches that "have deserved to have apostolic seats and to receive epistles" (2.8–9); a knowledge of the original languages of the Scriptures (He-
brew and Greek), or use of the best available Latin translations, preferably more
than one (2.11–15); and a knowledge of the "things" referred to in Scripture, such
as the natures of plants and animals, numerology, music, ancient Jewish customs
and institutions, history, medicine, astronomy, and various practical arts and crafts
(2.16–30). Understanding Scripture is a difficult project that requires a considerable command of the sort of erudition (and the philological resources, such as libraries) traditionally associated with advanced grammatical hermeneutics, especially the resolution of obscurities arising from literal and figurative expressions that
refer to "unknown things," or things outside the common person's frame of reference. In the fifth century, and even more so in later centuries, virtually no one outside the Church, and very few outside the major scholastic centers of Christianity,
would have access to such resources. Augustine in effect excludes all but the most
authoritative grammatical scholarship from valid scriptural interpretation, and the
Bible is rendered virtually as opaque as the Neoplatonic Homer.

The most important resources for solving scriptural obscurity and ambiguity,
however, are not the various knowledges of "things" but methods of "mental reasoning," among which the "ruling discipline" (*ubi regnat disciplina*) is that of "disputation and number" (*disputationis et numeri*; 2.31.48).[11] By "number" Augustine
seems to mean mathematical calculation as a model of formal reasoning—though
he says virtually nothing more about it—while by "disputation" he clearly means
dialectic, which he goes on to describe as the procedures for valid propositional reasoning and elenchic refutation (2.31–35). Augustine's key points are that the principles of valid inference are not human institutions but rules of nature "perpetually
instituted by God in the reasonable order of things" (2.32.50), that the truth of a
valid inference depends on the truth of the propositions it is derived from, and that
the truth of a proposition inheres in itself and is "a matter to be discovered in the
sacred books of the Church" (2.31.49; which leads back to the question of who is
qualified to read them). Thus he shows that the proposition "there is no resurrec-
tion of the dead" is necessarily false, since it entails a logically valid inference that
"Christ is not risen," which directly contradicts Scripture and therefore cannot be

true (2.32.50).[12] Received scriptural truth, in short, provides the anchor that guarantees the necessary truth or falsehood of interpretive inferences produced by valid logical procedures. At the same time, Augustine condemns sophistic antilogy and eristics, invoking the maxim of Ecclesiasticus (37.23) that "[h]e that speaketh sophistically is hateful." Making the lesser case the greater is disallowed; valid interpretation must confirm, and be confirmed by, the foundational premises recognized by orthodox authority. Once again: while Augustine may permit a multiplicity of readings as long as they accord with fundamental Christian principles (and are produced by valid means), what he offers is in fact a closed hermeneutic loop.

This becomes more evident in book 3, as Augustine turns to the problem of ambiguity, especially ambiguity caused by figural expressions. This requires an ability to understand when a sign is figural, and to read for the spirit rather than the letter of the Word (3.9–10). "And generally," Augustine says, "this method consists in this: that whatever appears in the divine Word that does not literally pertain to virtuous behavior or to the truth of faith, you must take to be figurative" (3.10.14). This can become a complex process and can involve some abstruse reasoning, but the key interpretive principle is that "what is read should be subjected to diligent scrutiny until an interpretation contributing to the reign of charity is produced" (3.15.23). What does not appear to fit orthodox Christian teaching must be *made to fit* by means of a figural interpretation supported by dialectical logic. Finally, Augustine notes that a knowledge of the tropes identified by the grammarians is useful for figural interpretation, since all of them are found in the Scriptures and some—he mentions *allêgoria, aenigma,* and *parabolê*—are actually referred to (3.29.40). He then finishes book 3 with a critique of Tyconius's book *Of Rules* for scriptural hermeneutics (3.30–37).

In sum, Augustine's hermeneutic principles in *De Doctrina* involve the traditional philological procedures of late antique *grammatica,* and the hyponoiac reading of "hidden meanings" derived by dialectical logic and figural interpretation, in order to "solve" the difficult, obscure, or ambiguous passages in Scripture and thereby keep the text in line with a predetermined Christian truth that is at once the ground and end of interpretation. The good interpreter finds what he knows in advance should be the proper lessons of the text, demonstrating by logically valid hyponoiac reasoning from infallible premises that *this is that.* This is an art of interpretive "invention" constituted wholly by grammar and dialectics. (It is worth noting that, in the incomplete *De Dialectica* attributed to the younger Augustine—supposedly composed a year or two before his conversion in Milan—the surviving chapters deal almost entirely with the signification of words, obscurity, and ambiguity; thus Augustine's concern with figural interpretation appears to be a component of dialectic, or is conjoined with dialectic in a general *grammatica* designed for scriptural interpretation.)[13]

Augustine's way of hyponoiac reading may not be as extreme as, say, Metrodorus's or "Plutarch's" ways of reading Homer—his general air of reasonability seems to put him closer to the soberer versions of Stoic hermeneutics, or to Plutarch in *How the Young Man Should Study Poetry*—though he may not be so far, in fact, from Neoplatonic ways of reading (with which he is contemporary). And at times he seems to stretch things fairly far. Augustine's most frequently remarked on (or most infamous) illustration of figural interpretation occurs in his discussion of the chastening and pleasure produced by the "most dense mist" of scriptural obscurity (2.6.7). His example is *Song of Solomon* 4.2:

> Thy teeth are like a flock of sheep that are even shorn, which came up from the washing; whereof every one bear twins, and none is barren among them.[14]

Since the *Song of Solomon* appears—at least on the surface—to be erotic poetry for all eight of its chapters, it certainly seems not to "literally pertain to virtuous behavior or to the truth of faith" and so is "obscure" in Augustine's terms and requires a figural interpretation to pierce its mists. According to Augustine, the basic meaning of this verse is that

> there are holy and perfect men with whose lives and customs as an exemplar the Church of Christ is able to destroy all sorts of superstitions in those who come to it and to incorporate them into itself, men of good faith, true servants of God, who . . . conceive through the Holy Spirit and produce the fruit of a twofold love of God and their neighbor.

But, as Augustine says, the *Song of Solomon* (or this verse in particular) conveys this notion figurally, through the device of praising the Church and its saints "as a beautiful woman" and thereby makes the basic meaning more pleasurable to contemplate:

> in a strange way, I contemplate the saints more pleasantly when I envisage them as the teeth of the Church cutting off men from their errors and transferring them to her body after their hardness has been softened as if by being bitten and chewed. I recognize them most pleasurably as shorn sheep having put aside the burden of the world like so much fleece, and as ascending from the washing, which is baptism, all to create twins, which are the two precepts of love, and I see no one of them sterile of this holy fruit. (2.6.7)

One can see how, with considerable and indeed sophistical ingenuity, Augustine could spin a homily from one verse of the *Song of Solomon*, or from anything; but it is apparent too that he is forcing onto the poetry—or out of the God-inspired *logos* that speaks through it—a meaning that old Solomon himself could not possibly have intended or foreseen, and one that modern readers have tended to regard as far-fetched at best.[15] But, of course, the reader who lacks the kinds of knowledge that Augustine requires for scriptural hermeneutics (and who is not already committed to the foundational truths of orthodox Christian faith) *is unqualified to say so.*

But now to rhetoric. There are also, Augustine says, "certain precepts for a more copious disputation" contained in the art of "rhetoric," or *eloquentia*: principles that involve, in essence, the effective presentation of arguments to audiences and that (like dialectic) are valid because they are not human inventions but part of the divinely instituted nature of things (2.36).[16] However, since these principles "are to be applied more in expressing those things that are understood than in the pursuit of understanding" (2.37.55), the precepts of "rhetoric" have no part in Augustine's account of invention and are deferred to the fourth and final book. Augustine there offers a spirited defense of "rhetoric's" utility for Christian culture—for who would wish the wicked to be more eloquent and more persuasive than "the defenders of truth"? (4.2.3)—but "rhetoric" as he describes it amounts to little more than what he calls "the practice of speaking most skillfully in copious words and verbal ornaments" (4.3.4) in order to effectively instruct, conciliate, and move one's audience by means of the plain, moderate, and grand styles.[17]

Augustine says that he will not give "the rules of rhetoric," which he presumes can be learned in secular schools (4.1.2) where the traditional forms of Roman education are still in place (though not for much longer, in the collapsing western empire). But the principles that Augustine does discuss suggest that he is thinking chiefly of the uses of rhythmic composition, schemes (such as accumulation, repetition, parallelism, and gradatio), and figures of discourse (such as question and answer or "entreaties and reproofs, exhortations and rebukes" [4.4.6]) for variety, drama, and emotional force. (At the same time, the homiletic speaker is to avoid recherché diction and excessive tropes.) Thus, for example, Augustine illustrates the "grand" style with this exhortative passage from Paul:

> Behold, now is the acceptable time; behold, now is the day of salvation.
> Giving no offense to any man, that our ministry not be blamed:
> But in all things let us exhibit ourselves as the ministers of God, in much patience, in tribulation, in necessities, in distresses,
> In stripes, in prisons, in seditions, in labors, in watchings, in fastings,
> In chastity, in knowledge, in long-suffering, in sweetness, in the Holy Ghost, in charity unfeigned,
> In the word of truth, in the power of God; by the armor of justice on the right hand and on the left;
> Through honor and dishonor, through evil report and good report; as deceivers, and yet true; as chastised, and not killed;
> As sorrowful, yet always rejoicing; as needy, yet enriching many; as having nothing, but possessing all things.
> Our mouth is open to you, O ye Corinthians, our heart is enlarged. (4.20.42)[18]

Or the "moderate" style, from Cyprian (in praise of virginity):

> Now we address ourselves to virgins, who because of their greater glory deserve our greater care.
> They are the flower and seed of the Church, the beauty and ornament of spiritual grace, the joyful inward nature of praise and honor, a whole and uncorrupted work, an image of God reflecting the sanctity of the Lord, the more illustrious part of the flock of Christ.
> The glorious fruitfulness of Mother Church rejoices in them and in them profusely flowers.
> The more glorious virginity adds to her number, the more the joy of the Mother increases. (4.21.47)[19]

Or the "plain" (or "subdued") style, again from Cyprian (explicating the sacrament of the chalice).

> You know that we have been admonished to follow the Lord's example in offering the chalice, and that nothing should be done by us other than that which the Lord first did for us, so that the chalice which is offered in His commemoration should contain water mixed with wine.

> For since Christ says, "I am the true vine," the blood of Christ is not water at all but wine.
>
> Nor can it be held that His blood, by which we are redeemed and vivified, is in the chalice when it contains no wine, through which the blood of Christ is shown, as is foretold by all the mysteries and testimonies of the Scriptures.
>
> Thus we find in Genesis . . . (4.21.45)[20]

And so forth; the passage goes on at greater length than I need consider here. Though Augustine's chief rhetorical authority is Cicero, what such examples illustrate is clearly a sophistic, even Asianistic, eloquence worthy of Gorgias and Aelius Aristides.

Augustine thus appears to be adapting the stylistic techniques of late antique sophistic declamation for lay preaching, which he justifies on appeal to Ciceronian authority and patristic examples, while he rejects the (to him) captious argumentation of sophistic antilogy. In this we might reasonably see, once again, at least a partial triumph of Isocratean rhetoric—or the Isocratean strand in Ciceronianism. But, again, Augustine reduces it considerably, and not only because he makes "rhetoric" merely the presentational servant of an inventional system constituted by grammatico-dialectical hermeneutics grounded in Christian doctrine.

For not only does Augustine decline to discuss the principles of rhetoric in detail, he also says that they are scarcely worth learning, even for those engaged in Christian homiletics. He does allow (4.3.4) that "it is enough that [the rules of eloquence] be the concern of youths," in which he is again presupposing the traditional forms of secular Roman education; but such study is beneath the dignity of "mature and grave" Christian men. Even for youths, rhetorical study is appropriate only for those "not pursuing some more urgent study" in preparation for service to the Church. Here Augustine seems to consign "rhetoric" (at least as taught in secular schools) to the sublunary realm that the Byzantine monk cited earlier likewise consigns it to: a useful and even necessary thing, admittedly, but not worth much serious attention. Further, Augustine holds that even for those who do wish to acquire eloquence to serve the Church, learning the precepts of rhetoric is hardly necessary. On one hand, as he says, "those with acute and eager minds more readily learn eloquence by reading and hearing the eloquent than by following the rules of eloquence," while those without talent will not be helped by the rules at all. On the other hand, "there is hardly a single eloquent man who can both speak well and think of the rules of eloquence while speaking." One need not know the rules to enact them, and knowing them doesn't really help; they only provide names for what an eloquent person intuitively does already. Thus, in Augustine's opinion, eloquence is acquired—by those who can acquire it at all—simply through *reading* and imitating (through reading out loud?) eloquent exemplars; and it usually is picked up, as he says, quickly or not at all (4.3.4–5; 4.7.21). Book 4, in consequence, is largely concerned with recommending suitable exemplars, such as Paul and Cyprian, and in general the Scriptures and the writings of patristic authors, which together constitute a Christian replacement for the traditional pagan literary canon. Explicitly "rhetorical" study is largely dismissed and in effect is made an epiphenomenon of Augustine's Christianized version of the grammatical *paideia*.

In this way, then, Augustine "saves" rhetoric for the Christian, literate elites of the Middle Ages, and for subsequent posterity, much as our Byzantine monk will do after him—by subordinating it to—or replacing it with—the verbal arts of dialectic logic and *grammatica* and reducing it to a knack for "copious words and verbal ornaments," which the talented will just pick up in the course of reading exemplary literature.

Rhetorical Poetics after the Middle Ages: Sidney's *Defense of Poetry*

> The grammarian speaketh only the rules of speech; and the rhetorician and logician, considering what in nature will soonest prove and persuade, thereon give artificial rules, which still are compassed within the circle of a question according to the proposed matter. (78)[21]

Sidney makes this statement in the course of amplifying his remark that "there is no art delivered to mankind that hath not the works of nature for his principal object" and on the way to his famous declaration that

> [o]nly the poet, disdaining to be tied to any such subjection, lifted up with the vigour of his own invention, doth grow in effect another nature . . . [so that] he goeth hand in hand with nature, not enclosed within the narrow warrant of her gifts, but freely ranging only within the zodiac of his own wit. (78)

The entire span of the Middle Ages separates Sidney from Augustine, and a few centuries separate him from the anonymous late medieval Byzantine synopsis writer. But at the risk of reductionism I want to suggest that in these statements, and in the *Defense of Poetry* more generally, Sidney reflects the transformations Augustine prefigured and, in his turn, prefigures many of the confusions that modernity has inherited—even as he presents a distinctly rhetorical poetics.

The history of medieval rhetoric is a complex story that has yet to be fully written, though probably the general outlines have been delineated, particularly with respect to the Latin West.[22] Rhetorical argumentation becomes conflated with, subordinated to, or simply replaced by, dialectical disputation, which is most typically identified with notions of "Aristotelian" logic.[23] The *stasis* systems still available from such texts as Cicero's *De Inventione*, the *Rhetoric to Herennius*, and (in the Byzantine world) Hermogenes' *On Stases*, come to be seen as supplements to dialectical logic providing topics of argument on secular, mundane matters or as parts of political or ethical philosophy (or "civil science"). But Aristotelian syllogistic logic is generally understood as the one, universal *method* of argumentation that applies in every case and subject matter, rather than a propaideutic exercise and basis for more advanced study in the complexities of rhetorical argumentation. Further, what comes to be understood as "rhetoric" proper is typically what we see in Augustine: an art of style, or presentation, the function of which is to embellish a predetermined subject matter (or "content") with a panoply of figural devices, in order to endow it with elegance, charm, and emotive force, or simply to render a clear and systematic exposition—so that "rhetoric" becomes in essence a part of grammar. Finally, *training* in rhetoric as a specific or separate discipline largely disappears or is absorbed into (or replaced by) the grammatical and logical curricula. Thus we find that the earliest recorded European university curriculum, from the University of Paris in 1215, specifies readings in grammar (Priscian), dialectic (Porphyry), and logic (Aristotle) but makes no mention of rhetoric at all.[24]

We see the effect of this general trend in the resurgent "rhetorics," or practical handbooks for specific verbal "arts," that began to proliferate between the twelfth and fourteenth centuries. These have long been recognized as falling into three main types: the *ars dictaminis* (for letter-writing), the *ars praedicandi* (for preaching), and the *ars poetriae* (for composing Latin verse).[25] It is often said that all these *artes* embody "Ciceronianism." What they chiefly reflect, however, is a formalism that betrays their derivation from "rhetoric" as conceptualized by the grammatical tradition. Each tends to prescribe a set of rules for the parts of each type of discourse, the topics to be covered in each part, and methods of embellishment, while argumentation and invention characteristically are given thin treatment or no treatment at all. Thus, for example, Geoffrey of Vinsauf's famous *Poetria Nova* (composed c. 1175) offers a forty two-line preface, some general and brief remarks on finding a subject matter (take something factual or make up a fable; lines 43–86); brief remarks on ways of arranging one's subject matter (begin from the beginning, begin from the end, begin from the middle, etc.; 87–202); and very lengthy discussions of amplification and abbreviation (219–736) and ornamentation (737–1968), based on the inventory of figures in the fourth book of the *Rhetoric to Herennius*. This is followed by a brief discussion of memory and delivery (1969–2065) and an epilogue (2066–2116). Similarly, the anonymous and typical *Rationes Dictandi* (c.1135) devotes about one page to defining "written composition," "letter," and the parts of a letter (salutation, securing good will, narration, petition, conclusion); about eight pages to different ways of handling the salutation, depending on the rank of the person addressed (with twenty examples); about one page each to the other parts; and about six pages on ways to rearrange and vary the basic formula for different circumstances. Another treatise of this type, the *Practica Sive Usus Dictaminis* of Lawrence of Aquilegia (c. 1300), identifies seven different types of letters (depending on the type of addressee) and offers tables of alternative locutions for each syntactic slot in each part of each type. The writer need only choose from menus of prefabricated phrases by some algorithm, or what amounts to a cut-and-paste operation—a formalistic tour de force that James Murphy has aptly described as "a rhetorical dead end unparalleled in the history of the arts of discourse."[26]

Or again, the typical *ars praedicandi* divided the "artistic" sermon into the "antetheme" (a prayer and some opening remarks), the "theme" or statement of the scriptural quotation to be expounded on, the "division" of the theme into parts, the "development" of each part by various kinds of amplification, and the conclusion. The forms of "development" typically included such things as "proof" by authority, allegory, example, syllogism, and "enthymeme" (which was understood in scholastic terms, or rather misunderstood, simply as an incomplete or defective syllogism).[27] Significantly, such "proofs" in a sermon functioned not so much as modes of argumentation as modes of explication, exposition, or confirmation of scriptural lessons that the audience was expected to receive. In Robert of Basevorn's *Forma Praedicandi* (1322)—perhaps the most fully developed example of this type of manual—reasoning by contraries, enthymemes, or examples is explicitly treated as a mode of "ampli-fication." The other modes of amplification are: discussing the meaning of a noun; di-vision; invoking "concordances" (with authorities); making comparisons; develop-ing metaphors; explication of hyponoiac meanings (via historical, allegorical, moral, or anagogic interpretation of scriptural passages); and discussion of causes and effects. These discursive moves are considered not as ways to discover an argument in rela-tion to some open question or to engage with an audience that is free to disagree but simply as ways to elaborate and illustrate a predetermined lesson. These modes of amplification are further abetted by such "ornaments" as digression, "correspon-dences" (parallelism in the arrangement and treatment of parts), "circuitous devel-opment" (in which the end of one part links to the beginning of another), "convolu-tion" (multiple relations between parts), "unification" (a sentence that sums up all the parts of the development that has preceded it), and the various ornaments of style and delivery (including cadences, "rhetorical" schemes and tropes, voice modula-tion, gesture, humor, allusions, multiple allusions, and "reflecting on the subject mat-ter"). The overwhelming impression is that Robert's "rhetoric" is in essence a ma-chine for churning out a copious, pedantically exhaustive, and systematically arranged and embellished explication of a scriptural quotation in terms of authorita-tive doctrine, in what is more like a lecture than a suasory encounter. All this comes close, already, to the "modes of exposition" featured in the drearily formalistic text-books of what has come to be called the current-traditional rhetoric purveyed in twentieth-century composition classrooms.[28]

All of this is background for Sidney's remark on grammar, rhetoric, and logic. So, of course, is the Renaissance rediscovery of the complete Quintilian, Cicero's *De Oratore*, and Aristotle's *Rhetoric* and *Poetics* and the revival of a more fully Ciceronian, even sophistic rhetoric in the humanist tradition—as well as the Ramist reaction in the sixteenth century, which effectively "reformed" rhetoric by making it again a technique merely of figural embellishment for presenting a subject matter systematically exfoliated and arranged already by "logic."[29] Indeed, Ramist "logic" can operate without reference to an audience at all: that is, it operates, as Sidney says, entirely "within the circle of a question according to the proposed mat-ter," exhaustively spinning out the entailments, correlatives, contraries, and what-not, of an initial proposition. So too for a "rhetoric" of presentational stylistics grounded in the argumentational procedures of Ramist "logic": insofar as it can operate as a grammar of elegance within its own system of rules, applying figures *suitable to the subject matter*, virtually no audience is required. (An audience that cannot recognize the elegance may be dismissed as ignorant and unrefined.)

Thus, on one hand, Sidney characterizes grammar, logic, and rhetoric as more or less mechanically rule-governed arts for producing properly literate discourse in speech or writing, for expounding a subject matter in a logically methodical way, and for embellishing the presentation with the tropes, schemes, and cadences re-quired for a particular type of style.[30] He is, in short, invoking presumptions famil-iar to his readers. On the other hand, however—and this is no news—Sidney's *De-fense* both embodies a fuller version of Ciceronianism (or Isocrateanism) than Ramist rhetoric would countenance and presents a rhetorical poetics meant to es-cape the formalism he ascribes to rhetoric, logic, and grammar. The *Defense* itself offers epideictic argumentation structured according to the parts of a Ciceronian oration and embodies the sort of dialogic argumentation that characterizes Ciceronian *inventio*. It certainly does not lay out the subject according to the divisions (and divisions of divisions) of an initial thesis, methodically "developing" each division in turn according to the rules of Ramist art; nor does it follow a dialectical procedure. Moreover, like Erasmus's *Praise of Folly*, or Apuleius's *Apologia*, or Aelius Aristides' *Against Plato Concerning Rhetoric*, and so forth, it operates very much in the spirit of a sophistic declamation and plays the game of making the weaker case the stronger as it replies to "them that, professing learning, inveigh against" poetry, "which from the highest estimation of learning is fallen to be the laughing-stock of children" (73–74). Sidney's *Defense of Poetry* is, in almost every respect, a spirited rhetorical performance worthy of its ancient predecessors. Indeed, just as Gorgias playfully concludes his *Helen* by calling it his *paignion*, "toy" (or "plaything"), Sidney concludes by calling his *Defense* "this ink-wasting toy of mine" (121).[31]

The *Defense* is generally understood to offer a poetics, derived from a conflation of Horace's *Ars Poetica*, Aristotle's *Poetics*, and Stoic theory, that makes poetry a medium of epideictic discourse whose end is moral suasion. For, as Sidney says, what he calls "right" poetry (as distinct from "divine" hymns and "philosophical" or didactic epic) works "both to delight and teach; and delight, to move men to take that goodness in hand, which without delight they would fly as from a stranger; and teach, to make them know that goodness whereunto they are moved" (81). From Aristotle he takes the notion that poetry is "more philosophical and more studiously serious" than history because it deals in *katholou* rather than particulars (88), and from the Stoic (and Neoplatonic) grammatical tradition he takes the notions of poetry as "first philosophy" and the poet as "the right popular philosopher" (87) who conveys by means of engaging tales and moving images what moral and natural philosophers will abstract as explicit doctrine. And indeed the genres of "right poetry" that Sidney identifies—pastoral, elegiac, iambic, satiric, comic, tragic, lyric, and (heroic) epic (94–98)—all take on the functions of traditional rhetorical genres. Thus pastoral, in showing "the misery of people under hard lords" and the "blessedness" the low can derive "from the goodness of them that sit highest" (94–95), embodies a kind of political-philosophical argument on just and unjust rulership and in effect provides an epideictic counterpart to "deliberative" or symbouleutic rhetoric. Likewise elegiac, iambic, satiric, and comic verse offer counterparts of dikanic argument: elegiac moves compassion and pity for unjust suffering (95); iambic makes "shame the trumpet of villainy with bold and open crying out against naughtiness" (95), thus functioning as accusation; and satiric and comic poetry, when rightly used, persuade their audiences to consider human vices in others and themselves as objects of shame and ridicule (95–96). Tragedy returns to the deliberative concerns of pastoral, by making "kings fear to be tyrants, and tyrants [to] manifest their tyrannical humors" and by teaching "the uncertainty of this world" (96). Lyric performs the traditional functions of encomium or panegyric rhetoric, rewarding "virtuous acts" with praise, giving moral precepts, and praising God (in which it reprises the "divine" concerns of hymnody); while "heroical" epic likewise stirs an emulative admiration for the "magnanimity and justice" displayed in noble actions (97–98) and thus is a form of panegyric history.

In all of this, Sidney clearly is conceiving poetry as epideictic rhetoric: it motivates both an Aristotelian recognition of *katholou* and an enthymematic judgment—embodied as a *pathos*, such as pity, admiration, or disgust—that constitutes, in effect, a rehearsal of an intentionality that is on the way to becoming part of a person's ethical repertoire. At the same time, however, precisely because Sidney derives his poetics from a conflation of Aristotelian, Horatian, and Stoic/Neoplatonic doctrines, he also commits himself to the sort of double vision we have observed already (in chapter 10) and thereby undercuts his argument.

Most crucially, Sidney follows the Aristotelian/Neoptolemic/Stoic tradition in defining poetry as, in essence, mimetic fabulation. This makes verse (or rhythmic prosody) an accidental and conventional rather than a defining feature of poetic discourse, although "the senate of poets" has chosen verse as the "fittest raiment" for it (81–82). As Sidney says, "verse" is "but an ornament and no cause to poetry" (81). But this definition, in its turn, at once sits oddly with Sidney's description of such lyric-argumentative genres as invective and encomium and—as with Aristotle, and the grammatical tradition—forces him in the direction of defining all poetry in dramatistic and allegorical terms. Indeed, Sidney's description of poetry as an art definable *in opposition to* the supposedly rule-governed operations of grammar, logic, and rhetoric (or literate discourse, syllogistic argument, and stylistic ornament) effectively leaves him without a means of describing it in terms of any well-recognized concept of argumentation that is, in the wake of a millennium of scholasticism, readily available to him or his Elizabethan reader.

A poem, as he says, is a "μίμησις . . . a representing, a counterfeiting, or figuring forth . . . a speaking picture" (79–80). As such, it is a "feigning" of "notable images of virtues, vices, or what else," through which the reader is given moral-philosophical instruction (81–82). This makes the lyric poem, once more, not so much a medium of argument but a dramatized representation of an emblematic scene—and the longer narrative a sort of extended allegory, as in Xenophon's "portraiture" of a just imperium "under the name of Cyrus" (81). To a certain extent, the notion of poetry as *figuring forth* moral concepts or *katholou*, when coupled with the notion of the poet "freely ranging . . . within the zodiac of his own wit," may suggest a kind of tropological fantasia, or an unsystematic system of poetical invention based on tropes (metaphor/allegory in particular) and constrained only by the limits of imagination. But this is not quite so. For "philosophy," and the authoritative moral truths identified by philosophy, provide the *materia* that preexists and in effect predetermines poetical invention. As Sidney says, "whatsoever the philosopher saith should be done, [the poet] giveth a perfect picture of it . . . so as he coupleth the general notion with the particular example" (83). In this, the poet is conceived, as in Stoic *grammatikē*, as a "right popular philosopher" who presents moral-philosophical *lessons* in a sweetened form, or an entertaining "masking raiment" (93), for those not capable of philosophy: [the poet] "doth intend the winning of the mind from wickedness to virtue, even as the child is often brought to take most wholesome things by hiding them in such other as have a pleasant taste" (92). Or again, when Sidney defends the poet against the Platonic (and later Christian) objection that poetry has "filled the world with wrong opinions of the gods," he resorts to the traditional Stoic explanation that the early poets "did not induce such opinions, but did imitate opinions already induced" (108). This makes the poet simply an articulator of the reigning *doxa* of his time and place. At no point does Sidney suggest that a poet might put in question what constitutes virtue and wickedness; these things seem to be givens.

As with Stoic and medieval grammar, then, poetry is conceived in such passages not as a medium of genuine invention or of ideological contestation but as a medium whose rhetorical and inventional possibilities are more or less limited to finding ways to ornament or "figure forth" already received opinion and authoritative dogma for nonphilosophic minds. Not only, then, is verse a "raiment" for poetry, but likewise poetry is itself a stylistic "raiment"—a figural ornamentation—for philosophical conceits. Sidney's poetry-reader, like Plutarch's boy, is to be presented with "notable images" of virtues, vices, and whatnot in order that he may be shown them clearly and memorably and may learn that "this is that."

This may not be what Sidney really means, or wants to mean; but he communicates it. Indeed I believe that what Sidney really has in view, if unsteadily, is a more thoroughly rhetorical poetics, one that is more consistent with the oft-remarked rhetoricity of his own poetic practices or of poetic and literary practices in the Renaissance generally.[32] Nevertheless, he also commits himself to what I have called the double vision implicit in the Aristotelian-Neoptolemic-Stoic-Horatian premises he grounds his discourse on and that he derives from the grammatical tradition from late antiquity through the Middle Ages—a double vision that he cannot escape entirely and in effect transmits.

Neither am I arguing that the grammaticalized rhetorical poetics Sidney both inherits and transmits is a description (or a fully adequate description) of actual poetic practices, either in the Renaissance or in the Middle Ages. As I suggested at the close of chapter 5, the poetics of the grammatical tradition are based on the institutionalization of poetry, or of "literature" in general, as a school subject and an object of philological and hermeneutic study. Insofar as poetry survives outside the school as a viable medium of public discourse, and continues to be experienced as such, it will tend to retain its character as offering a rhetorical, argumentative encounter to its audience—so that its practices will not necessarily be dominated, though they may be conditioned, by the grammatical tendency to conceive both "poetry" and "rhetoric" formalistically in terms of stylistic ornament for a predetermined "content" or to regard all texts as objects for scholastic exercises in the proper hyponoiac *ennarratio* (explication and paraphrase) of their "meanings" and "lessons."

Poetry certainly survived as a medium of public discourse, through the Middle Ages and Renaissance, and certainly continued to be experienced and understood as such, in both learned and vernacular traditions. This is perhaps most visible in the persistence of the versified panegyric history (or "heroic" narrative) and the romance; the survival of the popular mime in the *jongleur* tradition; and the continuing production of lyric odes, elegies, invectives, and encomia. Further, a long-prevailing attitude toward *grammatica* may be embodied in Martianus Capella's *Marriage of Philology and Mercury*, a fifth-century text that was widely read and used, from the ninth century to the Renaissance, as an encyclopedic overview of the liberal arts. In book 3, "Lady Grammatica" offers to the celestial wedding company an exposition on *grammatica* and on the wonders of poetic explication; but Minerva cuts her off before she finishes, because the gods are bored (*Marriage* 3.326).[33] In this we see, perhaps, a certain resistance to the ways that *grammatica* disciplined subjectivities or to the ways that it disciplined (or failed to discipline) responsiveness to the rhetorico-poetic practices available outside the school.

My point, however, is that Sidney participates in and transmits a conception of "poetry" and "rhetoric" that derives from *grammatica* and that has pervaded the scholastic tradition in Western literary culture from the Middle Ages to the present day. Both "poetry" and "rhetoric" tend to be cut off from notions of argumentation or "reason," which tends to be conceived in terms of the syllogistic arts of dialectic—and, from the Enlightenment onward, in terms of a Cartesian, calculative rationalism. "Rhetoric" tends *within this tradition* to be formalistically conceived as presentational stylistics and to be identified with a sublunary realm of practical communication, politics, and business. So conceived, it easily comes to be seen as an art of specious ornament, salesmanship, propaganda, and false consciousness at worst and as an art of effective or elegant "expression" at best. "Poetry," for its part, tends to be conceived in terms of a figural *mimêsis* that hyponoiacally signifies moral-philosophical *katholou* or that dramatistically represents them as models of subjectivity, to an audience that knows them and can recognize them already, saying "this is that": Cyrus is "just rulership," Aeneas is "heroic faithfulness to duty," and so forth. These tendencies have undoubtedly been intensified in the last two centuries by romantic ideologies and by the persisting romanticisms of modernist (and perhaps even postmodernist) thought. "Rhetoric" and "poetry" align with the practical and the aesthetic, the mundane and the ineffable, manipulation and truth, constraint and freedom, and so forth, in an almost endless and utterly familiar series of oppositions that all readers of this book can easily sketch out for themselves. This is a familiar, oft-told tale. Yet these oppositions are not, as is frequently supposed, the products of romanticism only, or of the Enlightenment, or of the "humanism" commonly identified with Enlightenment ideology. They are, as I hope I have suggested, the products of a much deeper, much older tradition that derives from late antiquity. And they have been with us for so long that we can scarcely see them as anything other than the shapes of eternal nature, even when we "undo" the epistemological assumptions of romanticism, humanism, and the Enlightenment.

Or so it seems, that is, if we have been trained in that deeper, older, yet more traditional way of thought. And all of us have. For my point is also that its products—grammaticalized rhetoric, grammaticalized rhetorical poetics, and grammaticalized poetics simply—have all been disseminated via the traditions of scholastic literary study and do not necessarily determine the possibilities of poetic practice *or the experience of poetic practices* in the civic or public space beyond the school. But insofar as "poetry," or high cultural *literary poetry*, must present itself to school-trained audiences whose conceptions and expectations have been formed by the grammatical tradition (in its various contemporary forms) and insofar as the poets themselves have been disciplined by it as well, then "poetry's" rhetorical possibilities correspondingly will be limited, to some degree, to reflecting back its audience's favored philosophical postulates in charmingly figured forms. Under such a circumstance poetry will tend to be limited to the rhetoric of what I have called

Notes

Preface

1. Some of the key, recent voices in this discussion—since 1990, and chiefly with reference to "classical" and medieval rhetoric—and representing a wide variety of positions—are: Bender and Wellbery 1990; Conley 1990a; Horner 1990; Murphy 1990; Cole 1991; Copeland 1991; Jarratt 1991; Morse 1991; Schiappa 1991a; Swearingen 1991; Enders 1992; Enos 1993 and 1995; Ochs 1993; Poulakos 1993; Garver 1994; Irvine 1994; Kennedy 1994; Neel 1994; Vitanza 1994; Worthington 1994b; Cohen 1995; Lunsford 1995; Poulakos 1995; Sinclair 1995; Eden 1997; Glenn 1997; Kastely 1997; Sloane 1997; and Atwill 1998. More or less recent classical scholarship that is relevant to reconsideration of the early history of rhetoric and poetry (in the West), and to revaluation of the sophists, includes Bundy 1986 (orig. 1962); Havelock 1963 and 1982; Bowersock 1969; De Romilly 1975 and 1992; Kerferd 1981; Russell 1983; Trimpi 1983; Woodman and West 1984; Gentili 1988; Kurke 1991; Brown 1992; Rose 1992; Anderson 1993; duBois 1995; Gleason 1995; and Stehle 1997.

1. Before the Beginnings

1. There are, of course, Homeric precedents or parallels to Hesiod's account, such as the description of the bard Demodocus's performance, and Odysseus's own account of the gift of eloquence, in book eight of the *Odyssey*, as well as scattered references elsewhere in both the *Iliad* and *Odyssey*; see Enos 1993 9–10. Hesiod, however, offers something more like an explicit theorizing of what is mostly implicit in Homer's passages. See Havelock 1963 97—98.

2. My translation here is based on the Greek text of the widely available Loeb edition, Evelyn-White 1914 84–87, and is adapted from the translations of Fraser 1983 27—28 and Lattimore 1959 127–129, as well as from Evelyn-White. See also Havelock 1963 107, 110.

3. This view is apparent in a number of widely used texts that can be seen to embody the current standard history, such as Kennedy 1980; Vickers 1988; Barilli 1989; and Bizzell and Herzberg 1990. See also Baldwin 1924, which can be seen as an earlier version, or a progenitor, of most of our current standard histories. Conley 1990a is probably the most iconoclastic, and most interesting, standard history now available. Recent revisionary histories of early or "preconceptual/predisciplinary" rhetoric include Jarratt 1991; Schiappa 1991a and 1992; Cole 1991; Enos 1993; and Poulakos 1995.

4. Gentili 1988 3; Cole 1991 p. 2; Schiappa 1991a 40–49.

5. Havelock 1963 108–109; Pucci 1977 17–18; Nagy 1990a 64. For recent analyses that are similar to the one offered here and in the next few paragraphs, see also Kirby 1992 34–60 and Gagarin 1992 61–76.

6. On rhetoric, Gorgias, and *goêteia,* see De Romilly 1975 6–22.

7. "Composition" here comprises both "arrangement" and "style." I am not suggesting that Hesiod is already distinguishing the "parts of rhetoric" identified in rhetoric manuals from the fourth century B.C. onward — but only that the theory embodied in those manuals can retrospectively see in Hesiod's account an embryonic anticipation of itself.

8. Havelock 1963 107, 161; Gentili 1988 184.

9. See Havelock 1963 chs. 3–6; Peabody 1975 31, 202, 206–215, 268–272; Oliver 1971 23–26; and Ong 1982 34.

10. See Havelock 1982 9–10, 187, 190; and Lamberton 1988 67. See also Thomas 1992 61–73.

11. See Chase 1961 293–300 and Carter 1991 209–232. On Aspasia, see Jarratt and Ong 1995 and Glenn 1997 36–44.

12. See Burgess 1902 92–102; Russell 1981 116–117; and Russell and Wilson 1981 xi–xxxiv. The key passage of Hermogenes is *On Types of Style (Peri Ideôn)* 403–412; translations are available in Russell and Winterbottom 1972 and Wooten 1987.

13. Perelman 1984 129–131.

14. It is sometimes asserted that Aristotle defines the audience of epideictic as "hearers," *akroatai,* as opposed to the *kritai* of pragmatic discourse. But Aristotle describes all audiences as *akroatai; akroatai* subdivide into *kritai* and *theôroi,* with *kritai* further subdivided into *dikastai, boulêtai,* and *ekklêsiastai* for dikanic and symbouleutic/demegoric discourse.

15. Perelman 1984 129–131.

16. See Perelman and Olbrechts-Tyteca 1969 47–62; Perelman 1982 18–21; and Perelman 1984 129–134. See also Oravec 1976 164–167, 171; Carter 1991 213–217; and Sullivan 1992 324, 327–329. On "identification" and epideictic, see Burke 1969 19–46, 49–59, 70–72.

17. See Nagy 1990a 38–40; Thomas 1989 21; and Havelock 1982 14, 19, 195. See also Gentili 1988 chs. 5, 6, 8.

18. See Jakobson 1960 350–377 and 1973 219–232; Finnegan 1977 25–26, 90–92, 108–109, 118–119, 127–133, 222–223; Fox 1975 127–128 and 1977; Abbot 1987 259; and Goldman 1983 62–63, 229–231. See also Bloch 1974 58–60 and 1975 45–64, 93–112, 141–161, 163–183, 185–203; Tambiah 1985 128, 132, 140; Zumthor 1990 126–140; and Kennedy 1998 ch. 4.

19. See, for example, Johnson 1982 199–200, n. 10.

20. Finnegan 1977 26, 118, 214–243.

21. Ong 1982 64–65, 78, 141.

22. See Meschonnic 1982; Attridge 1982 76–82, 285–315; Gregg 1984 106; Zumthor 1990 210–223; and Katz 1996 135–219. See also Burke 1968 29–45, 124–183, and 1973 1–137.

23. Rapoport 1979 217; see also Tambiah 1985 142, 145.

24. Bloch 1974 60–71.

25. Finnegan 1977 212–213, 242–243.

26. Tambiah 1985 155, 165–166.

27. Kennedy 1998 66–68.

28. Strathern 1975, Turton 1975.

29. Jennings et al. 1985 24, 27, 116. See also Chafe 1961 147–148 and 1993; and Hale 1883 in Tooker 1985 1: 51–58.

30. See Fenton in Jennings et al. 1985 4–7, 16–20, 28–30, 105–106, 111. See also Michelson 1980 26–40.

31. Goldman 1983 248–252.
32. Comaroff 1975 150–152.
33. Goldman 1983 228; Keenan 1975 97–99; and Turton 1975 174, 181.

2. *The Emergence of* Poiêsis, Logos, *and* Rhêtorikê

1. Starr 1986 69–74, 80–100; see also Havelock 1963; Solmsen 1975; Hansen 1987 and 1989, Starr 1990; and Meier 1990. Behind much of this thought lie Werner Jaeger's *Paideia* (vol. 1), and Bruno Snell's *The Discovery of the Mind in Greek Philosophy and Literature*. Newer perspectives, which usefully complicate the picture, are offered by Ober 1989, Jarratt 1991 1–61; Enos 1993; McGlew 1993; Cohen 1995; Harris 1995; Poulakos 1995 11–52; Ober and Hedrick 1996; and Yunis 1996.

2. Burke 1969 35–37.

3. My use of the term "literaturization" is obviously indebted to George Kennedy's influential discussion of *letteraturizzazione*, a term that Kennedy in turn adopts from Florescu 1971; see Kennedy 1980 4, 108–119.

4. Gentili 1988 3.

5. Gentili 1988 50.

6. Gentili 1988 32–36; De Romilly 1985 27, 228–229.

7. Nagy 1990a 17–51, 414–437. See also Edmonds 1931 1–31 and DeRomilly 1985 27–38.

8. The term "lyric," of course, was not in use during this period: it is a later, Alexandrian invention that applied originally to melic verse sung to the lyre but in modern usage has come to include not only melics but also elegiacs and iambics, or indeed any poem that is relatively short. I take up this topic in chapter 6.

9. De Romilly 1985 27.

10. Gentili 1988 61–62. See also Nagy 1990a 436–437.

11. Meier 1990 87–89; De Romilly 1985 47–48; and Nagy 1990a 382–413. On Sophocles' *Philoctetes* and Euripides' *Hecuba*, see also Kastely 1997 chs. 4–5.

12. On "modernism," see De Man 1983 142–165.

13. Nagy 1990a 19–30.

14. The image of "song" in those poems, however, may be only a conventional metaphor referring back to the old aoidic tradition, and in any case the shift to "spoken" delivery was probably incipient in *iambos* and *elegeia* from the start: Archilochus, for example, is credited with inventing the *parakatalogê*, an iambic delivery style "characterized by reduced rather than full melody" (Nagy 1990a 27), sometime in the mid–seventh century.

15. De Romilly 1985 48.

16. Nagy 1990b 29–31 and 1990a 36; Peabody 1975 30–31.

17. Nagy 1990a 46–47.

18. On this development, see Havelock 1982 180–181, 190–201, 369–391, and 1986 79–116; Thomas 1989 15–34 and 1992 52–73, 96–99 and Nagy 1990a 21–22.

19. Thomas 1992 72–73, 91, 119, 127, and 65–73, 88–127 generally; Thomas 1989 55; and Havelock 1982 198–201. See also Scribner and Cole 1981, which reports a four-year study of literacy among the Vai people of Liberia, and casts doubt on the notion of a special literate consciousness emerging with literacy acquisition in a formerly oral culture.

20. Ong 1982 78; Havelock 1986 109–110.

21. Freeman 1966 55, 457; Diels and Kranz 1951–1954 83, 89.

22. See Havelock 1982 234–236, 248–249, 240–242, 246.

23. Obviously, this position is close to that of Havelock 1963 concerning Plato's attack on poetry. My position here, however, is not that "philosophy" opposes "poetry" (as in

Havelock) but that a newer kind of "philosophical poetry" is in competition with an older one.

24. Thomas 1992 104, 111, 125; Havelock 1982 20–24, 148; Nagy 1990a 217–218. Here, and in this extract from Gorgias, I present both transliteration and translation in order to make the rhythmic structure of the style more visible; the original text, of course, is conventionally printed as continuous lines and paragraphs of prose.

25. Translation based partially on Kennedy, in Sprague 1972 48–49. Greek text transliterated from Diels and Kranz 1951–1954 285–286. See also Buchheim 1989 70–73. The bracketed phrases are hypothetical reconstructions (provided in Diels and Kranz) of gaps in the surviving text.

26. See Kerferd 1981 29 and Sprague 1972 35, 94–105.

27. Nagy 1990a 221–224.

28. The complete list of "older sophists" in Diels and Kranz 1951–1954 consists of Protagoras, Xeniades, Gorgias, Lycophron, Prodicus, Thrasymachus, Hippias, Antiphon, and Critias, plus the anonymous fragments known as the *Anonymous Iamblichi* and the *Dissoi Logoi*. The Diels-Kranz "canon," with the addition of Euthydemus of Chios, is available in English translation in Sprague 1972. As for the centrality of Protagoras, Gorgias, and Isocrates in histories of "sophistic rhetoric," see for example Conley 1990a 4–7, 17–20; Barilli 1989 3–6; and Kennedy 1980 25–36. If one were to include a fourth "central" figure it would most likely be Antiphon.

29. Russell 1981 118; Kennedy 1980 6–9. The *empeiria/technê* distinction is the basis of Kennedy's distinction between what he calls "traditional" and "conceptual" (or conceptualized) rhetoric.

30. See Schiappa 1991a 39–59, 209–210; Cole 1991 2, 121; and Jarratt 1991 13. In fact, the only known fourth-century use of the term *rhêtorikê* outside of Plato and Aristotle occurs in Alcidamas's *On the Sophists;* but, as Schiappa argues, this use in all probability postdates Plato's *Gorgias*.

31. Schiappa 1991b 5–8; Kerferd 1981 24; Anderson 1990 92, 103–104; Bowersock 1969 12–14; De Romilly 1975 11–15, 76–77. See also De Romilly 1992 and Poulakos 1995.

32. Anderson 1990 93–94, 96. As Anderson notes, Greek terms ending in *-ikê* have the resonance of modern English formations ending in "-ology."

33. Cited passages in Sprague 1972, 45–46, 51–53, 62.

34. Sprague 1972 3; Schiappa 1991a 126–127, 146–148. Brian Vickers, of course, has read the *Protagoras* as an unfair demolition of the famous sophist, but he also sees the portrait of Protagoras as accurate enough to be recognizable and plausible for Plato's audience (otherwise, of course, the demolition would not be credible or persuasive). Plato's intent is undoubtedly to show Socrates to advantage, but Vickers's reading may also be a bit extreme: we must take into account the possibility of some ironic distance between Plato and Socrates, Socrates' occasional boorishness in his interchanges with the older and more famous sophist, the generosity of spirit that is clearly accorded to Protagoras, the fact that *both* speakers get their positions turned around, and the evident respectfulness and friendliness with which they end their inconclusive dialogue. See Vickers 1988 121–128. On Plato's sometime sympathies and agreements with Protagoras, see De Romilly 1992 200–202.

35. Schiappa 1991a 56–59, 160–162; see also Jarratt 1991 31–62.

36. See Conley 1990 17, 22–23, 29–31; Schiappa 1991a 43 and 1995; Too 1995; and Poulakos 1997. See also Clark 1957 5–10; Jebb 1893 vol. 2 433; Norlin 1928–1929 1.xxix; and Kinneavy 1982.

37. For discussion of differences, see Kerferd 1981 68–82; Conley 1990a 5–7; Schiappa 1991a 64–85, 209–210, 1991b 8–10; De Romilly 1992 30–133; and Poulakos 1997 5–25. It is not clear to me that all the contrasts asserted between the presumed teachings of individual

sophists are sustainable by the available (and rather fragmentary) evidence, but there is no doubt that there were contrasts, some of them quite fundamental. Likewise, and as Schiappa in particular suggests, it is less than clear that the currently fashionable view of the sophists as emancipatory, democratic/liberal populists disseminating an "oppositional" mode of discourse to the masses is sustainable, though it might be true for a number of individual sophists. Most of the sophists that we know anything about were closely linked to the cultural and political elite. On the political philosophies of the sophists, see De Romilly 1992 213–233. On the social position and political connections of the sophists in later antiquity, see Bowersock 1969.

38. Schiappa 1991a 160; Clark 1957 146. See also Aristotle, *Sophistical Refutations* 33. 183b36.

39. Sprague 1972 241–270.

40. Russell 1983 1–20 and Kennedy 1963, 172–173. See also Clark 1957 213–261 and Clarke 1953 7, 17–21, 85–99.

41. See Cole 1991 chs. 5–6. This means that the supposedly lost *technê* of Isocrates may in fact be the surviving corpus of his writings. See Cahn 1989 and Too 1995 164–167.

42. On the term *rhêtôr*, see Schiappa 1991a 41 and Hansen 1987 50–69 and 1989 1–127.

43. Hansen 1987 55.

44. Hansen 1987 53, 56, 62–63; Arthurs 1994.

45. Hansen 1987 60, 66–69; Kennedy 1963 57–58. It is worth noting that *sykophantês* did not quite have the modern meaning of "sycophant": the literal meaning of the term is "one who brings figs to light," that is, by shaking the tree, and when applied to blackmailers and hired-gun accusers means something like the modern term "shakedown artist."

46. Schiappa 1991a 43. The surviving text of *Against the Sophists* is generally regarded as a fragment—so it is possible that Isocrates went on to use the term *rhêtoreia* in the rest of his argument. But for arguments that the text may be complete as it stands, see Cahn 1989 and Too 1995 151–199.

47. On the date of the *Gorgias*, see Dodds 1959 18–30.

48. Schiappa 1991a 40–48.

49. Schiappa 1991a 162–166; see also Kastely 1997 29–78 and Kerferd 1981 59–67.

50. Phaedrus's values and motives are different—for, as he tells Socrates, he would rather be eloquent than rich (228a). This fascination with beautiful *logos* is what qualifies him as a candidate for *philosophia*.

51. For an argument that the real target of the *Gorgias* is Isocrates, see Schiappa 1991a 45.

52. Kennedy 1991 4–6, 301.

53. On the meaning of *antistrophos*, see Green 1990.

54. On *ekklêsia*, *boulê*, *dikasterion*, and Areopagus, see Hansen 1987 14–19, 35–39, 119–120, 180 n. 687, 190 nn. 765, 771. See also Meier 1990 83, 146–148.

55. By way of comparison, consider Jürgen Habermas's notion of the "ideal speech-situation" as a model for rhetoric. See Habermas 1979 and 1984–1989. For summary and discussion of Habermas's position, see also Foss, Foss, and Trapp 1991 and Norris 1992 134–137.

56. Kennedy 1991 310–311.

57. See Garver 1994.

3. Hellenistic Rhetoric

1. Bowersock 1969 16; see also 10, 45, 58, 59–75, 116–117. See also Russell 1983 and 1990 and Anderson 1990 and 1993.

2. Notably, this spot is the scene of the final, elegiac chapter of Kennedy 1980.

3. Kennedy 1980 86.

4. Kennedy 1980 86–90, 1963 264–336; Russell 1981 3–4.

5. Clarke 1953 10–12; Kennedy 1972 3–71.

6. That is, the "Ten Attic Orators"—Aeschines, Andocides, Antiphon, Demosthenes, Dinarchus, Hyperides, Isaeus, Isocrates, Lycurgus, and Lysias—whose works were canonized as classics sometime between the third century B.C. and the second century A.D. For a discussion of this canon and its probable date of inception, see Worthington 1994a.

7. For examples of such documents, in translation, see Bagnall and Derow 1981; Austin 1981; and Burstein 1985. Cook 1962 191–195 cites and discusses some bylaws of the city of Pergamon, which were preserved in a stone inscription discovered in 1901, regulating roadway maintenance and the property rights of adjoining houses. For an account of the speeches reported in Polybius, see Kennedy 1972 32–37.

8. Brief overviews of Hellenistic rhetoric (and of the paucity of available evidence) are provided by Kennedy 1980 87–88 and Conley 1990a 29–33. For greater detail see also Kennedy 1963 264–336, 1972 114–126, 1989 200–219, and 1994 81–101, and Grube 1965 103–149, 193–206. On Cicero's teachers, see also Kennedy 1972 101–106. An English translation of what remains of Philodemus's treatise on rhetoric is available in Hubbell 1920; the Greek text is available in Sudhaus 1964 (a facsimile reprint of Sudhaus's original 1892–1896 three-volume edition).

9. Demetrius of Phaleron is mentioned as a student of Theophrastus in Diogenes Laertius's *Lives of the Philosophers* 5.39 and other sources; see Fortenbaugh et al. 1992 1: 66–69. The Demetrius of *On Style* may actually be Demetrius of Phaleron but may also be a later Peripatetic scholar at Alexandria with some connection to "the Phalerian" (if these were not the same person). On this point see Kennedy 1963 284–286 and Grube 1961 22–23, 39, 52–56. Conley 1990a 48 judges Grube's date of around 275 B.C. "hard to refute." On Ptolemy Soter and Demetrius, see also Smith 1974 2–4, 10–12.

10. On the *Rhetoric to Alexander*, see Rackham 1957 261–262 and Kennedy 1963 114–123. On *De Inventione* and the *Ad Herennium* and their Hellenistic sources, see Kennedy 1972 103–138. On the authorship of the *Ad Herennium*, see Caplan 1954 vii–xiv.

11. Usher 1985 translation. As it happens, Dionysius—who is a proponent of "Atticism" as opposed to "Asianism"—has a low opinion of Hegesias, whom he describes as the "high priest" of contrived style (4), a judgment he supports with a scathing critique of a passage from Hegesias's *History of Alexander* (18). Dionysius seems to regard Hegesias's contrivance as stemming from "ignorance" or from the provincial sensibility of the colonial Hellene or the Hellenized "barbarian" exaggeratedly emulating models that are really foreign to him. It seems highly probable that the eventual triumph of the "Atticists" in ancient literary-critical debate—a triumph won, ironically, at Rome—encouraged the nonpreservation of Hegesias's writings and other, once popular "Asianist" texts from this period. See Worthington 1994b 256–259.

12. See Walbank 1981 60–78. See also Fraser 1972 1: 101–102 and Samuel 1983 105–117, 119–122. Skopas of Aetolia turns up in Polybius 13.1–2, 16.18–19.

13. Athens, for example, was fully independent for a brief period under Demetrios Poliorketes I (307–294 B.C.), and even under Macedonian hegemony the city still could go its own way: in 200 B.C., King Philip V of Macedon besieged the city, unsuccessfully, for siding with Pergamon and Rome against him (Livy 31).

14. On Hellenistic city politics, see Cook 1962 180–199; Hansen 1971 179, 187–190, 202–203; Fraser 1972 1:93–99, 107–115; Smith 1974 2–3; Billows 1990 259–260; and Lund 1992 113–115, 138–140. For a general overview, see also Walbank 1981 chs. 5–8.

15. On Hellenistic royal administration, see Hansen 1971 189–199; Fraser 1972

1:101–107; Samuel 1983 105–117; Billows 1990 243–256, 268–285; and Lund 1992 178–182. For a general overview, again, see also Walbank 1981.

16. On rhetoric in Hellenistic education, see Conley 1990a 29–32; see also Marrou 1956 142–204; and Clark 1957 59–66. As Cook 1962 notes (p. 185), "[t]he Hellenistic cities maintained a regular establishment of paid teachers" who taught in the public gymnasia; some of these would have been rhetoric teachers. On this point, see also Harris 1989 129–146.

17. Rackham 1957 261. The major sources for this description of Anaximenes are Quintilian, *Institutio* 3.4.9, and the passage from Dionysius here cited.

18. Rackham 1957 261–262.

19. We can guess that the whole pretense of a book of instructions "from Aristotle to Alexander," combined with the "letter-writer's" bogus exhortations to prevent the book's being passed around and its lessons retailed by people like the "so-called Parian sophists," were meant to serve at least two other suasive functions: (1) to make the book, and the school lessons that went with it, seem worth the price; and (2) to discourage secondary resale of the book in order to maximize the publisher's (and the school's) profits.

20. Notably, Anaximenes/"Aristotle" says in his "letter" (1421a–b) that the lessons he will offer have been derived from two main sources: "the treatise that I wrote for Theodectes," meaning probably Aristotle's now lost *Theodectea* or possibly the also lost *Synagôgê Technôn*, a compendium of earlier sophistic *technai*; and a book by Corax, one of the two sophists of the fifth century B.C. reputed to have first taught a *technê* of speaking in law courts and political assemblies. On Aristotle's *Synagôgê Technôn* and the *Theodectea*, see Kennedy 1991 293–294, 243. In the *Rhetoric*, Aristotle cites the *Theodectea* when he is discussing the periodic style (3.9. 1410B) and he repeatedly cites examples from Theodectes' tragedies when he is discussing the "common topics" of enthymematic argument (2.23).

21. See Kennedy 1963 273–274 and Fortenbaugh et al. 1992 1:120–123 and 2:508–513.

22. These are the major headings used by Fortenbaugh et al. 1992. The estimate of 225 treatises in the Theophrastian corpus (Fortenbaugh et al. 1992 2) is based chiefly on the list of works given by Diogenes Laertius in *Lives of the Philosophers* (5.42–50), who also says Theophrastus's books "amount to 232,850 lines" (5.50). Some of these books must have been written by students or assistants under Theophrastus's supervision. It is worth noting here that both Aristotle and Theophrastus, in an effort to collect and systematically organize all available knowledge in the arts and sciences they studied, amassed a sizable library that was the forerunner of the great libraries of Alexandria and Pergamon; see Wycherly 1978 227.

23. For an overview, see De Romilly 1985 166–190.

24. On Hellenistic literacy, see Harris 1989 116–129, 325, 329; and Toohey 1994 163–164. On Alexandrian poetry, see Bing 1988 10–48, 56. See also Johnson 1982 96–98, and Davison 1962.

25. See Kennedy 1963 283. Demosthenes' famous declaration is widely repeated in antiquity, but probably the most widely available sources in English translation are Cicero, *De Oratore* 3.56.213, and Quintilian, *Institutio* 11.3.5–6. Of course, if Demosthenes visited Theophrastus's door, as reported in the pseudo-Lucian's *Encomium of Demosthenes*, then Theophrastus may actually be the source of the famous quip; see Fortenbaugh et al. 1992 1:71.

26. Quintilian's main discussions of this topic can be found in *Institutio* 10.7, 11.2–3.

27. Kennedy 1963 208–209, 262–263.

28. It is true that the *Ad Herennium* does seem at times to be training its student mainly for declamation exercises, fictional practice cases, but in early first-century Roman education the whole point of such exercise was realistic preparation for the career of a civic orator, and

especially for the career of a courtroom advocate; see Winterbottom 1982. Not until more than a century later, in the Imperial period, do we begin to hear complaints about extravagant declamation, or about declamation becoming a form of popular entertainment.

29. Hermagoras's division of questions into theses and hypotheses is more fully discussed by Quintilian, *Institutio* 3.5, which is the basis of my discussion here. See also Kennedy 1963 305–306.

30. For fuller descriptions of Hermagorean stasis-theory than I will offer here, see Kennedy 1963 306–314 and Conley 1990a 32–33. See also Nadeau 1959.

31. Kennedy 1963 310 and 1983 83; and Hubbell 1968 346. See also Nadeau 1959 and 1964. It seems at least possible, moreover, that Hermagoras' "negotiative" stasis may have had something to do with consultation on practical matters in "private discussions," as in a *synedrion*—where, in fact, juristic questions were a common preoccupation.

32. See Trimpi 1983 14–79, 243–348, for an extended discussion of the applications of stasis theory to poetics.

33. See Kennedy 1963 318, 320. On the lack of system in ancient Greek jurisprudence, see Frier 1985 130–131, and Gagarian 1986 145.

34. See Hubbell 1920 267, 269, 274, 284, 345, 348, 352–354, 356, 357, 359, 362. The relevant Greek fragments appear in Sudhaus 1964 vol. 1 9 col. 5, 19 col. 1, 50 col. 23–24, 122–123 col. 22; vol. 2 190–191 fr. 1, 209 col. 6, 234 col. 35, 241–243 col. 40–41, 245–246 col. 42–44, 256–257 col. 3a–4a, 261 col. 7a, 272 col. 15a–16a, 289 fr. 13a–b; suppl. 11–12, 61. On Philodemus's poetics, see Grube 1965 127, 193–199, 240–241; Kennedy 1989 204, 206, 216–217; and Greenberg 1990 274–276.

35. These were early prose writers, chiefly of the sixth century B.C.; Pherekydes of Samos was a cosmologist; Kadmos and Hekataios of Miletus were historians; Hermogenes (*On Types of Style* 2.12.411) says that Herodotus "learned much" from Hekataios's style, and improved on it.

36. On Neoptolemus and Eratosthenes, see Kennedy 1989 204, 205–206; and Grube 1965 127–128, 240–241.

37. It is often presumed that Philodemus is forcing his account of rhetoric onto Epicurus, though he does in fact cite, and sometimes quote, passages from Epicurus's *Peri Rhêtorikês* that indicate that Epicurus identified *rhêtorikê* with the sophistic practices of speechwriting, declamation, and panegyric, and that he considered it to produce *psychagôgia* in its listeners. Where Philodemus most probably departs from Epicurus—and finds himself at odds with Epicurean orthodoxy—is in his argument that sophistic is a genuine *technê*, or one worth learning or of possible benefit to the *polis*.

38. On Theophrastus's students, see Fortenbaugh et al. 1992 1: 1, 66–71. On Polybius, see Kennedy 1972 32–37; and De Romilly 1985 186–190. On the philosophers' embassy to Rome—they petitioned successfully for remission of a fine that had been levied on Athens (for pillaging Oropus, in Boeotia)—see Kennedy 1963 322 and 1972 53–54, 71; and Rackham 1977–1979 3: 310n. On the Scipionic circle, see Kennedy 1972 60–71. The key political figures in this circle were the younger Scipio—Publius Cornelius Scipio Aemilianus Africanus, the destroyer of Carthage—and his close friend, Gaius Laelius Sapiens; the principal literary figure was the comic dramatist Terence.

39. Anderson 1993 18–19. Hybreas and Potamon are mentioned in the Elder Seneca's *Controversiae* and *Suasoriae,* and in other sources; see also Bornecque 1902 172, 192. Philostratus the Egyptian—not to be confused with the more famous, later Philostratus who wrote the *Lives of the Sophists*—appears in Philostratus's *Lives* 486, and in Plutarch, *Life of Antony* 80.

40. Hubbell 1920 329, 356; Sudhaus 1964 2:46 (col. 45.33), 2:256–258 (col. 3a–col. 4a). Note that in Sudhaus's transcription of the original (and badly damaged) Greek text,

and in Hubbell, the open-quote following "Epicurus says" is not followed by any corresponding close-quote; it is impossible to say with certainty where Epicurus leaves off and Philodemus begins.

4. *"Rhetoric" from Cicero to the Second Sophistic*

1. In a letter of the following year, and in another of 45 B.C., Cicero claims that *De Oratore* was written in the manner of Aristotle's dialogues: see *Ad Familiares* 1.9.23 and *Ad Atticum* 13.19.4.

2. See Shackleton Bailey 1971 1–8; Lacey 1978 7–8; Mitchell 1979 1–6; and Fuhrmann 1992 4–9. The prime source for any and all accounts of Crassus's and Antonius's involvement in Cicero's boyhood education is Cicero's introduction to the second book of *De Oratore* (2.1.1–5).

3. On the series of events from the Gracchan reforms to Sulla's dictatorship, see Grant 1978 169–189. On Cicero's relation to these events, see Shackleton Bailey 1971 9–12; Lacey 1978 8–12; Mitchell 1979 11–41, 52–92; Fuhrmann 1992 13–18; and Rose 1995.

4. For a detailed account of this development, see Gruen 1984; see also Rostovzeff 1964 vol. 2. On the Roman assimilation, appropriation, and revision of Greek rhetoric, see Enos 1995.

5. Kennedy 1972 40, 55–56, 90–94, and 1994 107, 111, 115–116.

6. Lacey 1978 5–6.

7. Lacey 1978 14–15; Mitchell 1979 90–92; Fuhrmann 1992 27–29.

8. Lacey 1978 5–6; Bauman 1985 1–3; Bauman 1989 6–10; Frier 1985 127–128, 130–135, 157–163; Fuhrmann 1992 9–10.

9. Fuhrmann 1992 19–20; Enos 1995 15–38.

10. Frier 1985 131, 237, 251; see also Lacey 1978 6.

11. Bauman 1989 8–10.

12. For discussion of those problems, see Konstan 1993 22–23 and Rose 1995. See also Carter 1972; Crawford 1978; and Wood 1988.

13. Kennedy 1972 209–230. See also Hubbell 1914 and Solmsen 1941.

14. Leff 1986 313–318.

15. Concerning Theophrastus on rhythm, music, and prosody, see Barker 1985 and Fortenbaugh 1985b and 1994.

16. The usual view of Cicero's poetry has been, of course, that it was "mediocre" (Shackleton Bailey 1971 ix). However, as W. K. Lacey points out, "Plutarch says that Cicero's contemporaries rated him the best poet as well as the greatest orator. There is probably some exaggeration here; we know that some of his lines were made fun of in his lifetime, and that he gave up poetry after the age of forty-five or so; but we should not underestimate his contribution to Latin poetry" (1978 8). It's important to remember that Catullus, Horace, Propertius, Virgil, and Ovid all wrote after Cicero, and that Cicero was in effect a transitional figure for Latin verse. Manfred Fuhrmann describes him as "a precursor of Catullus and his circle" (Fuhrmann 1992 7). Little of Cicero's poetry survives, but it seems to have dealt mainly with Greek themes, as Fuhrmann says, in the manner of Hellenistic poetry; we know that in his youth Cicero published a tetrameter poem entitled *Pontius Glaucus* ("The Sea-God Glaucus"), which Plutarch mentions, and a Latin hexameter translation, of which 480 lines survive, of Aratus's philosophical epic the *Phainomena* (Fuhrmann 1992 7, 23–24). In the *Pro Archia Poeta*, of course, Cicero describes Archias as his poetry teacher. See Plutarch, *Cicero* 2.3–4.

17. See Kennedy 1972 239–258.

18. On Roman funeral discourse, see Ochs 1993 chs. 5 and 6.

19. This and the following anecdote of Heliodorus are discussed by Millar 1977 234; on Alexander Peloplaton's eventual appointment as *ab epistulis Graecis*, see also 91.

20. Wright 1921 308.

21. Aelius Aristides' *Monody for Smyrna* and his *Letter to the Emperors Concerning Smyrna* are extant (as the title suggests, the letter was addressed to both Marcus Aurelius and his coemperor Commodus), as are a great many of his writings; for translations, see Behr 1981 2:1–9. It is possible that by "monody" Philostratus means simply the letter, which incorporates most of the topoi from the *Monody*, and which contains the particular line that Philostratus quotes.

22. Behr 1981 2:361.

23. See Bowersock 1969; Russell 1983; Brown 1992; and Anderson 1993.

24. Millar 1981 52.

25. See Millar 1977 18–24, 59, 209–210, 275–278, 341–355; Jones 1964 1:321–322, 1:329–333.

26. See Millar 1977 3–6, 11, 60–61, 110–122; Jones 1964 1:333–341, 1:366–373, 1:563–606.

27. In the West, this means roughly the fifth century A.D.; in the east, of course, the empire survived in its Byzantine incarnation until the mid–fifteenth century. But in the reconfigured Byzantium that emerged from the disasters of the seventh century, the processes of feudalization shifted power to local military aristocracies with vast agrarian estates, whom the emperors at Constantinople had to deal with more or less as equals and could not always control. On Roman provincial administration, see Millar 1981 60–69, 79–80, 81–103; Millar 1977 251–252, 363–464; Braund 1988a and 1988b; Reynolds 1988; Jones 1964 1: 373–377, 406–410, 712–766; Brown 1992 9–30. On Byzantine provincial administration, see Maksimovic 1988; Kamer 1986; and Carney 1971.

28. Millar 1977 203–207.

29. Brown 1992 30–70; see also Bowersock 1969.

30. On imperial correspondence, see Millar 1977 203–274, 328–341, 537–550, 556–565.

31. See Farnsworth 1996.

32. Kennedy 1972 437 and 1994 194.

33. Kennedy 1972 435 and Garnsey 1970 5–6.

34. Millar 1977 61–66.

35. On the development of Roman law and legal studies under the emperors, see Millar 1977 3–4, 228–240, 466–467, 507; Bauman 1985; Honoré 1981 1–53; Jones 1964 1:470–522; and Frier 1985 286–287.

36. On the differential effects of social status in Roman law, see Garnsey 1970 and Jones 1964 1:516–522.

37. Kennedy 1972 437–442; Garnsey 1970 39–50; Bauman 1989 61, 105–106.

38. Kennedy 1972 442.

39. Winterbottom 1964 90.

40. Millar 1981 20.

41. Kennedy 1972 444–464 and 1994 186–189; Anderson 1990 99.

42. On the (mostly indeterminate) date and authorship of *On the Sublime*, see Fyfe 1973 xxi–xxii.

43. Brink 1989 473–482.

44. All these titles are from the Elder Seneca's *Controversiae*, tr. Winterbottom 1974 translation. On Greek declamation, see Russell 1983; on Roman declamation themes see also Winterbottom 1982.

45. Sinclair 1995 122–146; Winterbottom 1982.

46. Seneca the Elder, *Suasoriae* 7.

47. Brink 1989 480–482.

48. Kennedy 1972 465–481.

49. Afer's defense of Cloatilla, probably on *maiestas* and related charges—which Quintilian does refer to, if obliquely—may be a relevant model here; see Marshall 1993.

50. Kennedy 1994 182.

51. See, for example, Baldwin 1924 87–102; Vickers 1988 47; Barilli 1989 33; and Kennedy 1980 112–113, 1994 190–191. On the (long-disputed) date of the *Dialogus*, see Murgia 1985.

52. Syme 1958 2:670.

53. This assertion appears as early as Baldwin 1924 94, for example, and turns up again in Vickers 1988 47.

54. On Messalla and Quintilian, see Brink 1989 484–494.

55. Kennedy 1972 487–489, 492, 518, 523, 526.

56. Peterson and Winterbottom 1980 240 n. 1, 246 n. 1. Both figures are discussed in Tacitus's *Histories* (2.10, 53, 95; 4.6, 10, 41–42) and *Annals* (12.4; 13.33; 14.28; 16.22, 26, 28, 33).

57. Sinclair 1995 140–141.

58. Grant 1978 285–289.

59. Syme 1958 2:670–673.

60. Grant 1978 293–302.

61. It is not known who Curiatus Maternus really was, or even whether he is fictional, though it is perhaps worth noting that Dio mentions a certain "Maternus the sophist" being put to death by Domitian in 91; see Syme 1958 2:798–799.

62. See Conley 1990a 41; I am not persuaded, however, that Tacitus regrets that the Quintilianic version of the Ciceronian ideal is no longer possible under the principate, as Conley seems to argue.

63. On prosody and pathos in ancient theory, see Walker 2000 and Fortenbaugh 1985b and 1994.

64. The text is available in English translation, in the Loeb series, as *In Defence of Oratory*—a misleading title, since "oratory" cannot adequately translate *rhêtorikê* as Aristides uses it.

65. While there is a considerable surviving body of Aristides' writings, it represents only a fraction of his output, which apparently included over three hundred thousand lines to the god Asclepius; see Behr 1973 xv–xvi. There is also a *technê rhêtorikê* falsely ascribed to him, though the ascription suggests that he may have composed such a text, which is now lost. Aristides' surviving major writings—including forty six "oratorical" texts (speeches, letters, literary *logoi*) and the *Sacred Tales*—are available in translation in Behr 1973 and 1981. It should be added, here, that although Aristides did participate in politics through, for example, his letter to Marcus Aurelius and symbouleutic speeches to city assemblies, he repeatedly and successfully undertook lawsuits to resist appointments to public office—"liturgies," which were civic duties the officeholder undertook at his own expense (such as, for example, road maintenance) and thus were a form of taxation. Like most of the great sophists of his day, Aristides presented himself chiefly as an intellectual and literary figure and, in his devotion to the god Asclepius and in his prose hymns, as a religious figure also.

66. After Aristides, by the late third or early fourth century, hymns to deities seem to have become one of the standard divisions of epideictic prose, as can be seen in the fragmentary treatise(s) of "Menander Rhetor"; see *Menander Rhetor*, and Russell and Wilson's

introduction to their 1981 translation of this text. For the *Sarapis*, see Behr 1981 2:261–268 and 2:419 n. 1. Aristides' defense of prose hymns in *Sarapis* 1–14 is available also in Russell and Winterbottom 1972 558–560; for commentary, see Russell 1990b 199–219.

67. Although there is more or less universal acceptance of this biographical outline, there is also some doubt whether Philostratus's boy declaimer is the same Hermogenes who wrote the treatises: Philostratus makes no mention of Hermogenes' rhetorical treatises, and says that he lost his rhetorical powers on reaching manhood, that is around age sixteen, and "ended in advanced old age" (*eteleuta . . . en bathei gêrai*) accounted as "one of the many" (*eis de tôn pollôn nomizomenos*). It is possible that "advanced old age" is sarcastic, and—along with Philostratus's nonmention of Hermogenes' treatises and the relegation of him to "the many"—is the dismissive gesture of rivalry. Hermogenes' canonic status as a rhetorical authority was not established until the fifth century; his main competitor was Minucian, a now forgotten but then important figure who taught at Athens and would have influenced the sophists under whom Philostratus studied; Hermogenes, on the other hand, in Philostratus's time was influential mainly at Rome, Antioch, and Alexandria. See Kustas 1973 5–10.

68. Despite the fact that he was the chief rhetorical authority for the Byzantines, for a period of over a thousand years, and was then transmitted from Byzantium to the Renaissance—thus exerting a continuous influence much greater than that of Quintilian—there has been surprisingly little study of Hermogenes. (Nor, for that matter, has there been much study of the Byzantine rhetorical tradition.) For brief overviews of Hermogenes' career and extant writings, see Nadeau 1964 363–388; Kennedy 1972 619–633, 1980 164–166, and 1994 208–217; Wooten 1987 xi–xviii, 131–140; and Conley 1990a 54–59, 70. See also Kustas 1973; Kennedy 1983; and Conley 1990b. On Hermogenes in the Renaissance, see Patterson 1970 and Monfasani 1983. For translations of Hermogenes' *On Stases* and *On Types of Style*, see Nadeau 1964; Wooten 1987; and Heath 1995.

69. I am using the page numbers of Rabe 1913, on which Wooten's translation is based.

70. Wooten 1987 xi–xii, xvii, 133.

71. Wooten 1987 142–143 n. 15.

72. The standard source on the recovery of "Longinus" and theories of "sublimity" in the eighteenth century still is Monk 1935.

73. Tatum 1979 114.

74. All collected in the Teubner editions of Helm 1912–1931 and Moreschini 1991. *The Golden Ass* is currently available in numerous translations, including Lindsay 1960 and Gaselee 1971 (a Loeb reprint of Gaselee's 1915 revision of Adlington's translation of 1566); the *Apologia* and *Florida* are available in Butler 1909/1970; and the *Logic* (*Peri Hermêneias*) is available in Londay and Johansen 1987. *The God of Socrates* may be found in the anonymously translated 1869 *Works of Apuleius*.

75. See Butler 1909/1970 13–14.

76. Londey and Johanson 1987 37.

77. Toward the end of the final book of *The Golden Ass*, the hero, who suddenly becomes identified as "a native of Madaura" (though he begins the novel as a Greek), finances the cost of his stay at Rome by practicing as an advocate in the law courts (11.27–28); this reference is often taken as autobiographical.

78. Apuleius and Pudentilla seem, in fact, to have had a fruitful relationship. The fifth-century writer Sidonius describes them as one of the great literary couples in history (*Letters* 2.10.5), and from Apuleius's address to "my son Faustinus" in *On Plato* (2.1) it appears that he and Pudentilla produced at least one child (unless Faustinus was simply a disciple or student of Apuleius).

79. On the quarrels of sophists in this period, see Bowersock 1969 89–100.

80. On the matter of keeping or not keeping slaves, it is worth noting that book 9 of

Apuleius's *Golden Ass* contains one of the most powerfully negative representations of slavery in ancient literature.

81. Tatum 1979 112.

82. [N]un de hôs katêgoroi hêmôn kakoêtheis se anapeithousin, aiphnidion egeneto Apoleios magos, kai egô memageumai hup' autou kai erô. Evidently Apuleius's accusers have read out only the latter part of the sentence, beginning from *Apoleios magos*, which in isolation could be read as "Apuleius [is] a magician."

83. See Brown 1992. See also Bowersock 1969; and Anderson 1993. See Kennedy 1983 180–325 for a survey of Christian orators and rhetoricians in the late Roman and Byzantine empires from the third to the fifteenth centuries.

84. Schiappa 1995; Clark 1996; Poulakos 1997; and Atwill 1998 19–20, 27–28, 44–45, 58–59, 127.

85. Cohen 1995 38, 46.

86. See Cohen 1995 25–33, 34.

87. Translation of Smith 1919–1935.

88. Admittedly, this formulation applies chiefly to relations with other Greek *poleis*; Isocrates' lifelong dream of "liberating" Asia from the Persians and for the Greeks is frankly imperialistic. Isocrates, of course, invariably portrays the Persian Great King as unjust, morally corrupt, and wishing to extend his domination of the Asian Greek *poleis* to all of Greece, so that a PanHellenic campaign against the Persian empire would be an assertion of Greek rights.

89. See Poulakos 1995 53–73, which focuses on the notions of antilogy, *kairos*, and "the possible" as central to sophistic rhetoric as it emerged in the fifth to fourth centuries B.C.

90. Russell 1983 21–39; see also Anderson 1990 110.

5. Theognis's Octopus

1. On the dating of Theognis and the *Theognidea*, see Cobb-Stevens et al. 1985 1 and Nagy 1985 46–51. The verses of the *Theognidea* apparently refer to events as early as 640 B.C. and as late as 479; there seem to be no verses composed later than the fifth century B.C. There also are some verses in the collection ascribed to pre-Theognidean poets, suggesting that the "original" *Theognidea* may itself have been a compilation, consisting perhaps largely of Theognis's own verses but including also elements from a preexisting Megarian symposiastic tradition.

2. Lewis 1985 197; West 1974 43–45.

3. See Nagy 1979 301–304, 1990a 79–80, 363, 435–436, and 1996 chs. 1–4 and Miller 1994 9–36.

4. Figueira 1985a, 1985b. As Figueira notes, the dates for political events in archaic Megara are vague. Interestingly, and as Figueira also notes, there are some reasons to believe that comedic drama may have originated at Megara during its democratic period.

5. See McGlew 1993. On the tensions between oligarchic and populist (or "elite" and "middling") factions and ideologies in Greek *poleis* during this period, see also Morris 1996. The Athenian movement toward democracy can be understood as beginning with Solon's constitutional reforms, around 594–593 B.C., and culminating in the reforms of Ephialtes, the so-called "birth of democracy," around 462–461.

6. Translation of Levi 1979. Megara today is a modest and rather dull agricultural town off the side of the Athens-Corinth superhighway, just beyond the outskirts of the heavy industrial zone of Athens.

7. Nagy 1985 (see especially 41–46); Morris 1996 26, 37. In Theognis, see also, for example, 39–60, 145–148, 173–178, 183–192, 219–220, 279–292; 315–318, 363–370,

393–398, 797–800, 1081–1082, 1109–1114. Concerning Solon, see Aristotle's *Athenian Constitution* 5.

8. [E]*thos* and *thymos* are, respectively, neuter and masculine nouns, thus requiring the neuter and masculine forms of the adjective *poikilos* (*poikilon/poikilos*).

9. Gentili 1988 132–133; see also, more generally, 3, 115–154.

10. On defining "rhetoric" as an art of adapting discourse to its audience, see Perelman and Olbrechts-Tyteca 1969, 23–26 and Perelman 1982 13, 21.

11. See, for example, Theognis 309–315.

12. The basic meaning of *mythos*, according to Liddell and Scott, is "anything delivered by word of mouth"; it can be used to signify a speech made in an assembly, talk or conversation, advice or counsel, the subject matter of a speech, a resolve or plan, or a saying or proverb, as well as a rumor, legend, or story. Clearly, as Theognis is not a poet who tells stories but a gnomic poet who offers what Isocrates calls "suggestions needful for living," the sense of *mythos* in the *Theognidea* is closer to "speech" or "piece of advice."

13. It is worth noting here that Theognis's term for "judgment" is not *krisis*—the term that Aristotle will use in the *Rhetoric*, two centuries later, to signify the action of a "judge" (*kritês*) in response to an orator. Theognis's term is *gnomê*: judgment, the giving of opinion, the exercise of intelligence or thought. As he says at one point, "Gnomê, Kyrnos, is the finest thing gods give to mortal / men; *gnomê* holds the ends of everything" (1171–1172). In "Hearken to me, child," this exercise of judgment in response to persuasion is figured, significantly, as depending on the need to "discipline your wits," *damasas phrenas*. *Phrenas*, or *phren*, which literally signifies the "midriff" of the body as well as "heart" and "mind," is also the root of *phronêsis*, which typically signifies practical intelligence or judgment, and is Aristotle's term for "prudence." *Damasas*, interestingly, derives from the verb *damazô*, which means to "tame" (e.g., horses), "subdue," or "gain mastery over." In short, though his terminology is slightly different, Theognis, much like Aristotle after him, considers an exercise of judgment/*gnomê* in a rhetorical encounter to be, as well, as exercise of *phronêsis* grounded in the dispositions of a disciplined, skillful body. Just as Demonax must develop a *poikilos thymos* to manage the complexities of public life, young Kyrnos must train his *phren*.

14. Again, probably a Byzantine editor around 900 A.D.: Lewis 1985 197; West 1974 43–45.

15. On pederasty and *paideia*, see Lewis 1985. Such relations seem likely to have been common between older and younger upper-class females also. On aristocratic Greek female homoeroticism in early antiquity, as represented in the poetry of Sappho, see duBois 1995 7–15.

16. It is worth noting too that Pindar's word here for "persuasions," *parphamena*, is the same word that Hesiod uses in his "Hymn to the Muses" when he speaks of the people in assembly as "persuaded with gentle words," *malakoisi paraiphamenoi epéessin* (*Theogony* 1. 90). The root word is *paraphêmi*, which means to entreat, speak gently, persuade, advise, or speak deceitfully (*para-phêmi*, "speak-beside").

17. Sappho 1. See, again, duBois 1995 7–15; and Nagy 1996 97–100.

18. Nagy 1985 54–56; Nagy's discussion informs both this and the following paragraphs. See also Cobb-Stevens 1985.

19. See also, for example, Theognis 93–128.

20. Nagy 1985 41–46, 54.

21. I am using "narration" here in the sense of Paolo Freire's *Pedagogy of the Oppressed*, when he says that education suffers from "narration sickness" insofar as it reduces the didactic process to a monologic enumeration of facts, truths, principles, and so forth, treated as a body of information to be "deposited" in the student, who is in turn conceived as an empty receptacle. See Freire 1993 ch. 2.

22. See Walker 2000.

23. See Russell 1983.

24. Butler 1993 10; see also, more generally, 1–26.

25. On competition in archaic Greek poetry, and on the role of its audience as judge, see also Griffith 1990.

26. Translation is Kemp 1987 172.

27. Long 1992 44–45; Browning 1992 134, 137.

6. Lyric Enthymemes

1. Gentili 1988 3. As Gentili notes (3–4), much of this was noted as early as 1900 by Jacob Burckhardt but was mostly forgotten or ignored by subsequent critics of ancient poetry until fairly recently—as the shift inaugurated by Elroy Bundy's *Studia Pindarica* in the early 1960s did not really gather significant momentum until the 1980s. See Bundy 1986 (orig. 1962) 35; Johnson 1982; Kurke 1991; Miller 1994 1–8, 78–100; and Stehle 1997.

2. On the enthymeme in Aristotle and in ancient rhetorical theory, see Bitzer 1959; Delia 1970; Grimaldi 1972 53–82 and 1980; Boss 1979; Green 1980 and 1995; Gage 1983 and 1991; Conley 1984; and Walker 1994.

3. Plutarch credits Archilochus with inventing (among other things) the "spoken," recitative delivery set to musical accompaniment, and with being the first to alternate such delivery with singing (*Music* 28).

4. Miller 1994. This argument runs through the entire book, but see in particular 1–8, 52–76, 120–140. See also Cameron 1995 46.

5. Indeed, as Cameron 1995 makes abundantly clear (71–103), even the symposiastic performance or recital of epigrammatic poetry tended to be a competitive game, in which each turn-taker attempted to "cap" or outdo the verses of the person who had gone just before; this practice apparently continued at least through the Hellenistic period and probably into late antiquity. See also Griffith 1990.

6. Miller 1994 9–36.

7. Miller is, in short, overturning the view whose classic statement is Bruno Snell's *The Discovery of the Mind in Greek Philosophy and Literature;* see Snell 1982 (orig. 1953).

8. That is, the controlling mythologies shift from those of traditional religion and folklore to something like what Roland Barthes has called mythologies: the ideological paradigms and stereotyped scenarios by which human beings structure and interpret the "stories" of their own and others' lives. See Barthes 1972; see also Kermode 1968. On conventionalized types of Hellenistic women embodied in the poems of Asclepiades, see Cameron 1995 494–519. On lyric as framed within an assumed or tacit narrative, see Nathan 1986.

9. On Solon, see McGlew 1993 87–123 an Anhalt 1993. On Propertius's elegies, see Turner 1976; Radice 1985; and Stahl 1985.

10. It is likely, however, that Propertius's Cynthia was not wholly fictional, if we can believe Apuleius's statement (*Apologia* 10) that "Cynthia" was a pseudonym for a real woman named Hostia.

11. Corinna's defeat of Pindar is mentioned in Pausanias 9.22.3; Plutarch *Glory of Athens* 4; Aelian *Miscellaneous Histories* 13.25; Suidas *Lexicon;* and elsewhere; the testimonia are collected in Campbell 1992 18–25. The extant account of the "contest between Homer and Hesiod" dates from around 140 A.D. but appears to be based on an earlier life of Homer by the sophistic Alcidamas of the fifth-century B.C.; see Evelyn-White 1914 xli, 566–597, 625–627.

12. On such traditions, see Nagy 1990a and 1996; for a theoretical frame that helps to explain the development of rhapsodic traditions around an original or "founding" poet's

name and discourse, see Foucault 1977. It is not necessary, of course, that the name of the "founding" poet be "real." Rather, the name—Homer, Hesiod, Archilochus, Theognis, and so on—can just as well be a performance name, the name of a discourse that successive generations of performers reenact and even continue to develop.

13. And, as Finnegan 1977 shows, such limitation is not really characteristic of poetic discourse in the oral-traditional societies that modern, ethnological scholarship actually has been able to observe.

14. Indeed, as Morris 1996 32–35 suggests, Sappho speaks for the newer values of a "modern" seventh-century aristocracy that is far removed from "the brutal heroic age" and is coming to define itself in terms of cosmopolitan, "orientalized" refinement and luxury consumption. On value-hierarchies and argumentation, see Perelman and Olbrechts-Tyteca 1969 80–83.

15. See Rankin 1977 (esp. 1–9, 36–46, 74–84), who argues that Archilochus both represents a number of traditional, archaic values and undercuts or satirizes others, thereby presenting a distinctive, sometimes controversial *êthos* in agonistic tension with received traditions.

16. On ludic gaming and competition, see Lanham 1976 1–35.

17. For reconsiderations of orality and "primitive" thought, see, again, Finnegan 1977; Scribner and Cole 1981; Tambiah 1985; and Thomas 1992.

18. On early Greek law, see Gagarin 1986 and 1992. On classical Athenian law, see Todd 1993; Cohen 1995; and Foxhall and Lewis 1996.

19. As suggested by the famous Dipylon jar, which bears the earliest known Greek inscription (c. 720 B.C.)—"who now of all the dancers sports most playfully"—the dancers may have been competing too; for the jar with its clumsily scrawled inscription appears to have been awarded as a casual prize during a celebration of some kind in a private household. Havelock 1982 192–194 and Robb 1994 23–32.

20. There are historical instances of this sort of procedure in the archaic period, though in different contexts. As McGlew 1993 points out, for example, in 479 B.C. the tyrant Gelon of Syracuse—after winning an impressive victory over the Carthaginians—appeared before the Syracusan popular assembly "unarmed . . . and nearly naked," narrated an account of his achievements, and then proposed that he be removed from power. As McGlew says, "Gelon certainly intended to be shouted down, and the Syracusans did not disappoint him: in response to his offer to quit, they proclaimed him in a single voice their 'benefactor, savior, and king'" (137). The chief account of this episode appears in Diodorus 11.26.5–6.

21. Harold Bloom's now largely passé notions of the "anxiety of influence" and of poetic *agôn* are probably relevant here, though with Bloom these notions are generally framed within a poetics (or rather a psychoanalysis) of romantic subjectivity, which generally leaves out of consideration the poet's audience and occludes the notion of the poet's discourse as a rhetorical transaction with that audience. Bloom's poet seems to work out an Oedipal struggle in pristine solitude, in a private psychodrama. The archaic poet's agonistic differing with other (contemporary and traditional) voices is more a matter of public competition with those voices *for the attention and assent* of audiences and patrons, in order to with both reputation and a paying clientele. See Bloom 1973 and 1982.

22. This is, of course, an extremely brief general outline of the theory of argumentation presented in Perelman and Olbrechts-Tyteca 1969; see also Burke 1969 on "identification." Both theories remain extraordinarily fruitful as basic analytic frameworks and remain in my opinion unsurpassed (but see the more recent work overviewed in van Eemeren et al. 1996). For a recent restatement of this general framework, shifted into the vocabulary of poststructuralist philosophy and "performativity" theory, see Butler 1993 107, 241.

23. I do not mean to suggest, however, that the possibilities are unlimited. The value sets (or "ideologies"), social practices, and power arrangements already in place will make some "unconventionalities" more possible—more arguable—than others and will make others not only impossible to argue for (under a particular set of conditions) but also completely impossible for all participants even to conceive or enunciate (insofar as the conceptual grounding and/or the discursive operations necessary for such imagining and enunciating are not available); see Foucault 1972.

24. The notion of Homeric or Hesiodic epic as a master composition synthesized from shorter, "lyric" elements (as I am using that term) is of course traditional; probably the most forceful and copious contemporary argument for such a view is given in Nagy 1990a and 1996.

25. Peabody 1975 31. See also Dumézil 1943 56–80, 230–237; and Miller 1994 27–28.

26. Havelock 1982 150–165 offers an extended critical review of Peabody's argument (though Havelock mostly concentrates on Peabody's account of the evolution of the Greek hexameter, which does not concern me here); see in particular 163–164. I am not convinced, however, that Havelock's objections concerning chronology necessarily invalidate Peabody's most basic claims. Indeed, Havelock's suggestion that Homeric epic may be the most basic form of poetry, from which other genres derive, seems highly improbable insofar as it requires us to postulate the sudden appearance *ex nihilo* of a highly elaborated, complex, massively compendious epic poetry, followed by the development of shorter, simpler forms.

27. The best discussion of such framing commentary in extended narrative still is that of Booth 1983.

28. See Fish 1972 5–21, on Plato's *Phaedrus* as a "self-consuming artifact" that works by moving through a series of argumentative positions, each one in turn destabilized and displaced by its successor. Behind Fish's notion of "self-consuming artifacts" lies Kenneth Burke's much earlier notion of "psychology and form"; see Burke 1968 29–44, 123–183.

29. Miner 1990 7–7, 34, 83. See also Welsh 1978.

30. Miner 1990 235–236.

31. Miner 1990 234–235.

32. See Woodman and West 1984. See also, for comparison, the accounts of the political functions of early Japanese lyric provided by Levy 1984 and Marra 1993.

33. Culler 1988 292, 297–298.

34. See, for example, Winters 1957; Graff 1970 and 1979; Pinsky 1976 and 1987; Gage 1981; and Kertzer 1988. Some of these challenges, and that of Winters in particular, have taken the form of insisting that (lyric) poetry is an "exposition" of *statements* which must be judged by rational and moral criteria; this is not quite the same as explicitly treating lyric poetry as argumentation.

35. Hardy 1977 1–2.

36. Altieri 1984 19–21, 33. See also Altieri 1990 and 1992, where these ideas reassert themselves, and where lyricism and even art in general are thought of as, in essence, modeling or expressing forms of subjectivity; again, this is not the same as *arguing*.

37. Bernstein 1986 413–414, 360, 77; see 61–86, 217–236. See also Bernstein 1992 and the essays collected in Bernstein 1993, which, while not addressing this topic as explicitly as Bernstein 1986, nevertheless remain within (and more or less tacitly assume) the general position that the function of poetry is to resist, deconstruct, or speak outside of the prevailing structures of rationality; the idea that lyric poems might advance particular arguments for the reader's judgment remains largely outside the bounds of acceptable possibility.

38. The latter of these two problems is discussed at length in Graff 1970; see especially 13–17, 61–64, 112–137. My view differs from Graff's, however, in that Graff—working in

the tradition of Yvor Winters—tends to view the "argument" in a poem as a matter of an internal logic consisting of "ground-consequent" relations, the truth-value of which can be "objectively" assessed. The central problem with this formulation, from a rhetorical point of view, is that it leaves *audience* out of account.

39. Bernstein 1986 221, 228.

40. On the problems of contemporary identity politics, see Butler 1993 111–119. On closed-circuit rhetoric in modern poetry, see also Walker 1989a chs. 8–9.

41. See, for example, Bitzer 1959, which is the *locus classicus* for almost all contemporary notions of the enthymeme in rhetorical studies. See also Delia 1970; Grimaldi 1972 53–82; Miller and Bee 1972; Boss 1979; Green 1980 and 1995; Gage 1983 and 1991; Raymond 1984; and Conley 1984. Grimaldi, Conley, Gage, and Green have most informed the position that I take in Walker 1994 and that I will, with modifications, be taking here. For "Toulmin argument," see Toulmin 1958.

42. Green 1995.

43. Bitzer 1959; see also Gage 1984.

44. Quandahl 1986 133.

45. Green 1990 27.

46. See for example, Grimaldo 1972 69–82.

47. Compare *hôn enthymêthentes*, "being mindful of these things," Thucydides 1.42.1; or, from the funeral speech of Pericles, *enthymoumetha orthôs ta pragmata*, "we consider aright the facts," Thucydides 2.40.2

48. See Conley 1984; Raymond 1984; and Green 1995.

49. Grimaldi 1972 69. On the composition and original audience(s) of the *Rhetoric*, see Brandes 1989, 1–9 and Kennedy 1991 299–305.

50. Fortenbaugh 1975, 12–14, 17–18, 26–32, 57; Walker 2000.

51. For modern analogues to this account of emotion, see Solomon 1976; de Sousa 1987; and Tomkins 1991 3–108. For the notion of "intentionality" I am using here, see also Searle 1983.

52. Kosman 1980.

53. Miller and Bee 1972.

54. As I have noted before, the *Rhetoric to Alexander* is in fact a post-Aristotelian text, composed probably in the last quarter of the fourth century B.C., but is widely regarded as embodying earlier, fourth-century sophistic teachings, in part because it shows little or no Aristotelian influence.

55. Grimaldi 1972 67–82; Conley 1984.

56. On "identification," see Burke 1969 17–29, 55–59.

57. Perelman and Olbrechts-Tyteca 1969 115–120, 144–148.

58. On "adherence," see Perelman and Olbrechts-Tyteca 1969 1–44, 49–54, 104–110.

59. Conley 1984 171.

60. Grimaldi 1972 82.

61. Raymond 1984.

62. Grimaldi 1972 147–151 and 1980 349–356; Fortenbaugh 1975 11–18; and Conley 1982. Wisse 1989 20–29 presents a counterargument. The debate is summed up in Kennedy 1991 123. My views appear more fully in Walker 1992 and 2000 and are presented in condensed form here (and hereafter).

63. Kennedy 1991 123.

64. Walker 1992 and 20000.

65. As Aristotle notes in *Nichomachean Ethics*, the "conclusion" or will to act that arises from conflicting "premises" in the psyche will be determined by the "premises" that exert

most "energy" at the moment of decision (7.3 1147a; see also *Movement of Animals* 6 700b, 7 701a).

7. A *"Truest Paradigm for Western Lyric"*

1. Bloom 1979 10, 17, 20. Clearly, Bloom has an extremely reductive notion of the origins and history of rhetoric as well.

2. The best generally avaiable English translations of Pindar's odes are Lattimore 1976 and Race 1997: but see also Nisetich 1980, Bowra 1969, and the creaky Loeb Classical Library translation of Sandys 1919.

3. There has been some controversy, of late, over the specific circumstances and nature of epinician performance, most specifically regarding whether the poems were in fact performed chorally or by an individual singer (Pindar or a proxy) within the context of a *kômos*. In general I have retained what was in antiquity and still is now the predominant view, namely that the poems were performed by a *choros,* in the midst of (and as participants in) a *kômos,* though it is possible that some may have been performed by solo singers. Certainly, the poems could be and at later times probably were reperformed by individuals in symposiastic settings. See Slater 1984; Heath 1988; Lefkowitz 1988; Burnett 1989; Heath and Lefkowitz 1991; Carey 1989 and 1991; Kurke 1991 3–5; and Stehle 1997 16–17.

4. *Hestiasis* derives from *hestia,* "hearth/household/dwelling" or "altar/shrine," and from the verb *hestiaô,* "to receive at one's house, to entertain, to give a feast for some special occasion" (such as a marriage). A "public *hestiasis*" probably would take place at a shrine or some other civic or ritual space. The Olympian crown was a wreath of wild olive leaves; the Pythian crown was of bay leaves; the Isthmian crown was of celery; and the Nemean of dry celery.

5. Slater 2984 244–246, 246–247.

6. Heath 1988 191–192; Heath and Lefkowitz 1991 191.

7. Krummen 1990 33–94; discussed in Stehle 1997 56–57.

8. We should perhaps restrict this heterogeneous audience to male citizens, though it is not impossible that women would also have been present. Some of Pindar's odes for young victors (though not this one) make references to their desirability as candidates for marriage, suggesting that at least one aspect of a victory celebration could have involved the "presentation" of marriageable young people from (and to) the "best" families, as did—in other contexts—the performances of *parthenia* (processional "maiden-songs"); see Stehle 1997 30–39.

9. Kurke 1991, especially 257–262, from which the argument of most of this paragraph derives: Burnett 1987 and Goldhill 1991 108–166 offer similar lines of argument. See also Rose 1992 142–165, for a brief but very useful discussion of Pindar's relation to his social and political context.

10. It is worth noting that the so-called birth of democracy at Athens, marked by the tranference of sovereignty to the people's assembly (the *ekklêsia*), took place in 462–61 B.C. less than two decades after Melissos's double victory, when Pindar was about fifty-six years old. For discussion of these developments, see Ober 1989 and Ober and Hedrick 1996.

11. Kurke 1991 59.

12. It is worth remembering that the chief events at the great Panhellenic athletic festivals involved displays of what were mostly old-fashioned battlefield skills: horse and chariot racing; boxing, wrestling and pankration; discus and javelin (i.e., hurling rock and spear); and foot races, including races in full armor.

13. Kurke 1991 260; see also Gentili 1988 55–56.

14. Mullen 1982 3–45; Gentili 1988 115–154.

15. According to Stehle 1997 22–25, the scant information we have about the personnel for choral performances, especially in important public settings, and especially in the archaic period, suggests that the choreuts (*choreutai*) usually were nobles. Such performances gave the prominent a way to stage themselves as the leading, representative voices in and for the whole community.

16. Gentili 1988 162–163; Pindar's commission from the Athenians is reported in Isocrates, *Antidosis* 166.

17. Mullen 1982 167.

18. Todd 1993 197.

19. We probably should not, however, think of this exchange simply as "buying" and "selling" in a modern sense. As Kurke 1991 7–9, 166–167, points out, to project a modern, capitalistic model of market exchange or wage-hire onto archaic economic practices is anachronistic; Pindar's (and other poets') payment needs to be considered within the context of traditional systems of aristocratic gift exchange, guest-friendship, and so forth. Mapping the various economic practices within which Pindar's poetry is embedded is the burden of much of Kurke's book. On early Greek literary patronage, see also Gold 1987 15–38.

20. Rose 1992 151–173.

21. Rose 1992 158.

22. Rose 1992 151; Finley 1968 41.

23. Burnett 1987.

24. Stehle 1997 3–70 develops this basic point at length; concerning "psychological efficacy," see 19.

25. By "the *êthos* of the *polis*" I mean, of course, what the audience will recognize as such; since the citizen audience for public discourse is predominantly (or overwhelming) male-gendered in archaic Greek culture, "the *êthos* of the *polis*" is presumptively defined as male and freeborn—an identity that marginalizes the less fully "free male" identities of the poorest citizens, while excluding women and slaves. However, the notion of communal identity may shift somewhat, depending on the nature of the actual audience and occasion for any given type of performance. See Stehle 1997 30–39, 71–119.

26. Mullen 1982 41–42; Kurke 1991 5. The ode inscribed in golden letters was probably *Olympian* 7, which celebrates the voctory of a Rhodian boxer, one Diagoras, whose father Damagetos is also praised as "pleasing to Justice" (*hadonta Dikai*).

27. McGlew 1993 61–74.

28. Mullen 1982 164. Lucian wrote in the second century A.D.

29. The contemporary understanding of the function of mythical "digression" in Pindar derives, of course, from Bundy's *Studia Pindarica*. See also Carey 1981; Johnson 1982 24–75; Mullen 1982; Segal 1986; Burnett 1987; and Race 1990 141–164.

30. Bloom 1979 17.

31. Himera was a city on the north coast of Sicily. The joint glory of Gelon, Hieron, and their two other brothers (Polyzelos and Thrasyboulos) is celebrated in an epigram attributed to Simonides, which, according to the Pindaric scholia, was inscribed on a votive tripod at Delphi (the base of which may have been found); an apparently mutilated version of the epigram appears in the *Palatine Anthology* (6.214). See Molyneux 1992 221. Hieron would later win a great victory of his own over the Etruscans, in 474 B.C. in a naval battle at Cumae (Diodrus 11.51.1–2). Pindar celebrates the battle of Himera in another and later ode for Hieron, *Pythian* 1 (72–80), composed in 470.

32. Mullen 1982 167; see 164–184 for Mullen's detailed explication of *Olympian* 1.

33. This kind of city pride is reflected in an inscription (on a helmet, now in the British Museum) which commemorates Heiron's voctory over the Etruscans ("Tyrrhenians") at

Cumae: *Hiarôn ho Deinomeneos kai toi Syrakosioi tôi Di tyrran' apo kumas*: "Hieron the son of Deinomenes and the Syracusans [dedicate] to Zeus Tyrrhenian [spoils] from Cumae."

34. Kurke 1991 134, 135–162.

35. 1992 173, 182–183. Rose's chief theoretical frame for this argument is Jameson's distillation of Frankfurt school aesthetics (1971); See also Eagleton 1990 on the "ideology of the aesthetic," especially 366–417. For a treatment of Pindar that responds to Rose's deployment of a Jamesonian "double hermeneutic," see Segal 1986 123–152.

36. Rose 1992 183, 184. For Rose, this transcendent aesthetic power also makes Pindar more acceptable for modern readers living under the fragmented cultural regime of "late monopoly capitalism" (183).

37. Translation is Lattimore 1976 1.

38. Pausanias 5.7.1–3.

39. Pisa was the district around Olympia and was incorporated into the larger state of Elis.

40. Mullen 1982 166. As Mullen puts it, Syracuse—which had been founded about three hundred years before Pindar's time— was a sort of "New York" to mainland Greece's "Europe."

41. The games were thought to have been founded, originally, by Hercules, and according to Pausanias (5.8) were later held by Pelops, but were forgotten for some period of time and were not reinstituted as a regular Panhellenic festival until 776 B.C. (the starting point of Greek historical chronology). Pausanias also says (5.13) that Pelops was the chief hero worshiped at Olympia. Kurke 1991 133–134 suggests that the Pelops myth provided an *aition*, or origin story, for the horse-racing events at Olympia, and that the games (or at least the horse-races) may have been instituted as commemoration of the marriage of Pelops and Hippodameia. The name *Hippodameia* means sdomething like "Horse-taming."

42. Atreus outmaneuvered his brother Thyestes to gain the throne of Mycenae and subsequently killed Thyestes' sons and served their flesh to him at a banquet. Thyestes revenged himself by impregnating his own daughter, Pelopia, and then marrying her to Atreus; she gave birth to Aigisthos. Atreus was later succeeded by his son Agamemnon, who was murdered by his wife Klytaimnestra (in revenge for sacrificing their daughter Iphigenia) and by Aigisthos, who in turn were murdered by Orestes, Agamemnon's and Klytaimnestra's son. At this point, according to the *Oresteia*, the tragic cycle of blood revenge is ended through Athena's intervention and the creation of civil law. Atreus's other son, Menelaos, married Helen of Troy, from whom proceeded the disasters of the Trojan war.

43. In Xenophon's dialogue *Hieron*, Hieron denies (to his interlocutor Simonides) that the life of a tyrant is pleasant, and includes among his reasons an argument that "[m]any have slain their own children; many have themselves been murdered by their children; many brothers, partners in despotism, have perished by each other's hand; many have been destroyed even by their own wives, aye, and by comrades whom they accounted their closest friends" (*Heiron* 3.8, translation of Marchant 1968). While this statement is fictional and is meant to portray "the tyrant" as a general type, one wonders how much of the actual life Hieron of Syracuse is being "cited" here.

44. Mullen 1982 1709–172.

45. Pausanias, writing about seven centuries after Pindar, says (5.13.4–7) the miraculous shoulder bone had by his time crumbled away and disappeared but once had been of amazing size: before arriving at Olympia, it was lost in a shipwreck (off Euboia) and many years later was brought up in a fisherman's net and eventually reidentified by the Delphic oracle; Pausanias thinks the time the bone spent underwater was the cause of its decay.

46. Pausanias 5.7.1–3. The Alpheos-Arethusa link appears to have been part of Syra-

cuse's foundation-myth: it was revealed (says Pausanias) by the Delphic oracle as part of a command to Archias of Corinth to establish a new colony (Syracuse) on Ortygia.

8. Argumentation Indoors

1. For both Alcaeus and Sappho, I am using the Greek text provided in Campbell 1982; all my citations of fragments and testimonies follow Campbell's numbering. The epigraphs appear as Alcaeus testimony 20 and Sappho testimony 20.

2. On the images of Sappho perpetrated by male writers in antiquity (and after), see Gubar 1984; De jean 1989; Williamson 1995 5–33; and Stehle 1997 262–288. For a provocative reinterpretation of Sappho's place in the history of sexuality, see du Bois 1995 127–145.

3. Russell 1981 6.

4. The first of Alcaeus's ten books of poetry appears to have been devoted to hymns. See Campbell 1982 fr. 306C–311. For discussion of Alcaeus's hymns and heroic narratives, see Page 1955 244–290.

5. Stehle 1997 213–215, 264–265; Campbell 1982 fr. 160 and 142. *Hetaira* could also be taken to mean "courtesan" or prostitute, a sense that seems to have been applied to Sappho in at least certain strands of the biographical tradition, beginning probably with satiric portraits in Attic comedy (we know of several comedies whose titles included her name, all of them now lost). But Athenaeus, writing in the third century A.D., says that "even today free women (*eleutherai gynaikes*) and young girls (*parthenoi*) call their intimates *hetairai*, just as Sappho did" (*Deipnosophistai* 13.571d). "Small gathering" means, as Stehle remarks, about fourteen to twenty-two participants, as these are the numbers that could be accommodated by the traditional size and layout of the dining-rooms in which symposia were held.

6. Trapp 1997 xi–lv.

7. Likewise, as Havelock 1982 11 suggests, the "proto-intellectuals" who gathered at the courts of tyrants in the sixth and early fifth centuries were poets—such Pindar or Simonides at Heiron's court, or the poets that Pisistratus brought to Athens—but by the later fifth and early fourth centuries were sophists.

8. Burnett 1983 107–108.

9. Page 1955 243; quoted in Kurke 1994 67–68. In antiquity, however, Alcaeus was often viewed as a proponent of "liberty" or opposition to tyranny; see Campbell 1982 test. 7, 21.

10. For a fuller account, see Burnett 1983 107–120, to which my brief account is chiefly indebted; and Page 1955 149–243. See also Campbell 1982 xiii–xvii.

11. Page 1955 149; the translation here is Page's.

12. As Burnett 1983 109 n. 13 points out, the name Smerdis (which seems not to be an aristocratic name) may be evidence of a popular revolt against the Penthilids—or, more likely, of such a revolt being used by one or more of the noble clans as a means to seizing power.

13. Page 1955 177; Kurke 1994 76–77. *Damos* is the same as *dêmos*. As Kurke argues, the *damos* that Alcaeus speaks of is an increasingly wealthy landholding citizenry not limited to nobles—the *damos* who, in the seventh century, would assemble in the agora to hear the judgments and decrees of the *basileus* and aristocratic council.

14. McGlew 1993 79–81, 95–97. On Pittacus's popularity, see also Kurke 1994 90–92.

15. Page 1955 179–197; Burnett 1983 151–155; Gentili 1988 197–215.

16. Words appearing in brackets represent the conjectural restorations accepted in Campbell 1982 for damaged parts of the Greek text; suspension points represent parts of the Greek text lost beyond restoration. In some cases I have followed the readings of Lobel-Page 1955 and Page 1955.

17. Campbell 1982. See also fragment 306C(c), a second-century (A.D.) papyrus scrap from a badly crumbled commentary on Alcaeus, which also declares fragment 208 to be about Myrsilos.

18. Page 1955 179; Campbell 1982 fr. 114. Pyrrha was located on the opposite (western) side of Lesbos from Mytilene.

19. The allegorical nature of Alcaeus's "ship of state" poems is also recognized in a few bits of commentary preserved in papyrus fragments. See Campbell 1982 fr. 306.

20. Burnett 1983 156–181; Stehle 1997 216–218.

21. Gentili 1988 199, 202–203, 213–214; see also Kurke 1994 concerning Alcaeus's use (and violations) of traditional high poetic diction.

22. Page 1955 184–185.

23. Tradition says, of course, that Lycambes, who broke his oath with Archilochus—a marriage-contract in which he had promised his elder daughter to the poet—was driven to suicide, with his daughters, as a result of the damage that Archilochus did to their reputation. Even if we accept the notion that "Lycambes" may be a fictive name for a type, it seems likely that Archilochus had a target whom he was attacking through that figure, and that the story about a suicide may have some basis in actual events. See Miller 1994 9–36. It does appear, moreover, that there was an actual Lycambid family on Paros. See Rankin 1977 47–56.

24. Page 1955 210–223. See also Burnett 1983 124–126.

25. "Kronos's son" would be Zeus.

26. Campbell 1982 fr. 38A n. 2.

27. Translation of Campbell 1982. Fragment 38B consists of about one word each from five sequential lines and a single letter from a sixth.

28. On the archaic ideology of *habrosynê*, see Kurke 1992.

29. Page 1955 278–281.

30. Burnett 1983 190–198.

31. Burnett 1983 200.

32. See Page 1955 171–174 and Stehle 1997 234–237. In fragment 70, Alcaeus says "let [Pittacus], married into the family of the Atreidae, devour the city as he did in company with Myrsilos" (tr. Campbell); the Penthilidai claimed descent from the Atreidai—via Penthilus, the son of Orestes, the grandson of Atreus.

33. Page 1955 281.

34. Kurke 1994 90–92 comments on Alcaeus's alienation from and relative ineffectiveness with "the Lesbian *damos*, his intended audience and community."

35. For readings of this remarkable poem, see Page 1955 198–209; Burnett 1983 176–181; and Stehle 1997 230–234. The identities of Agesilaidas and Onomakles are unknown, though perhaps it is enough to recognize that Agesilaidas ("Leader of the people"?) is the poem's addressee and that Onomakles is an example of wretchedness in exile.

36. The chief sources for my rather brief discussion here are Page 1955 140–146; Burnett 1983 209–228; Williamson 1995 103–109; and Stehle 1997 262–278. On women's festivals in the ancient Greek world, see also Farnell 1896–1909; Detienne 1977; Burkert 1985; and Kraemer 1992.

37. Williamson 1995 105.

38. Stehle 1997 118.

39. It should be noted, however, that this "compulsory permission" had limited force, since only another man could prosecute the man who refused to pay for his wife's participation.

40. Stehle 1997 71–118.

41. Stehle 1997 32.

42. A perfumed oil; Campbell 1988 fr. 3 n. 6.

43. Campbell 1988 fr. 3 n. 2.

44. Burnett 1983 210–228. Stehle 1997 262–278 usefully complicates and partially refutes this picture in ways that I presently will be agreeing with.

45. Burnett 1983 226. The "consequences that mattered" involved virginity of brides (defined in terms of heterosexual penetration), reproduction, and the paternity of children.

46. Blundell 1995 83; see also duBois 1995 7–15.

47. On girls' names in Alcman's poetry—such as Hagesichora, "Chorus-leader"—see Calame 1995 179–183. For a detailed account of Spartan girl choruses, see also Calame 1977 vol. 2; which Stehle 1997 73–93 modifies.

48. Stehle 1997 73–93 remarks on the ways that Alcman's maiden-songs negotiate the problematics of this role, by having the *parthenoi* disavow the appearance of appropriating to themselves the otherwise "male" public authority and agency that properly belong to the speaker-function that the song projects them into. I am not sure, however, that at least some of these gestures cannot be treated as figures of aporia and aposiopesis that ultimately function as hyperbolic praise. One might also compare the chorus-speaker's gestures toward Astymeloisa to Sappho's famous, and similar, gesture in fragment 31—which no one reads as Sappho's avowal of her lack of agency.

49. Page 1955 140–142. On *thiasos* and symposium, see Gentili 1988 72–106.

50. Page 1955 60, 168–169.

51. Williamson 1995 107; see 106–109, 115, 126–128.

52. As Page 1955 60 remarks, there seems to have been a Lesbian version of the Troy-tale, in which Agamemnon—from whom the Penthilids claimed descent—and Menelaus stopped in Lesbos on the way back from Troy and together invoked the aid of Hera for their safe return. See Sappho fragment 17 and Alcaeus frragment 129. Sappho frragment 44 narrates the marriage of Hector and Andromache.

53. Fragment 44A may be part of a hymn to Artemis, though that is far from certain, and the attribution of the fragment to Sappho is itself doubtful.

54. Jarratt and Ong 1995; Swearingen 1995; Glenn 1997 36–49.

55. See Nagy 1990a, 1996.

56. Photius's *Library* does, however, mention "passages from Book 1 of the *Epitomes* of Pamphila, daughter of Soteridas" among the compilations of one Sopater the Sophist, a figure of the fourth or fifth century A.D. (test. 32; tr. Campbell 1982). Whether this Pamphila is a garbled version of Philostratus's Damophyla of Pamphylia—who would have lived a good ten centuries before Sopater, and even longer before Photius—I cannot say. Sopater's compilation apparently included also "Book 8 of Sappho," as well as the *Tales of the Exploits of Virtuous Women* by Artemon the Magnesian. Sopater seems to have been interested in distinguished women of the Aeolic/Ionic and "Asiatic" East Greek world.

57. Or, perhaps, a Deleuzian "rhizome"; see Deleuze and Guattari 1987 3–25.

58. Stehle 1997 283.

59. Williamson 1995 136–140.

60. Williamson 1995 106–107. If Sappho's circle met at her (or someone else's) house during the Adonia—or at any other time—they probably would not have met in the reception/dining room used for men's symposia, the *andrôn* (literally the "men's room"). They more probably would have met upstairs, in the women's quarters, the *gynaikônitis*. (Some of the Adonian activities also took place on rooftops.) If they met elsewhere in the house—such as the ground-floor family room or the central courtyard—they would have been in trafficked areas where other members of the household, including men, and others might come and go. Depending on their location in the house, then, the women at a gathering would have been accessible in varying degrees to male eavesdropping, overhearing, or direct observation, even if men were not explicitly included. I am here following the description of a

typical Greek house, based on excavations of fifth-century structures at Olynthos (near modern Thessalonika), described in Phylactopoulos 1975 2:456–459.

61. Jarratt and Ong 1995 15. Cicero *De Inventione* 1.31 includes an account of a "Socratic" conversation between Aspasia, Xenophon, and Xenophon's wife, from a now lost dialogue by a follower of Socrates named Aeschines. Aspasia was, of course, from Miletus (an Ionian Greek city on what is now the west coast of Turkey), which may suggest an East Greek tradition, going back at least to the time of Sappho, in which women played sophist-like roles with gatherings that could include men as well as women.

62. Nagy 1996 219.

63. Page 1955 26 considers this bracketed phrase, which appears in "Longinus," corrupt. Page also notes that the first part could be read as "[a]ll must be ventured (or endured)," or even "[a]ll has been ventured (or endured)," depending on the remainder of the sentence, which is missing. I have followed Snyder 1997 33 and Irwin 1974 67 in reading *chlôrotera de poias* as "more moist than grass" rather than the more usual "greener than grass."

64. Stehle 1997 288–318.

65. All three images are reproduced and discussed in Williamson 1995 6–7 and figs. 1, 2, 4.

66. In fragment 55, Sappho excoriates an uncultured woman, or perhaps a rival (such as Andromeda), saying that after death she will lie forgotten and unseen in Hades because "you have no share in the roses of Pieria" (tr. Campbell); it seems unlikely that this poem would have been delivered directly to the victim of its rather intense invective; it would have been presented, among Sappho's friends, as an apostrophe. This poem can be understood to promote group solidarity by projecting a blame-figure of "what we are not"; fragment 31 can be understood, conversely, to promote group identity by projecting a praise-figure of "what we love," like Astymeloisa in Alcman's maiden-song.

67. This discussion actually leads into, and introduces, "Longinus's" account of "amplification," *auxêsis*, which in *Peri Hypsous* is the figure of figures for "sublimity."

68. Burnett 1983 233; Stehle 1997 290.

69. In another fragment (44), which narrates the marriage of Hector and "elegant Andromache" (*abran Andromachan*), the scene ends in songs of praise for the "godlike" couple.

70. Burnett 1983 235–238. Burnett says that Sappho's "proof" of this contention is "almost Euclidean."

71. Page 1955 19; Campbell 1982 fr. 31; Stehle 1997 289.

72. Translation of Campbell 1982.

73. Snyder 1997 31–35, 38–44 discusses Sappho's representation of *erôs* as bodily disruption in these and other fragments.

74. Snyder 1997 34–35 notes that Sappho's evocation of "that man" as an "equal to the gods" parallels Odysseus's praise of Nausicaa at *Odyssey* 6.158–161: "That man is blessed in heart beyond all others, / whoever bestows upon you dowry gifts and takes you home. / Never have I seen such a one with my own eyes— / neither man nor woman. Awe takes hold of me as I gaze upon you" (tr. Snyder). Odysseus is, of course, attempting (successfully) to persuade Nausicaa to help him; he has just awakened, shipwrecked and naked, on the beach of Phaeacia. If Sappho's audience recognized this resonance, they would also see Sappho (or the speaker of the poem) in the role of an Odysseus-like persuader, exercising a kind of agency typically gendered as "male" in traditional Hellenic culture.

75. Stehle 1997 293–294, somewhat similarly, sees this poem as foregrounding and affirming the woman's agency, her ability to *present herself* effectively to others rather than be simply an object of their gaze, and so to "define the situation" rather than be the passive object of men's "willful desire."

76. DuBois 1995 163–194 argues that Sappho's poetry makes a case for the culture of

"Asianism" (as it would later be called), which has always stood as a disruptive, troubling "other" to the masculinist, "Atticizing" traditions of Western civilization. On Sappho's "subversion of tradition" and "challenge to the Homeric inheritance," see Snyder 1997 16–17, 63–77.

77. Page 1955 30.

78. Campbell 1982 fr. 55 n. 1; Page 1955 55.

79. Burnett 1983 281–290.

80. Campbell 1988 fr. 396. Campbell attaches a comment on this poem, from Demetrius *On Style* 5, that "the rhythm is exactly like a drunk old man." Campbell notes that the poem is cited not only by Demetrius but also by Athenaeus and appears as well, with a portrait of Anacreon, in a second-century (A.D.) mosaic in Autun; it apparently was widely popular. Cottabus was a game that involved casting the last wine-drops from one's cup at a target.

81. In another fragment (23, from the same papyrus as fr. 22, which bids Abanthis to sing of Gongyla), Sappho explicitly compares a lover (whose name is lost) to Helen: "[for when] I look at you face to face, [it seems to me that not even] Hermione [is] like you, and to compare you to fair-haired Helen [is not unfitting]." It may be that in Sappho's discourse (and perhaps in the discourse of Lesbian women generally) Helen figured as the paradigm of womanly excellence.

82. According to Campbell 1982 fr. 1 n. 1, "[s]ince Hephaestion uses [this] poem to illustrate the Sapphic stanza, it was probably the first poem of Book 1." It was preserved in its complete form by Dionysius of Halicarnassus, who cites it—along with a passage from Isocrates—to illustrate the "polished" (*glaphyra*) or middle style (*On Composition* 23). Both, in short, regard this poem as the embodiment of Sappho's distinctive or typical style. All modern editions of Sappho's poetry accept fragment 1 as poem 1 of book 1 of her verse. On what little is known of the contents and arrangement of the nine books of Sappho, see Page 1955 112–126. There are other examples of cletic hymns in Sappho's remaining fragments, for example. fragment 17, which is a hymn to Hera, but I think it is fair to say that these are not her most characteristic poems.

83. See, for example, the *Homeric Hymns,* many of which (especially though not necessarily only the shorter ones) seem to have had this function; Thucydides (3.104.4) refers to the *Homeric Hymn to Delian Apollo* as a "proëmium."

84. Jenkyns 1982 8–15; Burnett 1983 245–258; Williamson 1995 161–166;

85. My analysis here and hereafter is indebted to Nagy 1996 99–102.

86. Compare Hesiod's self-authorizing account of his encounter with the Muses (*Theogony* 22–35), which is given entirely as a third-person, past-tense narrative: "[a]nd once they taught Hesiod lovely song, as he was shepherding his lambs on holy Helicon," and so on.

87. In the Greek text as edited by Lobel-Page and Campbell as well.

88. The effect is even more extraordinary if Sappho is herself the performer, for when Aphrodite says, "Who, O Sappho, does you wrong?" Sappho as performer is delivering these lines and for the moment ceases to be Sappho: as in mediumistic "possession," Sappho is displaced by the goddess who speaks through her.

89. Page 1955 12–14; Jenkyns 1982 11.

90. To a certain degree, it is not clear that Sappho's voice "returns," since again there is nothing in the poem to clearly mark the transition. It is possible for the listening audience, at a performance, to regard the final strophe as a continuation of Aphrodite's speech or as a fusion of Aphrodite's and Sappho's voices—and as suddenly directed outward to the listeners themselves: *you* come, *you* fulfill my desires, *you* be my ally. These imperatives would then appear as Aphrodite's command *to them* in fulfillment of her promises to Sappho in the preceding strophe.

91. The *locus classicus* for speech-act theory is, of course, the work of J.L. Austin and John Searle, while its most notable recent iteration has been in the work of Judith Butler.

92. Stehle 1997 299 also remarks on this bardic, authorizing move, though she does not address the performative aspect of the poem. See also the discussion of this poem in Snyder 1997 7–25.

93. Page 1955 5. Snyder 1997 10 and 222 n. 5 points out that this is a distinct departure from Homer's usual epithets, such as "laughter-loving." Neuberger-Donath 1969 15–17 points out that *poikilothronos* does not occur elsewhere, while *poikilophronos* does occur in both Alcaeus and Euripides. Tinkler 1990 172–175 argues that Sappho's *poikilothron'* may not be from *thronos*, "throne," but *throna*, "drugs."

94. Page 1955 4–6; Jenkyns 1982 9; Burnett 1983 249–251. It is worth noting too that -*ploke* derives from *plekô*, which can mean not only "weave" (fabric, baskets, etc.) or "braid" (hair) but also to contrive, devise, plot, or complicate.

95. DuBois 1995 9.

96. Translation of Campbell 1988. Anacreon may be giving his thanks to Dionysus, though the text is damaged and the reading is uncertain. If Dionysus has "helped" him to break free of Aphrodite's bonds, he is in some sense "god-assisted," though what he may mean is simply that wine has helped him to forget.

97. Gentili 1988 95.

98. See McCloskey 1996, which offers a similar position. For that matter, see Hesiod at the beginning of *Works and Days* on the good and bad Strifes.

99. Burnett 1983 243 regards this poem as about, in part, the problems of courting "balky and changeable" young girls.

100. Williamson 1995 164–166 raises a similar line of argument.

101. These appear to be the last two lines of the poem; Campbell 1982 fr. 58 n. 3. The Greek text reads, *egô de philemm' abrosynan, . . . touto kai moi / to la[mpron eros tôelio kai to ka]lon le[l]onche*. Campbell reads *abrosynê* as "delicacy." He also regards the meaning of these lines as "uncertain" and conjectures that the sense is "love has kept me alive"; but it seems that *love of luxury* or "elegance," or the *erôs* that "elegance" calls forth, is what has kept the now white-haired Sappho going and indeed has brought her unsurpassable satisfactions.

102. Fragment 137, a dialogue-poem, is cited/preserved by Aristotle (*Rhetoric* 1.9. 1367a) as Sappho's reply to an indecent (or shameful) proposal by Alcaeus; and so it has traditionally been regarded. Modern scholars have doubted the identification of Alcaeus as the male speaker, although "Alcaeus's" speech is the only passage in Sappho's surviving poetry that uses Alcaic rhythm. If modern scholars are wrong, this fragment may be evidence that Alcaeus and Sappho belonged to the same or related groups.

9. *Solon* Sophôtatos

1. Johnson 1982 200. Johnson's definition of "lyric," like mine, does not depend on whether the poetry was actually performed (or meant to be performed) as song with lyre accompaniment; Archilochus is a "lyric" poet in Johnson's account, as are Catullus, Horace, and others whose verse can be regarded as strictly "literary."

2. Johnson 1982 4–5, 30–31, 197.

3. Hansen 1983 no. 28. Cited and discussed in Stehle 1997 315.

4. That is, like Hercules.

5. *Thesmophoriazusae* 528–530; an ancient commentary attributes it originally to Praxilla.

6. See Bing 1988 and Cameron 1995 71–103.

7. By "pious" here I mean not only traditional religious piety but what Kenneth Burke

describes in *Permanence and Change* (while borrowing from Santayana) as "piety"—"loyalty to the sources of our being"—which expands beyond the religious to a general and more or less traditionally determined sense of the proper, or of "what goes with what." See Burke 1984 71–79.

8. Traditional interpretation assumes these women are "hetairas," prostitutes; but Cameron 1995 494–519 suggests that this is not necessarily the case.

9. Simonides 22b in Campbell 1991; see also Page 1975 and 1981. This poem was actually inscribed on the marker of the Spartan grave-mound at Thermopylae; the marker is long gone, but the mound can still be seen.

10. Cameron 1995 20.

11. Nagy 1985 24, 26–29; see also Nagy 1979 238–242.

12. The term here is *leukon,* which can be read either as "white" or "clear."

13. That is, *kalê* and *aethliê* rather than *kalos* and *aethlios,* and *aposamenê* rather than *aposamenos.*

14. Edmonds 1931 259 n. 5.

15. For an illustration of the interpretive puzzles created by the basically elliptical, "coded" rhetoric of epigrammatic poetry, see Cameron's (1995) discussion of "Asclepiades's Girlfriends" (494–519).

16. Stehle 1997 61–63, 257–261.

17. I am following the numbering of Edmonds 1931 and West 1971–1992 and 1993. Unless otherwise indicated, the numberings of Edmonds and West are the same. My translations of Solon are based on the Greek text of West 1971–1992.

18. More literally, Solon says his shield is held or "thrown *over*" both sides; the point of the metaphor is that he has acted as the protector of both sides and the advocate of neither.

19. On the novelty of these images and on the ways they both appropriate and reconfigure Homeric precedents, see Anhalt 1993 124–138.

20. Stehle 1997 261.

21. Cameron 1995 44–46, 64, 78.

22. Anhalt 1993 7.

23. What is known is admirably summed up in Anhalt 1993 1–2. As Anhalt notes, accounts of Solon's life were written by Aristotle, Diodorus Siculus, Plutarch, and Diogenes Laertius—all of them derived, in varying degrees, from texts (or fragments) of Solon's legal code, Solon's poetry, and oral traditions. Of all these accounts Aristotle's is closest in time to Solon, though it is still two centuries removed, while Plutarch's is the fullest.

24. Edmonds 1931 28a; West 1971–1992 and 1993 4a.

25. Plutarch, *Solon* 16.1–2. As Plutarch later says (22.3), Solon—not having the absolute power of a tyrant—made his laws to fit the situation, rather than attempting to force the situation to fit his laws.

26. According to Plutarch (*Solon* 8.4–11.1) Solon won some impressive initial victories, but the war dragged on; eventually the Athenians and Megarians invited the Spartans to arbitrate the dispute. Solon presented the winning arguments and thereby won for himself prestige and prominence in Athenian politics.

27. As J. M. Edmonds's still current Loeb translation has it, "he had secretly written some elegiac verses and conned them till he could say them without book" (Edmonds 1931).

28. Writing was, of course, available to Solon; we know that his laws were preserved in writing, on painted, revolving boards (Aristotle, *Athenian Constitution* 7.1). But we also know that, according to Plutarch, he may have composed them as verses "before he published them"; and Plutarch gives what is purported to be the opening two lines, an invocation to Zeus as protector of laws (*Solon* 3.4). Solon's laws could, perhaps, have been recited like a Hesiodic poem of wisdom-lore. This suggests that Solon was, in some sense, transitionally

literate—still regarding oral composition and performance as the primary medium for significant public discourse, while using writing as a secondary medium of "recording" and preservation.

29. Peisistratus—Solon's younger contemporary and sometime friend—seized power at Athens, first, by inflicting wounds on himself and his mules and then riding into the agora claiming that he had been attacked; by this ruse he persuaded the *dêmos* to grant him a contingent of clubbearers, which he then used to make himself tyrant. Second, after he had lost the tyranny he regained it by staging a procession "featuring a tall country woman dressed to look like Athena and standing in a chariot, which was led by a herald loudly proclaiming that Athena was personally welcoming Peisistratus to her dwelling on the Athenian acropolis" (McGlew 1993 29; Herodotus 1.60; Aristotle, *Athenian Constitution* 14.3–4); according to Aristotle, the Athena lookalike was sufficiently convincing for the *dêmos* to be persuaded. Solon's "mad herald" performance is of a piece with such political theatrics.

30. Anhalt 1993 34.

31. Anhalt 1993 81–101.

32. I am following West's (and Edmonds's) line numbering, which does not include the three missing lines.

33. Anhalt 1993 67–68; see 67–114 for the full discussion.

34. See, for example, *Theognidea* 833–836.

35. *Prudently in balance* translates *artia kai pinuta*, which is not easily rendered. *Artia* can be rendered as "complete, perfect, right, suitable, sound" and suggests things put in their correct condition (a human body that is "sound" is *artia*) or arranged in appropriate and proper relation to each other. *Pinuta* can be rendered as "wise, prudent, discreet, understanding" and suggests being in accord with practical wisdom. So *artia kai pinuta* can also be rendered as "fitting and wise."

36. In *Rhetoric* 2.23, where he is discussing "common topics" on which enthymemes may be based, Aristotle cites examples from Theodectes' tragedies *Ajax, Alcmaeon, Orestes* and *Socrates*, and a panegyric speech entitled *Law*.

37. The reference here is not to Aristotle but to sophists and grammarians holding court and meeting with students in the Lyceum—the *Lykeion* gymnasium, east of the city wall of Athens near the Ilissos river. Isocrates composed the *Panathenaicus* around 342 B.C., during the twelve-year period when Aristotle was living abroad (in Asia Minor and Macedon) and some seven years before Aristotle founded his school in the *peripatos* of the Lyceum (in 335 B.C.); Kennedy 1991 6.

38. Trimpi 1983 25–63; see also Burke 1968 157–158. Obviously, Bakhtinian notions of "heteroglossia" in novelistic discourse are relevant here as well.

39. Miller 1994.

40. On the development of the "novel" in the Hellenistic and Roman worlds, see Hägg 1983 and Anderson 1984.

41. Gentili 1988 44–45, 55.

42. Johnson 1982 76–95.

43. Johnson 1982 90.

44. As he himself recognizes: Johnson 1982 ix.

45. For the surviving fragments of *On Imitation*, see Aujac 1978–1992 5:26–40 and Usener and Radermacher 1965 2:195–217.

10. Aristotelianism and Grammar

1. As Trypanis 1981 366 puts it, the period from 100 to 330 A.D. "was primarily the age of prose and . . . the decline of poetry and philosophy made the Sophists and rhetoricians

the educators of Greece and the carriers of its values," though I would argue that they were more than "carriers." Likewise, as Browning 1982 692 says, "[t]he Age of Hadrian, the Antonines and Septimius Serenus [sic] was one of prose." See also Bowie 1990. For the standard judgment on poetry in late antiquity, see De Romilly 1985 192; Trypanis 1981 384; Knox 1985 714–715; Browning 1982 698, 713; and Jones 1966 353. For an alternative (though not entirely opposed) view, however, see Cameron 1970's account of Claudian.

2. Kennedy 1994 242–270; Jones 1964 2:938–985.

3. For text and testimonies, see Campbell 1993 212–221. Hermeias was a eunuch who in 355 B.C. became tyrant of Atarneos (an Aeolian city on the coast of Asia Minor, opposite Lesbos) and was a close associate and patron of Aristotle and other philosophers; Aristotle married Hermeias's adopted niece. Hermeias was tortured and put to death by the Persian king Artaxerxes III in 341. According to Diogenes Laertius (*Lives* 5.5, 27) and Olympiodorus's commentary on Plato's *Gorgias*, Aristotle also composed at least one dedicatory epigram for a statue of Hermeias at Delphi, some hexameter poetry (apparently a hymn), elegiacs, and an encomium in praise of Plato.

4. [K]*atholou*, actually a compound of *kata holou* ("down from the whole; altogether"), functions adverbially with the meaning of "in general, generally"; when combined with the neuter definite article *to* (or *ta*, the plural), in Aristotle it becomes an abstract noun meaning literally "the in-general," or the way things usually are—or what is sometimes translated as "universals." Convincingly probable poetic *mythoi* persuade audiences that they embody *ta katholou*, as do rhetorical *paradeigmata*.

5. See Meijering 1987 99–133 and Trimpi 1983 25–63.

6. Trypanis 1981 318.

7. The notion of *katharsis* is, of course, something of a vexed issue in Aristotelian interpretation. For fuller discussion see Walker 2000; Nehamas 1994; Halliwell 1986 168–201 and 1987 89–91; and Nussbaum 1986 389–390.

8. Halliwell 1986 19–27.

9. *On the Fame of the Athenians* 5.348c; translation of Kennedy, in Sprague 1972 65.

10. This is, of course, the argument of Havelock 1963.

11. In the Hippocratic writings, medical *katharsis* is the forcing-out of substances from the body by means of drugs, *pharmaka*; see Hippocrates, *Aphorisms* 4; and Galen, *On the Natural Faculties* 1.13.40 and 3.13.188.

12. As Barker 1985 316–317 suggests, both Aristotle and Plato seem to have built on the theories of the fifth-century musicologist Damon, who held that "music influences character."

13. Else 1967 51, 304–306; see also Else 1986.

14. Else 1967 51; Halliwell 1987 19–27, 331–336,

15. Kosman 1980; Walker 2000.

16. Aristotle does not mention gender here, because it is not relevant to the all-male audience of the orator speaking in a political assembly or court of law; but elsewhere in his writings it is clear that he does consider gender as one determinant of ethical-emotional capabilities.

17. See also 249c, 275a, 275d.

18. See Halliwell 1987 176–180. As Halliwell notes, Aristotle's discussion is probably a condensed version of his earlier and much longer (and now lost) *Homeric Problems*.

19. See, for example, Johnson 1982 76–96.

20. As Cameron 1995 46 points out, "[m]any themes and genres that had been earlier treated in lyric [song meters] . . . were adapted to hexameters, elegiacs and iambics," which by the third century B.C. were the main forms of verse still available for public performance.

21. Johnson 1982 30–31.

22. As Oswald Ducrot and Jean-Claude Anscombre have argued, virtually every utterance (insofar as it predicates something) is characterized by "argumentivity": that is, it adumbrates a set of tacit presuppositions and implies likewise some set of inferences, which in effect are enthymematic "conclusions" that follow from it. This is not quite the same as my notion that the epigram—as a mode of epideictic rhetoric that asserts a *stance*—functions rhetorically as an enthymematic "cap" resting on a largely unstated (or minimally stated) set of warrants, which in more explicit argumentation would be developed by an "exetasis" leading to the statement of the enthymeme itself; and indeed an enthymeme is not really an enthymeme until it is overtly *presented* via an enthymematic gesture (of assertion or stance projection). But Ducrot and Anscombre's notion of linguistic "argumentivity," although it focuses chiefly on the *propositional* implicatures embodied in the linguistics and pragmatics of *sentences*, does provide a partial means of accounting for the tacit argumentation embodied (and asserted) by an epigram. See Ducrot 1980 and 1984 and Anscombre and Ducrot 1983 and 1989. All of this work (with the exception of Anscombre and Ducrot 1989) remains unavailable in English, but their position is given a concise summation in van Eemeren et al. 1996 315–322.

23. Most of this description of what became the standard grammatical *paideia* derives from Quintilian, *Institutio Oratoria* 1.1.15, 1.2.1, 1.4.2, 2.2.3. See also Harris 1989 96, 132–133, 233–248; Lamberton 1992a; and Irvine 1994 23–62.

24. Irvine 1994 24.

25. Kaster 1988 15, 17. All these phrases are Kaster's translations; the last is Kaster's paraphrase of Diomedes.

26. Irvine 1994 33; see also 30–33. While Irvine says that "Aristotelian theory on poetry became the standard equipment of the grammatical tradition," it is worth recalling that, after around 285 B.C., Aristotle's *Poetics* – like the *Rhetoric* and the rest of his lecture notes (the "treatises" that we have now)—"disappeared" for nearly all of the Hellenistic period. See Kennedy 1991 305–308 and Halliwell 1987 1.

27. The attribution derives from the scholiast Porphyrion's statement that "in this book [Horace] has brought together the precepts of Neoptolemus of Parium on poetic art, not indeed all but the most outstanding." See Brink 1963–1982 1:43. Brink's magisterial, three-volume study of Horace's literary epistles includes (1:43–152) what is still the fullest account and reconstruction of Neoptolemus's lost poetics from the surviving references to him, chiefly those in Philodemus of Gadara's *On Poems*. See also Porter 1995.

28. Brink 1963–1982 1:48–74; Porter 1995 98–117. Actually, with the appearance of prose fiction around the first century A.D., it eventually became possible to have *poiêsis* without *poiêma*—that is, a "fable" that was not a "poem"—though I am not aware of any ancient critic who makes such an observation.

29. Irvine 1994 34–38.

30. Diels and Kranz 1951–1954 2:411. An English translation is available in Sprague 1972 286. The *Dissoi Logoi* generally has been ascribed to the end of the fifth century B.C., as an "older sophistic" document; but for a cautionary note on this dating, see Conley 1986. Conley offers a fairly persuasive, speculative argument that the *Dissoi Logoi* could very well have been produced as a school exercise—one of the *progymnasmata,* for example, *kataskeuai-anaskeuai,* "arguments and refutations," or *antirrêsis,* "counterstatement"—written in a clumsy imitation of fifth-century literary Doric, by some Byzantine scholar. Even so, as Conley notes, the *mise-en-scène* of the exercise (as with many declamation exercises) is fifth-century Athens; the *Dissoi Logoi* writer is rehearsing the topics and arguments of that period.

31. This position is attributed to Neoptolemus by Philodemus of Gadara, in *On Poems* 5; see the translation of Armstrong 1995 260.

32. See Irvine 1994 34–38.

33. Lamberton 1992b.

34. Irvine 1994 38 calls this a kind of "deconstruction," by which analysis—especially etymological analysis—unlocked the "deeper" signifying potentials of a poet's discourse. We might compare Jacques Derrida's hyponoiac-etymological rereading of the *Phaedrus* in *Plato's Pharmacy;* we might also call this reading "allegorical" insofar as *allēgoria* means "other-saying"; see Derrida 1981 61–172.

35. The remarks of Tatian, Hesychius, Philodemus, and others on Metrodorus are collected in Diels and Kranz 1951–1954 2:49–50. See also Richardson 1975 69 and Long 1992 44–45.

36. As Long 1995 argues, the Stoics did not necessarily regard the myths of archaic poetry as encoding *true* wisdom—but they did regard them as embodying what the poets of early times (or their predecessors, the first inventors of the myths) thought to be true wisdom. Nevertheless, insofar as the poetry had to be preserved as a viable object of *paideia,* the poets still would have to be seen as transmitting genuine wisdoms in "primitive," poetic forms. On the development of grammatical and allegorical exegesis in the earlier second century B.C., particularly under the influences of the Alexandrian librarian, Aristarchus, and his contemporary and competitor the Pergamene librarian Crates of Mallos, see Porter 1992.

37. See Keaney and Lamberton 1996 1–28.

38. Translation of Keaney and Lamberton 1996. All subsequent citations of the *Essay* are from this translation.

39. Insofar as "Plutarch" gives us discussions of Homer the poet, the *lexis* of his poetry, and its *logos,* he may be said to be following Neoptolemus's division of "poetry" into poet, poem, and poesy.

40. Compare Aristotle, *Rhetoric* 2.2 and *On the Soul* 1.1 403a–b.

41. Keaney and Lamberton 1996 141 n. 1.

42. Lamberton 1992a xx. See also Lamberton 1986 and 1992b.

43. The quotations are from *Odyssey* 4.230 and *Iliad* 14.216–217.

44. The actual phrase here is *tēn praxin . . . hēs gegonen he mimēsis,* which might be read more literally as "the action . . . of which [or from which] the mimesis has arisen." That is, the mimesis is *based on* an action that it portrays or brings before the audience, while the true subject matter of the mimesis is the represented action's underlying *hypokeimenon.*

45. See, for example, the general overviews provided by Trypanis 1981 245–424; and Browning 1982 692–722. Heath 1989, likewise, provides a persuasive argument that "unity" (as typically understood by modern literary critics) had very little importance in ancient poetic practice.

46. The origins of mime are, in fact, more or less contemporary with classical Attic drama and with the older sophists. It seems to have originated in two forms: a "spoken" west-Dorian form (e.g., from Sicily and southern Italy), and a sung east-Ionian form (e.g., from the Aegean), though it may have had precursors in the Dorian cities of mainland Greece. The earliest mime composer we hear of is Sophron of Syracuse (c. 450 B.C.), whom Aristotle mentions (*Poetics* 1 1447b). Sophron is said to have composed in rhythmic prose—perhaps like that of his fellow Sicilian and contemporary Gorgias?—and may have been a model for the dialogues of Plato (as Aristotle suggests, by linking them). By the Hellenistic period, poetic mimes were being composed in verse for both "spoken" and sung performance in theaters, and literary mimes were being composed by such poets as Theocritus and Herodas. Mime, in sum, both coexists with and outlasts the full-fledged drama, is by far the most durable and popular form of dramatic poetry in antiquity, and is closely related to sophistic declamation. See Trypanis 1981 307–308. As Horsfall 1982 293 points out, in the late Roman republic the more lowbrow versions of the theatrical review might include—in addi-

tion to mimes—"songs, striptease, live sex and live animals on stage, imitations of beasts and humans," and topical satire.

47. See Trypanis 1981 308, 387, 747 n. 18; and Richter 1994a 105–124, 160–172, and 1994b ch. 4. On the rhetorical dimensions of late medieval drama, see Enders 1992.

48. On the rhetoric of Horatian lyric, for example, see Davis 1991; DuQuesnay 1984; Woodman 1984; and Johnson 1982 92–95, 123–145.

49. Cicero, *De Oratore* 2.173; and *Letters to Atticus* 14.2.1, 3.2. For standard (*Cambridge History of Classical Literature*) opinion on Roman mime and drama, see Horsfall 1982 293–294; Gratwick 1982 129; Rudd 1982 380; and Herrington 1982 519–520. It is probably fair to say that Horace's *Satires* owe more to mime than to Attic drama.

50. It is possible to interpret this injunction as meaning simply a coherent, unified presentation of a single subject matter (*materia*, 38); but the explicit, amplified focus on the fables represented in epic and tragedy (119–152) suggests more strongly that Aristotelian *mythos* is what is meant. Note here, as well, that Horace's own poetry, from his *Odes* and *Epodes* to his *Satires* and *Epistles*, is famous for its "impulsive meandering"; Davis 1991 10.

51. Cameron 1995 65. With Cameron, I take the view that in antiquity a poem's initial "publication" (like that of an oration) typically consisted of a public recitation, followed by manuscript circulation.

52. As more than one commentator has pointed out, Horace seems to ironize or subvert the very rules he enunciates. Thus Armstrong 1989 157: "[the *Ars Poetica*] is on the surface not just conversationally informal but joltingly arbitrary in its succession of topics. Its precepts taken one by one recommend the strictest sort of Aristotelian decorum. . . . But it is so audacious and shapeless in its structure and argument that it seems to express more sympathy than one would at first think with the wild and formless artwork and the mad poet it condemns with hilarious satire at the beginning and end." Brink 1963–1982, of course, has famously argued that the Neoptolemic triad of *poiêma-poiêsis-poiêtês* underlies the seeming arbitrariness, but the key point—which Brink discusses at some length—is that there has never been much agreement, among Horace's best commentators, about precisely what the structure the *Ars Poetica* has, if any; there are virtually as many analyses as there are commentators. For yet another structural analysis of the *Ars*, in terms of the rhetorical genre of *sermo*, the conversational "talk" (which permits a fairly loose *dispositio*), see Kilpatrick 1990 32–57.

53. Thus Russell and Winterbottom 1972 504; see also Grube 1965 327. All citations of this oration are in Russell and Winterbottom's 1972 translation (504–507).

54. Dio's description of his day, it should be noted, is also a portrait of refined, upper-class life: feeling unwell, he rises early and says his prayers, takes his carriage for "a number of turns on the racecourse [on his own estate?], driving as gently and quietly as possible," takes a walk and a little rest, oils himself, bathes, has a light meal, and then devotes the rest of his day to reading the tragedies (which he happens to have in his house, apparently)—"staging" them in his imagination, as a luxurious pleasure to console himself for being sick.

55. Translation of Wooten 1987, for this and all following quotations from *On Types of Style*.

56. In the edition/translation of Russell and Wilson 1981, there are two "treatises" ascribed to Menander, though both are incomplete, and possibly are parts of a single multivolume treatise. At the end of book 1 (on "hymns to the gods"), which is mostly complete, Menander announces his "launching-forth into the volumes," *eis tous tomous anagôgê*; the term *anagôgê* (literally "leading-up"), which is also a term for putting to sea, metaphorically suggests a lengthier treatise than the two books included in what is now called Treatise I. This transition also suggests that "hymns" were the only form of poetry included in the treatise, which seems to have been otherwise devoted to particular types of prose epideictic speeches for ceremonial occasions.

57. Translation of Russell and Wilson 1981, for this and all following quotations of Menander Rhetor.

58. On Claudian as a "propaganda" poet, see Cameron 1970, which is by far the best available and most complete account of this neglected poet's work.

59. On the life and career of Ausonius, see Green 1991 xv–xl; Sivan 1993, especially 74–96 and 119–141; Irvine 1994 84–87; and Evelyn-White 1919 vii–xli.

60. Green 1991 xvii; Grant 1990 183. See also Irvine 1994 84.

11. *Toward Modernity*

1. As cited by Syrianus, Apthonius, Planudes, and Sopater, in commentaries on Hermogenes. In Usener and Radermacher 1965 197–199. Most of the text of *On Imitation* has been lost.

2. In Walz 1968 3:461–462. Reprinted also in Usener and Radermacher 1965 2:199–200, with slight emendations.

3. The *pragmatikos topos* was subdivided into (a) *heuresis* and *krisis*, the discovery and judgment of arguments and (b) *oikonomia*, the management or "economy" of those arguments in a discourse. *Oikonomia*, in turn, included the "parts of an oration"—introduction, narration, and so on—that formed the usual sequence of discussion in sophistic handbooks. In addition to the *pragmatikos topos* there was the *lektikos topos*, which was subdivided into (a) *eklogê tôn onomatôn*, the "selection of words" (diction), which in turn was subdivided into *kuria phrasis*, proper expression, and *tropikê kataskeuê*, the use of figuration and (b) *synthesis tôn onomatôn*, the "composition of words" in prosodically effective phrases and sentences, the subject of Dionysius's most famous treatise. See Roberts 1901 9.

4. There is no surviving treatise on invention (the *pragmatikos topos*) from Dionysius, but it is significant that in *On Imitation* he discussed the use of enthymemes in history-writing; see Dionysius's *Letter to Gnaeus Pompeius* 3–6. For the phrase "mobile invention" I am indebted to Eric White; see White 1987.

5. The definition itself recurs in numerous Byzantine commentaries on Hermogenes and may have been invoked by Hermogenes himself. Again, see Usener and Radermacher 1965 2:197–199.

6. As Richard McKeon long ago remarked, rhetoric "has no history during the Middle Ages," at least not as a distinct subject matter. See McKeon 1942 and Murphy 1974 87, 300. A good recent overview of medieval rhetoric is provided by Conley 1990a 63–108.

7. Murphy 1974 47–63; Kennedy 1980 153–160 and 1994 265–270; Conley 1990a 74–78. See also Marrou 1949; Testard 1958; Brown 1969; and Cameron 1991.

8. Eden 1997 51–63; Irvine 1994 169–189. One might argue, however, as Eden does, that the interpretive methods of *grammatica* developed from the interpretive issues of the legal stasis. I think this is only partly true, but, even if it *is* true, it clearly is the case that by late antiquity the methods of grammatical hermeneutics had become a rather different thing.

9. Translation of Robertson 1958; unless otherwise indicated, all subsequent citations are from this translation. I am following the Latin text of Green 1995; Green's translation is in some respects superior to Robertson's (and offers some corrected readings), but my impression is that Robertson is generally closer to the Latin.

10. On the comparison to Plutarch, see Eden 1997 46–54.

11. My translation.

12. As Green 1995 112 n. 103 points out (following Jackson 1969), Augustine is using the procedures of Stoic logic in this demonstration.

13. See Jackson 1975.

14. King James translation.

15. See, for example, Robertson 1958 xi–xii.

16. My translation.

17. My translation.

18. 2 Corinthians 6.2–11 (Robertson's translation from Augustine's Latin).

19. *De Habitu Virginum* 3. I present this and the following example from Cyprian in "verse" form for comparison with the "verses" of 2 Corinthians just cited and to highlight the prosodic construction of the prose.

20. *Epistle* 63.2. Augustine quotes 63.2–4.

21. Duncan-Jones and Van Dorsten 1973. All further citations of Sidney's *Defense* are this edition.

22. By far the best and fullest general account still is Murphy 1974, though this is confined to the Latin tradition in western Europe. See also Baldwin 1928; Murphy 1978; Kennedy 1980 chs. 8–9; Vickers 1988 ch. 4; Conley 1990a ch. 4; Copeland 1991; Minnis and Scott 1991; Morse 1991; Brabant 1992; Enders 1992; Zumthor 1992; Mack 1993; Irvine 1994; Richter 1994a; Solterer 1995; Johnston 1996; and Reynolds 1996.

Byzantine rhetoric is a very large and mostly unexplored subject. Conley 1990a 63–71 offers an exceptionally useful if brief overview, from the sixth to fifteenth centuries. See also Kustas 1973; Monfasani 1976, 1983, and 1995; Kennedy 1980 ch. 8 and 1983; and Kazhdan 1984 and 1993.

23. "Aristotelian" logic was represented, most crucially, by Boethius's *De Differentiis Topicis,* Cicero's *Topica* (which purports to be a digest of Aristotle's *Topics,* and is one of Boethius's main sources), and parts of Aristotle's *Organon*—the *Categories* and *On Interpretation* (the so-called Old Logic) and later the *Prior Analytics, Posterior Analytics, Topics,* and *Sophistical Refutations* (the New Logic, which became available in Latin translation in the first quarter of the twelfth century).

24. Murphy 1974 105.

25. The standard and still best treatment of these three *artes* is Murphy 1974 chs. 4–6, on which my discussion here is chiefly based. See also Kennedy 1980 ch. 9 and Conley 1990a 93–108.

26. Murphy 1974 261.

27. Murphy 1974 303–355; on "enthymeme" in medieval scholastic thought, see Green 1995.

28. See Kitzhaber 1953; Berlin 1984 and 1987; and Crowley 1990.

29. On these developments, see McKeon 1952; Ong 1958; Vickers 1970 and 1988 ch. 5; Sloane 1974, 1985, 1993, and 1997; Lanham 1976; Kennedy 1980 ch. 10; Murphy 1983; Kahn 1985; Kinney 1986; Conley 1990a ch. 5; Green 1986; Struever 1992; Mack 1993; and Armstrong 1997.

30. In this respect, Hermogenes' *On Types of Style*—which had considerable influence on Renaissance stylistic theory—could be seen as offering a virtual set of recipes; see Patterson 1970.

31. *Helen* 21; *paignon* is literally the *Helen*'s final word. On neosophistry in Elizabethan humanism, see Kinney 1986 18–22, 304–362 (though Kinney's notion of sophistic is, in my view, too limited).

32. On this, again, see in particular Sloane 1974, 1985, 1993, and 1997; Kinney 1986 and 1989; and Armstrong 1997.

33. Irvine 1994 63. Rhetoric appears in book 5 of Capella's *Marriage,* following Grammar (book 3) and Dialectic (book 4); see Stahl et al. 1977 and Murphy 1974 44–46.

Works Cited

Abbot, Don Paul. 1987. "The Ancient Word: Rhetoric in Aztec Culture." *Rhetorica* 5.3:251–264.

Altieri, Charles. 1984. *Self and Sensibility in Contemporary American Poetry*. Cambridge: Cambridge University Press.

———. 1990. "The Powers and Limits of Oppositional Postmodernism." *American Literary History* 2.3:443–481.

———. 1992. "Contemporary Poetry as Philosophy: Subjective Agency in John Ashbery and C. K. Williams." *Contemporary Literature* 33.2:214–242.

Anderson, Graham. 1984. *Ancient Fiction: The Novel in the Graeco-Roman World*. London: Croon Helm.

———. 1990. "The Second Sophistic: Some Problems of Perspective." In Russell 1990.

———. 1993. *The Second Sophistic: A Cultural Phenomenon in the Roman Empire*. London: Routledge.

Anhalt, Emily Katz. 1993. *Solon the Singer: Politics and Poetics*. Lanham, Md.: Rowman and Littlefield.

Anscombre, Jean-Claude, and Oswald Ducrot. 1983. *L'Argumentation dans la Langue*. Liège: Pierre Mardaga.

———. 1989. "Argumentivity and Informativity." In *From Metaphysics to Rhetoric*, edited by Michel Meyer. Dordrecht: Kluwer.

Apuleius. *Works*. 1869. London: Bell and Daldy.

Armstrong, David. 1989. *Horace*. New Haven: Yale University Press.

———, tr. 1995. "Philodemus, *On Poems* Book 5." In Obbink 1995.

Armstrong, Edward. 1997. "A Ciceronian Sunburn: Humanist/ic Rhetoric and the Ethics of Spenserian Poetics." Ph.D. diss., Pennsylvania State University.

Arthurs, Jeffrey D. 1994. "The Term *Rhetor* in Fifth and Fourth-Century Greek Literature." *Rhetoric Society Quarterly* 23.3/4:1–10.

Attridge, Derek. 1982. *The Rhythms of English Poetry*. New York: Longman.

Atwill, Janet M. 1998. *Rhetoric Reclaimed: Aristotle and the Liberal Arts Tradition*. Ithaca: Cornell University Press.

Aujac, Germaine, tr. 1978–1992. *Denys d'Halicarnasse: Opuscules Rhétoriques*. 5 vols. Paris: Société d'Edition "Les Belles Lettres."

Austin, J. L. 1962. *How to Do Things with Words*. Cambridge: Harvard University Press.

Austin, M. M. 1981. *The Hellenistic World from Alexander to the Roman Conquest: A Selection of Ancient Sources*. Cambridge: Cambridge University Press.

Bagnall, Roger S., and Peter Derow. 1981. *Greek Historical Documents: The Hellenistic Period*. Chico, Calif.: Scholars Press.

Baldwin, Charles Sears. 1924. *Ancient Rhetoric and Poetic*. New York: MacMillan.

———. 1928. *Medieval Rhetoric and Poetic (to 1400), Interpreted from Representative Works*. New York: MacMillan.

Barilli, Renato. 1989. *Rhetoric*. Tr. Giuliana Menozzi. Minneapolis: University of Minnesota Press.

Barker, Andrew. 1985. "Theophrastus on Pitch and Melody." In Fortenbaugh 1985a.

Barthes, Roland. 1972. *Mythologies*. Tr. Annette Lavers. New York: Hill and Wang.

Bauman, Richard A. 1985. *Lawyers in Roman Transitional Politics: A Study of the Roman Jurists in their Political Setting in the Late Republic and Triumvirate*. Munich: Beck.

———. 1989. *Lawyers and Politics in the Early Roman Empire: A Study of Relations between the Roman Jurists and the Emperors from Augustus to Hadrian*. Munich: Beck.

Behr, Charles A., tr. 1981. *P. Aelius Aristides: The Complete Works*. 2 vols. Leiden: E. J. Brill.

———. 1973. *Aristides: In Defence of Oratory*. In *Aristides*. Vol. 1 of 4. Cambridge: Harvard University Press.

Bender, John, and David E. Wellbery. 1990. *The Ends of Rhetoric: History, Theory, Practice*. Stanford: Stanford University Press.

Berlin, James A. 1984. *Writing Instruction in Nineteenth-Century American Colleges*. Carbondale: Southern Illinois University Press.

———. 1987. *Rhetoric and Reality: Writing Instruction in American Colleges 1900–1985*. Carbondale: Southern Illinois University Press.

Bernstein, Charles. 1986. *Content's Dream: Essays 1975–1984*. Los Angeles: Sun and Moon.

———. 1992. *A Poetics*. Cambridge: Harvard University Press.

———, ed. 1993. *The Politics of Poetic Form: Poetry and Public Policy*. New York: Roof.

Billows, Richard A. 1990. *Antigonos the One-Eyed and the Creation of the Hellenistic State*. Berkeley: University of California Press.

Bing, Peter. 1988. *The Well-Read Muse: Present and Past in Callimachus and the Hellenistic Poets*. Gottingen: Vandenhoeck and Ruprecht.

Bitzer, Lloyd. 1959. "Aristotle's Enthymeme Revisited." *Quarterly Journal of Speech* 45:409–414.

Bizzell, Patricia, and Bruce Herzberg, eds. 1990. *The Rhetorical Tradition: Readings from Classical Times to the Present*. Boston: Bedford Books.

Bloch, Maurice. 1974. "Symbols, Song, Dance, and Features of Articulation, or, Is Religion an Extreme Form of Traditional Authority?" *Archives Européennes de Sociologie* 15.1:55–81.

———, ed. 1975. *Political Language and Oratory in Traditional Society*. New York: Academic Press.

Bloom, Harold. 1973. *The Anxiety of Influence: A Theory of Poetry*. New York: Oxford University Press.

———. 1979. "The Breaking of Form." In *Deconstruction and Criticism*. New York: Continuum.

———. 1982. *Agon: Towards a Theory of Revisionism*. New York: Oxford University Press.

Blundell, Sue. 1995. *Women in Ancient Greece*. London: British Museum Press.

Booth, Wayne. 1983. *The Rhetoric of Fiction*. 2nd ed. Chicago: University of Chicago Press.

Bornecque, H. 1902. *Les Déclamations et les Déclamateurs d'après Sénèque le Père*. Lille.

Boss, George P. 1979. "The Stereotype and Its Correspondence in Discourse to the Enthymeme." *Communication Quarterly* 27.2:22–27.

Bowersock, G. W. 1969. *Greek Sophists in the Roman Empire*. London: Oxford University Press.

Bowie, Ewen L. 1989. "Greek Sophists and Greek Poetry in the Second Sophistic." *Aufstieg und Neidergang der römischen Welt (ANRW)* 2.33.1. Berlin: de Gruyter.

———. 1990. "Greek Poetry in the Antonine Age." In Russell 1990.

Bowra, C. M., tr. 1969. *Pindar: The Odes*. New York: Penguin.

Brabant, Margaret, ed. 1992. *Politics, Gender, and Genre: The Political Thought of Christine de Pizan*. Boulder: Westview.

Brandes, Paul D. 1989. *A History of Aristotle's "Rhetoric."* Metuchen, N.J.: Scarecrow.

Braund, David C. 1988a. "The Growth of the Roman Empire." Introduction to Braund 1988.

———. 1988b. "Client Kings." In Braund 1988, 69–96.

———, ed. 1988. *The Administration of the Roman Empire, 241 B.C.–A.D. 193*. Exeter Studies in History no. 18. Exeter: University of Exeter Press.

Brink, C. O. 1963–1982. *Horace on Poetry*. 3 vols. Cambridge: Cambridge University Press.

———. 1989. "Quintilian's De Causis Corruptae Eloquentiae and Tacitus' Dialogus de Oratoribus." *Classical Quarterly* 39.2:472–503.

Brown, Peter. 1969. *Augustine of Hippo: A Biography*. Berkeley: University of California Press.

———. 1992. *Power and Persuasion in Late Antiquity: Towards a Christian Empire*. Madison: University of Wisconsin Press.

Browning, Robert. 1982. "Later Principate." In Kenney and Clausen 1982.

———. 1992. "The Byzantines and Homer." In Lamberton and Keaney 1992.

Bucheim, Thomas, tr. 1989. *Gorgias von Leontini: Reden, Fragmente und Testimonien*. Hamburg: Felix Meiner.

Bundy, Elroy. 1986. *Studia Pindarica*. Berkeley: University of California Press. (Orig. 1962.)

Burckhardt, Jacob. 1900. *Griechische Kulturgeschichte*. Ed. J. Oeri. Berlin.

Burgess, Theodore C. 1902. *Epideictic Literature*. Chicago: University of Chicago Press.

Burke, Kenneth. 1968. *Counter-Statement*. Berkeley: University of California Press. (Orig. 1931.)

———. 1969. *A Rhetoric of Motives*. Berkeley: University of California Press. (Orig. 1950.)

———. 1973. *The Philosophy of Literary Form*. Berkeley: University of California Press. (Orig. 1941.)

———. 1984. *Permanence and Change: An Anatomy of Purpose*. 3rd ed. Berkeley: University of California Press. (Orig. 1935, also 1954/1965.)

Burkert, Walter. 1985. *Greek Religion*. Tr. John Raffan. Cambridge: Harvard University Press.

Burnett, Anne. 1983. *Three Archaic Poets: Archilochus, Alcaeus, Sappho*. London: Duckworth.

———. 1987. "The Scrutiny of Song: Pindar, Politics and Poetry." *Critical Inquiry* 13.3:434–449.

———. 1989. "Performing Pindar's Odes." *Classical Philology* 84:283–293.

Burstein, Stanley M. 1985. *The Hellenistic Age: From the Battle of Ipsos to the Death of Kleopatra VII*. Cambridge: Cambridge University Press.

Butler, H. E., tr. 1909/1970. *The Apologia and Florida of Apuleius of Madaura*. Westport, Conn.: Greenwood. (Facsimile reprint; orig. Clarendon Press, Oxford).

———. 1920–1922. *Quintilian: Institutio Oratoria*. 4 vols. Cambridge: Harvard University Press.

Butler, Judith. 1993. *Bodies That Matter: On the Discursive Limits of "Sex."* New York: Routledge.

Cahn, Michael. 1989. "Reading Rhetoric Rhetorically: Isocrates and the Marketing of Insight." *Rhetorica* 7.2:121–144.

Calame, Claude. 1977. *Les Choeurs de Jeunes Filles en Grèce Archaïque*. 2 vols. Rome: Ateneo & Bizzarri.

———. 1995. *The Craft of Poetic Speech in Ancient Greece*, tr. Janice Orion. Ithaca: Cornell University Press.

Cameron, Alan. 1970. *Claudian: Poetry and Propaganda at the Court of Honorius*. Oxford: Oxford University Press.

———. 1995. *Callimachus and His Critics*. Princeton: Princeton University Press.

Cameron, Averil. 1991. *Christianity and the Rhetoric of Empire: The Development of Christian Discourse*. Berkeley: University of California Press.

Campbell, D. A., tr. 1982. *Greek Lyric I: Sappho and Alcaeus*. Cambridge: Harvard University Press.

———, tr. 1988. *Greek Lyric II: Anacreon, Anacreonta, Choral Lyric from Olympus to Alcman*. Cambridge: Harvard University Press.

———, tr. 1991. *Greek Lyric III: Stesichrous, Ibycus, Simonides, and Others*. Cambridge: Harvard University Press.

———, tr. 1992. *Greek Lyric IV: Bacchylides, Corinna, and Others*. Cambridge: Harvard University Press.

———, tr. 1993. *Greek Lyric V: The New School of Poetry ånd Anonymous Songs and Hymns*. Cambridge.: Harvard University Press.

Caplan, Harry, tr. 1954. *Rhetorica ad Herennium*. In *Cicero*. Vol. 1 of 28. Cambridge: Harvard University Press.

Carey, Christopher. 1981. *A Commentary on Five Odes of Pindar*. New York: Arno Press.

———. 1989. "The Performance of the Victory Ode." *American Journal of Philology* 110:545–565.

———. 1991. "The Victory Ode in Performance: The Case for the Chorus." *Classical Philology* 86.3:192–200.

Carney, Thomas F. 1971. *Bureaucracy in Traditional Society: Romano-Byzantine Bureaucracy, Viewed from Within*. Lawrence, Kan.: Coronado Press.

Carter, J. M. 1972. "Cicero: Politics and Philosophy." In *Cicero and Virgil: Studies in Honour of Harold Huntt*, edited by John R. C. Martin. Amsterdam: A. M. Hakkert.

Carter, Michael. 1991. "The Ritual Functions of Epideictic Rhetoric: The Case of Socrates' Funeral Oration." *Rhetorica* 9.3:209–232.

Chafe, Wallace. 1961. *Seneca Thanksgiving Rituals*. Bulletin 183. Washington, D.C.: Bureau of American Ethnology.

———. 1993. "Seneca Speaking Styles and the Location of Authority." In *Responsibility and Evidence in Oral Discourse*, edited by Jane Hill and Judith Irvine. Cambridge: Cambridge University Press.

Chase, Richard J. 1961. "The Classical Conception of the Epideictic." *Quarterly Journal of Speech* 47:293–300.

Clark, Donald L. 1957. *Rhetoric in Greco-Roman Education*. New York: Columbia University Press.

Clark, Norman. 1996. "The Critical Servant: An Isocratean Contribution to Critical Rhetoric." *Quarterly Journal of Speech* 82.2: 111–124.

Clarke, M. L. 1953. *Rhetoric at Rome: A Historical Survey*. London: Cohen and West.

———. 1971. *Higher Education in the Ancient World*. Albuquerque: University of New Mexico Press.

Cobb-Stevens, Veda. 1985. "Opposites, Reversals, and Ambiguities: The Unsettled World of Theognis." In Figueira and Nagy 1985.

Cobb-Stevens, Veda, Thomas J. Figueira, and Gregory Nagy. 1985. Introduction to Figueira and Nagy 1985.

Cohen, David. 1995. *Law, Violence and Community in Classical Athens.* Cambridge: Cambridge University Press 1995.

Cole, Thomas. 1991. *The Origins of Rhetoric in Ancient Greece.* Baltimore: Johns Hopkins University Press.

Comaroff, John. 1975. "Talking Politics: Oratory and Authority in a Tswana Chiefdom." In Bloch 1975.

Conley, Thomas M. 1982. "*Pathe* and *Pisteis:* Aristotle, *Rhet.* II.2–11." *Hermes* 110:300–315.

———— 1984. "The Enthymeme in Perspective." *Quarterly Journal of Speech* 70:168–187.

———— 1986. "On Dating the So-Called *Dissoi Logoi:* A Cautionary Note." *Ancient Philosophy* 5.1:59–65.

————. 1990a. *Rhetoric in the European Tradition.* New York: Longman.

————. 1990b. "Aristotle's *Rhetoric* in Byzantium." *Rhetorica* 8.1:29–44.

Cook, J. M. 1962. *The Greeks in Ionia and the East.* London: Thames and Hudson.

Copeland, Rita. 1991. *Rhetoric, Hermeneutics, and Translation in the Middle Ages: Academic Traditions and Vernacular Texts.* Cambridge: Cambridge University Press.

Cornford, Francis M., tr. 1980. *The Republic of Plato.* Oxford: Oxford University Press. (Orig. 1941.)

Crawford, Michael. 1978. *The Roman Republic.* London: Fontana.

Crowley, Sharon. 1990. *The Methodical Memory: Invention in Current-Traditional Rhetoric.* Carbondale: Southern Illinois University Press.

Culler, Jonathan. 1988. "The Modern Lyric: Generic Continuity and Critical Practice." In *The Comparative Perspective on Literature: Approaches to Theory and Practice,* edited by Clayton Koelb and Susan Noakes. Ithaca: Cornell University Press.

Davis, Gregson. 1991. *Polyhymnia: The Rhetoric of Horatian Lyric Discourse.* Berkeley: University of California Press.

Davison, J. A. 1962. "Literature and Literacy." *Phoenix* 16:219–233.

De Jean, Joan. 1989. *Fictions of Sappho 1546–1937.* Chicago: Chicago University Press.

De Man, Paul. 1983. *Blindness and Insight: Essays in the Rhetoric of Contemporary Criticism.* Minneapolis: University of Minnesota Press.

De Romilly, Jacqueline. 1975. *Magic and Rhetoric in Ancient Greece.* Cambridge: Harvard University Press.

————. 1985. *A Short History of Greek Literature.* Tr. Lillian Doherty. Chicago: University of Chicago Press.

————. 1992. *The Great Sophists in Periclean Athens.* Tr. Janet Lloyd. Oxford: Oxford University Press.

de Sousa, Ronald. 1987. *The Rationality of Emotion.* Cambridge, Mass.: MIT Press.

Deleuze, Gilles, and Felix Guattari. 1987. *A Thousand Plateaus: Capitalism and Schizophrenia.* Tr. Brian Massumi. Minneapolis: University of Minnesota Press.

Delia, Jesse G. 1970. "The Logic Fallacy, Cognitive Theory, and the Enthymeme: A Search for the Foundations of Reasoned Discourse." *Quarterly Journal of Speech* 56:140–148.

Derrida, Jacques. 1981. *Dissemination.* Tr. Barbara Johnson. Chicago: University of Chicago Press.

Detienne, Marcel. 1977. *The Gardens of Adonis: Spices in Greek Mythology.* Tr. Janet Lloyd. London: Harvester.

Diels, Hermann, and Walter Kranz, eds. 1951–1954. *Die Fragmente der Vorsokratiker.* 3 vols. Berlin: Weidmannsche.

Dodds, E. R. 1959. *Plato: Gorgias, A Revised Text with Introduction and Commentary.* Oxford: Oxford University Press.

Dougherty, Carol, and Leslie Kurke, eds. 1993. *Cultural Poetics in Archaic Greece: Cult, Performance, Politics.* Cambridge: Cambridge University Press.

duBois, Page. 1995. *Sappho Is Burning*. Chicago: University of Chicago Press.

Ducrot, Oswald. 1980. *Les Échelles Argumentatives*. Paris: Minuit.

———. 1984. *Le Dire et le Dit*. Paris: Minuit.

Dumézil, Georges. 1943. *Servius et la Fortune: Essai sur la Fonction Sociale de Louange et de Blâme et sur les Éléments Indo-Européens du Cens Romain*. Paris: Gallimard.

Duncan-Jones, Katherine, and Jan Van Dorsten, eds. 1973. *Miscellaneous Prose of Sir Philip Sidney*. Oxford: Oxford University Press.

DuQuesnay, I. M. Le M. 1984. "Horace and Maecenas: The Propaganda Value of *Sermones* I." In Woodman and West 1984.

Eagleton, Terry. 1990. *The Ideology of the Aesthetic*. Oxford: Basil Blackwell.

Easterling, P. E., and B. M. W. Knox, eds. 1985. *The Cambridge History of Classical Literature I: Greek Literature*. Cambridge: Cambridge University Press.

Eden, Kathy. 1997. *Hermeneutics and the Rhetorical Tradition: Chapters in the Ancient Legacy and Its Humanist Reception*. New Haven: Yale University Press.

Edmonds, J. M., tr. 1931. *Greek Elegy and Iambus*. 2 vols. Cambridge: Harvard University Press.

Else, Gerald. 1967. *Aristotle's Poetics: The Argument*. Cambridge: Harvard University Press.

———. 1986. *Plato and Aristotle on Poetry*. Chapel Hill: University of North Carolina Press.

Enders, Jody. 1992. *Rhetoric and the Origins of Medieval Drama*. Ithaca: Cornell University Press.

Enos, Richard Leo. 1993. *Greek Rhetoric before Aristotle*. Prospect Heights, Ill.: Waveland Press.

———. 1995. *Roman Rhetoric: Revolution and the Greek Influence*. Prospect Heights, Ill.: Waveland Press.

Evelyn-White H. G., tr. 1914. *Hesiod, the Homeric Hymns and Homerica*. Cambridge: Harvard University Press.

———, tr. 1919. *Ausonius*. Cambridge: Harvard University Press.

Fantham, Elaine. 1989. "The Growth of Literature and Criticism at Rome." In Kennedy 1989.

Farnell, L. R. 1896–1909. *The Cults of the Greek States*. 5 vols. Oxford: Oxford University Press.

Farnsworth, Rodney. 1996. "Contextualizing the Pliny/Trajan Letters: A Case for Crtiquing the (American) Myth of Deliberative Discourse in Roman Society." *Rhetoric Society Quarterly* 26.1:29–46.

Fenton, William. 1985. "Structure, Continuity and Change in the Process of Iroquois Treaty Making." In Jennings et al. 1985.

Figueira, Thomas. 1985a. "The Theognidea and Megarian Society." In Figueira and Nagy 1985.

———. 1985b. "Chronological Table: Archaic Megara, 800–500 b.c." In Figueira and Nagy 1985.

Figueira, Thomas, and Gregory Nagy, eds. 1985.*Theognis of Megara: Poetry and the Polis*. Baltimore: Johns Hopkins University Press.

Finley, Moses I. 1968. *Aspects of Antiquity: Discoveries and Controversies*. London: Chatto and Windus.

Finnegan, Ruth. 1977. *Oral Poetry: Its Nature, Significance, and Social Context*. Cambridge: Cambridge University Press.

Fish, Stanley. 1972. *Self-Consuming Artifacts: The Experience of Seventeenth-Century Literature*. Berkeley: University of California Press.

Florescu, Vasile. 1971. *La Retorica nel suo Sviluppo Storico*. Bologna: Il Mulino.

Fortenbaugh, William W. 1975. *Aristotle on Emotion*. London: Duckworth.

————. 1985b. "Theophrastus on Emotion" and "Theophrastus on Delivery." In Fortenbaugh 1985a.

————. 1994. "Quintilian 6.2.8–9: *Ethos and Pathos* and the Ancient Tradition." In *Peripatetic Rhetoric after Aristotle*, edited by William W. Fortenbaugh and David C. Mirhady. Rutgers University Studies in Classical Humanities. Vol. 4. New Brunswick, N.J.: Transaction Books.

————, ed. 1985a. *Theophrastus of Eresus: On His Life and Work*. Rutgers University Studies in Classical Humanities. Vol. 2. New Brunswick, N.J.: Transaction Books.

Fortenbaugh, William W, Pamela M. Huby, Robert W. Sharples, and Dimitri Gutas, eds. 1992. *Theophrastus of Eresus: Sources for His Life, Writings, Thought and Influence*. 2 vols. New York: E. J. Brill.

Foss, Sonia K., Karen A. Foss, and Robert Trapp. 1991. *Contemporary Perspectives on Rhetoric*. 2nd ed. Prospect Heights, Ill.: Waveland.

Foster, Michael K. 1985. "Another Look at the Function of Wampum in Iroquois-White Councils." In Jennings et al. 1985.

Foucault, Michel. 1972. *The Archaeology of Knowledge and The Discourse on Language*. Tr. A. M. Sheridan Smith. New York: Pantheon.

————. 1977. "What Is an Author?" Tr. Donald F. Bouchard and Sherry Simon. In *Language, Counter-Memory, Practice: Selected Interviews and Essays*, edited by Donald F. Bouchard. Ithaca: Cornell University Press.

Fowler, Harold North, tr. 1914. *Plato: Phaedrus*. In *Plato*. Vol. 1 of 12. Cambridge: Harvard University Press.

————, tr. 1921. *Plato: The Sophist*. In *Plato*. Vol. 7 of 12. Cambridge: Harvard University Press.

Fox, James J. 1975. "On Binary Categories and Primary Symbols." In *The Interpretation of Symbolism*, edited by Roy Willis. New York: Wiley.

————. 1977. "Roman Jakobson and the Comparative Study of Parallellism." In *Roman Jakobson: Echoes of His Scholarship*, edited by James J. Fox. Lisse: Peter de Redder.

Foxhall, Lin, and A. D. E. Lewis, eds. 1996. *Greek Law in its Political Setting: Justification not Justice*. New York: Oxford University Press.

Fraser, P. M. 1972. *Ptolemaic Alexandria*. 3 vols. Oxford: Oxford University Press.

————, tr. 1983. *The Poems of Hesiod*. Norman, Okla.: University of Oklahoma Press.

Freeman, Kathleen. 1966. *The Pre-Socratic Philosophers: A Companion to Diels*, Fragmente der Vorsokratiker. 2nd ed. Oxford: Basil Blackwell. (Orig. 1946.)

Freese. J. H., tr. 1926. *Aristotle: "Art" of Rhetoric*. In *Aristotle*. Vol. 22 of 23. Cambridge: Harvard University Press.

Freire, Paulo. 1993. *Pedagogy of the Oppressed*. Tr. Myra Bergman. New York: Continuum. (Orig. *Pedagogia del Oprimido* 1968.)

Frier, Bruce W. 1985. *The Rise of the Roman Jurists: Studies in Cicero's Pro Caecina*. Princeton: Princeton University Press.

Fuhrmann, Manfred. 1992. *Cicero and the Roman Republic*. Tr. W. E. Yuill. Oxford: Basil Blackwell.

Furley, David J., and Alexander Nehamas. 1994. *Aristotle's* Rhetoric: *Philosophical Essays*. Princeton: Princeton University Press.

Fyfe, W. Hamilton, tr. 1973. *Aristotle: The Poetics and "Longinus" On the Sublime*. In *Aristotle*. Vol. 23 of 23. Cambridge: Harvard University Press.

Gagarin, Michael. 1986. *Early Greek Law*. Berkeley: University of California Press.

————. 1992. "The Poetry of Justice: Hesiod and the Origins of Greek Law." *Ramus: Critical Studies in Greek and Roman Literature* 21.1:61–76.

Gage, John T. 1981. *In the Arresting Eye: The Rhetoric of Imagism*. Baton Rouge: Louisiana State University Press.

————. 1983. "Teaching the Enthymeme: Invention and Arrangement." *Rhetoric Review* 1:38–50.

————. 1984. "An Adequate Epistemology for Composition." In *Classical Rhetoric and Modern Discourse*, edited by Andrea Lunsford, Robert Connors, and Lisa Ede. Carbondale: Southern Illinois University Press.

————. 1991. "A General Theory of the Enthymeme for Advanced Composition." In *Teaching Advanced Composition: Why and How*, edited by Katherine H. Adams and John L. Adams. Portsmouth: Boynton/Cook.

Garnsey, Peter. 1970. *Social Status and Legal Privilege in the Roman Empire*. Oxford: Oxford University Press.

Garver, Eugene. 1994. *Aristotle's Rhetoric: An Art of Character*. Chicago: University of Chicago Press.

Gaselee, S., tr. 1971. *The Golden Ass: Being the Metamorphoses of Lucius Apuleius*. Cambridge: Harvard University Press. (Orig. 1915.)

Gentili, Bruno. 1988. *Poetry and Its Public in Ancient Greece: From Homer to the Fifth Century*. Tr. Thomas Cole. Baltimore: Johns Hopkins University Press. (Orig. *Poesia e pubblico nella Grecia antica: da Omero al V secolo* 1985).

Gleason, Maud W. 1995. *Making Men: Sophists and Self-Presentation in Ancient Rome*. Princeton: Princeton University Press.

Glenn, Cheryl. 1997. *Rhetoric Retold: Regendering the Tradition from Antiquity through the Renaissance*. Carbondale: Southern Illinois University Press.

Gold, Barbara K. 1987. *Literary Patronage in Greece and Rome*. Chapel Hill: University of North Carolina Press.

Golden, James L., and Joseph J. Pilotta, eds. 1986. *Practical Reasoning in Human Affairs: Studies in Honor of Chaim Perelman*. Dordrecht: D. Reidl.

Goldhill, Simon. 1991. *The Poet's Voice: Essays on Poetics and Greek Literature*. Cambridge: Cambridge University Press.

Goldman, Laurence. 1983. *Talk Never Dies: The Language of Huli Disputes*. London: Tavistock.

Graff, Gerald. 1970. *Poetic Statement and Critical Dogma*. Chicago: University of Chicago Press.

————. 1979. *Literature against Itself: Literary Ideas in Modern Society*. Chicago: University of Chicago Press.

Grant, Michael. 1978. *History of Rome*. New York: Scribner's.

————. 1990. *The Fall of the Roman Empire*. New York: Macmillan.

Gratwick, A. S. 1982. "Drama." In Kenney and Clausen 1982.

Green, Lawrence. 1980. "Enthymemic Invention and Structural Prediction." *College English* 41:623–634.

————. 1990. "Aristotelian Rhetoric, Dialectic, and the Traditions of *Antistrophos*." *Rhetorica* 8.1:5–27.

————. 1995. "Aristotle's Enthymeme and the Imperfect Syllogism." In *Rhetoric and Pedagogy: Its History, Philosophy, and Practice. Essays in Honor of James J. Murphy*, edited by Winifred Bryan Horner and Michael Leff. Mahwah, N.J.: Erlbaum.

————, ed. and tr. 1986. *John Rainolds's Oxford Lectures on Aristotle's Rhetoric*. London: Associated University Presses.

Green, R. P. H., ed. 1991. *The Works of Ausonius*. Oxford: Oxford University Press.

————, ed. and tr. 1995. *Augustine: De Doctrina Christiana*. Oxford: Oxford University Press.

Greenberg, Nathan. 1990. *The Poetic Theory of Philodemus*. New York: Garland.

Gregg, Richard. 1984. *Symbolic Inducement and Knowing: A Study in the Foundations of Rhetoric*. Columbia, S.C.: University of South Carolina Press.

Griffith, Mark. 1990. "Contest and Contradiction in Early Greek Poetry." In *Cabinet of the*

Muses: Essays on Classical and Comparative Literature in Honor of Thomas G. Rosenmeyer, edited by Mark Griffith and Donald J. Mastronarde. Atlanta: Scholars Press.

Grimaldi, William M. A. 1972. *Studies in the Philosophy of Aristotle's Rhetoric.* Weisbaden: Steiner.

———— 1980. *Aristotle, Rhetoric I: A Commentary.* New York: Fordham University Press.

Grube, G. M. A. 1961. *A Greek Critic: Demetrius on Style.* Toronto: University of Toronto Press.

————. 1965. *The Greek and Roman Critics.* London: Methuen.

Gruen, Erich S. 1984. *The Hellenistic World and the Coming of Rome.* 2 vols. Berkeley: University of California Press.

Gubar, Susan. 1984. "Sapphistries." *Signs* 10.1:43–62.

Habermas, Jürgen. 1979. *Communication and the Evolution of Society.* London: Heinemann.

————. 1984–1989. *The Theory of Communicative Action.* 2 vols. Boston: Beacon Press.

Hägg, Thomas. 1983. *The Novel in Antiquity.* London: Basil Blackwell.

Hale, Horatio. 1883. "An Iroquois Condoling Council." In *An Iroquois Source Book.* 1985. Edited by Elizabeth Tooker. Vol. 1 of 2. New York: Garland.

Halliwell, Stephen. 1986. *Aristotle's Poetics.* London: Duckworth.

————. 1987. *The Poetics of Aristotle: Translation and Commentary.* Chapel Hill: University of North Carolina Press.

Hansen, Esther V. 1971. *The Attalids of Pergamon.* 2nd ed. Ithaca: Cornell University Press.

Hansen, Mogens Herman. 1987. *The Athenian Assembly in the Age of Demosthenes.* London: Basil Blackwell.

————. 1989. *The Athenian Ecclesia II: A Collection of Articles 1983–1989.* Copenhagen: Museum Tusculanem.

————. 1991. *The Athenian Democracy in the Age of Demosthenes: Structure, Principles and Ideology.* Oxford: Blackwell.

Hansen, P. 1983. *Carmina Epigraphica Graeca Saeculorum VIII–V a.Chr.n.* Berlin: de Gruyter.

Hardy, Barbara. 1977. *The Advantage of Lyric.* Bloomington: Indiana University Press.

Harris, Edward M. 1995. *Aeschines and Athenian Politics.* Oxford: Oxford University Press.

Harris, W. V. 1989. *Ancient Literacy.* Cambridge: Harvard University Press.

Hartman, Charles O. 1980. *Free Verse: An Essay on Prosody.* Princeton: Princeton University Press.

Havelock, Eric A. 1963. *Preface to Plato.* Cambridge: Harvard University Press.

————. 1982. *The Literate Revolution in Greece and Its Cultural Consequences.* Princeton: Princeton University Press.

————. 1986. *The Muse Learns to Write: Reflections on Orality and Literacy from Antiquity to the Present.* New Haven: Yale University Press.

Heath, Malcolm. 1988. "Receiving the κωμος: The Context and Performance of Epinician." *American Journal of Philology* 109:180–195.

————. 1989. *Unity in Greek Poetics.* Oxford: Oxford University Press.

————, tr. 1995. *Hermogenes: On Issues.* Oxford: Oxford University Press.

Heath, Malcolm, and Mary Lefkowitz. 1991. "Epinician Performance." *Classical Philology* 86.3:173–191.

Helm, Rudolph, ed. 1912–1931. *Apulei Opera Quae Supersunt.* 3 vols. Leipzig: Teubner.

Helmbold, W. C., tr. 1952. *Plato: Gorgias.* Library of Liberal Arts. New York: Bobbs-Merill.

Helmbold, W. C., and W. G. Rabinowitz, trs. 1956. *Plato: Phaedrus.* Library of Liberal Arts. Indianapolis: Bobbs-Merrill.

Herrington, C. J. 1982. "Senecan Tragedy." In Kenney and Clausen 1982.

Honoré, Tony. 1981. *Emperors and Lawyers.* London: Duckworth.

Horner, Winifred B., ed. 1990. *The Present State of Scholarship in Historical and Contemporary Rhetoric*. Columbia: University of Missouri Press.

Horsfall, Nicholas. 1982. "Prose and Mime." In Kenney and Clausen 1982.

Hubbell, H. M. 1914. *The Influence of Isocrates on Cicero, Dionysius, and Aristides*. New Haven: Yale University Press.

———, tr. 1920. *The Rhetorica of Philodemus: Translation and Commentary*. In *Transactions of the Connecticut Academy of Arts and Sciences* 23.

———, tr. 1968. *Cicero: De Inventione*. In *Cicero*. Vol. 2 of 28. Cambridge: Harvard University Press.

Innes, Doreen C. 1989. "Philodemus." In Kennedy 1989.

Irvine, Martin. 1994. *The Making of Textual Culture: 'Grammatica' and Literary Theory, 350–1100*. Cambridge: Cambridge University Press.

Irwin, Eleanor. 1974. *Colour Terms in Greek Poetry*. Toronto: Hakkert.

Jackson, B.Darrell. 1969. "The Theory of Signs in Augustine's *De Doctrina Christiana*." *Revue des Études Augustiniennes* 15:99–108.

———, tr. 1975. *Augustine: De Dialectica*. Dordrecht: D. Reidl.

Jaeger, Werner. 1945. *Paideia: The Ideals of Greek Culture*. Tr. Gilbert Highet. 2nd ed., 3 vols. New York: Oxford University Press.

Jakobson, Roman, and Linda Waugh. 1960. "Closing Statement: Linguistics and Poetics." In *Style in Language*, edited by Thomas Sebeok. Cambridge, Mass.: MIT.

———. 1973. "Poésie de Grammaire et Grammaire de la Poésie." In *Questions de Poétique*. Paris: Éditions de Seuil.

———. 1979. *The Sound Shape of Language*. Bloomington: Indiana University Press.

Jameson, Fredric. 1971. *Marxism and Form: Twentieth-Century Dialectical Theories of Literature*. Princeton: Princeton University Press.

Jarratt, Susan C. 1991. *Rereading the Sophists: Classical Rhetoric Refigured*. Carbondale, Illinois: Southern Illinois University Press.

Jarratt, Susan C., and Rory, Ong. 1995. "Aspasia: Rhetoric, Gender, and Colonial Ideology." In Lunsford 1995.

Jebb, Sir Richard Claverhouse. 1893. *Selections from Attic Orators*. 2nd ed., 2 vols. New York: Macmillan.

Jenkyns, Richard. 1982. *Three Classical Poets: Sappho, Catullus, and Juvenal*. London: Duckworth.

Jennings, Francis, William N. Fenton, Mary A. Druke, and David R. Miller, eds. 1985. *The History and Culture of Iroquois Diplomacy: An Interdisciplinary Guide to the Treaties of the Six Nations and Their League*. Syracuse, N.Y.: Syracuse University Press.

Johnson, W. R. 1982. *The Idea of Lyric: Lyric Modes in Ancient and Modern Poetry*. Berkeley: University of California Press.

Johnston, Mark. 1996. *The Evangelical Rhetoric of Ramon Llull: Lay Learning and Piety in the Christian West around 1300*. New York: Oxford University Press.

Jones, Arnold Hugh Martin. 1964. *The Later Roman Empire, 284–602*. 3 vols. Norman, Okla.: University of Oklahoma Press.

———. 1966. *The Decline of the Ancient World*. New York: Holt, Rinehart and Winston.

Kahn, Victoria. 1985. *Rhetoric, Prudence, and Skepticism in the Renaissance*. Ithaca: Cornell University Press.

Kamer, Stephen Arnold. 1986. *Emperors and Aristocrats in Byzantium, 976–1081*. Ann Arbor: University Microfilms International.

Kastely, James L. 1997. *Rethinking the Rhetorical Tradition: From Plato to Postmodernism*. New Haven: Yale University Press.

Kaster, Robert A. 1988. *Guardians of Language: The Grammarian and Society in Late Antiquity*. Berkeley: University of California Press.

Katz, Steven B. 1996. *The Epistemic Music of Rhetoric: Toward the Temporal Dimension of Affect in Reader Response and Writing*. Carbondale: Southern Illinois University Press.

Kazhdan, Alexander. 1984. *Studies on Byzantine Literature of the Eleventh and Twelfth Centuries*. New York: Cambridge University Press.

———. 1993. *Authors and Texts in Byzantium*. Brookfield, Vt.: Variorum.

Keaney, J. J., and Robert Lamberton, eds. and trs. 1996. *[Plutarch]: Essay on the Life and Poetry of Homer*. American Philological Association: American Classical Studies no. 40. Atlanta: Scholars Press.

Keenan, Elinor. 1975. "A Sliding Sense of Obligatoriness: The Polystructure of Malagasy Oratory." In Bloch 1975.

Kellner, Hans. 1994. "After the Fall: Reflections on Histories of Rhetoric." In Vitanza 1994.

Kemp, Alan, tr. 1987. "The *Tekhnê Grammatikê* of Dionysius Thrax." In *The History of Linguistics in the Classical Period*, edited by Daniel J. Taylor. Amsterdam: John Benjamins.

Kennedy, George A. 1963. *The Art of Persuasion in Greece*. Princeton: Princeton University Press.

———. 1969. *Quintilian*. New York: Twayne.

———. 1972. *The Art of Rhetoric in the Roman World*. Princeton: Princeton University Press.

———. 1980. *Classical Rhetoric and Its Christian and Secular Tradition from Ancient to Modern Times*. Chapel Hill: University of North Carolina Press.

———. 1983. *Greek Rhetoric under Christian Emperors*. Princeton: Princeton University Press.

———. 1994. *A New History of Classical Rhetoric*. Princeton: Princeton University Press.

———. 1998. *Comparative Rhetoric: An Historical and Cross-Cultural Introduction*. New York: Oxford University Press.

———, ed. 1989. *The Cambridge History of Literary Criticism I: Classical Critricism*. Cambridge: Cambridge University Press.

———, tr. 1991. *Aristotle on Rhetoric: A Theory of Civic Discourse*. New York: Oxford University Press.

Kenney, E. J., and W. V. Clausen, eds. 1982. *The Cambridge History of Classical Literature II: Latin Literature*. Cambridge: Cambridge University Press.

Kerferd, G. B. 1981. *The Sophistic Movement*. Cambridge: Cambridge University Press.

Kermode, Frank. 1968. *The Sense of An Ending: Studies in The Theory of Fiction*. New York: Oxford University Press 1967.

Kertzer, Jonathan. 1988. *Poetic Argument: Studies in Modern Poetry*. Montreal: McGill-Queen's University Press.

Kilpatrick, Ross S. 1990. *The Poetry of Criticism: Horace*, Epistles 2 and Ars Poetica. Edmonton: University of Alberta Press.

Kinneavy, James L. 1982. "Restoring the Humanities: The Return of Rhetoric from Exile." In Murphy 1982.

Kinney, Arthur. 1986. *Humanist Poetics: Thought, Rhetoric, and Fiction in Sixteenth-Century England*. Amherst: University of Massachusetts Press.

———. 1989. *Continental Humanist Poetics: Studies in Erasmus, Castiglione, Marguerite de Navarre, Rabelais, and Cervantes*. Amherst: University of Massachusetts Press.

Kirby, John T. 1992. "Rhetoric and Poetics in Hesiod." *Ramus: Critical Studies in Greek and Roman Literature* 21.1:34–60.

Kitzhaber, Albert R. 1953. "Rhetoric in American Colleges 1850–1900." Ph.D. diss., University of Washington.

Knox, B. M.W. 1985. Epilogue to Easterling and Knox 1985.

Konstan, David. 1993. "Rhetoric and the Crisis of Legitimacy in Cicero's Catilinarian Orations." In Poulakos 1993.

Kosman, L. A. 1980. "Being Properly Affected: Virtues and Feelings in Aristotle's Ethics." In *Essays on Aristotle's Ethics*, edited by Amélie O. Rorty. Berkeley: University of California Press.

Kraemer, R. S. 1992. *Her Share of the Blessings*. Oxford: Oxford University Press.

Krummen, Eveline. 1990. *Pyrsos Hymnon: Festliche Gegenwart und mythische-rituelle Tradition als Voraussetzung einer Pindarinterpretation (Isthmie 4, Pythie 5, Olympie 1 und 3)*. Berlin: de Gruyter.

Kurke, Leslie. 1991. *The Traffic in Praise: Pindar and the Poetics of Social Economy*. Ithaca: Cornell University Press.

————. 1992. "The Politics of ἁβροσύνη in Archaic Greece." *Classical Antiquity* 11.1: 91–120.

————. 1994. "Crisis and Decorum in Sixth-Century Lesbos: Reading Alkaios Otherwise." *Quaderni Urbinati di Cultura Classica, Nuova Serie* 47.2:67–92.

Kustas, George. 1973. *Studies in Byzantine Rhetoric*. Thessaloniki: Patriarchal Institute for Patristic Studies.

Lacey, Walter K. 1978. *Cicero and the End of the Roman Republic*. New York: Barnes and Noble.

Lamb, W. R.M., tr. 1924. *Plato: Protagoras*. In *Plato*. Vol. 2 of 12. Cambridge: Harvard University Press.

————, tr. 1925. *Plato: Gorgias*. In *Plato*. Vol. 3 of 12. Cambridge: Harvard University Press.

Lamberton, Robert. 1986. *Homer the Theologian: Neoplatonist Allegorical Reading and the Growth of the Epic Tradition*. Berkeley: University of California Press.

Lamberton, Robert. 1988. *Hesiod*. New Haven: Yale University Press.

————. 1992a. Introduction to Lamberton and Keaney 1992.

————. 1992b. "The Neoplatonists and the Spritualization of Homer." In Lamberton and Keaney 1992.

Lamberton, Robert, and John J. Keaney, eds. 1992. *Homer's Ancient Readers: The Hermeneutics of Greek Epic's Earliest Exegetes*. Princeton: Princeton University Press.

Lanham, Richard A. 1976. *The Motives of Eloquence: Literary Rhetoric in the Renaissance*. Yale University Press.

Lattimore, Richmond, tr. 1959. *Hesiod: The Works and Days, Theogony, The Shield of Herakles*. Ann Arbor: University of Michigan Press.

————, tr. 1976.*The Odes of Pindar*. Chicago: University of Chicago Press.

Leff, Michael. 1986. "Genre and Paradigm in the Second Book of *De Oratore*." *Southern Speech Communication Journal* 51.4:308–325.

Lefkowitz, Mary. 1988. "Who Sang Pindar's Victory Odes?" *American Journal of Philology* 109:1–11.

Levi, Peter, tr. 1979. *Pausanias: Guide to Greece*. New York: Penguin.

Levy, Ian Hideo. 1984. *Hitomaro and the Birth of Japanese Lyricism*. Princeton: Princeton University Press.

Lewis, John M. 1985. "Eros and the Polis in Theognis Book II." In Figueira and Nagy 1985.

Lindsay, Jack, tr. 1960. *The Golden Ass by Apuleius*. Bloomington: Indiana University Press.

Lobel, E., and D. L. Page. 1955. *Poetarum Lesbiorum Fragmenta*. Oxford: Oxford University Press.

Londey, David, and Carmen Johanson, trs. and eds. 1987. *The Logic of Apuleius*. New York: E. J. Brill.

Long, A. A. 1992. "Stoic Readings of Homer." In Lamberton and Keaney 1992.

Lund, Helen S. 1992. *Lysimachus: A Study in Early Hellenistic Kingship*. London: Routledge.

Lunsford, Andrea, ed. 1995. *Reclaiming Rhetorica: Women in the Rhetorical Tradition*. Pittsburgh: University of Pittsburgh Press.

Mack, Peter. 1993. *Renaissance Argument: Valla and Agricola in the Traditions of Rhetoric and Dialectic*. Leiden: Brill.

Mailloux, Stephen, ed. 1995. *Rhetoric, Pragmatism, Sophistry*. Cambridge: Cambridge University Press.

Mailloux, Steven. 1989. *Rhetorical Power*. Ithaca: Cornell University Press.

Maksimovic, Ljubomir. 1988. *The Byzantine Provincial Administration under the Palaiologoi*. Amsterdam: Hakkert.

Marchant, E. C., tr. 1968. *Xenophon: Scripta Minora*. Cambridge, Harvard University Press.

Marra, Michele. 1993. *Representations of Power: The Literary Politics of Medieval Japan*. Honolulu: University of Hawaii Press.

Marrou, Henri-Irénée. 1949. *Saint Augustin et la Fin de la Culture Antique*. 2nd ed. Paris: E. de Bocard.

———. 1956. *A History of Education in Antiquity*. Tr. George Lamb. New York: Sheed and Ward.

Marshall, Anthony J. 1993. "The Case of Cloatilla: A Note on Quintilian's Quotations from the Defense Speech of Domitius Afer." *Ancient History Bulletin* 7.1:17–27.

McCloskey, Deirdre. 1996. "The Rhetoric of Liberty." *Rhetoric Society Quarterly* 26.1:9–27.

McGlew, James F. 1993. *Tyranny and Political Culture in Ancient Greece*. Ithaca: Cornell University Press.

McKeon, Richard 1942. "Rhetoric in the Middle Ages." *Speculum* 17:1–32.

———. 1952. "Poetry and Philosophy in the Twelfth Century: The Renaissance of Rhetoric." In *Critics and Criticism*, edited by R. S. Crane. Chicago: Chicago University Press.

Meier, Christian. 1990. *The Greek Discovery of Politics*. Tr. David McLintock. Cambridge: Harvard University Press.

Meiggs, Russell, and David Lewis. 1969. *A Selection of Greek Historical Inscriptions to the End of the Fifth Century* B.C.E. Oxford: Oxford University Press.

Meijering, Roos. 1987. *Literary and Rhetorical Theories in Greek Scholia*. Groningen: Egbert Forsten.

Meschonnic, Henri. 1982. *Critique du Rhythme: Anthropologie Historique du Langage*. Paris: Verdier.

Michelson, Karin E. 1980. "Mohawk Text: The Edge of the Forest Revisited." In *Northern Iroquoian Texts*. 1980. Edited by Marianne Mithun, and Hanni Woodbury. *International Journal of American Linguistics*, Native American Texts Series, monograph no. 4. Chicago: University of Chicago Press.

Millar, Fergus. 1977. *The Emperor in the Roman World* (31 B.C.–A.D. 337). London: Duckworth.

———. 1981. *The Roman Empire and Its Neighbours*. 2nd ed. London: Duckworth.

Miller, Arthur B., and John D. Bee. 1972. "Enthymeme: Body and Soul." *Philosophy and Rhetoric* 5:201–214.

Miller, Paul Allen. 1994. *Lyric Texts and Lyric Consciousness: The Birth of a Genre from Archaic Greece to Augustan Rome*. London: Routledge.

Miner, Earl. 1990. *Comparative Poetics: An Intercultural Essay on Theories of Literature*. Princeton: Princeton University Press.

Minnis, A. J., and A. B. Scott, eds. 1991. *Medieval Literary Theory and Criticism, c. 1100–c. 1375: The Commentary Tradition*. Oxford: Oxford University Press.

Mitchell, Thomas N. 1979. *Cicero: the Ascending Years*. New Haven: Yale University Press.

Molyneux, John H. 1992. *Simonides: A Historical Study.* Wauconda, Ill.: Bolchazy-Carducci.

Monfasani, John. 1976. *George of Trebizond: A Biography and Study of His Rhetoric and Logic.* Leiden: Brill.

———. 1983. "The Byzantine Rhetorical Tradition and the Renaissance." In Murphy 1983.

———. 1995. *Byzantine Scholars in Renaissance Italy: Cardinal Bessarion and Other Emigres: Selected Essays.* Brookfield, Vt.: Variorum.

Monk, Samuel H. 1935. *The Sublime: A Study of Critical Theories in Eighteenth-Century England.* New York: MLA.

Moreschini, C., ed. 1991. *Apulei Platonici Madaurensis Opera Quae Supersunt.* 3 vols. Stuttgart: Teubner.

Morris, Ian. 1993. "The Interpretation of Ritual Action in Archaic Greece." In Dougherty and Kurke 1993.

———. 1996. "The Strong Principle of Equality and the Archaic Origins of Greek Democracy." In Ober and Hedrick 1996.

Morse, Ruth. 1991. *Truth and Convention in the Middle Ages: Rhetoric, Representation and Reality.* Cambridge: Cambridge University Press.

Mullen, William. 1982. *Choreia: Pindar and Dance.* Princeton: Princeton University Press.

Murgia, Charles E. 1985. "Pliny's Letters and the *Dialogus.*" *Harvard Studies in Classical Philology* 89:171–206.

Murphy, James J. 1974. *Rhetoric in the Middle Ages: A History of Rhetorical Theory from St. Augustine to the Renaissance.* Berkeley: University of California Press.

———, ed. 1978. Berkeley: University of California Press. *Medieval Eloquence: Studies in the Theory and Practice of Medieval Rhetoric.* Berkeley: University of California Press.

———, ed. 1982. *The Rhetorical Tradition and Modern Writing.* New York: MLA.

———, ed. 1983. *Renaissance Eloquence: Studies in the Theory and Practice of Renaissance Rhetoric.* Berkeley: University of California Press.

———, ed. 1990. *A Short History of Writing Instruction.* Davis, Calif.: Hermagoras Press.

Nadeau, Ray. 1959. "Clasical Systems of Stases in Greek: Hermagoras to Hermogenes." *Greek, Roman and Byzantine Studies* 1:28–52.

———, tr. 1964. "Hermogenes: *On Staseis.*" *Speech Monographs* 31:361–424.

Nagy, Gregory. 1979. *The Best of the Achaeans: The Concept of the Hero in Archaic Greek Poetry.* Baltimore: Johns Hopkins University Press.

———. 1985. "Theognis and Megara: A Poet's Vision of His City." In Figueira and Nagy 1985.

———. 1990a. *Pindar's Homer: The Lyric Possession of an Epic Past.* Baltimore: Johns Hopkins University Press.

———. 1990b. *Greek Mythology and Poetics.* Ithaca: Cornell University Press.

———. 1996. *Poetry as Performance: Homer and Beyond.* Cambridge: Cambridge University Press.

Nathan, Leonard. 1986. "Putting the Lyric in Its Place." *Northwest Review* 24.3:77–83.

Neel, Jasper. 1994. *Aristotle's Voice: Rhetoric, Theory, and Writing in America.* Carbondale: Southern Illinois University Press.

Nehamas, Alexander. 1994. "Pity and Fear in the *Rhetoric* and the *Poetics.*" In Furley and Nehamas 1994.

Neuberger-Donath, Ruth. 1969. "Sappho Fr. 1.1: ΠΟΙΚΙΛΟΘΡΟΝ oder ΠΟΙΚΙΛΟΦΡΟΝ'." *Wiener Studien* 82:15–17.

Nisetich, F. J., tr. 1980. *Pindar's Victory Songs.* Baltimore: Johns Hopkins University Press.

Norlin, George, tr. 1928–1929. *Isocrates.* Vols. 1 and 2 of 3. Cambridge: Harvard University Press.

Norris, Christopher. 1992. *Uncritical Theory: Postmodernism, Intellectuals, and the Gulf War.* Amherst: University of Massachusetts Press.

Nussbaum, Martha. 1986. *The Fragility of Goodness.* Cambridge: Cambridge University Press.

Obbink, Dirk, ed. 1995. *Philodemus and Poetry: Poetic Theory and Practice in Lucretius, Philodemus, and Horace.* Oxford: Oxford University Press.

Ober, Josiah. 1989. *Mass and Elite in Democratic Athens: Rhetoric, Ideology, and the Power of the People.* Princeton: Princeton University Press.

Ober, Josiah, and Charles Hedrick, eds. 1996. *Dêmokratia: A Conversation on Democracies, Ancient and Modern.* Princeton: Princeton University Press.

Ochs, Donovan J. 1993. *Consolatory Rhetoric: Grief, Symbol and Ritual in the Greco-Roman Era.* Columbia: University of South Carolina Press.

Oliver, Robert T. 1971. *Communication and Culture in Ancient India and China.* Syracuse, N.Y.: Syracuse University Press.

Ong, Walter. 1958. *Ramus, Method, and the Decay of Dialogue.* Cambridge: Harvard University Press.

———. 1982. *Orality and Literacy: The Technologizing of the Word.* London: Methuen.

Oravec, Christine. 1976. "'Observation' in Aristotle's Theory of Epideictic." *Philosophy and Rhetoric* 9.3:162–174.

Page, Denys L. 1955. *Sappho and Alcaeus: An Introduction to the Study of Ancient Lesbian Poetry.* Oxford: Oxford University Press.

———. 1975. *Epigrammata Graeca.* Oxford: Oxford University Press.

———. 1981. *Further Greek Epigrams.* Cambridge: Cambridge University Press.

Patterson, Annabel. 1970. *Hermogenes and the Renaissance: Seven Ideas of Style.* Princeton: Princeton University Press.

Peabody, Berkeley. 1975. *The Winged Word: A Study in the Technique of Ancient Greek Oral Composition as Seen Principally through Hesiod's Works and Days.* Albany: SUNY Press.

Perelman, Chaim. 1982. *The Realm of Rhetoric.* Tr. William Kluback. Notre Dame: Notre Dame University Press.

———. 1984. "Rhetoric and Politics." *Philosophy and Rhetoric* 17.3:129–134.

———. 1986. "Address at the Ohio State University." In Golden and Pilotta 1986.

Perelman, Chaim, and Lucie Olbrechts-Tyteca. 1969. *The New Rhetoric: A Treatise on Argumentation.* Tr. John Wilkinson and Purcell Weaver. Notre Dame: Notre Dame University Press.

Peterson, Sir W., and Michael Winterbottom, trs. 1980. *Tacitus: Dialogus de Oratoribus.* In *Tacitus.* Vol. 1 of 5. Cambridge: Harvard University Press.

Phylactopoulos, George, ed. 1975. *History of the Hellenic World.* Tr.Philip Sherrard. 2 Vols. University Park: Pennsylvania State University Press. (Published originally in Greek [1971] as *Istoria tou Ellinikou Ethnous*.)

Pinsky, Robert. 1976. *The Situation of Poetry.* Princeton: Princeton University Press.

———. 1987. "The Responsibilities of the Poet." *Critical Inquiry* 13.3:421–433.

Porter, James. 1992. "Hermeneutic Lines and Circles: Aristarchus and Crates on the Exegesis of Homer." In Lamberton and Keaney 1992.

———. 1995. "Content and Form in Philodemus: The History of an Evasion." In Obbink 1995.

Poulakos, John. 1995. *Sophistical Rhetoric in Classical Greece.* Columbia: University of South Carolina Press.

Poulakos, Takis. 1997. *Speaking for the Polis: Isocrates' Rhetorical Education.* Columbia: University of South Carolina Press.

———, ed. 1993. *Rethinking the History of Rhetoric: Multidisciplinary Essays on the Rhetorical Tradition.* San Francisco: Westview.

Pucci, Pietro. 1977. *Hesiod and the Language of Poetry*. Baltimore: Johns Hopkins University Press.

Quandahl, Ellen. 1986. "Aristotle's Rhetoric: Reinterpreting Invention." *Rhetoric Review* 4:128–137.

Rabe, Hugo, ed. 1913. *Hermogenis Opera*. Leipzig: Teubner.

Race, William H. 1990. *Style and Rhetoric in Pindar's Odes*. Atlanta: Scholars Press.

Race, William H., tr. 1997. *Pindar*. 2 vols. Cambridge: Harvard University Press.

Rackham, H., tr. 1957. *"Aristotle's" Rhetoric to Alexander*. Cambridge: Harvard University Press.

———, tr. 1977–1979. *Cicero: De Oratore*. In *Cicero*. Vols. 3–4 of 28. Cambridge: Harvard University Press.

Radice, Betty. 1985. Introduction to *Propertius: The Poems*. Tr. W. G. Shepherd. New York: Penguin.

Rankin, H. D. 1977. *Archilochus of Paros*. Park Ridge, N.J.: Noyes.

Rapoport, Roy. 1979. *Ecology, Meaning, and Religion*. Richmond, Calif.: North Atlantic Books.

Raymond, James. 1984. "Enthymemes, Examples, and Rhetorical Method." In *Classical Rhetoric and Modern Discourse*, edited by Andrea Lunsford, Robert Connors, and Lisa Ede. Carbondale: Southern Illinois University Press.

Reynolds, Joyce. 1988. "Cities." In Braund 1988.

Reynolds, Susan. 1996. *Medieval Reading: Grammar, Rhetoric, and the Classical Text*. New York: Cambridge University Press.

Richardson, N. J. 1975. "Homeric Professors in the Age of the Sophists." *Proceedings of the Cambridge Philological Society* 21:65–81.

Richter, Michael. 1994a. *The Formation of the Medieval West*. New York: St. Martin's.

——— 1994b. *The Oral Tradition in the Early Medieval West*. Typologie des Sources du Moyen Age Occidental, fasc. 71. Turnhout: Brepols.

Robb, Kevin. 1994. *Literacy and Paideia in Ancient Greece*. New York: Oxford University Press.

Roberts, W. Rhys. 1901. *Dionysius of Halicarnassus: The Three Literary Letters*. Oxford: Oxford University Press.

———, tr. 1973. *Demetrius: On Style*. In *Aristotle*. Vol. 23 of 23. Cambridge: Harvard University Press.

Roberts, W. Rhys, and Ingram Bywater, trs. 1954. *The Rhetoric and The Poetics of Aristotle*. Modern Library. New York: Random House.

Robertson, D. W., Jr., tr. 1958. *Saint Agustine: On Christian Doctrine*. Indianapolis: Bobbs-Merrill.

Rose, Peter W. 1992. *Sons of the Gods, Children of the Earth: Ideology and Literary Form in Ancient Greece*. Ithaca: Cornell University Press.

———. 1995. "Cicero and the Rhetoric of Imperialism: Putting the Politics Back into Political Rhetoric." *Rhetorica* 13.4:359–400.

Rostovzeff, M. 1964. *The Social and Economic History of the Hellenistic World*. 3 vols. Oxford: Oxford University Press.

Rudd, Niall. 1982. "Horace." In Kenney and Clausen 1982.

Russell, D. A. 1981. *Criticism in Antiquity*. London: Duckworth.

———. 1983. *Greek Declamation*. Cambridge: Cambridge University Press.

———. 1990a. "Greek and Latin in Antonine Literature." In Russell 1990.

———. 1990b. "Aristides and the Prose Hymn." In Russell 1990.

———, ed. 1990. *Antonine Literature*. Oxford: Oxford University Press.

Russell, D. A., and N. G. Wilson, trs. 1981. *Menander Rhetor*. Oxford: Oxford University Press.

Russell, D. A., and M. Winterbottom, trs. 1972. *Ancient Literary Criticism: The Principal Texts in New Translations*. Clarendon Press. Oxford: Oxford University Press.

Samuel, Alan E. 1983. *From Athens to Alexandria: Hellenism and Social Goals in Ptolemaic Egypt*. In *Studia Hellenistica*. Vol. 26.

Sandys, John, Sir, tr. 1919. *The Odes of Pindar, Including the Principal Fragments*. New York: Putnam.

Schiappa, Edward. 1990. "History and Neo-Sophistic Criticism: A Reply to Poulakos." *Philosophy and Rhetoric* 23:307–315.

———. 1991a. *Protagoras and Logos: A Study in Greek Philosophy and Rhetoric*. Columbia: University of South Carolina Press.

———. 1991b. "Sophistic Rhetoric: Oasis or Mirage?" *Rhetoric Review* 10.1:5–18.

———. 1992. "*Rhêtorikê*: What's in a Name? Toward a Revised History of Early Greek Rhetorical Theory." *Quarterly Journal of Speech* 78.1:1–15.

———. 1995. "Isocrates' *Philosophia* and Contemporary Pragmatism." In Mailloux 1995.

Scribner, Sylvia, and Michael Cole. 1981. *The Psychology of Literacy*. Cambridge: Harvard University Press.

Searle, John R. 1969. *Speech Acts: An Essay in the Philosophy of Language*. London: Cambridge University Press.

———. 1979. *Expression and Meaning: Studies in the Theory of Speech Acts*. New York: Cambridge University Press.

———. 1983. *Intentionality: An Essay in the Philosophy of Mind*. Cambridge: Cambridge University Press.

Segal, Charles. 1986. *Pindar's Mythmaking: The Fourth Pythian Ode*. Princeton: Princeton University Press.

Shackleton Bailey, D. R. 1971. *Cicero*. New York: Scribner's.

Sinclair, Patrick. 1995. *Tacitus the Sententious Historian: A Sociology of Rhetoric in Annales 1–6*. University Park: Pennsylvania State University Press.

Sivan, Hagith. 1993. *Ausonius of Bordeaux: Genesis of a Gallic Aristocracy*. London: Routledge.

Slater, William J. 1984. "Nemean One: The Victor's Return in Poetry and Politics." In *Greek Poetry and Philosophy: Studies in Honour of Leonard Woodbury*, edited by Douglas E. Gerber. Chico, Calif.: Scholars Press.

Sloane, Thomas O. 1974. "The Crossing of Rhetoric and Poetry in the English Renaissance." In *The Rhetoric of Renaissance Poetry, from Wyatt to Milton*, edited by Thomas O. Sloane and Raymond Waddington. Berkeley: University of California Press.

———. 1985. *Donne, Milton, and the End of Humanist Rhetoric*. Berkeley: University of California Press.

———. 1993. "Rhetorical Education and Two-Sided Argument." In *Renaissance-Rhetorik*, edited by Heinrich F. Plett. Berlin: de Gruyter.

———. 1997. *On the Contrary: The Protocol of Traditional Rhetoric*. Washington, D. C.: Catholic University of America Press.

Smith, C. F., tr. 1919–1935. *Thucydides: History of the Peloponnesian War*. 4 vols. Cambridge: Harvard University Press.

Smith, Robert W. 1974. *The Art of Rhetoric in Alexandria: Its Theory and Practice in the Ancient World*. The Hague: Martinus Nijhoff.

Snell, Bruno. 1982. *The Discovery of the Mind in Greek Philosophy and Literature*. Tr. Thomas G. Rosenmeyer. New York: Dover. (Orig. 1953.)

Snyder, Jane McIntosh. 1997. *Lesbian Desire in the Lyrics of Sappho*. New York: Columbia University Press.

Solmsen, Friedrich. 1941. "The Aristotelian Tradition in Ancient Rhetoric." *American Journal of Philology* 62:35–50, 169–190.

———. 1975. *Intellectual Experiments of the Greek Enlightenment*. Princeton: Princeton University Press.

Solomon, Robert C. 1976.*The Passions*. Garden City, N.Y.: Anchor/Doubleday.

Solterer, Helen. 1995. *The Master and Minerva: Disputing Women in Medieval French Culture*. Berkeley: University of California Press.

Sprague, Rosamond Kent, ed. 1972. *The Older Sophists: A Complete Translation by Several Hands of the Fragments in Die Fragmente Der Vorsokratiker Edited by Diehls-Kranz, with a New Edition of Antiphon and of Euthydemus*. Columbia: University of South Carolina Press.

Stahl, Hans-Peter. 1985. *Propertius, "Love" and "War": Individual and State under Augustus*. Berkeley: University of California Press.

Stahl, William Harris, Richard Johnson, and E. L. Burge, trs. 1977. *Martianus Capella and the Seven Liberal Arts*. Vol. 2 of 2. *The Marriage of Philology and Mercury*. New York: Columbia University Press.

Starr, Chester G. 1986. *Individual and Community: The Rise of the Polis, 800–500* B.C. New York: Oxford University Press.

———. 1990. *The Birth of Athenian Democracy: The Assembly in the Fifth Century* B.C. New York: Oxford University Press.

Stehle, Eva. 1997. *Performance and Gender in Ancient Greece: Nondramatic Poetry in Its Setting*. Princeton: Princeton University Press.

Strathern, Andrew. 1975. "Veiled Speech in Mount Hagen." In Bloch 1975.

Struever, Nancy. 1992. *Theory as Practice: Ethical Inquiry in the Renaissance*. Chicago: University of Chicago Press.

Sudhaus, Siegfried, ed. 1964. *Philodemus: Volumina Rhetorica*. 3 vols. Amsterdam: Hakkert. (Reprint of the 1892–1896 Teubner edition.)

Sullivan, Dale L. 1992. "*Kairos* and the Rhetoric of Belief." *Quarterly Journal of Speech* 78:317–332.

Swearingen, C. Jan. 1991. *Rhetoric and Irony: Western Literacy and Western Lies*. New York: Oxford University Press.

———. 1995. "A Lover's Discourse: Diotima, Logos, and Desire." In Lunsford 1995.

Syme, Ronald. 1958.*Tacitus*. 2 vols. Oxford: Oxford University Press.

Tambiah, Stanley Jeyarajah. 1985. *Culture, Thought, and Social Action: An Anthropological Perspective*. Cambridge: Harvard University Press.

Tatum, James. 1979. *Apuleius and The Golden Ass*. Ithaca: Cornell University Press.

Testard, Maurice. 1958. *Saint Augustin et Cicéron*. Paris: Études Augustiniennes.

Thomas, Rosalind. 1989. *Oral Tradition and Written Record in Classical Athens*. Cambridge: Cambridge University Press.

———. 1992. *Literacy and Orality in Ancient Greece*. Cambridge: Cambridge University Press.

Tinkler, John. 1990. *The Constraints of Desire: The Anthropology of Sex and Gender in Ancient Greece*. New York: Routledge.

Todd, Marcus. 1985. *Greek Historical Inscriptions*. Chicago: Ares.

Todd, S. C. 1993. *The Shape of Athenian Law*. Oxford: Oxford University Press.

Tomkins, Silvan. 1991. *Affect, Imagery, Consciousness*. Vol. 3 of 4. New York: Springer.

Too, Yun Lee. 1995. *The Rhetoric of Identity in Isocrates: Text, Power, Pedagogy*. Cambridge: Cambridge University Press.

Toohey, Peter. 1994. "Epic and Rhetoric." In Worthington 1994b.

Tooker, Elisabeth, ed. 1985. *An Iroquois Source Book.* Vol. 1 (of 3). New York: Garland.

Toulmin, Stephen. 1958. *The Uses of Argument.* Cambridge: Cambridge University Press.

Trapp, M. B., tr. 1997. *Maximus of Tyre: The Philosophical Orations.* Oxford: Oxford University Press.

Trimpi, Wesley. 1983. *Muses of One Mind: The Literary Analysis of Experience and Its Continuity.* Princeton: Princeton University Press.

Trypanis, Constantine A. 1981. *Greek Poetry, from Homer to Seferis.* London: Faber and Faber.

Turner, Mark. 1976. "Propertius through the Looking Glass: A Fragmentary Glance at the Construction of Pound's Homage." *Paideuma* 5:241–65

Turton, David. 1975. "The Relationship between Oratory and the Exercise of Influence among the Mursi." In Bloch 1975.

Usener, H., and Radermacher, L. 1965. *Dionysii Halicarnasei, Opusculorum.* 2 vols. Stuttgart: Teubner.

Usher, Stephen, tr. 1985. *Dionysius of Halicarnassus: The Critical Essays.* 2 vols. Cambridge: Harvard University Press.

van Eemeren, Frans H., Rob Grootendorst, and Francisca Snoeck Henkemans. 1996. *Fundamentals of Argumentation Theory: A Handbook of Historical Backgrounds and Contemporary Developments.* Mahwah, N.J.: Erlbaum.

Van Hook, La Rue, tr. 1945. *Isocrates.* Vol. 3 of 3. Cambridge: Harvard University Press.

Vickers, Brian. 1970. *Classical Rhetoric in English Poetry.* Carbondale: Southern Illinois University Press.

———. 1988. *In Defence of Rhetoric.* Oxford: Oxford University Press.

Vitanza, Victor, ed. 1994. *Writing Histories of Rhetoric.* Carbondale: Southern Illinois University Press.

Walbank, F. W. 1981. *The Hellenistic World.* Atlantic Highlands, N.J.: Humanities Press.

Walker, Jeffrey. 1989a. *Bardic Ethos and the American Epic Poem.* Baton Rouge: Louisiana State University Press.

———. 1989b. "Aristotle's Lyric: Re-Imagining the Rhetoric of Epideictic Song." *College English* 51.1:5–28.

———. 1992. "Enthymemes of Anger in Cicero and Thomas Paine." In *Constructing Rhetorical Education,* edited by Marie Secor and Davida Charney. Carbondale: Southern Illinois University Press.

———. 1994. "The Body of Persuasion: A Theory of the Enthymeme." *College English* 56.1:46–65.

———. 1998. "Dionisio de Halicarnaso y la Idea de Crítica de la Retórica" (Dionysius of Halicarnassus and the notion of rhetorical criticism). *Anuario Filosófico* 31.2:581–601.

———. 2000. "*Pathos* and *Katharsis* in 'Aristotelian' Rhetoric: Some Implications." In *Rereading Aristotle's Rhetoric,* edited by Alan Gross and Arthur Walzer. Carbondale: Southern Illinois University Press.

Walz, Christian. 1968. *Rhetores Graeci.* 9 vols. Osnaburck: Zeller. (Facsimile reprint of 1832–1836 original.)

Watts, N. H., tr. 1961. *Cicero: Pro Archia Poeta.* In *Cicero.* Vol. 11 of 28. Cambridge: Harvard University Press.

Welsh, Andrew. 1978. *The Roots of Lyric: Primitive Poetry and Modern Poetics.* Princeton: Princeton University Press.

West, Martin L. 1974. *Studies in Greek Elegy and Iambus.* Berlin: de Gruyter.

———, ed. 1971–1992. *Iambi et Elegi Graeci, ante Alexandrum Cantati.* 2 vols. Oxford: Oxford University Press.

————, tr. 1993. *Greek Lyric Poetry: The Poems and Fragments of the Greek Iambic, Elegiac, and Melic Poets (Excluding Pindar and Bacchylides) down to 450 BC*. Oxford: Oxford University Press.

White, Eric Charles. 1987. *Kaironomia: On the Will-to-Invent*. Ithaca: Cornell University Press.

Williams, W. Glynn, tr. 1965. *Cicero: Letters to His Friends [Epistulae Ad Familiarem]*. 3 vols. Cambridge: Harvard University Press.

Williamson, Margaret. 1995. *Sappho's Immortal Daughters*. Cambridge: Harvard University Press.

Winkler, John J. 1985. *Auctor and Actor: A Narratological Reading of Apuleius's Golden Ass*. Berkeley: University of California Press.

Winterbottom, Michael. 1964. "Quintilian and the *Vir Bonus*." *Journal of Roman Studies* 54:90–97.

————. 1982. "Schoolroom and Courtroom." In *Rhetoric Revalued: Papers from the International Society for the History of Rhetoric*, edited by Brian Vickers. Binghamton, N.Y.: Center for Medieval and Early Renaissance Studies, State University of New York at Binghamton.

———— tr. 1974. *The Elder Seneca: Controversiae and Suasoriae*. 2 vols. Cambridge: Harvard University Press.

Winters, Yvor. 1957. *The Function of Criticism: Problems and Exercises*. Denver: Swallow.

Wisse, Jakob. 1989. *Ethos and Pathos from Aristotle to Cicero*. Amsterdam: Hakkert.

Wood, Neal. 1988. *Cicero's Social and Political Thought*. Berkeley: University of California Press.

Woodman, Tony. 1984. "Horace's First Roman Ode." In Woodman and West 1984.

Woodman, Tony, and David West, eds. 1984. *Poetry and Politics in the Age of Augustus*. New York: Cambridge University Press.

Wooten, Cecil.W., tr. 1987. *Hermogenes' On Types of Style*. Chapel Hill: University of North Carolina Press.

Worthington, Ian. 1994a. "The Canon of the Ten Attic Orators." In Worthington 1994b.

————. ed. 1994b. *Persuasion: Greek Rhetoric in Action*. London: Routledge.

Wright, W. C., tr. 1921 *Philostratus and Eunapius: Lives of the Sophists*. Cambridge: Harvard University Press.

Wycherly, R. E. 1978. *The Stones of Athens*. Princeton: Princeton University Press.

Yunis, Harvey. 1996. *Taming Democracy: Models of Political Rhetoric in Classical Athens*. Ithaca: Cornell University Press.

Zumthor, Paul. 1990. *Oral Poetry: An Introduction*. Tr. Kathryn Murphy-Judy. Minneapolis: University of Minnesota Press.

————. 1992. *Towards a Medieval Poetics*. Tr. Philip Bennett. Minneapolis: University of Minnesota Press.

Index